FOR THE DEAD REMEMBER

FOR THE DEAD REMEMBER

— THE LIFE OF M. R. JAMES —

DARRYL JONES

OXFORD
UNIVERSITY PRESS

OXFORD
UNIVERSITY PRESS

Great Clarendon Street, Oxford, OX2 6DP,
United Kingdom

Oxford University Press is a department of the University of Oxford.
It furthers the University's objective of excellence in research, scholarship,
and education by publishing worldwide. Oxford is a registered trade mark of
Oxford University Press in the UK and in certain other countries.

Published in the United States of America by Oxford University Press
198 Madison Avenue, New York, NY 10016, United States of America

British Library Cataloguing in Publication Data
Data available

Library of Congress Control Number: 2025945892

ISBN 9780198835233

DOI: 10.1093/oso/9780198835233.001.0001

Printed and bound by
CPI Group (UK) Ltd., Croydon, CR0 4YY

The manufacturer's authorized representative in the EU for product safety is
Oxford University Press España S.A. of Parque Empresarial San Fernando de Henares,
Avenida de Castilla, 2 – 28830 Madrid (www.oup.es/en or product.safety@oup.com).
OUP España S.A. also acts as importer into Spain of products made by the manufacturer.

MIX
Paper | Supporting responsible forestry
FSC® C013604

For Margaret and Morgan, with love

Preface

By the end of his life, he was able to sign himself 'M. R. James O.M., Litt.D., Hon D.C.L. Oxford, Hon. B.L.D. St. Andrews, V.B.A., F.S.A., etc. Provost of Eton, Sometime Provost of King's College Cambridge'—and, he might have added, Commandeur de l'Ordre de Léopold.[1] He was a man of massive academic and personal distinction—and many who met him thought he was a genuinely great man. The Liberal Party leader Jo Grimond, who had encountered him while a schoolboy at Eton, thought him 'the most impressive man I have ever met. It is impossible to compare him with Churchill or De Gaulle, wrapt about in the aura of their achievements. But in force of personality he struck me, perhaps because I was younger when I knew him, and knew him better, as more redoubtable than either.'[2] There is obviously an element of schoolboy hero-worship in this assessment—though Grimond was sixty-six when he published these words, at the end of a long and distinguished public career in which he had met many undeniably great men.

'The truth is', Montague Rhodes James wrote in 1922, 'I am a very immature creature, with not much clearer vision of life than I had when I left school.' He was writing to Gwendolen McBryde, the widow of the love of his life, James McBryde, who had died shockingly young in 1904. Gwen was perhaps the only real woman friend he ever had. His letter went on:

> It is a constant puzzle or if not puzzle, surprise, to me that I have never shared the ambitions or speculations about a career which ordinary people have, and ought to have, choice of profession, home of one's own, and all such. I believe there never was a time when I had more of a programme than to find out all I could about various matters and to make friends. Positions and objectives have been the same. I certainly never wanted to be Provost of King's, and when Eton seemed likely, I only welcomed it because it was Eton.[3]

His eminence was not, as he might have claimed, accidental, but it *was* unsystematic, more than a little chaotic, determinedly and even perversely idiosyncratic, and often infuriating. He loved jigsaw puzzles, mazes, cryptograms, codes and ciphers, crosswords, forgotten languages, unreadable manuscripts, imaginary books, and endless, complex, convoluted games. He knew things no one else knew, and never, ever forgot anything, in a manner that struck many people as simply uncanny. The Classical scholar Sir Roger Mynors recalled 'the feeling when you met him that he was slightly larger than life *and* could if necessary conjure a demon out of a brass bottle or tell you the names of the soldiers at the foot of the Cross'.[4] (He could certainly tell you the name of one of them: his study of *The Apocryphal New Testament* records that 'Longinus the soldier pierced [Christ's] side with a spear'. He also claimed to know the names of the shepherds attending at the birth of Christ.)[5] There's no doubt that he knew how to conjure demons. He knew all their names, their hierarchies and powers, what you could compel them to do on your behalf—but also why this was a terrible idea. He knew more, perhaps, than anyone alive about what he called 'the real Black Art, the Sorcery and Witchcraft of the Middle Ages'.[6] He was an insatiably curious man, who warned against the terrible consequences of curiosity.

Attempting to make sense of the jumble of his papers that were left in the care of the Colleges in which he spent his life, in 1972 the Eton librarian and archivist Patrick Strong wrote to his King's College Cambridge counterpart, A. N. L. Munby, observing that any future biographer 'will have maddeningly disjointed work'.[7] I can testify to that. How to make narrative sense of the many thousands of pages of correspondence, notebooks, lectures, sermons, not to mention the simply vast body of official, published work? He had at least three careers of enormous but overlapping distinction, like a Venn diagram (fittingly, he knew John Venn, who was just next door at Gonville and Caius). He was the most eminent anglophone codicologist of his day, the man who seemed to know almost all there was to know about medieval manuscripts—but also about Biblical apocrypha, ecclesiastical stained glass, and the occult. He was a very senior academic administrator—the Provost of King's College Cambridge; the Vice-Chancellor of Cambridge University, who very ably guided the university through the terrible early years of the Great War; and, in a kind of semi-retirement, he was the Provost of Eton. And, almost by way of an afterthought, he wrote ghost stories. He is, I firmly believe, the greatest ghost-story writer there has ever been, and the single most frightening writer I have ever read.

Montague Rhodes James was not an easy man. I think we need to be quite clear about this. He was a brilliant man, there's no doubt about that: unusually so, even for the circles in which he moved. He was unquestionably a sociable man, with a circle of lifelong friends to whom he was very loyal. He had, in a peculiar way, a charismatic personality: he had a profound effect on many of the people he encountered, some of whom, like Jo Grimond, thought he was a really great man. But you couldn't pin him down, and you still can't. For the most part, he had a tendency to deflect serious enquiry with a gentle wit or a disingenuous charm, or else slip into one of his many funny voices (he was a superb mimic, and a fine actor), or simply quote Dickens, much of which he knew by heart (he did have an astonishing memory): his conversation, we know, was habitually peppered with Dickensian references and allusions.[8] This is one of the things that Arthur Benson, one of his oldest and closest friends, and probably his most acute and sceptical observer, found most frustrating about him: his seemingly effortless ability to slip serious philosophical, political, existential, or psychological punches. He had, he insisted, 'no considered theories' on the ghost stories which are, no doubt to his considerable surprise, his most lasting legacy.[9]

When I first started writing about him, I described his as 'a curiously incomplete man'.[10] Many years, and many, many letters, archives, libraries, manuscripts, conversations, and friendships, have only served to intensify this belief. If he had an inner life at all (and I have sometimes wondered), it stayed resolutely inner. He held a series of *extremely* reactionary social views—most notably when it came to the education of women—and had a horror of progress and modernity which sometimes, some observers thought, amounted to a genuine fear of ideas and the intellectual life. Throughout this biography I am very clear that he was what several of his friends realized—a profoundly repressed and closeted homosexual man. But, while Arthur Benson or Oliffe Richmond or Gordon Carey knew this, it's very doubtful that he did, and certainly he never acknowledged it, probably even to himself. But there are times (never very openly, and never for very long) when one does encounter genuine passions: heartbreak, grief, despair, longing, loneliness, love. He once confessed to his beloved tutor and lifelong friend H. E. Luxmoore that 'I used to spend a great deal of time alone in the Chapel…It took away the sense of loneliness that was at times unbearable'.[11]

But Eton and King's, the institutions in which he lived his life—he lived his life *through* them—gave him support, meaning, community, and purpose. He never wanted them to change. As they structured his life, so they structure this book.

Acknowledgements

'I will be frank', Oliffe Richmond once wrote to Shane Leslie, who was planning a biography of M. R. James. 'In my opinion there is no need whatever for a biography of Monty.'[12] Richmond knew Leslie, and so knew that he could be credulous when it came to matters of the occult, and that he tended to play a little fast and loose with historical accuracy in the name of narrative. But Richmond, we shall see, was a man with secrets of his own, and he was wrong about a lot of things.

There will be mistakes here, no doubt, and they will certainly be mine. I've come to realise that writing a biography of M. R. James requires a range of expertise that no one person could possibly have. You need to be a codicologist, a historian of religion and scripture, a Classicist, a medievalist, an expert in stained glass, religious architecture, and iconography. It would help to know about twenty languages: all the major European ones, living and dead, plus Hebrew, and also Syriac, Coptic, Ancient Ethiopic, and probably a few others. You need to have a keen sense of the histories, structures, hierarchies, and rituals of universities. More generally, you need to be an educational historian, and a historian of class, masculinity, and sexuality. You need to know who the English establishment is and was, their networks and institutions. And you need to be a critic of supernatural literature, who knows something about the occult. Fortunately, I work in a university, and a university system, full of brilliant, helpful people who *do* know about these things, and who have been enormously generous in sharing what they know. (I haven't yet had to seek anyone out to translate some Ancient Ethiopic for me, but I'm sure I could find them.)

And so I want to record some of these debts:

At Oxford University Press, I would like to thank Luciana O'Flaherty for her enthusiasm and, most of all, her patience. I hope it was worth the wait! My thanks also to Judith Luna, who, almost two decades ago, wrote to me out of the blue to ask whether I would be interested in editing the *Collected Ghost Stories* of M. R. James, and so started me on the long road that leads—right here.

I am very grateful to Philip James and the James family for welcoming me to their family home in Skipness on the Mull of Kintyre, for putting me up, putting up with me, feeding me delicious food, and giving me access to suitcases and drawers full of the James family papers. My thanks to Philip James for permission to use the papers and photographs.

At Eton, my thanks to the Provost, the Lord Waldegrave of North Hill—or, if I may, more informally, to William and Caroline Waldegrave, for welcoming me to the Provost's Lodge, showing me around, and answering many questions. My thanks also to James O'Brien, Eton Housemaster, for taking such generous time to introduce me to Eton's life, customs, buildings, and history.

I owe an enormous debt of gratitude to Simon Goldhill of King's College Cambridge, who was always very enthusiastic in sharing with me his unparalleled knowledge of the Benson family, of the history of King's, and of the Classical Tripos, as well as his characteristic friendship and hospitality. My thanks too to Christopher Stray, who knows more than anyone about the history of Classics in Victorian universities, and was always very generous (that word again—I have encountered so much generosity) in sharing his knowledge.

Robert Lloyd Parry, a true scholar of the Cambridge ghost story, very kindly shared his notes on Anstey Guthrie's diaries at a time when they were unavailable at the British Library: although I got to see the diaries myself eventually, I certainly could not have written about Guthrie without his help and advice.

For a book of this kind, it's only fitting that I should have relied so heavily on the expertise and labours of many archivists and librarians. I can't name them all, but my thanks to: Georgina Robinson at Eton; Frank Bowles, Liam Sims, and their colleagues at Cambridge University Library; Patricia McGuire and Tom Davies at King's College Cambridge; Catherine Sutherland and Katy Green at the Pepys Library, Magdalene College Cambridge; Adam Green at the Wren Library, Trinity College Cambridge; Robin Payne and Katy Green (again) at Jesus College Cambridge; Ellen Gage at the Fitzwilliam Museum, Cambridge; Rafael Siodor at University College London Library; the librarians at the Lilly Library, Bloomington, Indiana; the Pierpont Morgan Library, New York; Trinity College Dublin Library; the East Sussex Record Office, Brighton; and the British Library.

In the School of English at Trinity College Dublin, I am blessed with great colleagues and students. My particular thanks to Jarlath Killeen, Bernice Murphy, and Eve Patten, my dear friends.

Helen Docking and I have known each other for more years than we care to admit, and she very kindly read the whole book, just to make sure it made some kind of sense.

My thanks also (I know why, though you may have forgotten) to: Marlene Arnese, Tamara Atkin, Chris Baldick, Rebecca Anne Barr, Kim and Martin Beazor, Molly Box, Scott Brewster, Ailise Bulfin, Anna Chahoud, Paul Chapman, Clare Clarke, John Connolly, Helen Conrad-O'Briain, Alice Crawford, Robert Crawford, Mark Cunningham, Nick Curwin, Nick Daly, Paul Delaney, Ana Orbegozo Desdentado, David Ditchburn, Ruth Doherty, Dara Downey, Beryl Dyson, Robert Edgar, John Exshaw, Christopher Frayling, Shoshana Goldhill, Zohar Hadromi-Allouche, Joe Harbison, Ross Harrison, Kate Hebblethwaite, Declan Hughes, Adrian Hunter, Wayne Johnson, Bob Jones, Celia Hilton Jones, Mark Jones, Maureen Jurkowski, Helen Kemp, Triona Kirby, Christopher Lee, Miles Link, Roger Luckhurst, Elizabeth McCarthy, Jenny McDonnell, Gail McElroy, Jane Mainley-Piddock, Michael Marsh, Jean-Michel Massing, Hannah Mathew, Andy Murphy, Patrick J. Murphy, Sorcha Ní Fhlainn, Björn Quiring, Rosemary Pardoe, Maria Parsons, Fred Porcheddu, Conor Reid, Ian Robertson, Victoria Rosner, John Scattergood, Brian J. Showers, Brenda Silver, Sam Slote, Andy Smith, Ann Kennedy Smith, Kevin Smith, Valerie Smith, Luke Thurston, Helen Twigge-Molecey, Martin Voracek, Tom Walker, Craig Wallace, Francis Young.

To my parents, Yvonne and Dewi Jones, my sister, Nerys Brown, and in memory of my beloved aunt, Molly Rice.

And, with all the love I have, my wife, Margaret Robson, and my daughter, Morgan Jones. This book is for them, of course.

Contents

Abbreviations

ACB	Arthur Christopher Benson
BL	British Library
BRJ	Herbert Ellison ('Ber') Rhodes James
CGS	*Collected Ghost Stories*
Cox	Michael Cox, *M. R. James: An Informal Portrait*
CUL	Cambridge University Library
E&K	*Eton and King's*
ECL	Eton College Library
GRJ	Grace Rhodes James
GSA	*Ghost Stories of an Antiquary*
HJ	Herbert James
JFP	James family papers, Skipness, Argyll
KCC	King's College Cambridge
LF	*Letters to a Friend*
LFMC	*Letters to a Friend* (Michael Cox's annotated edition)
MEJ	Mary Emily James
MGSA	*More Ghost Stories of an Antiquary*
MRJ	Montague Rhodes James
Notebooks	MRJ Notebooks, Fitzwilliam Museum, Cambridge
Pfaff	Richard William Pfaff, *Montague Rhodes James*
SRJ	Sydney Rhodes James
TG	*A Thin Ghost and Others*
WTC	*A Warning to the Curious*

Images

Cast of Characters

It is impossible to understand M. R. James without understanding the people amongst whom he lived his life. As the biography makes clear throughout, his ties of family, of class, and especially of institutions were unusually close, and so to tell his story is to tell their story too. Readers will almost certainly be unfamiliar with the great majority of the characters that swim into view, recede for a while, and then return again (and again) over the course of these pages, and so I thought it might be wise to begin with a *dramatis personae*.

The James Family

Grace Caroline Rhodes James (1859–1943): MRJ's sister.
Herbert James (1822–1909): MRJ's father; Rector of Great Livermere, Suffolk.
Herbert Ellison Rhodes James (1857–1939): MRJ's brother; military doctor, who served in Hong Kong and China.
Mary Emily James (née Horton) (1818–98): MRJ's mother.
Sydney James (1855–1934): MRJ's oldest brother; Eton master; Headmaster of Malvern College; Archdeacon of Dudley.

Friends and Colleagues

Cyril Alington (1872–1955): Headmaster of Eton to MRJ's Provost; later Dean of Durham.
Cecil Baring (1864–1934): MRJ's friend and travelling companion; banker.
A. C. (Arthur) Benson (1862–1925): close friend of MRJ; prolific man of letters; Eton master; Master of Magdalene College, Cambridge.
E. F. (Fred) Benson (1867–1940): friend and student of MRJ; high-profile novelist; brother of A. C. Benson.
Henry Bradshaw (1831–86): scholar and librarian; Fellow of King's; University Librarian; major influence on MRJ as a manuscript scholar.

William Bridgeman (1864–1935): lifelong friend of MRJ; Conservative MP and Home Secretary.

Henry Broadbent (1852–1935): Eton master and librarian; MRJ's teacher, friend, and later colleague.

Rupert Brooke (1887–1915): student and Fellow of King's; poet ('The Soldier').

Oscar Browning ('O.B.') (1837–1923): historian and man of letters; Eton master and Fellow of King's, where he was MRJ's institutional enemy.

Edward Montagu (Ted) Butler (1866–1948): MRJ's friend; Harrow master.

Gordon Carey (1886–1969): close friend of MRJ; student at Gonville and Caius; Fellow of Clare College; Headmaster of Eastbourne College.

J. H. (John Harold) Clapham (1873–1946): MRJ's King's colleague; College Tutor, and Professor of Economic History.

John Willis Clark ('J.') (1833–1910): friend of MRJ; architectural historian; Cambridge University Registrary [sic].

Sydney Cockerell (1867–1962): MRJ's friend and correspondent; his successor as Director of the Fitzwilliam Museum.

Mary Frances (Maisie) Cropper (1881–1973): wife of Walter Fletcher; sister of Billy Cropper.

Sibyl (Billy) Cropper (1890–1968): friend and correspondent of MRJ; youngest sister of Maisie Cropper.

Harry Cust (1861–1917): schoolfriend of MRJ; poet and literary editor; Conservative MP.

Goldsworthy Lowes Dickinson (1862–1932): MRJ's King's colleague; political philosopher and member of the Bloomsbury Group.

Marcus Dimsdale (1860–1919): MRJ's King's colleague; Fellow in Classics.

St. Clair Donaldson (1863–1935): close schoolfriend of MRJ; Archbishop of Brisbane and Bishop of Salisbury.

Walter Durnford (1847–1926): Eton master who taught MRJ; MRJ's successor as Provost of King's.

Walter Morley Fletcher (1873–1933): close friend of MRJ; physiologist, and major figure in the foundation of the Medical Research Council.

Lionel Ford (1865–1932): MRJ's lifelong friend; Headmaster of Repton and Harrow; Dean of York.

Stephen Gaselee (1882–1953): MRJ's student; librarian, diplomat, and Classical scholar.

Thomas Anstey Guthrie (F. Anstey) (1856–1934): MRJ's travelling companion; novelist and humorist.

Walter Headlam (1866–1908): MRJ's student friend and colleague; Fellow in Classics at King's.

Henry Jackson (1839–1921): MRJ's colleague; Regius Professor of Greek.

John Maynard Keynes (1883–1946): MRJ's institutional opponent; Economist; Fellow and Bursar of King's; major British intellectual of the twentieth century.

Augustus Austen Leigh (1840–1905): MRJ's predecessor as Provost of King's.

Shane Leslie (Sir John Randolph Leslie) (1885–1971): Anglo-Irish diplomat and man of letters; student of MRJ.

Cecil (Cis) Lubbock (1872–1956): MRJ's friend; Managing Director of Whitbread Brewers; Deputy Governor of Bank of England.

(Samuel) Gurney Lubbock (1873–1958): Eton housemaster; MRJ's friend, and first biographer.

Percy Lubbock (1879–1965): MRJ's friend; librarian, man of letters, and literary intellectual.

Henry Elford Luxmoore (1841–1926): MRJ's tutor at Eton, and close friend.

Gwendolen McBryde (1881–1958): widow of James McBryde; MRJ's closest woman friend, and longtime correspondent; illustrator.

James McBryde (1874–1904): student and beloved friend of MRJ; artist and illustrator.

Hugh Macnaghten (1862–1929): MRJ's major academic rival at Eton and King's; Eton housemaster.

Leopold Maxse (1864–1932): MRJ's student friend; extreme right-wing journalist and editor.

Eric Millar (1887–1966): MRJ's close friend and correspondent in his later years; art historian; Keeper of Manuscripts at the British Museum.

Eric Milner-White (1884–1963): MRJ's colleague; Dean and Chaplain of King's, and later Dean of York.

J. E. (John Edwin) Nixon (1840–1916): Fellow in Classics at King's, and beloved Cambridge eccentric.

Ronald Norman (1873–1963): MRJ's friend; Conservative politician and banker; Chairman of the Board of Governors of the BBC.

Allen Beville Ramsay ('Ram') (1872–1955): MRJ's most faithful friend and constant travelling companion; Eton master; Master of Magdalene College Cambridge, and sometime University Vice-Chancellor.

Oliffe Richmond (1881–1977): classicist; student of MRJ; Fellow of King's; Professor of Classics at Cardiff and Edinburgh.

(Joseph) Armitage Robinson (1858–1933): Professor of Divinity and Fellow of Christ's College; Dean of Westminster, and Dean of Wells; MRJ's colleague and collaborator, and sometime travelling companion.

A. F. (Alwyn Faber) Scholfield (1884–1969): MRJ's friend in his later years; Cambridge University Librarian.

Arthur Shipley (1861–1927): zoologist; Master of Christ's College and sometime Vice-Chancellor of Cambridge University; MRJ's colleague and travelling companion.

Henry Sidgwick (1838–1900): Knightsbridge Professor of Moral Philosophy, and major figure in late-Victorian Cambridge; co-founder of the Society for Psychical Research; MRJ's institutional opponent.

Henry Babington Smith (1863–1923): lifelong friend of MRJ; senior civil servant; Director of the Bank of England.

Owen Hugh Smith (1869–1958): MRJ's lifelong friend, a constant presence at ghost story evenings; Governor of the Bank of England.

Mark Sykes (1879–1919): MRJ's friend; student at Jesus College Cambridge; Conservative MP and diplomat, who played a major role in drawing the current political map of the Middle East.

William Ridgeway (1853–1926): MRJ's Cambridge colleague; Disney Professor of Archaeology.

Cecil Spring-Rice (1859–1919): MRJ's fagmaster at Eton; British Ambassador to US during the First World War; poet ('I Vow to Thee My Country').

J. K. (James Kenneth) Stephen (1859–1892): MRJ's student friend; poet and Fellow of King's; Virginia Woolf's cousin.

John Stirling-Maxwell (1866–1956): MRJ's friend; Scottish Conservative MP and landowner.

Will (William Johnson) Stone (1872–1900): MRJ's student, friend, and travelling companion to Scandinavia; public schoolmaster.

Eustace Talbot (1873–1905): MRJ's friend; student at Trinity College; medic.

Herbert Tatham (1861–1909): schoolfriend of MRJ; Eton master.

Charles Waldstein (Walston) (1856–1927): archaeologist; MRJ's undergraduate supervisor at King's; Director of the Fitzwilliam Museum.

Nathaniel Wedd (1864–1940): MRJ's colleague; classicist and Fellow of King's.

Vincent Yorke (1869–1957): MRJ's friend; businessman, banker, and county cricketer.

I

Port Royal, Jamaica, 1655

The James family of Jamaica were slave-owners. In 1887, Sydney Rhodes James, who had been looking through the family papers, informed his younger brother Montague that 'at one time we possessed 3160 slaves'.[1] The Jameses were, in fact, the oldest settler family in Jamaica: the 'original Jamaicans', according to one rather Anglocentric historian.[2] The people they enslaved worked sugar plantations in Hanover and Westmoreland counties, on the far west coast of the island. The Jameses soon intermarried with other local slave-owning settlers: the Rhodes family, and the Haughtons, who owned large plantations in Hanover and nearby Trelawny counties.

According to James family tradition, their ancestry was 'probably always Welsh'.[3] It was this, some friends thought, that gave the family a whiff of sulphur, a 'strain of devil-worship' shadowing their conspicuous, Evangelical godliness.[4] Richard Montague James, the first of the Jamaican Jameses, was certainly born in Glamorgan, around 1630, though his family actually hailed from Newport on the Isle of Wight. In the early 1650s, Richard Montague James and his wife, Margaret, left Wales, setting sail for Barbados in search of a new life. When the Anglo-Spanish War broke out in 1654, he volunteered as an officer in the invasion force led by Admiral William Penn and General Robert Venables, and took part in the failed siege of Santo Domingo in Hispaniola in April 1655, and the successful invasion of Jamaica the following month. He stayed on, settling in Port Royal, Kingston, and brought his pregnant wife over from Barbados. Their son, Richard, was born in Port Royal later that year. He seems to have been the first child born to British parents in Jamaica.

In 1678, Richard Montague James inherited land in Westmoreland County from his cousin, Captain William James. Richard Montague's son, Richard Jr—Colonel Richard James—lived to be 103, and attributed his long life to a diet of cocoa. As a Colonel in the Westmoreland Militias, he contrived to acquire large tracts of land in the county: at least 1020 acres, and probably much more. In 1734, Col. Richard settled in Davis Cove, Hanover County, and established a 'Plantation or Sugar Work'.[5] He died very old and very wealthy, leaving most of his estate to his son, Richard Haughton James, with a moiety of his Green Island property to his brother William, and £3000 to his daughter Sarah. Amongst his executors is 'my brother Montague James, Esq.'.[6]

Col. Richard married Frances, the daughter of Captain William Rhodes. *Their* son, William Rhodes James, sent his oldest boy, Montague, to Eton, and left instructions in his will that his younger sons, William and Thomas, were also to be 'sent to Old England by the first convenient opportunity to have their education there'.[7] Thus began the centuries-long connection between the James family and England's most prestigious public school. The future Brigadier the Hon. Montague James, who was born in 1713, may have been the first Jamaican James to attend Eton, but he was certainly not the last. When M. R. James went himself to Eton in 1876, he wasn't even the only Montague James in his year: his cousin Montague Vidal James arrived at the same time.[8] (The Vidals were another branch of the Jamaican Jameses, and their name pops up all over the family records.)

In 1927, E. N. Geijer, the Rouge Dragon Pursuivant of the College of Arms, wrote to Brigadier the Hon. Montague James's descendant, the Provost of Eton, to inform him that his ancestral namesake had been given a Grant of Arms in 1772:

> AZURE on a chevron between three Lions passant Guardant ERMINIOS as many ESCALLOPS GULES and for the Crest on a Wreath of the Colours a demi LION rampant ERMINIOS in the paws an ESCALLOP GULES as the same are in the margin hereof more plainly depicted to be borne and used for EVER by him the said Montague James Esquire and his descendants of his father Richard James Esquire and also by the descendants of his Uncle William James.[9]

These arms can be found on the James family tomb at Davis Cove.

When William Rhodes James died in 1744, instructions about sending his children to Eton were not the only provisions in his will. William Rhodes James of Hanover, Planter, left an estate of £3643.26, of which £2275 was the value of his sixty-three enslaved people. To each of his daughters, Rebecca and Ann, he left '£500 Jamaican currency at age 21 or marriage. Also her choice of one Negro girl out of my estate with a horse and saddle.'[10] In his own will of 1737, Haughton James of the Haughton Tower estate (Haughton James I) stipulated: 'I give & bequeath to my dear Wife, Mary James, all my Plate, Household Furniture, & the following Negroes, for ever, viz. Imoinda, Hamlet, Nanny, Elsy, Flora, Hercules, Neptune & Mary.'[11]

The Haughton Tower estate had a particular reputation for the cruel treatment of its slaves. In 1787, Haughton James II, temporarily back in England, wrote to his cousin in Jamaica: 'I have been shocked at hearing your name at the head of those noted for severity!'[12] Nevertheless, he was soon writing again: 'With regard to Negroes, my desire is that you will take the first opportunity that presents itself, to purchase a number of healthy and serviceable Negroes not exceeding 20, or at most 25 . . . The Abolition of the slave-trade is, I think, for the present quite out of the question, & the whole battle will end in some regulations in the mode of conducting it.'[13] In 1809, Mary Williamson, a Haughton Tower 'Brown woman' (this is what she called herself), wrote to complain that the estate's slaves were 'harrased, floged and drove past human strenght, without any redress [sic]'.[14] By 1835, in the wake of Abolition, Haughton Tower's 212 slaves had been formally recategorized as 'Apprenticed labourers'.[15]

The James family prospered in Jamaica until the nineteenth century, when a combination of personal tragedy and the consequences of the enactment of abolitionist legislation (the Slave Trade Act of 1807, and the Slavery Abolition Act of 1833) brought one of them, at least, home to England for good. William Rhodes James IV was born in Trelawny, Jamaica, in 1786, but came to England in 1815, following the deaths at sea of his wife, Mary, and their son, William. He settled initially in Marylebone, where he married his second wife, Caroline Pope, on 21 May 1819. Their second son, Herbert, was born in Woolhampton, Berkshire, on 26 October 1822. The Jameses moved to Suffolk, eventually settling in Wyndham House, a rather grand Georgian villa just off the High Street in the coastal town of Aldeburgh. A good burgher, in 1840 William donated a splendid water pump to the town. It was listed in 1996, and a nearby dedication stone, now barely legible, reads: 'This pump was erected for the use of the inhabitants of Aldeburgh by W. R. James 1840.'[16] Aldeburgh is a place to which we will be returning many times.

During his years at Aldeburgh, William Rhodes James IV continued to make large sums from his sugar plantations. In 1812, the Haughton Tower estate's income was £9705.11.1; the following year, the estate declared for tax purposes an income of £5697.10.9 for sales of sugar in London alone (to multiply the nineteenth-century pound by a hundred is a reasonable rule of thumb for its rough modern equivalent).[17] Amongst the James family papers there is a valuation of thirty-seven Haughton Tower slaves made in 1814: £3180.[18] In 1817, he bought thirty-six slaves from Mrs Ann Pawson.[19] In 1831, he inherited £4474.10.4 from the Haughton Tower estate, which had 236 enslaved people.[20]

He received £2731.6.0 from the Jamaica estates in 1834.[21] Haughton Tower receipts from the following July show sugar sales to the value of £3764.18.0.[22] That same year, 1835, he also inherited a share of the Steelfield Estate in Trelawny, valued at £4299.8.6, with 205 enslaved.[23] On his death in 1842, he left his entire estate to his wife, 'considering with great anxiety the present uncertain state of colonial interests'.[24]

* * *

Back in England, the James family continued to pursue 'colonial interests' of various kinds. William and Caroline had seven children—six boys and a girl, Caroline Mary, who died at sixteen. Their oldest son, William Rhodes James V, was born in Hanwell St. Mary in 1820. He was educated at Charterhouse, and then at Edinburgh University Medical School. On graduation in 1841, he joined the Indian Medical Service, where he was stationed in Madras. The climate affected his health badly. In January 1844, he wrote about this to his younger brother Herbert: Bombay and Bengal he found 'too unhealthy, and the regiments grow refractory when sent there.... My stomach is out of order . . . I have applied to Penang for a voyage & have been told that I am likely to go . . . I should indeed be fortunate as it is very healthy & a very pleasant station, lots of pay & no sick in hospital.'[25] But his health broke, and he was forced to return to England on board the S.S. Great Liverpool. On 4 July 1844, not long after the ship had left Alexandria, William Rhodes James V died.[26]

William's younger brother Tom went into the navy, and was variously stationed in Arabia, Bombay, and Singapore. 'I believe our next destination to be the Cape of Good Hope', he wrote excitedly to Herbert in 1849.[27] The next brother, Harry—Henry Haughton James—also went into the navy as a young Lieutenant, and spent his career in India: 'I have now spent six Christmas days in India, two of which have been in Bombay and the rest at sea', he wrote to Herbert in 1848. 'What happy times a sailor has!!!'[28] He retired from the Indian Navy in 1871 with the rank of Commander, and moved to Woodbridge, Suffolk, where he set himself up as a 'Coal Merchant and Maltster'.[29] Harry's daughter Minnie went on to play an important role in the history of librarianship, as Head Librarian of the People's Palace Library, now a part of Queen Mary University of London. In a manner that would certainly not have pleased her most distinguished cousin, she was one of the first women to occupy such a senior role.[30]

The sixth brother, Montagu James (the only member of the family to spell his name in this way), was another who led a short life of extraordinary colonial adventure. He studied at the East India Company Military Seminary at Addiscombe, Croydon, graduating seventh in his class in December 1849. By 1851, Second Lieutenant Montagu James was serving with the Royal Artillery in Dum-Dum, Calcutta. Before shipping out, he paid his bill for £178.18.0. to T. McBride, Military Tailor and Outfitter, Thomas St., Woolwich (including £4.15.6 for a 'Superfine Blue Cloak, lined, with cape, and Silk Velvet Collar').[31] Amongst the books he took with him were an English-Tamil phrasebook, a Persian grammar, a guide to Hindustani, a 'Fortification Atlas', and a copy of John Milton's *Paradise Lost*.[32] He saw action in the Anglo-Burmese War of 1852. In what sounds like an episode from *The Moonstone* or *The Sign of Four*, after the Battle of Rangoon in April he was arrested for wanton destruction, 'for the sake of plundering', of the Shwedagon Golden Pagoda. He narrowly escaped a court martial.[33] Soon after, Lieutenant Montagu James contracted dysentery while serving with the Bombay Horse Artillery in Bengal. The illness fatally weakened his health. He returned home to England, where he died on 8 March 1854, age twenty-three.[34]

Herbert, the second son, was the scholar of the family. He was educated at Temple Grove, an exclusive but, we shall see, very rough-and-ready preparatory school on the outskirts of London, and followed the family tradition by going on to Eton. There, he excelled, and won a scholarship to King's College, Cambridge. At Cambridge, he encountered several people we shall be meeting again in later chapters: he shared a set of rooms with Thomas Brocklebank, while Brooke Foss Westcott and J. E. B. Mayor were both contemporaries; later, he became friendly with Henry Bradshaw. Like most students of his generation, Herbert was a 'Poll Man', graduating without an honours degree in 1847. The same year, he was awarded the Crosse Scholarship for 'knowledge of the Holy Scriptures in the original tongues, Hebrew and Greek, of the earlier and later Heresies, and such other subjects of useful enquiry as may be thought most likely to assist in the formation of valuable characters, fitted to sustain and adorn "the cause of true religion"'.[35] As was the practice of the day, he was automatically awarded a Fellowship at King's.

William Rhodes James IV's oldest child, Haughton James III, the product of his first marriage, stayed on in Jamaica until his death in 1856, and continued to earn a sizeable fortune from the estate. But abolitionism had put an end to much of the family's source of income. Caroline's family believed that the estate had been paid £120,000 in reparations after abolitionism, but if so, this seems to have gone to Haughton James III's family in Jamaica.[36] Scholarships notwithstanding, Eton and Charterhouse, Cambridge and Edinburgh Medical

School did not come cheap, and nor did kitting oneself out with superfine silk-lined cloaks for service in the East India Company. The fortune of that branch of the James family was soon gone. And so, like many studious sons of the landless gentry, Herbert went into the Church. He was ordained as a Deacon of the Church of England in Norwich in 1847, and as a priest in 1849.

* * *

Herbert entered the Church of England during a period of extraordinary theological and intellectual ferment. There were sides to be taken, and he took one. Herbert James was, in the words of a friend and fellow priest, 'a Protestant Evangelical Clergyman'.[37] In its origins, the Evangelical movement within the Church of England was closely associated with Cambridge University, and most particularly with King's College. The Evangelical divine Charles Simeon, a major foundational figure in the movement, was a Fellow of King's.[38] Evangelical Anglicans often made common cause with the dissenting churches, whose observances and theologies resembled theirs in several ways: a focus on scripture, a love of (often very long) sermons, a distaste for ecclesiastical ornament and ritual. In the words of the King's theologian Alec R. Vidler, the Evangelicals 'attached primary importance to conversion and faith in the atoning death of Christ'.[39] The Evangelicals gained serious prominence in the Church of England in the 1850s, partly as a theological alternative to the Anglo-Catholicism of the Oxford Movement: the Evangelicals were often, in Vidler's words, 'fanatically anti-Catholic'.[40] Their sense of moral rectitude could be stifling, or harshly punitive. The great historian of the Victorian church Owen Chadwick writes: 'The Victorian parent was stern with his children. The evangelical parent, receiving biblical order not to spare the rod, was severe. [The Christian Socialist theologian F. D.] Maurice's sister used to put delicious puddings on the table before her child and just as he was expecting to eat would order him to carry them away to the poor of the village. Solitary confinement in a dark room was accepted punishment for the very young.'[41]

In a manner which is perhaps ironic, perhaps revealing, but never directly commented on by Herbert or his family, in the early decades of the nineteenth century the social conscience of the Evangelical movement was firmly associated with the abolitionist movement. The Clapham Sect, an Evangelical grouping centred around William Wilberforce, was viewed by George III as a collection of 'dangerous revolutionaries'.[42] Other critics accused the Clapham Sect of what Charles Dickens calls in *Bleak House* 'Telescopic Philanthropy', a focus on injustice in Africa or the West Indies combined with an inability to see the condition of the urban poor right in front of their eyes.[43]

Evangelical clergymen were admired, even by their opponents, for the labour of their individual commitment to their parishes.[44] This sense of commitment, and of a moral and pastoral seriousness, is very evident in Herbert's book, *The Country Clergyman and his Work*, which was based on a series of lectures he gave on pastoral theology to the Divinity School at Cambridge in May Term, 1889. Country ministry, Herbert told his students, '*offers work worthy of your highest powers*', as 'the battle of the Church has to be fought out in the country'.[45] 'It will be a good day for the Church of England', he thought, 'when she becomes, in the fullest sense of the word, a Missionary Church.'[46] Herbert recommends taking the fight to the people, delivering sermons and lessons in a 'cottage, or mission-room, or barn, or farmer's kitchen'.[47] The country clergyman should '*aim at that eloquence* which is found in *"earnest simplicity"*', avoiding issues of metaphysics or science.[48] Above all, he should '*Preach a Personal Christ*': 'He is no abstraction: no aggregate of doctrines, but a living, breathing, Divinely-human Person.'[49]

It would be very unwise, Herbert believed, to assume ignorance in one's country parishioners: 'They see further than you think. And you may be certain of this that whilst you are trying to gauge *their* powers, they are taking *your measure* with no little correctness.'[50] Their beliefs could surprise you. During his ministry, Herbert had encountered 'a family of Muggletonians in a secluded wood in Kent, and Swedenborgians in a smuggling parish in Suffolk, and Mormonites seeded about everywhere'.[51] In far-flung East Anglian villages, he had often encountered the survival of pre-Christian or extra-Christian beliefs, rituals, and practices, folklore and magic, cunning folk, 'the quasi-religious belief of some who have an esoteric confidence in witchcraft. For there are those who still betake themselves to the "wise man" or "wise woman". I can personally testify that the progress of the XIXth Century with all its boasted advancement has failed to explode this and kindred superstition.'[52]

Herbert's inordinately distinguished youngest son, who is the subject of this book, inherited many of his father's beliefs and attitudes. He revered 'the great Simeon', his Evangelical predecessor at King's.[53] He knew all about the survival of ancient practices in remote parishes, the pattern under the plough. He had a lifelong suspicion of intellectual abstractions, of metaphysics and science. As a schoolboy, one of his favourite poems was *Yesterday, To-day, and For Ever*, a monumental long (*very* long) poem by the future Bishop of Exeter Edward Henry Bickersteth, a leading Evangelical divine—'the most colourful and godly of the evangelical clergy', according to Chadwick.[54] He was particularly keen on Book X, 'The Millennial Sabbath', which, he informed his father, 'clears up some things about the Millennium which I cannot understand so well from other books.'[55] In this section of the poem, a pastoral English village, very much like his own Great Livermere, goes about its normal, peaceful business one sunny Sunday, when very suddenly the apocalypse happens: the sky turns blood red, and the hosts of darkness chant: 'Hail, Satan, Astaroth, and Baalim!! / Triunity of darkness, hail, all hail.'[56] The end of the world is here and now, at any moment. His good friend Percy Lubbock, the literary intellectual and theorist, wrote to him in 1923:

> of all the people I know you were the one who wd understand what *that* evangelicalism, the Christian sort (I believe there are other sorts) really meant. Probably there are not many of us left who do—& I am glad to think that something of it shd be caught & kept, to show the rest what it could be.[57]

* * *

In July 1854, Herbert married a distant relative, Mary Emily Horton. Herbert's letter announcing his engagement, written to his youngest brother, Lieut. Montagu, gives a good sense of this Protestant Evangelical clergyman's character and priorities:

> 'After mature deliberation' as the Queen said when she announced her choice of P. Albert, 'I have come to the resolve of selecting my cousin', Emily Horton, to be the future 'partner of my life'—and I think that when you [meet] her you will not think my choice an unwise one.
>
> That it has been made without much reference to certain things which the world call essentials I most readily admit. Youth—beauty to a certain extent—[seem to be] wanting—but if I may be allowed to take into consideration the . . . qualities of health, straightforwardness, unselfishness & wisdom—together with a hearty desire to serve God—I do not think that I am altogether a loser.[58]

Herbert was not one of life's romantics. But nor was Mary Emily. Some of her correspondence during their engagement is at times quite affectionate ('My own dearest Herbert', 'My precious one'), but from the moment of their marriage, she invariably signs herself with her full name, 'Mary Emily James', and evinces a recurring preoccupation with the efficacy of beef tea, which seems to be her favourite subject. The opening line of one of the first letters she wrote to him after their marriage is: 'Please leave your beef jelly open to the air, or it will turn sour.'[59] She was, for good reason, very concerned about making ends meet. She had a small interest in some property, but it didn't amount to much, and she gloomily told Herbert a few months after their wedding: 'Your share of the rent is just £10.4 but don't reckon on *having* it for expenses will come rather heavily I fear.'[60] Theirs was a long and happy marriage.

Mary Emily came from a naval family, which traced its ancestry back to Edward I (the Hortons were direct descendants).[61] Rear Admiral Joshua Sydney Horton, Mary Emily's father, was a distinguished veteran of the Napoleonic Wars. In February 1800, as commanding officer of the sloop HMS Fairy, he played an important part in the capture of the Pallas, a large French frigate, in an action fought off St. Aubyn's Bay, Jersey.[62] He captained several ships across the duration of the war, culminating in the command of the seventy-four-gun HMS Alfred in 1812. In July 1830, he was promoted to the rank of Rear Admiral of the White.[63] He died in France on 26 November 1835, after which his family returned to civilian life in Dover.[64]

Mary Emily's older brother, Sydney, joined the 14th Light Dragoons, and died in Bombay in 1844, aged twenty-eight.[65] Her second brother, William, retired from the navy with the rank of Rear Admiral, like his father before him.[66] Admiral Joshua Horton was stationed in Tours in the aftermath of the Napoleonic Wars, and it's there that Mary Emily was born in 1818. She and her family led an exotic, rather adventurous life. In the preface to one of Mary Emily's scrapbooks, her daughter Grace writes: 'She was born at Tours in 1822 [sic], & travelled with her mother & Aunt Mary Treacher in France and Italy for 20 or more years. She saw much French and Italian society, and in Sienna used to sing with a Musical Society. She had a fine contralto voice.'[67] It is sometimes difficult to reconcile the younger Mary Emily—a cosmopolitan young woman recording in her diary adventures in Naples, Siena, Rome, and Florence, and corresponding with friends in French and Italian; a fine artist with a gift for portraiture—with her older self, living in rural isolation, constantly worrying about the health of her family, and, in letter after letter, obsessed with beef tea.[68] Can they be the same person?

The Hortons' Kent and Channel Island connections came in very handy for Herbert and Mary Emily in the early years of their marriage. Herbert started off as an impecunious curate in Aldeburgh and then in Christ Church, Dover, which is where he met his future wife. Shortly before his marriage, Herbert was told that Sir Brook Bridges of Goodnestone House in Kent, sometime Conservative MP for East Kent and the future Baron Fitzwalter of Woodham Walter in Essex, had expressed 'strong desire of your becoming their clergyman'. He and Lady Bridges, Herbert was told, 'both speak in such high terms of your intended, that they feel quite happy in the prospect of having her associated with them at the Parish'.[69] The income was a great improvement: £200 a year, of which £15 was the cost of rent.[70] Herbert took up the Perpetual Curacy of Goodnestone in 1855, not long after his wedding.

Herbert and Mary Emily's first child, Sydney, was born at Wyndham House in Aldeburgh in 1855. Two more children, Herbert Ellison (known to his family as Bertie, or more simply Ber) and Grace Caroline, arrived in 1857 and 1859. And then, on 1 August 1862, their youngest child was born. Following a long-standing family tradition, the baby was christened Montague Rhodes James. The first we hear about him from his family is in February 1864, when Mary Emily wrote to Herbert, who was away at an Evangelical conference: 'Baby becomes more & more amusing. Last night he lay & talked at a prodigious rate till about ½ past 12—every now & then yawning & saying "Sleepy"!'[71]

And so Montague Rhodes James takes his place in our story. His family called him Toby. His friends called him Monty. More distant acquaintances tended to call him 'Dr. James', and then 'Provost'. Modern scholars quite properly refer to him as 'James'. What shall we call him? 'Monty' seems too chummy for this austere and august man, while the more formal 'James' seems too remote and stuffy for this friendly and sociable man. So we shall call him by the name he invariably used for himself in signing off his many, many letters: 'MRJ'.

* * *

Around 1865, Mary Emily's younger brother, William Horton, and his wife, Anna Maria, took up residence in the Hall, Little Livermere, Suffolk. Anna Maria's first husband, Charles Broke, was a landowner in Suffolk, and after Charles's death in 1855, the vacant living of Great and Little Livermere became part of the inheritance of their daughter, Jane Anne Broke, the future Lady de Saumarez of Sausmarez Manor, Guernsey. Jane's trustees agreed to present the living to Herbert.[72] It was more lucrative than Goodnestone, and came with an impressive rectory, a large whitewashed manor house set in grounds just near the flinty church and its graveyard, sheltered by a stand of trees. And so, in 1865, Herbert, Mary Emily and their children moved to the tiny hamlet of Great Livermere, a few miles from Bury St. Edmunds, deep in the Suffolk country-side. This is the place MRJ was brought up, the place to which he would return regularly until well into middle age. In 'A Vignette', an autobiographical fragment he wrote in the last months of his life, MRJ imaginatively revisited the place of his childhood:

> You are asked to think of the spacious garden of a country rectory, adjacent to a park of many acres and separated therefrom by a belt of trees of some age which we knew as the Plantation. It is but about thirty or forty yards broad. A close gate of split oak leads to it from the path encircling the garden, and when you enter it from that side you put your hand in a square hole cut in it and lift the hook to pass along to the iron gate which admits to the park from the Plantation.

> It has further to be added that from some windows of the rectory, which stands on a somewhat lower level than the Plantation, parts of the path leading thereto, and the oak gate itself can be seen.[73]

Great Livermere was the place which formed many of his sensibilities; a good place for a ghost-story writer. And young Montague Rhodes James grew up to be the greatest ghost-story writer there has ever been. This sense of place is fundamental to understanding the kind of writer MRJ was, with deep roots in a material locality. And so it's worth pausing to begin to understand exactly what it is MRJ took from Great Livermere, from Suffolk, and from East Anglia.

In the 1950s, the ethnologist George Ewart Evans began a series of investigations and interviews in East Anglia, with the aim of recording a rural life—a set of beliefs and rituals—which were, he thought, fast dying out under the pressure of twentieth-century modernity.[74] For Evans, 'the old rural community was essentially the true remnant of a primitive society that has lasted since historic times'.[75] Evans believed that this ancient way of life had survived in a particularly unchanged form in East Anglia for a number of reasons. Firstly, there was its location, effectively a land apart from the rest of England, cut off by inaccessible fens to the west, marshes to the south, and the North Sea itself to the north and east. Secondly, there was the soil and climate: 'The whole region has been more than once covered by the sea', and its mild climate and rich, chalky clay made for excellent arable farmland.[76] Its unique and isolated character gave East Anglia a particularly vivid folk culture, with a notably strong emphasis on ritual and magic. When in 2010 the film writer Rob Lewis wrote an influential early account of the resurgence of British rural horror cinema in the 60s and 70s, he borrowed his title from Evans's landmark 1966 study of East Anglian folk practices, *The Pattern Under the Plough*.[77]

Suffolk is rich with folkloric beliefs and supernatural traditions. In 1891, the folklorist Margaret Helen James, MRJ's cousin (she was the sister of the librarian, Minnie), published a compilation of local folklore, *Bogie Tales of East Anglia*. (Many years later, Margaret Helen compiled the index to MRJ's East Anglian antiquarian guidebook, *Suffolk and Norfolk*.) Many of M. H. James's East Anglian supernatural tales are located around Aldeburgh. To the north of the town, near the station, there lies a salt marsh, a mere, and a pine wood, set amongst sand dunes. The 'presiding bogie' of this landscape is a 'Hell Hound': 'a large black dog with fiery eyes, and a fierce appearance.'[78] This is Black Shuck, the particular East Anglian representative of a widespread folkloric phenomenon of supernatural black dogs, portents of death ('Shuck' is derived from the Old English *scucca*, 'devil').[79] In folklore and legend and superstition, dogs are often understood as liminal beings, mediators between two worlds: they guard or patrol the boundary between the material and the spirit world, this world and the next; they have a foot in both worlds.[80]

The East Anglian coast, Margaret Helen James writes

> was frequently ravaged by the Danes and other Northern pirate warriors. Many of these invaders were buried in mounds, or tumuli, which are to be found in every part, almost, of East Anglia; and in these mounds curious treasures have occasionally been found of armour, drinking vessels, and rings. These 'finds' have justified the legends of hidden treasure, presided over by animal spirits.[81]

(In April 1917, as we shall see in Chapter 10, Paxton, an over-curious archaeologist, excavated one of these burial mounds, a barrow hidden amongst those dunes and pine-trees to the north of Aldeburgh, not far from the station, and uncovered an ancient relic, an Anglo-Saxon crown. As to what happened next—well, he had been warned. . .)

Great Livermere was, by repute, the home of its own phantom dog, who haunted the Breck road towards Ampton, on the other side of the mere.[82] *Laefor-mere* is Old English for 'the lake where the rushes grow'.[83] From childhood, MRJ invested the mere itself with an uncanny, supernatural quality. There is some sense of this in a poem he wrote for his sister Grace in 1888:

> All through the rushes, and in the bushes
> Odd creatures slip in the dark
> And dusky owls with feathery cowls
> Go sweeping about the park....
>
> You heard a foot pass, it trailed over the grass
> You shivered, it came so near
> And was it the head of a man long dead
> That raised itself out of the mere?[84]

Even as an adult, he could be frightened by the stories of ghosts in nearby Honington Wood: 'I am very interested in the Honington Wood story', he wrote to his parents. 'These things always give me an impression of truth. I should be very unwilling to spend a night there, & heaven send I may not have to walk that way at six o'clock in November.'[85] The names of the local families whose graves people the Livermere churchyard—the Mothersoles, the Agers, the Worbys—found their way into his own ghost stories.

In 1914, a few years after Herbert's death, the Rev. Henry Dobrée assumed the living of Livermere (the Dobrées were a Guernsey family closely connected to Lord and Lady de Saumarez). Beryl Dyson, a lifelong Great Livermere resident and local folklorist, corresponded with the Rev. Dobrée's daughters, who told her that

> after a room that was once used as a nursery in the Rectory was made into a guest bedroom, guests using the room experienced most horrific dreams and nightmares and would not sleep in the room again. The two ladies could not remember exact details of the dreams, but, with great reserve, mentioned happenings appertaining to the slave trade. Consequently, that room was not used.[86]

Great Livermere rectory, then, according to at least some of its residents, was haunted by 'happenings appertaining to the slave trade'. In 'A Vignette', MRJ recalls how, as a child, he was haunted by the Rectory: 'I began to be visited by dreams which I would much rather not have had—which, in fact, I came to dread acutely; and the point round which they centred was the Plantation gate.'[87] As an old, dying man, was MRJ unconsciously conflating the plantation of Great Livermere with the plantations of Jamaica, which he certainly knew about? He was only one generation away from the slave-trade. But, as with many other difficult things in his life, he was mostly completely silent about it. Was MRJ troubled by his family's history in the slave-trade? There's no evidence that he was—except insofar as the ghost stories themselves might be said to show glimpses of a very troubled sensibility somewhere beneath his placid facade.

As a child, MRJ *was* troubled by nightmares. In a paper he delivered as a student in 1884, to the Cambridge University Chit-Chat Club, he confessed:

> A thought has often crossed my mind with regard to the dreams of . . . childhood. . . . I think that children are more easily susceptible than others to [supernatural] visitations . . . I was long subject to vivid dreams of a class totally different from any which now visit me. They consisted chiefly in alarming appearances—processions or dances of hideous larvae, coming suddenly, when one was barely asleep—not led up to in any way: unusually clear and dreadfully alarming. Certainly this is all perfectly explicable on physiological grounds: heavy supper, indifferent digestion, and the like. Yet is it not possible; very likely if any of the foregoing conclusion be true; that certain mischievous spirits of limited power may take delight in tormenting those who are not sufficiently strong minded to resist them.[88]

Even as an adult, these dreams continued from time to time. He recorded one in a poem he wrote in 1927:

> Why do these boys torment me so?
> I never did them any harm.
> They come to me when I'm in bed
> By thousands in a swarm.

There is one boy among the lot
His name is Great Big Joe
He has two rows of fossil teeth
All in his bottom jaw.[89]

The influence of his father's Evangelical Christianity gave him, as an intelligent and imaginative child, terrifying recurring visions of the end of the world:

> There was a time in my childhood when I thought that some night as I lay in bed I should be suddenly roused by a great sound of a trumpet, that I should run to the window & look out and see the whole sky slit across and lit up with a glaring flame: and that the next moment I and everybody else in the house would be caught up into the air & made to stand with countless other people before a judge seated on a throne with great books open before him; and he would ask me questions out of what was written in those books—whether I had done this or that: & then I should be told to take my place either on the right hand or the left.[90]

Readers of MRJ's ghost stories will recognize many of these preoccupations: the 'hideous larvae', transforming into terrifying wasps, flies, or (worst of all) spiders; the supernatural children and scary boys; the eschatological worries; the sense of a remorseless, inevitable supernatural judgement and retribution. These preoccupations will form a large part of the book you are about to read. It is the story of a brilliant, troubled, intellect and imagination contained within—finding a home within—a series of establishment institutions; of the troubled depths concealed beneath an unflappably conservative surface. To understand MRJ, we need to understand the worlds within which he moved, the people with whom he lived his life, the places in which he found a congenial home, the ideas and obsessions which drove him. This is his story, but it is also, and inevitably, theirs.

2

Temple Grove, 1873

Written for Christmas 1906, when MRJ was forty-four years old and already Provost of King's, 'A School Story' takes him, and us, back to his childhood, over thirty years earlier. The story was first read to a group of friends on Christmas Eve, but seems to have been written with the students of King's College School in mind: MRJ read it to them on 28 December. It begins with a discussion of 'The Folklore of Private Schools'—their ghost stories—and with a description of a place:

> The school I mean was near London. It was established in a large and fairly old house—a great white building with very fine grounds about it; there were large cedars in the garden, as there are in so many of the older gardens in the Thames valley, and ancient elms in the three or four fields which we used for our games. I think probably it was quite an attractive place, but boys seldom allow that their schools possess any tolerable features.
>
> I came to the school in September, soon after the year 1870 . . .[1]

This was Temple Grove Preparatory School, a school troubled—according to one of its headmasters—by 'persistent stories of marauding ghosts in the evening'.[2] It was troubled by other things too.

'Pick from the shelf any memoir or biography of an eminent Victorian and the chances are that its early pages will reveal him as a small boy making the journey by stagecoach to a distant boarding school in the early nineteenth century', writes the historian of prep schools Vyvyen Brendon.[3] Not just the early nineteenth century: as time went on, trains and then cars deposited little Victorians and Edwardians, eminent and obscure, to boarding schools whose regimes were generally Spartan, and often brutal. And so it was that on a rainy day in September 1873, sobbing uncontrollably, on what was to be 'one of the most lachrymose days of my life', the eleven-year-old MRJ was dropped off at Temple Grove Preparatory School in East Sheen, then a verdant, rather aristocratic Surrey village, and now a part of Richmond-upon-

Thames in Southwest London. By the time he arrived there, it had about 130 pupils, making it, he recalled, 'an alarmingly big community for a small boy to be pitchforked into'.[4]

It was compulsory for the pupils to write home on Sundays. His earliest letters to his parents are full of information about his new environment—his lessons, his teachers, his classmates. The first term seems to have gone well—but then, returning to school after the Christmas holidays, he had a wobble, writing to his parents: 'I did not feel very nice after you were gone. Please, if you find time to write, tell me if I shall be fetched back this term.'[5] Things got worse, and he wrote to his mother on 24 January 1874:

> Dear Mamma. You can't think how I hate being here. I cry every night in bed, and if some one does not come to see me soon, I don't know what I shall do . . . I have only about two whom I can call my friends . . .
>
> I wish I was at Home
> I hate school[6]

His mother wrote back on 27 January:

> My darling old Mons,
>
> Cheer up, & look up! I felt very sad when I read your note, and wished I could give you a hug & a tickling! But, my darling, I trust the soreness of leaving home has already a little diminished and that it will yet do so. Every one says the second term always seems the worst for schoolboys, at first. We all think of you, & pray for you—& I am sure you do not forget to pray for yourself, darling. Try to be brave, & cheerful, & the very trying will do you good . . .
>
> Do not cry, but try to count up some of your mercies & comforts, & remember this is not a long term.[7]

Grace also chipped in with support—'I am sorry to hear that you do not like the school as well as you did last term, however I dare say you will like it better later on in the term'—and cheered her younger brother up with fantasies about the lives of their cats, who attend one another's weddings, serve each other dishes of mud, and plot to steal the family's beef pie.[8] Next week's letter home finds him putting a brave face on things: 'I like it better than I did.'[9]

Though there was to be the odd moment of bad behaviour and trouble, this is the last we hear from MRJ of any real homesickness or unhappiness at Temple Grove. But nevertheless it obviously stuck in his mind. A fragment of a story written around 1885 seems to confirm this. In the story, entitled 'The Beginning of Secular', a young boy, Michael Desent, is in 'a highly emotional frame of mind' at the prospect of starting school the following day:

> People who do not know much about it—who were never boys of twelve or were such stupid ones that they have forgotten it on purpose—such people will not believe how excruciatingly sentimental boys of that age are apt to become on certain occasions—notably when leaving home: but so it is, and it is not by any means a bad trait in their characters. However pleasant the school they are going back to, you very rarely find a normal boy with a happy home really anxious to rejoin his young friends. . .[10]

He got over his homesickness, as we might have expected. But there was one thing about Temple Grove that young MRJ never really got over, that he would carry with him for the rest of his life. The place was full of spiders. 'We find very large spiders about here, mostly in our basins', he wrote to his mother. 'There are also a whole lot of wasps, flies etc.'[11] Readers of the ghost stories will recognize these anxieties, played out in monstrous form. MRJ was a lifelong arachnophobe: 'He had a horror of spiders', his friend Gwendolen McBryde wrote, 'especially large ones, and of the lone spider which will unaccountably turn up in the bath.'[12] Spider-monsters of various kinds figure heavily in his fiction, particularly in his earlier stories. The demon of 'Canon Alberic's Scrap-book' is like 'one of the awful bird-catching spiders of South America translated into human form'—a hominid tarantula.[13] In 'The Ash-Tree', Mrs Mothersole carries out her supernatural vengeance through the agency of gigantic, 'veinous' spiders. (When MRJ first wrote this story, he called it simply 'The Spiders'.)[14] In 'The Tractate Middoth', the ghost of Dr Rant has 'eyes [which] were very deep-sunk; and over them, from the eyebrows to the cheek-bone, there were *cobwebs*—thick', and the untrustworthy Mr Eldred meets a horrible end when he is smothered by a swarm of spiders.[15] Infestations of flies, and their master, Beelzebub, Lord of Flies, feature memorably in both 'The Residence at Whitminster', and 'An Evening's Entertainment'. 'Mr. Humphreys and his Inheritance' climaxes with one of MRJ's most unforgettably repulsive apparitions:

> Nearer and nearer it came, and it was of a blackish-grey colour with more than one dark hole. It took shape as a face—a human face—a *burnt* human face: and with the odious writhings of a wasp creeping out of a rotten apple there clambered forth an appearance of a form, waving black arms prepared to clasp the head that was bending over them.[16]

* * *

Temple Grove was amongst the most venerable of English prep schools. 'It had the reputation for being the oldest private school in England', MRJ wrote; 'could be traced back to 1792, when a certain Dr Pinckney had it.'[17] Unusually for him, almost everything in this sentence is wrong. Temple Grove was actually founded in 1810 by William Pearson, a close friend of Prime Minister Spencer Perceval, in Sheen Grove, a large Jacobean Mansion surrounded by fourteen acres of grounds.[18] Formerly owned by Viscount Palmerston, Temple Grove was described by the celebrated musicologist Charles Burney (father of the novelist Frances Burney) as 'a prodigious great magnificent old-fashioned house'. It was fitted out as a school with no expense spared. A manifesto written by Pearson and his two assistants, both of whom in turn succeeded him as headmaster, assured Temple Grove's pupils that 'you will daily experience those advantages which distinguish the polished gentleman from the rustic clown'. In its early years, Temple Grove in fact had few rivals, and a high reputation as a school (in the words of Lady Charleville, whose friend's son was a pupil) 'where Greek is first taught, and many other things in the new fangl'd mode'. In what must have been a significant coup for the school, in the 1810s the Duke of Wellington sent both his sons to Temple Grove, following a positive report from Sir John Murray, his Chief of Staff during the Peninsular War, whose nephew was a pupil there. This began a relationship between Temple Grove and the Wellesley family which was to last right through the nineteenth century.[19]

Temple Grove was never cheap. By the time MRJ arrived, the fees were 100 guineas a year for 'all ordinary school charges with French, Drilling and Laundry'. On top of this, students were expected to pay for their books, plus a guinea a year for the doctor (a questionable investment, we shall see), and fifteen shillings to the church. German, music, and drawing lessons cost two guineas a year each, and carpentry one guinea. For the recently introduced optional extra of cold baths in the morning (particularly popular, apparently, amongst Scottish pupils), the charge was ten shillings a term.[20] This was a struggle for the James family, who were not (or no longer) rich. One of the great social and educational advantages of Temple Grove was that it had developed a superb record in educating scholarship students for the major public schools. Young MRJ was an academic prodigy, and this was just as well: an Eton scholarship was worth £100 a year, but even with this, his education would be a financial stretch for the family.

In 1828, at age six, MRJ's father had himself been sent to Temple Grove. The headmaster at the time was indeed that Rev. Dr J. H. Pinckney. He was, it seems, an obsequious social climber who was fond of a drink—and he was not the only Victorian private school headmaster with a reputation for sadism and brutality. Benjamin Disraeli's younger brother James was a pupil under him at Temple Grove; the future Prime Minister came to loathe 'that wretched

Pinckney', and offered a brief but damning portrait of the school in his 1844 novel *Coningsby*:

> [Coningsby] was sent to a fashionable school preparatory to Eton, where he found about two hundred youths of noble families and connections lodged in a magnificent villa, that had once been the retreat of a minister, superintended by a sycophantic Doctor of Divinity, already well beneficed, and not despairing of a bishopric by favouring the children of great nobles. The doctor's lady clothed in cashmeres, sometimes inquired after their health, and occasionally received a report as to their linen.[21]

The travel writer and religious freethinker Henry J. Coke, who went to Temple Grove in 1834 at age seven, was even more damning of Pinckney and his regime: 'We were half-starved, we were exceedingly dirty, we were systematically bullied, we were flogged and caned as though the master's pleasure was in inverse ratio to ours.'[22]

How unusual was this? And what treatment did the young MRJ receive at Temple Grove? His own account in *Eton and King's* is characteristically unforthcoming, but we can piece together a picture from his letters home, from the accounts of his contemporaries at the school, and from the many other accounts we have of nineteenth-century boarding school life.

* * *

To begin with, there were the beatings from the masters and the bullying from the pupils to which Henry Coke attests. Again, it sometimes seems that there is scarcely a memoir or a biography of a figure from the period that does *not* include some accounts of horrifying brutality. A. C. Benson, a lifelong friend and exact contemporary of MRJ, and our best source for the experience of life at Temple Grove, believed that in Victorian boarding schools 'obedience . . . was maintained by ceaseless flagellation, while the younger boys were, to use an ugly old phrase, remorselessly licked into shape by the upper boys'.[23] George Croke Rowden, Temple Grove's headmaster in the 1850s, was, according to one of his pupils, 'an austere, bad-tempered man and an awful bully . . . who turned round the heavy ring on his little finger, so that it raised a bump on your head when he boxed your ears', and who deployed the birch 'just for exercise'.[24]

Several theories have been put forward to explain the prevalence of repressive physical violence in Victorian boarding schools, none of which necessarily contradicts any of the others. There is no doubt, firstly, that these punitive regimes were *structural* to the school system. (Although there are significant differences, it does not do to separate preparatory schools and public schools too rigidly from one another; both were governed by the same ideology, and many of the issues I discuss here hold for Temple Grove at the beginning of MRJ's schooldays and, later, for Eton.) The Clarendon Commission report of 1864, which investigated English boarding schools, has a detailed chapter on the punishment regimes of the schools, and most particularly on the public school practice of allowing older boys to beat their younger schoolmates: 'This system appears to have taken root very early in English schools. Outlines of it are found in the Statutes framed for Winchester, the oldest of them, by William of Wykeham, and the traditional forms which are attached to it at that school would be enough to denote the antiquity of that practice.'[25] Furthermore, the heavy reliance on corporal punishment seems to have been, if not quite a uniquely then certainly a distinctively British educational characteristic, right the way through the twentieth century: Italy had never practised corporal punishment in schools; France outlawed it in 1881; in the US its use continued in primary, though not secondary schools into the 1960s.[26] The United Kingdom did not outlaw corporal punishment in all schools until 1998.

Although concerns about bullying were certainly common in pre- and post-Clarendon boarding schools, from a modern perspective it can be difficult to disentangle the licit violence administered by masters and prefects from the illicit violence of bullying. Both are part of the system. Boarding school ideology produced a culture of taboo and *omerta* which taught the boys, and their parents, never to report brutality to the authorities, however shocking.[27] H. E. Luxmoore, MRJ's beloved tutor at Eton, proclaimed: 'I constantly preach—not secretly but openly to all—that tale-bearing is inadmissible in schoolboy matters, and that even in cases of bullying, a boy should bear his knocks or defend himself or another.'[28] In that greatest of all documents of the nineteenth-century public school, *Tom Brown's Schooldays*, the captain of Rugby School announces to his fellow pupils that reporting incidents of violence or bullying to the masters was 'against public morality and the school tradition', and 'resolved that the practice must be stopped at once'. Any boy caught going to the masters 'should be thrashed publicly, and sent to Coventry'.[29]

The Clarendon Report was written in response to concerns about the conditions at Eton, in particular, and it led to the Public Schools Act of 1868, which legislated for the government regulation of seven prominent English boarding schools. The Commissioners worried that 'any [punishment] system of this kind should be exposed to some risks and open to some objections': most egregiously that 'it should be abused from defect of temper or judgement' by the 'imperious and tyrannical', and that in 'unfit hands, it should become an instrument of positive evil'.[30] There is ample testimony that this is indeed exactly what happened all too often, but the Commissioners finally came down strongly on the side of the status quo. Public school education, they asserted, was fundamentally 'an instrument for the training of character'.[31]

Physical punishment, then, is unquestionably a major component in the education of the Victorian ruling class—especially given the extraordinary limitations of the formal classroom curriculum, which sometimes seems as though it was deliberately designed as a kind of mind-narrowing anti-education from which, as a matter of policy, nothing could be learned. (Charles Darwin summed up his time at prep school thus: 'The school as a means of education for me was simply a blank.')[32] But to imagine the Victorian boarding school as an institution for the provision of education in any modern sense is to make a category mistake. Better, perhaps, to accept the account of the educational historian John Honey: 'learning to endure pain and know his place, the boy was tested and re-tested in a process of prolonged and constantly renewed attrition, by which a new social personality was formed.' This produced, in the words of the twentieth-century Wykehamist (Winchester College) novelist Nicholas Monsarrat, author of *The Cruel Sea*, 'a breed of almost compulsive conformists: brilliant yet safe men'.[33]

Institutional violence has been understood as one part of a Spartan regime designed to produce men with the appropriate levels of physical, emotional, and psychological toughness to thrive in the far-flung warzones and frontier conditions of the Victorian British Empire: hard and pitiless men who simply did not have the mental equipment to ask serious political and philosophical questions about the moral mission of that Empire.[34] William Hodson, previously a draconian Head Boy at Rugby, carried the methods he had learned there to a horrific conclusion during his service as a military officer in the Indian war of 1857, burning twenty-three sepoys alive in a building to which they had fled, and summarily executing the sons of the Mughal, who had surrendered to him at Humayun's Tomb in Delhi. He ordered them to strip, shot them himself, and threw their bodies in a cart. His fellow-officers seem to have been untroubled by this.[35] 'Prep school boys', a Temple Grove headmaster confirms, 'were great conformists.'[36]

Institutional violence has also been read as a component of the muscular Christianity that underpinned Victorian social morality, in which 'physical courage in the mêlée' was the most highly regarded social virtue.[37] And, in a line of argument we should take seriously, it has been read as an aspect of the

'English Vice', a sado-masochistic love of flogging into which aspects of Victorian sexual desire were channelled.[38] The English Vice was certainly a feature of the highest levels of Victorian society: the Old Etonian Lord Melbourne has been described as 'an obsessive flagellant', who told Queen Victoria that he did not think he had been flogged *enough* at school, since 'flogging had an amazing effect on him'; Gladstone, also an Old Etonian, recorded his own scourging and flagellation in his diary.[39]

All of these explanations no doubt hold for Temple Grove, a school which one of its headmasters called a 'Cradle of Empire', producing an entire establishment class of 'admirals, generals, statesmen, bishops, judges, and colonial administrators'.[40] One Temple Grove teacher had a personal motto permanently written on the blackboard: *Oderint dum metuant*. 'Let them hate so long as they fear.'[41]

Even the most sympathetic historians of boarding school life recognize that the first half of the nineteenth century was the 'nadir' of English education, in which discipline was enforced by 'ferocious' methods.[42] Henry Coke certainly thought that Dickens's Dotheboys Hall, presided over in *Nicholas Nickleby* by the archetypical sadistic headmaster, Wackford Squeers, was the 'photograph' of Temple Grove.[43] The man of letters Leigh Hunt, in school around 1800, was punched in the face and had his teeth knocked out by a teacher who was exasperated by his stammering.[44] On his first day in Westminster School in the late 1820s, the historian and novelist James Anthony Froude failed in his fagging duties of firelighting and coffee-making and 'was severely flogged by the older boys—the first of countless beatings he was to receive at their hands'.[45] Froude's brother Robert was beaten 'senseless' by the Classics master.[46] 'I have been woke many times by the hot points of cigars in my face', Froude recalled. Older boys set him on fire, 'to make me dance'.[47] In 1832, a particularly sadistic episode of bullying at Eton led to one boy, Rowland Williams, being 'completely scalped as with a tomahawk, the scalp hanging down over the neck and suspended only by a small piece of skin'.[48] In the same school, half a century later, the politician and diplomat Robert Cecil had his mouth burned with a lighted candle, and begged his parents to be taken away from 'this horrid place'.[49] In the 1890s, the novelist Hugh Walpole (later a close friend of Arthur Benson) was subjected to a variety of tortures by school bullies, including sticking pins and pen nibs in his genitals. He later confessed that he found the experience of the Great War less traumatic than boarding school (he served as a stretcher-bearer on the Russian Front, and was awarded the Cross of St. George for bravery).[50] Thackeray, Tennyson, Bulwer-Lytton, Lewis Carroll, Cardinal

Manning, Yeats, Kipling, A. A. Milne, and very many others had horrendous experiences of violence at school, either from teachers or fellow-pupils or both. Anthony Trollope seriously contemplated suicide at Westminster, where one of his bullies was his brother, who thrashed him every day.[51] Winston Churchill never forgave the savage beatings he got at St. George's, Ascot, at the hands of its headmaster, the Rev. Henry Sneyd-Kynnersley. Roger Fry, a few years older than Churchill, was convinced that Sneyd-Kynnersley was aroused by the flogging, which could be so uncontrolled as to leave his study splashed with blood and shit.[52] Algernon Charles Swinburne, that unusual case, looked back on his canings, administered by his Classics master, with great affection.[53] One account of prep school floggings in the 1890s records the Headmaster's ritual injunction: 'Be a man! TAKE DOWN YOUR BREECHES LIKE A MAN!'[54]

Boarding school could more generally be a world of brutal physical violence, in which, in the words of one historian, 'little short of death seems to have been taken much notice of, and not always that'.[55] Boys were expected, and even encouraged, to sort out their differences with their fists. Throughout the eighteenth and nineteenth centuries, boxing had become understood as a defining characteristic of a certain kind of English masculinity.[56] From Tom Jones to Sherlock Holmes, the English gentleman was handy with his fists. Bare knuckle fights could go on for hours, until one or both combatants was in no state to continue. This could end very badly. In 1825 at Eton, Francis Ashley, younger son of the Sixth Earl of Shaftesbury, was beaten to death in a fight with an older boy. Francis's older brother witnessed the fight but refused to intercede as he felt this would be unsporting (repeatedly asked to break up the fight, he instead urged his brother on with cries of 'one more round, one more, for the honour of the Ashleys'). No charges of any kind were brought against the participants or the school.[57] The Victorian public school world was, in the words of the enlightened educationalist Edward Thring, graduate of Eton and King's and Headmaster of Uppingham, 'a land of misrule . . . Rough and ready was the life we led; cruel at times the suffering and wrong'.[58]

* * *

By the time MRJ arrived in Temple Grove, it was run by the formidable and despotic Ottiwell Charles Waterfield—known to pupils as 'The Cow' (a jumbled version of his initials, OCW). Waterfield was by absolutely all accounts a phenomenally forceful personality, exercising an unforgettable influence on all his pupils, who responded to him in equal measures with awe, terror, and admiration. To modern eyes, he seems domineering, overbearing, megalomaniacal, sadistic, and emotionally unstable. In fact, he often seems like a monster. Even the Temple Grove Trust's own website describes him equivocally, as 'a great teacher and a great beater'.[59] He was certainly a great beater.

Like everyone else, MRJ was awestruck by the headmaster. 'Waterfield', he recalls, 'was Olympian both in appearance and manner, and could discharge his bolts with stunning force and unexpectedness'.[60] The son of a society barrister, O. C. Waterfield was a man of some intellectual distinction.[61] A Scholar of Eton and a graduate and Fellow of King's, he was for a time a teacher at Eton in the 1850s, but it was clear that his masterful personality would not allow him to be subservient to any external order for long. By the time we meet him in 1873, he is a forty-two-year-old married man, tall and bearded, with grizzled hair cut after the fashion of Charles Dickens. He wears a silk gown, walks with a limp, and carries with him a whiff of Havana cigars. He has unusually piercing eyes, and a wart on his nose.

This description of Waterfield I owe largely to Arthur Benson, who dedicates a whole chapter to the headmaster in his memoirs, and writes about him with terrible intensity.[62] In a manner very characteristic of Arthur's writing more generally, his description of Waterfield offers a startling disjunction between mimesis and diegesis, showing and telling. Arthur's editorial statements about Waterfield are impeccably respectful, entirely befitting a man who was an old friend of his father the Archbishop of Canterbury. He was 'really a great teacher, extremely clear and forcible, and it was from him that I first learnt it was possible to be intellectually interested' (in a similar vein, Arthur Benson's younger brother Fred, the novelist E. F. Benson, thought him 'the best private schoolmaster that ever lived').[63] But this official, diegetic version of Waterfield is powerfully countermanded by the practice of reading Arthur's memoir, which mimetically conjures up, through the eyes of a frightened child, an ogre.

Waterfield, Arthur writes, 'struck terror into our souls. I have never in my life been so afraid of a human being as I was of him.'[64] It should be noted that the Benson family grew up in the shadow of a patriarch who was notably domineering and critical, even by Victorian standards.[65] It should also be noted that, by the time Arthur writes these words, he is in his sixties, a successful and highly respected man of letters, and the Master of Magdalene College, Cambridge. But he is still clearly in awe of his former headmaster—and petrified of him: 'Waterfield . . . permeated and controlled the whole place in a very extraordinary manner, without effort or intervention, in an inflexible and inevitable way of which only natural rulers have the secret. . . . Waterfield was the one central and all-important *fact* of the place, pervading and dominating visibly and invisibly the school and all its concerns with an unaccountable sense of supremacy.'[66] MRJ called this 'a good picture' of Waterfield and Temple Grove.[67]

Far too much of an establishment figure to offer the kind of systematic criticism of Temple Grove that writers such as Dickens, Coke, or, later, George Orwell were to offer of the viciousness of the English private school system, Arthur's careful summation is: 'I am sure that Waterfield was in no sense of the word a cruel or heartless man.' 'But', he adds, 'he was too severe, and punished a good deal, believed in caning and flogging—I still shudder at the sound of his bunch of keys, when he unlocked a drawer in his writing table and pulled out a cane.'[68] At Temple Grove, Waterfield held the monopoly on institutional violence: 'No other master was allowed the cane', Arthur wrote.[69] When he stepped down in 1880, his successor, J. H. Edgar, who had been his deputy since 1863, wrote a pamphlet of guidelines for school staff which reiterated this: 'No Master is on any account permitted to strike or to wilfully hurt a boy.'[70] Only the Headmaster could do this.

Waterfield's weapon of choice was a cane made of rhinoceros hide: ordinary wooden canes had a habit of shattering due to the violence of his assault, leaving dazed pupils picking up splinters from the floor while Waterfield administered further strokes. When he got really angry, a former pupil recalled, the wart on his nose 'swelled up enormous'. Having finished the beating, he would embrace and kiss his victims—apparently to show that they were forgiven—and say, 'Well, that's all over, my boy.' He was known to burst into tears if he came to believe that he had punished a child unfairly.[71]

Institutional violence was all around him on a daily basis, but was MRJ ever beaten by Waterfield? We have no direct evidence that he was, but we do know that on occasion at Temple Grove he behaved in ways that could only have led to beatings. Most particularly, he was accused of bullying.

The details of this are very unclear. In November 1874—that is, towards the start of his second year at Temple Grove—Waterfield wrote to MRJ's father:

> There is a serious complaint of bullying against your boy.
>
> If you have any doubt of the fact—and I freely admit that had I heard the story without proofs I should entirely have disbelieved it—I should wish you to see the condition in which the sufferer is. Arms and legs are covered with bruises.[72]

What was this about? There are no surviving letters from Herbert James to his son about this, so we can only speculate. It's certainly the case that MRJ was much given, well into adulthood, to 'ragging' and other forms of physical horseplay. It's also certainly the case there were other occasions in which this got him into trouble with the Headmaster. At the very end of his time at Temple Grove, in July 1876, he wrote to his mother:

> I and 2 other fellows . . . humbugged J. Cartwell Esqre round the grounds this morning and tumbled him on the grass put grass in his face etc. and at length he commenced to shed tears more from rage than pain. In this plight he was seen by one of the masters and thus it came to the ears of O.C.W. We three went up of our own accord to tell him and he didn't mind much but spoke to us on the subject and I think the only consequence of the affair will be to make us feel rather silly in our own eyes and to think carefully in future how we carry on a bit of fun.[73]

Whether the November 1874 episode was innocent play gone wrong, or deliberate bullying, or a combination of both, it seems to have blown over quickly. In his next letter to his mother, MRJ is relieved to say that 'At present I am in most people's good books'; she replies, 'I am most thankful that the "bother", as you called it, is over. I was sure you were sorry for the anxiety it had caused.'[74] Before the end of term, he interrupts a letter to his father 'to have a wrestle in which I licked'.[75]

* * *

The 'thunderbolts' that MRJ recalled Waterfield delivering were not only physical. He was given to bursting into classes to spot-check the boys' Latin—and, in the words of William Brown, an older contemporary of MRJ at Temple Grove, 'Waterfield acted on the principle that if you did not know your lesson you were insulting him'.[76] One particularly browbeating occasion obviously seared itself into Arthur Benson's memory as he recalled how the headmaster 'would say to a dull boy palpitating with terror, and returning, in the extremity of despair, to the same lumpish answer, time after time, to Waterfield's brisk queries, "Don't bully me, sir—I'm not going to sit here half the morning to be bullied by you like this!"'[77] (Psychological projection is a real thing.) Lionel Byrne, a younger contemporary of MRJ at Temple Grove and Eton, and future Eton master, had a very similar story:

> Of course the masters varied in efficiency, but all were kept up to the mark by the knowledge that at any moment their class might be summoned to the Headmaster's study to have its lesson heard. These were occasions of terror, for not only was the Headmaster a formidable figure in himself, but he had a way of ejaculating as the victim shuffled and stammered, "Don't bully me, sir!", and at the same time rattling the keys of a drawer in his table where a long ebony ruler reposed, ready to leap forth and do dire execution on the sluggard.[78]

Byrne and his co-author E. L. Churchill, both Eton masters, drew heavily for their account of Temple Grove on MRJ's 'valuable reminiscences . . . of his preparatory school'.[79] It is entirely possible that this story about Waterfield comes from MRJ's own memory.

Waterfield was also rather unpleasant to his wife, Ada, whom Arthur Benson recalls as a remarkable woman. He was given to speaking impatiently, ironically, 'and even abruptly' to her in front of the pupils, and to offering trenchant public criticism of her behaviour, which she dismissed as 'only his way'. Ada Waterfield nevertheless clearly had a degree of fellow-feeling and empathy for the sufferings of Temple Grove's pupils. One evening at dinner, Waterfield caught one boy mixing mustard, salt, gravy, and beer in a glass. He summoned the boy to the front of the dining hall and commanded, 'Drink it up, sir!'. The boy stood there helpless and embarrassed, for as long as twenty minutes by one account, with the Headmaster and the whole school glaring at him in silence. Unable to bear it any longer, Mrs Waterfield grabbed the glass and drank it down herself in one go. And then, with her handkerchief to her mouth, she fled the room, and was violently sick in the passage outside.[80]

* * *

'Medical methods have advanced in sixty years, but it is hard not to believe that even for those days the treatment at this particular school was rough.'[81] Byrne and Churchill's account of healthcare and hygiene at Temple Grove is borne out by the reminiscences of others. Coke, we remember, complained about being 'exceedingly dirty'. He went on to elaborate:

> As to cleanliness, I never had a bath, never bathed (at the school) during the two years I was there. On Saturday nights, before bed, our feet were washed by the housemaids, in tubs round which half a dozen of us sat at a time. Woe to the late comers! for the water was never changed.[82]

Filth and malnutrition broke his health. Pale, and obviously seriously ill, he was removed by his parents from Temple Grove. It took six months' rest at home for his health to return.

The ordinarily unwell were confined to the Sick Room—Number 19, a cold, bare room on the top floor—where they were given birch twigs immersed in vinegar and brine to suck on. More serious cases were isolated in the Sick Cottage and purged with laxative Gregory's Powder, which one pupil remembered being 'utterly and completely loathsome'.[83] (Temple Grove's only surviving medical records from the nineteenth century relate to orders of Gregory's Powder.) When the entire football team came down with mumps, their sole treatment was bandages around their necks. Arthur Benson recalled a period of illness in the Sick Cottage as the happiest time he spent in Temple Grove.[84]

In MRJ's time, under Waterfield, Temple Grove was prone to theories of healthcare which could be frankly insane. When the Benson brothers contracted whooping cough, the treatment was fumigation in the local gas-works, where they stood amongst the refuse from the retorts, breathing in the mephitic fumes given off by smouldering offal. In another gesture of solidarity, Mrs Waterfield joined them in the gasworks, chatting to them and telling them stories to keep up their spirits while they all coughed and spluttered and retched. Such was the stink that she could never wear her dress again.[85]

Further cranky medical strictures in MRJ's time at Temple Grove forbade the drinking of water during the summer, except at mealtimes. The school's taps were turned off to enforce this. On hot days, the boys were parched, and devised elaborate methods to get a drink. These involved blowing residue water out of the brass lavatory taps and into a waiting tin can, or dropping a bottle on a string down a covered well. It came up very murky, and full of leeches and beetles, which were strained out before the boys enthusiastically drank the water.[86]

MRJ's only bout of serious illness at Temple Grove was in November 1875 when, along with most of the rest of his class, he caught measles. His back was covered in spots, and he complained to his mother about the boredom:

> I think I'd better come home as quick as possible, for I don't get on well here with nothing to read, do, say, or think about. My lips are very dry and sore and bleed at intervals . . . They put GREASE (ugh!) on my lips which doesn't do them any good whatever, and I believe they're sore from having no cold water to drink.[87]

The fever and boredom, however, produced a burst of literary creativity, and the letter goes on to give a surreal account of an interminable lesson given by a 'stupid dunderheaded idiot' at 'the Juvenile Church Missionary Society's meetings at Stockton-cum-Podgers', which MRJ follows with what seems to be his first-ever ghost story. As such, it's worth quoting at length:

> I . . . went homewards, calling in at the Black Bull on the way for I was rather thirsty. I asked for a bed and was told that they were all occupied but the one in the haunted room so I said I'll stop there. 'The ghost's very awful', said the landlord 'you'd better not sir.' 'I tell you I will', I said. So I took a light and my walking stick and went upstairs. The first thing I did was to spoil the walls by making holes in them with my walking stick so as to let the ghosts out if they did get in: and if the ghosts had been Freemasons they would have got out the best way they could. Well, and they *were* Freemasons and now I'll tell you what they did. The moment I heard them coming I knew they were Freemasons so I got under the bed and hid there. And I could see out very nicely. Well, so the Freemasons set the doorkeepers at the door to look if there was any one coming, so then they took off their jackets and waistcoats and togging and they made the Demons light a fire in the middle

> of the room and they danced around it. Suddenly one of them turned round and saw me!!!!!! The tortures I underwent that night would have undermined Hector's constitution. Imagine me in the morning after having undergone a series of treatment from Freemasons!!!!! Well, now, after having suffered all those tortures, while in my arm chair meditating, who should come in but my old friend, the Archbishop of Canterbury. He looked terribly worn out, poor fellow! and he sat down with a sigh and said I can't shake hands all the servants here have [all gone] away and I spilt some whitewash over my gown and I couldn't go to dinner like that and I'd lost the clothesbrush so I took the blacking and my hair-brush and I've been blacking my gown and my hands too: and then I forgot I'd done it with the hair brush and I brushed my hair just before I came to see you and it's very uncomfortable. So I said Well my dear Archbishop I should have said it *was* slightly uncomfortable to have a lot of boot-blacking on one's hair. he said 'It is. But that isn't all. I have been meditating on an epic poem on The Building of Canterbury Cathedral, in 12 books price 3s. 6d!'

Many of the regular features of MRJ's ghost stories can be found here, in embryo form. There's the ecclesiastical history, of course, and the arcane supernaturalism (the Freemason ghosts). But most strikingly of all is the setup of the solitary traveller spending a night at a haunted inn, a classic Jamesian trope which recurs in many of his best stories, from 'Canon Alberic's Scrap-Book' to 'Number 13' to 'Oh, Whistle, and I'll Come to You, My Lad' to 'Rats'.

* * *

We have a very good sense of what the school day was like at Temple Grove across the nineteenth century. Here is Temple Grove's daily timetable, as MRJ would have experienced it:

6.30	Get up
7.0	Get boots . . .
7.15-8.30	Work
8.30	Prayers and breakfast
9.30-10.45	Work
[10.45]	Drill
11.15	Work
12.30	Play
1.0	Dinner . . .
4.0-6.0	Work
6.0	Tea . . .
7.0-8.0	Work
8.0	Prayers
8.30	Bed

Before bed, the boys had supper, 'a very simple snack'.[88]

The boys were largely housed in dorms in the main building, each supervised by a matron. The dorms were large rooms 'cut up', as one pupil recalled, 'into rows of horsebox-like bunks.'[89] After lights out, it was absolutely forbidden to leave one's cubicle, though of course that didn't stop the boys. Fred Benson wrote of 'going on tiptoe into the next dormitory, and, after waking up my special friend, sitting on his bed, propped up with pillows and talking in whispers till there came the sound of the dressing-bell, which portended the entrance of matron'.[90] Because the size of the school had grown since its establishment, new accommodation had to be found for the extra boarders. In 1871, Waterfield leased Wedderlie, a house ten minutes' walk from Temple Grove, as an extra accommodation block. Every morning and evening, the boarders would process from Wedderlie to Temple Grove and back again in a convoy, to protect against attacks from the local village children.

Perhaps unsurprisingly, former pupils had a lot to say about the food—which Arthur Benson thought 'wholesome and good, but hardly adequate, according to modern ideas'.[91] Others disagreed as to the wholesomeness, though not about the adequacy of the portions. One former pupil, Norman Macleod, knew that 'it was not good for young boys to be quite hungry as we were'. Another fostered a particular hatred for the sausages: 'it was a point of honour not to eat a single mouthful of this garbage.'[92] The contents of food parcels from home—ham or turkey or tongue or jam—were shared out amongst the dorm. On one such occasion, MRJ wrote to his sister to inform her that a pig's head and a chicken had been smuggled into the dorm at night: 'We had a feast but some of the tongue was left. Accordingly some fellows went over to our schoolroom where we were not allowed on Sunday and disposed of the rest. I wasn't there.'[93]

Henry Coke is adamant that in Pinckney's time the Temple Grove school day began 'with two large spoonfuls of Sulphur and treacle', administered as an appetite-suppressant.[94] This is a detail which Coke quite consciously shares with *Nicholas Nickleby*, where Mrs Squeers ladles out the nauseating stuff every morning, but that does not mean he's making it up—brimstone and treacle was widely used for various medicinal purposes. Eton had its own recipe, dating from the seventeenth century, and used as a painkiller 'to Coore the Eche' (to cure the ache), whose ingredients included 'A hanfull of wormwood' and 'A pound of Lard'.[95] The popular Victorian household manual *The Dictionary of Daily Wants*, first published in 1859, recommends brimstone and treacle as an 'excellent and efficacious' purgative for children.[96]

Thankfully, this practice seems to have subsided by the time MRJ was at Temple Grove. Before the formal schoolday started at 7.30, he and his contemporaries were each instead given a Captain's Biscuit. This was a hardtack biscuit, a notoriously molar-destroying cracker made of wheatflour, salt, and water, and long a staple of military campaigns on account of its durability (it was as indestructible as it was inedible—though also infamously prone to insect infestation). The Temple Grove Captain's Biscuits were five inches in diameter and three-quarters of an inch thick, and rock hard—and so tended to be used for currency as much as food. Six Captain's Biscuits could get you three tea-sucks—sugar tubes used as straws in cups of tea.

At 7.15 a.m., the school would congregate in the large room for an hour's lessons before prayers and a breakfast of bread and butter with tea or coffee (in Coke's day it was unbuttered bread and watered-down milk, which the pupils called 'skyblue').[97] The main meal of the day was lunch—meat and a pudding, served with beer or porter. Coke, who was definitely not having a good time, swears that the pudding was served first, 'to save the butcher's bill', while one particularly awful but regularly served beef pudding was nicknamed 'resurrection-bolly' as it was believed to be 'composed of all the scraps left on . . . plates during the last week'.[98] Tea with bread and butter was at 6 p.m., followed by prayers and supper at eight. Unlike the Captain's Biscuits, supper biscuits were 'highly sought after'.[99]

Lionel Byrne's memories of lunch, a 'turbulent ceremony lasting nearly half an hour', were particularly intense, not to say downright disgusting:

> The bread was stale, the meat roughly cooked and still more roughly served, and the pudding often consisted of greasy suet with a little rhubarb or marmalade thrown in . . . The ordinary food was so uneatable that the boys brought in pieces of paper, wrapped up their dinner and hid it in the grounds or threw it down the drains except during one term when rats ate a large hole under one of the tables and waited in hordes for the food eagerly passed down to them. As boys had either to clear their plates or be punished, this simplified matters considerably.[100]

Both Byrne and Fred Benson recalled the punishment of the 'pig-table' to which Waterfield sentenced particularly unruly boys as a punishment for their 'swinish habits'.[101] This was a small serving-table in the middle of the room, at which the boys were made to stand and eat whatever they could grab from passing serving-maids.

These accounts of unappetizing (or even nauseating) food served in insanitary (or even rat-infested) conditions are quite characteristic of the boarding-school experience. J. A. Froude complained that at Westminster 'I was nearly starved', to the extent that his work suffered, which just made the beatings worse.[102] Thackeray vividly recalled the rotten food at his boarding school. College food seems to have been no improvement. When Arthur Gray, later Master of the College, went up to Jesus College, Cambridge in the 1870s, he encountered 'the bleeding bullock's hearts that were put before us twice a week . . . Frozen gravy and caterpillars supplied with the vegetables were principal constituents in our diet'.[103]

* * *

In MRJ's time, Temple Grove's 130 pupils were divided into six classes. Four of these (it had until recently been five) were taught simultaneously in the large schoolroom, while another was taught in 'a sort of passage'.[104] The sixth class was in a spotless building, with new lockers and furniture.

The teachers were a variable lot, and poorly paid. One or two were men of genuine ability, and even distinction. Sir Arthur Sullivan had begun his career as a music teacher in Temple Grove, and kept up his connections with the school. MRJ remembers him coming to hear the choir sing—though he was more interested in the cake, served to the choristers with 'a curious kind of pineapple jam', than he was in the music, or indeed in Sir Arthur.[105] A bearded, one-armed Irishman, Charles Geoghegan (known as 'Geege'), who had studied at Trinity College Dublin, was generally thought to be the school's best teacher, and remembered warmly as someone with a real understanding for the boys—and whose missing arm was the source of many rumours. MRJ's early letters home record various attempts to spell his name—'Ghegegan', 'Gaergen'.[106]

Others not so much. It was, in fact, notoriously difficult to get well-qualified teachers to work in preparatory schools. In an article entitled 'The Assistant Master, Past, Present and Future', which appeared in the first issue of *The Preparatory Schools Review* in 1895, W. T. Sutthery records the advice of his college tutor: 'Never have anything to do with a preparatory school if you want to get on.'[107] One educational historian describes prep schools as the refuge of 'gentlemanly failures'.[108] At Temple Grove, there were shared memories of one particularly comic and useless teacher, a bewhiskered writing master, Mr Prior, who lived in mortal terror of Waterfield and spent his time sharing his rich fantasy life with the boys: MRJ has memories of him recounting slaying a dragon at a wealthy uncle's castle in the North of England while taking the class on a school walk.[109] It is likely that MRJ summons up memories of Mr Geoghegan and Mr Prior in the person of the haunted teacher Mr Sampson in

'A School Story'—a bearded Irishman who 'had travelled a good deal, and had stories which amused us on our school walks'.[110]

With an acute eye for the preposterousness of authority, at the beginning of his second year MRJ wrote a vivid account of his teachers to his sister Grace:

> I will now tell you the masters, and what I think of them. Beginning with COW otherwise Mr. Waterfield (but when the boys speak of him, they always call him COW), Rawlins (don't know him) Gaergen who has one arm (pretty fair) Marshall (don't mind him), Bullock (a pig, a wretch) Luckman (don't know him well) Davy (nice) Prescott (pretty good) Prior (the writing master and a pig) Hásé (nice) (Boudin) the French master (fair), and I think that is all.[111]

William Bullock—the pig, the wretch—was certainly out of favour around this time. A letter to his parents, also from Autumn 1874, has a cartoon of a bearded man under which is written 'Waxy Molock alias Bullock'.[112] Lionel Byrne remembered him as 'horrid but efficient'.[113] J. H. Edgar, Waterfield's deputy and successor, also had a nickname, MRJ's letters home reveal, but 'If you were to tell Mr Edgar that we all call him Blacky, of course he would be dreadfully angry'.[114]

Temple Grove was, Disraeli reminds us, 'a school preparatory to Eton'. This is, of course, the original definition and purpose of a preparatory school—to *prepare* pupils for entry into one of the great public schools. Since 1904, this has been through the independent school Common Entrance examination system. In MRJ's day it was through an often arcane series of scholarship examinations, all of which had one thing in common: a heavy, if not total, reliance on the Classics as the benchmark of educational achievement. These were often marked by university dons (decades later, MRJ remembered his own examiners: Charles Old Goodford, Provost of Eton; the historian Sir Edward Creasy; and the mathematician Sir Philip Gregory—all were graduates of Eton and King's). Byrne and Churchill flatly state that boys of MRJ's generation went to prep school simply to learn Latin and Greek, 'all other subjects being of quite secondary importance'.[115] The modern historian of Temple Grove Simon Wright suggests that, even by Victorian standards, the school represented 'an extreme example of the worship of classics', alongside 'a neglect of mathematics' and an attitude to the arts 'which must be reckoned abysmal'.[116]

At the heart of the Temple Grove education was a Latin grammar, the *Principia Latina*, which boys were expected to learn by heart, and which Lionel Byrne believed was written by Waterfield himself.[117] The school's Latin curriculum included Cornelius Nepos, Caesar, and Virgil; its Greek curriculum began with the Eton anthology *Sertum* (from primary text to explanatory notes, this book does not contain *a single word* written in English), followed by Xenophon's *Anabasis* and Homer's *Odyssey*.[118] As a matter of fundamental principle, this was a vocationally useless education: the purpose of being taught the Classics in boarding school was not that they had any intrinsic educational or intellectual value, but because they symbolized the gentlemanly education.[119] The great Dr Thomas Arnold of Rugby considered science 'only fit for earning a livelihood, of no educational significance as a preparative for power'.[120]

This was certainly how the perennially frustrated Henry Coke viewed his Temple Grove education:

> Did we learn much at Temple Grove? Let others answer for themselves. Acquaintance with the classics was the staple of liberal education in those times. Temple Grove was the *atrium* to Eton, and gerund grinding was its *raison d'être*. Before I was nine years old I daresay I could repeat—parrot, that is—several hundred lines of the Æneid.[121]

Others did answer for themselves, and said the same kinds of things. Arthur Benson always did well at school, but 'never took the smallest interest or pleasure in the work itself'.[122] Five years younger than MRJ, the critic G. S. Street mostly recalled 'rendering Longfellow into Latin Elegaics'. The Clarendon Commission (made up entirely of men who had themselves had a Classical education) had reported that 'Natural Science . . . is practically excluded from the education of the higher classes in England', and, concerned that this put the nation at a particular disadvantage next to Germany, where science was an established part of the educational curriculum, recommended its introduction.[123] (This disadvantage would be a greater concern after the Franco-Prussian War of 1871, which made Germany Britain's major European rival.) This does not seem to have occurred in any wholesale way. The colonial administrator Sir Ronald Storrs wrote that, even as late as the 1890s when he was a pupil at Temple Grove, science was 'not only never taught: it was never mentioned'.[124]

MRJ was a spectacularly successful product of this education system—which accounts for both his preternatural intellectual abilities and his conspicuous intellectual weaknesses. In an obituary notice, the librarian Stephen Gaselee wrote of him: 'there has never been before, and probably there will never be again, a single man with the same accomplishment and combination of memory, palaeography, mediaeval learning, and artistic knowledge.'[125] But even his closest friends could find him infuriatingly anti-intellectual, his mind closed to philosophical thinking, to new developments—or even, some thought, to ideas themselves.

Yet even MRJ himself, better suited than almost anyone to thrive under such a curriculum, could find it frustrating. His memoir, *Eton and King's*, effectively begins with an account of what is obviously an existentially horrendous bollocking (that is the only word for it) he once got from 'the tremendous Waterfield': 'a dreadful explosion took place at breakfast, when it appeared that I had put the subject of the sentence into the ablative absolute.' He likens this to the dressing down given by his teacher to the protagonist of Thackeray's *Pendennis*: 'A boy who construes δε *and* instead of δε *but* is guilty not merely of folly, and ignorance, and dullness inconceivable but of crime, of deadly crime, of filial ingratitude, which I tremble to contemplate.'[126]

Temple Grove sent parents monthly reports on the progress of their sons. In MRJ's first one, from October 1873, he is placed first out of nine in his division. His Latin and Greek are both 'good' ('very good' is the highest category), while his performance in Mathematics (always by far his weakest subject), hovers on the border between 'poor' and 'bad'. His conduct, both in and out of school, is 'very good'. Waterfield comments on the report that 'I have no fault whatever to find with James other than he ought to know more in order to make an Eton scholar . . . He appears to be a thoroughly good boy.'[127] By the end of the year, he is winning the Class Prize and the French Prize. 'I am thoroughly satisfied with James', Waterfield writes. 'He works extremely well and I am doubting whether I shall not give him a double remove so as to ensure a longer preparation for the Eton examination next year.' His performance in Mathematics has improved, to 'tolerable' (which is as good as it ever got).[128]

But then something happened in February 1875, when it is reported that his Latin was only 'fair' and his Greek 'tolerable', placing him eighth out of eleven in his division: 'He is not working well', Waterfield writes '—does not show up his exercises—and makes endless excuses'.[129] This episode looms rather large in the James family correspondence for a while, though it is difficult to judge exactly what happened. It seems to have been a case of translation homework not submitted—MRJ was adamant that he had done the work, but mislaid it, and also claimed (justly, it seems) to be suffering from a sore throat. It was considered sufficiently serious for Waterfield to write personally to MRJ's father: 'No other boy in his division is behaving in the same way—and though this is a point on which schoolmasters are liable to err—I think that the other boys' faces plainly showed their disapproval.'[130] By the following week, Waterfield writes, the matter has been cleared up: 'He admitted the nature of his excuses . . . and he promises to work differently in future . . . You will I hope fully understand that I do not suppose him capable of direct untruth—though I do think he has allowed himself to press unsound excuses.'[131] On the same day, 5 March 1875, MRJ writes a letter home to his father which is full of defensiveness and wounded pride:

> Dear Papa. I don't want to talk about it, but the last thing I should like to do would be to cause you to write another letter of the same kind as the last, but I don't like to talk upon it.
>
> Mr. W. has told me he thinks it is all right now.[132]

The letter from his father which occasioned this response is lost—perhaps it was too painful to keep—though we do have Herbert's next letter:

> For this week has been one of much discomfort to us by reason of what we heard not only of the original misdoing, but of the after indifference. I do thank God very heartily that this is now over, and as heartily I pray that we may never have occasion to hear of anything like it in future.[133]

Much ado about nothing? To a modern sensibility, perhaps. But here, as in many of Herbert's letters, we see the anxieties of a Victorian father—painfully religiously earnest, a little socially marginal, and in danger of getting out of his depth financially, but desperate for his intellectually gifted son to do well at school. When the dust had settled, MRJ wrote again to his father:

> I will tell you about the making up [with Waterfield]. We again had verses with W. Being last I was alone when I showed mine up. They were good and he was pleased. He asked me whether I was sorry for the other copy of verses. I said I wd. do anything to prevent its happening again or words to that effect. He said he thought I must have been in a bad temper and that prevented my doing the verses. I said very likely I had been. Then we embraced and he said tho' he might have occasion to scold me he should always be able to trust me. Then he took the old bad copy of verses which he had kept and tore them up saying he knew he should have no occasion to keep them longer.
>
> And that is all.[134]

There appears to be a lot going on here.

However dramatic this episode may have seemed at the time for the James family, it soon blew over, and young MRJ was soon back up vying for the top of the class. His competitors for the top spot were two boys in particular, Edward Grey and Ernest Swen David Goldschmidt. His letters home are peppered with references to these boys: 'Grey and Goldschmidt are rather strong for me at present. However I have hopes', he wrote in Autumn 1876.[135] Grey, the future Viscount Grey of Fallodon, was to become the British Foreign Secretary at the outbreak of the First World War, and famously made the prophetic utterance

'The lamps are going out all over Europe. We shall not see them lit again in our life-time.'[136] Goldschmidt, whom MRJ remembered as 'a nice boy', was the son of the Swedish singing star Jenny Lind: 'One day she came to see him, and he presented me to her as his friend.'[137]

End-of-year exams in Classics were conducted and marked by external examiners, whose reports survive in the Temple Grove archive in the East Sussex Record Office in Brighton. In the 1874 exams, Goldschmidt is joint first in division IIβ and Grey is joint 3rd in IIβ; while MRJ is below them in IIIα, and places second. The following year, in the exams after the scare of March 1875, the examiner, Edward Woolley Bowling of St. John's College Cambridge, has MRJ 'decidedly first in my marks'. He is two marks ahead of Grey, and fourteen ahead of Goldschmidt. By the end of his final year, MRJ was miles ahead of anyone else, with 290 marks to Grey's next-placed 258. 'James's verses', the examiner (H. W. Paul of Corpus Christi Oxford) wrote, 'were remarkably good . . . James translated best into English'.[138] 'I am still top. I have licked Grey in exams', he wrote to his father.[139]

* * *

In his autobiography, Arthur Benson summoned up the 'sense of delicious escape' he felt on leaving Temple Grove, 'with its dull work, its frozen intercourse, its unappetizing meals':

> I had not any sentiment except that of unfeigned satisfaction. I never wanted to see the place, or its masters, or the boys again. I wanted to cast it all behind me, and forget it as soon as I could; and the last sight of the high-walled, sinister house, as we drove away, gave me a thrill of intense pleasure, as though one had left a land of bondage.[140]

In his diary, he was blunter: 'I hated the place . . . and said goodbye to it with joy.'[141]

Things were different for MRJ. In fact, though he may not have known it at the time, perhaps the most important lesson he learned at Temple Grove was the recognition that he was in his element inside institutions, and could flourish there. Unlike Coke or Benson, he was generally happy at prep school, and excelled both academically and socially. By the time he left Temple Grove in 1876, he was Captain of the School, and also captain of the Second XI cricket team. Like many bookish, scholarly schoolboys, he was fairly useless at cricket, and all sports: one of his letters home gives an account of a cricket match in which 'I made one run and was bowled. Our side [was] licked, of course, because I was there.'[142] 'I did it because I had to do it', he later said about sport:

'constantly, unwillingly, and badly.'[143] Furthermore, his sporting prowess, such as it was, was rather hampered by a tendency to lose his glasses in the long grass: sixty years later, Lionel Byrne could still recall the 'feel of those spectacles triumphantly extracted from the coarse dry grass' as he scrabbled around on his hands and knees to find them.[144] MRJ tended not to be paying much attention anyway: one of his classmates observed him reading a copy of Aristophanes during a game of cricket, chuckling away, oblivious to the match.[145] Herbert James, whose letters to Waterfield are frequent and full of anxieties, worried that his son was not shaping up to be a particularly muscular Christian: 'He has grown into such a *weed*.'[146]

While even MRJ may have chafed (very) occasionally against the formal curriculum, he nevertheless found Temple Grove an intellectually rewarding place. It was there that he really forged his lifetime's habit of voracious and highly idiosyncratic reading, and his fascination with cultural obscurities. This tendency had been apparent from a very young age. He once told his friend Gurney Lubbock that, at his first children's party, he had burst into tears, but 'was easily comforted by being taken to the library and left there'. When he was six years old and suffering from bronchitis, 'he expressed a longing to see a certain seventeenth-century Dutch Bible, which he had heard was in the possession of his father's friend, Bishop Ryle'. The Bible was sent to him, and Grace remembered him 'sitting up in bed, in a red dressing gown, poring happily over it'.[147]

In his lessons and lectures at Temple Grove, Waterfield would occasionally veer off topic and discourse on such *outré* matters as Ogham inscriptions in Brittany—exactly the kind of thing that captivated MRJ's imagination. In Temple Grove library, which he always remembered as 'a blessed place', he read the travel writer and codicologist Robert Curzon's *Visits to Monasteries in the Levant* (1849), 'which I believe first inspired me with a curiosity about manuscripts'.[148] (It was in fact the first book he ever borrowed from the school library, on 16 September 1873.)[149]

With its Orientalist traveller's tales of Albanian bandits, harem girls, the Nile in flood, and the deaths of four hundred pilgrims by suffocation in the Church of the Holy Sepulchre in Jerusalem (from which mass panic Curzon barely escapes with his life), this book is a riveting read, and certainly makes the life of a manuscript collector seem like one long, exciting adventure. Most significantly of all, Curzon's book contains a chapter on manuscripts and the supernatural which reads for all the world like an antiquarian ghost story. In Egypt, Curzon encounters a Coptic carpenter-magus, who tells him of a forbidden library long kept secret from Muslim invaders. The pair journey across the Plain of Thebes in search of the library:

> Skulls and bones were strewed on our path, and often at the mouths of tombs the night wind would raise up fragments of the bandages which the sacrilegious hand of the Frankish spoilers of the dead had torn from the bodies of the Egyptian mummies in search of the scarabæi, amulets, and ornaments which are found upon the breast of the deceased subjects of the Pharaohs.[150]

Secreted in a tomb in the midst of a necropolis is a collection of ancient Coptic manuscripts. The tomb was originally a temple dedicated to the worship of 'the gods of the infernal regions—Kneph, Khonso, and Osiris', and later used for worship by Coptic Christians, who 'painted the grim figures of St. George and various old frightful saints and hermits, whose uncouth forms would almost give one the idea of their having served for a system of idolatry much less refined than the worship of the ancient gods of the heathen, whose places they have usurped in these gigantic temples'.[151] Examining the manuscripts, Curzon becomes aware of a presence, a sense that they are not alone:

> 'No one knows of this tomb or of the holy manuscripts which it contains. Surely there can be nothing here to make a noise, for are we not here alone, a hundred feet under the earth, in a place where no one comes?—It is nothing: certainly it is nothing.' . . . The carpenter and I looked at one another: he turned pale—perhaps I did so too and we looked over our shoulders in a sort of anxious, nervous kind of way, expecting to see something—we did not know what.[152]

Readers of 'Canon Alberic's Scrap-book', whose demon-haunted manuscript is guarded by a sacristan with 'a curious furtive, or rather hunted and oppressed air . . . He was perpetually half glancing behind him', might feel they are on familiar territory.[153]

At Temple Grove, the young MRJ kept a record of his antiquarian reading 'in a plaid-covered notebook . . . which contains most of my precious hagiological research'.[154] He is eleven years old when he writes this. Increasingly, these matters preoccupy his letters home. At the end of his first year he writes to his father that 'I desire above all things to make an Archaeological research into the Antiquities of Suffolk'.[155] June 1875 finds him reading a book about manuscripts 'which did not tell me very much except about stichoi & also about titloi, Kephalaia, and Eusebian canons and Ammonian sections et cetera. It talked about spurious apocryphal works though not much.'[156] Already, at twelve, he is an accomplished codicologist.

Recognizing his interests, his Aunt Rachel sent him 'a relic from Abyssinia', and his uncle gave him a present of 'a silver coin of Vonones II, King of Parthia', which MRJ kept in a carved box, but lost one day on a half-holiday outing to Richmond.[157] Like much else from his Temple Grove days, this coin may have found itself imaginatively reconfigured in 'A School Story', where Mr Sampson wears a watch-fob made of 'a gold Byzantine coin . . . [with] an effigy of some absurd emperor on one side . . . Yes, I can see it now: he told me he had picked it up in Constantinople'.[158] It is this coin which identifies Mr Sampson's body when it is disinterred from an Irish well at the end of the story.

He was also beginning to develop a serious interest in the supernatural, an interest which, as it would throughout his life, grew directly out of his scholarly researches. 'I want to know what LEPRECHAUNES and CLURICAUNES are', he wrote to his father from Temple Grove. 'They are a kind of supernatural beings but that is all I know about them. I suppose they are something like kobolds . . . I have checked about 200 apocryphal works Old and New Tests . . . There used to be 72 O.T. apocryphal works. Of these I can only find 57.'[159]

MRJ's prodigious and weird erudition certainly made an impression on his schoolmates. Arthur Benson's clearest memory of his friend at Temple Grove was of 'his showing me an immense list of Roman saints, with mysterious symbols appended'.[160] Writing to MRJ in 1918 as he was returning to Eton, Lionel Byrne recalled how 'you stood towards many of us even then in the position of a philosopher, stored with infinite knowledge'.[161] In a long passage of memoirs at the end of his chapter on Temple Grove, MRJ himself summed up his time at the school as, in essence, laying the foundations for his future scholarly life:

> When I left Temple Grove for Eton, it was with a very miscellaneous stock of general information and plenty of hobbies in the bookish line; I collected martyrdoms of Saints—the more atrocious the better—and Biblical legends, and by gifts of friends and purchase had accumulated a number of old classics, such as Aelian. A happy chance threw some second-hand book catalogues—of David Nutt and Elijah Johnson—in my way, and from them I learnt names of obscure authors, all of whom it was my ambition—for no definite reason—to read. At this time, in fact, all antique knowledge seemed immensely desirable; and so did what I called Archaeology, which meant exploring every accessible church in the holidays and writing notes on everything I saw. It all sounds dreadfully priggish, and I have no doubt my Divinity papers at Temple Grove and my Sunday Questions at Eton were a sad blend of ignorance and blobs of misplaced erudition; but to me it was all fresh and delightful. Nothing could be more inspiring than to discover that St. Livinus had his tongue cut out and was beheaded, or that David's mother was called Nitzeneth.[162]

We have a copy, in fact, of MRJ's first ever Divinity paper at Temple Grove, since MRJ sent it home to his parents. It is full of interesting pointers towards the direction of his growing intellectual interests. The last two questions are 'How does Christ refute the accusation that He was casting out devils through Beelzebub?' and 'What does our Church say of the Books of the Apocrypha?'[163]

His letters home also confirm his interest in hagiographical martyrdoms, which provided the impulse for some pretty gruesome illustrations: one particularly ghoulish letter comes with 'splendid specimens of original art', including 'St. Frederick after death' (his severed head dripping blood), a 'Roman martyr having his eyes screwed out from behind', and 'An ancient and sagacious Abbot with one hand cut off'.[164]

As well as having an insatiable appetite for apocrypha and arcana, MRJ was also a lifelong reader of the classier end of popular fiction, from Dickens to Dorothy L. Sayers. Before going to Temple Grove, he was a devotee of Frederic Farrar's popular school stories, which he used as a template for understanding prep school. Arthur Benson reminded MRJ, he thought, of Power in Farrar's *St. Winifred's, or The World of School* (1862). There is an interesting spot of hero-worship in this analogy, perhaps unconsciously revelatory about the attitudes of the young schoolboy (though only four months older than MRJ, Benson was in the year above him). Power is one of the 'very best boys' in St. Winifred's school, 'most attractive', if somewhat cold and reserved, and marked by an 'unvarying success in all school competitions', who comes to the rescue of the protagonist, Walter Evson, by carrying him to the shore when Walter is caught unawares on a rock by the advancing tide.[165]

At Temple Grove, novel-reading was tolerated, but grudgingly, and with exceptions. A notice sent out to parents made this clear: 'Mr Waterfield particularly wishes that inferior novels should not be introduced into the school.'[166] *Jane Eyre* was confiscated from one boy. Both Dickens and Thackeray were forbidden, and all novels were totally banned on Sundays. This stricture is evoked in a genuinely shocking scene in *David Blaize*, Fred Benson's thinly fictionalized schoolboy novel, when a teacher is caught by the Head secretly reading De Maupassant on a Sunday. In front of a class, the Head tears 'this stinking—yes, sir, stinking—carrion' into pieces, stamps the pages into the ground, 'and then, with an indescribable ejaculation of disgust, threw the mutilated remains into the fireplace'.[167]

In the Temple Grove library, MRJ avoided Walter Scott (an author he came to admire greatly much later in life) but was a keen reader of both Charles Kingsley and his brother Henry. He was captivated by works of fantasy, from George Macdonald's classic *At the Back of the North Wind* to George Meredith's Orientalist *The Shaving of Shagpat: An Arabian Tale*. He enjoyed William Gilbert's nautical adventure *King George's Middy*, and the school stories of the prolific Ascott R. Hope, author of *Oudendale: A Story of Schoolboy Life*. At some point 'in the early seventies' he also first encountered the great Dublin master of the supernatural tale, Joseph Sheridan Le Fanu.[168] This was the beginning of a lifelong fascination. Purely as a writer of ghost stories, Le Fanu was MRJ's greatest influence, and the writer he came to think of as the great model for the genre. Of all writers of ghost stories, he wrote as late as 1931, 'Who do I think has best realized their possibilities? I have no hesitation in saying that it is Joseph Sheridan Le Fanu.'[169]

But his favourite writer as a prep school boy was R. M. Ballantyne, author of the Victorian children's classic *The Coral Island* and many others. Even late in life he wanted his Temple Grove classmate Orlebar minor to know 'that I have not forgotten, and doubt if I have forgiven, his losing my copy of *The Norsemen in the West*'. (That said, Beauchamp Orlando Chichele Orlebar is not a name one was likely to forget anyway.) He was particularly fond of Ballantyne's annual Christmas volume, and came to recognize its list of stock characters: 'A comic Irishman, a dear old lady, an irascible old gentleman, an adventurous boy (sometimes a charming girl), a skilled hunter (or engine-driver, or fireman, or sailor).'[170] It is tempting to speculate that this is where MRJ got his understanding of literary character from: certainly his malapropic servants and loquacious tradesmen are not significantly more sophisticated than this (in fiction, it is fair to say, his interests lay elsewhere).

On Sundays, Temple Grove's reading was confined to works of religious improvement, of which MRJ particularly enjoyed John Mason Neale's series of stories from church history for children, and found his *The Quay of the Dioscuri: A History of Nicene Times* 'really entrancing' (here, the child truly is father to the man). Works such as the Rev. William Adams's *Sacred Allegories*, or Bishop Samuel Wilberforce's collection of sermons *Agathos and Other Sunday Stories* (they are as exciting as they sound) were read aloud by masters in the big schoolroom. Best of all were the occasions when Waterfield himself read to the First Class in his drawing room:

> This we very much enjoyed; to see Waterfield in a milder light, to feel that he unbent to some extent, was highly interesting. Besides, he was a very good reader. Stanley's *Lectures on the Jewish Church*, Farrar's *Life of Christ* (in which I remember his sharply criticizing faults of taste) and the *Pilgrim's Progress* were the books I heard him read. Some of us who knew the text of *Pilgrim* were agog to see whether in the episode of Doubting Castle he would give us the author's words and say 'that lock went damnable hard'. When he came to the point, he checked slightly, and said 'desperate hard'.[171]

Crisis averted.

* * *

The annual Classical Examiners' reports ended with a list of the previous year's Temple Grove public school scholarships. Headmasters like Waterfield prized these, and prized Eton scholarships highest of all. They were always the first items on the list. From the very beginning—from, as we have seen, his first school report, just a month after he arrived at Temple Grove—MRJ was marked out as a boy with the potential to get one of these great treasures.

'I hope to leave this hole next term', MRJ wrote to Ber in 1875. 'I am going up for Eton and Charterhouse I believe.'[172] His first attempt at an Eton scholarship ended in one of his rare academic failures. He was placed eleventh: high enough to be accepted, but just not high enough for one of the ten scholarship places on offer. (Arthur Benson, a year above him, *did* get an Eton scholarship in 1875.) MRJ seems to have approached this 1875 examination fairly nonchalantly—'I think on the whole I should like Charterhouse better than Eton', he told his father.[173] This certainly seems to have had Waterfield worried: 'Your boy has gone in for his first paper. His work has shown ability, but he had been in a very careless mood, and he has made blunders against which I specifically warned him.' Worst of all, MRJ, the future Provost of both Eton and King's, 'used ablatives absolute as the subjects of sentences . . . The examiners are the Provosts of Eton and King's. This sort of thing will make their hair stand on end in horror.'[174]

Waterfield's next letter found him in a more philosophical mood, and determined that MRJ should try again next year: 'I am so accustomed to find that boys require a lesson which failure gives that I am not in the least disheartened . . . I am quite certain of your boy's powers.'[175] Herbert was not so sure: 'It seems to me that a good place at Eton may be a little beyond him', he wrote, and proposed trying him for Charterhouse, or for Haileybury, where his older brother Sydney had gone, and where he would no doubt get a scholarship with ease (he also consulted Sydney about the possibility of sending MRJ to Winchester or Repton).[176] Characteristically, there are a number of anxieties at play in this suggestion, and in the following exchange of letters, on both sides. For Herbert, there are social anxieties, but also financial ones: any scholarship is better than none, and he confesses that 'My chief reason to having him prepared for it [the Eton scholarship] was the financial one. But . . . even with scholarships, the expenses of Eton, Charterhouse and Haileybury amount to much the same viz. £50/ann.'[177] For Waterfield, it is the knowledge of what maintaining its record of scholarships to the very best public schools meant for Temple Grove's prestige. And so he wrote Herbert a long and detailed letter, patiently laying out the financial implications of the various scholarships: Haileybury offered two scholarships at £30, a further two at £20, with little or nothing by way of university scholarships to follow; Charterhouse offered ten scholarships of £90, with access to university scholarships; Eton offered ten scholarships of £100, with access to King's and similar scholarships in the future.[178]

This seems to have worked, and in July 1876, MRJ went to Eton once again to have a go at the scholarship exam. This time, it was a much more positive experience. He was shown round the school by Arthur Ryle, a family friend (the brother of Herbert James's godson) who would go on to be his fagmaster (that is to say, the sixth former for whom the younger boy acts as a fag, or servant). He sat his exam in the Lower School; on the wall in the passage he noticed his father's name, and the names of other relatives. The exam paper had questions on Diocletian and Justinian, to which he gave very full answers. 'I think the exam got on very well', he wrote.[179] He was right. On 21 July, Waterfield got the results. 'I need not say that the boy's success gives me great pleasure', he wrote in MRJ's last school report.[180] Waterfield kept a Name Book, with the names and addresses of all Temple Grove's boys, along with the date they arrived. Next to MRJ's details, he added proudly: 'Eton Scholarships. Second. July 1876.'[181]

A new chapter was about to begin in his life. Montague Rhodes James was going to Eton.

3

Eton, 1876

Henry Elford Luxmoore came to teach at Eton in 1864. The son of a Barnstaple vicar, he had himself, like many of his ancestors before him, been a pupil at the school (where he fagged for MRJ's future Vice-Provost at King's, Fred Whitting), before going on to Pembroke College, Oxford, where he graduated with Firsts in both the 'Mods' and 'Greats' examinations, the two parts of which traditionally comprised the Oxford *Literae Humaniores* (Classics) degree. On graduation, he returned immediately to work as an Assistant Master at Eton, where he was to remain until his death in 1926. He was a shy man, and a modest one, but intellectually serious and highly cultured, and very committed to the life of the school he loved. At Eton, he soon gained a reputation as a superb housemaster and Tutor, whose house pupils, it was said, 'regarded themselves as a race apart', albeit that they themselves, like their housemaster, were sometimes regarded as a little priggish.[1] The novelist Anthony Powell, who encountered Luxmoore at Eton in the early 1920s, certainly thought so: he remembered 'that sanctimonious old stick H. E. Luxmoore . . . always ready to improve the occasion with some piety'.[2]

A reputation for priggishness or sanctimony would not have bothered the Evangelical Rev. Herbert James, who, once MRJ's place at Eton was secure, contacted Luxmoore to ask him to be the boy's Tutor. 'I am able to receive your son & shall have great pleasure in doing so', he replied on 16 September. And so H. E. Luxmoore became MRJ's Tutor at Eton: this was the beginning of a lifelong friendship, one of the most important in both their lives. 'I, as a shrinking little Colleger', MRJ said in a 1921 address, 'became your pupil, and passed . . . through the three stages of unmitigated terror, tremulous awe and admiration, and intimate and life-long devotion, tempered by a disposition to criticise, which I firmly believe you encouraged'.[3] When, in 1929, MRJ wrote the preface to a posthumous edition of Luxmoore's correspondence, he still habitually referred to him as 'my tutor'.[4]

Over many years, MRJ and Luxmoore developed and reinforced one another's intense cultural conservatism, utterly loyal institutionalism, and propensity to distrust and resist all change: 'you and I are both early Victorians', MRJ once told Luxmoore; and, as the narrator remarks at the beginning of MRJ's story 'A Neighbour's Landmark': 'Remember if you please . . . that I am a Victorian by birth and education, and that the Victorian tree may not unreasonably be expected to bear Victorian fruit'.[5] As a young man, Luxmoore had connections with the Pre-Raphaelite movement, and with John Ruskin, of whom he remained a lifelong disciple. From Ruskin, Luxmoore learned a hostility to industrial modernity, a belief that 'happiness and goodness are not consistent with the ugly restlessness, the callous defacement, the joyless herding, the strident screaming, hooting and foulness of a mechanical age'.[6] In its obituary in 1926, the *Times* summed him up as 'a man of extraordinarily fine perceptions, an artist in life, and a scorner of materialism in all its forms'.[7] Both men, Luxmoore and MRJ, master and pupil, were Victorians, increasingly at sea in, and at odds with, the modern world.

But Luxmoore could only just squeeze the young boy in as his tutee because the school's Governing Body had recently agreed to relax the number of students a Tutor could accept in his Pupil Room, and he hoped that 'it may hereafter be a subject of congratulation that he entered Eton'.[8] A few days later, on his first day at Eton, MRJ, accompanied by his father, stepped into the drawing room of his Tutor for the first time. He had recently turned 14, and this was, he later recognized, 'one of the very few pivot days of my life'.[9] In an obituary of MRJ written for the *Eton College Chronicle*, Henry Kennett Marten, his Vice-Provost, wrote: 'From the day on which he first came to Eton in 1876, until his death he loved Eton with an undying love.'[10] 'The very heart of England was Eton', MRJ believed, and the school 'inspires [its] sons with a love that lasts out their lives'.[11]

This love was deep and immediate. 'Eton is simply heavenly in the Summer Half', he wrote to his father towards the end of his first year. 'Evenings are a terrestrial Paradise, especially in the Playing-Fields & at (Romney) Locks.'[12] But his 'undying love' could also have its sinister side. MRJ only wrote two ghost stories with Eton settings. Both are quite late, relatively slight, but rather revealing works.

'After Dark in the Playing Fields' (1924) is a phantasmagoric tale, in which MRJ's encounter with a talking owl reveals the grounds of Eton transformed from a 'terrestrial Paradise' into a supernatural landscape, with overtones of *A Midsummer Night's Dream*—'*Come not near our fairy queen*', the owl says—and of *The Merry Wives of Windsor*, in which Herne the Hunter and the fairy folk haunt nearby Windsor Great Forest. (These were his two favourite Shakespeare plays, which he often read aloud to friends.)[13] The story closes with MRJ confessing a new awareness of the uncanny reality underlying Eton:

> You see—no, you do not, but I see—such curious faces: and the people to whom they belong flit about so oddly, often at your elbow when you least expect it, and looking close into your face, as if they were searching for someone—who may be thankful, I think, if they do not find him. 'Where do they come from?' Why, some, I think, out of the water, and some out of the ground. They look like that. But I am sure it is best to take no notice of them, and not to touch them.[14]

His other Eton tale, 'Wailing Well', is a story whose grimness is belied by its initially jocular tone, and it plays with reality in a manner which verges on the sadistic. This is a literal campfire tale, which MRJ read to Eton Boy Scouts in Warbarrow, Dorset, on 27 July 1927. Stanley Judkins, a rebellious Eton schoolboy, ignores the warnings of an old shepherd, wanders away from the Scout Camp, and meets a horrible end at the hands of a group of skeletal figures, three women and a man. After 'awful screaming', his corpse is discovered hanging from a tree: 'There was not a drop of blood in the body.'[15] To add verisimilitude, MRJ peoples the story with actual Eton staff members—Kennett Marten, William Hope-Jones, A. C. Beasley Robinson, Henry Ley, Julian Lambart—and the Provost himself. In his obituary, Marten singles out 'Wailing Well' as a particularly 'gruesome' tale, and recalls that, after hearing it 'several boys had a somewhat disturbed night as the scene of the story was quite close to the Camp'.[16]

A couple of years earlier, in *Eton and King's*, MRJ confessed his own recurring Eton nightmare:

> Nowadays there is an interval of three or four minutes' silence on the part of the bell, during which Chapel fills: but there is still the quickened beat at the end—a dreadful sound to some wretched boy who finds himself on Barnes Pool Bridge or somewhere down Keate's Lane. It is still the subject of nightmares with me: I am at the further end of the College, looking feverishly for my surplice, and I hear the Bell say 'bang-bang-bang', and despair fills my breast.[17]

Ostensibly, this is an anxiety-dream about being late for Chapel—but the intensity of the language and the experience hints at something deeper and weirder.

* * *

The Eton to which MRJ went in 1876 was an ancient institution undergoing dramatic change. Built on 'a dreary swamp' much prone to flooding, the College was founded in 1440 by Henry VI, as 'The Kynge's College of Our Ladye of Eton besyde Wyndesore'.[18] The school was originally established to provide clerical training for the children of the middle class: Henry, a scholarly and devout man, wanted to build 'A College of sad priests'. His proposed statutes for Eton included provision for 25 'poor and indigent scholars'—a number later raised to seventy when the actual statutes were drawn up. These were the original Eton scholars, the Commensals or Collegers whose number MRJ joined more than four centuries later. The original statutes forbade students growing long hair or a beard, and keeping various beasts—and also practising heresy, simony, or magic.[19]

Henry's provision for scholars living on site marks the beginning of an important Etonian division, between the 'Collegers' on the one hand, and the 'Oppidans', who lived and boarded in the town, on the other. This division almost amounted to the simultaneous coexistence of two separate schools within the same institution, each with their unique histories and traditions—almost, in fact, it has been suggested, amounting, to 'two races apart'.[20] In 1871, the *Cornhill Magazine* published an Etonian story entitled 'Collegers v. Oppidans'.[21] Shane Leslie, the Irish diplomat and writer, who became friendly with MRJ in his later years, called his own Etonian *bildungsroman The Oppidan*.[22] A letter of 1877 has MRJ, in his first year at Eton, worrying that his classmate Godding 'goes about with oppidans'.[23] This suspicion was reciprocated. An Oppidan Eton contemporary, E. C. Chambers, wrote to MRJ in 1926:

> I have read your book [*Eton and King's*]. It held me. It emphasizes the extreme difference between Colleger & Oppidan. More than ever I felt the gap yawning. It is inevitable that Collegers—who to us meant so little—loom so large. . . . We have been at two such different schools that it is impossible we should have similar views.[24]

Because of its close connection with Henry VI, Eton faced a precarious future during the Wars of the Roses, sometimes in favour with the political mood of the day, sometimes not. But the school endured, and became an institution emphatically associated with royalty in the eighteenth century owing to the patronage of George III, who resided in nearby Windsor Castle and was often to be seen around the school grounds, characteristically greeting the boys with a cheery 'Well, well, my boy, when were you flogged last, eh?'[25]

The answer to George III's question was quite likely to be 'Very recently'. In the late seventeenth century, Headmaster John Rosewall resigned after flogging a boy to death and falling into a state of 'melancholy madness'. One of his successors, George Heath (Headmaster, 1792–1802), was bedridden for a week with exhaustion after flogging seventy boys in one go. The celebrated and notorious John Keate (Headmaster, 1809–34) had an addiction to flogging which can only be described as pathological. He proudly claimed that his basic philosophy was to believe that boys never told the truth, and once flogged eighty boys at a sitting while being pelted with eggs.[26] (I'm amazed he wasn't beaten to death by his own pupils.)

This is the world into which Herbert James arrived in 1830, at age eight, as a (very) young Etonian fresh out of Temple Grove: a world of barbaric anarchy, savage beatings, and boy republics.[27] In 1834, while Herbert was there, the Old Etonian E. S. Creasy wrote in the *Quarterly Journal of Education* that 'the inmates of a work-house or gaol are better fed and lodged than the Scholars of Eton'. Collegers, he asserted, had to undergo 'privations that might have broken down a cabin boy or would be thought inhuman if inflicted on a galley-slave'.[28] Herbert's experience of Eton in the 1830s, as recounted in Sydney's autobiography, is certainly startling:

> Life in College was incredibly rough, and food was most inadequate both in quality and quantity. Some ancient cronies were allowed into Hall to gather for their own consumption whatever scraps were left: they sometimes tried to snatch morsels from the tables during the meal, and my father once saw a boy drive his fork into a too-intrusive hand.[29]

This was not, it should be noted, any consequence of Eton's financial hardship, but rather a matter of policy and ideology. The school went out of its way to refuse to improve the food, which was served with beer which one former pupil described as 'vile, villainous and detestable'. Faced with starvation, the boys resorted to eating candlewax or raw turnips, or went foraging for nuts. The Long Chamber, where the Collegers slept, was infested with rats, which swarmed through the room after lights out. If they could catch them, the boys nailed rat-skins to the walls as trophies.[30]

Educationally, things weren't much better. Eton had used the same Latin textbook, the *Eton Latin Grammar*, for 300 years.[31] Charles Allix Wilkinson, a contemporary of Herbert's at Eton, begins his *Reminiscences of Eton* (1888) with a long jeremiad on the Eton education:

> I think it was simply disgraceful that, in return for all that was paid for us, and after many years of the curriculum of the time, we should—or might, as some did—come away without writing a respectable hand; without any knowledge of the etymology of our language, or, in simpler terms, without being able to spell; without knowing how to do a rule-of-three sum, without any acquaintance with common geography not only of the world, but not even of Great Britain, scarcely

> perhaps of England; without knowing whether the sun went round the earth, or the earth round the sun, or whether the moon was made of green cheese; without any knowledge of history except the stories they learnt at home in the nursery . . .[32]

Addressing a dinner of Old Etonians in 1916, General Herbert Plumer, who left Eton just as MRJ arrived in 1876, observed with rueful humour: 'We are often told that they taught us nothing at Eton. It may be so, *but I think they taught it very well*.'[33]

Eton began to teach Mathematics, very tentatively, in 1836, when Stephen Hawtrey, who had graduated Eleventh Wrangler (that is, in eleventh place amongst the first-class degree results) in the Cambridge Mathematical Tripos in 1832, was given permission to teach a little Maths as an extra, on the side, though outside regular school hours and with the strict permission of parents. (Until 1824 the Mathematical Tripos was Cambridge University's only degree. The Classical Tripos—that is, the degree based on the only subject taught at public school—was introduced initially only for those who had already taken the Mathematical Tripos, and for the sons of peers. In other words, the *only* subject taught at public school had nothing whatsoever to do with the *only* subject taught at university. How did the British ever achieve anything?) In 1851, Mathematics was incorporated into the regular work of the school, with an extra charge of four guineas a year. Hawtrey built the Rotunda, the circular building in which Mathematics was taught, out of his own funds, and was given permission to appoint six additional Mathematics Masters, although these initially had a lower standing (and salary) than the Classical Masters, akin to the Fencing or Drawing Masters. A small amount of Science and Modern Languages teaching was to follow, but nevertheless the curriculum remained overwhelmingly Classical. Even as late as the 1920s, some boys could spend as many as twenty out of twenty-three weekly periods studying Classics.[34]

Teaching conditions were basic, even during MRJ's time. In the Upper School, five divisions were taught in the same room. The boys sat on benches, with no facilities for writing.[35] John Maude, at Eton in the 1860s, recalled that at least six or seven of the other classrooms were 'disgracefully primitive and uncomfortable'; George Nugent-Bankes, a contemporary of MRJ's, came particularly to 'abominate' the mathematics classrooms: 'They are small, close, and in many cases let the rain in.'[36]

On a full day (Mondays, Wednesdays, and Fridays; Tuesdays, Thursdays, and Saturdays were half-holidays or shorter days), there were four formal lessons a day, at 7 or 7.30 a.m., 11 a.m., 3 p.m., and 5 p.m. Much of the rest of the day was spent in the Pupil Room, working with one's Tutor. This was where much of the real teaching was done, with the Tutor looking over the boys' written exercises individually, or construing Latin texts in small groups; and this largely explains the very close relationship between boys and their Tutors.[37] This could often grow, as it did with MRJ and Luxmoore, into a lasting friendship.

There was little doubt that Eton needed reform. Critical letters began to appear in the press from 1860, attacking Eton for its understaffing, its greedy Fellows, its incestuous over-reliance on graduates of King's College Cambridge. In 1861, the *Westminster Review* accused the school of 'self-love . . . moral childishness and snobbery': it was not preparing its pupils for the realities of the modern world.[38] But the school's very place at the heart of the establishment was precisely what could make reform difficult. Even modest proposals for change were often met with a volley of outraged correspondence to the *Times*. The Fellows were notorious for blocking any change they could. Edward Balston, whom MRJ considered 'rather a tragic figure' (and a very boring speaker), resigned the Headship of Eton rather than submit to the yoke of the 1868 Public Schools Act, while the Vice Provost, George Dupuis, threatened to repel the Clarendon Commissioners with dog whips if they set foot in Eton. In the face of public criticism of the excesses of corporal punishment, one commentator writes, 'Eton cheerfully flogged on'.[39]

When change did come to Eton, it came at the hands of a series of reforming Headmasters, beginning with James John Hornby (Headmaster, 1868–84) and his successor Edmond Warre (Headmaster, 1884–1905). Hornby began by reforming the curriculum, in ways which were modest but meaningful. On top of the three weekly periods already given over to Mathematics, for the Upper Division he assigned a further two to French, and, for some pupils, two more for Science; and he added further periods of 'Extra Study', outside the curriculum, for senior boys. Warre modified this further still, replacing Greek with German in the Upper School for those boys with no aptitude for Classics. In 1874, just before MRJ arrived, Hornby introduced the Higher School Certificate, for which assessment Classics carried 1260 marks, Mathematics 500, and Divinity and History 200 each. While boys could sit papers in Modern Languages and Science, these did not count towards the overall grade. The numbers of Masters doubled, from thirty-one in 1868 to sixty-one in 1905.[40]

Eton also embarked on a significant building programme. Hornby doubled the number of schoolrooms—including building some much-needed new Mathematics classrooms, which opened in 1877, just after MRJ arrived (not that he got much joy out of them). Sydney, who came to teach in Eton in 1879, and who liked Warre very much and admired 'the general uplifting of "tone"' which he brought to the school, was greatly struck by his 'grandiose building schemes': 'An old Etonian who had not visited the place for forty years would be simply thunderstruck by what he would see.'[41] Writing *in medias res*, Nugent-Bankes in 1877 observed the 'building mania' that was taking place: the College seemed to be covered in scaffolding.[42]

* * *

MRJ and his classmates were formally admitted into Eton by the Provost in 'a little ceremony conducted in the College Library'. (Years later, MRJ would conduct this ceremony himself, and wrote his own Latin greeting.) Only then was he allowed to wear his gown, and put on 'an entirely new costume'.[43] (Eton did not have a uniform, as such, but it did have a dress code, and only the older boys could wear the high collars known to them as 'stick ups'.) Rite of passage over, he was ready to begin a new life.

MRJ moved into a partitioned stall at the north-west corner of the once-notorious Eton Long Chamber, along with his new belongings: an armchair, a bureau (which Eton slang rendered as 'burry'), and, at his mother's insistence, a bath. Luckily for him, his stall, at the very top of the room, was next to the gaslight, kept lit all night, which meant that he could lie in bed reading long after the other boys were asleep. As he read, he listened to the boys talking in their sleep: 'It had an uncanny effect; one could never hear what they said, there was merely a curious oppressed babbling.'[44]

As a new boy, MRJ soon settled into his fagging duties. He was very fortunate in his fagmasters. The first was Arthur Ryle, the boy who had shown him round and looked after him when he came to sit the scholarship exam in July. Ryle was the son of Herbert's friend and Eton contemporary John Charles Ryle, the Evangelical Bishop of Liverpool, who was Sydney's godfather. After Arthur Ryle left Eton, MRJ fagged for Cecil Spring-Rice, the future diplomat who became British Ambassador to the US during the First World War. He was not ill-treated by either. Ryle, in particular, he remembered, was 'very kind and patient', and allowed him the use of his room to work in. Likewise, he told his parents, 'Spring-Rice is very well, and I like him very much'.[45] (Arthur Benson was hopelessly in love with Spring-Rice: 'I adored him at a distance when I was at Eton.')[46] MRJ thought himself a pretty useless fag: he couldn't cook anything, not even toast with any reliability, so his fagging duties amounted to little more than waking Ryle up, drawing his bath, making his tea, and running a few errands.[47] Nevertheless, a letter home notes, the threat of harsh treatment was never far off: 'Punishment with a siphon will be henceforth adopted in

Chamber, since the Sixth Form object to the previously established [practice] of punishment with a brush for a bad fire.'[48] The practice of beating with a siphon—a length of rubber hose generally used for filling a bath—seems to have been a characteristically Etonian punishment, and one which, in the opinion of one Eton memoirist, 'hurts considerably more than a caning'.[49] (Years later, J. M. Barrie wrote to MRJ informing him that 'I am interested to find that Jas Hook was a contemporary of yours at Eton'. The future pirate captain had a 'strange, agonising' time at the school, which no doubt explains a lot.)[50]

Very shortly after arriving at Eton, MRJ fell ill, and was off school for three weeks. He had suffered a 'bilious attack', a common Victorian illness which, according to the medical literature of the period, belonged 'to popular rather than scientific pathology', but was nevertheless nasty, characterized by 'fever, vomiting, headache, constipation, and perhaps some abdominal pain'.[51] He thought it may have been food poisoning, and blamed it on 'cold sausages from a tin'.[52] Unsurprisingly, MRJ found this 'displeasing, not to say horrid'; it left him feeling 'altogether limp and nondescript'. All he could do was read the copy of *Vanity Fair* which Ryle had lent him. 'I dare say the sausage illness threw you back', Grace commented.[53] Mary Emily, always acutely sensitive to illness, wrote, full of sympathy: 'Few things are more trying than what is termed a "bilious attack"—one feels so utterly unable to do anything but be physically miserable.'[54]

Mary Emily's letters to her youngest son from around this time are full of concerns about his health and wellbeing ('I hope you are mindful of your cod-liver oil').[55] There were good grounds for this, especially in his first year—the bilious attack laid him low for three weeks in October 1876; worse still, in March 1877 there was a minor outbreak of smallpox amongst the Oppidans, which had MRJ writing home to ask whether he'd already been vaccinated. Around this time, Mary Emily is particularly keen to make sure he bathes regularly, a subject to which she returns numerous times in her letters of 1876–7: 'I hope you are prudent & are enjoying your one bathe in the day & have learnt to *dry* yourself.'[56] She also worries that he is eating properly, and on 19 March goes to the Co-Op grocer's and places an order for what seems to be the first appearance in MRJ's Eton life of that public school classic, the food parcel:

1 – Tongue ('Picnic') in a tin
2 – Pots Potted Ham
2 – Tins bloater Paste
2 – Pots strawberry Jam
1 – Jam Apricot.[57]

All this sounds delicious compared to the tin of Cumberland Roast Chicken which his schoolmate Herbert Tatham once had, 'which defied all tin openers for a long time and was battered into a shapeless mess. When at last an opening was effected, a sigh of fetid air came from it, and the contents rose in a fountain through the aperture.'[58]

The first new acquaintance MRJ made at Eton was James Godding, a diminutive and vulnerable boy from Hayes, Middlesex, who slept in the next stall; Mrs Godding, visiting her son when MRJ was convalescing after his bilious attack, was kind enough to bring him some grapes. Ryle took to calling Godding 'Zacchaeus' on account of his tiny stature, 'only that he wouldn't have climbed up the tree'.[59] Godding was also hapless, or perhaps just odd: he set fire to his stall (inadvertently, MRJ thought), the flames consuming 'his shirts and an umbrella and several socks!!!!!!!'[60] His size and strangeness made Godding an obvious target for bullies. In the earliest surviving letter to his parents from Eton, written in February 1877, MRJ tells them that Godding 'has taken to weeping at the least thing now. I don't think it answers.' A little later, he starts getting exasperated: 'Godding is getting most awfully loathsome. It is quite impossible to protect him.' Fortunately, by the beginning of the next school year, MRJ is able to report that 'Godding gets on well and is a well-known character in Eton'.[61]

Godding and MRJ were both sufficiently well-known new boys, in fact, to make an appearance in lightly fictionalized form in Nugent-Bankes's *A Day of My Life; or, Every Day Experiences of Eton*, a novel by an older boy which was something of a bestseller when published in 1877. Godding is Dollard, the 'small-tug' who 'stands about three foot in his thickest boots' and gets 'considerably humbugged', while MRJ has a cameo as an anonymous 'very small boy with a very big head. He looks as if he thought a good deal.'[62] MRJ read the book, of course, as soon as it came out, and declared it 'Rather stupid altogether'; but by the time he came to write his memoirs in 1926, he had come to think of it as 'most truthful and excellent reading'.[63]

From the beginning, MRJ was very thick with Ion Thynne. His earliest surviving Eton letter to his parents informs them that 'Thynne has been swiped, or swished. Poor Thynne!' John Alexander Roger ('Ion') Thynne was the son of Lord Henry Thynne, a Tory MP who had served in Disraeli's government. After graduating with a 'Gentleman's Third' (the lowest class of honours degree) from New College, Oxford, Ion Thynne led a colourful life, which included a period sheep farming in South Africa. Theirs was a friendship which would get them both in trouble within a couple of years. But in their first year, the pair took long walks together: on one memorable sunny day in May they walked the four miles or so to Runnymede and climbed to the top of the Round Tower, from where they could see the Crystal Palace and the Chiltern Hundreds.[64]

This was, in fact, a small and in many ways a closed world. At Eton, MRJ met some of the people with whom he was to lead the rest of his life. Arthur Benson had gone there from Temple Grove a year ahead of him, of course, and it was at Eton that the pair were to become firm friends, 'on intimate terms'.[65] 'Lately', he wrote at the beginning of his third year, 'I have also improved the acquaintance of Benson, who is a very superior party. I like him extremely. His chief topic is the Collegiate Church and Ecclesiastical Constitutions generally.'[66] Arthur was much more interesting than MRJ makes him sound, and for decades afterwards they would be very close friends whose lives intersected at very many points. Many of our most revealing glimpses of MRJ are seen through Benson's eyes—he was an unusually acute observer, by turns sharply critical and warmly generous—who, as a member of a notably graphomaniac family, always wrote everything down.[67] Without being too allegorical or schematic, one of the reasons, as we will see again and again, why Arthur and MRJ were so close is because each seems to fill a lack in the other. Arthur was a successful and high-profile man of letters, but could at times be intensely jealous of MRJ's scholarly and institutional success. Arthur, as his diaries attest, was a man with far too much interiority; MRJ, it sometimes seems, was a man with no interior life at all.

St. Clair Donaldson, the son of a high-ranking colonial administrator, who arrived at Eton with MRJ in 1876, though as an Oppidan, was also to become one of his closest friends: St. Clair was later to call MRJ 'my first, and dearest, & finest friend'.[68] As with Benson, this was a friendship which deepened over their time at school and afterwards. Over the years, MRJ grew very close to the whole Donaldson family, and was a frequent visitor to Bère Court, their home in Pangbourne, Berkshire. Like many of MRJ's friends, St. Clair was an overachiever. After Eton and Trinity (where he gained Firsts in both the Classical Tripos in 1885, and in Theology in 1887), he went into the Anglican Church, and was enthroned as the Bishop of Brisbane in 1904; the following year, he became its inaugural Archbishop. He returned to England in 1921 to become Bishop of Salisbury.

There are others. Henry Babington Smith came to Eton from his family estate of Jordanhill, Renfrewshire, the year before MRJ. Universally known as 'HB', Babington Smith left Eton for a sensational career in Trinity (Firsts in both parts of the Classical Tripos) and the Civil Service, serving in India, South Africa, and Constantinople, before returning to England in 1906 to take charge of the Post Office. 'Never what you would call frolicsome, he was in youth and later one who never seemed externally to get any older', was how MRJ remembered him after his death in 1923, though he actually seems to have been quite an intrepid schoolboy.[69] MRJ recalled him dropping confiscated pistol cartridges, one by one, into the fire in the Headmaster's study, 'just behind the magisterial chair, with results very discomposing to us all, but most to the occupant'. When the pair went bat-hunting after dark in the College cloisters, only Babington Smith would brave climbing across the 'battlemented wall with nothing behind it'.[70]

Of all his Eton schoolfriends, MRJ thought, it was Harry Cust—like St. Clair, an Oppidan—who seemed most obviously destined for greatness, 'predestined to succeed in whatever he undertook', according to his classmate Hugh Macnaghten.[71] Cust was extremely good-looking—most everyone remarked on his intense, sapphire-blue eyes—and he seemed to excel at everything, from scholarship to sports to acting. 'I don't think there was *anyone* so entirely brilliant, on whom we laid our money so certainly as H. C.', Arthur Benson wrote. (Cust was another of Arthur's unrequited loves, about whom he wrote the passionate poem 'Utrumque Nostrum'—'Both of Us'.)[72] 'Nobody came nearer to the conception of the Admirable Crichton', MRJ wrote of Cust. 'Any degree of intimacy with him at Eton was an honour and a delight.'[73] Dazzlingly well-dressed, a brilliant conversationalist, and an orator of 'sparkling ability' according to his Eton contemporaries, Cust was also very vigorously and wide-rangingly heterosexual—extremely attractive, and attracted, to women.[74] In 1890 he was elected Conservative MP for Stamford, Lincolnshire, but resigned his seat five years later in a sex scandal; in 1900, he was re-elected as MP for Bermondsey. In between, he edited the *Pall Mall Gazette*, where he published Wells, Kipling, and others. Cust was also a minor poet of some note: at one point, his poem 'Non Nobis, Domine' was included in *The Oxford Book of English Verse*.

* * *

As far as it was possible to do so, MRJ lived his life in an exclusively male world. The institutions which gave his life shape and meaning were obviously all-male—and as he grew older, he used his growing institutional power to make sure that they stayed that way. His friendships with men were deep and often extremely loyal. But what was the nature of these friendships? This is the time to begin to talk about the complicated and obscure matter of MRJ's sexuality.

After all, his friends did. Arthur Benson's biographer, David Newsome, tells us that Arthur went on holidays during the First World War with his friends Frank Salter and Oliffe Richmond (a Classicist colleague of MRJ's at King's, and a gay man): they spent the evenings 'composing limericks and discussing Monty James's mysterious love life'.[75] 'I don't myself think that Monty is at all a marriageable man', Arthur wrote, in a powerfully resonant phrase which simultaneously reveals and conceals its meaning, as was Arthur's wont. Richmond actually thought he had twice been 'on the verge' of marriage (once with Sibyl Cropper, whom we shall meet later).[76] 'He likes beautiful graceful people', Arthur wrote in 1904, meaning men.[77] 'These things are mysteries', he concluded.[78] Anthony Powell, always a very well-connected observer, remarked: 'I myself have heard it suggested that James's (of course platonic) love affairs were in fact fascinating to watch.'[79] Interviewed in 2013, Adrian Carey, the son of MRJ's good friend Gordon Carey, told Mark Gatiss that he thought MRJ was drawn to Gordon, who came up to Cambridge as a scholar of Gonville and Caius in 1906, because of his good looks, and added: 'I remember my father saying of him long after his death, "I suppose he was what would nowadays be called a non-practising homosexual."'[80]

Nowadays, yes; but not then. At least, certainly not in MRJ's schooldays. For one thing, the word 'homosexual' would have had no meaning in 1880, because it did not exist—though it would soon gain some valency as a sexological, or even a pathological, category after the publication of Krafft-Ebing's *Psychopathia Sexualis* in 1886 (C. G. Chaddock's 1892 translation is the earliest recorded use of the English word 'homosexuality'), and especially in the wake of the Oscar Wilde trial in 1895.[81] Arthur Benson, whose life was characterized by a series of intensely passionate, sexually unrequited attachments, only used the newfangled word 'homosexual' (first used as an adjective in 1892, and as a noun in 1894) twice in the many volumes of his diary, and then only in the last year of his life, 1925.[82] Expressions of intimacy, and even of passion, between men clearly meant something different to a man of MRJ's generation than they would today, and understanding exactly what they meant is complex. Nevertheless, when, say, MRJ's friend and travelling companion Willie Bridgeman (the future Home Secretary, First Lord of the Admiralty, and Chairman of the BBC) writes in 1888, 'what day could be more appropriate for writing to you than this—Valentine's day'—or when his very close friend Walter Fletcher writes across various letters, 'I want to see you badly', 'I itch to see you again', 'I want *badly* to spend some hours with you'—we might fairly think that the world in which MRJ moved was a *queer* one, in which same-sex desire was able to be understood, expressed, but also contained within institutions.[83]

Nobody could argue that MRJ inhabited an environment unaware of same-sex relationships. And while there is no direct evidence of any sexual relationship between MRJ and, well, anybody, this is in part because we have so little direct evidence of *any* aspect of the emotional or interior life of this unusual man. For whole areas of MRJ's life, what we have are gaps, silences, absences. These are significant in themselves. MRJ was a celibate gay man whose desires were almost certainly unacknowledged and unarticulated, even to himself. He lived his life surrounded by many other gay men, some of whom were as open about their sexuality as an Edwardian could be, some very sexually active, and others (notably Arthur Benson) tormented by the nature of their desires. MRJ seems to have been none of these things.

For MRJ and others, their sexual identities were shaped by the institutions that had given form to their lives and personalities since adolescence. Same-sex relationships were a feature—some might say, a characteristic—of boarding-school life, between the boys themselves and, on occasion, between the staff and the boys. In fact, when MRJ entered Eton in 1876, the school had recently been rocked by a rather public series of sex scandals. Edward Lyttelton, the future Headmaster who had been a pupil at Eton a few years before MRJ (he arrived in 1868), recalled 'a hideous amount of vice' in the Eton of the 1870s.[84] William Johnson, an Eton contemporary of Herbert's who went on to be the most brilliant and influential Eton master of the mid-nineteenth century (he was Luxmoore's Tutor, and MRJ thought him 'a great Eton tutor'), certainly cultivated very intimate friendships with (and between) his pupils, and was dismissed by Hornby in 1872 for writing what has been euphemistically termed 'an indiscreet letter' to a boy, after which he relocated to Madeira and changed his name to William Cory.[85] Johnson's sacking was followed two years later by the dismissal of another high-profile Eton master, Oscar Browning, for intimate relations (they certainly shared a bed, 'spooning') with George Curzon, the future Viceroy of India. O.B., as he was generally known, was not universally liked—one colleague considered him 'very insubordinate and unscrupulous, playing with honesty and sailing very near the wind'—but he was very well-connected and notably sensationalist, and so, perhaps fearing too much scandal, Hornby actually fired him on a technicality, for having too many boys in his Pupil Room: 'I have not charged him with *immorality* is the ordinary sense of the word', Hornby insisted.[86] O.B. retreated to a Fellowship at King's, which drastically reduced his earnings, from a princely £3000 a year to a modest £300 a year, the basic salary of a King's Fellow.[87] At King's, he spent years irritating and exasperating MRJ, who hated him: 'That man, believe me, is the worst I know', he wrote in 1889, after witnessing a particularly egregious example of O.B.'s bad behaviour.[88]

Drawing on his many years' experience teaching at Eton, in 1906 Luxmoore wrote a pamphlet about preparing boys for Communion during 'the critical years of passage from childhood to adolescence', which is full of alarms about the need to control and direct burgeoning schoolboy sexuality.[89] The 'wild beast that lurks without', he believed, is always eager to crash through 'that natural hedge of modesty'; and 'the organs of sex . . . [are] so delicate that to rub, misuse, handle them so as to set up an inflammatory action may produce disastrous effects for life'.[90] This is pretty clearly an injunction against masturbation, but it soon takes Luxmoore onto familiar territory:

> Some sudden temptation, unsuspected, misunderstood, comes to the half-ignorant lad; the gap has been made by his own fault, and in a moment the irreparable harm is wrought. If it is not the beginning of the end, at least he can never again be what God intended him to be. . . . [C]ases of moral corruption are outside the pale, and must be, and ought to be reported, because they are *physical*, and spread like small-pox.[91]

It should be noted that not all commentators viewed public school same-sex desire with the same censoriousness: a long letter to the *Journal of Education* in March 1882, signed 'Olim Etonensis' ['Once an Etonian'], argued that adolescent homosexual practices were transient, and did no lasting harm, and counselled educationalists to 'let well alone'.[92] But most did. Victorian writers of schoolboy fiction were much given to stern pronouncements or horrified warnings about homosexuality, though these could be couched in terms so abstract as to elude ready understanding. *Tom Brown's Schooldays* makes direct reference to 'the small friend system', where older boys took up with younger, good-looking ones, and offers this ominous, if vague, warning:

> He was one of the miserable little pretty white-handed curly-headed boys, petted and pampered by some of the big fellows, who wrote their verses for them, taught them to drink and use bad language, and did everything they could to spoil them for everything in this world and the next.[93]

Eric; or Little by Little (1858), the best-known novel by MRJ's childhood favourite F. W. Farrar, dedicates two chapters to the dangers of 'the "taking-up" system . . . when a big fellow takes up a little one'. The second of the two chapters, meaningfully entitled 'Dead Flies', closes with a genuinely dire passage:

> Many and many a young Englishman has perished there! Many and many a happy English boy, the jewel of his mother's heart,—brave and beautiful and strong,—lies buried there. . . . May every schoolboy who reads this page be warned by the waving of their wasted hands, from that burning marle of passion, where they found nothing but shame and ruin, polluted affections, and an early grave.[94]

In *St. Winifred's*, MRJ's favourite Farrar novel, Walter Evson's friend Kenrick turns 'degenerate' when he seeks 'the adulation of younger boys', leading to 'ruined beauty' and 'the shame of the unclean'.[95] 'Books like *St. Winifred's* and *Tom Brown's Schooldays*', George Orwell—very much a product of the public school system—recognized, 'were heavy with homosexual feeling'.[96]

Headmasters were particularly keen on these kinds of warnings. Edward White Benson, Arthur and Fred's father, and erstwhile Headmaster of Wellington, was a leading light in the Church of England Purity Society, dedicated to stamping out sexual immorality. He tended to refer to homosexuality as 'the abominable'.[97] Before Arthur went off to Eton, he was given a lecture by his father 'to set me on my guard against impure temptation'. But, Arthur confessed, 'he spoke so guardedly that I had not the least idea what he was alluding to, having passed through my private school in complete and virginal innocence'.[98] In *David Blaize*, Fred's schoolboy hero, just about to leave the thinly disguised Temple Grove for a thinly disguised Marlborough, is warned by the Headmaster that 'there are worse things than stealing. Things than damn the soul, David.'[99] As Headmaster of Eton, Warre warned new boys in his opening address 'to keep clear of the evil thing, that which defiles, and shun the abomination in our midst. . . . Have none of it, don't touch it, stamp it out.'[100] Meanwhile, at Uppingham, Edward Thring warned boys that 'the poisonous breath of sin keeps tainting and corrupting all the freshness and purity of young life', after which 'the wretched victim finds an early grave, killed by his own foul passions'.[101]

MRJ himself only commented explicitly once, late in his life, on the dangers of desire and the temptations of the flesh, in a sermon he delivered to the boys at Eton in 1928. This is a very revealing utterance, which takes as its text the First Epistle of St. John, with whose author MRJ seems closely to identify: 'Well, he *was* old. . . .. And he had never lived in the gay world, though he had watched it, and was wise enough to gauge the kinds of things that went on in it.' In essence, he was talking about himself here. 'The gay world' is the world of bodily desires, and it is this which the boys of Eton must shun:

> Taking it so, I do not think you can deny that he is right when he says that uncontrolled indulgence of the appetites of the body & of the eye, & the smartness, the swagger . . . of life are not what God . . . has thought best for man, but what some men have though best for themselves. Not all men, for ever since we began emerging out of the state of beasts, there has been dawning before some of our race the conviction that it is not best for us to do all we can do. . . . Indulge every desire & every appetite that comes to you and you become a beast again.[102]

* * *

For the most part, MRJ unsurprisingly sailed through his school work in his first year at Eton: 'Everything seems to go well in College, where he is both happy & quiet', Luxmoore wrote reassuringly to Herbert.[103] His Division Master was Frank Rawlins (later to become a close friend of Sydney's), 'a good beak to be up to. I like him.'[104] Early in 1877, he was pleased to be able to tell his parents, 'I am at present, and have been for some time, first in school-work'.[105] He was. Rawlins's first school report, dated March 1877, is glowing:

> James was away for three weeks at the beginning of the School time, but soon took his place as 1st in the Division, & has kept it since. The work is obviously too easy for him, but he is not careless. He is always ready with his answers in school. His one fault is unpunctuality. I am much pleased on the whole. Place (by average), 1st of 36.[106]

Rawlins's report makes reference to MRJ's illness of Autumn 1876, as a result of which he found himself, as he recalled, 'detached from the rest of my Election' (that is, his cohort of 1876), and temporarily taught by Walter Durnford. In later years, MRJ and Durnford came to know each other well and worked closely together (Durnford was in fact his successor as Provost of King's), but viewed through twelve-year-old eyes Durnford was a fearsome character, 'the possessor of an extensive and richly coloured vocabulary: and when he did not like a thing, the division were left in no doubt.'[107] But the young scholar flourished at Eton. Rawlins thought him 'the best and most promising boy I have known', and his next report, from H. A. Chignell, is downright incandescent:

> Your boy goes on a good course. It is long since I have had a boy whose very presence gives me so much satisfaction & pleasure. . . . His tutor never ceases to say kind things about him. I think we both envy you such a son.[108]

As Rawlins intimated, punctuality was always a problem for MRJ. It is at the root of his recurring Eton nightmare about being late for Chapel. In part, this is because his tendency to work late into the night meant that he was very bad at getting up in the morning. This was the case throughout his life: his friend Ronny Norman once signed off a letter, 'I hope this will find you out of bed (it hasn't a chance if it comes before 11AM)'.[109] As a schoolboy, he was often punished for this, but regarded writing lines as 'a small price to pay for the pleasure of saying to oneself on a particularly dark and cold morning, "Well I'm blowed if I'll go into school", and turning over in bed.'[110] These complaints recur throughout his school reports: R. F. Rumsey, his Mathematics teacher (with whom he had a difficult relationship), thought him 'Unpunctual or Irregular'; in 1877 he was placed in Class III for Punctuality, with a grade lower than 'Tolerable'; the following year, G. E. Marindin commented, 'His only *fault has been unpunctuality*.'[111] 'Irregularity in shewing up' and 'Staying out' were two of Edmond Warre's criticisms when he came to write his own school report for MRJ in 1879.

The third was an old favourite—a recurring lament with which anyone who has ever studied MRJ's letters and manuscripts will strongly sympathize: 'Execrable handwriting.'[112] MRJ was perversely proud of his illegible handwriting, and certainly did nothing to improve it, in the face of repeated warnings in report after report that this was potentially suicidal for someone who lived and died by written examinations: 'The great question of calligraphy is not to be forgotten', Luxmoore warned in a letter to Herbert: 'it is quite certain that this will be a very great hindrance to success in any exam in a boy whose future must depend on examn. [examination] to force himself to this preliminary.'[113] Indeed, Luxmoore thought it had already begun to do him harm. Hugh Macnaghten, long his most serious academic competitor at Eton and King's, did rather better than him in the examinations of 1879. Luxmoore knew that Macnaghten was far 'inferior in intellectual sympathy and interest' to MRJ, but thought that 'there is no doubt Monty's handwriting contributes much to competitive inequality, if it does not even create it'.[114] MRJ was well aware of this, and wrote 'There has always been some curious twist in the minds of my teachers an examiners—nay, of so-called friends as well—which leads them to disparage my handwriting'.[115]

Complaints about his handwriting, in fact, dogged him throughout his life. A friend complained to him in 1885:

> I have been shown a piece of paper covered over with an almost entirely illegible scrawl: it purports to be a letter from one—Montague Rhodes James—I know him by repute as a bounder of the deepest dye—but I did not know how hard it was to make anything of "James—His Mark" before I went down to Eton.[116]

In 1925, he wrote an essay for a memorial volume of reminiscences of Arthur Benson, but the typist returned it to the editor, E. H. Ryle, in disgust, 'with a note to the effect that she wished these "University Gentlemen" could write better—and that she, at any rate wouldn't send any son of her's [sic] to the University—pure waste of money in her opinion'.[117] My sympathies are all with the typist here, but MRJ never had any intention of doing anything about his handwriting, and even claimed that he modelled it on Luxmoore's. (He didn't. Luxmoore's writing is perfectly legible.)

Handwriting notwithstanding, he was getting off to a wonderful start; but the success wasn't universal. MRJ was never any kind of mathematician, and from the beginning this was the only aspect of his school work he seems to have found genuinely challenging. 'I have kept ahead in Classics', he wrote home in May 1877, 'but Maths not so good as I cd. wish.'[118] That December, he was 'disgusted with himself' at finishing only fifth in his year in the trials (exams), 'But I know exactly what it was that lost me: 1. Mathematics . . . 2. Science. Which came unexpectedly. 3. The slowness of my handwriting'. He was, he wrote bitterly, particularly 'surprised and disgusted at being beaten by Hitchcock, whom I detest'.[119] The detested Hitchcock is the future Rev. George Edward Hitchcock, Vicar of Hale, Surrey; MRJ's dislike of him adds a rather sadistic edge to a letter he had sent to Grace a few weeks earlier:

> I have just been . . . with Hitchcock mi[nor] to see him have his tooth out with laughing gas of which he took 10 gallons. It is rather a painless process. When he had finished inhaling the gas, he began waving his hands about. The tooth was very neatly drawn. It came out with a squelch. It was a large one.[120]

(Teeth would have their revenge on MRJ down the line.)

He developed a strong dislike for his Maths teacher, the Rev. Robert Frederick Rumsey: 'Rumsey alias Clumsy alias Grumsey alias anything else ending in -umsey is gradually deteriorating as the end of the half approaches', he wrote to his parents at the end of the first year.[121] He got off to a bad start with Rumsey, who caught him cribbing Godding's homework within the first fortnight, and gave him a Georgic (that is, copying out 500 hexameters of Latin verse) for punishment: 'The offence was not repeated', MRJ recalled, 'but my distaste for Mathematics was not lessened.'[122] As if teaching Mathematics wasn't bad enough, Rumsey was also 'a confirmed Ritualist', an Anglo-Catholic whose Oxford Movement sympathies put him at odds with the James family's Evangelical leanings.[123] The dislike may have been mutual. Amongst Herbert's Eton correspondence is a torn fragment of a school report, unsigned and undated, which stands in jarring contrast to almost all MRJ's other school reports (he would get another stinker from his sixth form Maths master: there is a pattern here). It's entirely likely that this is from Rumsey, one of the few Eton Masters with whom MRJ had any real issues: 'James is a silent member of society—slipshod in his work. I think understanding it; but taking no delight in it. 6th of 12.'[124] When MRJ heard the news in March 1878 that 'Rumsey the Measly One' was leaving Eton to take up the living of Burnham in Buckinghamshire, he was delighted.[125]

* * *

One gets the sense, though, that the real intellectual benefit MRJ got from Eton was the opportunity to develop the arcane and obscure course of reading which he had started in Temple Grove, and which was to define the rest of his life. Whenever he got to London, he headed straight for the bookshops of Charing Cross Road, or for his particular favourite, the antiquarian specialist J. M. Stark in William Street: on his first visit there in July 1877, he 'examined a Fabricius . . . and Lawrence's Book of Enoch, Ascension of Isaiah, etc.'[126] 'I hope father will not be alarmed', he confided to Grace, 'I shall not get any hurtful publications from Mr Stark.'[127] Around this time, he starts writing to antiquarian booksellers all over London, requesting copies of their catalogues: 'Certainly catalogues are an enticing form of literature', he wrote prophetically to his father.[128] Unlike most fifteen-year-olds, this is how he spends his money: 'I have got 5 new Apocryphal Books. Psalms of Solomon, I and iv Esdras, Revelations of Baruch, Ascension of Moses, for 3/, which I consider an acquisition.'[129] His horrible handwriting meant that the catalogues would arrive having been addressed to a variety of people and places, 'all honouring me with a "Revd". And one called me Games and another represents me living at Kew Buildings.'[130]

From early on, we can detect the mischievous, playful attitude towards learning and sources which characterizes his fiction. Since MRJ always knew more than anyone else about his subjects (in fairness, he was the only person interested enough to find out about many of them), he could delight in perpetrating scholarly hoaxes. In October 1878, he tells his father, 'I forged an interesting MS on a fragment of old paper which was stuck on one of the real MSS containing revelations as to the whereabouts of two chests full of gold which were buried in Rome at the Via Appia in 1569.' His division master, the generous H. A. Chignell, was completely deceived by this, and went into raptures at the prospect of these chests of buried treasure—as did Luxmoore, who, when the forgery was revealed, claimed that he had known it all along. 'Which', MRJ slyly adds, 'was not true.'[131]

His second year finds him reading Isaac D'Israeli's *Curiosities of Literature*, and having his first encounter with a book which was to interest him for the rest of his life (he edited an edition in 1914, and produced a translation in 1923), Walter Map's twelfth-century compendium of 'Courtier's Trifles', *De Nugis Curialium*, 'which contains some extraordinary stories about Ghosts, Vampires, Wood-nymphs, etc.'[132] In early 1878 he started to learn German with Luxmoore. Languages always came preposterously easily to MRJ, and within a few weeks he is already reading the great philologist Max Müller's 5-volume *Chips from a German Workshop*. Around this time, he also read J. L. Petit's *Architectural Studies in France*, and was dazzled by its brilliant illustrations. This marked the beginning of a deep fascination with French ecclesiastical architecture. On his regular visits to France he would always make a bee-line for the nearest cathedral, where he would keep detailed records of what he saw, in his notebooks and his letters. By the end of his life, he claimed to have visited all but two of France's cathedrals (he put the number at 143; Nice and Toulon were the ones he missed).[133] One of the first he sought out, St. Bertrand de Comminges, a strange Romanesque cathedral high in the foothills of the Pyrenees, has a very special place in our story.

MRJ's extracurricular reading during his first years at Eton wasn't confined to the abstruse and unusual. He read normal things too. As we've seen, he got through *Vanity Fair* while convalescing after his bilious attack. He also read Farrar (again), Bulwer-Lytton, and Charles Kingsley; later on he would read William Morris and, with great enthusiasm, Wilkie Collins (he particularly loved *The Moonstone*). Most importantly, in the Autumn of 1877 he read *Sketches by Boz*. This was the beginning of a lifelong love of Dickens, the author he read more than any other. There was no Dickens at home in Great Livermere, but the College Library had a complete set, onto which 'I fastened like a leech'.[134] For the rest of his life, not many months would go by without his returning to Dickens (the only book he could never get on with was *A Child's History of England*). His conversation, his friend Gurney Lubbock attests, was habitually peppered with Dickensian references: 'Mine like Mr. Pecksniff's is a forgiving nature' was one of his recurring catchphrases.[135] 'I imagine he knew most of Dickens by heart', Gwen McBryde thought.[136] One of his favourite party pieces was to recite from memory the whole of the trial scene of Bardell v. Pickwick from *The Pickwick Papers*: this was, Shane Leslie remembered, 'Monty's most splendid recital'.[137] Fred Benson thought that, for MRJ,

'Dickens was the St. Peter who held the keys of the heavenly kingdom of literature'.[138] A. E. Housman wrote to MRJ asking him to track down an obscure Dickensian quotation: 'Probably you can answer straight away.'[139] The ghost stories are scattered with Dickensian allusions, from Mr Rogers in 'Oh, Whistle, and I'll Come to You, My Lad', who misquotes *Dombey and Son*, to the *Edwin Drood*-reading Principal Verger of 'An Episode of Cathedral History', to the landlord of 'The Story of a Disappearance and an Appearance', 'who really requires the pen of a Boz to do him justice', to the epigraph of 'Rats', which quotes from 'Tom Tiddler's Ground'.[140]

Many years later, back in Eton as its Provost, MRJ insisted on writing the exam paper for the 1926 Remove English Literature Prize. It is difficult to imagine a more Jamesian document than this. The exam has thirteen questions (you had to answer them all), every single one of them on *The Pickwick Papers*. The questions range from the straightforward ('1. When was Charles Dickens born, and when did he die?') to the abstruse ('9. What did Mr. Jingle mean when he said: "Smart chap that cabman—handled his fives well; but if I'd been your friend in the green jemmy—punch his head 'cod I would—pig's whisper—no gammon"?') Quite properly, students were expected to have memorized the entirety of Mrs Leo Hunter's poem, 'Expiring Frog', to know who won the Eatanswill byelection (and what party they represented), and to recount what happened to the Pickwickians at Bury St. Edmunds.[141] 'I put Charles Dickens', he wrote in *Eton and King's*, 'at the forefront of the accessions to my pleasure which Eton gave, for it was wholly new.'[142]

* * *

While MRJ was forging a new life for himself at Eton, the old family life was going on in Livermere. Mary Emily, we know, was always keen to talk about health issues, her own and the family's. While Herbert and the boys were generally fairly robust, Grace's physical and mental health was always a concern. What this meant was that she and Mary Emily would, on occasion, spend time apart from Herbert, for seaside rest cures. May 1877 finds them at Lowestoft—'I hope it will do her good', Mary Emily confides to MRJ, but Grace was less sure: 'We don't want to go much but it is for the good of my health and I daresay I shall like it'.[143] A few months later she tries to persuade Herbert to take Grace to Cromer. This idea didn't get anywhere, and nor did the later suggestion that Mary Emily and Grace spend six months in the South of France.

Sydney went from Haileybury up to Trinity College, Cambridge, where he excelled as a sportsman and a scholar. He was elected a Bell Scholar in 1875, and graduated with a First (the highest rank of degree in British Universities) in the Classical Tripos. But Sydney's real distinction was that he was an outstanding rugby player, who went on to captain the university rugby team. In May 1879 he was appointed as an Assistant Master at Eton, while his youngest brother was still a pupil there. A couple of months later, he was called in to help after MRJ, as a bet, had held his breath for too long and then become dizzy and fallen against a stone mantelpiece. 'How foolish Toby has been cutting his head open', Sydney wrote to their parents; 'he has marked myself for life . . . cutting his forehead to the bone in a diagonal direction above the eye.'[144] (You can still see the scar on some photographs of MRJ.) Perhaps fortunately for both, he never taught him, though they managed to find themselves joining Eton's Officer Training Corps together, with Sydney covering the expenses for both of them. In fact, scar aside, Sydney's only memory of MRJ at Eton seems to have been encountering his little brother on his way into a class on Thucydides, carrying an enormous, teetering pile of books. Typically, none of them had anything to do with Thucydides.[145]

Ber had gone to study medicine at Charing Cross Hospital—which gave MRJ a pretext for semi-regular visits to London, during which he would head immediately for the bookshops, and sometimes try to catch a cricket match at Lord's. 'Have you seen any operations yet?' MRJ wrote to him. 'If so, please write and tell me all about it.'[146] Ber's vocation certainly made him a ghoulish correspondent, in a way which greatly pleased his younger brother, whether commenting on the deformities of some of the patients he encountered (complete with graphic illustrations), writing excitedly about a combination revolver-dagger-knuckleduster he saw in a shop window ('It would be very useful in the colonies'), or describing the sad demise of the family cat, which he had to shoot owing to terminal illness: 'Chummy has died of loss of brains from the passage of an ounce ball through her skull.'[147]

Ber and MRJ were very distinctive correspondents. From childhood, they had developed the twin personae of Geo. William Johnson (Ber) and Bardolf Barker (MRJ), a pair of rival tradesmen. The brothers carried out their entire correspondence, and a large part of their relationship, through these alter egos. Often, entire long letters, or exchanges of letter, happen without slipping out of character. Gurney Lubbock, who knew the James family well, describes the relationship wonderfully:

> Herbert was Johnson, a butcher, and Monty was a grocer called Barker; and it must be understood that they were Barker and Johnson to each other and no one else. A jealous and intense rivalry was understood to exist between the two

> characters; they crabbed each other and made the darkest insinuations: Barker would suggest to Johnson that he tampered with his weights, to be accused in turn of putting sand in his sugar. All this began in private school, and was renewed whenever they met.[148]

One of MRJ's earliest surviving letters to Ber is sent from 'Etonn Collidge':

> Der Jonnsn
>
> I oap as you are krwite wel i am wel. Many thancks fore yewer littur as i gott to day. Ow is yur edd getin on from the varse raick as marry you was a kramin it with the larst time as I seen yu—I add 2 cards from you some weaks back whitch I did nott arnswear.[149]

When MRJ went down with sausage-related food poisoning during his first weeks at Eton, Ber/Johnson sent him a postcard to cheer him up:

> Wot Bardof sed
> Ow I wish I ad not eat
> Eny off that orrid meat
> Now I cannot tuch the pudin
> An it looks a putty goodun.[150]

(One of the ongoing jokes is that neither correspondent can spell Barker's first name, which appears in a number of inventive forms. The Bardolfs were local nobility, an aristocratic Norfolk dynasty.) We can see here quite clearly the origins of the many loquacious working-class characters who people MRJ's stories. Lubbock recalled how MRJ would often slip into the character of Barker, even when Ber wasn't around:

> The *alter ego* which was shaped thus in boyhood remained, modified by circumstances but essentially unchanged, to the end; and at any moment the appropriate situation or right word might call Barker to life, 'slow in the uptake', yet volubly argumentative at times, with an eager yet puzzled interest in all human things. Barker would often take a rich, elemental interest in some entertainment, which must have been stupidly dull to M. R. James; and the worst sort of film would be enlivened by the running comment that Barker whispered into one's ear—in an accent that was Suffolk, of course, in origin, but later on had surely acquired the peculiar *timbre* of Cambridge.

The very Provost of Eton could sometimes find himself possessed by the spirit of Barker, once informing a group of visitors that a recently erected statue of Perseus was in fact 'a statue of our Blessed Founder King Henry the Eighth: he is 'olding the 'ead of one of his wives. We don't know which it is, but we think it must be Anne Boleyn.' As time went on, MRJ took on other personae, and was particularly prone to slipping into 'an ignorant but rather self-satisfied verger'. There are a few of these in his stories, too.[151]

* * *

Eton offered opportunities beyond the narrowly academic. The school's glittering roster of alumni were always keen to return to the *alma mater*, and in his second year perhaps the most celebrated living Etonian of them all came down 'like a wolf on the fold' to deliver a lecture on Homer. This was Prime Minister William Ewart Gladstone, who had gone to Eton in 1821. Although admittedly out of office in 1878, he nevertheless had time to deliver what was obviously a well-prepared and wide-ranging lecture which took in the connections between Greek mythology and Genesis, the topography of the plain of Troy, Latin misrepresentations of Homer, and the politics of Homer's legacy, 'and ended with the highest encomiums of Eton'. MRJ was quite surprised to hear him pronounce Homer as 'Oomy'.[152] A few days later, he resolved to write to the great man and ask for his autograph.

MRJ was never much of a sportsman, though he enjoyed watching cricket, especially the annual Eton-Harrow match played in July at Lord's. He never really played Fives, though he did play tennis. He was rather keen on the Eton Wall Game. 'The origin of the Wall Game is hidden in mystery', the Eton historian R. A. Austen Leigh wrote.[153] For the uninitiated, its rules are scarcely less obscure. Vaguely resembling rugby, the Wall Game is played on the school grounds between two goals, one being the door of the Lower Master's garden wall (known as 'Good Calx'), the other an ancient elm tree near Fellows' Pond ('Bad Calx'), whose stump was finally removed in 1994. (In 'After Dark in the Playing Fields', the owl lives in the Bad Calx tree, and is irritated at its appropriation: "Ow should I know what silly names you call it?')[154] The annual Collegers v. Oppidans Wall game, played on St. Andrew's Day, is one of the highlights of the Eton sporting calendar. In MRJ's time, the Collegers were enjoying an unbroken winning run. In his second year, he wrote home with a match report for the 1877 Wall Game:

> The chief news is that to-day the great Wall Match of Collegers v. Oppidans was played, resulting as usual in a complete victory for the Collegers 10 shies to nothing. You would have been delighted, I assure you, with the savage and furious hacks and 'flicks' given to the shins of both parties.[155]

MRJ was, he thought, pretty good at the Wall Game, and it was a source of minor regret that he never actually got to play for the Collegers—Twelfth Man in his last year, 1881, was the nearest he came, and 'I shall always say when occasion offers that but for a bad knee and a crumpled ear—both accruing from friction against the Wall (I still have the ear)—I should have played for College that year.'[156]

MRJ's mode of being with boys could sometimes be physical, and even rough. He grew into a large, burly man: even in his sixties, Anthony Powell recalled, 'he was a big man of striking presence . . . you were immediately aware of something powerful and unusual'.[157] His fondness for unbridled horseplay, which was to continue well into his adult life, could sometimes get him into trouble. Once or twice this did have an unpleasant edge. He once put a dead frog in his classmate Henry Wood's bed, a creature of which Wood had 'an almost superstitious horror'.[158] We've seen that he was accused of bullying and 'humbugging' in Temple Grove. In his third year at Eton, he came rather to dislike one of his classmates, Ernest Brooks, a very bright but solitary boy who was given to laughing loudly to himself. 'Brooks is not nice, and is a convenient object for venting one's superfluous energies upon', he wrote to his mother.[159] Brooks wrote to his father about some of the humbugging he had received, and the affair ended with Chignell giving MRJ (who was adamant that the whole affair was exaggerated) and nine of his classmates a dressing down. Luxmoore certainly took 'that unfortunate & to me mysterious affair' seriously enough to write to Herbert about it: 'I only feel as if the boy was rather more of a problem than I thought.'[160]

Gurney Lubbock, at Eton about ten years after MRJ, is quite forthright about this side of his character:

> We used to accuse him of having bullied a certain distinguished contemporary, and he never quite denied the charge; and it was always said that he was 'complained of' for something of this kind, and that Sydney, by then a Master at Eton, did nothing to avert the complaint.[161]

MRJ himself admitted this. His travelling companion Thomas Anstey Guthrie recorded in his diary a conversation the pair had in Viborg in 1906: 'M.R.J. at school a bully.' He told Guthrie about a boy 'whose arms they used to twist, delicate skin, arms black and blue. M's parents called for.'[162] It's also worth noting that on those relatively few occasions when MRJ seems to have been in trouble at either Temple Grove or Eton, there are letters missing from the correspondence; it's not always easy to reconstruct events. Lubbock may be conflating things here, but on its face this is not an account of the 'row about Brooks', which took place in November 1878, before Sydney arrived at Eton.[163] Besides, Brooks was not really a 'distinguished contemporary': though he did brilliantly at Cambridge, he went on to a quiet career in the British Museum. But MRJ could certainly be unkind: 'I can't stand Forster much longer', he wrote in 1881. 'I shall discard him in favour of I don't quite know who. His appearance and manners are very much against him. He lives at Great Chesterford and his Pa is the Rev. C. T. Forster who I think wrote an idiot book about the Sinaitic Inscriptions.' (This letter was written in a bad humour: he begins by railing against one of his teachers, 'that little idiot Vaughan'.)[164] MRJ himself may be getting things wrong here: the Rev. Charles Forster certainly did publish a philological study of the Sinaitic Inscriptions, but didn't have a son at Eton at the same time as MRJ. But there *were* a couple of Forsters at Eton with him, the more distinguished of whom was Henry Forster, a future Tory MP who served in several governments and became Governor-General of Australia in 1920.

* * *

As his time at Eton progressed, MRJ began to gain a serious reputation for scholarship. Luxmoore recognized from his first term that he had a prodigy on his hands: 'I never knew a boy see his way so quickly & surely through a difficult passage.'[165] At the end of his second year, Edward Austen Leigh wrote in his report: 'James "facile princeps" [easily first] in my division.... His theology is far deeper than mine, and I am no judge of it'; though he worried a little about 'his zeal in reading more recondite authors to the neglect of the best models' (which is exactly what MRJ made a career of).[166] 'James is a real student, and a born scholar', says Warre's school report for 1879.[167] John Fortescue, future Royal Librarian at Windsor, and one of Sydney's pupils at Eton, wrote to MRJ years later that 'your brother Sydney told me with reverence & awe that he was as naught compared with his younger brother'.[168] Even while MRJ was still a pupil at Eton, and Sydney a teacher, Luxmoore was adamant that he was 'so much the senior of his elder brother'.[169] Another of the 'pivot days' in MRJ's life surely took place in the autumn of 1879, when he and Henry Babington Smith 'wheedled' the keys to the Fellows' Library out of Vice-Provost George Dupuis, 'and for the first time we were able to handle actual manuscripts. . . . The Eton collection of manuscripts was the first in which I was able to browse untrammelled'.[170] (MRJ and Babington Smith were the first pupils afforded this honour since the sixteenth century.) Stephen Gaselee, who followed in MRJ's footsteps from Temple Grove to Eton to King's twenty years later, recalled that 'there was still a legend of him as the learned boy' when Gaselee arrived at Eton in 1896.[171] Stark, the antiquarian book dealer, began to send him fragments of manuscripts, which, like the biblioclastic demonologist Canon Alberic de Mauléon, he kept in a scrap book.

Warre thought that MRJ's learning amounted to 'a voyage to an unknown country'.[172] In January 1879, he began to teach himself Ancient Ethiopic, 'without a grammar and with only an alphabet and glossary which I recently purchased in an Ethiopic reading book'.[173] This book was the Orientalist August Dillmann's *Chrestomathia Aethiopica* (1866, and entirely in Latin), which he had picked up for seven or eight shillings at Elijah Johnson's bookshop in Trinity Street, Cambridge. Over the next few months, he set about learning the language. The notebook on which he records his Ethiopic studies opens with the 'Alphabetum Æthiopicum', and moves systematically through suffixes, pronouns, interrogatives, nouns, verbs. Before long, he is working on an Ethiopic text of the Acts of the Apostles.[174] The teetering pile of books which Sydney found him carrying on the way to his class on Thucydides 'were on the Ethiopic language, or some equally recondite subject'.[175] The first item in Dillmann's book was an apocryphal *Book of Baruch*, and even at sixteen, 'anything like a fresh apocryphal book was meat and drink to me'.[176] Somehow, he managed to rope Ion Thynne into working with him on a translation of this work—though the final version lists the translation as by MRJ alone ('Liber hic traductio est ex Æthopica lingua in Anglicani a M. R. James').[177] His interest in Ancient Ethiopic seems to have amounted, in the early part of 1879, to something of an obsession. Luxmoore was 'very much struck' with MRJ's latest interest, while Herbert seems to have been worried that it would distract from his school work. In a letter partly written in Ancient Ethiopic, MRJ had to reassure him that 'You need not be alarmed about my Ethiopic as I mean to let it rest for a while after I have finished the third Book of Baruch'.[178]

But he didn't let it rest, and what happened next is strange—one of those episodes in MRJ's early life which seem significant, but in a manner that is difficult to grasp. Having finished the translation, MRJ and Thynne decided that they wanted to dedicate it to Queen Victoria, and so they wrote 'a very polite letter to Her Majesty, beseeching us to accept the Dedication of our work'.[179] On the face of it, this seems like a harmless, if precocious and eccentric, thing to do—but it appears to have been considered a breach of protocol. The request was read by Queen Victoria's Private Secretary, Major General Sir Henry Ponsonby, who wrote a stern letter to Hornby, demanding that the boys be punished for their 'impertinent joke'. Hornby, in turn, was 'excessively annoyed by the conceit & bad taste of the proceeding', while Luxmoore warned

Herbert that 'he must be on his guard against what may do him social harm if misinterpreted into conceit'.[180]

There is more going on here than meets the eye. MRJ was certainly ill in March 1879, and wrote a long letter to his father which is, for him at least, rather manic and strident. He apologized for this, claiming to be 'slightly disarranged in the intellect' owing to the 'combined effects of too much reading and too much East Wind'. He was certainly doing some intense reading, even by his standards: 'I think the last straw that broke my back was reading a lot of the Orphic Hymns (fifty of them) at a sitting. They taught me a good many words, so I will not repent of my evil ways.'[181] Around this time, he was also working on an Ethiopic translation of the Gospel of St. Mark, and took it upon himself to learn Ancient Egyptian hieroglyphics.[182] One effect of this disarrangement was that he developed a temporary fixation on the Royal Family, which seems to have been brought about by the wedding of the Duke of Connaught and Princess Louise Marguerite of Prussia on 13 March, which took place at St. George's Chapel in nearby Windsor Castle. He went to the railway station to cheer the arrival of the Princess, and watched the Prince of Wales and the young princes saying goodbye to the Provost and Headmaster 'through my faithful spy glass'. 'The streets of Eton and Windsor were most gay', he recorded. Luxmoore, too, got swept up in events, exclaiming to the boys, 'The Queen's a dear!' 'I lived last week quite in an atmosphere of royalty,' he wrote—and one consequence of this was that he developed 'a badgering tendency . . . to think of nothing but the Queen'.[183]

Luxmoore wrote a worried letter to Herbert: 'I was made rather uneasy by your boy's complaining on Monday that his head failed him at work & he said he had a fixed idea & cd. not rid his brain of "the Queen", & cd. not sleep.'[184] Herbert thought that Hornby was handling the affair badly, and over-reacting, telling Luxmoore that he thought the offence was 'a comparatively venial one'. He engaged Sydney—then still in Cambridge studying for a Fellowship in Trinity—to go and see Hornby to 'smooth the matter down a bit'.[185] This seems to have worked—MRJ and Thynne certainly escaped a thrashing, and Hornby was sufficiently impressed by Sydney that he wrote to him out of the blue a few weeks later offering him a job.

This manic episode was succeeded by a brief period of depression, in which the school doctor told Luxmoore that 'he is in a low way'.[186] In his next letter home, on 2 April, MRJ tells Herbert that 'I wrote to the Queen as a consequence of being ill. . . . I look upon it as a purely idiotic act'. He resolved things, as he tended to do when faced with emotional difficulty, by declaring the matter closed in his mind and refusing to talk about it further: 'But henceforth with your leave I will say farewell to this subject, as it only badgers me unnecessarily.'[187]

In the long run, this episode may even have served MRJ rather well. He eventually published a loose translation of *Baruch*, as well as a more scholarly study.[188] He drew on the memory of the Orphic Hymns in the early 1890s when he came to write the story 'Lost Hearts', in which the occultist Mr Abney's library 'contained all the then available books bearing on the Mysteries, the Orphic Poems, the worship of Mithras, and the Neo-Platonists'.[189]

During his years at Eton, MRJ's 'recondite' explorations into unknown countries of reading are staggering. 'I was charging about into literature ancient and modern like a bull in a china shop', he later realized.[190] Luxmoore wrote, a little anxiously, to Herbert, worrying about his 'dilettante habits of reading': 'He dredges the deeps of literature for refuse'.[191] For MRJ, the lure of the marginal, the apocryphal, the irrelevant, the forgotten—or indeed the forbidden, the rejected, and the occult—would always be irresistible. His notebooks contain records of his reading, and while we don't have them all for his Eton years, we do know, for example, that in 1878–9, he was researching (amongst much else), 'Notable Feasts in Synaxarion Augusti', 'Abdias, lib. iv De S. Iacobo Majore', 'Ausonius of Burdigala d. 394', 'Hermes Trismegistus', and 'Syriac MSS from the Monastery of St Mary Deipara or the Nitrian Monasteries'.[192]

The presence here of the legendary magus Hermes Trismegistus, a major figure in the history of magic and hermetic philosophy, signals the beginnings of a serious engagement with the occult. Although he had promised not to obtain any 'hurtful publications' on his bibliographic expeditions, in 1879, in David Nutt's bookshop, he first encountered 'an appalling book', Collin de Plancy's notorious *Dictionnaire Infernal*, which 'had the most dreadful tales and illustrations in it'.[193] This taxonomy of the hierarchies and powers of demons was first published in 1818, though MRJ was captivated here by the 1863 sixth edition, with celebrated illustrations by Louis Le Breton. These included, famously, a powerful image of Beelzebub as a gigantic wasp-like fly, which was to influence a number of the ghost stories, notably 'Mr. Humphreys and his Inheritance', in which the ghost of an occultist manifests 'with the odious writhings of a wasp creeping out of a rotten apple', and 'The Residence at Whitminster' and 'An Evening's Entertainment', both of which contain supernatural infestations of flies ('"Lord of flies, sir," and no more would he say').[194] MRJ told his father that he was going to buy the book as soon as he could afford it.

In the late 1870s, he took to visiting Stewart's booksellers in King William Street, next door to Stark's. Stewart's specialized in occult literature, and it was here that MRJ first encountered grimoires and other books of magic, most notably Francis Barrett's *The Magus*, which made a deep impression on him.[195] Barrett's occult classic, first published in 1801, is full of portraits of demons—Apollyon, Belial, Theutis, Asmodeus, 'The Incubus', Ophis, 'The Spirit Antichrist', Astaroth, Abaddon, Mammon—reproduced in hand-tinted colour plates and, as MRJ might have said, 'drawn from the life'.[196] His class-mates began to notice the uniquely sinister territory into which he directed his energies, and to appreciate it. On 4 December 1878, with the winter nights closed in, he concludes a letter to his parents: 'I must depart for awhile as I am engaged for a "dark séance" i.e. a telling of ghost stories in which capacity I am rather popular just now.'[197] Down the years, there would be plenty more of these 'dark séances' on long, cold December nights.

The supernatural was very much on his mind in his later teens. In early 1880, Arthur Benson got MRJ involved in the production of a magazine, *The Eton Rambler*. He worried that this would take up too much of his time, but set about writing an essay on 'Ghost Stories': 'I think it is rot,' he wrote when it was done, 'but the editors appear to like it.'[198] He ended up writing two inter-linked essays, which together amount to a knowledgeable survey, with pastiches, of some of the major tropes of the ghost story. The first opens with a revealing passage:

> Everyone, I think, has an innate love of the supernatural. Everyone can remember a time when he has carefully searched his curtains—and poked in the dark corners of his room before retiring to rest—with a sort of pleasurable uncertainty as to whether there might not be a saucer-eyed skeleton or a skinny sheeted ghost in hiding somewhere. I invariably go through this ceremony myself. Of course we all know there are no such things,—but some one might be going to play us a trick, you know, and anyhow it's best to be quite sure. People do tell such very odd stories.[199]

The second essay offers some general guidelines for the ghost story:

> It is desirable, too, that the teller of these tales should assume the tone of one who believes in the truth of what he is relating. . . . And he should stoop occasionally to the incredible, by which I mean the sort of tale that deals in blood and bones, and sheeted spectres, and other phenomena in the nature of walking undertakers' advertisements . . .[200]

MRJ's broader literary interests were beginning to develop. He was elected to the Literary Society in the Spring of 1880, and eventually succeeded Arthur Benson as its President in September 1881. In 1880, he was also one of the founding members of the Shakespeare Society, dedicated to reading the plays aloud, whose numbers were strictly limited to six Collegers and six Oppidans: Luxmoore soon became its President, and remained so until his death. MRJ's letters from this time are full of details about the Shakespeare plays he read from the Globe edition which he used for the rest of his life: *Much Ado About Nothing* was first, then *Richard II*, *Henry VI Part 2*, *The Merchant of Venice* (with MRJ in comic form as Launcelot Gobbo), *Henry V* ('an excellent play'), *As You Like It*, *The Tempest*, and *A Midsummer Night's Dream*, which saw him cast as one of the Rude Mechanicals: 'I shall do it Barker-wise', he promised. More generally, around this time he read and enjoyed Mark Twain's *The Prince and the Pauper*, and Joel Chandler Harris's *Uncle Remus Stories*, which occasioned several pages of pastiche in which 'Brer Hornby' sets 'Brer James' and 'Brer Benson' a long and exhausting passage of Terence ('he waz Lat'n') to translate, leaving them 'des 'bout fa'rly tuckered out'.[201]

In 1881, he became one of the editors of the *Eton College Chronicle*, the newspaper written and organized by the boys. There was even a modest salary of fifteen shillings per edition. He was, on the whole, embarrassed by his stint as editor of the *Chronicle*—'Some devastating attempts at humour are to be found—but I hope no one will look for them—in my numbers'.[202] No doubt he had in mind pieces such as 'Clarence *Mi.*'s Dream', a dialogue between a fourth-form boy who has failed to do his homework, and his exasperated tutor.[203] Some of MRJ's articles very obviously come from his own particular perspective. In 'Things Not Generally Known at Eton', for example, he writes: 'The College Library . . . is a place not merely unexplored, but, to some, unknown even by report; and yet there are few who would not be interested, one way or another, in the objects it contains.'[204] MRJ was always glad of having taken up the editorship because it brought him close to his co-editor, St. Clair Donaldson: the pair had been classmates since the beginning, but only now became friends.[205]

The Literary Society organized talks, given by a variety of luminaries. Gladstone came again (when he was Prime Minister for the second time), and once again ended his talk with a 'glowing panegyric' on Eton, 'the queen of all the schools of the world' (within a few weeks, to MRJ's annoyance, he had given speeches in Wellington and Marlborough, where he had disparaged Eton!).[206] The great John Ruskin came twice. The highlight of the first talk, ostensibly on the English Lakes, was 'a tremendous denunciation of Gustave Doré'. The second, on Amiens and its Cathedral, was a real eye-opener: 'For the first time I learnt what might be read, and in what spirit, in the imagery of a great church: and what the thirteenth century had to say to the nineteenth.'[207]

Francis Galton, founder of the eugenics movement, came to give a talk on the 'Features, Strength, Height, etc. of Boys', and proposed keeping a photographic archive of Eton boys, for eugenic purposes (no doubt as contrast to the photographic archives of 'murderers . . . or idiots' which he also proposed).[208] MRJ also heard talks by the philosopher Henry Sidgwick, on Carlyle, and the classicist F. W. H. Myers, on Nelson: Myers's lecture he thought 'the most eloquent, the most ornate that we ever listened to'.[209] Sidgwick and Myers, both based at Trinity College Cambridge, would in 1882 become founder members of the Society for Psychical Research, an organization of which MRJ was to become very sceptical.

'Suppose I shall have to read a paper!' he wrote on election to the Literary Society.[210] On Saturday 5 February 1881, the *Eton College Chronicle* reported:

> M. R. James read a most instructive and amusing paper on the 'Occult Sciences.' He traced the growth of these from the earliest times, through the middle ages, and discussed the history and characteristic of several Demons. The reader displayed surprising knowledge, though the paper was perhaps slightly disjointed owing to the necessary curtailment, due to its length.[211]

Beginning with Collin de Plancy, but moving far beyond it, 'Occult Sciences' is in essence a digest of MRJ's magical and demonological research up to this point. This reading laid some of the foundations for his future scholarly and creative output. The paper begins by defining 'magic' narrowly, as 'the calling up of spirits and rendering them subservient to one's own power'.[212] One of the major sources for 'Occult Sciences' was the French scholar François Lenormant's *Chaldean Magic* (1874), which contains a detailed account of the hierarchies of demons, who inhabited 'uncultivated wilds and deserts . . . the bleak summits of mountains, the pestilential marshes, and the sea'.[213] Lenormant argues that Chaldean demonology found its way into the thinking of some Old Testament prophets, and quotes Isaiah 34:13–14, on the destruction of Edom, in support of this:

> And thorns shall come up in her palaces, nettles and brambles in the fortresses thereof: and it shall be an habitation of dragons *and* a court for owls.
>
> The wild beasts of the desert shall also meet with the wild beasts of the island, and the satyr shall cry to his fellow, and the screech owl shall rest there and find for herself a place of rest.

As Lenormant points out, some versions translate the King James's 'screech owl' as 'Night Monster' (the RSV has 'night hag'). This is a singularly important passage for MRJ's fiction. He draws on it for his first published story,

'Canon Alberic's Scrap-Book': 'Isaiah was a very sensible man: doesn't he say something about night monsters living in the ruins of Babylon?' says Dennistoun, who has witnessed the manifestation of a demon.[214] 'Occult Sciences provides a further gloss on this passage. 'Screech owl', 'night monster', and night hag' are all translations of the Hebrew *lî-lît*, Lilith, which MRJ glosses: 'Lilith . . . is a prominent person in Jewish magic and demonology. . . . She was originally the wife of Adam before Eve's creation, but was tempted by Satan and became a demon. In Isaiah the name occurs and is translated as owl.'[215] MRJ famously forgot nothing, and years later he brought this to mind again while writing 'An Episode of Cathedral History', which he first read in May 1913. In the story, Canon Lyall has a sleepless night, caused by the wailing of a demon: 'rather too much Isaiah 34. 14 for me . . . "the satyr shall cry to his fellow".' 'Cathedral History's demon is explicitly female, and the tomb which had imprisoned her is marked by a cross with an inscription 'from the Vulgate of Isaiah xxxiv . . . IBI CUBAVIT LAMIA'.[216] This translates as 'HERE LIES A LAMIA', and is taken from the Latin Vulgate translation of the exact same passage from Isaiah 34: 'et occurrent daemonia onocentauris et pilosus clamabit alter ad alterum ibi cubavit lamia et invenit sibi requiem'. United by these verses from Isaiah, MRJ's two demons, male and female, cry to each other across the decades.

In the researches that led up to 'Occult Sciences', MRJ also read another work of the occult to which he would return many times over many years.[217] This was *The Testament of Solomon*, a classic of demonology in which King Solomon commands a variety of demons, including Beelzebub himself, and makes them do his bidding, which includes building the Temple in Jerusalem. In 'Canon Alberic', the horrifying 'sepia drawing' which Dennistoun finds (and later burns) of King Solomon commanding a demon is evidently an illustration from *The Testament of Solomon*.[218]

'Occult Sciences' also contains a passage on the 'diabolic magic' of 'divination by pouring ink into the hand of a boy, who sees in it the description of any person called for'.[219] In writing this, he may have been inspired by his beloved *The Moonstone*, in which Collins's Indian mystics practise similar forms of divination (Dickens also alludes to this practice in *The Mystery of Edwin Drood*, another work which was very important to MRJ). Almost forty years later, MRJ drew on this for his own tale of divination and black magic, 'The Residence at Whitminster': 'Frank was looking earnestly at something in the palm of his hand. Saul stood behind him, and seemed to be listening.' The occult forces Lord Saul Kildonan unleashes are so powerful that they seem to have summoned

Beelzebub himself, as MRJ remembered him from the 'appalling' illustrations to Collin de Plancy: 'I tore at the curtain and let in enough light to be able to see something waving which I knew was an insect's leg, by the shape of it: but, Lord, what a size! Why, the beast must have been as tall as I am.'[220]

His second paper for the Literary Society, delivered the following October, was equally characteristic. His subject was 'The Lives of the Saints', and the Literary Society Journal entry records that he gave the subject his own inimitable slant, a particular interest in 'the fabulous and the grotesque—giving a considerable portion of his space to the martyr-legends'. MRJ, we know, enjoyed this gruesome stuff, and his audience seems to have too (they were teenage boys, after all): 'the paper afforded amusement as well as instruction', the Journal records.[221]

MRJ's scholarship was also beginning to take on a more formal aspect. In the spring of 1879, he made what he considered to be a startling discovery:

> Yesterday I found in looking over my note-book, and aided by a subtle process of reasoning terminating in absolute certainty, that a MS fragment at Bury, no. 135 in S. James's Library at the right hand corner as you go in, bottom shelf, a white vellum book contains the Preface to and beginning of a Latin translation of Plutarch's Life of Sertorius, in a hand of the 9th or 10th century.[222]

As is apparent from the tone ('absolute certainty'), this discovery was part of the manic episode that included sending the translation of *Baruch* to the Queen. Rather against Luxmoore's better judgement, MRJ sent news of his discovery to C. E. Doble, editor of the *Academy*, who responded positively: 'if you are quite sure of the age of the MS. We shall have pleasure in publishing your interesting communication'.[223] This sent MRJ into overdrive:

> Next week, or at any rate sometime soon, I shall have an article in the Academy, perhaps a series. The first is a fragment of Plutarch out of a Bury MS which the Editor will insert. The series, if he will take it, will be Apocryphal. I have sent the first one which is the Assumption of Moses and 3rd book of Baruch. The next one will be Asenath Joseph's wife and the Testament of Job if I can get it. I have also had a shot at the Graphic which I think they will take, as they have not returned it.[224]

The article, 'A Latin Fragment of Plutarch's Sertorius', was published in the *Academy* in July 1879—this is MRJ's first scholarly publication, age sixteen.[225] It's a remarkable intellectual achievement, but also a remarkable *performance.* As one of MRJ's earlier biographers, Richard William Pfaff, writes, 'the impression given is of a middle-aged, perhaps even elderly, antiquary, very like a character from one of MRJ's ghost stories'.[226] Unfortunately, his grandiose scheme for a series of Apocryphal publications came to nothing, at least for now—Doble rejected his next article as 'scarcely critical enough for our purpose', and the article he sent to the *Graphic* was also turned down.[227] Years later, he wryly owned up that he thought his first publication was founded on a mistake: 'I suppose it now to have been from a fifteenth century humanist version: at the time I believed it to have been much older.'[228]

July 1880 saw MRJ elected to the College Debating Society, in whose weekly meetings he was a keen participant. The following July saw him elected to the exclusive Eton Society, commonly known as 'Pop'. Pop was, in part, another Debating Society—but more than this it was a self-conscious and self-selecting Etonian inner circle, an elite within an elite. Eric Parker, whose *Eton in the 'Eighties* MRJ singled out at the best book on the Eton of his time, thought that 'If you were in Pop, the whole world of Eton was yours.'[229] MRJ's contemporary E. C. Chambers hated Pop, and thought it a cradle of vice: 'In fact I can't see how Pop is allowed to continue', he wrote in 1926. 'The reason probably is that in College the evil is not seen because the Captain of the College must be in Pop.'[230] (He doesn't go into detail as to the nature of this 'evil'—Chambers was a man of pronounced right-wing views—but one suspects fears of sexual immorality.) Accounts vary as to how Pop got its name, though all imply a sort of café origin: it seems either to derive from 'Popina', or 'cook shop', or from the fact that its meetings were originally held in Mrs Hatton's lollipop shop.[231]

The records of the Debating Society and Pop debates are illuminating. In them we can begin to see the formulation of MRJ's highly conservative political character. He rarely made any kind of overt political statement, and certainly not publicly, but his politics unquestionably informed his institutional life at every stage, and to an extent also guided his personal life (he knew lots of Conservative politicians, which may not be particularly unusual for a well-connected Old Etonian, and was good friends with at least one figure of the extreme political right, Leo Maxse). As early as the autumn of 1878, in an extra-curricular 'Sunday Questions' session, MRJ held forth on communism:

> In more recent times this word has been applied to the opinions (if they can be said to have any opinions at all) of an abominable set of people who rendered themselves objects of abhorrence to every well-balanced mind in the last Franco-Prussian War by destroying a vast number of priceless treasures of art and antiquity by means of petroleum and other detestable compounds.

'I am sure this is virulent enough even for you', he wrote to his mother.[232] In September 1880, MRJ spoke for the first time in an Eton debate, discussing the motion 'That the present condition of Ireland is desperate'. He was 'in favour of complete Home Rule and entire isolation of Ireland from England, if practicable'. There was nothing progressive about his position in this argument, though: it was founded on his belief that the Irish were 'a radically vicious people' who should best be left to themselves.[233] More straightforwardly, in another debate on Home Rule a few months later (it was the burning political topic of the moment), MRJ 'expressed his entire disapprobation of the system of Home Rule from Conservative principles leading him to resent such an extensive innovation'.[234] Characteristically, he opposed a motion in October 1881 that 'The distinctive dress of Collegers should be abolished', arguing that, as well as being 'an act of simple ingratitude' against the founder of the College, the 'statues had been sufficiently tampered with already. The Fellows had been wellnigh abolished—any miserable man—Bradlaugh or Huxley—might be Provost.'[235] There is a whole, intensely conservative institutional and intellectual worldview enfolded within this argument, one to which MRJ was to adhere unchangingly for the rest of his life. Charles Bradlaugh was a notoriously atheist Liberal MP. The great agnostic materialist T. H. Huxley, against whom MRJ nursed a long-running grievance, sat for a number of years as the Royal Society's nominee on Eton's Governing Board (an imposition of the Clarendon Report and the Public Schools Act which MRJ considered 'a flagrant violation of our pious and royal Founder's wishes'), and may in fact have been in the running to succeed Charles Old Goodford as Provost in 1884 (MRJ, we shall see, was very unhappy about this).[236] MRJ closed his peroration with a statement of defiance: 'were the Governing Body to abolish his gown—a feat for them by no means impossible—he himself should continue to wear it every day and all day'.[237]

On 19 March 1881, MRJ proposed the motion 'That higher female education is objectionable'. This debate was his idea, and is his first real foray into one of the major political debates of his professional life. It's worth quoting his speech at length here: his views on this subject never changed, but this is the first and only time he really gives them full articulation:

> Before bringing forward my reasons for objecting to the higher education of women I will sketch the area over which I consider the list of a lady's accomplishments ought to extend. She should know the 3 leading modern languages, French, German & Italian. Should be somewhat of a musician and be able to draw. History, Geography and English literature she should be acquainted with and as to Mathematics should know enough Arithmetic to keep accounts. Almost the most important of all is that she should be well acquainted with house-keeping duties. Such an education should make her a pleasant member of society and a competent help-meet for her man. Which is the end where to she was created.

> Now for a women to go through an elaborate course of University reading and attain the highest standard in Classics or Mathematics seems to me a contravention of the laws of Providence. It must unfit her for any domestic position. Besides a woman who has passed the standard of a Senior Classic or a Senior Wrangler has done no more than fit herself for a lecturer, and women lecturers will not be in request while men are to be had. What are we supposed to gain by throwing open all the professions to women as well as men. It seems to me that the technical education a woman would have to undergo to be a lawyer or doctor would [make her] cease in great degree to be womanly. And hereby we should lose an element of undoubted value for the sake of gaining one whole worth is not nearly so appreciable.

Women graduates might lead to 'female suffrage, and . . . women speaking in public assemblies—both radically bad, I am certain'.[238]

Other debates were nearer his scholarly interests. In February 1882, the motion was 'That we need not believe in ghosts'. It was all, MRJ suggested, a matter of what one meant by 'belief'; for himself 'he could not but believe in anything and everything when in bed'—but that if he truly believed the stories he read, 'he should never know what a quiet night was again'. Perhaps ninety out of a hundred ghost stories, he suggested, could be dismissed—but to dismiss them all would be tantamount to a refusal to believe in the afterlife, and a denial of the evidence of the Bible, in which ghost certainly appear. People tended to dismiss the very possibility of ghosts, he thought, merely because they 'don't like the idea of such things happening'.[239] Another debate concerned a matter which was to become very close to MRJ's heart, and on which had very firm views: the restoration of ancient buildings. His position on this, which again did not change for the rest of his life, was heavily influenced by Ruskin: 'it was only our duty to preserve them for posterity if we could do so without altering them. *Restoration* was unjustifiable, *reparation* was beneficial'.[240] This was a debate in which the older MRJ took an active part, as a recognized authority on, for example, ecclesiastical architecture, or medieval stained glass; the ghost stories are dotted with asides on the depredations of modern restoration, or on the shortcomings of the Gothic revival.

* * *

'I like being in the VIth form', MRJ told his parents in September 1880.[241] The sixth form certainly had its benefits. He moved into better rooms, and in his last year got to live in the top room in the Tower, with his own staircase. This was a particularly idyllic place to be in spring and summer, when he could smell 'the perfume of the lime blossom in the Long Walk', and hear the water rushing through Romney Weir, and the peeling bells of the clock towers: he was particularly fond of hearing St. George's Bells in the Curfew Tower ringing out St. David's, the psalm tune: 'How blest the man who ne'er consents By ill advice to walk Nor stands in sinners' ways nor sits Where men profanely talk.'[242] This tune, and these memories, obviously meant a lot to MRJ, and he invokes them poetically in 'After Dark in the Playing Fields':

> First the thin voice of the pavilion clock, then the deeper sound from the Castle quadrangle, then Lupton's Tower, drowning the Curfew Tower by its nearness. . . . The Curfew Tower was still playing St. David's tune and the little chime that follows, for the third and last time, but the other bells had finished what they had to say, and now there was silence, and again the 'restless changing weir' was the only thing that broke—no, that emphasized it.[243]

As a sixth former, the food definitely improved. Nugent-Bankes's sixth-form fare included a first course of rabbit or veal with potatoes, followed by beefsteak pudding, with the invariable jam roly-poly for pudding, all accompanied by beer. A typical meal for MRJ would be a cold joint of meat, followed by apple pie, with Stilton to finish.[244]

He got his own fag, Robert Edward Myddelton-Biddulph, whose family owned Chirk Castle in Denbighshire. On leaving Eton, Myddelton (he dropped the Biddulph) got a commission in the Royal Welsh Fusiliers, and was decorated for his service in the Boer War and the First World War, rising to the rank of Colonel. As a fag, MRJ thought him 'Rather big with a fat face & black hair—slightly yellow complexion. Rather slow, but makes very good toast'. Before supper, there might be a 'working off'—that is, caning a smaller boy for some malefaction—but only on 'rare occasions'.[245]

Classics lessons were in Hornby's study, with the Headmaster sat behind an octagonal table. Hornby wasn't an inspiring teacher—the endless construing of Latin verses had the boys perpetually on the lookout for diversions (as when Babington Smith set off the cartridges in his fire)—but he was well liked, and MRJ was happy in his classes. The same couldn't be said for Edward Rouse, the Maths master: 'He is a sort of fiend', MRJ thought. 'Rouse is hanxious that we should learn by 'eart the Sixth Book of Heuclid. But it will be of no use to us hereafter.'[246] In 1881, Rouse was responsible for what is unquestionably MRJ's worst-ever school report:

> James K.S. last in the same set. Much too sleepy in school. Seems to get no good from class teaching, and without class teaching (when there is no taste or aptitude for the study) mathematics become an undigested mass of formulae from which no mental food can be extracted.[247]

Perhaps as revenge against Rouse, MRJ and St. Clair Donaldson argued forcefully in a Pop debate for the uselessness of Mathematics, which MRJ dismissed as 'degenerating into a nasty quibbling accuracy about x's and y's'—another view he was to hold, without much further reflection, for the rest of his life.[248]

There were regular visits to London. In January 1880, he went with Luxmoore, and they visited the Wren and Hawksmoor churches in the City, climbed to the top of the Monument ('foggy but fun'), and went to see a Holbein exhibition. In the afternoon, they went to a performance of *H.M.S. Pinafore* at the Opera Comique off the Strand. MRJ was enraptured: 'We had a stage box. I had my glass with me, and saw beautifully. I don't think I ever enjoyed myself quite so much before.... I now rank H.M.S. Pinafore on a level with the Messiah.'[249] (Well, he *was* seventeen.)

In the box at the Opera Comique, he met J. K. Stephen, then an undergraduate at King's, for the first time. At Eton, Stephen (who was Virginia Woolf's cousin) had gained the reputation for being 'the king among schoolboys' because he was so good at everything—an outstanding scholar, a superb sportsman (by far the best player of the Wall Game of his generation), handsome, funny, and extraordinarily charismatic.[250] Stephen is the kind of figure around whom legends swirl. Oscar Browning, very much a mentor, thought that he was 'the most brilliant young man with whom I ever came into contact, and was regarded by all his contemporaries as an intellectual giant'.[251] Arthur Benson thought him the best Cambridge undergraduate of his time, 'at the very top of his reputation, and certainly the most marked man of the younger generation'.[252] On his one visit to King's, Oscar Wilde was said to have swapped repartee with Stephen like a pair of tennis players.[253] As a Fellow of King's, he was employed as tutor to Prince Albert Victor ('Eddy'), the Duke of Clarence, the son of the future King Edward VII, with whom it's entirely possible that he had a sexual relationship.[254] It's less possible that Stephen was Jack the Ripper, though he has been fingered for that role—as has the Duke of Clarence.[255] MRJ was drawn into Stephen's circle for a time in Cambridge, and saw quite a lot of Prince Eddy as a consequence. But Stephen suffered from a bipolar condition, which seemingly worsened after a head injury in December 1886. A series of psychotic episodes saw him confined to an asylum in Nottingham, where he was diagnosed as suffering from 'Extreme depression—almost mute'. He died there shortly afterwards in 1892, age 32: cause of death was recorded as 'Mania', 'Refusal of Food', and 'Exhaustion'.[256] Almost the last thing Stephen did was to complete a volume of poetry, *Lapsus Calami* ('A Slip of the Pen'), which was published in 1891 (to some acclaim and success: it went through four editions in 1891 alone; a second volume of poetry appeared in November 1891).

Arthur found the Eton poem 'The Old School List' so moving that he couldn't bear to read it. Another poem, the Latin ode to King's, 'Coll. Regal.', closes with a stanza which ties together JKS and MRJ:

> Vivat J. K. Stephanus,
> Humilis poeta!
> Vivat Monty Jamesius,
> Vivat A, B, C, D, E
> Et totus Alphabeta![257]

('Long live J. K. Stephen, / Humble poet! / Long live Monty James, / Long live A, B, C, D, E / And all the alphabet!')

There were more prosaic affairs, too, in this trip to London. MRJ needed to get his teeth fixed. They had been troubling him for a while, and would do so for years to come, until he eventually capitulated to the entreaties of friends and family and got himself a set of dentures. In December 1879, he had an abscessed tooth removed, and two fillings. On the London trip with Luxmoore the following month, he had five more teeth filled. Luxmoore thought he had 'teeth like Egyptian finances' (because it would take so long to get them straight).[258]

In his earlier years at Eton, Luxmoore didn't think MRJ was doing himself justice in the round. He was undeniably a scholarly phenomenon, though most observers recognized that his erudition was, in many senses of the word, weird. But he was hardly the kind of all-round prodigy of a boy that Eton prided itself on producing—no J. K. Stephen, certainly, nor a Harry Cust. 'I think him rather under valued in College', Luxmoore confided to Herbert in 1879. 'He is not of course a boys' boy nor a very forceful character, but I think he ought to have his fair share of influence & have never quite seen to what fault on whose side it is owing that [he] appears not quite to get it.'[259] One gets the sense that it is really in the sixth form that MRJ begins to come into his own as a schoolboy, widening his circle of friends and getting quite heavily involved in Eton's cultural life. He was, in his way, a very sociable man, and this sociability starts in earnest once he gets into the sixth form.

It's around this time that MRJ really begins the series of visits to the homes of friends that would take up much of his leisure time over the years. July 1881 finds him with Arthur at Lis Escop, Bishop Benson's episcopal palace in Truro. Things got off to a comic start at breakfast the first morning, when the bishop mistook MRJ for a Mr Arthur James, and so assumed he must know his old friend Mrs Rogers (he didn't). MRJ found the great man 'exceedingly funny in appearance with a tremendous head, long hair, and no hair on his face' (unlike, one supposes, Herbert James, to whom MRJ wrote these words, who had one of those enormous, floribundant Victorian beards).[260] For MRJ, the best thing about Bishop Benson was that he told ghost stories of an evening. This was an interest he obviously passed on to his sons: Arthur and Hugh Benson were both accomplished writers of ghost stories, and Fred a stupendous one.

The following summer, he visited the Donaldson family in Pangbourne, in the wake of a tragedy. Seton, St. Clair's younger brother, was drowned in an awful boating accident in the Thames at Eton on 28 May. He had gone out boating with his friend Charles Fergusson, and the boat capsized as they were changing places. Seton's legs were caught in the boat line, which dragged him under: Fergusson held his head above water for a quarter of an hour, until he could hold him no longer, and was nearly drowned himself in the process (he was dragged out of the water by boys from a neighbouring school, and went on to live a long and successful life, eventually becoming Governor-General of New Zealand). MRJ went to the funeral in Sulham church, two miles from Bère Court, and, as editor of the *Chronicle* dedicated an entire issue to a long and powerful eulogy for Seton, which he wrote himself: 'Most boys are brave and manly, but none braver or manlier than he'. 'Verily', it closed, 'it is well with him now.'[261] Lady Donaldson, the boys' mother, was a widow who lived at Bère Court with her sister and a young companion, and MRJ's visit was obviously much appreciated: 'Lady Donaldson makes you feel you would cut your throat in five minutes if it would afford her any relief', he told Babington Smith.[262] Seton's death brought MRJ close to the whole family. 'I cannot suppose Lady Donaldson will ever recover', he wrote; and when St. Clair returned to Eton, MRJ thought, 'he hardly knows where he is'. The oldest Donaldson brother, Stuart, was a master at Eton, and a good friend of Sydney's; it was Sydney, in fact, who broke the news of Seton's death to Stuart. St. Clair, Sydney thought, was 'nearly mad' with grief.[263] For years afterwards, MRJ would find a home at Bère Court.

Later that summer of 1882, immediately after leaving Eton, MRJ went on holidays to Switzerland and the Italian Tyrol with St. Clair and Stuart Donaldson, who were haunted by their brother's loss, and had terribly upsetting dreams: 'Stuart had the most pathetic dream I ever remember the other night at Constance', he told Babington Smith, 'about bringing Seton back—wonderfully vivid.'[264]

'I did not know him well myself', MRJ admitted to his parents at the time about Seton; later he confessed 'I had never spoken to him'. But over the years, because it 'deepened and solidified' his closeness to the Donaldson family 'to my great gain' (he adored Lady Donaldson), the death acquired an enormous symbolic importance for him: 'The name of Seton Donaldson remains among the sacred things.' [265]

* * *

In the summer of 1880, MRJ sat the Newcastle Scholarship exams. The Newcastle was and remains Eton's most prestigious award, established in 1829 from the benefaction of the Duke of Newcastle, with an annual award of £250 (an enormous amount in the nineteenth century). Scholarships, prizes, and awards were important to MRJ and his family not only for existential reasons (he was the kind of boy who got them), but also out of financial necessity. The educational course on which MRJ set sail did not come cheap. Even with his King's Scholarship of £100 a year at Eton, costs mounted up. On top of the fees, there were annual payments to the Headmaster and the Tutor (ten guineas a year for Collegers, twenty for Oppidans), plus what could be very considerable tradesmen's bills necessary to maintain the lifestyle of an institution which was, by the nineteenth century, 'narrowly a school for the rich'.[266] MRJ's letters home characteristically open with either requests for money or thanks on the arrival of the latest cheque or postal order. Over the summer of 1879, he wrote to the editor of the *Windsor Gazette*, asking for paid work.[267]

MRJ didn't get the Newcastle in 1880—the prize was awarded to Walter Hobhouse, future Oxford don and Headmaster of Durham School, who was three years above MRJ. But he was placed in the select, the list of runners-up, along with Arthur, Babington Smith, and Hugh Macnaghten. As a reward for this, Luxmoore organized a holiday to France for MRJ and James Pixley, who was a year behind him. French holidays would become more-or-less annual events for MRJ, and this is where it all starts, 'my introduction to medieval glass and sculpture, but above all to the sacred soil of France.' On the way, they stayed in the 'really luxurious' Lord Warden Hotel in Dover—where, over thirty years later, Harrington and Dunning stay in their pursuit of Karswell in 'Casting the Runes'. The channel crossing was like a millpond, and on the other side, at Abbeville, they visited St. Wulfram's Church—where MRJ has Karswell meeting his nasty end. At Amiens, he was very struck by the Cathedral, with its two towers, spire, and 'vast Rose Window'. In Paris, they visited the Louvre, where MRJ saw the Venus de Milo, and Notre Dame, and sat in cafes drinking coffee and watching 'Trapeze Gymnastics at which ma's hair would have curled'. His first visit to 'Furrin Parts', as he wrote to his parents from the Hotel Castiglione in Paris, had him hungry for more.[268]

He sat for the Newcastle again in 1881, and again placed in the Select, along with Arthur, Babington Smith, and Harry Cust (Macnaghten won it that year). Luxmoore worried that his mind wasn't on his schoolwork that term, and that he was 'loafing': 'his place is not maintained against others & there is more mention of sufficiency than of brilliance or effort', he wrote to Herbert.[269] He was certainly very wrapped up in his arcane researches around this time, which is when he wrote 'Occult Sciences'.

By January 1882, when he sat the scholarship exam for King's, he had certainly got himself together. He was the highest-placed of all the Classics applicants, joint first overall alongside a brilliant mathematician. He beat the runner up, the future judge Sidney Rowlatt (author of the notorious Rowlatt Act of 1919, which violently suppressed the Indian nationalist movement) by one mark, 464 to 463, though Rowlatt was a second-year undergraduate at the time. The examiner, J. E. C. Welldon, was astonished by the standard of the field that year, which 'was larger and intellectually stronger than any we have had within my memory, I may say than any we have ever had. [MRJ's] total of marks was higher than Inge's three years ago, and he beat Rowlatt who was considered an exceptional scholar when we elected him in 1880.' (William Ralph Inge, winner of the Chancellor's Medal in 1883, went on to become Lady Margaret Professor of Divinity at Cambridge, and the anti-modern 'Gloomy' Dean of St. Paul's.) But, Welldon warned Herbert,

> If I have any remark to make it is that I could wish his style were equal to his knowledge. Nobody can examine him and not conceive a great respect for his ability; yet I thought his work would often be more telling if he did not seem to fling down information in a slapdash, almost defiant manner without much effort to order or marshal it, to present his facts in relation to each other and make his composition effective as a whole.[270]

The 'almost defiant manner' Welldon identifies here seems very characteristic of the way in which MRJ insisted on carrying out his intellectual life, from his pride in his horrible handwriting to his absolute insistence on eccentric and arcane forms of knowledge. Herbert Ryle, writing with his congratulations, also thought that 'Montie more strong & rough than polished as a scholar'.[271] Luxmoore wrote to MRJ, warning him that 'your danger . . . [is] of miscellanious [sic] accumulation, without enough sorting & coordinating to leave room for the original to grow'.[272] One of the few surviving examples of MRJ's Eton school work, a Latin translation, comes with Luxmoore's comments: he thought it 'Good', but 'too elaborate'.[273] But Luxmoore confessed to Herbert that he thought himself somewhat to blame for this: 'I am always convinced that more incisive criticism of pure scholarship than I had to give would have presented M's work in a rather more chastened form to the examiner's eye, & breeds the misgiving that I am not all he wants.'[274]

This scholarship result put MRJ in a good place for sitting the Newcastle again that Easter. This time, there would be no 'loafing'. He spent long days working towards the examinations, and was placed first. MRJ 'cd. not have got more Eton distinction', Luxmoore thought, adding: 'Had the boy been other than he is, I might plume myself on a friendship which I value, but where there is so much frankness & so little repulsion, I cannot say the difficulty of the task has been equal to the pleasure of the recall: so I cannot claim much credit on that score.'[275] Writing from the South Camp, Aldershot, Geo. William Johnson sent his congratulations:

> Hit a long wile sin I roat to you befour. But i want ter congrattilate you for avin gott thee Noocassil. I allus sed, hif you wos to cum an ax me hoo will git hit, I wil say Baldolf Barker.[276]

To celebrate, Luxmoore took MRJ and St. Clair, who had been placed in the Select, to Italy. The boys took the train to London, 'accompanied by heat and babies', and met Luxmoore in the Savile Club. In Florence, they visited the Uffizi and the Academy, and MRJ became 'a confirmed Botticellian by contemplation of that artist's picture of spring'. And then, on an 'exquisite' afternoon, the boys walked to Fiesole: 'There is I suppose no place anything at all like Florence', MRJ told his parents. In Bologna, they climbed the Torre degli Asinelli, and went to a performance of *The Barber of Seville*. From Bologna they went to Venice, where they took the train home via Simplon, taking what would, the following year, be the route of the newly launched Orient Express. At Simplon, the pass was blocked by a snowfall. The passengers had to get out and continue their way by sledge, where they were 'nearly wiped out' by a series of avalanches crashing over them, one of which left MRJ entangled with another passenger, a fat, red-faced Frenchman.[277] 'We were very nearly carried over a precipice', he wrote excitedly.[278]

The tragedy of Seton Donaldson's death fell over the summer of 1882. But there were happy moments too, in what was a gloriously sunny season. Bathing, for MRJ, 'was always a joy': 'Clad in a simple towel, one basked on the Acropolis and looked at the Castle shimmering in the heat, and, with the smell of the river in one's own nose, was conscious of complete happiness.'[279] (Later, on his French holidays, we find MRJ plunging naked into a river at any opportunity.) At Sydney's instigation, in 1879 he had joined the Eton Corps of Rifle

Volunteers. He was, he realized, pretty useless at the militaristic aspect of things, and never wanted to take a peep in their artillery room. He was perversely proud of the fact that his promotion to Lance-Corporal represented the limits of his military ambitions and abilities.[280] But this did allow him, in the 'perfect weather' of the late summer of 1882, to go camping with Babington Smith to Ashridge Park in the Chilterns. There, he saw the Chapel, whose stained glass was to make an appearance in 'The Treasure of Abbot Thomas'.

The camping trip 'softened the pangs of leaving', but it was time to go.[281] In August 1882, he was 20 years old. Tim Card, the Eton historian and former Vice-Provost, believes MRJ 'may have been the oldest boy in the history of the school'.[282] He returned to Eton for the 'dreadful business of packing up': 'It is worse leaving one's room I think than almost anything else', he told Babington Smith.[283] 'Well dear old boy', Herbert wrote to him, 'years come and years go, but it will take a long time to get the taste of Eton out of our mouths—and for you, at least, there is not much bitter in that taste'. But King's College Cambridge, as Herbert recognized, meant the chance to live 'life in a larger sphere'.[284] 'I expect you will enjoy King's tremendously', Arthur Benson wrote to MRJ not long before he went up. 'I doubt if you will ever leave it for the rest of your life.'[285]

4

King's, 1882

In October 1882, MRJ moved into his new rooms in King's Lane in Cambridge. After unpacking his books, he went in search of company:

> I then called on St. Clair . . . He eventually came to my rooms & I speedily originated a rag by hanging his hat on the coal scuttle. Marshall & Thomas thought my bookcases were falling & came to see if they could render any assistance. We were at that moment somewhat mixed on the hearthrug. I was about to lift him up with my hands but the interruption frustrated me.[1]

This looks like business as usual for MRJ, a continuation of the Eton schoolboy life with its eroticized male friendships and physical horseplay. And in many ways it was. MRJ certainly found a ready-made community in Cambridge, which was full of people he already knew. St. Clair Donaldson was just down the road at Trinity, as were Harry Cust and Henry Babington Smith. Arthur Benson was a year above him at King's. Many other classmates and contemporaries were around and about.

One of the first things he did on arriving at King's, in fact, was to join the Pitt Club—very much the preserve of Old Etonians at the time, 'exclusive and aristocratic, and it is a social honour to be elected to membership', according to MRJ's King's colleague Nathaniel Wedd—along with St. Clair and in fact most of the Etonian freshmen at Cambridge.[2] The Pitt Club is located in a fine Neoclassical building on Jesus Lane, and MRJ spent a lot of time there: for much of the 1880s, the greater part of his correspondence was written from the Pitt Club; he was elected President of the Pitt in 1887.

There was, MRJ thought, a 'rift' at King's between Etonians and non-Etonians, and 'undeniably an Eton clique', who thought that 'their old sacred preserve was being laid waste by revolutionaries'.[3] Nathaniel Wedd, very much *not* an Old Etonian, who came up to King's in 1883 from the City of London School and became a Fellow in 1888, agreed that the College was divided between what he called the 'Best Set'—predominantly but not exclusively Old

Etonian—and the 'Outsiders' or 'Scallywags', of whom he was definitely one. 'The dominant personality in the best set was Arthur Benson. He decided who was, or who was not, to be known, and his word was law in the best circles.'[4] Benson, Wedd believed, had drawn up a 'black list' of 'those whom it was permissible to know, and those who must be regarded as beyond the pale'.[5] ('What brutes we've been!', Herbert Ryle exclaimed, when an Outsider friend confessed his unhappiness at being blacklisted and ignored.)[6] This was a schism which lasted throughout the decade.[7] MRJ would unquestionably have been one of the Best Set. That said, he was the *only* Etonian in his Freshman cohort at King's in the autumn of 1882. What was going on?

* * *

For all its atmosphere of familiarity and safety, MRJ had arrived at a college, and a university, which were undergoing serious changes, the product of the same forces which had brought change to Eton, but with even more profound and far-reaching consequences.

The King's College of Our Lady and St. Nicholas (to give it its full name) has long had, according to one of its historians, 'a reputation for peculiarity'.[8] MRJ himself thought it 'an odd mixture of medieval formalism and, I should say, slackness'.[9] Historically, it stood at an angle to the university of which it was a part, and to which it had a rather different relationship from that of all the other colleges. Until as recently as 1861, King's had been a closed corporation, admitting only Etonians. Founded in 1441 by Henry VI, Eton and King's were twinned from the start. Henry wished King's to be comprised of a 'scanty band of white-robed scholars', seventy in total—a mystical number, with its origins in Christ's 'other seventy' disciples as recorded in Luke's Gospel—and it was very consciously set up as an institution for the mass production of clergymen.[10] King's was initially exempted from the University's jurisdiction by a papal bull, and for centuries awarded its own degrees without recourse to university examinations. The College was exempt from these until as late as 1851, although it did institute its own annual exams in 1829, and its own independent finals exams in 1836.[11] Eton scholars succeeded automatically to Fellowship of King's—a sinecure for life, terminable only by death, apostasy, or marriage—without having necessarily sat any kind of competitive examination since secondary school. Perhaps unsurprisingly, owing to its sense of self-containment (and self-satisfaction) and intellectual isolation, by the mid-eighteenth-century King's had come to be regarded as the worst of the Cambridge colleges, dubbed by contemporaries 'a splendid cenotaph of learning', or 'the grave of talent'.[12]

What King's did have, though, in abundance, was money, and social standing—along with Eton, it was at the heart of the establishment. From 1814–50, it was presided over by the extraordinarily reactionary Provost George Thackeray, who simply blocked all change.

But the University was changing. 'It might be said, with some exaggeration, that in 1870 the University of Cambridge was a provincial seminary.' These are the words of the Cambridge historian Christopher Brooke—they are, in fact, the opening words of his volume of the definitive, authorized history of the University. But things were changing, slowly: 'Cambridge in 1870 was only just beginning to grow once again into a distinguished academy of learning.'[13] Most startlingly, women's colleges were opening: Girton in 1869, Newnham in 1871. There will be much to say about women students and scholars in due course, but for now it is enough to note that for many years the Girton and Newnham students were not full members of the University in that they were not eligible to take degrees. The first woman graduate of the University was Queen Elizabeth, the future Queen Mother, awarded an honorary degree at the head of the first female graduating class in 1948. MRJ did his significant bit to ensure that Cambridge was, by over a quarter of a century, the last of the ancient universities of Britain and Ireland to award degrees to women (the Scottish universities awarded them in the 1890s, Trinity College Dublin in 1905, Oxford in 1920).

'Nobody comes to the university in order to learn', wrote Virginia Woolf's father, Leslie Stephen—soon to decamp to Bloomsbury, but then a Fellow of Trinity Hall—in 1865. He was exaggerating, of course, but not by very much. Stephen's *Sketches from Cambridge* presents a withering picture of entitled Fellows spending their lives 'laying down a cellar of sound port wine', of 'third-rate lectures in Latin and Greek', of an 'intrinsically useless' curriculum, of Senate elections on important issues dominated by backwoodsmen ('a crowd of rarely seen barristers and country parsons') who are in reality far more interested in rowing than in education—as are many of the students.[14] Students who graduated with ordinary (non-honours) degrees were known as 'Poll Men', which the university's own library website defines thus: 'From the Greek, *hoi polloi*: the many: used for the great majority of undergraduates who did not achieve, and often did not aspire to, honours in the tripos.'[15] (What this meant was that many of Cambridge's most distinguished alumni were Poll Men, graduating without honours: Wordsworth and Coleridge, for example, or Darwin.)

It's certainly the case that College Fellows at Cambridge up to Leslie Stephen's time weren't exactly overburdened: 'College fellows had few *necessary* duties', writes Peter Searby in his own volume in the official Cambridge university history; a Fellow 'valued his right to employ his time as he saw fit'.[16] Fellows weren't obliged to teach, and were not required to do any significant research—though many, but by no means all of them, did. Stephen remarked ruefully that College Fellows 'have passed the best years of their lives within our walls, . . . have imbibed our prejudices and our creeds with their daily food, and . . . have, as it were, taken the very shape of the walls in which they live'.[17] He could have been talking about MRJ. In essence, he *was*.

By the middle of the century, there was a strong feeling that both Oxford and Cambridge Universities had been passed by, their scholarship obsolete, their curricula damagingly narrow.[18] A petition for reforming Cambridge University was signed by luminaries including Erasmus and Charles Darwin, W. M. Thackeray, and Charles Babbage. In 1849, Prime Minister Lord John Russell (who, uniquely amongst Prime Ministers up to that point, had been a student at Edinburgh—because his father believed an Oxbridge education to be a waste of time and money) appointed a 'Royal Commission of Enquiry into the best methods of securing the improvements of the Universities of Oxford and Cambridge', chaired by John Graham, former Master of Christ's College, and now Bishop of Chester. Cambridge initially refused to co-operate with the Commission, believing it unconstitutional, but Russell held firm—though some of the Colleges remained obstructive or unforthcoming, and the Masters of Jesus and Clare refused to participate. Like the Clarendon Commission Report a few years later, Graham's report (which came out in 1850) was full of very modest proposals for reform, which many saw as barely adequate to the moment.[19] (Russell himself was certainly not satisfied with the report.) Nevertheless, they were greeted in some quarters with rage and anguish. Realizing that the University would not reform itself, the government eventually imposed reforms: the Cambridge University Act of 1856 led to the promulgation of new university statutes in 1861, which vested the University's power in its Senate.

Among the Commission's proposals for Cambridge was an expansion of the University's curriculum. This was sorely needed. By the time MRJ arrived in King's in 1882, the Cambridge curriculum—the very idea of what constituted an undergraduate education—was moving towards the end of a long and often difficult process of expansion, which the Graham Report had hastened along. The Mathematical Tripos had been established in 1748, and was for years Cambridge's only degree subject. In the late eighteenth century, the University had eight endowed Chairs in the sciences, though it did not teach science. There had been a Regius Professor of Greek since 1540, and the Chancellor's

Classical Medals were instituted in 1751 (these were among the University's most prestigious awards; MRJ was awarded one in 1886)—but the Classical Tripos itself was not established until 1824, and until 1849 it was only available to students who had already passed the Mathematical Tripos (until 1854, students still needed an ordinary degree first). A flurry of new Triposes were created in the wake of Graham: Moral Science (1851), Natural Science (1851), Law (1858), Theology (1874), History (1875), Semitic Languages (1878), Indian Languages (1879), Medieval and Modern Languages (1886), Mechanical Sciences (1894), Economics (1905). For real conservatives, Christopher Brooke writes, these new Triposes were 'the damnable intrusion of modern secular civilization, tending to the destruction of all that was most precious in Cambridge'.[20]

In the wake of Graham, and for perhaps the first time in its history, King's found itself in tune with the times, and ahead of the rest of the University. The man primarily responsible for this was Augustus Austen Leigh. Part of a venerable Eton and King's dynasty (and Jane Austen's great-nephew), Austen Leigh was the College Tutor from 1868–81, where he spearheaded some really significant reform, most particularly in his insistence that students at King's, uniquely amongst Cambridge colleges, had to enroll in honours Triposes.[21] No other men's college had this regulation until after the Second World War, which meant that King's did disproportionately well in the Triposes, and most particularly in the Classical Tripos and the newly established Historical Tripos. King's began to produce an intellectual elite, seriously bent on achieving the highest honours.[22] In 1874, for example, every Kingsman bar one graduated with a First.[23]

The other major reform sweeping the University was the abolition of religious tests, according to which holders of any public office had to swear allegiance to the Church of England. This was the key episode in the secularization of the University, its transformation from a *de facto* seminary to a research institution. The Cambridge University Act of 1856 stipulated that no religious test or declaration of faith was necessary for any degree except Divinity. But it also specified that membership of the Senate, the University's governing body, was confined to those 'who had declared themselves to be *bona fide* members of the Church of England'.[24] For the next fifteen years, in the universities and in parliament, a fierce political battle was fought over the remaining tests.[25] The casualties of this battle included Leslie Stephen. In stereotypical Victorian intellectual fashion, he had lost his faith after reading *The Origin of Species*, and became a champion of agnosticism. Unable to reconcile this with an adherence to religious tests, he resigned his Fellowship at Trinity Hall and moved to a house in Bloomsbury, not far from the British Museum in Central London. The intellectual and artistic history of twentieth-century Britain might have been very different had he stayed on in Cambridge. Henry Sidgwick, the great intellectual powerhouse of late-Victorian Cambridge, and one of the founders of both Newnham College and the Society for Psychical Research, resigned his Fellowship at Trinity in 1869. Two years later, the religious tests were finally abolished. Sidgwick, who had retained his lectureship in Moral Philosophy, was made an Honorary Fellow of Trinity in 1881. We shall be meeting both Henry Sidgwick and the Bloomsbury Group again—the path MRJ's life took intersected with theirs in many places, and not often happily.

By tradition, Cambridge colleges had been populated not only by clergymen but by *celibate* clergymen. From the 1830s, Heads of Colleges, and Professors (who were employed by the University rather than the colleges) were allowed to marry, but not College Fellows. Fellows were formally permitted to marry in 1882—at which point, it was said, an army of mysterious wives appeared from their hiding places all over England—though in reality the statute requiring celibacy was removed in 1860, after which individual colleges changed their practices piecemeal.[26] In 1865, Stephen observed that 'The married Fellow—a few years ago as strange a monster as a hippogriff—already swarms in our courts', though he acknowledged that this was a 'dangerous topic' to raise.[27] In 1881, the Classicist A. H. Cooke became King's first married Fellow.[28] In *Eton and King's*, MRJ, who never married, looked back on this changing world with some regret: 'Most of them [Fellows] are married, and live normal family lives, which is no doubt an excellent thing, but if I may air a grievance, makes Collegiate life a very different and rather difficult affair . . . The centre of gravity of [a Fellow's] affections runs a great risk of being shifted from the College to the villa.'[29]

These are the historical tides by which MRJ was caught at Cambridge: gender-equality, secularization, professionalization, scholarly rigour, the social mission of the universities, a gradual widening of access. Some he tried to resist; sometimes he was successful in this. MRJ stands, Janus-faced, on the boundary between two different historical conceptions of the academic and scholarly life.[30] As a celibate bachelor don he would have been at home in, say, the King's of the seventeenth century—except that he never took Holy Orders, and, as we shall see, resisted some pretty strong moral pressure over several years from his father to go into the Church. As a scholar and a publishing industry he was a phenomenon, who simply knew more things than anybody else, and knew them differently. And yet his interests range so widely that they fit into no academic discipline that I can think of. MRJ's own preferred term, 'antiquary', is accurate, but has no place in a modern university, being a term which belongs most properly to the intellectual life of the seventeenth century.[31] It is no accident that many of his ghost stories have a seventeenth-century setting or background: 'The Ash-Tree', 'Martin's Close', 'The Diary of Mr. Poynter', 'The Uncommon Prayer Book', 'A Neighbour's Landmark'.

* * *

One of the first letters MRJ got from home was from his mother. It is a very strange and troubling letter, quite unique amongst their extensive correspondence:

> You told me to write fully of myself—of my soul I cannot say much besides my usual complaint . . . I *loathe myself* sometimes—but I cannot dwell on this just now—& I don't know that it is profitable to say such things even to you—but that I know you will pray for me.[32]

The handwriting for this letter is much shakier than usual, and the letter is often difficult to decipher; there are many underlinings. What is this? Mary Emily's habitual concerns with the state of her own and her family's health can sometimes seem obsessive, bespeaking real underlying anxieties. In the case of Grace's mental and physical health, she had good cause to be anxious. But there is a real feeling here of something being let out.

This was no doubt exacerbated by an opportunity that had recently come Herbert's way for a new and much more lucrative parish, a King's living. The problem was that it was hundreds of miles away in Prescot, Lancashire, just outside Liverpool.[33] (Herbert's good friend J. C. Ryle had a couple of years previously been enthroned Bishop of Liverpool, so may have had a hand in this idea; Herbert made regular trips to Liverpool on Evangelical business.) Understandably, this dominates the family correspondence for a while. Sydney, for one, was rather keen on the idea: 'Prescot looms more probable? Eh?' he wrote to MRJ on 16 October, two days before Mary Emily's letter. When Herbert declined the offer, largely on the grounds of Grace's health, Sydney thought it 'rather a pity in some ways', but acknowledged 'I guess it wd. have proved a beastly hole to live in'.[34] Grace herself was mightily relieved:

> We ain't going to Prescot after all. It is a beastly squalid place. The house is in very bad repair and the atmosphere nasty . . . I wish I were not a consideration in the matter, but I cannot help not being stronger, and fortunately it is not only on my account that Father declines.[35]

Mary Emily and Grace drew up plans for a rest cure on the French Riviera, though in the end these fell through, and they ended up spending Christmas 1882 in Torquay.

Ber, meanwhile, spent the autumn of 1882 stationed in the military barracks at Aldershot, waiting for a posting. 'Have you seen the comet?' he asked MRJ in November.[36] The Great Comet of 1882, visible to the naked eye from September to December, was causing consternation amongst troops returning from Egypt, who blamed it for an enormous outbreak of dysentery, which affected 70 per cent of the army; a medical orderly, meanwhile, had committed suicide by cutting his throat 'from ear to ear' (Ber loved grim details like this). The following years found him stationed in China, but at the time it looked likely that India would be his destination, at least according to Geo. W. Johnson: 'India is a five years stashun. Wot I ses—sen me hout wile young an let me hav sum spawt. Oos afrayd? Tygers an wails an lyons an hipotocemious, drat hem hal. Jonson? Not known to feer.'[37]

But the thing that seemed most to preoccupy Ber's letters around this time was the fact that MRJ arrived home after his first term in Cambridge sporting a moustache—and even, for a time, a beard (items which had until 1859 been forbidden to King's students—it was the duty of a College porter to shave them).[38] This development amused Ber no end, and his letters from 1883 are full of illustrations of cut-throat razors, shaving brushes, and bristly faces of various kinds, and are addressed to 'Shavey Bardorf' or 'a party by the name of Bardof sumthink Shavey'.[39] Bardolf Barker was a stubborn fellow, though, and the moustache remained unshorn for the duration of MRJ's undergraduate years.

* * *

MRJ studied for the Classical Tripos. His tutors at King's were George Prothero and J. E. C. Welldon. Prothero, the College's Senior Tutor, was a distinguished historian who had done more than anyone to put King's on the map as an institution for the study of History.[40] Welldon was an outstanding classicist, who walked into a position at King's immediately after graduating as Senior Classic and Chancellor's Medallist in 1877. At the end of MRJ's first year, Welldon left King's to take up the Headship of Dulwich College and then of Harrow, before moving on to become Bishop of Calcutta, and then Dean of Manchester and finally of Durham. (It was Welldon, we remember, who had written to Herbert the previous January to inform him of MRJ's unprecedented performance in the scholarship exams.) MRJ thought him 'an excellent

Tutor'.[41] The feeling was mutual, with Welldon confiding in Herbert that 'Intellectually and morally he is all I could wish'.[42]

There were lectures in the morning, but these were optional and often stupefying. The phenomenal classicist Walter Headlam, one of MRJ's undergraduate friends, found lectures a 'waste of time'.[43] MRJ himself didn't benefit much from lectures, either, certainly not in his formal subject of Classics, and characteristically maintained that 'for making acquaintance with the ancient literature I felt I was best left to myself'.[44] When, in his second year, he signed up for a course of lectures on Seneca's letters given by J. E. B. Mayor, the notoriously eccentric and parsimonious (his living expenses came to two pennies a day) Professor of Latin, he was the only person in the audience. (This would not be the only time Mayor delivered a course of lectures to an audience of one.)[45] 'The thing became a nightmare', he remembered, but at the time he found Mayor's lectures 'wonderfully learned' (his very copious notes for the series take up nearly a whole large notebook, with the occasional doodle), and the pair often ended up back in Mayor's rooms: 'He is a keen Vegetarian you know.'[46]

Brooke Foss Westcott's lectures were never sparsely attended. One of the foremost English theologians of his generation, Westcott was Regius Professor of Divinity and a Professorial Fellow of King's (and, from 1890, Bishop of Durham). While university lecture courses were not generally as poorly attended as Mayor's, the norm was a meagre 10–20 students. Westcott's lectures regularly drew audiences of 300. 'Every place in the hall is occupied', Arthur Benson wrote; 'there are dons, ladies, undergraduates, students from Girton and Newnham.'[47] MRJ went too, but he didn't approve of Westcott or his lectures. He found them 'Socialistic'.[48] In reality, Westcott was no radical: 'deeply conservative by instinct, and worried by the possible outcome of scholarly enquiry', according to one commentator.[49] Perhaps it was all the women in the audience that bothered MRJ, all those Girton and Newnham students. Perhaps it was Westcott's complex theology, which tended towards mysticism, metaphysics, and intellectual obscurity—not qualities MRJ particularly valued. Perhaps it was his sense of social mission: he gave lectures to Durham miners, and was soon to publish *Social Aspects of Christianity*.[50] Even Herbert—given to railing in print against the dangers of the 'Socialist wind-bag'—thought MRJ a little harsh on Westcott, though he acknowledged his 'wideness'.[51]

In his first term at King's, MRJ also got to know a number of the other Fellows. As we've seen, Oscar Browning had fled to King's after his dismissal from Eton in 1874. 'O.B.'s attentions are persistent', he wrote to his father in his second term.[52] Persistent, but not particularly welcome. MRJ was wary of him from the start, not least because O.B. never passed up an opportunity to trash Eton. However justified he personally may have felt his 'unremitting abuse of Eton' was, MRJ thought, 'it alienated us, and nothing after that could make us perfectly easy with him'.[53] O.B. held gatherings of students in his rooms on Sunday evenings—MRJ did go along occasionally, but preferred heading round to Trinity for a 'Hell' in Harry Cust's rooms.[54]

O.B. is the *only* person MRJ treats at all equivocally in his memoir, *Eton and King's*:

> I did learn to admire O.B. for many things: for the kindnesses he did to people who could make no return, for his abilities, which sometimes reminded one of genius, for his big ideas. *But*—the but is very large. I owe to him . . . a profound distaste for anything in the nature of a business meeting. Oh, the prolixity, the quarrelsomeness, the relentless plying of the grindstone for his own particular axe![55]

The reality is that O.B. *was* an equivocal character, on a number of fronts. Arthur Benson responded to his 'leering, satyr-like' fawning over young men with a kind of sexual terror: 'there is a kind of flesh-creeping feeling about the man', he thought, 'I don't know what, as though there was, or might be, something horrible in his mind.'[56] He was certainly a vain, arrogant egotist who lived on gossip and name-dropping. He was rumoured to throw away any book which did not mention him in its index (this joke seems to have been widely circulated: the 'Select Index' to the King's magazine *Basileon* contains the entry 'Oscar, Mr. Browning, No mention of').[57] O.B. could certainly be, as MRJ suggests, an impossible colleague. On the back of the menu for the King's Founder's Day dinner of 1885 (eight courses, including Golden Plovers), MRJ drew a caricature of O.B., and wrote out the verse from 'God save the Queen' which includes the lines 'Confound their politicks / Frustrate their knavish tricks'.[58]

O.B. graduated in 1860 with outstanding results in the Classical Tripos (Fourth Classic), but he was no one's idea of a great scholar. That said, he certainly was a man of letters, and there were plenty of those around in Victorian and Edwardian Cambridge, from Charles Kingsley to Edmund Gosse to E. M. Forster to Arthur Benson. Oscar Wilde believed him 'everything that is kind and pleasant'.[59] He could be an impressive advocate of righteous causes, and often found himself supporting progressive issues. He was, most notably, a champion of teacher education, instrumental in setting up and running Cambridge's Principal Day Training College. He supported the right of Jewish students to be exempt from taking the compulsory paper on Paley's *Evidences of Christianity* in the Cambridge Previous Examination. He was one of the founders of the Cambridge Home Rule Society, which took an unpopular line on the Irish Question in a Conservative institution (he once invited the Irish nationalist leader John Dillon to dine in Hall at Kings, and maintained at the dinner that 'it would be the proudest moment of his life, if he were thrown into prison on behalf of the suffering Irish').[60] Ironically, and quite characteristically, he was an advocate of women's education while being primarily remembered today for his appearance in Virginia Woolf's *A Room of One's Own*, where he is the subject of withering criticism for his belief that 'after looking over any set of examination papers . . . irrespective of any marks he might give, the best woman was intellectually the inferior of the worst man'.[61] Though they had very different reasons for doing so, a dislike of Oscar Browning might have been just about the only thing on which MRJ and Virginia Woolf would have agreed.

Even by the academic standards of the time, J. E. Nixon was an eccentric man. MRJ's friend Gordon Carey, who had been a pupil at King's College Choir School, remembered Nixon as 'small in stature, flurried in manner, with goatee beard, one false arm, one glass eye, and three pairs of spectacles in procession down the slope of his nose'.[62] In a story that must have delighted MRJ, it was rumoured that Nixon was actually compounded of two separate dons, who had been unfortunately compacted together as the result of a train accident near Euston.[63] A distinguished Classicist, he had returned to King's from King's College London, where he was Gresham Professor of Rhetoric (a position which he continued to hold at Cambridge). At Eton, Nixon had been bullied because of his disability, and no doubt also for class reasons (his father was a small tradesman in next-door Windsor), and this, MRJ thought, had made him 'a champion of the oppressed', whose many acts of kindness were as characteristic as his eccentricity, and much less exasperating.[64] 'The mind', MRJ recalled of Nixon, 'was like no one else's. It worked like a clock with the pendulum taken off, or an electric fan out of order.' At meetings, he was up and down 'like an insane Jack-in-the Box', and once demanded the right of reply to his own motion, which he then disagreed with profoundly and voted against (his was the only dissenting vote).

Nixon was also bizarrely accident prone. He was given to riding around King's on a tricycle: under normal circumstances, this would be unwise, but for a man like Nixon this constituted a real danger: he once ploughed into a student right outside MRJ's rooms in the Gibbs Building.[65] Fred Benson once wrote a mock-heroic ode to 'Pnyxon', winner of the tricycle race, which had

MRJ in stitches every time he recalled it.[66] MRJ himself wrote a comic interlude on the same subject, in which the tricycling Nixon encounters the heroine, Anne, and asks 'Is that you, Browning?'[67] Throughout his life, in fact, MRJ loved telling and hearing stories about Nixon, of which there was a seemingly endless number. In spite of only having one hand, he was a keen pianist, and once played a duet with Fred in which his playing got so demonstrative that his false hand flew off; he carried on regardless, pounding the keys with his stump.[68] (He travelled with a spare false hand in his suitcase, much to the surprise of a variety of hotel chambermaids.)[69] MRJ was much given to embellishing, and often to inventing, stories about Nixon. Nixon had once had a 'terrible experience', MRJ recalled, while on holiday with the Bishop of Durham, Brooke Foss Westcott, when he found 'a plethora of wasps in both boots which had had their orifices stopped up in some unexplained fashion'. (The Bishop, he added, 'was quite at a loss to account for it'.)[70] Nixon, in fact, MRJ claimed, lived in perpetual fear of Westcott, whom he thought of as his nemesis, a Professor Moriarty figure, out to get him. MRJ had great fun with this, spreading mischievous rumours about 'the relentless cruelty' of Westcott and the 'cheerful endurance' of Nixon.[71] The pair certainly had history—at least, according to MRJ. Nixon was, he insisted, romantically involved with his first cousin, Amelia Bugbird, but Bishop Westcott objected to this relationship so strongly that it led to a furious argument between the two dons. 'I have never quite credited the persistent rumour that blows passed', MRJ commented.[72]

Of all the dons he encountered as an undergraduate at King's, it was Henry Bradshaw who had the greatest effect on MRJ. In spite of having graduated in 1854 with a middling second-class degree, Bradshaw was widely recognized as one of Cambridge's greatest scholars—the one time they met, the great German sage Theodor Mommsen 'was more impressed by Henry Bradshaw than any other man he'd met in England', and said he wished he'd had a stenographer present to record the conversation.[73] Bradshaw, who had studied at Temple Grove, Eton, and King's, was appointed Assistant Librarian at Cambridge in 1856, Superintendent of Manuscripts in 1859, during which time he completely reformed the University's manuscript department, and then University Librarian from 1867 to his death in 1886. Bradshaw's practice as a cataloguer, particularly of incunabula, was revolutionary, focusing on all aspects of the catalogued book, from illustration to bindings to provenance.[74] In 1895, one of MRJ's first and most personal catalogues, of the manuscript collection of King's, paid tribute to Bradshaw for the 'brilliance and thoroughness of his work'.[75]

In the wake of the Graham Report and the Cambridge University Act, Bradshaw, then a young Fellow, had been a major proponent for the reform of King's. Later in life, he became an instrumental figure in uniting the College's different factions, modernizers and Old Etonian traditionalists. He achieved this in part through becoming himself a model of welcoming sociability. His rooms were one of the best sets in King's, and, a colleague wrote, 'his society was open to all'.[76] Rather strangely, Bradshaw derived great pleasure from getting undergraduates (including MRJ) to tickle the palms of his hands, while he 'sat and purred'.[77] In his memoirs, MRJ paints a worshipful picture of Bradshaw: 'You felt there was nothing little about him, and the reverence and love he inspired needed no explanation.'[78]

MRJ also shared with Bradshaw a suspicion of abstract intellectual theorizing. Bradshaw's biographer, MRJ's tutor George Prothero, puts it well:

> One class of men he was shy of—'intellects', he used to call them; the men who dwell habitually on 'higher ground', and deal only with the loftiest topics of conversation. With such persons he was seldom himself; he became reserved, ungenial, sometimes even waspish, or took refuge in a chilling silence.[79]

Henry Sidgwick, T. H. Huxley, J. G. Frazer, Jane Harrison, John Maynard Keynes, Bertrand Russell, J. B. S. Haldane: the list of 'intellects' with whom MRJ clashed, or of whom he disapproved, is a long one.

* * *

MRJ had an enjoyable first term at King's. Charles Waldstein, just arrived from New York to take up his post as Reader in Classical Archaeology and Director of the Fitzwilliam Museum, directed what was to be the first of an ongoing series of Greek plays, Sophocles's *Ajax*, with J. K. Stephen in commanding form in the title role, ably supported by Harry Cust. MRJ enjoyed this so much that he vowed to get involved next time. In November, he had a surprise visit from an old acquaintance, the terrifying O. C. Waterfield, in Cambridge visiting his old friend Henry Bradshaw. They had breakfast together, and the Cow regaled MRJ with tales of Mahdist insurrection from his recent time in Egypt.

Viewing ecclesiastical architecture was always a favourite pursuit, and he and St. Clair (who saw each other every day) had a good time visiting various college chapels—in the first week alone, they went to the chapels of Peterhouse, Christ's, Jesus, and Emmanuel. And then there was King's College Chapel itself, the finest of all Cambridge's chapels, a marvel of fifteenth-century perpendicular Gothic. Attendance at daily 8 a.m. chapel services in King's was compulsory (as it was in all colleges until the First World War)—though MRJ, never an early riser, bunked off as many of the morning services as he could get away with, or sometimes signed in but then went straight back to bed. On one occasion, he was 'gated' (confined to the precincts of the College) for this, and summoned to see Provost Richard Okes (an old friend of Herbert's), who told him, 'When I was your age I used to get up at five o'clock every morning and make myself a cup of cocoa and do a couple of hours' work before Chapel. Now couldn't you resolve to do something of the same kind?'[80] Unsurprisingly, this had no effect, and from time to time MRJ would receive beautifully written 'letters of regret' from Austen Leigh, by that time Vice-Provost, reminding him of his duties.[81]

In December he sat his first series of examinations, the Previous Examination, or 'Little-go'. This was a general exam which students had traditionally, since its introduction in the 1820s, sat towards the end of their second year, but which since the 1870s had been open to first-year students. 'They treat you like the beasts that perish in the Littlego', MRJ told his parents. He found the prospect of the exams 'very dreadful', largely because, for the last time ever, he would be forced to take Mathematics papers. The exams took place in the Corn Exchange, 'a hideous place with a glass roof which sins against all imaginable rules of architecture'. The compulsory paper on Paley's *Evidences of Christianity* he found 'dull fare'. He was five minutes late for his Euclid paper, and was fined a shilling. His desk for the algebra paper was directly underneath a drip from the roof, which added insult to injury. In general, he found the whole experience 'disgusting beyond all description'.[82] The compulsory Maths meant that he was never going to shine in the Little-go, but when the results came out next term he achieved a creditable Second Class (of his immediate circle, only St. Clair Donaldson attained a First in the Little-go that year), with outstanding results in Classics: 'It is Mathematical as well as Classical', he explained to Herbert. 'As I told you, I believe I was first in the latter branch.'[83] And that, for MRJ and Mathematics, was that.

He spent the first part of the Christmas vacation visiting the Bensons in Truro. He was present for some momentous news. Edward White Benson was to be made Archbishop of Canterbury. He was a very intimidating man, and the news had MRJ wondering how to respond: 'What would one say? "I congratulate you", or "Well I'm sure", or "I never should have thought of it" or, with Sarah [the James family maid], "The hidear of such a thing".'[84] 'What I did say must be left to imagination', he wrote to Babington Smith.[85] On the 22nd he travelled to Torquay to spend a couple of days with Grace, before heading back to Cambridge for Christmas (carols at Trinity on Christmas Eve).[86]

On Boxing Day, on his way home to Livermere he stopped off for a night with the Donaldsons in Bére Court, but was persuaded to stay longer by the grief-stricken Lady Donaldson, for whom 'I am afraid Christmas has brought with it other than cheerful thoughts: I do not know that I ever feel half so mean and small as when brought face to face with Seton's memory.'[87]

Returning to King's after Christmas, he had one of his periodic health scares. MRJ himself wrote to Luxmoore complaining of a 'twinge', and Luxmoore replied warning him 'to guard against weak action of heart'.[88] In his first term, remarkably, MRJ had won the Carus Greek Testament Prize (value £11, paid in books). Welldon told Sydney that MRJ 'had walked in for the Carus' (Sydney added to his brother, 'I hope you will treat the examiners for the Littlego with equal contempt').[89] He had then put himself forward for the Chancellor's Medal (which realistically, as a first-year, he didn't have a hope of winning), the Craven Scholarship, and either the Porson Prize or the Porson Scholarship (this is unclear: both were awards for achievement in Greek, and both were awarded in 1883). He was obviously working too hard. This illness seems to have been reasonably serious, sufficiently so for Welldon to feel the need to write to Herbert to let him know that 'he has suffered from palpitation of the heart. I am afraid he is delicate and wants much care.'[90] This arrhythmia seems to have been brought on by the stress of overwork and exhaustion: 'no man, however strong, can stand such trifling with his health, and I hope he will never be so unwise again', Welldon counselled.[91] 'I write just a line to set your mind at rest with regard to my Elth', MRJ reassured Herbert. 'I am very well now and have been all week.'[92] (As it transpired, apart from the Carus he didn't get any of the awards he went in for that term, though he was placed very highly in all of them, to his father's great delight.)

Obviously, the family were worried about his health. Sydney came up with an idea, and the next day—28 January 1883—he wrote to his youngest brother: 'I have a proposal to put to you.'[93] Syd had been planning a Greek holiday that Easter, along with Stuart Donaldson and Walter Durnford. Would MRJ and St. Clair like to come too? The holiday would be expensive, but between them Syd and his friends would pay for MRJ, so he needn't worry about the cost (it ended up costing over £80 a head). Cecil Baring—scion of the famous banking family—who was an Etonian chum of MRJ and St. Clair now studying at Oxford, also came along, making it a party of six.

They travelled to Brindisi, and from there by steamer to Corfu, Patras, Corinth, and Athens.[94] For this Classically educated party, the holiday was a journey of wonders, and they packed it all in: Delphi, Thebes, Eleusis, Nauplia,

Mycenae, Tripolitza, Megalopolis, Andritsaina, Bassae, Olympia. MRJ thought Tiryns particularly splendid, was taken aback by the sculptures of Cephisodotus, and particularly by a Gorgon's head. At Argos, they were defeated by a local delicacy, 'a large cuttle-fish, stewed in some viscous fluid, surrounded by what looked like brown rosettes, which turned out to be suckers'. They passed a sleepless night being bitten to death in Aegina—and in the morning, between them, collected eighty specimens of bedbug. At Athens, they met Heinrich Schliemann, the archaeological titan who had excavated Troy, and who was then working on his third excavation of Mycenae, and they encountered the Greek royal family during a visit to 'the hideous new Cathedral' (these are Sydney's words). MRJ himself was particularly taken by the beautiful town of Andritsaina in the far west of the Peloponnese: 'This is the spot I should feel inclined to haunt', he thought, many years later.[95]

The holiday seems to have worked, and this is the last we hear of the heart palpitations. The spring of 1883 finds him back at King's, enthusiastically reading *Piers Plowman*, 'a work of real genius' whose complex manuscript history he found particularly fascinating. This is normal for MRJ. Women were not; and, rather to his dismay, they began to intrude upon his social circle in a romantic fashion: 'Miss Holden with the soapy eye is up here. Tilley is much fascinated by her. I, not.' He preferred to spend his time performing a 'musical sketch' with Arthur Benson, or attending 'a paper on medieval army ironwork'.[96]

Around this time, he began to get seriously interested in the King's College Chapel stained glass, a subject which was to engross him for the rest of his life. 'I assure you I shall end by writing a large book about the windows', he wrote to Mary Emily. 'Illustrated by chromolithography—a nice work of mine it would be too.'[97] MRJ's engagement with medieval stained glass was deeply scholarly—sufficiently so for him to have been *the* authoritative voice in the resetting of the windows of York Minster, for example—but it was also, as readers of 'The Treasure of Abbot Thomas' will recall, imaginative and playful. MRJ never did write his 'large book' about the King's Chapel windows, but he did publish a short book in 1899, *A Guide to the Windows of King's College Chapel*, and in 1892 wrote an anonymous article on them for the *Cambridge Review*.[98] Out of this article materialized his earliest extant ghost story, 'A Night in King's College Chapel'.[99] The story opens with MRJ falling asleep in the stalls while writing a paragraph from the *Cambridge Review* article, and waking up after dark, alone in the locked chapel. Though very much in the comic vein, the story is certainly revealing about some of MRJ's recurring preoccupations and anxieties. The figures from the windows come to life. Job's wife scolds her husband 'assisted by a hideous demon', while St. Luke, a doctor, proposes giving Enoch a 'filthy purge' compounded of 'dust from the altar, and frankincense and a fat chapel spider'. Women and domesticity, demons, spiders: this is the recurring stuff of MRJ's ghost stories.

On 27 January 1883, MRJ was elected to the Chit-Chat Club: 'I am going to an institution called the Chitchat', he wrote to his father a few weeks later. 'Benson, Cust, HB and others are members, but it is not a large society at all, only about 11 people and the subjects terrible deep sometimes.'[100] Set up by the Trinity law student Alsager Hay Hill in 1860, the Chit-Chat was an informal discussion group for 'the promotion of rational conversation', whose members were invited to present 'any original paper on any interesting topic by which conversation is likely to be promoted'.[101] It was initially centred around students from Trinity Hall and Sidney Sussex colleges, but by MRJ's time was largely the province of Trinity and King's. Members would gather at 9.45 p.m. on Saturday nights to hear papers, accompanied by coffee, 'whales' (anchovy toast), and snuff from a snuffbox presented to the club by F. W. Maitland. MRJ addressed the Chit-Chat many times during his undergraduate years. Very typically for him, his first paper, delivered in May 1883, was entitled 'Useless Knowledge'.[102] The title of this paper not only stands as a manifesto *for* MRJ's intellectual and institutional commitment to certain forms of highly privileged knowledge (the 'vocationally useless' education of Eton and King's and the larger system they represented in ideal form), but also would have been understood as a manifesto *against* the Society for the Diffusion of Useful Knowledge, the Whig society founded by Henry Brougham in 1826 with the express aim of making scientific and mechanical knowledge available to a working-class readership.[103]

But there's more to 'Useless Knowledge' than this, and it's worth dwelling on this talk as it is indicative of the way MRJ's mind worked—the often bizarre, perverse, or infuriating positions he could take. In classic debating society fashion, he begins by putting the strongest case he can muster against his subject, and offers a fairly withering critique of the whole system of classical education:

> I have read more literature of a type which I consider as nearly as possible absolutely useless than anybody is this room . . . How much of the actual knowledge which has hitherto been my life's object to acquire, is likely to affect me, or anyone else, for good? . . . I fancy I am within my rights in asking whether, when all that is good & noble in a classical education has been deducted, there does not remain a very large mass of information which the learner has been made to believe essential, and which yet neither has as a matter of fact helped him, nor is calculated to do so . . . Is this a healthy condition of mind? I am afraid not.[104]

MRJ dismisses one of the usual vindications of the classical education, its 'effects . . . in the character'. What might this leave? The answer for MRJ is nothing. He offers *no defence at all* for the useless knowledge on which he was to build his career. Even by 1883, he had already amassed a formidable expertise in the Apocrypha of the New Testament, the subject on which he was to write his brilliant Fellowship dissertation a few years later. 'Useless Knowledge' devotes a large section to these books, on which MRJ concludes: 'I have been thus prolix on New Testament Apocrypha, because I think that in a fair measure they are the pattern for useless literature and because I think they have as a body deserved immortality less than any books I know.' We can't simply write this off as youthful rhetorical brio (he didn't really mean it, he's overstating his case, letting his language and the occasion run away with him). Over forty years later, he published one of his very greatest scholarly achievements, his 1924 Oxford edition of *The Apocryphal New Testament*—a collection of marginal or excluded scriptural texts whose intrinsic worth, he concluded, was highly dubious: 'It will very quickly be seen that there is no question of any one's having excluded [the Apocryphal Gospels] from the New Testament. They have done that for themselves.'[105] It may be that MRJ believed that even to engage with utilitarian critiques of a classical education would be to give these critiques a validity he was not prepared to countenance. But it seems more likely to me that he simply delighted in the intrinsic uselessness of what he did.

He followed this up next spring with a paper on 'Art Magic'—what is more commonly known as Ceremonial or Ritual Magic. The paper on 'Art Magic' survives in the Fitzwilliam Museum, under the title 'Magic. Its Possibilities'—it is written in the same notebook as his notes on Mayor's lectures. In this paper, MRJ warns against spirit conjuration and the summoning of demons—practices in whose reality he seems implicitly to believe: 'That communication with spirits is desirable I should certainly deny: for neither can I imagine a man of the highest intelligence devoting himself to the establishment of it: nor any spirit who would produce the results recorded except in playfulness, folly, or spite.' In a manner which anticipates 'Canon Alberic's Scrap-book' and many of his other stories, he warns that only 'a malignant spirit would be very likely to take any handle offered it which could lead to communication with mankind'.[106]

Down the years he would deliver many more Chit-Chat papers, generally on very characteristic subjects, from Walter Map to Sheridan Le Fanu, church portals to the grotesque.[107] His address on 'The Education of a Gentleman', given as part of a symposium on the subject in November 1889, was unsurprisingly entirely

Classical in its framework, apart from the occasional sideswipes at mathematicians and medics.[108]

Over the years, many of MRJ's Cambridge circle would become members of the Chit-Chat Club—Charles Waldstein, Arthur and Fred Benson, Harry Cust, Walter Headlam, Lionel Ford, Willie Bridgeman, Johnnie Maxwell, Vincent Yorke, and several others. The Chit-Chat finally petered out in 1897, 'in which year', he wrote, 'the Club, though never formally wound up, might be said to have expired of inanition due I fear to the failure of the secretary to summon meetings, & to the apathy of the members'.[109] But he was faithful to the last, and was present at its final meeting on 8 May 1897, to hear Lord Lytton give a paper on 'King Poppy'.[110] He kept Maitland's snuffbox.

Membership of the Chit-Chat was widely understood as preparation for the Conversazione Society, better known as the Apostles, Cambridge's foremost intellectual society. (Its very name is a modest undercutting of the self-importance and pomposity of the Apostles: Chit-Chat rather than Conversazione.) Promising members of the Chit-Chat Club would be taken for a walk by an Apostle, in what was essentially an interview; Babington Smith was invited to join, but MRJ never was. 'You could be found wanting', he thought: 'if the experiment was ever tried on me, as to which I am in doubt, that certainly was the result.' Why did MRJ never join the Apostles? The answer is simultaneously puzzling and obvious. No one would have denied that he was amongst the outstanding scholars of his generation at Cambridge; but the purpose of the Apostles interview, he thought, was to 'probe your capacity for philosophic speculation', an arena for which MRJ had little aptitude and less interest.[111] The Apostles were very much a gathering of 'intellects', and formed a nucleus for the Bloomsbury Group. While some of his friends were Apostles (Babington Smith, J. K. Stephen, Herbert Tatham, Rupert Brooke), a roster of the society's prominent members often simply reads like MRJ's enemies list: O. B., Sidgwick, Westcott, Maynard Keynes, Bertrand Russell, Lytton Strachey.

* * *

MRJ remembered Michaelmas Term 1883 he as the most enjoyable time of his undergraduate life. He moved into a much nicer set of rooms, in Staircase H on the ground floor of the Gibbs Building, next to the chapel. He had inherited them from Arthur Benson, who had gone straight from King's to an Assistant Mastership at Eton (a position for which Mary Emily worried that he was 'too dreamy').[112] These were to be MRJ's rooms for over a decade, until he moved to a set of rooms on the top floor of the Wilkins Building in January 1895. Arthur had done some interior decorating 'after his own fashion with mottoes and other designs of uncertain import'. On a cupboard door was painted, in blue, a nude man on a rock, with a beam of light striking his bow, and a Greek inscription which read 'I saw the light and was afraid'.[113] No doubt inspired by his surroundings, in a rare moment of aestheticism (if not decadence) MRJ went to London and bought an Oriental rug at Liberty's, 'much the nicest shop I ever was in, full of nothing but Eastern fabrics of gorgeous hue'.[114] He hired an upright piano from the Cambridge music shop on Regent Street owned by F. R. Leavis's father, which he ended up keeping for so long that the shop eventually just gave it to him.[115] The composer Arthur Somervell, a King's contemporary, thought that this cheap and not very tuneful piano had cost him £600 in rent.[116] He wasn't much of a pianist, and his playing was hampered by his insistence on starting over again every time he made a mistake, which was often—a practice which infuriated Arthur Benson.

The Gibbs Building was, MRJ came to suspect, haunted. Sometimes, a 'ghostly cry' could be heard at nights, coming from one of the bedrooms on the next staircase. MRJ never heard the cry himself, but one Christmas Luxmoore was staying in these rooms, and had an awful sleepless night, which he told MRJ all about at breakfast the next morning. MRJ asked a couple of the older King's Fellows, Fred Whitting and Felix Cobbold, whether they knew anything about this. They certainly did—it was the voice of someone who had died in 1878.[117] That was as far as MRJ was prepared to go in print—but there are leads we can follow to identify the Gibbs Building ghost. In the margin notes to his copy of *Eton and King's*, which is in the Eton archives, Shane Leslie identifies this figure as Thomas Brocklebank, 'the bursar—by suicide, after a supposed intrigue with a chorister. [According] to A. F. Scholfield [University Librarian, 1923–49] there was a Mr King who said it was a very lamentable thing to be turned out of the College at 70 and above all to be turned out for fornication!'[118] Leslie claims that he got the name of Brocklebank from MRJ himself at the very end of his life, during Leslie's last visit to the Provost's Lodge at Eton on Founder's Day 1935: 'A Fellow called Brocklebank died there in great trouble. He was the College ghost.'[119] Shane Leslie is always interesting, but not always reliable, and so we can't be absolutely sure here—but there certainly was a Thomas Brocklebank, a King's Scholar from Eton, who was Fellow, Bursar, and Vice-Provost of King's, and who did die in 1878, though age fifty-three rather than seventy. MRJ unquestionably knew all about Brocklebank, who was a friend and contemporary of his father at both Eton and King's, where they shared a set of rooms in the Gibbs Building. When Herbert left King's for Aldeburgh in 1853, Brocklebank arranged for a valuation of the furniture in their rooms: it was valued at £38, of which the greater part (£30.5) was owing to Herbert.[120] We know this because MRJ kept at least some of the correspondence between Brocklebank and Herbert: this inventory, and an accompanying letter, plus a long and chatty earlier letter about Brocklebank's Christmas visit to London in 1846, full of details about Drury Lane pantomimes, and Dickensian references.[121] In 1896, MRJ's King's colleague W. H. Macaulay wrote to MRJ telling him that he'd bumped into an old chorister who'd shared a story about Brocklebank making sure that the College choir got extra pudding on his birthday.[122]

Thomas Brocklebank was also a friend of William Johnson Cory (dismissed from Eton, we remember, in the wake of a sex scandal involving a pupil), who wrote about him warmly in his diary: '[Brocklebank] is so full of plain, wholesome interest in plain, humdrum people, such as our tenants, incumbents, and choristers; with him I feel that King's College is my parish and my county.'[123] The interest in choristers, in particular, seems to have been his undoing.

Figures like Brocklebank and Cory, and others in our story—Oscar Browning, for example, or Oliffe Richmond, or the Cambridge librarian Charles Sayle, and even perhaps Arthur Benson—are best understood in the context of a 'Uranian' tendency or movement in late-Victorian and Edwardian same-sex male desire.[124] Uranianism very clearly grew out of the all-male public school world and its veneration of the Classics, and was characterized by the intense desire of older men for adolescent boys or much younger adults, often young men in whom they were in some position of authority or control. Arthur's diaries, for example, record 'an intimate talk about romantic friendships' with his friend D. A. Winstanley, the great historian of Cambridge University: 'we agreed that to be a Don and not to care, romantically, for the young men was a very chilly affair'.[125] Uranianism is a difficult topic for a twenty-first-century commentator to write about, or even to think clearly about, as it runs so obviously counter to contemporary sensibilities, to what we now know about exploitative sexual behaviour and the manipulation of power relations, about grooming and predation. It also provides a disturbing context within which to read one of MRJ's most celebrated stories, 'Lost Hearts', the tale of an older scholar preying on his young wards.

To complicate the story of Thomas Brocklebank, in 1926 MRJ received an anguished letter from Oliver Vassall-Phillips, an author and Catholic priest who had been a close friend of J. K. Stephen. Vassall-Phillips, a military chaplain, had read *Eton and King's* on board a troop-ship carrying his regiment to India, and wrote immediately to MRJ, from on board the S.S. Nevassa, to ask whether the Gibbs Building ghost was actually that of his friend James Wilson, who had committed suicide 'in ghastly circumstances arising out of a visit to me at Oxford'. What happened at Oxford is not discussed, though Vassall-Phillips's letter talks at some length about the subject of J. J. Hornby sacking Oscar Browning from Eton after Browning's relations with the young Lord Curzon—so we can guess. The shift in subject from Wilson's death to Browning's dismissal is only superficially tangential: Vassall-Philips was a devoted pupil of O.B.'s at Eton, and wrote to him in the wake of the Curzon affair, lamenting 'Altogether I miss you DREADFULLY' (Vassall-Philips was nineteen at the time).[126] Wilson threw himself under a train near Taplow in Buckinghamshire, but before killing himself he wrote Vassall-Phillips 'a terrible and most pathetic letter . . . Forty-eight years have passed since then, but every word of that letter burned its way into my heart so that I can never forget it as long as I remember anything'.[127] And so Father Vassall-Phillips wrote his own desperate letter to MRJ, in the hope that he could help him somehow to lay his own ghosts.

We need to be cautious when dealing with the story of the ghost of Thomas Brocklebank (is there a ghost? was it Brocklebank? did he commit suicide? was there a gay sex scandal? did it involve choristers?)—but there is much that could be said here about ghosts, homosexuality, concealment, encoded speech, and silence.

In his second year, MRJ began to play a much fuller part in the life of the College. Spurred on by the *Ajax* in his first year, he signed up for that year's Greek play, Aristophanes's *The Birds*, again directed by Waldstein.[128] Perhaps to everyone's surprise, he landed the lead role, Peisthetairos—for which he grew the splendid beard which Ber found so amusing. This was scarcely an amateur production in the normal sense. It was performed in the Theatre Royal in late November and early December (MRJ made sure to book accommodation for his parents for the opening night), with a celebrated score by Hubert Parry. The Irish composer Charles Villiers Stanford, soon to become Professor of Music, was also involved as conductor, and was particularly struck by John O'Connor's 'strikingly original' stage designs: 'He painted a bird's eye view of the earth as seen through the clouds which formed the wings, and gave the impression to the audience that they were looking down a funnel of vapour, across which the chorus of birds would fly at intervals.'[129] (Thirty-five years later, Stanford would still be addressing MRJ as 'Peisthetairos'.)[130]

The production, and MRJ's performance in particular, got excellent reviews (understandably, he kept the clippings): 'Mr. James', said the *Standard*, 'performed an astonishing feat in thus reciting eight hundred lines of Greek with perfect familiarity, and almost without a moment's hesitation from beginning to end. His admirable acting was the backbone of the performance.' He was particularly effective, the *Athenæum* thought, at conveying his character's 'fussy self-importance'. The *Daily Telegraph* thought his performance 'a distinguished success'.[131] The same couldn't be said for Harry Cust as Prometheus, who had terrible trouble learning his lines, and got by through MRJ's prompts (he seems to have memorized the entire play), 'filling in the gaps with improvisation in an unknown tongue'.[132] Arthur Benson and Leo Maxse were also in the cast. After the last performance on December 7th, the cast gathered in Christ's College for a group photograph all dressed in their stage costumes, with MRJ 'in my wedding dress (and nothing else)'.[133] As this might suggest, the whole performance was something of a revelation for him. The vivid, blazing sunsets that term, caused by the explosion of Krakatoa on 27 August, emphasized the sense of a heightened, magical time, which left him with 'a halo in memory'.[134]

The new academic year brought new friends into his life, or made friends of old acquaintances. In *The Birds*, he met John Willis Clark, Fellow of Trinity, University Registrary (his formal title), architectural historian, and antiquary. Though Clark was thirty years older, the pair obviously had a lot in common—including a shared love of popular culture. They would go to Drury Lane together to watch the music-hall comedians Dan Leno and Little Tich, and would happily read Conan Doyle's Sherlock Holmes stories to each other in their rooms. With his long white mane and beard, his flowing silk gown, his colourful assembly of speech impediments (Arthur Benson phonetically transcribed his pronunciation of 'the library' and 'ver yibewrwawy'), and his notoriously quick temper—'extreme testiness and ironical frankness', said Arthur, who also had a role in *The Birds*—'J.' Clark cut an odd, intimidating figure.[135] (Luxmoore had got an irascible response from Clark after writing persistently to all concerned, as was his wont, in his attempt to get *The Birds* performed at Eton.) But Clark and MRJ warmed to one another immediately. He recognized the young undergraduate as a real scholar, and even asked him to look at the proofs of his magnum opus, the multi-volume *Architectural History of the University of Cambridge* (1886), to 'correct the grosser blunders': there weren't any, of course, and MRJ discovered in them 'a new view of the way in which the scientific method could be applied to the study of the history of buildings'.[136] Clark was a mainstay of the College's Amateur Dramatic Club (ADC), and was keen to get MRJ involved; but he was also a scholar of sufficient standing to be able to reassure Herbert that, no, theatrical performances would not inevitably damage his son's academic career. Like MRJ, Clark was the kind of Cambridge don who knew what he liked, and definitely knew what he didn't like. When he went to see a performance by the Abbey Theatre, he was apoplectic, telling MRJ, 'Have you been to see vese Irish Players? . . . Well, I have, and my advice to you is, Don't. It's nuffing more van a parcel of incompetent amateurs muttering unintelligible nonsense in ve dark.'[137] MRJ didn't approve of the Abbey either, and complained that Lady Gregory's *The Workhouse Ward* was 'full of the vilest language'.[138]

Lionel Ford came up to King's on a scholarship from Repton. At Cambridge, he and MRJ 'became inseparable'.[139] A future pillar of the establishment, Ford was very much one of MRJ's overachieving friends, graduating with a First in the Classical Tripos, and winning the Chancellor's Medal the year after MRJ, in 1887. He was also a top-notch cricketer (he played for Buckinghamshire), something which must have stood him in good stead for getting an Assistant Mastership at Eton immediately after graduating, before moving on to the Headships of Repton and then of Harrow, and ending up as Dean of York (his memorial is in the Zouche Chapel at York Minster). As a student, Ford was fond of practical jokes, whether dropping sugar lumps onto Westcott's hat as he walked under the window, engrossed in thought, or writing 'O.B.' in large letters in the snow on King's lawn (MRJ thought the Great Ego might have been impressed by this tribute, but he wasn't). Lionel and MRJ often sang duets of Handel together late into the night, with Lionel singing bass and MRJ treble. They weren't very good, and were once stopped by 'the voice of an inmate crying out as if in great extremity, "O *do* shut up!"'[140] 'He was the centre of our group', Lionel said of MRJ, 'never seeking people out, but letting people find him, and then with apparently endless time at their disposal.'[141] This was Fred Benson's view of his older brother's circle at King's, too: 'at the head of this vivid group was certainly Monty James'.[142]

If Lionel Ford was an excellent scholar, Water Headlam was a brilliant one: 'a prince among scholars', MRJ thought; 'perhaps the finest Greek scholar that Cambridge has ever produced', in Fred Benson's view; the best writer of Greek since the Ancient Greeks themselves, according to his student Rupert Brooke.[143] Headlam was particularly close to the Stephen family—he was a good friend of J. K., and seems to have had some kind of romantic relationship (or at least flirtation) with the young Virginia Stephen.[144] At Cambridge, his abilities as a classical writer and translator were soon recognized—between 1885 and 1887 he won an unprecedented seven Browne Medals for composition (four of these were awarded each year, and he won a medal in each category;

while he never swept the board in any given year, he did win three out of four in 1887), and carried off the Porson Prize in 1887. As a Fellow of King's, he gained an international reputation as a scholar and editor of Aeschylus and Herodas—though also a reputation amongst his students as a terrible teacher. He often didn't bother turning up for lectures, or got so absorbed in his work that he just forgot about them—and when he did show up, in the words of a student, 'his actual lectures are beyond despair'.[145] For all his abilities, he also had a commensurately self-damaging streak of intellectual arrogance and political naivety, a tendency to pick intellectual fights with established senior scholars, which he sometimes conducted in vituperatively personal terms: '"The man doesn't know Greek"', he would often sneer about his colleagues, accompanied by 'peals of cackling laughter'.[146] Headlam, who had a lifelong terror of death, dropped dead in a London hotel in 1908, age forty-two, from an 'accidental twist of the intestine', after spending the day watching the cricket at Lord's.[147] In 1912, MRJ wrote an entry for his old friend in the *Dictionary of National Biography*, which praised 'his fastidious taste and keen sensibility to all beauty . . . coupled with an almost unrivalled sense of the genius of the Greek language'.[148] Virginia Woolf wrote after his death: 'There was something very charming about him, but he was difficult, and I think he had quarrelled with most of the people at Cambridge.'[149]

Through Headlam, MRJ got more involved with J. K. Stephen. The pair became members of Stephen's T.A.F. (Twice a Fortnight) dining club, which met on Sunday nights for conversation, drinks, games, amateur dramatics (with MRJ providing the funny voices and mimicry—he did particularly good impressions of O.B., Mrs Gamp, and 'that interesting fellow, George Eliot')—and general japes. These could sometimes get out of hand: Lionel Ford recalled MRJ and St. Clair rolling around on the floor at one T.A.F. evening, 'with Monty James's long fingers grasping at his vitals'. (It's worth pointing out that this is a tableau of the future Headmaster of Harrow, the future Archbishop of Brisbane, and the future Vice-Chancellor of Cambridge University, as recorded in a book published by the Society for Promoting Christian Knowledge, written by the future Headmaster of Eton, Cyril Alington, who declined to go into any further details about this episode 'for reasons of piety'.)[150]

In 1883, Stephen got the job of tutor to Prince Eddy, the Duke of Clarence, who went up to Trinity that year. And so it was that, for a time, MRJ was drawn into the orbit of 'The Pragga', as his circle called Eddy. The Pragga makes fairly regular appearances in MRJ's correspondence over the next couple of years, and was given to popping up unannounced in his rooms: 'He is not at all formidable', MRJ told his parents, 'but I hate presenting people to him.'[151] Through the Pragga, the powerfully monarchist MRJ even got to meet the Prince of Wales, who was up visiting his son in Trinity: 'he isn't at all bad & tries to make it pleasant for one', he reassured his mother.[152]

Willie Bridgeman had been at Eton with MRJ, but the pair really got to know each other through the ADC. Bridgeman went on to have the kind of great public career that MRJ and Arthur Benson had foreseen for Harry Cust. Elected MP for Oswestry (Conservative, naturally) in 1906, Bridgeman was a close ally of Stanley Baldwin, and became a notably hardline Home Secretary in Baldwin's government in the 1920s, as well as serving as First Lord of the Admiralty and Chairman of the BBC. In Trinity, Bridgeman shared rooms with two other friends, Johnnie Maxwell and Albert Baillie. Sir John Stirling-Maxwell later became Tory MP for Glasgow College, and a powerful voice in Scottish politics; nothing was done north of the border, it was said, without consulting Johnnie Maxwell first.[153] Albert Baillie, President of the ADC, was obviously very fond of MRJ, and thought him 'without peer as a social companion. He was a first-rate singer of humorous songs and an admirable actor'.[154] (Gwendolen McBryde, who knew him well later in his life, confirms this: 'M. R. J. was a born actor', she thought, and a particularly brilliant Falstaff.)[155] After Cambridge, Baillie went into the Church, beginning his ministry in very deprived areas of Tyneside and London, before ending his career as Dean of Windsor, just down the road from MRJ at Eton. The two of them corresponded right up to the 1930s.

If Willie Bridgeman was a reactionary Tory, Leo Maxse was a right-wing radical. In 1887, shortly after leaving King's, he abandoned Gladstonian liberalism in disgust at what he saw as the Prime Minister's capitulation to Irish Home Rule—writing to MRJ that 'Mr. Gladstone has equivocated over the Irish question as he has never equivocated before'—and set out on his ever-rightward political journey.[156] Maxse was hilarious company (he is by far MRJ's funniest correspondent), wildly extroverted, reckless, even dangerous, 'a continuously active squib introduced into our calm academic life'.[157] (He once contrived to lock Oscar Browning and the Pragga into O.B.'s bathroom.)[158] But the pair hit it off from the start, and even formed their own dining club, the King's Cross, with a uniform, an insignia, a Greek motto, and a bound Book of Rules which limited the membership to the two of them. Maxse's wildness, though, had a nasty edge: he once rode one of the Pragga's horses to death, just for the hell of it. Through his friendship with a Trinity student,

Herbert Vivian, Maxse became involved with the ultra-monarchist Neo-Jacobite movement and its periodical *The Whirlwind* (which MRJ, in fairness, considered 'a ridiculous paper—edited by a ridiculous man', Vivian).[159] Maxse was disgusted by what he saw as a culture of effeminacy pervading King's, in particular, and in his last year at Cambridge wrote to MRJ in his characteristic, colourfully denunciatory register, 'King's is damnable, there is no other word for it, a cesspool of all that is abominable with a thin diminishing layer of something better'.[160] For years afterwards, he refused to return to Cambridge.

After leaving King's without attending his graduation ceremony (he got a second-class degree in History), Maxse became a celebrated journalist and provocateur, and from 1893 was the editor of the *National Review*, a Conservative newspaper which he steered to the extreme right, ending up as pro-Fascist by the 1920s.[161] The *National Review* plays a significant cameo role in our story: MRJ's first published ghost story, initially entitled 'A Curious Book', and then retitled 'The Scrap-Book of Canon Alberic', appeared there in August 1895. (In one of many moments of interconnection, Maxse married Virginia Woolf's old schoolfriend Kitty Lushington, who was the model for Clarissa Dalloway.)

MRJ acquired another friend in the spring of 1884, and very unusually she was female. Miss Dorothea Bridget Antigone Celia Muriel Motts was a ten-week-old tabby cat, who slept in MRJ's rooms swaddled in flannel in an upended litter bin. Miss Motts seems to have been quite the focus of attention for MRJ for a while (she is given a 'handsome collar' as a present; his letters are full of news about her), and he took to walking round King's with the kitten perched atop his hat. Miss Motts went missing a few weeks later: 'she will be cried by the town crier tomorrow... I should be quite [worried] if I did not think she would turn up yet'.[162] She didn't turn up, though, and in due course he got another cat, which sat in his windowbox, and died from falling out of the window—exactly what Mrs. Smith, his bedmaker, has warned him would happen.[163] (Many years later, MRJ would write a famous tale of feline vengeance, 'The Stalls of Barchester Cathedral'—originally entitled 'The Cat of Death'!) He kept pet cats for the rest of his life, many of them, and believed he understood their language, but was puzzled by their manners.[164] They generally lived.

All this fun he was having didn't come cheap. Being at Cambridge was an expensive business anyway. In 1893, an article in *The Cambridge Review* maintained that the 'average estimate' annual expenditure at Cambridge was £202 a year, although a student could live 'in reasonable comfort' for £150.[165] But total costs of about £250 a year were perfectly normal, and MRJ found himself keeping pretty fast company.[166] It's no exaggeration to say that at times during his undergraduate years, most of his letters home begin either with requests for money or with thanks for sending money. By early 1883, he was having to write to J. J. Hornby, Headmaster of Eton, to ask for an advance on the forthcoming instalment of his Newcastle Scholarship (Hornby sent him £10).[167] Michaelmas Term 1883, when he was in *The Birds* and hanging out with the Pragga, seems to have been a particularly expensive time: no sooner had Herbert sent him a cheque in December to pay his bills, than another set of bills arrived, for a hefty £11. These Herbert duly paid, only to receive yet another request in January to pay another of MRJ's bills.

MRJ was living beyond his means, and his family's means. This in part explains why he applied for so many prizes and scholarships. There was the academic honour and glory, of course there was; but there was also the money. Fortunately, MRJ was the kind of student to whom prizes and scholarships came easily. In 1883, he won one of two Bell Scholarships, worth £50 a year for four years, and open only to the sons of clergymen. Better still, in February 1884 he was able to send a telegraph to Livermere informing his family that he'd been awarded a Craven Scholarship. This was a big deal. The Craven Scholarships were founded in 1649, with a specific remit of giving 'preference to poor scholars', and by the time MRJ won his, the value was a significant £80 a year for seven years.[168] The Craven, according to Nathaniel Wedd (who didn't win it), was 'the Blue Riband of Classical Honours', and St. Clair thought that even MRJ's degree result 'is bound to feel rather flat after the Craven'.[169] Grace, back from Torquay in January, but now in Guernsey for the sake of her health (she and her mother were staying with Mary Emily's sister, Jane, Lady de Saumarez), wrote to her little brother with 'hearty congratulations on your truly delightful success—It is scrumptious'.[170]

As winter turned into spring in 1884, MRJ began to turn his attention towards the looming academic challenge of Part I of the Classical Tripos. Under new regulations, the Cambridge Tripos system had formally been split into two parts in 1880-81, with the view of accommodating the possibility of 'Double Honours' students.[171] One of the consequences of this decision was that, in the Classical Tripos, degree results were displayed by class, but listed alphabetically within classes: the title of 'Senior Classic' for the top-ranked student no longer obtained (in 1878, Sydney had graduated Seventh Classic), though the Wranglers list for First Class Mathematicians, which had a rich history and provenance, remained. It's also worth noting here that, from 1882, women students sat the same exams as the men, though their results were classified separately (and in 1887, Agnata Ramsay got the highest marks in Part I of the Classical Tripos, doing better than both Lionel Ford and Walter Headlam; she was in fact the only candidate that year placed in the First Division of the First Class).

It was relatively unusual to take Part I of the Classical Tripos in one's second year (Arthur Benson, Walter Headlam, Lionel Ford, and Agnata Ramsay all sat it in their third year, and none of them went on to do Part II), but that is what MRJ decided to do. 'I don't think it is much fun having a Tripos', he wrote to Herbert in May, up to his eyes in Greek grammar revisions. He sat the exams over a week at the end of the month, and thought his performance in the Grammar and History papers 'will about do'. The last paper, Greek and Latin Translation, on the Saturday, went 'all right'. After the exams, he relaxed by playing the piano, by returning to his Ancient Ethiopic and to Walter Map, and by learning a new language, Coptic, which Albert Baillie considered 'something dreadful to think of', but which by 6 June MRJ could read 'with a certain amount of ease'.[172]

The results when they came out were better than 'all right'. He had got a First in Part I of the Tripos. He was, in fact, one of three names listed alphabetically in Division 1 of the First Class (unusually, there were four First Class divisions that year), alongside John Haydon of King's and Montague Rendall of Trinity (the future Headmaster of Winchester). It was only years later he definitively discovered quite how well he had done: in 1900, A. H. Cooke, one of the examiners back in 1884, showed him the list of marks for that year. His were the highest, with Haydon second and Rendall third. 'I am quite amused to find I was top, which I had never known before', he told Herbert.[173] This seems to have been a little disingenuous. He certainly had a good idea of his results, and had told his parents. In March 1885, Provost Richard Okes, who was behind the times, wrote to Herbert that he looked forward to seeing the family over the summer, 'when [MRJ] takes his degree as Senior Classic'.[174] '*Why* don't they name a senior classic as they name wranglers???' Mary Emily protested, worried that her son's momentous achievement would not publicly be recognized for what it was.[175]

While he was revising for his exams, news arrived from Eton of the death of Provost Charles Old Goodford. The appointment of a new Provost of Eton was always an intensely political affair, and MRJ was naturally interested in the outcome. Leo Maxse, that Lord of Misrule, had written a straight-faced letter to the *Pall Mall Magazine* proposing Oscar Browning for the post: 'O. B. suspects nothing and is highly pleased', MRJ wrote. In turn, MRJ thought that O. B. himself may have been behind the proposed nomination of T. H. Huxley, a member of the Eton Governing Body, for the position, a prospect which filled him with horror: 'However little respect for Henry VI the governing body may have, I don't think people would stand a lay Provost at once—not to say a secularist, and a coarse 19th century stinks man like Huxley don't do.'[176] Even if Huxley had been offered the job, it's quite unlikely that he would have accepted it: he was made President of the Royal Society in 1883, and 'From this time forward the burden of ill-health grew slowly and steadily', his son Leonard wrote, becoming increasingly debilitating.[177] Anyway, as it transpired, he didn't do: the Headmaster, J. J. Hornby, was offered the post.

In one very specific way, Hugh Childers's friendship was to have a huge influence on the course of MRJ's life, as it took him on his first bicycling holiday. The pair had known each other since Eton, and at Cambridge discovered a mutual curiosity about cycling (though MRJ never really got to grips with the penny farthing). They drew up plans for a trip around northern France at the end of June. They hired a Cheylesmore double tricycle—an extraordinary contraption with two enormous front wheels, in which the cyclists sat abreast high up front, and steered by way of a pair of handles. They cycled the Cheylesmore into King's to a round of applause from Henry Bradshaw and J. W. Clark, and then set off for the Port of London, en route to Boulogne. One of the Cheylesmore's many spokes got damaged during the crossing, and so the pair were constantly on the lookout for a 'velocipédiste' to repair it, though generally had to rely on village blacksmiths for a quick fix.[178]

The plan was to visit as many cathedrals as possible over the course of about four weeks. They spent the first night in Abbeville, which MRJ knew from his holiday with Luxmoore in 1880. From there, they cycled to Amiens, where MRJ admired the colossal cathedral. As Picquigny, he was irritated by their dining companions at the hotel, three Anglican priests, including 'one fat one and one loquacious with an awful wife'.[179] The cathedral at Noyon he thought 'charming and severe', though he lamented that 'the Revolutionists have planed off all the sculpture [and] taken away the statues'. From there to Chauny—'a nasty manufacturing place'—before cycling through the Forêt de Coucy Basse and into Laon, which 'stands on a high isolated hill. The cathedral has 5 towers and is lovely.' They spent the night of the 28th in Reims, in a hotel room with amazing views of the cathedral.[180]

The weather was hot, and the Cheylesmore was hell whenever the going was uphill, so they cooled down by plunging into rivers wherever they could—always a favourite activity for MRJ. His diary entry for 6 July reads: 'Bathe. Cathedral. Bathe again. Cathedral again', which pretty much sums things up.[181] One such dip at Vatry, on the road between Chalons and Auxerre, was particularly welcome, and had MRJ waxing unusually poetical: 'Early next evening a garçon took us to bathe in the delightful Aube. The clock of the church struck 6 while we were in the water. The banks were covered in aspen and scented bay.' ('Has it occurred to you to have a *warm* bath in any French town?' Mary Emily wrote back.)[182]

His letters and postcards home rarely pass up an opportunity to write about the stained glass he's seen. At Voué, he admired the thirteenth-century windows, with their depictions of St. Joseph, Tobit, Daniel, Peter, and St. Nizier—though the window depicting St. Urban was 'under restoration of the most dreadful kind' (modern ecclesiastical restoration was another recurring bugbear for MRJ). At St. Florentin, they visited 'a late 15th century church with the most perfect stained glass'.[183] At Auxerre, they turned round and began to make their way back to the coast, via Versailles and Chartres, whose cathedral MRJ found simply overwhelming.

* * *

In the wake of MRJ's Part I results, his former tutor, J. E. C. Welldon, was very firmly of the opinion that MRJ had 'a very great future' before him, 'to do wonders both for Science & the Church, such as has not been done for years': he was 'one of the very few . . . . who can work out a scheme of "Comparative Religion" (i.e. comparison of legends & cults of all religion) with ability and devotion'. But first, Welldon thought, 'In Archaeology you are to teach Cambridge'.[184] And so it was that in Michaelmas Term 1884, MRJ was back in King's working towards Part II of the Tripos. His new neighbour across the staircase in the Gibbs Building, Cecil Knatchbull-Hugessen, took a similarly serious attitude to his work (he graduated with a First in 1886), and the pair spent happy evenings that autumn studying together (they had known each other since Eton, where they were in the Debating Society together). MRJ decided to go in for the Jeremie Septuagint Prize, awarded for 'a critical study of the Septuagint Version of the Old Testament, and such other Hellenistic literature as may serve to illustrate the New Testament' (value £17).[185] He won it, of course.

Part II of the Classical Tripos was a highly specialized course of study, undertaken by relatively few (just over 10 per cent of Part I graduates went on to Part II between 1882 and 1914). The majority of honours students were happy to leave after Part I, graduating with a BA: Arthur Benson, Walter Headlam, Lionel Ford, Agnata Ramsay, and Cecil Knatchbull-Hugessen all got Firsts in Part I of the Classical Tripos and left it at that. (Similarly, from 1882 the list of Mathematics Wranglers was drawn from the results in Part I; a number of celebrated Wranglers, including Russell and Keynes, did not go on to take Part II.) Unusually, St. Clair Donaldson took Part I of the Classical Tripos in 1885, and then Part I of the Theological Tripos in 1888. Of MRJ's close circle, only Henry Babington Smith also did both parts of the Classical Tripos.

Part II of the Classical Tripos was comprised of five strands or 'Groups': Language and Literature (Group A), Philosophy (B), Ancient History (C), Archaeology (D), and Comparative Philology (E). In the 1880s, students could take up to three of these strands. In practice, different colleges, because of the expertise of their staff, tended to specialize in different areas. Trinity, for example was particularly strong in Philosophy, an area MRJ wouldn't have touched with a bargepole: 'Technical philosophy was not to be mastered', he realized; or at least not by him. 'Large regions of Aristotle and Plato had to be left unexplored.'[186] When he first read Plato's *Republic* in 1882, he found it 'oppressively deep'.[187] Though he did sit exams in Language and Literature (this was compulsory until 1895), the overwhelming focus of MRJ's studies for Part II was on Archaeology. In the 1880s, 'Archaeology' at Cambridge encompassed a broad range of study: categories for examination included 'The History of Art', 'Special Sites', 'Numismatics', 'Inscriptions', 'Mythology', 'Religion', and '(Domestic) Antiquities'.[188] This was a breadth of field which strongly appealed to MRJ: '*Sculpture*, *painting*, *coins*, *inscriptions*, *mythology*, *gems*—each of these implies a good deal of reading', he wrote to Mary Emily.[189]

Specializing in Archaeology meant that he got to work very closely with Charles Waldstein. Waldstein arrived in Cambridge in 1880, and—enjoying the patronage of both Sidgwick and Bradshaw—had been promoted to a newly created Readership in Classical Archaeology in 1883. At the same time, he was appointed Director of the Fitzwilliam Museum, Cambridge's museum of fine art and antiquities. A flamboyant, cosmopolitan Jew with degrees from Columbia and Heidelberg, Waldstein was not universally popular: 'I wish that German-American-Jew would go back to his respective countries', Charles Villiers Stanford is said to have remarked during the rehearsals for one of the Greek plays Waldstein directed.[190] (Albert Baillie, who took part in one of these productions, testified that Waldstein, Stanford, and J. W. Clark, all 'men of hot temper and decided opinions', were given to having 'quite violent quarrels'.)[191] But Waldstein and MRJ got on very well (the age difference was only six years between them): 'His teaching', he thought, 'was the most stimulating that I experienced at the University.'[192] As the year went on, it was certainly intensive:

'Most evenings I go to Waldstein, and am coached by him in various things', he wrote in May 1885.[193] Mary Emily worried that he was working too hard again that year, and advised him to get more 'fresh air & exercise'.[194]

Most importantly, Waldstein gave MRJ his first proper taste of manuscript cataloguing. He put him to work cataloguing the Fitzwilliam's medieval manuscripts, something he found endlessly absorbing, all-consuming. There were 130 MSS in the Fitzwilliam's collection, and his original plan was to get through about half of them in that academic year. In practice, the process took a little longer, and he eventually published *A Descriptive Catalogue of the Manuscripts in the Fitzwilliam Museum* in 1895.

The Part II examinations came in June. Cecil Baring joked that '3 examiners had been reading hard for a year with the view of finding something you didn't know'.[195] If so, they didn't succeed. MRJ doesn't seem to have found his Part II exams particularly challenging, merely observing to his parents that his Greek translation paper, which he sat on 19 June, was 'nothing very interesting . . . but plenty of room for mistakes'.[196] He didn't really make any, though. When the results came out they were sensational, and he celebrated by taking a group of friends, including Babington Smith, Lionel Ford, and St. Clair, out to dinner, where they drank champagne. Indeed, there was an unspoken agreement, according to St. Clair, that, whenever he won a prize, MRJ would take T.A.F. members out for dinner, where he would read them an original composition. 'I am not at all sure', he thought, 'that his bad habit of writing ghost stories was not fostered by the encouragement we gave him in those formative days.'[197]

While the Part I results could be ranked, as all candidates were taking the same exams, the individual pathways, combinations, and weightings of Part II made different candidates' marks incommensurable. The results were posted alphabetically within an overall class, with first-class performances in a given strand noted by appending in brackets the letter by which that strand was known. An asterisk after the letter denoted 'special distinction'. MRJ did his Part II in the compulsory Language and Literature (A), and in Archaeology (D). His degree results read 'James (*a**, *d**)'.[198] They literally could not have been any better.

5

Fellow of King's, 1887

There was never any doubt that MRJ would return to King's to work towards a Fellowship. He may have claimed with hindsight that he never had any definite professional ambitions or direction, no sense of a career, but in the summer of 1885 he knew exactly what he wanted to do next.

By this time, the days of automatic Fellowship for Etonian King's Scholars were over (W. P. Brooke, the father of the poet Rupert Brooke, was elected the first non-Etonian Fellow in 1873). In fact, MRJ was applying for his Fellowship under a new regime. From 1882, King's Fellowships were limited to a term of six years, unless the holders occupied specific teaching or administrative positions in the College or University (this helped to solve the problem of College policy being dictated by change-blocking backwoodsmen). From 1885, Fellowships were awarded competitively, by dissertation.[1] What this meant was that the award of a Fellowship was by no means a certainty, even for highly gifted scholars. While MRJ and Walter Headlam both got Fellowships, Lionel Ford (a Chancellor's Medallist) did not. In E. M. Forster's *künstlerroman The Longest Journey* (1907), which draws heavily on his undergraduate years in King's, Stewart Ansell, the outstanding philosophy student of his day, is twice thwarted in his application for a King's Fellowship.

Furthermore, by the 1880s the value of a Fellowship had dropped significantly. In King's and the other Cambridge colleges, Fellows' stipends were paid out of the rental income from college properties. In the 1860s, Leslie Stephen estimated that a Fellowship was worth about £2500 (which, added to other opportunities for income, made a First-class Cambridge degree potentially worth, he thought, about £5000).[2] The agricultural depression of the 1880s greatly reduced the value of the properties, and thus of the Fellows' stipends. The depression affected colleges differently, depending on the nature of their property portfolios, but King's was badly hit. Between the 1870s and the 1890s, the value of a King's stipend was reduced from about £300 a year to about £80. It did not rise above £130 until

1913.[3] In 1907, shortly after MRJ became Provost, King's was so short of cash that MRJ contemplated discontinuing the Chapel services, which cost £2500 a year; they were 'an expensive luxury', he complained to Arthur, but getting rid of the services would make the Chapel 'a voiceless corpse'. Fellowships in 1907 were worth £100 a year.[4] (You can see why so many talented participants in MRJ's story—Luxmoore, O.B., Sydney, Welldon, Arthur, Lionel Ford—chose school teaching over academia. Relatively speaking, it was where the money was.)

MRJ decided to write his Fellowship dissertation on *The Apocalypse of Peter*. This is a significant choice (and not a little perverse), for a couple of reasons. First, notwithstanding the breadth of his formal specialism in Classical Archaeology, it took him very far from his undergraduate degree subject. In spite of his astonishing results in the Classical Tripos, MRJ was never really a Classicist—certainly not in the way that, say, Walter Headlam was. No single academic discipline could ever contain him, but his dissertation was where at least some of his actual intellectual interests lay. Second, and most importantly, he chose to write his dissertation on a non-existent book. More precisely, *The Apocalypse of Peter* was a lost work whose contents could be conjectured and reconstructed from about half a dozen surviving references and quotations, in the works of Clement of Alexandria, Theodotus, Sozomen, and the seventh- to eighth-century *Canon Muratori*.[5] 'For myself', MRJ wrote of these scattered references, 'they had always possessed a curious interest as being the remains of a book once highly prized in several important Christian communities.'[6] 'These six lines, however', he commented elsewhere, 'contained enough clues to suggest what the subject of the book had been, and I wove about them a web of considerable size.'[7] He seems to have begun weaving this web perhaps as early as 1884, when he was still an undergraduate. Notes on the Greek New Testament in a notebook dated that year find him wondering whether Theodotus's work might not be 'full of quotations from the Apocalypse of Peter'.[8] William Smith's *Dictionary of the Bible* (1860), the standard reference work for the later nineteenth century, calls *The Apocalypse of Peter* 'spurious', 'wholly devoid of historical worth', and 'mischievous', and concludes: 'From the fragments and notices it appears to have consisted chiefly of denunciations against the Jews, and predictions of the fall of Jerusalem, and to have been of a wild fantastical character.'[9] One can see exactly why it would have appealed to MRJ.

* * *

In June 1885, Cecil Baring wrote to MRJ with a proposition. Would he be interested in spending a few weeks over the summer travelling around Europe as tutor to Lord Paisley, eldest son of the Marquis of Hamilton? 'The youth Paisley' was an Oppidan at Eton, in Water Durnford's house, and would, Baring thought, 'be amenable enough to discipline'.[10] At a loose end for the summer, generally short of money, and always keen on European travel, MRJ said yes. At the end of July, he went to the Grosvenor Hotel in London, to meet Hamilton, who did not impress him: 'he is a shopkeeper's assistant—small, with a black moustache joining his whiskers and a frock coat. He is not interesting in conversation either, being more fussy than anything else.' MRJ was content to 'let him wash in idle fury round my base'.[11] He thought Paisley was lazy and had nothing to say for himself, but they got on fine.

The pair headed for Brussels, and from there to Strasbourg, where MRJ made sure to visit the cathedral (he thought the spire 'very ugly', but admired the West Front).[12] They spent a few days at Lake Silvaplana in Switzerland, and from there went to Salzburg, where MRJ had a fantastic time in the nearby Berchtesgaden salt mine:

> The salt mine is very good fun. They make you put on a hat & coat & trousers & leather flap behind... The females appear in a cap & coat & white trousers, which thrilled me with horror but they seemed to like it. I could have spent hours whizzing down the wooden slides (but you only do it twice) and there was a most fascinating inclined plane railway which took one out of the mine.

Less fun was the Ethnographical Museum, where they saw

> a Japanese exhibition with Japanese shops & Japs working in them. Paisley is fond of all Ethnographical & Fiji & such things... P. is very fond of savage curiosities so he was delighted with the Japs. They rather bore me, do Jap things, but with certain reservations I can be happy anywhere and was so among the Japs on this occasion.

Rather grumpily, he thought that 'The Cathedral and nearly all churches in Salzburg... are of that particular style which makes me quite ill'.[13]

MRJ found his stint as a tutor and companion to aristocratic offspring generally enjoyable and stress-free (and lucrative: Hamilton paid him £75.13.0 for his tutoring duties, including expenses).[14] The following January, he and Leo Maxse put a notice in *The Times* advertising their service as tutors for the following summer—'We have long intended to try for some nouveaux riches', he told Grace.[15] The Duchess of Abercorn, Lord Paisley's mother, wrote to him 'to ask if you would feel inclined to escort a youth around the continent this summer', but he turned her down as 'I cannot give up next term at Cambridge'.[16] Tutoring of this kind was agreeable enough in its way, but it wasn't really for him. At some point later, he got a remarkably honest letter from Francis Ford, Lionel's brother, who had himself taken up this sort of tutoring position, and was in search of a replacement: 'He should have my sort of qualifications: a little brain as the work is very easy—athletic inclination—above all, a good chap; as companionship to an only son is the chief requirement.'[17]

By October 1885, MRJ was back in his rooms in the Gibbs Building. He spent most of his days in the Fitzwilliam, working on the catalogue, and a year or so later Charles Waldstein proposed to the Fitzwilliam Syndicate that a post be created for him, of Assistant Director, with a modest salary of £100 a year ('bottlewasher' was MRJ's diffident description of the job).[18] He loved cataloguing. It gave a kind of boundless free rein to his scholarship and his unsystematic curiosity, and was the best opportunity to collect and show off those 'blobs of misplaced erudition' he prized so much.[19] 'My dear old bookworm', his friend Ted Butler wrote to him in 1887, 'you could only talk about Greek Testament and Fitzwilliam dust. But I believe you thrive on it, so I won't say anything against it.'[20] He certainly did thrive on it. He began to draw up plans which he would spend the rest of his life carrying out, largely successfully. 'Having now got a description together of about 6000 illustrations in the Fitzwilliam I want to go gradually on and include all the Cambridge libraries', he told his parents.[21] As well as the Fitzwilliam, he went on to catalogue the manuscript collections of sixteen of the twenty-one Cambridge colleges that then existed. In 1926, he embarked on his most ambitious project, a catalogue of the entire medieval manuscript collection of Cambridge University Library—an endeavour so vast that it remained unfinished, and was never published.

Cataloguing was a labour of love, and a kind of obsession, but it could also be a handy source of extra income when he was asked to catalogue the manuscript holdings of private collections like the Pierpont Morgan Library or the extraordinary collection of Henry Yates Thompson, publisher of the *Pall Mall Gazette* and the greatest living collector of illuminated manuscripts. Arthur Benson thought that MRJ brought in an extra £2000 a year from cataloguing, 'earned in odd moments'.[22] This is an astronomical sum, and must surely be an enormous exaggeration, but we know that he charged Yates Thompson five guineas per manuscript, and that his five-volume catalogue (1898–1912) contained descriptions of 144 manuscripts in total.[23]

Waldstein also got him involved in that year's King's Greek Play, Aeschylus's *Eumenides*. He seems to have had a small role (though his name doesn't appear in the surviving promotional material), alongside Albert Baillie, who had a major part (this was the production where he witnessed Waldstein, Clark, and Stanford having their furious rows), and Lionel Ford in the Chorus. Amazingly, there was actually a woman on the stage: the Girton Classicist Janet Case, who later taught Virginia Woolf, played Athena. She was the only woman to appear in a Cambridge Greek Play until 1950. The production was a success, and Willie Bridgeman wrote to him in March to ask whether he'd write a parody of the *Eumenides* for the ADC.[24] That same month he went down to London to see the theatrical superstar Henry Irving performing in his signature role as Mephistopheles in *Faust* at the Lyceum. It was, he thought, 'a magnificent spectacle'.[25]

There was to be no Greek play in 1886, but in 1887 MRJ trod the boards one last time in Waldstein's production of Sophocles's *Oedipus Tyrannus*, in which he, Lionel, and Babington Smith all played supporting roles (MRJ was the Messenger from Corinth). In a guardedly positive review, the *Telegraph* reserved its praise for them: 'These minor parts rank, as a matter of fact, among the most satisfactory features of the representation.'[26]

'I should like to have a term without any examination', he wrote in October 1885, explaining to his father why he didn't want to go in for the Carus Prize that year (and besides, he'd won it back in 1882).[27] But in the autumn of 1885 he did decide to have another go at the Chancellor's Medal, the major Cambridge gong which he'd just missed out on in his first year as an undergraduate, awarded since 1751 for 'the best appearance in Classical Learning'.[28] Two medals were given annually, in ranked order, and the exams began for MRJ on 18 January, so he started to work seriously towards them in December. 'I didn't perform to my satisfaction in the exam', he confided to his parents when they were over; but when the results came out in March, the news was good all round: not only had MRJ come top, but Henry Babington Smith was the second Chancellor's Medallist that year. Mary Emily wrote with 'heartfelt "felicitations" on this fresh honour!' Cecil Baring chipped in from Balliol: 'my eye is now getting accustomed to see lists of all kinds in the newspaper headed by your name.'[29]

At the beginning of January 1886, with MRJ just back in Cambridge after Christmas and studying hard for his Chancellor's Medal exams, he got a telegram from Sydney. Edmond Warre, the Headmaster of Eton, had asked Syd to get in touch, to see whether his brother would be interested in filling in for a sick teacher, William Lane Hitchcock. It wasn't the first time he'd got an offer of this sort—a few months earlier, Welldon had written from Harrow asking whether he'd teach there for a term. MRJ turned him down, notwithstanding the £100 salary on offer.[30] But Eton was another story. And so it was that on 25 January, a few days after taking the Chancellor's Medal exam, he wrote to his parents, 'You now behold me in my new capacity as an Usher'. He'd travelled to Eton with Lionel Ford on the Saturday after finishing the exams, and had his first class on the Monday morning, 'which was not so formidable as I expected... I am told I have the nicest division in the school'. On the whole, he enjoyed his time as an Eton Master: 'I am very happy, and quite busy', he wrote; 'The Division is well, & thoroughly able to keep up a brisk general conversation on any subject.'[31] But he knew that teaching was not for him: he managed successfully to avoid teaching undergraduates for most of his long university career, something he happily acknowledged later in life:

> You may perhaps imagine that because I am in some sense the head of a great educational establishment, I have spent my life educating young people. That is not the case. I did once spend six weeks taking a division of small boys at Eton & for a few years did a little lecturing at Cambridge; that is the extent of my experience.[32]

And so MRJ was back in Cambridge come April, and never again expressed any desire to return to Eton as a Master.

MRJ spent his Eton salary that Easter on a holiday to France and Italy with Luxmoore. On the eve of their departure, he was detained in the Charing Cross Hotel: 'was much tried by OB who not only took me to his room for over an hour last night for the purpose of abusing Eton, but sat at my bedside for half an hour this morning jawing like all possessed'.[33] As a compulsive name-dropper, Oscar Browning was keen to tell MRJ about all the people he should visit while in Italy; MRJ was equally keen to visit none of them.

The plan was to get to Rome for Good Friday. En route, they visited Milan for the Palm Sunday procession, and then travelled to Pisa, where MRJ admired Benozzo Gozzoli's Old Testament frescoes at the Campo Santo. Journeying onward via Lucca, they arrived in Rome on Maundy Thursday. MRJ was suitably impressed by St. Peter's, the Pantheon, and the Colosseum. They went to a service at the Lateran Basilica, lit by a dozen wax candles, where 'the voice of the male trebles is something extraordinary'.[34] At Santa Croce in Gerusalemme, they witnessed the Rite of the Presanctified, the litany performed during Lenten weekdays. On the return journey, they stopped at Orvieto, which brought out the archaeologist in MRJ as he visited 'various little sweet churches: the last had 13th & 14th century frescoes peeping through the plaster all over it—only uncovered here & there. What joy to scrape for a day.' As often, foreign travel brought out MRJ's poetic side, as he wrote of 'a lovely sunset, a silver crescent in a pink sky over purple Apennines, and pale green over that' from his sleeping car to Lake Maggiore; at the lake itself, he went for a walk amongst 'chestnut trees, narcissi, streams, blue lake, sun on mountains'.[35] And so home, via the Simplon Pass (where MRJ revisited the site of the avalanche of 1882) and Dijon.

* * *

Arthur Benson thought that MRJ, 'in refreshing contrast with the majority of the human race, possesses strongly marked characteristics. He knows exactly the sort of life that suits him, and exactly what he likes.'[36] What this meant also is that MRJ always had a very strong sense of what he *didn't* want to do—and generally, he didn't do it. As we've seen, although he loved both Eton and King's, and their schoolboys and undergraduates, he definitely didn't want to teach. Nor did he ever display the slightest desire to go into the Church. He loved *churches*, of course, and was, in his way, a very devout man. He very much enjoyed church services, and even enjoyed, when called on to do so in a professional capacity, delivering sermons. Clerics of various kinds were all around him, naturally, in his family (Herbert, Sydney) and amongst his friends—St. Clair and Lionel, two of his very closest friends, both went into the Church, as did Albert Baillie and several others. Traditionally, old-school dons were always clergymen, and MRJ had a strong sense of the relationship between the Church and the educational institutions he loved. He took strong objection to the possibility of T. H. Huxley's appointment as Provost of Eton on the grounds that 'I don't think people would stand a lay Provost'—and yet, in 1918 he himself was to become the first-ever lay Provost of Eton.[37]

Why did MRJ not take Holy Orders? It's been suggested that it may be because his lifelong engagement with the occult and the supernatural, with black magic, was actually more profound and authentic than has been supposed, or that his researches had led him to a form of pantheism which he found impossible to reconcile with a formal Christian vocation.[38] These are arguments we should take seriously: they tell us something real about MRJ, and have the great virtue of taking his scholarly interests at face value. But in the end, I don't think they can be right. MRJ didn't go into the Church because he didn't want to. It didn't suit him.

There may also be a deeper and more troubled explanation, one which MRJ himself would never articulate other than in highly displaced forms. In a notebook of 1883, around the time that taking Holy Orders was becoming a real possibility for him, he relates the following anecdote:

> The narrator was of the last generation. I don't know if he is still living. But he used to say that at one time he was sorely troubled with temptations to resign all religious and moral sanctions: and at such times—particularly when alone in his room and thinking over the matter—he was conscious of the presence of an old man—his costume of the last century—with an expression indescribably abominable and evil. I cannot learn that this being definitely spoke to him; rather he seemed to be superintending the mental process of temptation.[39]

Malignant faces in period costume recur across MRJ's fiction, from the cobwebby spectre in old-fashioned clerical vestments in 'The Tractate Middoth' to the 'malevolent' figure in 'white linen drapery' in 'A Vignette'.[40] Might these figures be somehow 'superintending the mental process of temptation'? Does MRJ himself feel the burden of the solitary scholar, 'sorely troubled with temptations to resign all moral and religious sanctions'?

He came under quite a lot of pressure, though, to take Holy Orders. His father certainly wanted—and perhaps expected—him to become an Anglican clergyman. On 31 July 1886, the eve of his twenty-fourth birthday, Herbert wrote him a long letter:

> I want—God knows how much and how dearly I want—to see you coming out more and more for Christ, and taking your place as a rallying-point for Him. Do, my darling son, let yourself be fully persuaded of his real true love for you, and of his readiness to fill yr. whole heart with this purest of all forms of joy. This love to Him comes easily, and in His love, His loving service. And I am sure I need hardly remind you that... your powers are all the more free for such objects as may call to them.[41]

This is one of a series of similar exhortations which Herbert sent MRJ on his birthday, almost annually across the 1880s, from the time he came of age in 1883, when, on his son's twenty-first birthday, he wrote, 'You have had your stirrings of heart, and your desires after spiritual good... You know *where* they wd. lead you and *how*. Follow them up.' Herbert seems to have enlisted Luxmoore in this campaign, who asked MRJ in February 1889 'whether you are quite satisfied to let the question of H[oly] Orders wait'.[42] It seems to have dawned on Herbert eventually that this wasn't getting through: he had his last go in 1891, on MRJ's twenty-ninth birthday, when he expressed his hope that his son would become 'a moulder of men'. 'But', he writes, 'for this there must be a closer union with Christ'.[43] Sadly for Herbert, this closer union never came to pass.

* * *

MRJ rounded off the summer of 1886 in sociable form, with a shooting party at Willie Bridgeman's family home in Shifnal, Shropshire. Bridgeman worried about 'the dormouse-like torpor to which you resign yourself every vacation', and so invited him along to this annual event. He travelled there circuitously, via Northamptonshire and Nottinghamshire, taking in a few country churches as he went. MRJ wasn't much of a shot, but he did enjoy going to the local church to play the organ in the mornings.[44]

Back in Cambridge, his social circle was widening further still. He joined the Union—largely, he claimed, for the opportunity to work as the librarian of its newly established library. But almost all his Cambridge friends, old and new, still came from the same King's-Trinity axis. At Trinity, there was Ted Butler, to whom MRJ was not a little attracted. Ted was, he thought, 'the admirable Crichton of this age…a tall dark youth straight as a poplar with curly hair & dark eyes…I think he is quite a magnificent being, not spoilt by his success'.[45] Ted was the son of Henry Montagu Butler, who in 1886 was elected Master of Trinity, having previously served as Headmaster of Harrow and, briefly, as Dean of Gloucester. In 1888, Montagu Butler married the Classical prodigy Agnata Ramsay, over thirty years his junior. MRJ became very friendly with Montagu Butler, and over the next few decades was a frequent dinner guest at the Trinity Master's Lodge. Not once, as far as I can see, does he mention the Master's wife in his correspondence, notwithstanding the fact that her achievements in the Classical Tripos were of a similar calibre to his own.

Fred Benson, already an old friend, arrived up at King's in 1887. Like many of his friends down the years, Fred found MRJ's personality strangely magnetic: 'the clan of friends met, so to speak, under the informal hegemony of Monty James. Intellectually (or perhaps aesthetically) I, like many others, made an unconditional surrender to his tastes'.[46] Archbishop Benson, obsessed by rectitude and always with eyes peeled for 'the abominable', asked MRJ to keep an eye on Fred at Cambridge, to make sure he didn't stray.[47] At King's, Fred fell in love with another of MRJ's social circle, the very glamorous Vincent Yorke, with whom he shared a set of rooms in the Gibbs Building ('I feel perfectly mad about him just now. But I hope & believe it will soon be all right. Ah if he only he knew, and yet I think he does', Fred wrote in his diary).[48] The son of a Conservative MP and a Dutch aristocrat (Baroness Sophie Matilda de Tuyll de Serooskerken, no less), Yorke was obviously quite something: he got Firsts in both parts of the Classical Tripos, played first-class cricket for Gloucestershire, was a captain in the Royal Gloucestershire Hussars, made a fortune in business, and ended up as Director of the Westminster Bank.

Owen Hugh Smith arrived in Trinity in 1888. Yet another figure from a firmly establishment family, his father was Hugh Colin Smith, then a Director of the Bank of England, and its future Governor. Owen would follow in his father's footsteps. Over the years, MRJ would spend many happy weekends at the Smiths' home, Mount Clare near Roehampton in Surrey, and the pair would often take off for bicycling expeditions at weekends, 'which I...look upon', Smith insisted, 'as institutions that must be maintained.'[49] Down the years, Owen Hugh Smith would be present at more of MRJ's Christmas ghost story readings than anyone else.

* * *

MRJ finished the first draft of his Fellowship dissertation in October 1886. Then he spent a couple of months going back and forth to Oxford, chasing up references and making new discoveries in the Bodleian and in Balliol library, where he got to examine an apocryphal Gnostic *Testament of Abraham*, of which he published an edition in 1892. As well as the Latin, Greek, French, German, Coptic, and Ethiopic which he already had, for his dissertation he learned Syriac, which was fine, and Hebrew, which unusually he found a real challenge (he got some help, and a long reading list, from the Scottish Arabic scholar Ion Keith-Falconer).[50] He began a correspondence (in Latin and French) with a young French scholar, Pierre Batiffol, who he had discovered was preparing a Greek edition of the story of Asenath: when Batiffol's edition was published in 1899, it was dedicated to MRJ.[51] 'In the course of my investigations', MRJ wrote of *The Apocalypse of Peter*,

> it became clear that the book must have contained at least two elements, one a prophetic or predictive section, relating to the end of the world, the other a narrative of visions; and more particularly a vision of the torments of the wicked, in which various classes of sinners were represented as punished in a manner suitable to their offences.[52]

The inhabitants of Hell, its demons and its sufferers, always held a particular fascination for MRJ, and he came to believe that *The Apocalypse of Peter* had been a material influence on Dante's *Divine Comedy*.

The dissertation was examined by the Dublin theologian F. J. A. Hort, the Hulsean and Lady Margaret's Professor of Divinity, a close friend and collaborator of both Brooke Foss Westcott and Edward White Benson. Hort was not an easy man to impress—he had a reputation for 'the minutest accuracy and the most cautious utterances', and he was quite dismissive of Batiffol, whom he thought 'young, industrious & energetic, but a poor scholar & very inaccurate'—but he was very impressed by MRJ.[53] MRJ was, in his turn, even more impressed by Hort, whom he thought 'really was comparable to Origen for the range of his learning and the powers of his mind'.[54] The Fellowship committee agreed unanimously to award MRJ his Fellowship, all thirteen members rising together in acclamation when his name was called out. It was formally conferred on 15 March 1887. Two days later, Hort wrote to congratulate him personally: 'The course is now clear to you for endless important & interesting work.'[55] Leo Maxse, who hated King's, wrote from Australia with congratulations of his own: 'I feel that I lose a certain amount of caste by writing to or in any way communicating with anyone who has in so barefaced a manner as yourself donned the livery of hell.'[56]

Alas, MRJ's actual dissertation seems no longer to exist: it would have been instructive to read it, and to read Holt's comments and assessment. But we do have his notes, and his one-page 'Plan of Dissertation on Apoc. Peter'.[57] Many of MRJ's conjectures about the contents of *The Apocalypse of Peter* were to be borne out within a few years, with the discovery in 1892 of a large part of the work in an eighth-century Greek fragment unearthed in a Christian grave at Akhmîm in Egypt. The text was transcribed and published by its discoverer, the French Egyptologist Urbain Bouriant, alongside the text of the apocryphal *Gospel of Peter*, which was part of the same fragment. At Cambridge, MRJ and his Christ's colleague J. Armitage Robinson gave a pair of lectures on these texts, which were soon published by Cambridge University Press, alongside the original Greek texts, in a volume dedicated to Hort, who died shortly before publication. A subsequent discovery in 1910 by Sylvain Grébaut of an Ethiopic fragment of *The Apocalypse of Peter* meant that MRJ was able to publish a (conjecturally) full translation in his 1924 edition of *The Apocryphal New Testament*.[58] Sourcing and reconstructing this text had taken him almost forty years.

* * *

While he was writing his dissertation, MRJ also had more prosaic matters to contend with. His teeth were playing him up again, very badly, to the extent that he was finding it difficult to eat. Mary Emily thought his chronic bad teeth were caused, or exacerbated, by his late nights, his bad diet, and his very heavy smoking. 'I wish I could feel that you were a more ordinary person as to your ways and that took in less smoke and more good wholesome food!!' she worried in November 1886. 'If you are deprived of eating proper food by the state of your teeth, it is a real duty to have them seen to *at once*.'[59] It was the best part of a month before he finally capitulated and went to a dentist in King's Lynn to have a large, abscessed tooth removed. It wouldn't be too long before another one was causing him pain: 'I hope your tooth is quiescent—or removed!' Mary

Emily writes the following October. (What *must* the inside of his mouth have looked like?)

As soon as he had submitted his dissertation, MRJ was drawing up his next French holiday. The plan was to go with Willie Bridgeman and another Trinity friend, George Duckworth, and much of the arranging was done during a visit to the Bloomsbury home of Duckworth's stepfather, Leslie Stephen—where MRJ would quite likely have first encountered George's little half-sister, the five-year-old Virginia. The initial idea was 'to make a shot for St. Bertrand de Comminges', the tiny habitation high in the foothills of the Pyrenees dominated (overwhelmed) by a magnificently uncanny twelfth-century Romanesque cathedral.[60] That proved impractical in the end, though the trio got as far as Narbonne, via St. Etienne ('a loathesome hole... all iron works'), a staggeringly steep cycle ride up to Lepuy, and then Langogne, and Rodez, whose church had the finest organ MRJ had yet seen. Best of all was Albi, which he thought had the most magnificent cathedral he'd ever visited.[61] As was his wont, he made extensive notes of all the cathedrals he visited, and the notes for Albi include an *extremely* complex and elaborately drafted full-page representation of the cathedral's roof.[62] Bridgeman kept the accounts for the holiday, which set the three of them back £27.10.0 a head. He thought the whole adventure 'a complete success'.[63]

The newly elected Fellow of King's spent the spring of 1887 working on the Fitzwilliam catalogue, and beginning the research for his latest project, a catalogue of the Trinity manuscripts. He was also back in the Bodleian, where he indulged his sense of codicological mischief: 'I forged a 14th-cent. English account of the Parthenon by a traveller of the time, which deceived Waldstein. I begin to fear that anything I do find will be discredited.'[64] *Athens in the Fourteenth Century* by 'Professor E. S. Merganser' is MRJ's most elaborate hoax (a merganser is a breed of fish-eating duck), and obviously the product of a man who feels a scholarly burden lifted from his shoulders. It was published as a pamphlet in 1887.[65] Through Professor Merganser, MRJ parodies via over-literal translation a certain kind of Germanic scholarly discourse, but also, more straightforwardly, indulges his mimic's love for funny voices and silly accents:

> I shall from the upset beg to excuse me, for all these that through misluck and an over-weening foreknowledge of the English speech mistakenhoods may befall ye, my good-heart readers. Ever must my plea of an amateur be that I have in my studies of the foresaid only so far as the early twelfth yearhundreds beginning bestrided. And this last, is it from our today's times forgettinghood or our much

> to be bewailed speechshapelearningness's unwisdomship, is to a nineteenth year-hundred period's togethergatheringreceivingsaloon sad unbefitted.

Athens in the Fourteenth Century purports to be a fragment from the writings of the fourteenth-century traveller Sir John Mandeville, taken from 'the Rhodes MS. No. 17', found in the library of 'a private house in Suffolk'. The preface is written by one 'George J. Barker'.[66]

In October 1886, Arthur Tilley, Fellow and Junior Tutor at King's, told MRJ that 'in a year or two they would offer me Herbert Ryle's lectureship'.[67] Ryle (who was Herbert's godson, we remember), had just accepted the post of Principal of St. David's College in Lampeter. The vacant position was a Lectureship in Divinity, and it came MRJ's way sooner than he had been led to expect. The following May, Augustus Austen Leigh, by now Vice-Provost of King's, wrote to offer him the post, for two years in the first instance, and with an annual stipend of £100. 'The proper stipend is £200 but this is rather too much to give for a first appointment', Austen Leigh added.[68]

'I do not think that lecturing was ever my *forte*, as it was certainly never one of my pleasures', MRJ confessed.[69] 'I do not think anyone will come', he worried before his first lecture; but in the event some eight or nine students showed up.[70] He wasn't exactly packing them in like Westcott, but at least he drew a larger crowd than Mayor. In the event, MRJ held this lectureship until 1893, when he left to take over as Director of the Fitzwilliam. He rarely mentions his lectures in his correspondence, and then only in passing, but we know that by 1889 he was lecturing eight to ten hours a week. We also have a list of the topics on which he lectured. It is a long list, but it includes a few old favourites: Petrine and Clementine Apocrypha (*The Apocalypse of Peter*), Apocryphal literature of the Old Testament, the Sibylline Oracles, Introduction to Apocalypse, Apocalypse i–iii. MRJ's lectures on the fifth-century *Clementine Recognitions* were so detailed that Hort wrote to him asking whether there was any need for him to give his own scheduled lectures on this abstruse subject, since MRJ seemed to have covered everything.[71]

It was in the *Clementine Recognitions* that MRJ read something very specific about Simon Magus, the heretical Samaritan sorcerer who makes an appearance in the Acts of the Apostles:

> Now when Niceta and I asked him how these things could be effected by magic art, and what was the nature of that thing, Simon began thus to explain it to us as his associates. 'I have', said he, 'made the soul of a boy, unsullied and violently slain, and invoked by unutterable adjurations, to assist me, and by it all is done that I command.'[72]

Around 1893, he wrote one of his first and best ghost stories, 'Lost Hearts', in which the occultist Mr. Abney commits the serial murder of children in pursuit of his investigations, because 'It is recorded of Simon Magus that he was able to fly in the air, to become invisible, or to assume any form he pleased, by the agency of the soul of a boy whom, to use the libellous phrase employed by the author of the "Clementine Recognitions", he had "murdered"'.[73] So, something came out of the lectures he disliked giving, after all.

* * *

Very occasionally, the world of scholarship offered the possibility of the kind of excitement and adventure MRJ had first read about when he borrowed Robert Curzon's *Visits to Monasteries in the Levant* from Temple Grove Library back in 1873. The real reason he was staying with Leslie Stephen in Bloomsbury in March 1887 was because he had a meeting with Sidney Colvin, Waldstein's predecessor as Director of the Fitzwilliam, who had moved on to become Keeper of Prints and Drawings at the British Museum. Colvin had just met an extraordinary man, an Albanian called Alexitch, who told him an even more extraordinary story. In the remote valley of the Drin, fifty miles from the nearest civilization, 'a secret part of the country visited only by shepherds', a landslip had uncovered what appeared to be a complete, undiscovered Greek temple. Alexitch had gone to investigate when he heard reports that a shepherd retrieving some sheep that had fallen into a hole on the ground, which legends told was haunted, and had 'reported strange things at the bottom'. And so Alexitch made his way to London, to share his findings with the British Museum—or so he claimed. Colvin proposed that Henry Babington Smith travel out to Albania to investigate 'a sight which no mortal eye has yet beheld', and Henry suggested that MRJ should go too, given his archaeological and antiquarian expertise. 'If Alexitch does not lie', MRJ told his parents, 'the theory is that the edifice is a heroön [a shrine to a hero] or a family shrine of Alexander's time... On the whole it is one of the most exciting things I have heard—beats King Solomon's Mines.'[74]

Alas, the escapade never came to pass—Colvin received a telegram to the effect that Alexitch was not to be trusted, and that was that. But the following December found MRJ setting out on a real archaeological adventure, to Cyprus. Again, this was thanks to Babington Smith, who had turned down a job on an archaeological dig because he'd landed a post in the civil service, and had recommended MRJ to take his place. And so, with the approval of King's, the Fitzwilliam, and the University Council, he got a few months off to go to excavate Kouklia (Old Paphos), a major excavation on the south-western tip of Cyprus, and Leontari Vouno, a remote mountain village in the far north of the island. The dig was led by Ernest Gardner, the archaeologist and Fellow of Gonville and Caius who had just been appointed Director of the British School of Archaeology at Athens. MRJ knew Gardner a little, as they'd both been part of the cast for the 1883 production of *The Birds*. Gardner was ill for much of the time, though, and so in practice the supervisor was D. G. Hogarth, Fellow of Magdalen College, Oxford, and later a close friend and collaborator of T. E. Lawrence.

The prospect of the Cyprus trip made Herbert very apprehensive—'I don't know that, under the circs. of your College work, I wd. have wished you to "go foreign"...I confess that I wd. have liked to see you settling down to steady work on the lines already drawn out for you.' But he was reassured that MRJ would not forfeit his lectureship. Besides, the trip would give him the chance to meet up with Ber, who was then stationed at Limassol, where he complained to Bardolf Barker that 'The people heer does not noe how to speak excep siliness'.[75] 'Don't forget good, useful boots', Herbert is soon advising, while warning against 'diarrhoea, chills, &c.' Mary Emily chimes in, 'I think that in your outfit a good travelling cap, with ears to tie down, has a place—not only for travelling but for camping out at night in Cyprus', and reminds him not to forget his binoculars. Herbert lent him £10 towards his various travelling expenses, and Sydney lent him £50 (there's no record of either of them ever having been paid back).[76]

On 12 December, on board ship from Brindisi to Alexandria, MRJ wrote a long and excited letter to his parents. His journey so far sounds like something out of John Buchan or Graham Greene. He shared a sleeping car from Paris to Brindisi with a Greek traveller, who he initially worried was going to murder him in his sleep. But the pair bonded over shared cigarettes, and discussed Demosthenes and Cicero ('much in favour of the former'). 'The upshot was', he writes, 'that he entrusted me with an engraved gem of some value to be presented for inspection at the Museum of London in the month of April.' (At the time of writing, he still had the gem, which he thought might be 'a really good one'.) At some point in their journey, the pair were joined by a third companion, a Levantine. This is where things got really interesting:

> Just before Brindisi, the Levantine asked if I had any arms about my person, & on my replying no, produced, ah heaven, a revolver from his pocket, but his intentions were honest & I took an early opportunity of assuring him that if I disappeared, the Continent would instantly be plunged into all the horrors of

> a European war. However, with others I think it will be best to say that I always carry dynamite.[77]

In some part of his fantasy life—the part that read Ballantyne or Wilkie Collins or Rider Haggard—MRJ, with his prodigious linguistic skills and store of arcane knowledge, obviously enjoyed thinking of himself as a Richard Burton or a Sandy Arbuthnot figure, an Imperial Orientalist or a player of the Great Game. St. Clair, about to move to a parish in Stepney, wrote reassuringly that 'Except for the "high probability"...that your Levantine Robbers will blow your brains out, they are no worse than East Londoners'.[78]

The voyage by boat from Brindisi to Nicosia, via Alexandria, Port Said, Joppa (Jaffa), and Beirut was every bit as enthralling. He had a number of conversations in Latin with a pair of Capuchin monks, one a Belgian en route to China via Jerusalem, and the other an Italian Professor of Philosophy at Bethlehem: 'he argues with great skill, on the slightest provocation, in the Socratic method', MRJ wrote to Sydney. On deck, he witnessed

> an encounter between the Boatswain or someone & a fiery southern mariner. The former after some altercation flew at the latter from sixteen yards off & hit him a most tremendous smacking blow on the head...I was again sorry for the sailor & felt myself compelled to plaster his head with honey,—thus fostering a revolutionary spirit. But again it may stand one in good stead when the crew rise in mutiny on the high seas & murder the passengers in their berths.[79]

Travelling was exotic and exciting, but it was also dislocating and frightening. MRJ was a man used to familiar institutions full of friends, and there in the sleeper compartment to Brindisi, surrounded by menacing-seeming foreigners, he appears to have succumbed to a bout of loneliness, self-doubt, and anxiety, which he confided to Lionel Ford in a letter which was evidently rather anguished. The pride MRJ had long taken in the intrinsic uselessness of his work suddenly seemed to him misplaced, empty. We no longer have this letter, but we do have Lionel's reply:

> Dear old chap, I know the kind of feeling that comes over one in a railway carriage, when each moment carries one further from all that one loves. I don't wonder at your being despondent and thinking of your unworthiness. Only that you mustn't say that your life is wasted: if there was nobody except me left of your many friends, I should know well enough it isn't so. How much I owe to you I can't say, but I do feel with all my heart that in starting on what is probably my lifework, I start with aims and hopes which you have largely created.[80]

Lionel showed the letter to Ted Butler, who was also worried by it, and wrote a long letter of reassurance and comfort: 'I hated to see the way you wrote about yourself, for I am quite sure that you are quite wrong: I mean as to your saying that your life must be a useless one. Why need it be?'[81] MRJ obviously conveyed something of the same mood to Luxmoore, whose response, as befitting a public schoolmaster, was more phlegmatic and Stiff Upper Lip, promising that 'a decent gloss you may be sure [will] be drawn over the analysis of sickness & anatomy of choly on board the Brindisi boat'.[82]

From Brindisi he sailed to Alexandria, and from Alexandria to Limassol. On these voyages, he whiled away the time reading Thackeray's *Irish Sketchbook*, and fell in with an English crowd, some of whom he liked, but one of whom he found particularly irritating. With a very few exceptions (Lady Donaldson, Gwen McBryde, Sibyl Cropper), he was never comfortable around women, and generally found their presence irksome. 'There is a woman here', he wrote on the ship, 'playing the worst kind of music, an imitation of Haydn—perhaps Haydn himself. It couldn't be worse. And the beast was knitting during dinner.'[83]

He landed in Limassol on the morning of 22 December. That evening, he met up with Ber, and the pair spent the next couple of weeks together, hanging out in the United Services Club, playing cribbage and drinking with the Chief of Police, Captain Bor. One gets the strong sense that, for MRJ, the only real problem with Cyprus was (again) the presence of women: 'But there are enough decent people about to last for some time. The island is as full of scandal & gossip as possible & I am very glad I live in a bachelor society for the most part.' At Limassol, he stayed with the family of the late Col. Warner, who had been Chief Secretary to the High Commissioner, and while he appreciated their kindness (they put him up for Christmas), he found Mrs Warner intensely annoying: 'Nobody could mean better, but the irritation she causes me is entirely disproportionate to the cause (or causeuse).' He thought Lady Bovill, the widow of the judge Sir William Bovill, 'a ghastly woman'. When Ernest Gardner turned up with his wife, he complained to Mary Emily, 'I really don't know what Mrs. Gardner expects to do here... You will see that I consider her somewhat of a nuisance. She objects to smoking, with far less reason than you, for what is one to do of an evening if not smoke?' 'I could easily argue with Mrs G', he wrote later, 'who dresses in terracotta & thinks she can argue. She is Scotch, used to teach at the High School in Oxford, used the phrase internally subjective lately, and takes a pride in being unconventional... Why on earth did he bring her here? I expect he hadn't much voice in the matter.'[84]

When January came, he was relieved to get out to Old Paphos to join Hogarth on the dig: 'He is a good sort I think.' MRJ liked Paphos: he stayed in a large, airy room with nine unglazed windows, and travelled to the dig every morning by mule. He found himself in charge of thirteen men, excavating a large stone building of mysterious origin, the Temple of Aphrodite.[85] It looked, he thought, 'like Solomon's Temple'.[86] He wrote letters home sitting amongst the tombs on the hillside. MRJ found the Temple 'more perplexing every day... a puzzle'; 'the people who made all these things are not Greeks nor yet it wd. seem Phoenicians but nobody knows.' They uncovered strange carvings shaped like poppy heads ('What are they?'), carved animals, black glazed pots, and graves full of vases and 'coiled rings of copper'. They dug into the large, many-chambered tombs of the Kings of Paphos, all 'quite empty now'.[87] The findings, on the whole, were not spectacular. Luxmoore was near the truth when he wrote that, instead of uncovering 'a colossal finger of the finest bronze', leading to the discovery of a statue with 'jewels for eyes', MRJ would find 'only the dullest of illegible inscriptions & endless articles for Hellenic journals'.[88] Hogarth later admitted that he, MRJ, and Gardner, all young and inexperienced (they were all born in 1862), really didn't know what they were doing on this dig, being 'so raw as not to know if there were any science of the spade at all'.[89]

MRJ got to see a bit of the island while he was there. He saw the ruins of Tamassos at Politiko. He went to Famagusta and Nicosia, and passed a leper colony whose inhabitants kept 'dogs as large as donkeys'. He visited the monastery of the Cypriot Saint Mnason, which he found 'in a frightful state'.[90] This was a particular disappointment, as Lionel had pictured MRJ 'in a monastery, uprooting a Papias from a bundle of dull old manuscripts'.[91] This was something the pair had evidently discussed, as Papias was one of MRJ's recurring preoccupations, which took on an almost talismanic significance for him as the supreme prize for the manuscript-hunter. When he had first heard of the possibility of going to Cyprus back in November, he had confided to his parents that 'if a copy of Papias turns up I shall be all the better pleased'.[92] In his first published story, the actual scrapbook which Canon Alberic de Mauléon has compiled from his plundered sources is a compendium of codicological wonders, including 'a fragment of the copy of Papias "On the Words of Our Lord," which was known to have existed as late as the twelfth century at Nîmes'.[93] Like Dennistoun in 'Canon Alberic', in 1905 MRJ's colleague and former student Oliffe Richmond *did* claim to have discovered and transcribed an 'imperfect palimpsest' of Papias at the monastery of Alcobaça in Portugal—though this was in reality just a codicological in-joke ('I like being quiet over my little finds', he told MRJ).[94] In his 1919 monograph on codicology, *The Wanderings and*

Homes of Manuscripts, he returned to this particular manuscript, writing: 'It is almost a relief that catalogues [of ancient English libraries] do not tell us of supremely desirable things such as Papias on the Oracles of the Lord or the complete Histories and Annals of Tacitus.'[95]

MRJ left Cyprus on 4 April, and travelled home via Paris. He missed out on some of the archaeological fun: just after he left, Hogarth discovered the temple of the phallic god Opaon Malanthios at Amargeti (what would MRJ have made of that?).[96] But, back in London, he had a celebrity encounter. He was taken to lunch in the Savile Club in Mayfair by John Henry Middleton, the recently appointed Slade Professor of Fine Art at Cambridge and future Director of the Fitzwilliam. The pair dined with Edmund Gosse and Thomas Hardy, who was then at the height of his success and fame as a novelist. In years to come, Hardy would be a great admirer of MRJ's ghost stories, sending him appreciative notes. Gosse was a Cambridge acquaintance, and a good friend of Arthur Benson's. Then Lecturer in English at Trinity, he was known at the time as an art critic and a minor poet; the extraordinary memoir of his upbringing amongst the Plymouth Brethren, *Father and Son*, for which he is best remembered now, was not published until 1907 (Arthur, who had commensurate father issues of his own, admired *Father and Son* beyond words, and wished he'd written it).[97] They all seem to have got on well that day, and Hardy proposed MRJ for membership of the Savile Club. This was the great London preserve of the literary establishment, whose membership around the turn of the century included, as well as Hardy and MRJ, Henry James, H. G. Wells, Rudyard Kipling, Max Beerbohm, Rider Haggard, W. B. Yeats, Robert Louis Stevenson, and many others. While he was happy to be a member of the Savile, this was not really a scene that MRJ much enjoyed. Down the years, whenever he was in London, he tended to make for his other club, the Protestant-only National Club in Whitehall Gardens.

That summer, he and his friend Ted Sanderson, an Old Harrovian who had come up to Trinity in 1886, went to stay with George Duckworth's family (the Leslie Stephens) at their summer home in St. Ives, Cornwall. There they met George's sister Stella, whom MRJ thought 'extremely beautiful'. 'I think I should have stopped a little longer at St. Ives but it was becoming dangerous', he wrote to his family.[98] It's worth pausing on this, as it is the *only* time when MRJ seems seriously to have acknowledged the attractiveness of a woman. Certainly this was marked enough to worry Mary Emily, who thought the stepdaughter of a notorious agnostic and freethinking metropolitan intellectual a most unsuitable match. She was very relieved to discover that it was actually Ted Sanderson who had fallen in love with Stella Duckworth:

> I felt there was something 'in the air', though I did not imagine that the something was chiefly on account of your friend.—I *do* sympathise with him—and with you.—But if I may speak out my mind, I am relieved that the lovely Miss D. is his choice, & not yours!—I am persuaded of her amiable & attractive qualities but I should be deeply grieved, & very anxious if you married a woman who did not distinctly hold the Christian faith & hope. Miss D's surroundings, even, as I understand, her mother, do *not* hold this, & therefore I conclude that she herself is, at best, a sheet of white paper as regards religion. This does not do to live or die upon, as I am happy to think you yourself feel & believe.—I can but pray & trust that you will be guided in your own choice, whether it be an early or a later one, to a wife whose training at any rate has been Christian—God only can make that training & teaching effectual.[99]

'The beautiful Stella', as he insisted on calling her, seems to have held quite a fascination for MRJ's circle.[100] As well as Ted Sanderson, J. K. Stephen was an unwelcome suitor: he was a large, imposing man with serious mental health issues, and his behaviour around her was certainly scary, and even, according to one account, 'violent and sexually threatening'.[101] Also unwelcome was Walter Headlam, of whom she wrote, 'I cannot think of him without a shudder and yet he is much to be pitied—it is awful'. ('What can he have done?' asks Virginia Woolf's biographer Hermione Lee; Walter certainly had form when it came to this family, and a few years later would be turning his attentions to young Virginia herself).[102] With what is surely a strong aftertaste of sour grapes, Walter wrote to MRJ calling Stella 'vacca divina' (a divine cow), and maintaining 'I am sure she is simple; and cool'. He was 'convinced that for Ted it couldn't possibly do'.[103]

Whatever the nature or degree of the feelings Stella Duckworth may have aroused in MRJ (and it's highly doubtful that there were any), she was very much an anomaly. The following year, he met Leo Maxse's sisters at the family's new home in Dorking, and found them 'very taking—very French or rather so in appearance—but speaking very slowly and with a slight drawl like Leo'. He signed off cheekily to his mother, 'Please add them to my list of fiancees'.[104] He assured Leo that he was 'a don and a dean and a confirmed bachelor'.[105]

It's fair to say that, with one or two exceptions, MRJ simply did not like women, and avoided their company. This was certainly the reputation he cultivated. A 'beautiful and accomplished lady' once said to Arthur Benson over dinner 'with a graceful air of judgment that she had but one fault to find with [MRJ], and that was that he hated women'.[106] He once refused to congratulate a colleague on his engagement, on the grounds that he hadn't been told about it in advance. Mindful of this, a colleague and former student, J. H. Clapham, wrote anxiously to MRJ on the occasion of his own engagement: 'I know you have definite tastes and that you don't accept all your friends' views of women.'[107] Another colleague, Oliffe Richmond, once described MRJ (in a letter to the man himself!) as 'orthodox & woman-hater'.[108] Owen Hugh Smith once made the mistake of inviting MRJ to a social gathering in which there would be *two* women present, and had to apologize profusely; 'How glad you will be to be free of the female sex', he wrote when, perhaps understandably, the women decided not to come.[109] Gwen McBryde, by far his closest women friend, wrote that 'It was the fashion in [his] clique to proclaim themselves misogynists'. For MRJ himself, she thought, this was not a pose: 'I think perhaps his friends had been right' to believe that he disliked women; 'Even in later days they were chary of bringing their women folk when they looked in on him.'[110]

* * *

King's was full of excitement and consternation as 1889 dawned. Provost Richard Okes had died in November 1888, just short of his 91st birthday. He had been Provost of King's since 1850. As a Fellow, MRJ was one of the electors for the new Provost, and when the vote came in February, it was a two-horse race between the Vice-Provost, Augustus Austen Leigh, and the great Cambridge modernizer Henry Sidgwick. There was never any doubt which way MRJ would vote. Like T. H. Huxley, Sidgwick was an 'intellect', one of those nineteenth-century stinks men who didn't do. He had helped found a women's college! In the event, Austen Leigh was elected by a comfortable majority. Eleven Fellows voted for Sidgwick. Of these, MRJ told Herbert, three were 'decent people afflicted with morbid consciences', who had made a 'wrongheaded' decision. Some of the others were 'Social Democrats', while others still were simply 'monstrosities'. The last Sidgwick supporter, the eccentric J. E. Nixon, he considered 'in a class by himself'.[111]

With the election of a new Provost came the beginnings of a new administration, which in turn brought new possibilities for MRJ, as he explained to Herbert: 'The deans Nixon and Stearn are incompatible & one will have to go. The greater part of the College would like to get rid of both, & it is not inconceivable that Douty might be made one dean & myself another.'[112] Deanship was a broadly disciplinary and pastoral position, not enormously onerous but carrying a modest stipend of £125, and with the real advantage that it was one of those administrative positions that would allow MRJ to continue his Fellowship beyond the normal six-year limit. He was definitely interested. But there was a problem: the other name suggested, E. H. Douty, a gynaecological surgeon who taught in the Anatomy Department, was not a Fellow; in order to make him Dean, King's would have to fast-track his Fellowship.

What happened next is very troubling. *The Granta*, a newly formed Cambridge magazine, got hold of the story and, sensing an opportunity to make mischief and draw attention to itself, published an article entitled 'The Coming Dean':

> A rumour has reached us on very good authority of another plan of the 'Stupid Party', as they are termed in King's. It is proposed to elect Mr. Douty to one of the vacant Fellowships, and to confer upon him the somewhat degrading office of Dean. That obsolete anachronism, attended as it is with so much odium and opprobrium, is naturally shirked by competent men in the college, and they are ready to make anyone Dean who is willing to do the dirty work.[113]

Nor did MRJ escape *The Granta*'s gaze. A subsequent article, entitled 'Those in Authority', describes him, rather acutely it seems to me, as 'Faultily faultless, icily regular... There are some lives whose brilliancy and cleverness serve to dazzle rather than to lighten the eyes of the critic and biographer. It is a well-known scientific fact that an excess of light is much more impenetrable than an excess of darkness.' He had dedicated himself, the article maintained, to 'a gallant though possibly injudicious attempt to maintain the pre-eminence of his old school in every branch of College life'.[114] MRJ was understandably annoyed at this, telling his friends at the Chit-Chat Club that 'The *Granta* has been very severe on cliques of late... What I rather object to is its assertion that cliques are bad... you might as well say that friendship is bad'.[115] But things were about to get worse.

The national media got hold of the Douty story. The *Pall Mall Gazette* wrote:

> The Fellows of King's, Cambridge, are about to give a striking proof of the extent to which their conception of the College is divorced from any idea of educational responsibility or duty to the public... [Mr Douty's] academic achievements are summed up in a second-class in the elementary part of the Science Tripos... He has not competed for a fellowship by dissertation, nor is he (that would be a little too absurd) to be elected as a 'distinguished person'... Mr Douty is understood to be a very good fellow, who is deservedly popular, 'goes out riding with the dons, you know', belongs to the old social Etonian set, and altogether is just the man who *should* be elected if the college is to be regarded as a kind of pleasant social club.[116]

The original *Granta* article had also proposed Oscar Browning as a candidate for Vice-Provost, and MRJ detected O.B.'s hand behind the whole thing: 'The Coming Dean' singled out for praise 'Mr. Oscar Browning [who] has done his best to eliminate the dead level of academic mediocrity which has been the curse of many colleges beside King's'.[117] The article was written by Robbie Ross, a Canadian Freshman and 'a great protégé of O.B.'s'.[118] Ross is best known as the devoted friend of Oscar Wilde in his later years, though he was already romantically involved with Wilde when he came up to Cambridge as an undergraduate: it was Wilde who first introduced Ross to O.B. In a Union debate, Ross spoke powerfully against Douty's candidature for Dean. A chain of events led to Ross's being thrown into the fountain at King's by a group of six undergraduates ('hired bravos', according to *The Granta*)[119], including Ted Sanderson, Fred Benson, and Francis Ford, seemingly at the instigation of the Junior Tutor, Arthur Tilley—Fred's diary for March 1888 refers to this cryptically as the 'Ross scheme'.[120] MRJ, who was, as we know, rather fond of physical horseplay and had even been prone to bullying as a schoolboy, confessed that 'the idea pleased me a good deal'. Given Ross's fragile health, this kind of manhandling and ducking could have had serious consequences: it may either have caused or exacerbated a serious bout of pneumonia. The College was thrown into uproar, with O.B., 'nearly mad with rage', threatening legal action: 'Oscar Browning I suppose told a hundred lies if he told one. (& one I can pretty well swear to)', MRJ wrote. Leo Maxse sent a telegram advising MRJ, 'If they are summoned for assault mind to employ counsel. I will get a barrister to come down if they want one.'[121] O.B., in his turn, wrote a letter of protest to the Governing Body of Kings: 'an outrage was committed in College, the result of which was to deprive an Undergraduate temporarily of his reason, and to ruin his University career'.[122] Nixon, still nominally Dean and acutely sensitive to bullying, wrote a detailed report in which he recommended severe punishment for the perpetrators. Francis Ford never forgave 'that little Twist-About' Nixon for this, though no action seems to have been taken.[123] Nixon also wrote a long letter to MRJ in his tiny handwriting, intimating darkly that 'a plot or conspiracy or combination if you prefer the word was surely going on to oust me from office', by nameless colleagues who were 'maintaining outwardly the most friendly relations with me'.[124] MRJ 'had a tête-á-tête with Mr. Ross, the author of the obnoxious article, & found him quite reasonable & sorry for what he had done'. The editor of *The Granta* came to see MRJ to demand Francis Ford's expulsion from the Pitt Club, a request that was firmly refused. The next edition condemned 'the dastardly outrage which has caused a feeling of resentment amongst all right thinking men', and the paper's editorial team challenged the perpetrators 'to combat in the manner of law-abiding Englishmen with the gloves of the boxer'.[125]

Tilley, who had not only encouraged the ducking, but dined with the perpetrators afterwards, was forced to apologize publicly in front of the College, and resigned his Junior Tutorship.

In the event, the proposal to award Douty a Fellowship was defeated by one vote. MRJ voted in favour. In the furore that followed, he got to his feet and made perhaps the most unexpected institutional intervention of his life. Nathaniel Wedd, recently elected a Fellow and by no stretch of the imagination a man of ideological sympathy with MRJ, discusses this in his unpublished memoirs:

> The leading mind among the Exclusives, taking stock of the position, concluded that the lines of exclusiveness were wrong, and that for the future, he and all whom he could influence, would have no more to do with them. With great moral courage, he asked all undergraduates to meet at the reading room, and there expounded the conclusion at which he had arrived, and his determination to act on different lines in the future. This was succeeded by a general reconciliation and in the position of the Dean, to which the great reconciler was shortly afterwards appointed, the policy of equalization got its chance and proved completely successful.[126]

In spite of the fact that MRJ had also urged his audience not to read *The Granta* ('Blessed is the man that endureth temptation, for when he is tried he shall receive the crown of King's', he was reported as saying), it was, that paper concluded, 'an oration to the College á la Mark Antony'.[127]

'It must have cost him a great deal', J. H. Clapham thought, 'but he did it.'[128] Although it has been read as the moment 'he now began to lay all shows of partisanship aside', this should not be seen as some kind of Damascene conversion.[129] His own analysis at the time was that 'Personally I am quite in sympathy with the fountain-people: but it was a mistake in policy inasmuch as it was regarded by the College at large as an act of revenge coming from the "Eton" set'. His institutional instincts remained always conservative, and at times reactionary, and he certainly never lost his sense of primary affiliation to Eton. But nevertheless, he was conscious that something had changed: 'It has been most unpleasant throughout. I [hope] the net result will be nothing but good (I spent a couple of hours with Wedd the other evening as one consequence).'[130] The Old Etonian Tory and the Fabian 'Scallywag' could find some common ground after this, and worked together reasonably happily for decades.

* * *

The Deanship was formally conferred on MRJ at the end of November 1889. In the event, his fellow Dean was A. H. Cooke, the College's first married

Fellow. As a Dean, MRJ's duties were not onerous: one Old Kingsman recalled him breaking up a football match being played on King's Great Court by saying gently, 'I do wish you fellows would go to bed'.[131] (They did.)

The other major event of that term for him was a vacancy for Director of the Fitzwilliam. This was no surprise: Waldstein had been offered the post of Director of the American School of Classical Studies in Athens in January 1887; he eventually accepted it in the autumn of 1889. This position had the great advantage of putting Waldstein at the heart of the material culture of his academic research, and over the next few years he oversaw excavations at Plataea, Eretria (where he believed he had found the tomb of Aristotle), and the Heraion of Argos. He returned to Cambridge in 1895 as Slade Professor of Fine Art, a position he held until his retirement in 1911, shortly after which he was knighted. He also went on to enjoy an interesting public intellectual career, writing critiques of the idea of the 'Jewish Question', and of the application of racial theory to eugenics.[132] At the end of the First World War, fearful of popular anti-German feeling, he anglicized his surname to Walston. He also found time to represent the USA in the 1896 Olympic Games at Athens, where he competed in the rifle-shooting event, and seems to have done rather well.

This change at the top potentially put MRJ in a difficult position. His job at the Fitzwilliam was tied to Waldstein's directorship, and was quite likely to lapse when he left. It was always on the cards that John Henry Middleton would succeed Waldstein. By training an architect, Middleton had worked alongside George Gilbert Scott, and had led a genuinely colourful life. In his memoirs, MRJ conjures a picture of Middleton as the kind of scholarly Orientalist that he himself had occasional fantasies of being:

> Clad in a dressing-gown or a velveteen coat, and a skull-cap, and smoking a kind of shag [tobacco] (as I should call it) named 'Golden Returns', he sat and retailed in a level voice, with frequent slight dramatic pauses, the most startling personal experiences... He had seen Bomba arrive, fleeing for refuge, at the Italian convent where he was at school: he remembered well the promulgation of the Dogma of the Immaculate Conception. He had fished for alms out of the window of a prison in Aleppo, had had an audience with the Sultan at Fez, advancing with some trepidation along the hall to where the Sultan sat flanked by two live lions—unattached: he had slept or not slept in the native home of the bed-bug in a Central American forest: had seen, on the broad and boundless Perearers [prairees], Apaches transfix American soldiers with arrows shot from horseback: had also seen the celebrated rope-trick.[133]

MRJ liked Middleton, was dazzled by him, but by no means thought he should be Director of the Fitzwilliam. 'To tell you true, I am a little frightened at the prospect of Middleton in his relation to the staff and I think it is inevitable that he should succeed Waldstein... I am afraid it won't do', he wrote to Francis Jenkinson, Fellow of Trinity and soon to become University Librarian. MRJ proposed that the Fitzwilliam Syndicate (of which Jenkinson was a member) should also appoint a deputy, so that 'a complete change could be obviated'—presumably, he meant himself.[134] Middleton was a fascinating man and a fine scholar, but also a depressive (one particularly serious episode as a student led to his effectively locking himself in his room for six years) and a chronic morphine addict, a habit which would eventually kill him in 1896.[135] Lionel Ford strongly urged MRJ to go for the job himself ('you must apply for the Fitzbilly')—lest he find himself out of a job he liked doing; Ted Butler advised the same, noting 'if you were beaten, you wouldn't feel very much being beaten by a man of Middleton's position'. 'I do not want to break the connection between myself & the Museum', he told Herbert, 'so I think it most likely that I should stand.' But he recognized that his chances were 'problematical—I may say very small'.[136] Middleton of course got the job, and in the event almost his first decision was to extend MRJ's contract by three years. Montagu Butler, the Master of Trinity, who was the chair of the Fitzwilliam Syndicate, wrote reassuringly to MRJ in the aftermath of the decision: 'your claims are universally spoken of with the highest respect and, apart from the claims of your distinguished competitor, there was not one of the Electors who would not gladly have seen you at the head of the great Museum'.[137] MRJ was still only twenty-eight: there would be other times.

* * *

Throughout these years, Mary Emily's letters to MRJ are peppered with her concerns about Grace's health. 'I wish I could see Gracie look better', she wrote to him in May 1889, 'she is thinner than I remember her, excepting perhaps after her worst attack of bronchitis.'[138] To take her out of herself, and to give her something to look forward to, MRJ had the idea of inviting his sister to a dance at King's that August, which Ted Sanderson was organizing on behalf of the T.A.F. club. This was a radical departure for both of them. 'Your enterprising a dance is something amazing!' Mary Emily told him—and it was.[139] '*I shall not dance myself*', he assured Grace, 'but there will be supper I believe, & I will chaperone you... I shall be greatly annoyed if you do not come to this the only dance you are likely to see me at for some time. I consider it a settled thing then.'[140] Grace sent him a formal reply:

> Dear Monty James
> I should very much like to come to your dance: I perhaps will chaperone Gertrude & Milly if their mother does not care to come, & in that case I shall not be expected to dance but look after them. I should very much like to see all your beautiful young ladies dressed for the evening.

'You are quite sufficient chaperone for me anywhere', she wrote in her next letter.[141] When August came, and perhaps to nobody's surprise, Grace didn't turn up for the dance. 'I was not very sorry not to go, as I was not feeling well', she said curtly, and that was that.[142]

The year to come was a lively and social one for MRJ. Straight after the T.A.F. dance, he mounted his tricycle and headed for France for a couple of weeks, taking in Beauvais, Nantes, Chartres, Dijon, and Troyes. Back in England, he collected Luxmoore and the pair went for an antiquarian tour of Buckinghamshire before heading to Pangbourne for one of many visits to the Donaldsons. By this point, Lionel Ford had joined Sydney on the staff at Eton, so he often popped over to see them. With E. C. Austen Leigh he went to stay at the family seat at Chawton, where he visited Jane Austen's house and wandered around Selborne in the footsteps of the naturalist Gilbert White.

In the Easter holidays of 1890 he was back in France, this time with Fred Benson. This was the Archbishop's idea. He feared that Fred, who was clever but unfocused, wasn't in the right frame of mind for his impending finals, 'in danger of growing stale through sheer industry'.[143] He thought that a couple of weeks away from Cambridge in the company of an eminent scholar might do his son good. They took in Rouen, Caen, Bayeux, and Lisieux, and ended up in Amiens and Beauvais. It was on this holiday that Fred amused MRJ by composing his Pindaric Ode to 'Pnyxon, Winner in the Tricycle Race'.[144] The holiday may have worked; at least it allayed the Archbishop's anxieties. Despite Fred's protestations that he 'knew nothing whatever' about classical history, all of which he says he had to bone up on the night before the exam, he got a First in Part I of the Tripos.[145] Unlike Arthur, he stayed on for Part II, under the supervision of J. H. Middleton, and got a First in that, too.

MRJ continued to find manuscript-hunting an exciting business, and in 1890, an old friend of his father's, F. R. Chapman, Archdeacon of Sudbury in Suffolk, tipped him off about six manuscripts in nearby Brent Eleigh, the survivors of a significant collection bequeathed to the parish in 1700. MRJ went to investigate: 'I found them housed in a dank building in the churchyard.'[146]

While this was not exactly the treasure-trove of codicological wonders that his fictional counterpart, Mr Dennistoun of the Wentworth Collection, was soon to discover in the far-flung cathedral of St. Bertrand de Comminges, the Brent Eleigh collection contained some important finds—enough for MRJ immediately to secure purchase of the manuscripts for the University Library.[147]

Most notably, at Brent Eleigh he found 'a volume containing the long-lost life of William of Norwich (a boy supposed to have been kidnapped and crucified by Jews in 1124)'.[148] Studying this manuscript brought him into correspondence with the indefatigable Dr Augustus Jessopp, vicar of Scarning in Norfolk, and a prominent antiquary, who told MRJ that 'your "find" is a really important literary discovery'.[149] The celebrated folklorist Joseph Jacobs thought so too—he heard of MRJ's discovery, and wrote to him in a spirit of 'despairing envy' asking if he could excerpt a part of the manuscript for his forthcoming history of Jews in England in the Middle Ages.[150] MRJ agreed, though against Jessopp's advice, who thought Jacobs 'a very slippery and unscrupulous personage with whom the less one has to do the better'.[151]

Augustus Jessopp was interested in the supernatural—a subject about which he could claim personal experience. In 1880, he published an article in the *Athenaeum* recounting a visit he had paid to Manningham Hall in Norfolk, to examine and take notes on 'some very rare books in Lord Orford's library'. What happens next is irresistibly familiar to any reader of 'Canon Alberic's Scrap-Book': '*as I was actually writing*, I saw a large hand within a foot of my elbow'. The hand belongs not to an arachnoid demon, but to a figure 'dressed in what I can only I can only describe as a kind of ecclesiastical habit of thick corded silk'. Even more irresistibly, Jessopp's *Athenaeum* article is entitled 'An Antiquary's Ghost Story'.[152]

MRJ and Jessopp worked together on an edition of Thomas of Monmouth's *The Life and Miracles of William of Norwich*, which they published in 1896 (though Jessopp was adamant that 'you deserve all the laurels').[153] The story of St. William, they write, 'is the starting-point...in the history of the myth of Jewish ritual murders'.[154] While MRJ in his sections of the Introduction is at great pains to debunk the historical reality of 'blood libel' (the antisemitic smear which accuses Jews of murdering Christian children to use their blood in various religious rites), we know that he was fascinated by stories of occult ritual sacrifice, particularly of children. MRJ traces blood libel narratives back to an account of the crucifixion of a Christian child by Jews in Inmestar, Syria, in 415, as recounted by the church historian Socrates Scholasticus.[155] Socrates's *Church History* also records that, in Alexandria, 'the pagans had formerly celebrated their mysteries, and sacrificed human beings to Mithra'.[156] Mr Abney, we remember, the child-sacrificing occultist of 'Lost Hearts', possesses 'all the then available books bearing on the Mysteries, the Orphic poems, the worship of Mithras, and the neo-Platonists. In [his] marble-paved hall stood a fine group of Mithras slaying a bull, which had been imported from the Levant at great expense by the owner.'[157] Mr Abney plans to sacrifice his young cousin Stephen on 24 March, which, MRJ notes in *William of Norwich*, the Norwich Consuetudinary manuscript at Corpus Christi, Cambridge, identified as William's feast day: 'The calendar of the MS. places the "Passio S. Willelmi matriris" on Mar. 24.'[158] MRJ's fathomless memory was storing all this up.

* * *

That autumn of 1890, tragedy struck the Benson family. Arthur and Fred's sister Nelly worked as a social worker in the East End, where she contracted diphtheria from some of the local children. It was all over in a matter of days. She was only twenty-six. 'I am sure she would have made a considerable mark on the world had she lived', MRJ wrote.[159] Arthur and Fred took Nelly's death very hard. 'It was a horrible, dreary time', Arthur remembered. 'We wrote innumerable letters and tried to be cheerful.'[160] When spring came, MRJ took the Benson brothers to Aldeburgh for a few days, to stay at the White Lion. This worked so well that they all went to Bruges and Antwerp together the following month.

The following academic year saw the return of an old friend to King's. J. K. Stephen moved back onto MRJ's staircase in the Gibbs Building, and started giving lectures in History. But this was hardly the same man as the golden undergraduate of a few years back. Stephen's bipolar disorder had worsened dramatically after an accident in 1886 when he was hit on the head by a pump-engine windmill vane. 'He is much the better for being at Cambridge, I think. The worst symptom about him is that he spends a lot of money', MRJ wrote in February.[161] But things soon got much worse, as Stephen had a very serious manic episode.[162] He began to write unstoppably. 1891 was the year in which he published two volumes of verse. He edited an Eton miscellany, *Keate's Lane Papers*, and wrote *The Living Languages: A Defence of the Compulsory Study of Greek at Cambridge*, a short book on a subject near to MRJ's heart. He also published a pamphlet denouncing his doctor, George Savage, who had diagnosed his mental illness, and wrote a 6000-line 'Swiftlike satire' on Gladstone, which he composed while visiting Ireland over the long vacation. By the spring, his behaviour was so erratic that the doormen at the Savile Club, of which he was a member, had been instructed to prevent him from entering the building. Back in Cambridge for Michaelmas Term, Walter Headlam found Stephen stark naked in his rooms in November 1891, throwing all his belongings out of the window and singing.[163] It was at this point that he was sectioned to an asylum in Northampton. In January he began to refuse food, and on 2 February he collapsed, and died the following day. He had starved himself to death.

Stephen's defence of compulsory Greek was his contribution to an ongoing discussion. In 1891, the University proposed 'a Syndicate in order to suggest an alternative to Greek as a compulsory subject in the Previous [Entrance] Examination'.[164] This was a debate which had been rumbling in Cambridge for years, and its latest manifestation was in belated response to a report of 1880 which concluded, very controversially, that 'the existing obligation to satisfy the examiners for the Previous Examination both in Greek and Latin excludes from the University a number of able and industrious students'.[165] Arthur Benson wrestled with this issue, and eventually came down on the other side from Stephen: he feared a 'drift away' from Oxford and Cambridge, which would inevitably get 'left behind' within a generation, and so with great reluctance came to the conclusion that 'it seems to me that Greek must go'.[166] Even the Chit-Chat Club, hardly a progressive bastion, had in 1887 voted 5–4 in favour of a motion 'that Greek should be made optional in the Previous Examination' (present that evening were MRJ and several friends—Lionel Ford, Walter Headlam, Arthur Tilley, Ted Butler, Marcus Dimsdale—some of these must have voted in favour of the motion).[167] In 1891, the opposition to this tendency was led by the Regius Professor of Greek, Richard Claverhouse Jebb, who convened a meeting in his house to form an organized resistance to the Syndicate. One of Jebb's confederates in this movement was the Emmanuel Classicist James Adam, who enlisted MRJ to the cause on grounds which were essentially pushing at an open door: his dislike of Henry Sidgwick, one of the major proponents of reform. As a broadside in the debate, Sidgwick wrote 'that elementary acquaintance with Greek, now required by the Previous Examination, is useless as a means of acquiring knowledge, and valueless as a source of literary culture'.[168] Rhetoric like this was obviously a red rag to MRJ, with his suspicion of all change and his total and lifelong commitment to 'Useless Knowledge'. So long as Sidgwick was on the Syndicate, Adam wrote to him, 'as he is sure to be, the Wolf will reappear in sheep's clothing... [and] the next concession will be to abolish Greek'.[169]

* * *

In March of 1892, MRJ was in France again, travelling with Armitage Robinson of Christ's, with whom he was shortly to begin work on the Akhmîm manuscript of the *Gospel and Apocalypse of Peter*, plus Robinson's Christ's colleague Arthur Shipley, Lecturer in Morphology—'a teacher of Biology but a very nice little man'—and George Hamilton-Gordon, an undergraduate at Trinity whose father, Sir Arthur Hamilton-Gordon, a keen and knowledgeable antiquarian, had recently returned to the family home at Corrour Lodge near Fort William from a period spent as Governor-General of Ceylon.[170]

The party travelled though the south of France in the direction of the Pyrenees, visiting Orleans, Tours, Bordeaux, Agen, Auch, and Tarbes. But these were all, for MRJ, the prelude to the one place he really wanted to visit—a place he'd wanted to see for years:

> On Tuesday the rain turned to snow & we set out in snow & took the train to Montrejeau, & thence to Loures on a branch line. Here at 10 o'clock in the morning we had a simple repast of Madeira & biscuits & drove in a close fly to St. Bertrand de Comminges. It is a tiny walled town on a steep hill. But the snow which was some inches deep prevented our walking round about it. We could only examine the Cathedral: it is a splendid church, without aisles & short. You see the whole length from the door. There is no proper nave. The stalls which are like those at Auch form a separate inclosure inside the church into wh. you can't see. In the corner of the nave is a splendid organ case on XVI cent with nearly all the inside gone. A splendid 14th-century cope of *English* work in the treasury with all sorts of scenes on it. Beautiful cloisters & altogether a sweet place. But the snow was very much against one.[171]

MRJ was fascinated by the weirdness of St. Bertrand: its location, high on a remote Pyrenean mountainside; the dusty stuffed crocodile hanging above the font, a souvenir brought back by some returning Crusader; St. Bertrand's crozier in the Treasury, made from a carved narwhal tusk; the broken tomb at the north-west angle of the cloister (what had got out?); the enormous choir screen and with its sixty-seven stalls—one of which depicted, he noted during his visit, 'the devil in short cape, with clawed feet, & pointed ears'—and its elaborate Tree of Jesse carved for Bishop Jean de Mauléon (a name to remember; a name to conjure with).[172] 'A sweet place'? At some point within the next eighteen months, MRJ's imagination would transform the Cathedral of St. Bertrand into a habitation of demons. His first published story opens with these words:

> St. Bertrand de Comminges is a decayed town on the spurs of the Pyrenees, not very far from Toulouse, and still nearer to Bagnères-de-Luchon. It was the site of a Bishopric until the Revolution, and has a cathedral which is visited by a certain number of tourists. In the spring of 1883 an Englishman arrived at this old-world place—I can hardly dignify it with the name of city, for there are not a thousand inhabitants. He was a Cambridge man. . .[173]

* * *

Back from his posting in Cyprus, Ber was shipped out almost immediately to Ireland. MRJ went to visit him there in July. It was a memorable trip, and a very boozy one. He docked at 6 a.m. after an overnight crossing, and that morning Ber took him to see his friend Father Dunne, who plied them with whiskey before lunch and then sherry with their meal. That afternoon, Ber showed MRJ something that, like the Cathedral of St. Bertrand, would haunt his imagination: 'the Doctor took me to the horrid vaults of St. Michan's Church which have the properties of preserving bodies in a dry & dusty state for centuries. Anyhow we did see them & they are a nightmare.'[174] Perhaps unconsciously as of yet, the early ghost stories were beginning to shape themselves in his mind. The mummified corpses he saw in St. Michan's combined with years of intensive occult study in 'Lost Hearts', where young Stephen Elliott, the ward of the occultist Mr Abney (whose reading is essentially MRJ's own research), encounters an awful figure lying in the bath:

> His description of what he saw next reminds me of what I once beheld myself in the famous vaults of St. Michan's Church in Dublin, which possess the horrid property of preserving corpses from decay for centuries. A figure inexpressibly thin and pathetic, of a dusty leaden colour, enveloped in a shroud-like garment, the thin lips crooked into a faint and dreadful smile, the hands pressed tightly over the region of the heart.
>
> As he looked upon it, a distant, almost inaudible moan seemed to issue from its lips, and the arms began to stir.[175]

The next day, the pair headed across country to Westport, County Mayo, where Ber was garrisoned. Yet again, they had a bibulous time of it: 'Whisky [sic] before lunch. Whisky at lunch. Call at the Mess (whisky there). Dinner at 5.30!!!! with four or five or more other guests. Champagne there. Hot whisky afterwards, then a short stroll. Then more whisky.' They visited Moyne Abbey and Turlough Abbey, saw the High Cross of Tuam, and climbed Croagh Patrick. From Athlone they sailed down the Shannon to Clonmacnoise. Back in Dublin, MRJ spent a full day in Trinity College Library, where he was amazed by its greatest codicological treasure: 'The beauty & minuteness of the ornament of the Book of Kells exceeds anything you can imagine. It is physically impossible for anyone to copy it.'

MRJ had arrived in Ireland at a time of great nationalist ferment, and he could hardly be expected not to have encountered some aspects of this. The issue of Irish Home Rule had undone the third Gladstone government in 1886. At the very time MRJ was in Ireland, a general election was held in which Gladstone ran on a platform which included Irish Home Rule—and this was the rock on which, two years later, his fourth and last government was to founder. While in the West of Ireland, MRJ visited Galway, where he encountered 'a good deal of Parnellite enthusiasm':

> They call Parnell the murdered chief for some reason best known to themselves. But I am forgetting on Monday evening when we found no less than four Irish members in the Presbytery. John Dillon, Condon, Crilly, & Deasey. John Dillon was the only one who could be called a gentleman. The others are second or 3rd or 5th raters. Dillon is an honest man but a fanatic. We heard many amusing & distinctive things & parted good friends.

'I have no patience with . . . Home Rulers', MRJ had written in 1888, and his visit to Ireland did nothing to change his mind.[176] 'Ireland is a depressing society I conclude', he wrote to Mary Emily. 'I think some concessions in the way of altering Land Laws are necessary: but Home Rule is ridiculous.'

6

Director of the Fitzwilliam Museum, 1893

On 'a fine summer morning' in May or June of 1893, MRJ was walking in the Fellows' Garden of King's when he encountered two young students, both members of the University Athletic Team.[1] One he already knew: Gurney Lubbock was from a family with whom MRJ was to have close connections throughout his adult life, whose members we shall be meeting many times in these pages. The other was to become one of his closest and most intimate friends. His name was Walter Morley Fletcher.

As with many of MRJ's friendships, this was obviously an extremely rewarding relationship for both men. For Fletcher, MRJ was 'the man whose friendship, all through his life, was to mean most to him'. But Walter Fletcher was quite unlike most of the rest of MRJ's circle. He was not, as his wife Maisie testified, 'cast into the public school mould'.[2] He was also a lifelong Liberal Party supporter. Walter was the ninth of ten children, the son of a Liverpool chemist who came up in the world and relocated to Gordon Square, Bloomsbury (the Leslie Stephens were their neighbours). His parents were both proud Nonconformists, and his father had studied at the so-called 'Godless' University College London because he refused to subscribe to the religious tests still compulsory in Oxford and Cambridge. Walter himself came up from University College School in Hampstead to study Natural Sciences at Trinity, eventually graduating with firsts in both parts of the Tripos (his high academic achievement *is* characteristic of most of MRJ's friends), and going on to a very distinguished career in public administration, notably as one of the founders, and first Secretary (Chief Executive), of the Medical Research Council from its formation in 1913. When Walter was up for a Fellowship in Trinity in 1896, he had the honour of getting a good luck message from MRJ's alter ego Bardolf Barker himself:

> Sir i am not much used to righting but I felt I must out with these Few lines Sir in the event whitch you being the successful Competittor as we all opes no Doubt but what you will come Down ansum they ses no but I ses what hever Mr. fletcher's failings may be he as always behaved the gentleman by me and so you have done sir

Walter got the Fellowship. But Barker had fallen on hard times—his health was 'very bad with the indigestion and palpitations', and his grocery business had gone under; he was 'through no fault of my hown throwed out of work and completely Destute'. Could Mr Fletcher spare him even 'a Poundpiece'?[3]

Walter was also a gifted athlete: he once took MRJ to the Guildhall to watch a cinematograph of him competing in an athletics meet (he won the hammer throw, but was pipped at the post in the hurdles). More sedately, the pair enjoyed playing bowls together, and had a particularly intense rivalry at cards. They embarked on a lifelong game of piquet: the first to a million points. They got nowhere near that, but kept score quite jealously. In June 1905, MRJ writes in one of his notebooks that he is just ahead, 58,231–58,226.[4] (These piquet scores, plus the scores of the innumerable games of cribbage he played with whoever was to hand, can be found throughout MRJ's notebooks, and written on the backs of letters, often punctuating earnest and arcane scholarly enquiries.) The final score, according to Walter's calculation, was Walter Fletcher 100,180—MRJ 96,460; though MRJ was adamant that they had unfinished business on this one. Walter was in the lead, granted, but he hadn't won yet, not by a long shot. ('How many wives have suffered . . . for the picquet [sic] habit ingrained by Monty in the young', Oliffe Richmond once wondered.)[5] In a brief reminiscence written after Walter's death, MRJ captured this aspect of their friendship with warmth and humour:

> Working days we did not pass together. He was kept busy by his laboratory and I by some library, but at the ends of such days, meetings were regular enough, whether in my rooms or his, either tête-à-tête or in good company. The backbone of such evenings was furnished by piquet. We had envisaged a match of a million points—as the years passed on we were to become Heads of Houses, sans eyes, sans ears, sans teeth, sans everything; conveyed night after night by faithful retainers to our respective Lodges, and ever and anon wrangling feebly over situations which neither could be made to comprehend; until finally a day came when the million limit was passed, and the unsuccessful member collapsed with an inarticulate cry and arrangements for the inquest set in.[6]

Walter himself, much more emotionally direct and open, wrote to MRJ in 1918, 'I owe more to you than I can express; your friendship is one of the biggest things in my life, and without it I should have been beggared'.[7]

As Dean of King's, MRJ hosted a gathering of students and colleagues every Sunday evening, in which his rooms were invariably packed. But he also kept an informal open house in his rooms most evenings, so that it was common to find half a dozen or so young men slouched on various chairs or leaning against the mantelpiece, drinking whisky and soda, smoking, talking and gossiping, singing, reading stories, performing skits, and playing cards: forging and solidifying a remarkably coherent group identity. In this, he was following the model of intellectual sociability laid down by his King's idol Henry Bradshaw. It's from these years, the fifteen years or so either side of 1900, that we get our most vivid pictures of MRJ the don. This is how Cambridge immortalized him.

His rooms, first in the Gibbs Building and later in the Wilkins, were a chaos of papers and books, opened letters strewn everywhere, pipes and tobacco tins (Sun Dew brand was his favourite), cigarettes and ashtrays (always full), academic gowns and discarded clothes, Mr Leavis's ancient piano in the corner, a china cat on the mantelpiece and its furry counterpart prowling around somewhere. 'It would kill me!', the more fastidious Arthur Benson thought after a visit to MRJ's rooms.[8] In the midst of all this pandemonium, evening callers would generally find MRJ sitting at an old card-table, working or playing solitaire. This was the only available surface not piled high with books and papers in what one correspondent ominously called 'that room with the dark corners'.[9] 'He is commonly known as Monty', *The Granta* wrote in a profile of 1905, 'and is glad to see anyone at any hour of the evening, and will brush aside many thousand pounds' worth of illuminated manuscripts to clear a space for his favourite game. He has possessed no watch since he took his degree, and doesn't want one.'[10]

It is from these gatherings that we have our best single physical account of MRJ, from the Kingsman-turned-industrialist Sir Charles Tennyson. Here is MRJ, as encountered in the 1890s:

> He was tall, dark and rather heavily built, with straight black hair and features which were clear cut without sharpness or aquilinity. He moved silently and with deliberation, spoke softly, seldom laughed but often chuckled, and when he read aloud, as he was fond of doing—generally tales of humour or horror—he seemed able to make dramatic effects without raising his voice or exceeding a purely conversational emphasis. By a pause, and the slightest variation in tone—perhaps the raising of an eyebrow or forefinger—he made his audience realize all that he himself realized in the passage and all that the author had intended it to convey. . .
>
> There were no invitations and no obvious effort at hospitality. Whisky and soda water, cigarettes and tobacco were on the table. The host lay back in his chair, smoking. He seemed to have no fear of silences, but spoke low and intermittently, turning from one to another and presenting to each in turn the friendly

> transparency of his large round spectacles. Now and then he would throw back his head and laugh with a sharp barking sound at some quip or anecdote. Sometimes he would let fall a dry witticism as he padded softly across to the mantelpiece to fetch a spill or fill his large curving pipe at the tobacco jar.

There was always, Tennyson concluded, 'a curious feeling of intimacy about the gathering, which made one realize why it was that Monty James made more friends amongst the fleeting Cambridge generations than any other of the dons and kept those friends longer'.[11]

Several of MRJ's friends and visitors are, like Tennyson, keen to emphasize MRJ's great talents as a mimic and performer—and particularly as a comic. Arthur Benson's diaries are dotted with accounts of hilarious evenings in MRJ's rooms:

> Afterwards went and acted charades! in MRJ's rooms. The worst is that MRJ is such a born actor he puts everyone else out of court. To hear him go to the window & ask an imaginary man where he put his hat was ineffably ludicrous.[12]

After another such 'thoroughly irresponsible evening' at MRJ's, Arthur records, 'I went away shattered with laughter; head aching behind the ears'.[13] He would lapse into one of his variety of comic personae, often mid-sentence. He was regularly to be heard talking to himself, generally in some regional voice or other. He was fond of repeating, at inopportune moments or apropos of nothing, favourite advertising slogans: 'Like those who mid error scarce know how to grope / Perplexed by the merits of Monkey Brand soap'. Shane Leslie recalls him walking around muttering to himself, 'Won't wash clothes'.[14] He was much given to raucously sincere renditions of music hall songs like 'O Miss Bailey, Unfortunate Miss Bailey' or 'I'm a Man Wot's Done Wrong to Me Parents'.[15]

Arthur Benson, who knew a lot about concealment (his diaries were stored under embargo for fifty years after his death), suspected that this comic tendency was a form of deflection: 'Monty is a delightful companion, so long as you keep to the lawn & the shrubberies.'[16] No straying, in other words, into the wilderness, either emotional or intellectual:

> He is *very* humorous too—but after that his mind is the mind of a nice child—he hates & fears all problems, all *speculation*, all originality or novelty of view. His spirit is both timid and unadventurous. He is *much* abler than I am, much better, much more effective—but I feel that he is a kind of child.[17]

This is, in part, the suspicion and hostility towards 'intellects' that MRJ got from Henry Bradshaw, an aspect of his own intense institutional conservatism.

But there is something more here, something uniquely personal and psychological, which amounted at times to a genuine terror of ideas. Oscar Browning, admittedly not a sympathetic observer, put it about that 'James hates thought'.[18] But friendlier voices concurred. J. H. Clapham thought that 'Monty was unspeculative and exceedingly non-political' (he was certainly the former).[19] In MRJ's company, Nathaniel Wedd wrote, 'humour, learning, and laughter flowed in a sparkling and not always shallow stream':

> But there was one line of conversation which was always discouraged—no metaphysics were allowed. The jargon displeased and the theories disturbed. On one occasion two young men were heard discussing some philosophic problem. [MRJ] rapped sharply on the table with his pipe, and called out: 'No thinking, gentlemen, please!' 'Thought' in this sense really did disturb Monty throughout his life.[20]

'The theories disturbed.' This, we will see, is a strong element of what drew him to the ghost story, and what made him such a brilliant writer in the genre.

In his memoir of Walter Fletcher, MRJ lists some of the people who tended to congregate in his rooms along with Walter: 'Gurney Lubbock, Eustace Talbot, James McBryde, Arthur Jelf, W. G. Hemmingway and many more'.[21] Tucked away in the middle of this list, as it were concealed, so you might not notice it, is the love of MRJ's life. This is James McBryde.

McBryde hailed from St. Helen's in Lancashire, and came up from Shrewsbury to King's in 1893 to study Natural Sciences. His family intended him to go into medicine, though he was not academically gifted and had no real aptitude for the subject (he thought he'd only got into King's because the Mathematics paper in the entrance exam happened to be the same one as the sample paper he'd used for revision). He was, though, a talented illustrator, and as the decade went on it became clearer and clearer to him that the visual arts were his real vocation. People liked James McBryde: he was open, honest, trusting, and good-looking in a fresh-faced way; an uncomplicated, outdoorsy type, fond of fishing and shooting, cycling and rambling. 'McB. made his way into our hearts through sheer natural goodness', MRJ recalled. 'In person he was not tall, had light curly hair, and a kind smile: in short, he conciliated goodwill.'[22] He was 'entirely unspoilt . . . childlike, modest, amusing to the last degree, good in every way'.[23] 'I am anxious', MRJ wrote, 'to keep him as he is in the matter of simplicity and goodness.'[24]

The pair were close from the start: 'ever since our first meeting, [I] have found his friendship an unfailing source of content', MRJ wrote:

> No one whom I have known could enlist the warmest affection more easily, or retain it more surely. There was no companion who so completed a circle, - no one who, even when he supposed himself to be out of spirits, brought so much enjoyment into an expedition. A smile will never be far off when friends speak of him.[25]

Over the next decade or so, McBryde became MRJ's most cherished friend and correspondent—of all the thousands of correspondents he had, including the large handful of people whom we would call his very close friends (Arthur Benson, St. Clair Donaldson, Walter Fletcher, H. E. Luxmoore, Gordon Carey, A. B. Ramsay, and a few others), McBryde is the *only* one whose correspondence he numbers and annotates. This means something. For a man as emotionally reticent as MRJ, this means a lot.

What was the nature of their relationship? On MRJ's part, we might call it a chaste gay love affair—though this was not, of course, a language available to him or his contemporaries. Many on the outside saw it as fundamentally paternal. Maisie Fletcher thought that McBryde 'to Monty James had become almost like an adopted son'.[26] There are certainly elements of this when McBryde's actual father died. MRJ was the first person to whom McBryde wrote immediately after his father's death in March 1898: 'half an hour ago I was with my dear old father when he died'.[27] More than eighteen months later, almost the only surviving letter from MRJ to McBryde (why?) is on what must have been a recurring note of consolation, in what sounds remarkably close to the language of Victorian spiritualism:

> I like to think—and indeed it is more than thinking—that people when they go into the next world lose all the weakness & bodily trouble in which we have known them, and are young again, and see others whom they have been missing for a long time, and are at their best—growing to be more perfect instead of weaker. . . . [It] is my belief that instead of being cut off & separated from you by immeasurable distance, he has as living an interest in you and your doings as ever.

The letter concludes: 'I think you know how much I value you, my dear thing.'[28]

* * *

On 28 October 1893, the minutes of the Chit-Chat Club record that something momentous happened at a meeting in MRJ's rooms in the Gibbs Building: 'Mr James read "Two Ghost Stories".'[29] These were the stories that became 'Canon Alberic's Scrap-book' and 'Lost Hearts', two stories that we've seen MRJ patiently creating from the raw material of his scholarship and his travels. In a notebook of November 1888, MRJ discusses his reading of *The Testament of Solomon*, one of the classic works of demonology, in which King Solomon commands various demons to do his bidding by means of a magic ring. *The Testament of Solomon*'s principal demon is 'Ornias, the fierce demon . . . offspring of the archangel Uriel', who kills his victims by strangulation.[30] MRJ's notes comment: 'Ornias the demon *sucks the thumb* of his victim. A human form. Dark. Fiery eyes.'[31]

MRJ seems to have named Canon Alberic's scholar-protagonist, Dennistoun, after James Dennistoun, the compiler of a well-known nineteenth-century album (scrap-book) of medieval manuscripts.[32] Leafing through the priceless volume he has been given in St. Bertrand de Comminges, Dennistoun finds 'a sepia drawing at the end of the seventeenth century', representing King Solomon commanding a demon, 'a mass of coarse black matted hair . . . hideously taloned. The eyes, touched in with a burning yellow, had intensely black pupils.'[33] The same year that MRJ composed 'Canon Alberic', 1893, Arthur Shipley, the morphology lecturer who had accompanied him to St. Bertrand, published *Zoology of the Invertebrata*, a study whose section on arachnids opens with an account of 'the gigantic South American *Mygale avicularia*', whose prey 'often takes the form of small birds'.[34] 'Imagine', MRJ writes in 'Canon Alberic', 'one of the awful bird-catching spiders of South America translated into human form. . . . . And you will have some faint conception of the terror inspired by the appalling effigy'. The narrator shows the image of the demon to 'a lecturer on morphology—a person of, I was going to say, abnormally sane and unimaginative habits of mind. He absolutely refused to be alone for the rest of the evening, and told me afterwards that for many nights he had not dared to put out his light before going to sleep.'[35]

In the same 1888 notebook, MRJ writes, 'First I would remind you that our forefathers had one method of amusement open to them which is closed to us. And that was, telling stories. There are a few people who can tell ghost stories . . . '[36] With his vast stores of arcane knowledge and his natural gifts as an actor, MRJ was one of these people, and across the later 1890s and early 1900s, the reading of an MRJ ghost story would begin to take shape as a Christmas ritual in his rooms in King's, in front of a select group of friends, colleagues, and students: almost always Luxmoore, Owen Hugh Smith, and the Eton Master A. C. Ainger, plus close colleagues like Walter Durnford and A. B. Ramsay, Oliffe Richmond and Nathaniel Wedd, Walter Fletcher and James McBryde, one or more of the Lubbock family (Gurney, Cis, Percy, or Harold—MRJ was close to them all), the College chaplains E. G. Swain and

F. E. Hutchinson, Arthur Benson whenever he could make it, and a revolving cast of whoever happened to be around.[37]

Every evening leading up to Christmas, the party went for dinner at High Table in the Hall at King's, with hot spiced beer, and the accompaniment of the choir singing carols in the gallery. On Christmas Eve itself, MRJ and his friends would gather in the Chapel—always full and always dark—for the service, a 'gravely cheerful' occasion. The 'faint musical hum' as the Choir took up the note for the first carol, 'Once in Royal David's City', struck MRJ as 'the very spirit of Christmas'. For the second verse, the congregation joined in: 'I do not know what has moved me more than this did, and still does when I recall it', MRJ wrote. 'All very pedestrian and Anglican and Victorian and everything else that it ought not to be: but I should like well enough to have it over again.'[38]

After the Chapel and the dinner, the party would retire to the Combination Room (the Common Room) for after-dinner drinks and cards, and from there over to MRJ's rooms, talking, laughing and smoking, drinking port or whisky and soda as usual. Sometimes, someone would play a few bars on the piano, but always hesitantly and never for long (it was not, we know, a very tuneful piano, and besides, their minds were on other things). MRJ himself would generally disappear into the bedroom to finish his story, 'composed at fever heat', and it was usually well after eleven by the time he emerged, the ink still wet on the sheets of paper covered in his spidery, impossible handwriting. He would blow out all the candles but one, and begin to read (to *perform*) his latest ghost story, his clear, confident voice cutting through the dark and the December chill. After the story, a silence would fall on the party.[39]

'There is nothing so good as Xmas at King's', Luxmoore thought; 'Really, there is nothing like it—let alone the ghost story'; 'Chapel, Combination Room & the Lodge is a combination no where else attained. The club, the country house &—well, the chapel for to that there is no parallel—all rolled into one with the added freedom—may I say it? we are alone—of a single sex.'[40] One of Luxmoore's accounts of MRJ's Christmas ghost stories, from 1902, is particularly revealing: 'Last night Monty James read us a new Xmas story of most blood curdling character, after which those played animal grab who did not mind having their clothes torn to pieces & their hands nailscored.'[41] (The story was almost certainly 'Count Magnus', very blood-curdling indeed.) Animal Grab, 'An Interesting and Amusing Round Game', is a Victorian variant of Snap, in which the players lunge for paired cards while making animal noises ('Tig-Tig' for a pig, 'Hobble-Gobble' for a turkey, 'Moo-Moo' for a cow, etc.).[42]

To an extent, this seems exemplary of the 'Theory of Permanent Adolescence' which the Old Etonian writer Cyril Connolly believed damaged 'boys of the great public schools', serving 'to dominate their lives and to arrest their development'. It is a further aspect, in other words, of MRJ's fondness for 'ragging' and other forms of physical horseplay, well into adulthood. Connolly also believed that Permanent Adolescence made public schoolboys 'in the last analysis homosexual'.[43] While this is an impressionistic statement, perhaps, it does bespeak a certain truth about MRJ and his circle, and the relations between men which the institutions in which he lived encouraged. 'For there is no doubt', Connolly concluded of his Etonian education, 'that homosexuality formed an ingredient in the ancient wisdom. It was the forbidden tree round which our little Eden dizzily revolved.'[44]

This last observation of Luxmoore's does imply an inherent connection between the stories themselves and public school sexuality: an all-male community, all of whose activities seem sexualized. It also implies that the ghost story and the Animal Grab were two different (but related) kinds of all-male game or entertainment which took place in this institutional setting. The torn clothes and nailscorings which Luxmoore thought a feature of Animal Grab as played by MRJ and his friends are also a recurring feature in MRJ's ghost stories, and play a significant role in both the stories he read to the Chit-Chat in 1893. The demon who looms up from behind Dennistoun in his hotel room at the end of 'Canon Alberic' has 'nails rising from the ends of the fingers and curving sharply down and forward, grey, horny and wrinkled'; it is these taloned hands which Dennistoun first sees while sitting at his desk, and which reach out to grab (or Grab) at his head, or his throat.[45] Giovanni, the vengeful ghost boy of 'Lost Hearts' (a story about an older scholar preying on his young wards), has 'fearfully long', translucent nails, which scratch 'long, parallel slits, about six inches in length, some of them not quite piercing the texture of the linen' of young Stephen Elliott's nightgown, and leave 'marks and scratches... for all the world like a Chinaman's fingernails' down his bedroom door.[46] It is with these nails that he tears open the chest of his murderer, Mr Abney.[47] Like much in MRJ's stories, this may have its deep origins in his research. One of his notebooks for 1878 enumerates the contents of a bestiary he had been compiling. In amongst the various dragons and harpies, camelopards, unicorns, and griffins, there is a reference to a 'Clawed boy'.[48]

We can't be precise about the exact order and dates for MRJ's readings at this period. 'Canon Alberic' and 'Lost Hearts', as we've seen, were not initially read in 1893 as Christmas stories. On 24 December 1896, his colleague

W. H. Macaulay writes 'to offer my congratulations to you and your company on last night's performance . . . I seldom have been as well entertained'.[49] Macaulay goes on to recount an anecdote he'd just heard from an old chorister about Thomas Brocklebank, the King's College ghost. It may be more likely that Macaulay is referring here not to a ghost story, but to MRJ's pantomime, *Alex Barber*, performed that Christmas. But if it *was* a ghost story, it seems likely that this 1896 performance was either 'The Mezzotint' (in which Dennistoun makes a cameo reappearance), or else 'The Ash-Tree'. The next reading we know about with certainty is 1902, in which MRJ seems to have read 'Count Magnus'. The following year, 1903, was a bumper occasion, as Luxmoore records:

> a ghost story of diabolical eeriness is written and read most evenings. Dr. James led off with 'No. 13' & 'Fur flebis' ['Oh, Whistle, and I'll Come to You, My Lad'] Arthur Benson followed with the 'House at Trehele' wh[ich] lasted two nights—& Percy Lubbock's fragment of the School Inspector drew up the curtain on a lurid scene only to drop it again hastily.[50]

Arthur, whose friendship with MRJ was always tinged with a certain jealousy—professionally and intellectually, he was particularly aware in these years that he was playing second fiddle in the relationship—was typically a little equivocal about the occasion, feeling that his own story, 'meant to be read aloud' and published as 'Basil Netherby', was rather put in the shade: 'MRJ read us one of his medieval ghost stories—this is a pleasant habit of his—the local colouring is excellent, & the stories grim—but there is a certain want of depth about them. The people are like elderly dons.'[51]

As Arthur and Percy Lubbock's participation in 1903 testifies, 'Mr. James read "Two Ghost Stories"' is significant not only because it properly marks the beginning of MRJ's career as a writer of ghost stories, but also because it inaugurates a whole tradition of what we might call the Cambridge Ghost Story. The Benson family had their own tradition of telling ghost stories, which MRJ witnessed at Lis Escop in Truro back in 1881, so Arthur's stories were able to fit nicely into the occasion. Fred was an even better writer of ghost stories than Arthur, and their younger brother Hugh, a Trinity graduate, also wrote them. All three Benson brothers were members of the Chit-Chat Club (Fred was actually present on the fateful evening in October 1893). Percy Lubbock had a ghost story to tell that Christmas, and E. G. Swain, the King's Chaplain, published his own volume of ghost stories, *The Stoneground Ghost Tales*, in 1912. The Old Etonian and Kingsman R. H. Malden, who graduated in 1902 with firsts in both parts of the Classical Tripos, collected his own ghost stories as *Nine Ghosts* in 1942. The Master of Jesus College, Arthur Gray, published his collection, *Tedious Brief Tales of Granta and Gramarye*, under the pseudonym 'Ingulphus' in 1919. Many of the Chit-Chatters also tried their hand with the genre.[52] Bringing up the rear, chronologically at least, the King's librarian A. N. L. Munby published his own remarkable collection, *The Alabaster Hand*, in 1949.

MRJ's own publishing career began almost immediately after he read the ghost stories to the Chit-Chat. In August 1893, Leo Maxse took over the editorship of the *National Review*, a magazine founded in 1883 with close links to the Conservative Party. Leo had written to MRJ in November 1893 asking whether he could get the Pitt Club, the Union, and the ADC to subscribe to the magazine. One thing led to another, and after Christmas MRJ sent 'Canon Alberic' (then entitled 'A Curious Book') and 'Lost Hearts' to Leo, with a view to getting them published in the *National Review*. Leo wrote back on 8 January. He was certain he wanted a story by MRJ, though he didn't like 'Lost Hearts' and was initially ambivalent about 'Canon Alberic'. Then, later the same day, he sent a second letter:

> On carefully thinking over your second story 'A Curious Book' I should like to have it for the National Review provided you will give me the benefit of your name by signing and will not mind a delay of two or three months in its appearance. . . . I am sorry to say the National Review is only able at present to offer you 10s. a page for stories, perhaps you will think this too mean.[53]

He didn't think it too mean, though the process took a bit longer than Leo had promised. MRJ returned the final revised proofs in December 1894, and 'A Curious Book', retitled 'The Scrap-Book of Canon Alberic', appeared in the *National Review* in March 1895.[54] This was MRJ's first published ghost story, and it appeared, not exactly accidentally and certainly not uncharacteristically, in a Conservative Party organ.

One *National Review* reader, in particular, was deeply enthused by what he read. Arthur Machen, the great writer of weird fiction whose masterpiece, *The Great God Pan*, had appeared the previous year, wrote to MRJ 'to congratulate you on a marvellous piece of work. . . . I have seen nothing for a very long time that is half as good as the "Scrap Book"'.[55]

MRJ constantly encountered the ghostly and the supernatural in his scholarly and imaginative life. He knew more about demons and spirits, curses and grimoires than more or less anyone else. But did he believe in them? This is an unusually complex and revealing question to ask of a Victorian.[56]

Like MRJ himself, the ghost story is a characteristic product of nineteenth-century forces. It is a reaction to the secular, materialist, industrial modernity that animated the dominant, progressivist Victorian utilitarian ideology. As such it has clear relations with spiritualism and occultism (and their scientific off-shoot, psychical research), the belief that the worlds of matter and of spirit inter-penetrated, or were separated only by a thin veil, which could readily be pulled aside (by clairvoyants or mediums, for example) to allow communication with the Other World. Spiritualism was extraordinarily widespread and permeated all sections of society, and was *the* main Victorian response to secular modernity.[57] Debates about spiritualism and the occult were at the very centre of Victorian public and intellectual life: 'No major Victorian thinker or writer', Jarlath Killeen writes in his history of nineteenth-century Gothic fiction, 'from the Brontës to the Brownings, from Dickens to Darwin, was unconcerned about the occult.' 'The ghost', Killeen concludes, 'represents a breach in historical progression: in a stark reproach to the Victorian investment in notions of linearity and progress, the ghost is a manifestation of the "past-in-the-present".'[58]

MRJ's own position on the reality of the supernatural was typically ambivalent, or contradictory—or perhaps, as some have suggested, he was simply undisturbed by (or even unaware of) the implications of what he wrote.[59] ('No thinking, gentlemen, please!') Towards the end of his life, writing the Preface to the *Collected Ghost Stories* (1931), he asked: 'Do I believe in ghosts? To which I answer that I am prepared to consider evidence and accept it if it satisfies me.'[60] It is difficult to know which is more striking about this remark, its brevity or its evasiveness. MRJ had little interest in psychical research, that attempt by some of the foremost intellectuals of his own generation to establish a basis for discovering the veracity of the supernatural, and to test it according to tough-minded empirical standards. The Society for Psychical Research, in fact, had its home in Trinity College Cambridge, where it was founded in 1882, with Henry Sidgwick as its first President. MRJ was no admirer of Sidgwick, and the SPR itself makes a disguised appearance in 'The Mezzotint' as the 'Phasmatological Society', a collection of busybodies from whom news of the story's supernatural illustration must be kept at all costs (the Phasmatological Society was a real forerunner of the SPR, with its base in Balliol College, Oxford). In his scattered writings on supernatural fiction, MRJ policed the boundaries between his own stories and the possible reality of an Other World quite rigorously: 'I have not sought to embody in [my stories] any well-considered scheme of "psychical" theory. . . . I feel that the technical terms of "occultism", if they are not very carefully handled, tend to put the mere ghost story (which is all I am attempting) upon a quasi-scientific plane, and to call into play faculties other than the imaginative.'[61] While he believed that it was appropriate for a ghost story to express an uncanny sense of epistemological indeterminacy—'a loophole for a natural explanation; but, I would say, let the loophole be so narrow as not to be quite practicable'—this is quite clearly an aesthetic judgement on the ghost story rather than a statement about the existence of the supernatural.[62] In one of his late essays on the ghost story, 'Ghosts—Treat Them Gently!', he makes the distinction very plain: 'I am speaking of the literary ghost story here. The story that claims to be "veridical" (in the language of the Society of Psychical Research) is a very different affair.'[63]

This is what MRJ professed to believe, and certainly how he wanted to present his beliefs to his readers. But it isn't necessarily how those who knew him saw things. MRJ and Arthur Benson once had what was, for them, a heated argument during a cycling trip about 'the prolongation of identity or consciousness'—what the spiritualists would call the survival of the human personality after death. MRJ believed in the reality of this phenomenon, for which Arthur thought there was 'not a shred or tittle of evidence' (though he *was* open to the possibility of telepathy)—at which MRJ became 'pettish and out of temper'.[64] A. B. Ramsay, a long-time friend, colleague, and travelling companion, and a frequent presence at the ghost-story readings, was clear that MRJ 'believed in ghosts and would have liked to believe in fairies'.[65] Shane Leslie, very much a believer himself, maintained that 'Monty never attended séances, though silently attracted', and that his ghost stories were not 'a side hobby', but rather 'his relief from a secret madness in his inner soul'.[66] Nathaniel Wedd developed a whole theory of MRJ's engagement with the supernatural, heavily influenced by Arnoldian conceptions of 'Celtic magic', drawing inferences from his Welsh ancestry:

> The fact is that Monty had the Celtic instinct for speculation and the Celtic sense of the unseen world. That's why he was so interested in ghosts. He could never really disbelieve in them. For years I lived in my rooms beneath his in Fellows' [Gibbs] Building. At about two a.m. I used to knock the ashes of my pipe put by tapping on the mantel-piece. Monty told me how often and often when in bed he heard the tap, tap tap, he used to lie shivering with horror. He couldn't believe it wasn't a ghost in his outer room, though he knew all the time exactly how the sounds were produced. At heart he believed in ghosts and their malevolence. There the strain of devil-worship derived from his Welsh ancestry came in, and his ghost-stories may be regarded as a means of getting his obsession off his chest. It saved him from madness . . .[67]

As the critic Peter Davidson has astutely observed, MRJ was 'a troubled man, in perfect control of his public manner'.[68] The second part of this observation is certainly true, and has understandably led many observers to assume the first.

Wedd unquestionably thought that the ghost stories sprang from 'repressed instincts'.[69] What darker depths did the benign and sociable surface manner conceal? Behind 'the friendly transparency of his large round spectacles', what had those eyes seen?

MRJ's world is one of forces that need to be kept at bay. Sometimes these are social and political forces—the upheavals to his world that MRJ dreaded and fought: the presence of women in the university; threats to the stability of the curriculum and of the whole worldview it embodied and upheld; the whole complex of terrors encapsulated for him in the word 'thought' ('the theories disturbed'). His real dislike of Oscar Browning, for example, was based not only on personal animosity, a clash of very different characters, but because O.B. presented himself, in however self-regarding, ostentatious, or insincere a fashion, as King's foremost advocate of progressive causes. 'I . . . owe to him', MRJ wrote, 'the pernicious distaste of theorists, especially educational theorists, which I can never hope to unlearn.'[70]

But these dangerous forces are also, and for the same reasons, metaphysical ones. As we see again and again, MRJ's ghost stories enact the perils of the very research he himself did every day. As 'Canon Alberic' was taking shape in his mind, he was also working away cataloguing the Fitzwilliam manuscript collection. Both works—the manuscript catalogue and the story of the researcher who discovers a manuscript which unleashes a demon—were published in 1895. Like most of his codicological work, the Fitzwilliam catalogue contains dozens of descriptions of the various devils and demons he encountered in the collection. In the Death of Judas, for example, in MS 20 24a.27, 'A black devil flying down from R[ight] draws his (nude) soul out of his stomach'.[71] An illustration from the *Legenda Aurea* in MS 22 p. 24. 55 has 'Black clouds. Devils on earth. Men in eaves mourning: hell-hounds running about hills. Lurid sky'; while another at MS 22 p. 194. 153 has 'Egeus prostrate with staff; a devil strangles him behind'.[72] Often, these devils are described as being 'shaggy', or 'hairy'.[73] 'Canon Alberic''s demon is covered in 'coarse, matted black hair'.[74]

Materialist sceptics tend to come rather badly out of MRJ's stories. In 'Oh, Whistle, and I'll Come to You, My Lad', Professor Parkins's scientific materialism is put to the test and exposed as empty dogma. 'The Mezzotint' closes with a brief portrait of 'the Sadducean Professor of Ophiology', whose snide dismissal of the supernatural is 'met with the reception it deserved'.[75] The allusions in this academic title are to the New Testament. The Sadducees were a priestly Jewish caste 'which say that there is no resurrection' (Matthew 22: 23) and who believed in 'neither angel nor spirit' (Acts 23: 8). 'Ophiology' is the study of serpents, and alludes to Matthew 4: 7: 'But when [John the Baptist] saw the Pharisees and Sadducees, he said unto them, O generation of vipers, who hath warned you to flee from the wrath to come?' Throughout his life, MRJ was fascinated and disturbed by Sadducees ancient and modern, rational materialists who tried to reconcile their outlook with religious faith. He came to believe, for example, that the book of Ecclesiastes was written by 'a serious-minded Sadducee'—which was why, he thought, non-Christians and even atheists tend to find it so appealing, as it proposes a Deistical God, 'who plays no part in the world'.[76] While one looks in vain for much sense of redemption or forgiveness in MRJ's stories, they present at every turn a thoroughly interventionist supernatural order, vengeful and malign. Perhaps surprisingly to himself, MRJ might have found himself in agreement on this matter with the great Harvard psychologist and SPR member William James, when he wrote a few years later in *Varieties of Religious Experience* (1902):

> Were one asked to characterize the life of religion in the broadest and most general terms possible, one might say that it consists of the belief that there is an unseen order, and that our supreme good lies in harmoniously adjusting ourselves thereunto.[77]

In all of MRJ's stories, perhaps the only thing we can say with certainty is that there is 'an unseen order', and, if we know what's good for us, we need to stay on the right side of it, and preferably leave it alone.

The ritual of MRJ's ghost story evenings *contained* these terrors, transforming them into entertainments, social occasions. But, as the silence that fell after the readings suggests—and as anyone who reads the ghost stories knows—the dread remains.

* * *

Back home in Great Livermere in the mid-1890s, Mary Emily was still worrying about MRJ's health. She was concerned about the state of his digestion ('your "internal mechanism"'), and sent him 'the wherewithal for some beef tea—a small tea spoonful . . . mixed with *quite boiling* water'. She urged him to 'Get a bottle of Eucalyptus smelling salts—do!'[78] Cambridge, she thought, had 'a reputation of being a most cold-giving place'.[79]

Ber continued to travel the world. He had heard late in 1892 that he was to be posted to the China Station, and by March 1894 had been sent from Ireland to Hong Kong. He initially spent his time shooting partridges in Macao—but he soon found himself in the middle of an outbreak of the plague. During his time in Hong Kong and China, he treated a variety of tropical diseases—malaria, smallpox, leprosy, beriberi. Bubonic plague, though, was 'an annual visitor, coming in spring, and disappearing in late summer'.[80] Ber's formal report on the outbreak estimates 3000 fatalities in Hong Kong alone, and 150,000 in Canton more generally. He encountered the decomposing corpses of victims in bales of dried fish, or being eaten in the streets and villages by pigs and dogs.[81] If poor digestion and toothache in the family gave Mary Emily sleepless nights, one can only imagine the effect news of the bubonic plague had on her: 'I am afraid the family is in a fuss about Hong Kong but it doesn't seem to touch the European population', Sydney reassured MRJ.[82] For his work treating what became several outbreaks of the plague, Ber was awarded the Chinese Double Dragon Medal, 'which is about the size of a soup plate!'

Ber obviously relished his time in Hong Kong and China. He enjoyed an expedition to the Yangtze to shoot pheasants, and went on a tiger-hunt. He slept in temples which doubled as guest-houses, tying one end of his hammock to the high altar. He loved the food, writing excitedly about dining on sole, crab, oysters, and curried frog. He even started to learn Mandarin, a language at which he became quite adept. On the fringes of his correspondence from China, relayed back to MRJ via Mary Emily, one gets the sense of the febrile political climate leading up to the Boxer Rebellion of 1899, of growing fear amongst the European concessions of Chinese cities. In Tianjin, which was seized by the Boxers in 1900, he saw 'English, German, French, and Russian gunboats in the harbour for the protection of foreign residents'.[83]

Sydney's major news of these years was his engagement in 1897 to Linda Hoare. Linda was the third daughter of Henry Hoare of Staplehurst, Kent, a member of a prominent English banking dynasty. 'The Hoares were and are a great Eton family', Sydney wrote in his memoirs.[84] Sydney's diary for 1897 isn't really giving much away. Around the time of his proposal, his entries are extraordinarily terse, one-word utterances: 'Idiot.' 'Misery.' 'Yes.' 'The news out, L. ill.'[85] Linda's diary for the same time is a little more forthcoming: 'As I woke up early when my breakfast was brought I saw on the tray a letter with strange writing & Windsor p. mark. I guessed directly who it was from & what it was. I trembled from head to foot for a moment. I opened & read. It was a proposal from S.J. I was much agitated but *v.* happy.'[86] Shortly after their marriage, the pair relocated to Malvern College, a grand public school in Worcestershire. As Headmaster of Malvern, Sydney had a reputation as 'a benevolent autocrat', and one can see this in the astute recommendation of one of his referees for the post, Arthur Benson: 'I do not know anyone among my colleagues whose authority is so absolutely unquestioned. He has the power of imposing his will on all who are subordinated to him.'[87]

Everyone liked Linda, and from her correspondence one can see why. She was a lively and good-humoured presence, rather given to malapropisms: 'You old secretian!', she exclaimed when it turned out that Sydney had been hiding something from her; 'You've just damped my curiosity'; 'It's only four miles as the cock crows'; 'a man who likes to have a voice in every pie'.[88] Linda took a particular interest in the woeful state of MRJ's teeth, which just kept getting worse and worse: in April 1901, he lost one of his front teeth biting into a hard French croissant (how hard can a croissant be?). Linda wrote to him in 1904:

> My cook has teeth just like yours! So I hasten to write and tell you her experiences. She has just had the last out. She had 12 out last time, & she tells me that she did not mind at all, but is thankful to be rid of them. The dentist tells me she will be much better in consequence. So there! Go & do the same, & don't lose any time.[89]

Linda's follow-up letter opens with an illustration of a person in a dentist's chair, having their teeth pulled out, and the words 'Dear Montague. My cook has. Have you been?'[90] He hadn't, and it would be 1913 before he got his first set of dentures. But Linda's attentions to his teeth continued: 'Linda SRJ Dentist active', he wrote, gnomically, in a diary entry in 1925.[91]

Grace's mental and physical health—always fragile—was getting worse. As early as 1888, Lionel Ford witnessed some of her disturbing behaviour, and wrote to MRJ: 'Do you remember that terrible scar she got, trying to push her head through the door panel in a fit of ungovernable rage? Alas, that disfigurement will I fear be permanent.'[92] After another episode the next year she went to stay with the Lushington family in Tunbridge Wells, and was soon 'very much like her old self, except for getting too easily tired'.[93] But things deteriorated across the 1890s, especially given the ailing health of her elderly parents, no longer able to look after her as before. She lost weight: a friend described her as 'the daughter of Babylon, wasted with misery'.[94] In May 1903, apparently completely out of the blue, she wrote a very strange and troubling letter to MRJ. On the front of the envelope was written 'Last wishes of G. C. Rhodes James May 1903', and on the back 'Make sure that I am dead, as directed inside'. The letter contained these instructions: 'Let the little finger of my left hand (top joint) be *severed* with a knife, to see that I really am dead, & let everything be done to absolutely ascertain this, as I have a horror of being buried alive.'[95] (Hugh Benson left similar instructions for after his death, which his brother Arthur carried out: Hugh wanted one of his arteries opened.)[96]

In 1905, Grace collapsed completely, with what MRJ called an 'attack', which may have been a seizure while running for a train, or a panic attack. MRJ arranged for a nurse, and hoped that a relapse could 'be *completely* avoided by being good'.[97] But later that year Grace was ill again, and the doctor informed MRJ 'Your sister is suffering from slight palpitation of the heart and noises in her head; this necessarily makes her nervous, and one cannot help feeling rather anxious after her former illness'.[98]

* * *

In November 1892, MRJ decided to apply for the vacant Disney Chair of Archaeology at Cambridge. He had very little field experience as an archaeologist (his trip to Cyprus in 1887 was it), but his formal qualifications in Part II of the Tripos were in archaeology, and they were unparalleled. His work on the tombs and, later, the bones at Bury St. Edmunds Abbey was a distinguished success. MRJ's academic specialism, at least in his early career, up to about 1900, can be described as 'Christian archaeology', and this is clearly what he had in mind when applying for the Disney Chair.[99] He wrote to Francis Jenkinson, the University Librarian, a potential referee:

> I enter on the Medieval ticket principally, but I should be glad to help the students of Classical Archaeology as far as I can. . . . If I were elected I should try to utilize a considerable mass of material collected in the twelve years to throw light on Christian art—most especially what people call Iconography.[100]

In his formal application to the Vice-Chancellor, he wrote:

> During the last twelve years I have accumulated a large mass of material illustrative of Christian Art and Iconography. This material consists in the main of description as full and accurate as I could make them, of sculpture, painted glass, pictures, and illuminated MSS existing in a very considerable number of English and foreign Churches, Libraries, galleries, and Museums. . . . My object in all this has been to trace, as far as I could, the historical development of sacred art from the points of view of selection and treatment of subjects, and to bring it into connexion with the literature and legends to which the artists had access. In other words, I have worked with the view of applying to Christian art those methods which are applied nowadays to the remains of Classical sculpture & painting.[101]

The competition for the Disney Chair was very stiff: the other candidates were Charles Waldstein, William Ridgeway, Ernest Gardner, with whom MRJ had worked in Cyprus, Lionel Cust, later to be appointed Director of the National Portrait Gallery, William St. John Hope, the distinguished antiquary, and

MRJ's King's colleague Arthur Tilley, the rank outsider.[102] (Waldstein, Ridgeway, Cust, and Hope all went on to be knighted for their achievements, while Gardner finished his career as Vice-Chancellor of the University of London.) MRJ was a credible candidate for the Disney Chair, but in the event it was given to Ridgeway, an eminent senior Classical archaeologist (and an irascible reactionary), who held it until his death in 1926. Ridgeway, an Irishman and a graduate of both Trinity College Dublin and Gonville and Caius, was at the time Professor of Classics at University College Cork (Queen's College, as it was called then). His application and appointment are indicative of the changes that were taking place in academia. Ridgeway put together a formidably professional portfolio in application for the post, published as a hefty booklet by Cambridge University Press. He gathered incandescent references from a whole establishment cadre of senior academics and intellectuals, including Francis Jenkinson (who declined to give MRJ a reference), Henry Jackson, R. C. Jebb, J. G. Frazer, John Venn, J. H. Middleton, A. W. Verrall, and many others, which he also included in his application booklet. In contrast, MRJ wrote a handwritten letter to the Vice-Chancellor, and was very diffident about his achievements and future plans. 'Should I be elected, I should propose to make the development of Christian art, and its connection with Christian literature and legend, the subject of my public lectures', he wrote. 'Besides this, I should be glad to give such help to students of Classical Archaeology as my previous studies would qualify me to bestow.'[103] His referees were Middleton, Augustus Jessopp, the Norfolk antiquary with whom he had worked on William of Norwich, Robert Burn, Fellow of Trinity and University Praelector in Roman Literature and Archaeology, and Mandell Creighton, Bishop of Peterborough and former Dixie Professor of Ecclesiastical History. While Burn, who had himself graduated Senior Classic back in 1852, wrote glowingly about MRJ's academic achievements—'He is a *very* good scholar'—Jessopp's reference seems to belong to a bygone age:

> Among ye younger Cambridge men with whom I have been brought into relations—I know no one from whom I expect so much as I do from Mr. James; I can feel no doubt that he will justify ye Great Expectations that his friends entertain regarding him—or that his career can be other than a brilliant one.[104]

MRJ, it should be said, didn't like William Ridgeway. He thought him 'a *bad* man—unscrupulous, quarrelsome, mischief-making'.[105] The Disney was the only university chair for which MRJ ever applied. (But with a certain historical irony, in July 1926 he was on the panel which appointed Ridgway's successor, Ellis Mimms.)[106]

In 1892, J. H. Middleton left the Fitzwilliam to take up the post of Director of the Art Collections at the South Kensington Museum (now the Victoria and Albert Museum). The following year, MRJ was elected unopposed to the vacant Directorship of the Fitzwilliam, a position he held until 1908. The Directorship of the Fitzwilliam was a full-time post, but MRJ proposed juggling it with his various King's commitments:

> I am very sorry [Middleton] is going: it raises, too, several questions. As far as I can count my chickens, this appears to be the situation. I shall probably stand for this place. If I were elected, I should have to resign one of my posts here. Dean or Lecturer?[107]

'You will have your hands full in either case, either at the Fitz: or at K.C.', Herbert thought.[108] Middleton himself wrote to MRJ that 'I do not think there can be any doubt as to your election', but warned him that 'the only objection I have heard from any one was that you are already very fully occupied'.[109] MRJ thought he should give up his Lectureship. The very competent Alan England Brooke was ready to take over from him (in 1926, Brooke became one of MRJ's successors as Provost of King's), and besides, he thought, the Deanship was still a delicate role, and he could see no other obvious candidate. Not to mention the fact that, at £300 a year, the Director's salary was meagre. He needed his King's income.

MRJ was not a very successful museum director. As the twentieth century dawned, running a largish museum was no job for a part-timer, and it was obvious that his primary commitments were to King's and to his own scholarship. 'I suppose it will still leave your evenings free for those poor old doggrell-mongers of the third century on whom you expend (notice! I don't say *waste*) what was meant for mankind?', Edmund Gosse wrote on hearing of MRJ's appointment.[110] Sydney Cockerell, MRJ's successor at the Fitzwilliam (who liked him very much, and admired his scholarship enormously), thought that he wasn't up to the job: 'he had absolutely *no* taste whatsoever (you had only to look at his house to see that), and he hadn't the *least* idea how to run a museum. He just looked in occasionally to see if there were any letters.'[111] 'The business of the place is simple enough' was MRJ's only advice to his successor when he took over.[112]

For all his shortcomings, MRJ turned out to be a competent enough administrator, with the great virtue of being able to inspire loyalty in his staff.[113] He did secure a number of very important acquisitions to the Museum, though these tended to be in the manuscript collections. His preface to the 1895 Fitzwilliam catalogue contained a plea that 'some collector who should make use of my work might be led to think of the Fitzwilliam as a place where his manuscripts would be choicely valued, religiously preserved, and minutely investigated'.[114] The Trinity astronomer and collector Frank McClean responded to MRJ's invitation, and on his death in 1904 bequeathed his enormous collection of manuscripts to the Fitzwilliam, and also his gems, ivories, rare books, coins, and art collection.[115] True to his word back in 1895, MRJ set about cataloguing the McClean collection; the catalogue was published in 1912.

It wasn't all manuscripts. William Ridgeway, the Disney Professor, continuously badgered MRJ as Fitzwilliam Director with requests, often for money to conduct his research, with the promise of Egyptian artefacts in return. From time to time, his Chit-Chat friend R. C. Bosanquet, now Professor of Classical Archaeology at the University of Liverpool, would write with outlandish suggestions and updates, from smuggling Bronze Age antiquities through Greek customs in his luggage—'a simpler, cheaper, more dangerous & less moral method of exportation'—to sending the Fitzwilliam 'the most strident bagpipes that ever were—Cretan—for the anthropological collection'.[116]

On occasion, the opportunity arose to acquire some 'curious prints' for himself or for the Fitzwilliam—such as the illustration of the disinterred coffin and skeleton (six feet three and a half inches) of Edward IV, made by 'an ancestor, Mr. Evelyn' during the restoration of St. George's Chapel, Windsor, in the eighteenth century, or the sketchbook of Thomas Stothard and a series of sketches of William Harvey, all of which he secured for the Fitzwilliam in 1895.[117] At around the same time, Mr Williams, 'the gentleman who presided over an art museum at another University', was offered the chance to buy (at the rather expensive price of £2.2.0) an 'Interesting mezzotint: View of a manor-house, early part of the century. 15 by 10 inches; black frame', from the reputable dealer J. W. Britnell. This turned out, after some investigation, to be a depiction of Anningley Hall in Essex—and, what was that figure, 'just on the edge in front'?[118] Has it moved? 'The Mezzotint', with its moving ghostly figure, is among the creepiest of MRJ's stories.

As his work with Augustus Jessopp on the Brent Eleigh manuscripts and William of Norwich shows, MRJ was always fascinated by East Anglian antiquarian mysteries. In the years around 1900, he got involved in a particularly absorbing one. The year 1895 was a time of extraordinary publishing fervour, even by MRJ's standards. As well as the Fitzwilliam Catalogue, he published catalogues of the manuscripts at Eton, King's, Jesus, and Sidney Sussex Colleges. He also published, amongst many other things, a study of the sculptures in the Lady Chapel at Ely, and a monograph on Bury St. Edmunds Abbey.[119]

This latter work brought him into contact with the economist and antiquarian Sir Ernest Clarke, Gilbey Lecturer in the History and Economics of Agriculture at Cambridge. Clarke had become preoccupied by 'the alleged removal of St. Edmund's body to Toulouse in 1216'. MRJ was sceptical: he had found a reference in an abbey register at Douai in Northern France to the possible location of remains at St. Edmunds Abbey. The pair set about gaining permission from the Marquess of Bristol, who owned the land on which Bury Abbey stood, to conduct an excavation. This process took several years, but Clarke was utterly indefatigable. A formal proposal for the dig in the Chapter House was written on 20 May 1902: 'Dr James has undertaken to give the excavations, if decided upon, his general supervision, and to pay such visits to the sight as may prove to be necessary.'[120] The excavation, in December and January, uncovered six skeletons of abbots, whose remains were examined by the physiologist Alexander Macalister. There was some public interest in this, and MRJ wrote a letter to the *Times*, in which he identified the six abbots.[121] Writing years later in *Suffolk and Norfolk*, MRJ added: 'The crypt has never been explored: no monastic site in England needs investigation more or, probably, would repay it better. Here it is quite possible that the bones of St. Edmund may rest.'[122]

Meanwhile, back at King's, business somehow managed to go on more or less as usual for MRJ. He attended a lot of boring meetings, during which he often amused himself by composing comic skits and interludes. On the back of an exam paper in 1890, he wrote a description of 'Nixon and Julia: A Pastoral Serenata', with characters including 'Julia. A nymph', 'Nixon. A swain', 'Browning. A giant', and 'Westcott. A Bishop'.[123] In 1893, he wrote a whole libretto for a comic operetta on the back of the Classical Tripos Part II Section D exam paper, set in an interminable College meeting in which O.B. does much of the talking:

> The Vice-Provost [aside]:
> That feller Browning—he's a funny chap
> You never quite know what he's driving at.
> Mr Browning:
> Really, sir, if this bullying goes on
> For bullying it is—I shall sit down.

The meeting begins at ten, whereupon Browning and Nixon launch into a series of objections to the minutes. By half-past one 'We've not begun / Even to deal / With motion one'.[124]

More and more academic and professional recognition came his way. In the summer of 1894, Cambridge awarded him the degree of Litt.D. on the strength of his research. 'The General Board have approved me, which is the last step', he wrote to Herbert.[125] For the rest of his life, he would formally and professionally be known as 'Dr. James' ('The 1st letter I ever wrote to a Dr.', said the impressed Owen Hugh Smith).[126] In 1895, Middleton wrote to tell him that the Royal Society of Antiquaries 'are clamouring that you should become a member'.[127] Academically and institutionally, MRJ was a made man.

* * *

In 1893, Fred Benson's life was transformed by the publication and runaway success of his first novel, *Dodo*—'the most modern and up-to-date book that has yet appeared', according to the *Bookman*.[128] Subtitled 'A Detail of the Day', *Dodo* is the story of Dorothea Vane, a beautiful, vacuous society princess, and the circle in which she moves. The novel is a lightly fictionalized account of a very influential cadre who called themselves 'The Souls', a group which included A. J. Balfour, H. H. Asquith, George Curzon, and Harry Cust—who seems to have been Fred's source for much of *Dodo*'s biographical material.[129] Dodo herself was modelled on Margot Asquith, who later protested at being fictively represented as 'a pretentious donkey with the heart and brains of a linnet'.[130]

Dodo was an ostentatiously attention-grabbing novel, and its publication caused something of a sensation. Arthur Benson, who sometimes thought of his younger brother as a nihilistic dilettante, incapable of taking anything seriously, did not approve of *Dodo*—not least, one suspects, because of wounded pride when people kept congratulating *him* on having written such a success.[131] Owen Hugh Smith, who read *Dodo* before it was published, wrote to MRJ worrying that the book was 'much too personal . . . it is a pity that he shd get people's backs up with his first book by being personal'.[132] When MRJ himself read *Dodo*, he was so appalled by its seeming moral laxity, bad taste, and general air of being 'modern and up-to-date' that he confronted Fred about it in Cambridge. The pair argued, apparently quite vociferously, with Fred growing progressively more arrogant and obnoxious in response to his friend's evident disapproval. Arthur felt he had to step in, writing to MRJ to explain that Fred had become increasingly defensive about criticism of *Dodo*'s morality, while offering a measured, equivocal (those very Arthur Bensonian words) defence of his brother:

> I was myself . . . hoping that he had been less spoilt than a young man who had sold 13,000 copies of a novel had every right to be. I thought he kept his balance wonderfully on the whole. You may be sure that I have spoken to him very plainly about writing no more at present & so have others—& also about some

> of his friends whom I hold in high detestation. . . . I do not myself mind his being a little Bohemian as long as he is not disreputable, & I think he has no inclinations that way.[133]

That Christmas, he went to Felixstowe. Throughout the 1890s, in fact, and well into the 1900s, MRJ went on a series of Christmas (and occasionally summer) holidays to Felixstowe, a seaside town and port on the Suffolk coast. He seems first to have gone there with Sydney in 1890. Clambering across the black groynes on the beach at Felixstowe, built to protect the land against the erosion that is a particular feature of the East Anglian coast, obviously sparked something in his mind. And so it was that on 21 December 1903—the winter solstice and the Christian Feast of St. Thomas; the shortest day and the day of doubt—he told the story of Parkins, the rational materialist Professor of Ontography (the study of reality) at a fictitious Oxbridge College, St. James's, who spends a few days before Christmas in the Globe Hotel at 'Burnstow'. Parkins's colleague, the archaeologist Disney (MRJ hadn't forgotten), asks him to check out a nearby Templar's Preceptory, to see whether 'it would be any good to have a dig there in the summer'.[134] On St. Thomas's Day, he unearths an ancient artefact, a whistle which summons up a supernatural entity. Taking its title from the refrain of a Burns poem, the story, one of MRJ's best, was published as 'Oh, Whistle, and I'll Come to You, My Lad'.

Disney warns that 'The sea has encroached tremendously . . . all along that bit of coast'.[135] Here and elsewhere, MRJ's ghostly East Anglia is an unstable, shifting, eroding landscape, a liminal space; many of his most celebrated stories will be played out in this territory of sand-dunes, black groynes, and drowned villages.[136] Walking home along the beach near Burnstow after having found the ruins of an ancient Templar church and graveyard partly reclaimed by the sand, and struggling over the groynes every few yards, Professor Parkins cannot shake a growing feeling of unease: 'company, he began to think, would be very welcome on that lonely shore, if only you could choose your companion. In his unenlightened days he had read of meetings in such places which even now would hardly bear thinking of.'[137] He has terrifying nightmares of a man being pursued over the groynes by a spectral creature. On this borderland between two worlds (the land and the sea, the material and the supernatural), there is no sure footing. Literally and epistemologically, MRJ's characters stand on an uncertain ground of being. This is a terrain of ambiguity they share with many of the landmark works of British and Irish Gothic, haunted by marshes, bogs, quicksands, Great Grimpen Mires.[138] Furthermore, in its very solitariness, 'Oh, Whistle' selfconsciously rejects the familial ideology—hearth and home—

which underpinned the traditional Dickensian ghost story. When domesticity intrudes upon the story, it does so as a locus of terror: the whistle summons up a ghost which takes the form of a bedsheet which rises from the bed next to Parkins, with 'a horrible, an intensely horrible face *of crumpled linen*'.[139] There is about 'Oh, Whistle, and I'll Come to You, My Lad' a terrible, desolating sense of loneliness. It is a Christmas ghost story like no other.

After he got back from Felixstowe, MRJ spent Christmas of 1893 in King's, and then headed to Great Livermere for the New Year. Early in January he continued what was to become another festive ritual, the 'annual pantomime excursion', which he seems to have inaugurated with Cecil Knatchbull-Hugessen in the 1880s.[140] In January 1894 he went with Owen Hugh Smith and Percy Lubbock to London to see *Hansel and Gretel*. Pantomimes were a 'gorgeous entertainment' which spoke to MRJ's love of a certain variety of English popular culture, and this one 'fully answered all expectations'.[141] On the stage in London during these years, he also went to see Buffalo Bill's Wild West Show. In fact, he enjoyed it so much he went twice.

He also had several goes at writing types of pantomime. He took to writing skits which were performed at Christmas for the boys in King's College Choir. His good friend Gordon Carey went to King's College Choir School in 1897, age 10, and had vivid memories of Christmas 'blow-outs', including a 'topical play' written by MRJ and 'enacted for our benefit by him and others, in which certain College notables were for once identifiably guyed'. (When the Chaplain, E. G. Swain, took over the writing duties, the results were 'rather less scurrilous'.)[142]

More ambitiously, he wrote a pair of full-length pieces for the Amateur Dramatic Club. On 21 December 1895, the ADC performed *The Dismal Tragedy of Henry Blew Beard*, with MRJ in the title role as a London sausage-merchant, supported by Gurney Lubbock, Will Stone, E. G. Swain, and the hulking rugby international L. F. Giblin, mostly in drag roles. It's a genuinely funny play, and the programme came with a series of 'Opinions of Critics', including 'W. Shakespeare': 'Dear Dr James, You seem to me to have touched, nay, surmounted—the height which I was trying to reach (but alas! did not) in my play of *Hamlet*. But I bear you no ill-feeling.'[143] (G. F. Handel, Henry Irving, and Ellen Terry all chipped in with equally laudatory remarks.) This was followed up in 1896 with the *Historia de Alexandro Barberio et XL Latronibus*, rendered in English as 'Alex Barber and the Forty Thieves', which allowed MRJ (again in the lead) to indulge his fondness for comic accents—'Well, Sarah, what's for dinner today? Somethink tasty, I ope, for I'm peckish, mind yer.' *Alex Barber* is set in a modern-day Cambridge, in which 'them Old Fellers' take to crime to supplement their measly salaries: 'When I was made a Fellow / Of Cambridge College here, / I gave my lectures regularly / On eighty pounds a year. / Till I took up with Robbing. . . '[144] A scholar had to make a living somehow.

* * *

As MRJ entered middle age, the circle of people with whom he lived his life grew wider, while staying essentially the same in its character. There were the students—and for as long as he was in Cambridge, young men would find a welcome in his rooms, and be drawn into his life, his beliefs, and his intellectual interests. From children to students, he always enjoyed the company of young people, who brought out his own childlikeness, his irresponsibility, his sense of never quite having grown up. Other, more adult figures—friends and colleagues—also swim into view in these years.

Allen Beville Ramsay, 'Ram', was a constant in MRJ's life from this period onwards, a particularly faithful friend and companion, often there at Christmas or accompanying MRJ on various bicycling holidays. Ram graduated from King's with a First in the Classical Tripos in 1894, and was immediately appointed to a position at Eton, where he remained until 1925, when he succeeded Arthur Benson as Master of Magdalene. Arthur himself thought Ram 'an odd fellow', whose 'profound admiration for Monty James & his mind' came far too close to adulation for his own more ambiguous sense of things.[145] Shane Leslie, not beyond a spot of adulation himself, thought Ramsay 'Monty's favourite disciple in every way'.[146]

Ramsay himself is a slightly spectral presence in MRJ's life—often there, his presence always recorded, but never much speaking or being spoken about. We do, however, have from him one splendid account of MRJ's reading habits, gleaned from many years as a travelling companion:

> He seemed to hold it unnecessary to make enquiries about the merits of authors and their works; he read them all, old and new, good and bad. Before a journey to Cornwall he would buy an armful of detective stories at the Paddington bookstall and at the journey's end he had them finished. Of some the chapters would be read in reverse order, for variety of effect.[147]

'Marcus Dimsdale is another figure of the middle years', MRJ wrote in his memoirs. Dimsdale and MRJ had moved in overlapping company for years: Dimsdale was an Old Etonian and a Fellow in Classics at King's. But it isn't really until the turn of the century that they became friends, seeing one another every day, 'never without pleasure'.[148] Dimsdale was the third son of Robert, sixth Baron Dimsdale of the Russian Empire (an ancestor had been ennobled by Catherine the Great after inoculating her against smallpox). He was very much a Fellow of the old school: a country gentleman, apparently more interested in fishing than in scholarship.[149] Dimsdale was 'erratic and charming', in the words of one friend—and notoriously absent-minded. He often seemed to forget what he'd gone outside for, and once overlooked the existence of the King's fountain, and walked straight into it.[150]

It was, in fact, as a light essayist rather than a scholar that MRJ most valued Dimsdale. 'On Shaving with a Bradshaw' was his favourite, and this essay, a discussion of the meaning of English place names, does show how the two King's Fellows' minds could sometimes move along parallel tracks. Noting the frequency of Lincolnshire place-names ending in -by, Dimsdale finds them 'dimly reminiscent of Norse mythology'.[151] One of the names Dimsdale singles out is Aswarby, a place MRJ had already fictively visited in the opening sentence of 'Lost Hearts': 'It was, as far as I can ascertain, in September of the year 1811 that a postchaise drew up before the door of Aswarby Hall in Lincolnshire.'[152]

Eustace Talbot was a Wykehamist who came up to Trinity in 1892, and was close friends with his fellow medical student Walter Fletcher. MRJ first met Eustace when he came to his rooms with Walter and another friend, Ronny Norman (a member of the great English banking family), and was astonished by his good looks: 'The life and beauty of his face and all his outward self—notable then as always—began by attracting and prepared you to like him', MRJ remembered of that first meeting. 'It was a pleasure, as always, to look at him.'[153] Eustace followed MRJ into the T.A.F. and Chit-Chat Clubs, and acquired a reputation as a charming idler. He was, even according to Walter, who knew him best, 'a magnificent mystery', 'a striking personality', certainly, but one who could come across as 'overbearing', and who often left people with 'an uncomfortable feeling that something in him was only half-tolerant of them'.[154] He graduated with an Ordinary (non-honours) degree, and began a career as a junior doctor in St. Bartholomew's Hospital in London.

Mark Sykes—Colonel Sir Tatton Benvenuto Mark Sykes—led a short but extraordinary life. The son of a very wealthy Yorkshire landowner, and a Roman Catholic, Sykes was a student at Jesus (not a good one—he never graduated). He was introduced to MRJ by E. G. Swain, and the pair hit it off straight away. They shared a sense of humour and a talent for mimicry (Yorkshire accents were Sykes's speciality), and an interest in ghost stories. Sykes was, by absolutely all accounts, a fantastically entertaining companion.

He was often to be found round at MRJ's rooms of an evening. 'I think he told me a great deal more than I told him', MRJ recalled; 'certainly he was most times the central figure'.[155] Sykes had no interest whatsoever in his studies, and left Cambridge in 1897, still only eighteen years old, for a commission in the Green Howards (the Yorkshire Regiment). He saw action in the Second Boer War, and in the early 1900s travelled extensively in the Middle East, and joined the diplomatic service as Attaché to the British Consulate in Constantinople. 'This house is full of scorpions', he wrote to MRJ from the Summer Consulate in Tarabya, on the banks of the Bosphorus.[156] Sykes was elected Unionist MP for Kingston-upon-Hull Central in 1911, and was the leading political authority on Turkish and Middle Eastern affairs. A close friend of Arthur Balfour, and a convert to the Zionist cause, Sykes was one of the architects of the Balfour Declaration of 1917, which declared the British government's support for the creation of a Jewish homeland in Palestine.

Mark Sykes died in February 1919, age thirty-nine, a victim of the Spanish Flu pandemic. Throughout his adult life, he kept up a detailed and lively correspondence with MRJ, often taking him to task for his tardy replies: 'You are a pig of pigs! You would not answer my letters.'[157] Summing up his friendship with Sykes, MRJ wrote: 'he was not that detestable thing, a cosmopolitan: he was very English, very robust, totally without affectation: keenly alive to absurdities wherever met: at the same time profoundly serious about his religion.'[158]

In his biography of Sykes, the Anglo-Irish aristocrat Shane Leslie, another Old Etonian and Kingsman, gives a vivid flavour of the evenings they spent in MRJ's rooms:

> Dr. James seemed to work outside the usual bounds of time and space, and accordingly he had leisure to entertain those who were wise enough to invite themselves to his rooms. The frequentation of Dr. James's famous suite on the great court at King's was a semi-social process known among Old Etonians as 'keeping Montem'. On the impressionable Mark this process made a great impression. Here was a striking contrast to the official pedant, for Dr. James's rooms were neither didactic nor dreary. Manuscripts and priceless texts often strewed the table amid pipes and siphons, but the humorous yarn and the thrilling ghost story filled the longer pauses.[159]

'Keeping Montem' is an Old Etonian pun, and furthermore one that draws attention to MRJ's backward-lookingness. Until discontinued in 1847, Montem was an annual Eton festivity, in which the school gathered at Whitsuntide at the Montem Mound, an Anglo-Saxon burial mound in nearby Slough. It had its origins in the sixteenth century: William Malim, a headmaster in the 1560s, described a procession of the boys to Montem 'to give glory there to Apollo and the Muses, they praise it in song. . . . Here the novices or newcomers . . . are at first seasoned with salt, and then shrewdly hit off in rhyme'.[160] By the eighteenth century, the salt had become metaphorical: at Montem, money was collected to fund the expenses of the School Captain when he went up to King's.[161]

In 1900, Charles Tennyson and R. H. Malden founded a King's College magazine, *Basileion*. A 1909 article, 'The Fresher's Guide to College Clubs and Societies', concludes:

The remainder of the College affect one of these three groups:

1. The Sheppard's flock.
2. The Dicken's sons.
3. They who keep Montem.[162]

The other figures alluded to here are the Classicist John Tressider Sheppard, a future Provost of King's, and the philosopher and Bloomsburyite Goldsworthy Lowes Dickinson. It's worth noting that these three representative, prominent Kingsmen are all gay men. Noel Annan, another future King's Provost (and a married gay man), explicitly links Sheppard and Dickinson when discussing different types of King's College homosexuality in his book *The Dons*:

> Sheppard, when a young fellow . . . went about proclaiming his infatuation with various young men, and tried to convince Lytton Strachey that to fall for a philistine was not necessarily evidence of a bad state of mind. Lowes Dickinson was different. He fully understood his temperament, submissive and ardent, regarding himself as crippled by his homosexuality but distinguishing between his condition, which by the laws and conventions of his country was tragic, and his actions, which were not, he thought, base.[163]

Annan identified Sheppard and Dickinson, as well as a number of other people who feature in MRJ's story—most notably Arthur Benson, but also William Johnson Cory, A. E. Housman, Maynard Keynes, Edward Dent, Charles Sayle, and several others—as prominent figures in what he calls 'The Cult of Homosexuality' in English cultural life from 1850 to 1950.[164] If that cult had a centre, it was King's College Cambridge.[165]

* * *

'I pass my days tranquilly with MSS', MRJ wrote to his parents.[166] Reading his correspondence really gives a sense of what a full-time obsession manuscript studies were for him. By the 1890s, even his letters to his family dealt largely (and at times, almost exclusively) with manuscripts. 'Monty, what's the good of spending all your time with those old manuscripts?' a friend once asked him.[167] He could often be overheard talking to the manuscripts, which talked back: Maisie Fletcher remembered a beheaded saint lamenting his fate in a thick Cockney accent.[168] In 1896, he was approached by Lord Acton, recently appointed as Regius Professor of History at Cambridge, to ask whether he would write a chapter on 'The Christian Renaissance' for the proposed *Cambridge Modern History*, 'written by the best experts the English world affords'.[169] Acton was stunned by MRJ's scholarly habits, as the economic historian J. H. Clapham recalled:

> When Monty James was in his early thirties, Lord Acton came here [to King's]... 'You know Montague James?' he asked a King's man. 'Yes, I know him.' 'Is it true that he is ready to spend every evening playing games or talking with undergraduates?' 'Yes, the evenings and more.' 'And do you know that in knowledge of MSS he is already third or fourth in Europe?' 'I am interested to hear you say so, Sir?' 'Then how does he manage it?' 'We have not yet found out.'[170]

Acton was scarcely less impressed by the chapter MRJ wrote for him. 'Your chapter is a corner stone', he told him. 'I have nothing else that is so solid.'[171]

'Who shall duly celebrate the excellences of the push bike tour in France, particularly in the years before the War? Over thirty times I did it, so I do not speak without knowledge', MRJ wrote.[172] In September 1895, he went on the first of a series of holidays with James McBryde, which were to become cherished memories for him—and were, in time, to provide the inspiration for some of his best early stories. This was a bicycling holiday which the pair undertook, along with Gurney Lubbock, from Dieppe to Munich.[173] This was the furthest MRJ ever cycled. Gurney had persuaded him—after some pestering, as he was 'always conservative and not very adventurous in such matters'—to invest in a brand new, pneumatic-tyred 'safety bicycle', a vast improvement on the old Cheylesmore.[174]

Cycling by moonlight across Northern France was an eerie experience, and brought out MRJ's always vivid awareness of the spectral and supernatural aspects of landscape:

> We started again about 5. & after a good deal of losing our way on the dark, & something approaching despair on my part, we got into a strange, fearfully flat & featureless, treeless country; with nothing to be seen but the skyline, the white road, & the moon ... all the time the breeze made curious moaning sounds, as if the country were full of wandering souls.[175]

As with his native East Anglia, it is the *flatness* of the landscape—'fearfully flat & featureless'—that makes it so uncanny. Even more alarming for MRJ were the encounters with gigantic continental spiders: McBryde came to his rescue when he 'seize[d] by its sinewy leg the largest spider I have ever seen in a derelict bath in Verdun'.[176]

The holiday gave MRJ licence for one of his favourite rhetorical activities—venting his frustration with railway officials and other bureaucrats. He wrote his parents a long, exasperated rant about 'what incredible, unimaginable, effete, inadequate, conceited, incompetent, muddle-headed, unintelligent, fussy, infernal imbeciles all & every single person in the whole of France in any way connected with luggage is or are'.[177] Thirty years later, he was still fuming at 'the phenomenal perennial pigheadedness of French railwaymen about luggage'.[178]

Other French holidays followed. In September and October 1896 he travelled in real style when he journeyed through the Dordogne with Arthur Hamilton-Gordon, spending nights in a variety of Grand Hotels (with very expensive headed notepaper). Arthur Hamilton-Gordon, Baron Stanmore, was a prominent Liberal politician and high-ranking colonial administrator: he had been Governor of New Zealand and of Ceylon. He was the father of MRJ's Trinity chum George Hamilton-Gordon, and he shared with his son's friend a serious interest in French ecclesiastical architecture. He was never happier than when visiting French cathedrals, and the pair kept up an intense rivalry over which of them had visited more—though Hamilton-Gordon eventually admitted defeat, confessing in 1901 that 'You have clearly distanced me now as to French cathedrals'.[179] The pair had begun planning a French holiday together in 1894, and this solidified when Hamilton-Gordon read 'Canon Alberic':

> Taking the other day, casually, an old number of a periodical, I saw in it a tale of *diablerie* by you, the scene of which was laid at St. Bertrand de Comminges. Is it pure invention, or is there a groundwork of local legend? I ask because I have heard of a similar diabolic connection with a book in the East.[180]

The pair travelled from Perigueux through the valley of the Dordogne to the spectacular Rocamadour. In Souillac, they stayed for several days with the Marquis de Cardaillac and his family in the astonishing Chateau de la Treyne, 'at the top of a sheer rock over the Dordogne: a small house with two towers'. The Marquis was keen to drive them around his estate, to see his vineyards and his truffle-beds. Characteristically, while MRJ found the Marquis 'an oldish man with plenty to say for himself', he thought 'the wife not very interesting, nor yet his aunt Mme. de Pardoux'.[181]

Earlier in the summer of 1896, MRJ went on a Welsh holiday. He travelled via Llangollen and Bala to Snowdonia. There he met up with McBryde, and they went to see Beaumaris, Caernarfon, and Harlech Castles, three of the four mighty fortresses Edward I built to secure English colonial rule in North Wales after the death of Llywelyn, the last indigenous Prince of Wales, in 1282 (Conwy, the fourth castle, is also nearby, though MRJ doesn't mention visiting it). In Tremadoc, at the entrance to the Llyn Peninsula, the pair joined Arthur Benson and others for a few days at Tan-yr-Allt, Howard Sturgis's holiday home. 'Howdie' Sturgis was an Old Etonian and Trinity graduate of American ancestry and independent means, a modestly successful novelist, and a friend of Henry James, Edith Wharton, and E. M. Forster. 'Howard in his infinite Howardism', Henry James exclaimed. 'Our dear Howard is like a cake—a richly sugared cake—always on the table. We sit round him in a circle and help ourselves.'[182] Sturgis was as near as you could get to being an openly homosexual man around 1900. His novel of schoolboy life, *Tim* (1891), now reads like a ground-breaking work of gay fiction. This was certainly how Arthur Benson's friend Henry Havelock Ellis, the pioneering Victorian psychologist and sexologist, understood it, commenting that it was written 'in order that the emotional and romantic character of the [homosexual] relationships described may appear more natural'.[183] Sturgis's long-term partner, William Haynes-Smith, was known to friends as 'The Babe', a nickname Fred Benson seems to have borrowed for his 1897 novel of Cambridge life, *The Babe, B.A.*

None of this seems to have caused much scandal or opprobrium, though all accounts of Sturgis are as clear about his sexuality as late Victorian and Edwardian language could be. Sydney, MRJ's foursquare, rugby-playing older brother, was a good friend and a frequent visitor to Tan-yr-Allt. Sydney thought Sturgis 'by far the best actor of female parts that the A.D.C. produced for a long series of years, if not ever. He was curiously feminine in his tastes, *e.g.*, he used to embroider his mother's nightgowns.'[184] The Spanish-American philosopher George Santayana, a close friend and annual visitor to Sturgis's home, was also very taken by the way in which Sturgis had 'learned to sew, to embroider, to knit, and to do crochet', and thought that he had been sent to Eton by his family 'to cure him of his girlishness. A cruel remedy, it might seem, as if he had been sent to sea before the mast. . . . Young Howard calmly defied all those school-boys with his feminine habits and arts, which he never dreamt of disguising.'[185] Arthur Benson was friends with Sturgis for over thirty years. His initial impression of Sturgis, from his first visit to Tan-yr-Allt in the 1890s, was of 'a sort of fairy-prince', and he remembered his regular visits to Sturgis's bedroom before dinner, where Howdie would place a flower in his buttonhole. That summer, Arthur found Howard Sturgis 'particularly nice and affectionate'.[186] His 'delicate improprieties', Arthur thought, 'were tactfully calculated to give a prim mind rather a sense of glorious tolerance at *not* being shocked than of any moral disapproval.'[187] In his diaries, the never-not-conflicted Arthur *was* shocked, and rather disgusted, at seeing Sturgis and Percy Lubbock having 'a long and lover-like kiss', and registered his discomfort at his friends' 'emotional flirtations' at Tan-yr-Allt, 'making little overtures and whinneyings, like dogs and horses' to one another.[188] One friend, though, certainly did not partake in these flirtations. Arthur's diary for the visit also records 'M. R. James there imitating all things'.[189]

* * *

By the 1890s, Cambridge's two women's colleges, Girton and Newnham, were well established.[190] The presence of women as Cambridge students, though always controversial, was becoming accepted. Dons began to open their lectures to women students: as early as 1873, twenty-two out of the thirty-four Cambridge professors declared themselves prepared to admit women into their lectures, though women had no automatic right to attend. In 1881, a proposal to open examinations to women was overwhelmingly passed in the Senate, by 366 votes to 32—Henry Sidgwick was one of the guiding forces behind this decision, and a member of the Syndicate which came up with the report on which the vote was based. But these women students were hardly recognized as full members of the university, and were certainly not allowed to take degrees, whatever their examination results. In spite of enormous inbuilt disadvantages (the entire public school system was geared towards the Classical Tripos and its Oxford equivalent), women began to perform on an equal footing with men. In 1880, before women's performance in exams was officially recognized, Charlotte Scott from Girton was informally bracketed with the Eighth Wrangler in the Mathematical Tripos. In 1887 Agnata Ramsay was the only candidate placed in the First Division of the First Class of the Classical Tripos (Chancellor's Medallist Lionel Ford was in the Second Division; Walter Headlam, whom many thought the finest Classical scholar of his generation, was down in the Third). In 1890, Philippa Fawcett of Newnham was placed 'above the Senior Wrangler' in the Mathematical Tripos.[191] It was difficult to see what the intellectual argument might be for refusing degrees to women.

Calls for serious reform had been rumbling since 1881, and by the middle of the 1890s the pressure was formidable. In 1895, 2000 Cambridge men signed a Memorial advocating degrees for women. Senior conservative figures in the university began to marshal their forces in opposition to this. On 22 February

1896, Augustus Austen Leigh, Provost of King's, chaired a meeting of the opposition to degrees for women; Alfred Marshall, Professor of Economics, was one of the leading voices resisting change; Brooke Foss Wescott was another of the opponents.[192] When a Syndicate was drawn up to produce a new report on degrees for women, its proposed membership included Henry Sidgwick—an archetypal university insider who knew exactly how to operate institutional machinery to get the results he wanted. But, in an unprecedented move, the great Cambridge reformer's appointment to the Syndicate was rejected—he was felt to be too evidently biased in favour of women. MRJ, in fact, was instrumental in this rejection, as one of nine signatories (William Ridgeway and Arthur Shipley were two others), who gave 'Notice of a Non Placet' (a negative vote) to the Senate on 9 March, on the grounds that they believed it improper that the proposed Syndicate 'should contain so many declared partisans amongst its numbers'.[193] So, Henry Sidgwick was not on the Syndicate—but MRJ was. This was most likely at Austen Leigh's suggestion, to give the Syndicate a strong voice in opposition to reform. There was never any doubt where MRJ would fall on this issue: 'How are you, old man?' Cis Lubbock wrote to him around this time. 'Flourishing, I hope and still unhurt by the machinations of your foes, the would-be Lady M.A.'s.'[194]

The Syndicate, chaired by the Vice-Chancellor, the mathematician Charles Smith of Sidney Sussex College, was bitterly divided, and could not arrive at a consensus. The majority report, signed by the Vice-Chancellor and eight others, recommended awarding BA and MA degrees to women, though declined to go as far as proposing full university membership.[195] MRJ dissociated himself completely from this report, which he refused to sign in any of its forms. Instead, he and four others (including his friend and collaborator Armitage Robinson) produced a minority report of their own, proposing what they clearly thought was an ingenious wheeze (though it just seems mean-spirited to me). Women students, they suggested, should be awarded the degrees of MLitt and MSc—which all sounds very impressive, except that neither of these awards was recognized by the university.[196] MRJ was also one of many signatories of a letter of protest against the proposals, a letter endorsed by virtually the entire conservative establishment of the University, which closed with an ominous rhetorical flourish: 'The present position may be the parting of the ways for women's education; it certainly is the parting of the ways for Cambridge herself. The future of the University lies in the hands of the members of the Senate.'[197]

A three-day debate was held on the report in the University Senate, on 13, 15, and 16 March 1897. MRJ was one of the speakers, and he kept a copy of his speech. His argument does not engage at all with the merits of women's education. Rather, it warns darkly of the end of a traditional public school Cambridge. 'How many times in recent years have we noticed, or been told', he asked, 'that "Oxford gets the pick of the public school boys"?':

> Now what I would ask the Senate to consider is this. How are the proposals before us going to affect the minds of boys and parents in these circumstances? Are they likely to be attracted or repelled by the news that the University is offering additional inducements to women students, and that it is placing them more nearly on a level with men?

A whole social and political system was in danger of being overthrown, he maintained, and Cambridge University with it. He closed his speech on a note of frankly outrageous hyperbole: 'If [the proposals] are answered in the affirmative, we shall have to prepare ourselves all the sooner to become not a mixed but a women's university.'[198]

The students had no formal voice in this vote, though they very much took matters into their own hands. Over 2000 students petitioned the Senate to keep women out of the University—this must mean that three-quarters of the students who signed the memorandum calling for reform in 1895 had changed their minds eighteen months later.[199] The petition was organized by *The Granta*, the Cambridge magazine which had form when it came to mischief-making, whose editorial declared that 'the harpies are upon us, and this time with a vengeance'. The magazine ran an ongoing series of fake war reportage from 'The Women's War'. An undergraduate debate organized in parallel with the Senate House debate came down heavily against degrees for women, 1083 votes to 38.[200]

Cambridge was swept up in this debate, with everyone taking sides. Arthur Berry, the King's mathematician, was a tireless activist and campaigner for women's education, and dedicated a lot of his time to teaching at Girton. J. E. Nixon was also a supporter of the cause of degrees for women, and of full membership of the university 'without distinction of sex', warning against 'reactionists who would like to undo all the progress that has been made in this direction, and whose programme has no finality but that of severing our connection with women's education'.[201] On this and most other issues, there was no greater 'reactionist' than MRJ. But not all of his friends agreed with him. Walter Headlam and Charles Waldstein both voted yes, as did the august Montagu Butler, Master of Trinity.[202] Ronny Norman, a regular presence at gatherings in MRJ's rooms, was a supporter of degrees for women. James McBryde, however, was not, and the affair seems to have given him a lasting loathing of women students. Studying art at the Slade five years later, he found his female classmates 'fat and hideous', without 'the least spark of intelligence to suggest any subject for themselves'. He thought that the proponents of women's education at King's might benefit from meeting them: 'Berry & Wedd should be sent there to see them apropos of their women's degree ideas for Cambridge.'[203]

The vote itself was scheduled for 21 May. By this time, the whole affair had been taken up by the national press. The *Times* and the *Morning Post* ran articles condemning the prospect of awarding degrees to women, though without engaging in any way with the issues: as the historian of women at Cambridge Ann Kennedy Smith writes, 'it was simply held to be self-evident' that women should not be awarded degrees.[204] Opponents of the proposal put up posters declaring 'No Gowns for the Girtonites! Non Plus the Newnhamites!! Frustrate the Feminine Fanatics!!!'[205] The No campaign was ferociously well organized and funded: special 'Non Placet' trains were laid on, to make sure that the No voters got to Cambridge for the vote.

On the day of the vote, King's Parade in central Cambridge was thronged by thousands of protestors and spectators—a crowd largely made up of young men in straw boaters. An effigy of a woman student, wearing a white blouse, blue bloomers, and striped stockings, and sat on a bicycle, was hung (by the neck) above the entrance to Macmillan and Bowes' bookshop: 'It's a misogynistic caricature of a female student that represents everything that over ten thousand men have gathered on King's Parade to protest against on 21 May 1897', Kennedy Smith writes.[206] MRJ kept his own memento of that day, which he later gave to Gwen McBryde: a photograph of protestors massed outside Senate House under a large banner with an adapted quotation from *Much Ado About Nothing*: 'Get You To Girton, Beatrice, Get You To Newnham. Here's No Place For You Maids'.[207] As the vote was taking place, dons, corralled outside Senate House waiting for the result, were pelted with rotten eggs and firecrackers thrown from the windows of Gonville and Caius College.

When the result was announced, it was a landslide: 661 Yes—1707 No.[208] Of all the Colleges, only Emmanuel's electors had returned a majority vote in favour of granting degrees for women. The effigy of the woman student was taken down and ritually burnt on a bonfire in Market Square. A small riot broke out. Some of the protestors marched over to Newnham and smashed windows. The *Cambridgeshire Weekly News* published an 'Extra Special Edition' entitled *Triumph of Man!*[209] 'I never thought of accusing you personally on the score of women's degrees', Ronny Norman wrote to MRJ, 'but I was none the less pained to read of the decision.'[210] The reactionists had had their way. It would be over fifty years before women were finally granted full membership of Cambridge University.

* * *

In March 1898, Mary Emily wrote to MRJ to let him know that Ber had come home, and was now stationed in Aldershot, 'dry and healthy'.[211] About six weeks later, on 9 May, she wrote again, discussing the ongoing Spanish-American War and, on a more domestic level, giving him the news about a family christening, and worrying about Herbert's health. He was getting less mobile, and they had recently purchased a small Exmoor pony to pull him around in his bath chair when he was out and about. He had developed bad toothache. This was the last letter she ever wrote to him.

Mary Emily died in September 1898. She was eighty years old, and her health had been failing for some time. 'I feel for you in this horrible V-shaped depression of the barometer, but I am afraid I can hardly get over to you', MRJ wrote in his last letter to her, a few days before her death.[212] Gurney Lubbock, who knew all the James family, wrote that Mary Emily 'had the deep, far-reaching unselfishness of character which, for all her gentleness, was strong and incisive'.[213] Given MRJ's emotional reticence, he was scarcely likely to verbalize his feelings at length, though he did write in reply to one letter of sympathy that he believed Mary Emily had led 'the most perfect life I have known'.[214] In her last years, Mary Emily went deaf, and MRJ told Owen Hugh Smith 'how great the pleasure was to think of her having her hearing restored to her'.[215]

A few days later, MRJ went to York. He had been invited to Yorkshire to address a Church Congress in Bradford—but his real reason for going north was to tour the medieval churches of York and study their remarkable collection of stained glass. It is worth dwelling on what MRJ saw on this visit because it resonated so powerfully with his own intellectual preoccupations with apocalypses and demons, and because deciphering the riddles of stained glass is the central theme of one of his best-known early stories, 'The Treasure of Abbot Thomas'.

'York is the paradise of the student of old glass', Frederick Harrison, Librarian of the Dean and Chapter Library of York Minster, wrote in *The Painted Glass of York* (1927), a book whose acknowledgements single out MRJ for his assistance 'in my study of old glass'.[216] The city's churches contain perhaps as much as 75% of England's surviving medieval stained glass. Most particularly, MRJ wanted to look at the extraordinarily apocalyptic Prick of Conscience window in All Saints, North Street. This is widely recognized as a masterpiece: 'a window without parallel in medieval glass', according to Harrison; 'without doubt one of the most treasured possessions of European stained glass', according to the Minster's chief glazier, Peter Gibson; 'unique in European art', according to the All Saints historian Allan B. Barton.[217] The window is a rendering of a section of *The Prick of Conscience*, a long homiletic poem of the first half of the fourteenth century recounting the last fifteen days of the earth, one of whose manuscripts is in the McClean collection which MRJ secured for the Fitzwilliam.[218] The window follows the poem's chronology fairly closely, beginning with Day One, in which 'þe se sal ryse, als þa bukes says, / Abowen þe heght of ilka mountayne' (4759–560: 'The sea shall rise, as all the books say, / Above the height of every mountain'), and ending with Day Fifteen: 'Alle þe worlde sal bryn on ilk syde' (4813: 'All the world shall burn on every side'). Memorably, the window renders Day Five's 'wondreful fisshes of þe se' as a group of grotesque sea-monsters; on the twelfth day, the stars fall from the sky, and on the thirteenth the dead arise from their graves.

The iconography of St. John the Evangelist often includes a chalice containing a serpent, an allusion to John's drinking of the poison chalice in his encounter with the high priest Aristodemus of Ephesus. In *The Golden Legend*, Jacobus de Voragine recounts the tale:

> 'If you want me to believe in your God, I will give you poison to drink. If it does you no harm, it will be clear that your master is the true God.' . . . Then the apostle took the cup, armed himself with the sign of the cross, drained the drink, and suffered no harm; and all present began to praise God.[219]

In the depiction of St. John in the stained glass of Holy Trinity, Goodramgate, which MRJ viewed on 1 October, the chalice contains what looks very like a cephalopod—though on closer examination is actually a serpent covered in octopus-like suckers. It is tempting to think that MRJ, who was irresistibly drawn towards the exceptional and the particular, and who forgot nothing, remembered this when he came to write 'Count Magnus' in 1901 or 1902. All that can be seen of the flesh-sucking demon which the vampiric Swedish count brings back with him from the Black Pilgrimage to Chorazin is something like 'the tentacle of a devil-fish'[220]—that is, according to the *OED*, 'the octopus, cuttlefish, or other cephalopod'. The subsequent history of weird fiction, from H. P. Lovecraft's 'The Call of Cthulhu' to China Miéville's *Kraken*, would have been very different without cephalopod morphology, to which the genre returns obsessively. 'Count Magnus' was, unsurprisingly, Lovecraft's favourite MRJ story.[221]

St. Denys Walmgate, another of the churches he visited, has a more conventional St. John, depicted, MRJ noted, with 'Poison cup & dragon'. But, very unconventionally, MRJ's notebooks also point out a window containing

'Many angels with musical instruments. At top one with organ. Below on L[eft] two, one with stringed instrument, the other with hurdy gurdy'.[222] This is followed by his sketch of the St. Denys hurdy-gurdy—which is, as the church's historian observes, 'very rare'.[223] It was surely not only the rarity of the hurdy-gurdy that attracted MRJ's attention, but also the fact that the instrument had already made a memorable cameo appearance in 'Lost Hearts', where it belongs to one of Mr Abney's victims, Giovanni, who 'come a tweaking his 'urdy-gurdy round and about the drive one winter's day'.[224]

But most of all, St. Denys's is full of demons. They are everywhere in its stained glass. Most notably, there is a striking roundel of a red devil with a tail, dating from c.1200: this is an image of St. Michael preventing the demons from escaping from Hell.[225] Elsewhere in the church, an angel and a demon whisper counsel into the ears of a Pope, and demonic faces leer from restored fragments of glass. On his travels in the 1898 visit, MRJ also saw 'the descent of Lucifer', and 'fragments, including demons' in St. Michael, Spurriergate. In St. Martin's, Coney Street, he saw 'a horned beast above a lady praying', and 'St. Martin as a bishop, holding a cross-staff and exorcising a fiend'.[226]

* * *

Back in King's, MRJ had the opportunity of a new, more lucrative, but also more demanding job. The Senior Tutor of the College was in overall charge of undergraduate education. In the right hands, this was an opportunity to effect momentous change: Augustus Austen Leigh had completely revolutionized King's whole pedagogical and intellectual outlook during his time as Tutor. In November 1899, A. H. Cooke, the current Tutor, took up the Headmastership of Aldenham School in Hertfordshire. Provost Austen Leigh was in no doubt as to who he thought should succeed him: 'More than one of our Fellows has told me that you *ought* to succeed Cooke; and I know of no other way in which we can escape probable disaster', he told MRJ. 'I can only say it would be very much to the advantage of the College if you would do so. A Tutor need not do much teaching.'[227] MRJ knew what this meant: 'the fat is in the fire', he wrote to Herbert; 'if I am asked, I must not say no.'[228]

MRJ made it very clear that he wouldn't give up the Fitzwilliam, and so he found himself standing down as Dean, a role he rather liked and was quite good at, to become Tutor, a job he hated and for which he was not suited. He had become, Oliffe Richmond thought, 'an unwilling victim of the administrative machine'.[229] While he was generally interested in undergraduates and their lives, he had never had any interest in education, and gave lectures very reluctantly. He undertook the role of Tutor, he told HB, 'with real disinclination'.[230] By the end of 1900 he had had enough—'the prospect of an indefinite period of arranging examinations', and all the other tedious and fiddly duties of the role, he thought, 'is one which I cannot face with equanimity: and I can rather easily find twenty other things which I should otherwise be doing'.[231] After little more than a year in the role, he told Austen Leigh he wanted to resign. 'It is always difficult to know how far one ought to ask others to sacrifice themselves for the good of the community', Austen Leigh replied; but he urged MRJ to give it another year, for three reasons:

1. We should have a less distinguished man.
2. We should probably have a Tutor who would be less human, less able to understand & be understood by the undergraduates.
3. We should have someone whose religious influence and example would be at best nil, & therefore mischievous.[232]

As the final point here makes clear, Austen Leigh was appealing to MRJ as a prominent voice in the resistance against the forces of modernization. This is the burden behind Austen Leigh's original entreaty that 'I know no other way in which we can escape probable disaster', and his invocation of the language of self-sacrifice 'for the good of the community'. Austen Leigh also forwarded MRJ a letter from A. H. Cooke, written in the same vein: 'It would be a terrible calamity to put one of the ungodly party—like Wedd or Berry or even Macaulay—in [MRJ's] place. I should move heaven & earth to prevent the scandal of the College, which possesses King's Chapel, having a Tutor who never entered it.'[233] MRJ could not resist such arguments, and slumped on, most unwillingly, for another year. He resigned the role in May 1902, and was replaced by W. H. Macaulay, one of the people Cooke had warned against. Macaulay was a very distinguished success as Tutor.[234]

Between 1899 and 1901, MRJ went on a trio of Scandinavian holidays, to Denmark and Sweden, which were to have an enormous influence on his life and his work. The most important thing was that James McBryde was there. Travelling with them in 1899 was Will Stone, another Kingsman, who had gone on to teach at Radley, and was just about to take up a new post at Marlborough—and whom we last met back in 1895 as one of the cast of *Henry Blew Beard*. MRJ found in Stone 'what one asks for in a travelling companion, affection and humour and a power of simple enjoyment and a willingness to be pleased'.[235] The voyage to Esbjerg was choppy, and Stone and MRJ were both badly seasick. MRJ, who was a great devotee of Hans Christian Andersen, found Denmark 'a land of romance':

> The first evening we spent there fully answered expectation, as we lay on the edge of the river in the big meadow by Ribe and watched the behaviour of the storks on the housetops over against us, with Ribe cathedral tower in the background, and a most radiant sunset sky.[236]

In Copenhagen the three of them hired bicycles and headed along the coast to Helsingör (Elsinore), stopping en route for 'a wonderful good bathe' at Rungsted. From there, they crossed over to Helsingborg in Sweden. At Visby, on the Swedish island of Gotland, they visited the Bronze Age Trojaborg maze ('Troy Town' is also a common name for ancient mazes in England and across Northern Europe). They also went to the circus: MRJ was horrified to find that the big top was full of 'truculent' spiders running around their feet.[237] In the Royal Library at Stockholm, MRJ inspected the Codex Aureus, a lavish Gospel illustrated in Canterbury, which he thought 'magnificent'; and, right up his street, the Codex Gigas or Devil's Bible, 'a Bohemian MS about a yard high', which has as its star attraction 'a large picture of the devil'. [238]

The Scandinavian holiday of 1899 brought out James McBryde's creative side. As soon as he got back, he began work on an illustrated children's book, *The Story of a Troll-hunt*. The book opens with three pipe-smoking Englishmen sitting on the back lawn of King's, on the banks of the Cam, with the Chapel in the background, and planning 'an expedition to Denmark with the object of bringing back a live specimen of a Troll for the Fitzwilliam Museum'.[239]

The holiday was a great success, and the trio began to draw up plans to repeat it again the following year. It had improved MRJ's Danish, a language he could read with ease, but which he had initially found incomprehensible when spoken by actual Danes, as he had learnt it from a dictionary.[240] He had also begun to learn Swedish, with the aid of a grammar and a long train journey. For the 1900 trip, he was furnished with letters of introduction from the Danish Legation, compliments of Charles Waldstein. This holiday was to provide the inspiration for another classic ghost story, 'Number 13', in which a Danish scholar, Mr Anderson, is troubled by the presence of a supernatural hotel guest in the nonexistent room next door.

Disembarking in Esbjerg after another choppy voyage (this time, McBryde was sick), the trio headed to Endrup, where they cycled through a beautiful beech wood and lunched at a watermill. At Vejle, they sailed across the fjord in a steamer and had tea in the Munkebjerg hotel, high up in the woods overlooking the fjord. At Jelling, they visited the 'great Runic stones' on the barrow of King Gorm and Queen Thyra.[241]

'Among the towns in Jutland, Viborg justly holds a high place.' This is the opening sentence of 'Number 13'. 'There are good hotels in Viborg—Preisler's and the Phoenix are all that can be desired.'[242] MRJ, Stone, and McBryde spent several nights in Preisler's Hotel in August 1900; there is no Hotel Phoenix in Viborg, though the friends had stayed in the Phoenix in Skanderborg a few nights earlier. Unfortunately, Mr Anderson, the protagonist of 'Number 13', stays in neither of these fine places, but chooses instead the Golden Lion, an obvious mistake.

In Viborg, MRJ met the local schoolmaster, Herr Mickelson. The pair fell into an intense discussion of the occult, 'which is his real subject' (Mickelson was the author of a prizewinning study of the medieval mystic Meister Eckhart).[243] It's likely that it was Mickelson who told MRJ the story of Daniel Salthenius, the eighteenth-century scholar who had sold his soul to the Devil. The contracts, signed in Salthenius's blood, could still be seen at the museum of Uppsala: MRJ made a mental note of this for his next Scandinavian visit. Mickelson introduced him to a former pupil, an artist called Jensen, who also happened to be staying at Preisler's. MRJ again took a mental note of that name, which he used for Mr Anderson's fellow-guest in 'Number 13', the lawyer who ends up sharing a double-bedded room with Mr Anderson after both have been disturbed by the nocturnal activities of the man in Number 13, Magister Nicholas Francken.

In Dronninglund, in the far north of Denmark, Waldstein's letters got them a welcome at Voergaard Castle, whose owner, Peder Brønnum Scavenius, furnished MRJ with a resonant name for the archivist in 'Number 13'. MRJ was very struck by Voergaard and its location, which gave him yet more ideas:

> The situation in a wide lonely moor is also a most curious thing. Nothing else like this moated grange can be imagined. It was built by a very wicked old lady who is all about the place still, & has an enormous monument in the church.[244]

In a letter to his sister, Will Stone filled in some of the details:

> Built by Fru Ingeborg Skael in 1588. This exciting woman after she had paid for one wing found the expenses too great and so when the ships bringing building materials came, had the cables cut just before the storm: the ships were wrecked and she claimed the cargoes as a lady of the manor. The architect's bill was too heavy. He was requested to appear with the keys and his bill receipted. She would go through the rooms with him first and threw the heavy keys round his neck. After going the round they stood on the drawbridge. Fru Ingeborg called attention to the view and pushed the poor man into the moat, where the heavy keys dragged him to the bottom. She then called assistance. Naturally she walked after death and had to be exorcised into a neighbouring marsh. Every year she advances one cock's step toward the house; the marks are said to be visible because of course the grass won't grow: when she reaches the house it falls down.[245]

But the remote mausoleum of a wicked Scandinavian aristocrat whose spirit continued to haunt the land would be a story for another day.

After they got back, Will Stone was particularly keen to hear the new ghost story MRJ had written in the wake of the holiday: 'No. 13 must be finished before you come to Marlborough', he urged.[246] He wrote to his sister: 'You ask about Denmark. It was glorious—M. R. James, storks, Cathedrals, old towns, handsome people, lakes (lots), plenty to eat, Danish ballads to read.'[247] He and MRJ began to correspond in Danish. And then, in February 1901, there was an outbreak of infectious pneumonia in Marlborough, which saw the 'sick-house overflowing into a classroom'. 'I am perfectly well', he assured his father on 16 February.[248] Ten days later, he was dead. 'For myself, it is the first time I have lost a companion of that age & those associations and I do not at all know what to make of it. He is a dear youth', MRJ wrote to Herbert.[249] A week later, he and McBryde travelled together to Will Stone's funeral in the village of Preshute, just outside Marlborough. Preshute is overlooked by one of the English landscape's famous white horses. This is the kind of thing from which MRJ drew comfort.

That summer, MRJ and McBryde headed for Sweden, just the two of them. On the crossing from Hull to Gothenburg, they drank whisky and soda and played innumerable games of hangman. At the southern tip of Sweden, they visited the cathedral city of Skåne, and the nearby town of Trollhätten ('Trolls' Hoods'), another name MRJ found irresistible. Further north, on the shores of Lake Vänern, they visited Råbäck, another name that stuck in his mind. At Husaby, the pair saw the oldest church in Sweden, the burial place of Olaf Skötkonung, the first Christian King of Sweden. Husaby's altarpiece, MRJ was fascinated to discover, was donated to the church in 1679 by Magnus Gabriel De la Gardie, Lord High Chancellor of Sweden. In Roglösa, they visited another church, 'which is covered with iron work representing Michael and the dragon, hunting scenes, & devils, a very odd, early production'.[250]

By now, the elements of MRJ's second Scandinavian ghost story, the terrifying 'Count Magnus', were beginning to assemble themselves in his mind. The hapless researcher Mr Wraxall, 'near being a Fellow of his College at Oxford—Brasenose, as I judge from the Calendar' (nearly a Fellow, but not *really* a Fellow), writing a 'chatty' guidebook to Sweden (again, a work of *semi*-scholarship), becomes fascinated by the tomb of Count Magnus De la Gardie in Råbäck, which is covered in grim images of battles, and of a man 'running at full speed' away from a mysterious hooded creature, from whose garment can be seen protruding something that looks like 'the tentacle of a devil-fish', watched over by a cloaked man standing on a hill.[251] Count Magnus has been on the Black Pilgrimage to Chorazin, birthplace of the Antichrist: 'What did the Count bring back with him?'[252]

MRJ was particularly keen to get to Uppsala, to see the Daniel Salthenius contract with the Devil, and on 18 August he wrote home: 'I saw the two contacts with the devil written (& signed in blood) in 1718 by Daniel Salthenius, who was condemned to death for writing them. He escaped this & he died Professor of Divinity at Konigsberg.'[253] The contracts can still be seen at the University of Uppsala library. This is what MRJ read:

> I, Daniel Salthenius, desire from you, O Devil, the following items which you shall give me in exchange for payment.
>
> 1. You shall now at this time give me a purse which shall never run out of purely minted money, and that money shall remain in my possession or in that of the one I give it to.
>
> 2. You shall grant me particular success in the world with gentlemen and ladies of high station, as well as success in hunting and fishing, so that I never return empty-handed.
>
> 3. That all the arts already I have learned, or later shall learn, I shall retain.
>
> 4. That I now receive from you the Black Book.
>
> 5. That I can become visible or invisible, whenever I wish.
>
> 6. You shall now give me that thing, whatever it may be, that has the quality, that when I have it about my person, I may immediately come to any place I name. In return I promise to serve you during my lifetime as best I can and after my death to belong to you, body and soul. Anno 1718, this I affirm with my signature and blood.[254]

When Salthenius's crime was discovered, he was initially sentenced to death by beheading, but the sentence was commuted to eight days' imprisonment due to the extenuating circumstance of his age: he was a fifteen-year-old student at the time.

MRJ was now able to put the finishing touches to 'Number 13', which draws to a close with a retelling of the Salthenius story:

> I had the whole story from [Mr. Anderson] a few months later, as we sat in a wood near Uppsala, after the visit to the library there, where we—or, rather, I—had laughed over the contract by which Daniel Salthenius (in later life, Professor of Hebrew at Königsberg) sold himself to Satan. Anderson was not really amused.
>
> 'Young idiot', said he, meaning Salthenius, who was only an undergraduate when he committed that indiscretion, 'how did he know what company he was courting?'[255]

Image 1 The James family, outside Great Livermere, *c.* 1882. l to r: MRJ, Ber, Mary Emily, Herbert, Sydney, Grace. Reproduced by permission of Philip James.

Image 2 MRJ as a young schoolboy. Reproduced by permission of Philip James.

Image 3 Eton Pop, July 1882. MRJ seated at centre. Also in the photograph: St. Clair Donaldson (front row, first from left); Herbert Tatham (second row, standing at right); Henry Babington Smith (second row, second from right). Reproduced by permission of Philip James.

Image 4 MRJ as Peisthetairos in *The Birds*, 1883. Archive Centre, King's College Cambridge: MRJ/F/5/4a-f.

Image 5 MRJ, self-portrait from Notebooks, 13.1. Photograph © The Fitzwilliam Museum, University of Cambridge.

Image 6 James McBryde, Will Stone, and MRJ, on holiday in Denmark, 1899. Reproduced by permission of Philip James.

A HAND LIKE THE HAND IN THAT PICTURE.

Image 7 James McBryde's illustration of 'Canon Alberic's Scrapbook' (1904), with MRJ as Dennistoun. Author's collection.

THE GRANTA SPECIAL MAY WEEK NUMBER.

Photo by J. Palmer Clarke.

The Provost of King's.

Image 8 The Provost of King's, *The Granta,* XVIII (8 June 1905). Archive Centre, King's College Cambridge: MRJ/F/5/49.

Image 9 MRJ and friends on holiday in Germany, 1911: l. to r. unknown man, MRJ, A. E. Conybeare, Thomas Anstey Guthrie, A. B. Ramsay. Archive Centre, King's College Cambridge: MRJ/F/8/1.

Image 10 Burlinson and Grylls, Eton College Chapel Memorial Chapel Window (North), from a design suggested by MRJ (1924). Author's photograph. Reproduced by permission of the Provost and Fellows of Eton College.

Image 11 MRJ *c.* 1930. Reproduced by permission of the Provost and Fellows of Eton College.

Image 12 The last photograph ever taken of MRJ, 4 June 1936. Reproduced by permission of Philip James.

7

Provost of King's, 1905

In the first years of the twentieth century, the bachelor idyll MRJ had built around him in King's began to show signs of cracking, as one by one his friends started to get married. Most dramatically, James McBryde married Gwendolen Grotrian, a young artist from Yorkshire, the daughter of Frederick Brent Grotrian, Conservative MP for Kingston-upon-Hull East, and the founder of the *Hull Daily Mail*. Gwen first met McBryde at the home of a family friend, and in May Week of 1896 or 1897 (her memory of the exact date was a little unclear), he invited her to a ball at King's. It was during this visit that she first encountered MRJ, and her impressions of their first meeting are worth recording: 'For the first time I wished that I had been born a boy, with the chance of living quite differently, even if I could not have arrived inside the charmed circle.'[1] Not long afterwards, Gwen and James got engaged.

The pair were married on 15 July, 1903, in the Grotrian family home in Hessle, in what was then the East Riding of Yorkshire. 'I am simply bursting to hear how McB's wedding went off & whether you had a good or only a strenuous time', Walter Fletcher wrote from Marburg.[2] MRJ had had a strenuous time. 'In the afternoon was the wedding reception', he wrote to Grace. 'The first mistake I made was in never going to look at the presents. The whole function was most offensive & I fled as soon as I decently could & slept at York.'[3]

MRJ spent a lot of that summer of 1903 in the company of his friend Percy Lubbock, who didn't seem likely to get married any time soon (although even he did, eventually). When news reached him in June of McBryde's impending marriage, he wrote to Herbert: 'Hideous weather, requiring all one's exertion to subdue the growing tendency to depression! . . . I fled the gay scene on Friday with P. Lubbock & went to Wisbech, the marchland churches & Lincoln.'[4] Percy Lubbock, a Fellow of Magdalene and the College's Pepys Librarian from 1906, was a significant voice in the history of gay letters in the early twentieth century, a friend and confidant of Howard Sturgis and E. M. Forster, and author of the seminal work of Modernist aesthetics, *The Craft of Fiction* (1921). In the aftermath of the wedding, he and MRJ went for a holiday together on Kent, where they visited Canterbury and MRJ's birthplace, Goodnestone. At Rye, they had an encounter with Percy's most influential literary friend, Henry James: 'a very pleasant man he is', MRJ told Herbert, 'talking just as he writes with punctilious effort to use exactly the word he wants: looks like a respectable butler.'[5]

In January 1904, Gwen wrote to MRJ to let him know that James McBryde had been ill with 'a touch of . . . appendicitis', but that he was on the mend.[6] But the condition flared up again the following month, which had MRJ worrying that 'McB & his wife are not out of the woods yet'.[7] He went to visit the McBrydes for a few days that spring, and this was the last time he saw James McBryde. On 6 June, he got a letter from McBryde's sister:

> He had another attack of appendicitis the week before last—was successfully operated on last Tuesday. His wife wrote every day—each day he seemed to be getting better & this morning I got a telegram just saying
> 'James died last night.'[8]

MRJ was 'quite broken-hearted'.[9] He wrote an anguished letter to Arthur Benson, quoting lines from Henry Vaughan's 'The Garland':

> Flowers gather'd in this world die here; if thou
> Would'st have a wreath that fades not, let them grow,
> And grow for thee. Who spares them here, shall find
> A garland, where comes neither rain, nor wind.[10]

We no longer have this letter, unfortunately, but we do have Arthur's long reply. MRJ's life of arcane scholarship and antiquarianism, and even of hospitable sociability, Arthur worries, won't sustain him during a period of genuine crisis, with which he is emotionally ill-equipped to deal. MRJ was now, Arthur thought, brought face-to-face with aspects of his life he had long sought to deny:

> I am much moved by your letter. This is the first I had heard of the death of McBryde. I did not know he was ill. It was the other day only that I was looking at his picture in your rooms & asking Percy Lubbock about him . . .
>
> I wonder if what you say about sentiment is quite true? If you mean sentimentality it is of course entirely so; but I sometimes wonder if in steering clear of that which one instinctively dislikes, & grows to dislike more & more, we don't perhaps err by over-repression, & keep our feelings so close & dissemble them so completely that they tend to die of inanition. I don't think that Fitzgerald . . . Newman & Thackeray, people of very different types—were ashamed of caring

> very much about their friends, & even of saying so, on occasions. One wants to know that people *care*—that is one of the few things that endures. Companionship over champagne & cigars—& even over ruined abbeys—is not very sustaining.[11]

In his diary, as he tended to, Arthur wrote more revealingly:

> A sad & moving letter from MRJ telling me of McBryde's death . . . Monty's letter touched me very much, for he called me his oldest friend. But there seemed a curious effort in the letters not to let himself go, not to dive deep; to take the thing as lightly as was consistent with feeling it very much—not to let it be a sad remembrance. He spoke strongly of McB as being a friend who didn't want sentiment, by which I think he meant sentimentality. But here I believe Monty a little deceives himself. He likes young beautiful graceful people & what is that but a refined sentimentality. He is not demonstrative & thinks that unsentimental.[12]

A few days earlier, stunned from McBryde's death, MRJ had driven past Arthur in a hansom cab, 'looking very grave & sad'.[13] Arthur tried to call to him, but he was lost in his own thoughts.

MRJ's friends rallied round. 'I know how much it must mean to you', Lionel Ford wrote.[14] Luxmoore recognized a difficult truth about the life he and many of his friends had chosen: 'Those who have no wife and home circle of their own give hostages to fortune perhaps in greater dependence on and closeness to their friends, and to you this means a very deep and painful wound.'[15] Others, more introspective and emotionally articulate than MRJ, registered their own sense of shock, in terms he would have found difficult to acknowledge, let alone give voice to. 'The blow is a bitter one to me', a shaken Gurney Lubbock wrote the day after McBryde's death, 'for I begin to realize more fully how much happiness I have always had from my friends & how little they have had from me. How selfish, how utterly selfish, one has been.'[16] Most open of all, Johnnie Maxwell wrote to share his own feelings at the death of his close friend John Scott, Viscount Enscombe a few years earlier, after '5 years of closest friendship, every hour enjoyed and remembered':

> Only a slave wd. be resigned to a friend's death, but slowly I have learnt that there is a sordid something about sorrow which is all right for small things but all wrong for big things. . . . Love slowly regrets a mood so inappropriate. What is left is not, thank God, resignation but a part of life's experience not to be highly despised, lonely, but full of happy echos [sic].[17]

McBryde's funeral took place on 8 June, at his family home in St. Helen's, Lancashire. MRJ travelled up from Cambridge with Walter Fletcher, taking a garland of his own, roses, lilac, and honeysuckle, which he had picked from the

Fellows' Garden at King's. After the service was over and the other mourners had left, he stood alone at the graveside, and threw the flowers onto the coffin. In this moment, and this gesture, one can read MRJ's genuine, heartbroken passion. Victorian floriography, its symbolic language of flowers, was widely understood.[18] Roses and honeysuckle both signified love; lilacs innocence, or first love: *my love dies with you*.

But, as MRJ told Walter Fletcher, 'it doesn't end here'.[19] As a memorial to McBryde, MRJ used his considerable influence to persuade Cambridge University Press, that venerable and august publisher, to publish McBryde's illustrated children's book, *The Story of a Troll Hunt*. McBryde's family were touched and delighted. Gwen ordered a dozen copies. Julia, his sister, was particularly taken by MRJ's Introduction: 'you seem to me to have said just the right things & what one feels', she told him.[20] MRJ closes the Introduction by remembering his holidays in Denmark and Sweden with McBryde and Will Stone—both of them, he says, quoting Ephesians, 'now no longer sojourners but citizens'. This, finally, was what MRJ said about McBryde: 'The intercourse of eleven years—of late minutely recalled,—has left no single act or word of his which I could wish to forget.'[21] MRJ quotes again from Henry Vaughan in remembering McBryde—the opening two stanzas of Vaughan's poem 'As time one day by me did pass'. What he did *not* say, but what he certainly knew, were the words of the poem's final stanza:

> Sleep, happy ashes! (blessed sleep!)
>   While hapless I still weep;
>   Weep that I have out-lived
>   My life, and unrelieved
> Must (soul-less shadow!) so live on,
> Though life be dead, and my joys gone.[22]

In telling Walter that 'it doesn't end here', MRJ said more than he knew. Gwen was pregnant, and on 27 November she gave birth to a baby daughter, Jane. 'I told you a Miss McBryde was born last week perhaps, or you saw it in the paper', MRJ told Herbert. 'I rather regret its sex, but it must be as it may.'[23] Walter was Jane's godfather, and MRJ—regretted sex notwithstanding—agreed to be her guardian: 'she will need someone to look up to as much as a boy would have, so you will forgive my having troubled you, I had no choice in the matter, for I did not want anyone else.'[24] 'I wonder when I shall find a moment to look in, and make its (her, I beg pardon) acquaintance', MRJ replied, in his first-ever letter to Gwen. 'Convey my blessing, seriously, to my ward. I greatly appreciate the responsibility.'[25]

Thus began what was to be one of the enduring friendships of MRJ's life, and by far the closest friendship he ever had with a woman. There seems no doubt that, initially at least, his friendship with Gwen was a way of continuing his relationship with James by other means, keeping his memory alive, being close to him. But over time, Gwen and Jane became vital parts of his life, another kind of family. The McBrydes moved into The Woodlands, a house in Dippersmoor, Herefordshire, right on the Welsh border, and MRJ first went there in June 1905, 'to make acquaintance with Miss Jane McBryde'.[26] From then on, he would visit every summer, and often in the New Year, and at other times, generally unannounced; the McBrydes, in their turn, were as often to be found visiting MRJ in King's. He loved the Herefordshire countryside, which gave him what several friends believed to be a genuine mystical fulfilment. He thought of it as Beulah, the heaven on earth in *The Pilgrim's Progress*: 'It's like that, isn't it?' he told Maisie Fletcher, as the pair watched the sun set over the Black Mountains.[27] Dippersmoor Manor itself he thought 'like an enchanted mansion in a Hans Andersen fairy tale'.[28] He spent long, idyllic July afternoons in the garden at Woodlands, doing crosswords, reading detective stories, playing croquet, and eating wild strawberries.

He took his role as Jane's guardian seriously, and was very good at it. He liked children, and understood them on their own terms without irony, in a way that is unusual for adults. Oliffe Richmond, generally a detached and rather cynical observer of events and people, saw MRJ's 'childish side, so beloved of children', and thought him 'infinitely kind' to little Jane.[29] 'Would you like me to call you "Black Mouse"?' Jane asked MRJ on her first visit to King's. 'Madam, I should be honoured', he replied, and from that moment on Gwen and Jane always called him Mouse.[30] He started a long correspondence with Jane: 'Dear Mouse', 'Dear Mrs. Cat' (his name for her). Often this was written about, and sometimes from, their various cats: MRJ, we remember, claimed to know the language of cats, and was on terms of particular understanding with his cat Tabby, who thought small dogs ridiculous, looked forward to the annual Harvest Mousing Campaign, and worried about her wayward nephew, Pyramus.[31]

* * *

One by one across these years, MRJ's friends were getting married: Johnnie Maxwell in 1901, Mark Sykes in 1903, Lionel Ford in 1904, J. H. Clapham in 1905. While the prospect of these marriages often produced reflexive dismay and performative groans on his part, he tended to like his friends' new wives and families. Johnnie's wife, Christian, was a lively and regular correspondent, who shared MRJ's arachnophobia, and wrote delightedly horrified letters about finding giant spiders in the bath. She was so terrified by 'The Ash-Tree', his great arachnophobic tale, that she could no longer sleep with her bedroom window open 'because of horrible spiders creeping in'.[32] He thought Lionel's wife, Mary, 'really a splendid person', and enjoyed visiting the pair at Repton, where Lionel had become headmaster, and where they would play duets on Lionel's new organ.[33] (Arthur Benson was *very* taken by Mary Ford, writing, 'Good God, what would not one give to care for anyone like that!'.)[34] He was godfather to Clapham's daughter, who called him 'God the Father'.[35]

More importantly, in June 1904 Walter Fletcher got married to Maisie Cropper, a member of a prominent Quaker family from Ellergreen in Kendal, in the far northwest of England. Walter's college friend Jem Cropper introduced him to his sister at a Trinity Ball in 1899 with the words 'Look here, old chap, if you'll dance with my sister, I swear I'll dance with your cousin'.[36] Maisie's first impression of Walter was of 'the difficult don', but he became an increasingly regular visitor to Ellergreen, and in 1902 the pair got engaged.[37] Eustace Talbot was the best man, and MRJ travelled up to Westmoreland for the wedding with Johnnie Maxwell and Owen Hugh Smith. Unusually for such events, he seems genuinely to have enjoyed himself: 'The wedding was extremely well thought out', he wrote to Herbert. 'Every thing was quite punctual, the church not over decorated, the congregation extremely large and well behaved, the singing excellent. . . .. These weddings are a fearful strain on the emotions, but nothing could have been better done than this one. All the same, the bridegroom was a sad sight between one and two o'clock just before the ceremony.'[38]

Walter was very keen that MRJ and Maisie should become friends: 'Oh my dear, you must really like him for my sake, and I'm sure you will for his own', he wrote to her. In Cambridge, he took her 'almost tremblingly to lunch' with MRJ. She was nervous because of his 'reputation of being a woman hater', but he soon had her reduced 'almost to tears of laughter' with his repertoire of funny voices. He was in the middle of an impersonation of the Vice-Provost Fred Whitting, who had no roof to his mouth, when Whitting himself walked in to offer his congratulations to Walter and Maisie.[39]

MRJ, in fact, grew fond of the whole Cropper family, whom he visited often. They were a lively, rambunctious clan, and he spent his evenings there singing Westmoreland ballads and music hall songs with Maisie's father. On his first visit to Ellergreen, he was met off the train by the Cropper sisters, who found him on the platform talking to himself in a Cockney accent: 'I don't see no flags a-flying. I don't 'ear no bands a-playing. I don't see no triumphal arch.'[40] It was the Croppers who were the first to hear him read 'Oh, Whistle, and I'll Come to You, My Lad', in Ellergreen (did he write it there?). But he was particularly close to Maisie's thirteen-year-old sister Sibyl, whom everyone called Billy.

The pair hit it off so well that he took her to see Buffalo Bill's Wild West Show (one of his favourites) in London in January 1903. 'Monty James is *actually* (and really I shall have nothing left to be astonished at) coming to his hated London on the 21st in order to go to Buffalo Bill because Billy has asked him to. I pretended not to be surprised when he admitted it but inwardly I gasped', Walter wrote.[41] They enjoyed a long and riotously inventive correspondence, largely written from the perspective of various animals—cats, of course, but also drunken owls, or Archy the talking archaeopteryx, who eats the family cat and lays an egg from which a turkey hatches. Bardolf Barker himself occasionally joined in the correspondence, disguised as a chatty owl:

> dere cropper
>
> i rite to tell you that I must postpone my visit to hellergreen till a later date has I ham ditaned it ome for a munth
>
> yrumbleservant
>
> Barn howl[42]

Billy was well up for this, and capable of responding in kind, in a manner that must have delighted MRJ: 'I'm sure that Dr James 'e says that 'e would recommend you to me leastwise me to 'im leastwise 'im to you leastwise 'im to you leastwise you to 'im leastwise.'[43] As well as comedy voices and Buffalo Bill, the pair shared an enthusiasm for the Sherlock Holmes stories ('Aren't they ripping?'), and swapped conspiratorial anecdotes about the necessity of keeping a pistol on one's person at all times.[44]

Years later, Oliffe Richmond told Arthur Benson that he thought MRJ had been 'on the verge' of marriage to Sibyl. But this seems hardly likely based either on their extensive correspondence nor on the recollections of any other friends or family members—plus, there was an age-gap of almost thirty years (unusual, though certainly not unheard of in a Victorian marriage). Besides, Richmond was an inveterate gossip, much given to discussing his friends' love-lives. Arthur, who knew MRJ much better, concluded: 'I do not myself think that Monty is at all a marriageable man.'[45] (Richmond also thought that he might have married Eton headmaster Edward Lyttelton's daughter Nora, which seems even less likely: Nora was even younger than Billy. Arthur himself believed that Nora's mother was 'quite shamelessly' trying to match her daughter and MRJ, with a complete lack of success which he found amusing.)[46]

Oliffe Richmond himself really swims into view in MRJ's life around now. (Or rather, cycles, as he, MRJ, and Percy Lubbock were given to taking long bicycling excursions together.) An Old Etonian and a pupil of Luxmoore's, Richmond was an excellent Classicist with a particular flair for manuscript studies. He was, in fact, one the very few people who could actually be said to have studied under MRJ, who avoided teaching wherever he could. MRJ took him on a manuscript-hunting holiday to Wolfenbüttel in Lower Saxony after he finished Part I of the Classical Tripos in 1903, and supervised the manuscript research he did for Part II the following year. It probably helped that he was very good looking, 'O. Richmond a good deal in evidence', Arthur wrote in his diary during the 1903 festive ghost story marathon, 'his personal beauty is the most attractive thing about him; & he is full of enthusiasm & friendliness; but he seems curiously devoid of tact'.[47] Luxmoore, his former tutor, agreed: 'He is very egotistical, & very tactless, & I can't help seeing how like in action to OB.'[48] MRJ once took Richmond to task for making a derogatory joke about an old friend: 'I wish you wouldn't say such things at all—& in any case not in other people's houses & to other people's guests.'[49] He was known, not necessarily kindly, as 'The Golden Olive'.[50]

Richmond was the first person elected to a King's Fellowship during MRJ's Provostship—and he thought MRJ had been instrumental in getting him the position.[51] Not being tactful, he spent a couple of years lobbying MRJ quite intently in the cause of career advancement: 'Of course, a Craven & Fellowship together would be ideal: but a Fellowship alone would lead me straight into bankruptcy', he complained, shortly before getting both awards; 'I cannot live at King's decently without taking hack work.'[52] (He seems to have recruited his mother in this endeavour, too: she wrote MRJ several letters in support of her son's career: 'It *is* nice of you all at Kings to appreciate our boy as you must do'.)[53] But his enthusiasm for manuscripts was real, and (as we've seen) he once jokingly wrote to MRJ about his discovery of an 'imperfect palimpsest' of MRJ's most prized lost manuscript, Papias's *Life of Christ*, unearthed at a Portuguese monastery—'but I like being quiet about my little finds'.[54]

But it wasn't only his tactlessness that led Luxmoore to compare Richmond to Oscar Browning. Richmond had a particular fondness for younger boys, in a manner which troubled some of his colleagues. 'He told me a long story about his old adventure with the King's choir-boy, and his recent attempts as a Don to frequent the choir-school', Arthur Benson wrote. 'The odd thing is that he tries to disguise his motive in the matter. He makes out that he would like to help and befriend the choristers—whereas he really has a sentimental interest in boys.'[55] 'O.R. has a morbid predilection for *boys*—it is a sort of sexuality, an erotic mania', Arthur worried, though he added that he thought Richmond's behaviour was 'wholly pure and good', presumably because Arthur believed he did not act on his desires. Nevertheless, Arthur, who knew a lot about forbidden sexual temptation, felt bound to warn Richmond: 'I told O.R. he must drop these boys or that he would for ever be misrepresented. . . . I told him today that it *was* a sexual perversion.'[56] This is remarkably frank language for the usually circumspect Arthur, and his warnings were to prove prophetic. In 1912, Richmond was caught up in a sex scandal, when one of the choirboys complained about the nature of his attentions, and he was instructed to keep away from the school. MRJ as Provost had to deal with this. 'If this had happened to me, it wd drive me from Cambridge', Arthur wrote, 'but R. takes it with a sort of mild vexation, unintelligible to me.'[57] Luxmoore wrote a long, fascinating letter to MRJ, in equivocal defence of Richmond:

> I mean that he interferes in matters for wh. he is not made responsible, especially in matters of morals & young people & has great confidence that he can always set things right better than other people. So was OB at Eton & he did a great deal of good by it, & I sympathised with a great many of his efforts: but there always was about OB just something a bit greasy wh. made one feel insecure of the complete cleanness of his sincerity & motives. I don't set up to be a good judge of character & may be wrong but I know Oliffe longer & better than most people & the thing that most attracted me to him was that I believed him singularly clean minded. I know the circumstances that have been against him at King's in the way of his dealings with the young ones—& I think (will you mind me saying so?) that it wd be a good thing if you would hear his account of them—I mean of course if he is right in thinking that you *do not* know the *complete* circumstances & have never heard—shall I say his defence? Or his side of the story? It is well possible that you have heard him 100 times and are tired of it. But he thinks & says that he has had no opportunity of clearing himself with you & that is what he professes to be the source of 'these tears'.[58]

Not long afterwards, Richmond gave up his Fellowship and left King's, to become Professor of Latin at University College, Cardiff and, later, at Edinburgh University. He never returned to Cambridge in a professional capacity.

* * *

Lyndhurst Falkiner Giblin, the King's mathematician and England rugby player whom we last met in 1895, done up in drag for the Christmas production of *Henry Blew Beard*, had had a colourful few years. After graduating from

King's in 1896, he took himself off gold-mining in the Klondike. By 1903, he realized that this wasn't going to work, and so headed home to Tasmania, where his father ran the government. In 1905, armed with a reference from MRJ, he got himself a job mining in the Solomon Islands. That wasn't a great success, either, and so, back in Tasmania, he variously tried his hand at farming, fruit-growing, and politics in the years leading up to the First World War. After the War, he got a job as the Government Statistician in Tasmania—he stuck with this, and in 1929 was appointed Ritchie Professor of Economics at the University of Melbourne and then, from 1935, Director of the Commonwealth Bank. They don't make economists like L. F. Giblin anymore.

On his way home from the Klondike, Giblin stopped off at King's for Christmas 1903, and so found himself in attendance at that year's monumental festival of ghost stories, listening to MRJ read 'Oh, Whistle'. It was Giblin, in fact, who first suggested that MRJ should publish a volume of his ghost stories, with illustrations by James McBryde. In March 1904, just before leaving for Tasmania, he sent a reminder: 'Have you had in mind the scheme planned at Christmas of publishing your Christmas stories with illustrations by McB? Don't let it drop.'[59]

But who might publish these ghost stories? In November 1902, Edward Arnold had written to MRJ asking whether he would be interested in writing a book on 'Learning in England' in the Middle Ages: 'we find the idea most attractive. It is just the sort of book we enjoy publishing'.[60] Edward Arnold was a member of a great Victorian dynasty (Thomas Arnold of Rugby was his grandfather; Matthew Arnold was his uncle), and his publishing house specialized in educational books (and in the high end of imperial travel writing). It made sense that Arnold should approach MRJ with a proposal like this, especially given that the first volume of Lord Acton's very high-profile *Cambridge Modern History*, with MRJ's chapter on 'The Christian Renaissance', had just come out that year.[61] This proposed book didn't come to pass, and nor did Arnold's suggestion the following year that MRJ might write 'a volume on "Chapters of Learning in England" during the Renaissance'.[62] But the pair stayed in touch, and in the spring of 1904 Arnold agreed to publish MRJ's first volume of ghost stories. Arnold initially suggested H. J. Ford as an illustrator (at a cost of £4.4.0 per drawing, with the author to pay), but Giblin had already spoken to McBryde '& suggested my illustrating your stories, with a view to their publication'.[63] MRJ talked Arnold round, though not till July. (Ford, however, did make a reappearance in MRJ's publishing life nine years later, with an incredibly beautiful series of Pre-Raphaelite-influenced illustrations for *Old Testament Legends* in 1913.)[64]

But there were problems. MRJ's initial manuscript was not long enough. In March 1904, he wrote to McBryde:

> The ones I thought of printing were –
>
> 1. One that came out in the National Review of '94. A man goes to S. Bertrand de Comminges, spends a day in the church . . . & buys a book from the sacristan in the evening. There is a very odd picture in the book of Solomon on his throne & a demon strangling one of his bodyguard. When my man is in his room looking over his book at night he sees a hairy hand on the table by him & finds the demon in [the] picture standing behind him & just going to pounce. Of course he is rescued.
> 2. the mezzotint
> 3. the spiders
> 4. the No 13 story
> 5. the Swedish story about Count Magnus
> 6. the one about the whistle
>
> I don't think I have any others that will do.[65]

'Are there any more of the Ghost-stories?' Arnold asked him. 'Those sent would only make a slim volume, and if there was half as much again it would be a great advantage.'[66] The manuscript was currently 38,000 words, and so the book would be sold at three shillings and sixpence a volume; at 60,000 words, Arnold could charge six shillings: 'we never find books "go" as well as 3s/6, so we are obliged to make you alternative offers according to the price we may be able to ask.' At 6/-, the royalties would be 10% on the published price of all copies up to 500, 15% from 500–3000, and 20% over 3000. But at 3/6, the royalties were much less: 10% for the first 1000, 15% thereafter, plus two-and-a-half pennies per copy for sales in the colonies. And so, Arnold asked, 'We should be extremely glad if you could torture your brains and extract some horrors so as to make up the volume to 6s/- length.'[67] He added an ingeniously wrong-headed suggestion: 'Mumm thinks he remembers having once read a very good story by your brother, and it occurred to us whether it might be possible to work a joint volume.'[68] There is no evidence that either Syd or Ber ever wrote ghost stories, let alone published them. It seems likely that Mumm had somehow got it into his head that *Henry* James was in fact MRJ's brother![69]

MRJ did have one other story, 'Lost Hearts', 'but I don't care much about it'.[70] (It's one of his best stories, but Leo Maxse hadn't liked it much either, and had turned it down for the *National Review*, though the *Pall Mall Magazine* had published it for Christmas 1895.) He agreed to add that, and then set about writing the volume's only original story, 'The Treasure of Abbot Thomas', in which a scholar attempts to decipher the meaning of stained-glass windows, and ends up unleashing a very slimy supernatural entity in a German well. It is worth dwelling on this story, as it opens up vistas into some of MRJ's lasting preoccupations, with ecclesiastical stained glass, and with the restoration of churches.

* * *

By this point, MRJ was a recognized authority on medieval stained glass—a 'true expert', according to Richmond.[71] Ever since his undergraduate days, he had been fascinated by the stained glass at King's Chapel. 'One of the angels', he wrote to Herbert in 1883, '—a delightful being in himself—holds a sword with the following very unseraphic inscription "Egrede egrede iur sangrinam et uir Belial!" It is of course apropos of the adjacent representation of Shimei cursing David, but it amused me.'[72] (This is an inscription from 2 Samuel 16: 7: 'Come out, come out, thou bloody man, and thou man of Belial'.)

'The most famous building in Cambridge, and its greatest work of the Middle Ages', Nikolaus Pevsner writes of King's College Chapel, one of the landmark works of the ecclesiastical perpendicular. 'There is nothing else in English architecture quite like this huge single fan-vaulted chamber of stone.'[73] The agreement between the estate of Henry VII and King's College for the building of a chapel stipulated a series of windows to be glazed with 'images, storis, armys, bagis [badges], and other devises'. 'It is so evident', Willis and Clark write in their *Architectural History* of Cambridge University, 'that the building was designed for the exhibition of pictures in glass on a grand scale.'[74] The windows were begun by the German-born glazier Barnard Flower in 1515, and completed in 1531 by a group of six London-based glaziers.[75] There are twelve windows each on the north and south sides, showing New Testament scenes beginning with the birth of the Virgin Mary and ending with her assumption and coronation, each accompanied by their Old Testament analogues or antitypes. On the East Window is the Crucifixion, and on the West Christ on the Throne of Judgement.[76]

One of the recurring complaints of MRJ's own *Guide to the Windows of King's College Chapel, Cambridge* (1899) is about the restoration of some of the windows, undertaken by John Pike Hedgeland in the 1840s, which he considered 'conspicuously bad'.[77] By the time MRJ arrived at King's, Hedgeland was generally thought to have treated the windows 'pretty severely', and so between 1893 and 1906, they were all releaded. 'Great was the excitement', MRJ wrote, 'when a fresh window was thus made accessible, of going over it, settling what mistakes must be rectified, what glaring modern patches should be taken out and replaced by neutral-tinted glass.'[78] Nineteenth-century glass restorers, he came to think, 'have sinned against light'.[79]

MRJ took a consistent and firm stance against the modern restoration of ecclesiastical art and architecture. Around the same time that he wrote his study of the King's Chapel glass, Arthur Gray, a Fellow of Jesus College, and a man whose life and career has several parallels with MRJ's (he became Master of Jesus; he was a notable writer of ghost stories; he was a conspicuously conservative institutionalist), wrote asking whether MRJ would make a study of the stained glass in Jesus Chapel, which he worried had succumbed to 'the barbarities of this century' (Jesus Chapel has some magnificent Victorian stained glass, by William Morris and Edward Burne-Jones).[80] This anti-restorationalism was a position MRJ likely got from Luxmoore originally; in his turn, Luxmoore got it from Ruskin, who, in *The Seven Lamps of Architecture* (1849) damned restoration as 'the most total destruction a building can suffer . . . Do not let us deceive ourselves in this important matter: it is *impossible*, as impossible as to raise the dead, to restore anything that has ever been great or beautiful in architecture'.[81] In setting his face against modern restoration, MRJ was very self-consciously participating in a significant Victorian cultural and political debate. In the words of one commentator, 'restoration and reconstruction became central metaphors for Victorian thinking'.[82] Like many Victorian debates, this was at its heart a debate about religion, as ecclesiastical restoration, and the Gothic Revival of which it was one aspect, were closely associated with Oxford Movement Ritualism: 'The Restoration of Churches is the Restoration of Popery', in the words of one incensed critic, the Evangelical pamphleteer Francis Close.[83] MRJ's extreme anti-restorationalism, then, is entirely congruent with both his religious and cultural background, and means much more than just a set of aesthetic preferences about the way churches look.

MRJ laid out his beliefs most fully in a long and detailed letter to Raymond Pelly, Vicar of Great Malvern in Worcestershire, who had written to him for advice on restoring his church windows:

> I do not and cannot tolerate the idea of replacing any portion of a defective picture in modern coloured glass: still less, that of drawing new heads and figures to fill in gaps in the design . . . I see no logical distinction between completing the Malvern windows & repainting & restoring a faded fresco whether on the walls of an English country church or of an Italian monastery: whether the work of a nameless monk, or of Leonardo da Vinci . . . I say, then, rearrange & relead but do not dream of restoring.[84]

(MRJ proposed reordering the glass at Malvern, which brought him into conflict with the Society for the Preservation of Ancient Buildings, and with William Morris, who advised against it for fear of damaging the windows.)[85] This is an aesthetic sensibility which very clearly informs some of the ghost stories. In 'An Episode of Cathedral History', a demon is released during the Victorian restoration of a late-medieval perpendicular Cathedral: 'It was in 1840 that the wave of the Gothic revival smote the Cathedral of Southminster.'[86] Leave well alone.

'The Treasure of Abbot Thomas' opens with lines in Latin from the '*Sertum Steinfeldense Norbertinum* . . . An account of the Premonstratensian Abbey of Steinfeld, in the Eiffel, published in Cologne in 1712 by Christian Albert Erhard'.[87] This is an invented book, but characteristically it comes out of real research. In the summer of 1903, the Norfolk antiquary Dundas Harford wrote to MRJ about a recent tour he had made of the Eifel Mountains in Germany. Visiting the abbey of Mariawald in Heimbach, Harford was interested to learn about its stained glass, which had been removed and scattered in the aftermath of the French Revolution. Some of it, he believed, had found its way to his own church, St. Stephen's in Norwich. Would MRJ be interested in examining the glass?[88] In 1904, MRJ was asked by Lord Brownlow of Ashridge House in Hertfordshire (which MRJ had visited with Babington Smith just before leaving Eton) to catalogue the stained glass in his chapel.[89] Lord Brownlow knew that the glass had been imported from Germany in the nineteenth century, but could say no more about its provenance. MRJ believed that the glass 'probably came from one church, the Abbatial Church of Steinfeld in the Eiffel district', and published his findings in *Notes of Glass in Ashridge Chapel* (1906).[90]

In September 1908, MRJ received a letter from a German priest, Father Nikola Reinartz, who had heard about 'The Treasure of Abbot Thomas' in a scholarly German article written in 1907 by a Dr Förster, who wrote that 'the Englishman M. R. James tells a ghost story from Steinfeld in his agreeably written book *Ghost Stories of an Antiquary*'.[91] In London for an ecclesiastical conference, he went to a bookseller in Charing Cross Road to buy the book (the bookseller couldn't locate it, but then fortuitously Reinartz saw that his hand had been resting on a copy all along). 'I went to Cambridge', he wrote in his shaky English, 'to see the author of the story of Abbot Thomas. Steinfeld is my native country and I am much interested to know where have gone the famous glass windows and librarie of the Abbey.'[92] The correspondence between the pair continued: 'It almost appeared to me that the author of the "Story of Abbot Thomas" was setting me a new problem to solve; the key of which I am unable to find, owing to the fact that my petition for permission to see the Chapel windows at Ashridge has remained unanswered.'[93] But Father Reinartz was a doggedly persistent man, and so decided just to show up at Ashridge with a letter of introduction from MRJ. His study of the windows led to a series of articles which revised MRJ's original assertion. Drawing on Reinartz's work, Bernard Rackham has maintained that the Ashridge glass was not, as MRJ had thought, from Steinfeld alone, but was an amalgamation of the missing glass from both Steinfeld and Mariawald.[94] For readers who want to have a go at solving the mystery themselves, the Ashridge Glass is now on display at the Victoria and Albert Museum in London (it was donated to the museum by Ernest Edward Cook, the grandson of the travel agent Thomas Cook). The V&A's curators maintain that the glass comes solely from Mariawald, and that it was first bought by John Christopher Hampp of Norwich, before being sold on to Lord Brownlow.[95]

The Ashridge Glass itself, Reinartz wrote, was chaos: 'a shamble. . . . Only a brilliant ruin has remained.'[96] 'The Treasure of Abbot Thomas' is a story about solving the riddle of stained glass; about learning how to read it. MRJ's notebooks are full of this kind of thing—attempts to decode the meaning of stained-glass windows (or sometimes church doors), which he evidently understood as a form of cryptography, puzzles to decipher.[97] In 1921, MRJ was asked to advise on the renovation of the glass in York Minster. He believed that the glass panels in the Minster's East Window were ordered incorrectly, thus making no narrative sense, and proposed a new ordering: 'The present order is not correct: displacements occur in rows i–iv, vi, vi.'[98] Frederick Harrison, the great authority on York Minster, accepted James's reordering, and reproduces it as an appendix to *The Painted Glass of York*.[99] During the Second World War, much of the Minster's glass was removed for safekeeping. Subsequently, the glass was replaced, and the Great East Window's panels reordered according to MRJ's schema. It is estimated that the Minster's windows would have been releaded every 120–150 years, each releading causing the possibility of mistakes in the replacement of the glass, or of loss—further exacerbated by the fires of 1829 and 1840. In 1945, prior to the postwar replacement, the Minster's glass was described as 'the largest jig-saw puzzle in the world'.[100] This is a statement which would obviously have appealed to MRJ, who saw medieval stained glass in part as an interpretive challenge, a code to be deciphered, a matter of *order*—and who also loved jigsaws (Maisie and Billy Cropper's brother Charles drew him working at a jigsaw in 1912, with the inscription: 'M.R.J. A jigsaw puzzle. Worse than a manuscript.')[101] The 1945 renovation of the glass was overseen by the Dean of York Minster, Eric Milner-White, who had been a student and then a colleague of MRJ's at King's. In his account of York's stained glass, Peter Gibson (one of the glaziers who worked with Milner-White on the postwar releading) notes that

> under the guidance of Dean Milner-White, one very important underlying principle was observed. The restorative work would be governed by the *re-arrangement* of the existing medieval glass. That meant that where pieces were missing if no ancient replacement were available then pot-metal glass would be used but with no attempt to paint upon its surface.[102]

'The right sequence was worked out by the late M. R. James, exactly following the Biblical text; we have now restored it: the opportunity was a duty', Milner-White wrote in 1950.[103] This was not the first time that Milner-White had drawn on MRJ's expertise for a stained glass project. During his time as chaplain, Milner-White renovated a part of King's College Chapel, adding 'a large stock' of old glass that MRJ himself had collected.[104]

* * *

With 'The Treasure of Abbot Thomas', the book of ghost stories was complete. But what to call it? 'I want a *title*', Arnold wrote on 18 July 1904, 'so that I may announce the volume in our new list.'[105] As we can see from the list of stories he gave to McBryde on 13 March, MRJ was not good with titles. The only firm titles he had at this time were 'The Mezzotint', and the one story he *didn't* want to include, 'Lost Hearts'. The others are all placeholders or vague descriptions ('The one about the whistle'), or else the intriguingly rejected 'The Spiders' (too close to home, but possibly a better title than the one he went for, 'The Ash-Tree'). 'Canon Alberic's Scrap-book', which had already gone through two different titles, both eventually rejected, has at this point no title at all.

He went for *Ghost Stories of an Antiquary*, a brilliant—and brilliantly revealing—title. Like most literary genres, the ghost story is capacious. Its borders are fuzzy, and its best practitioners often exploit this sense of categorical ambiguity. MRJ is probably the greatest ghost story specialist of them all—but are his stories really 'ghost stories'? 'Canon Alberic' is unambiguously a tale of occult demonology, and 'Count Magnus' is essentially a vampire story. Elsewhere, we have a variety of supernatural entities—octopeds and octopodes, spirits of the wind—and cursed or haunted artefacts—whistles, hotel rooms, illustrations. The representation of ghosts underwent serious changes in the second half of the nineteenth century, in part due to the widespread influence of spiritualism.[106] Traditionally, the appearance of ghosts had served a narrative or moral purpose, a telos: to right wrongs, correct injustices, impart information, or atone for crimes (the ghosts of Banquo, Hamlet's father, or Jacob Marley all perform one or more of these functions).[107] In his influential 1894 work on spirits and the supernatural, *Cock Lane and Common Sense*, the folklorist Andrew Lang maintained that, conversely, 'the modern ghost is a purposeless creature':

> He appears nobody knows why; he has no message to deliver, no secret crime to reveal, no appointment to keep, no treasure to disclose, no commissions to be executed, and, as an almost invariable rule, he does not speak, even if you speak to him.[108]

('Speak to me' is Hamlet's repeated injunction to his father's ghost.)[109] 'Abbot Thomas's slimy entity protects rather than discloses its treasure, and the only story in *Ghost Stories of an Antiquary* that fully conforms to this traditional model is 'Lost Hearts', with its vengeful ghost-children. MRJ was developing and adapting the genre even as he claimed it for his own.

More revealing still is that these are the stories 'of an Antiquary'. The antiquary, a connoisseur or collector of the informational or material minutiae of an often intensely local history, was by the time MRJ was writing very much an outmoded intellectual category, hearkening back in its specifically English context to a golden age in the seventeenth century.[110] Antiquarianism was itself antiquated. It was viewed as amateurish, superseded by modern systematic archaeological and historical scholarship.[111] MRJ, as we've seen many times, liked to position himself right on the border between old-fashioned antiquarianism and modern scholarship, with a foot in both camps. With his fascination for the exceptional, the particular, the apocryphal, and the occult, he was himself one of the last of the antiquaries, rooting around unsystematically in the material stuff of the past, from bones to legends to manuscripts to iconography (to whistles, windows, mezzotints, mazes, Anglo-Saxon crowns, binoculars, choir stalls, curtains, and any number of books and papers), even while he had an unassailable international reputation as an academic scholar, 'already third or fourth in Europe' by his early thirties. You can see exactly why he chose to ask the antiquary Augustus Jessopp (author, we remember, of 'An Antiquary's Ghost Story') for a reference for the Disney Chair of Archaeology, at the same as you can see why this was a terrible idea in a modernizing university (William Ridgeway, who got the job, had a reference from the archetypal Victorian systematic scholar, J. G. Frazer).

So, *Ghost Stories of an Antiquary* it was, and Arnold drew up a contract on 25 July, with an astonishingly quick turnaround time: 'The MS. shall be delivered to the Publisher, complete and in a condition ready for Press, not later than July 31st 1904.'[112] Six days were allowed.

On 21 October, he wrote to Herbert: 'Proofs of my book just beginning to come in. I suppose that it is meant to be out by Xmas. I shall be rather amused at correcting proofs of so different a character to my catalogues.'[113] (This is the first we hear of the ghost stories in any of his many letters to his family, and comes at the end of a letter in which he has discussed working on the St. John's College manuscripts, an upcoming visit to Eton for a meeting of the Committee of Taste, and the possibility of Lionel Ford succeeding Warre as Eton headmaster. The stories are a long way down his list of priorities.) 'I see rumours of a book of Ghost stories', Sydney wrote from his new job as Headmaster of Malvern on 6 November, by which time MRJ had more or less finished the proofs.[114] The book was published in time for Christmas.

Ghost Stories of an Antiquary came with a short preface by MRJ, which is in effect a dedication and a memorial to James McBryde:

> I wrote these stories at long intervals, and most of them were read to patient friends, usually at the season of Christmas. One of these friends offered to illustrate them, and it was agreed that if he would do that, I would consider the question of publishing them. Four pictures he completed, which will be found in this volume, and then, very quickly and unexpectedly, he was taken away. This is the reason why the greater part of the stories are not provided with illustrations. Those who knew the artist will understand how much I wished to give a permanent form to even a fragment of his work; others will appreciate the fact that here a remembrance is made of one in whom many friendships centred.[115]

The strong suggestion here is that book was *only* published on the understanding that McBryde would do the illustrations, and that it is *primarily* being published as a vehicle for McBryde's illustrations, and as a memorial to the man and his friendship.

McBryde was only able to complete four illustrations for the book. Two are for 'Canon Alberic'—Dennistoun 'deep in his notebook' in the cathedral of St. Bertrand (which McBryde drew from photographs), and Dennistoun in his room at night with the scrap-book, happily smoking his pipe and yet to notice the demon that has appeared behind him. In both cases, Dennistoun is clearly based on MRJ himself: the drawing in the Cathedral is, Gurney Lubbock averred, 'an easily recognizable sketch of Monty himself: the bend of the knee alone would identify it'.[116] The other two were from 'Oh, Whistle'—a brilliant representation of Parkins cowering behind a groyne, with a sheeted spirit pursuing in the distance, and one of Parkins menaced by the ghost in his hotel room. 'I don't think I ever liked anything better than illustrating your stories', McBryde wrote, in the last letter he ever sent MRJ. 'To begin with I sat down and learned advanced perspective and the laws of shadows, etc etc.' He drew the images very large, on 'yards of paper', and thought that the drawing of Parkins behind the groyne 'is certainly the best thing I've ever done'.[117] 'My dear boy . . . I like the etching very much. You have evidently got hold of the thing, & I expect will make a great success of it', MRJ wrote when he saw some of the preliminary sketches.[118] He had begun a few more of these preliminary sketches, which Gwen gathered together for MRJ: one for 'Number 13', two for 'Count Magnus', and one for 'The Ash-Tree', in which 'The spider tree was to be from an Ingmanthorpe work'—a sketch of a tree James had come across in the grounds of a Yorkshire manor house.[119] For 'Count Magnus', James had begun a sketch of the Count's sarcophagus, with Mr Wraxall stooping to pick up a padlock. But, he wrote, 'I think the best picture will be Mr. Wraxall seeing two figures standing in the moonlight at the crossroads while driving in his closed fly'. His last words are mysterious, tantalizing: 'Didn't you once write a story about a troglodyte?'[120]

MRJ's friends loved the book, of course. 'I hear you have published a book of ghost stories wh. I must procure. They must be a pleasant change from apocryphal gospels, & both alike are children of your fantasy', Ronny Norman wrote, rather astutely, on 18 December.[121] Arthur Benson didn't like the book's cover, which he thought looked like 'sackcloth' (it does, rather), but confessed that 'my blood freezes pleasantly as I peep'.[122] 'They have terrified me', Herbert Tatham said, listing 'Count Magnus' as his favourite.[123] Eustace Talbot wrote on 26 December:

> I have also read with much pleasure & no little trembling the Ghost Stories. You have succeeded in giving me two bad nights & one jumpy walk on a dark foggy evening in the country when every tree became possessed of horrible long arms & every step was dogged by hideous echoes about 10 yards behind! So I think you may be congratulated on your result.[124]

Maisie Cropper's sister Edith wrote to tell MRJ that the whole family had been reading *Ghost Stories of an Antiquary*: 'I have shivered over "Lost Hearts" . . . We all like the pictures—especially the man tumbling over the breakwater.'[125] 'I do like your ghost stories', Billy Cropper wrote:

> I think the best of them as one reads them, and the worst of them, when one [has] blown out the candle, is that they begin with such trifling little things.

> Anything might make a beginning. If the bed squeaks louder than usual or the cistern outside my door, it may be an incident in a blood-curdling story.[126]

Arthur Hamilton-Gordon, his travelling companion to French cathedrals, was particularly interested in 'Canon Alberic', but thought 'you make a mistake in giving a picture of the St. Bertrand Devil. His precise form and the terrors of his hand are best left to the imagination.'[127] While he was writing 'The Treasure of Abbot Thomas', MRJ had written to Mark Sykes for suggestions. 'As regards your ghost in the well, I suggest a weir-wolf, which you have not got—Cerberus in fact.' He thought that the hellhound should appear to the sound of the 'Dies Irae'.[128] Undaunted by the fact that MRJ had completely ignored his advice, he wrote with further suggestions for future ghost stories: 'what about a mechanical man ghost, i. e. a copper man with a bad spirit attached—held in by a word of power, or by [a pentangle]—or with seven metals in seven holes in his chest, each of great talismanic power.'[129] (He'd obviously been giving this quite a lot of thought. MRJ ignored this suggestion, too.)

Beyond MRJ's immediate circle, the book was warmly received. The Prince of Wales, the future Edward VIII, let MRJ know, via an Oxford intermediary, that he was an admirer.[130] The Director of the Cambridge Observatory arranged an evening of MRJ's ghost stories, in which the Observatory's lights were dimmed so that they could be read aloud by candlelight.[131] Reading with a specialist's eye, William Kirk Dickson, a librarian at Edinburgh University Library, Keeper of the Advocates' Library, and future Librarian of the National Library of Scotland, was particularly appreciative of 'Canon Alberic': 'Perhaps it makes a more intimate appeal to a librarian! We have one or two pretty devilish MSS. in the Library. I shall keep a more careful eye on them in future.'[132] A. E. Housman thought the stories 'not like any others that I know, and very satisfactorily appalling'. A few years later, in November 1913, he sent a copy of *Ghost Stories of an Antiquary* to Thomas Hardy, particularly recommending 'Oh, Whistle' and 'Count Magnus': 'I hope that you may find some pleasure in them, if read in broad daylight.' Hardy replied that 'I was agreeably sensible of their eeriness, even though the precaution was taken of reading them at a safe distance from bed-time'.[133] That Christmas, Hardy sent a MRJ congratulatory Christmas card, 'in a fit of enthusiasm', after reading the ghost stories with his wife.[134]

Reviews in the press were mixed, with some readers not quite sure what to make of the book. *The Athenaeum*, an augustly self-important cultural organ, was out of the gates quickly with a very positive review:

> Read in suitable circumstances, *Ghost Stories of an Antiquary*, by M. R. James (Arnold), cannot fail to produce a series of thrills. Dr. James uses his multifarious erudition with effect to produce a background of vraisemblance. We see no reason to lament the fact that the stories are scholarly in their setting rather than journalistic . . . In fact, the whole thing is done in the best way—the way to carry conviction. The best story, to our thinking, is 'O whistle and I'll come to you, my lad', but all the eight maintain a very level quality of excellence, and do credit to Dr. James's imagination.[135]

The Spectator's reviewer affirmed that the stories were 'things to be read by *daylight*'.[136] The reviewer in the *New York Times* was rather more equivocal: 'Mr James manages at times to give you a pretty well-defined creepy feeling—but his ghost stories are not quite the real thing in spite of the pains he takes to pile up detail in the setting and leave the horror itself as undefined, shapeless, and elusive as may be.'[137]

But the last word on the matter surely belonged to Bardolf Barker, who sent his alter-ego an unsigned review of *Ghost Stories of an Antiquary*. Barker's was one of a series of fake reviews MRJ fabricated for the book, including ones from the *Daily Express* ('THE FLESH CREEPS! . . . AN ATTACK ON SCIENCE') and the *Sketch* ('A new light has sprung into the ranks of the Mystics . . . Dr James is a bold young man, he may go far').[138] But Barker surpassed them all:

> Proffessor James in "His Ghost Stories of an Antiquarian" has made a startling contribution to modern Spiritist fiction of the hair lifting order—
>
> Proffessor James is better know in Classic circles rather than in the realms of Literature—but he has a distinct and vigorous style all his own none the worse perhaps for a sprinkling of old world knoledge rich in legend, fact and fancy—in the course of his entertaining little work, the Proffessor introduces some delightful touches from his varied palette, his scintillating descriptions breath the air of the scholar worthy of the combination room of one of our most venerable Alma maters—

Barker's final judgement is surely definitive: 'Readers will do well to do more than skip this little work.'[139]

* * *

As his letters home suggest, the publication of the ghost stories was hardly MRJ's top priority in the busy year of 1904. By 1900, he had already published his manuscript catalogues of King's, Sidney Sussex, Jesus (all 1895), and Peterhouse (1899). He had spent a large part of the new century cataloguing the manuscripts of Trinity College, and the results were published in four volumes, 1901–1904. In 1904, he also published a manuscript catalogue of the library of

Emmanuel College. 1905 saw the publication of the catalogues of Christ's, Pembroke, Queens', and Clare Colleges. 1907 was Gonville and Caius (with a second volume in 1908) and Trinity Hall; 1909, Magdalene; 1913, St. John's; and, a straggler, in 1925, St. Catharine's. As Lord Acton had asked: how did he do it?

In March 1903, he had been elected to the British Academy, one of the second cohort of members following its establishment in 1902. In December of that year, he wrote to the Academy's Secretary, Israel Gollancz, proposing a gargantuan cataloguing project, to include catalogues of the manuscripts of all cathedral libraries, all the great London institutions (Lambeth Palace, the Inns of Court, Westminster Abbey, and many others), the Scottish Universities, Marsh's Library in Dublin, 'the great private collections, as far as possible', the collections of the public schools, of municipalities, and of parish churches. 'I am of the opinion', he concluded, 'that the work, if rightly organized, could be brought to a successful issue within a very few years.'[140] This project was absurdly ambitious for any one scholar, but he managed an amazing amount of it, cataloguing Lambeth Palace (four volumes), Westminster Abbey, the John Rylands Library at Manchester, Aberdeen University Library, and very much else besides.

He also made some headway with 'the great private collections', including those of Frank McClean and J. Pierpont Morgan, who shipped his MSS to MRJ across the Atlantic in a specially made locked box, for cataloguing.[141] Most importantly, he worked on the collection of Henry Yates Thompson, the preeminent living English manuscript collector. The son of a wealthy Liverpool banker, Thompson was the publisher of the *Pall Mall Gazette* (whose offshoot, the *Pall Mall Magazine*, had—perhaps not coincidentally—published 'Lost Hearts' in 1895). He was also a serious scholar, who graduated with a First in the Classical Tripos in 1862 (part of the same graduating class as R. C. Jebb and Henry Jackson), and won the Porson Prize, and the Browne Medal twice. In 1893, he had set about collecting the finest private manuscript collection in the world, and in 1896 he employed MRJ to catalogue it, often travelling to Cambridge to bring him the manuscripts in person.[142] Thompson had a unique philosophy of collecting: he would at all times limit his collection to one hundred manuscripts, of only the finest and rarest kind. Whenever he acquired a new one, he sold one of his collection to make room for it.[143] Between 1898 and 1912, MRJ published four volumes of catalogues of the Thompson collection.

Outside the world of scholarship, in late 1904 MRJ once again found himself embroiled in institutional politics, and (again, not for the first or the last time) in direct competition with one of his oldest friends. His own account of things, in a letter to his father of 22 November, is rather offhand: 'Arthur

Benson & I have lately been put forward as candidates to represent the assistant masters on the [Eton] Governing Body: but finding that the election was being run on party lines, we both agreed to withdraw: a good deal to my relief.'[144] MRJ is being characteristically diffident, though probably not disingenuous; but nevertheless, there was a lot more going on here, certainly as far as Arthur was concerned. As his biographer, David Newsome, writes, this seat on the Governing Body was something that 'Arthur wanted unreservedly. It would give him a real position at Eton and a chance of prosecuting the reforms he really wanted to see.'[145] In particular, Arthur had long dreamed of removing, or at least softening, the requirement for compulsory Greek in the Eton curriculum. This, as we saw in Chapter 5, was a highly controversial matter for educators of Arthur's generation, and so the election to the Governing Body became a proxy war for larger political issues. MRJ was approached to see whether he would run. Hugh Macnaghten, a contemporary of both Arthur and MRJ since their schooldays, and now an Assistant Master at Eton, wrote to Arthur telling him that he was 'supposed to represent the anti-tutorial, anti-Classical system'. The Classicists, Arthur thought, would vote 'en bloc' for MRJ: 'He has been chosen as a Tory, without any reference to his fitness to represent the Liberal element, which is after all in a majority.'[146] Arthur, in fact, thought MRJ would be a terrible choice all round:

> M.R.J. is in education a strong reactionary; but I don't think he wd. be a good person as he is a bad man of business &c, never wd. answer letters, & would, I think, take no further trouble except to throw his influence strongly against all modernizing of curriculum.[147]

At Herbert Tatham's suggestion, MRJ and Arthur met privately to discuss things. They went for a drive together and decided that both should withdraw their names, 'MRJ . . . feeling, as I did, that the thing must not be run on party lines'.[148] Recognizing the public, political nature of this debate, Arthur went so far as to print and circulate a withdrawal of his candidature:

> But it only came home to me in the course of the last few days that the election was beginning to be viewed as a party matter; and that a large and important minority, including many of my best and oldest friends, whose views I regard with much respect, were definitely of the opinion that I had taken too pronounced a side on practical politics, and expressed opinions of too liberal a character to be regarded as a comprehensive or impartial representative.[149]

Arthur found the whole affair 'humiliating and mortifying': 'I have missed the one thing I desired, a seat on the G.B.—though assured to me by a majority.'[150] Arthur's mental health was never strong, and he began to have real problems sleeping. The second half of his life was blighted by a series of extraordinarily debilitating breakdowns that sometimes lasted for years at a time. One of the worst of these took place between 1907 and 1910, though one can see the beginnings of it around this time. The causes of Arthur's breakdowns are complex: his own individual psychological makeup, in which the pressures of conformity and respectability were pushed beyond their limits; his outrageously dysfunctional family history; his increasingly tormented awareness of his own sexuality: 'I don't think I am an entirely conventional person', he wrote in January 1905.[151] But the depression seems also to have stemmed from his growing sense of being publicly and professionally thwarted, of never quite achieving the institutional recognition that was his due. He felt, he confessed to Luxmoore, 'wounded and sore'.[152]

It's no accident that it's from around this time that we get some of Arthur's most bitterly critical observations of MRJ, a close friend whose intellectual and institutional status was far more assured, but who didn't seem unduly to care about matters which caused Arthur enormous anguish. 'The more I see of him', Arthur wrote, 'the more I feel what a funny comfortable little paddock Monty's mind is—every year the hedge grows a little higher.'[153]

> Monty has *no* intellectual, religious, or philosophical interests really. He just has some aesthetic perceptions, antiquarian tastes, & a wonderful memory. But there has never been any stress or wrestling. He has just gone peaceably on, in his natural & simple instincts. It is a beautiful way of life, in a way, but a superficial one when all is said.[154]

Arthur's life contained a lot of 'stress or wrestling'. He found other people's admiration for MRJ increasingly irksome, or even mystifying. When A. B. Ramsay 'talked with profound admiration of Monty James, & his mind', Arthur reflected in his diary:

> Now I don't think Monty James is in the Palace at all—he seems to me to be nothing but a servant in an antechamber, handing things to those who go in. MRJ has an immense & accurate memory for details . . . but not the least constructive or practical power. He is *very* humorous too—but after all his mind is the mind of a nice child—he hates & fears all problems, all *speculation*, all originality or novelty of view. His spirit is both timid and unadventurous. He is *much* abler than I am, much better, much more effective—but I feel that he is a kind of child.[155]

Arthur Shipley and Stephen Gaselee were both convinced that MRJ was 'a man of genius, among the 4 greatest of Cambridge men'. Arthur strongly disagreed: 'Monty's knowledge is extraordinarily accurate & minute; but mainly concerned with unimportant matters, & his mind has *nothing* constructive in it. He seems to me to be an almost perfect instance of high talent; a perfect second-rate man.'[156] Things got worse in 1905 when MRJ was elected Provost of King's, another position Arthur dreamed of.

* * *

'To me', MRJ wrote in *Eton and King's*, 'the game of political intrigue on a small (or large) scale has never been interesting.'[157] Perhaps not, but he was remarkably good at it. No political innocent has ever been elected head of an Oxbridge college.

To everyone's shock, Augustus Austen Leigh dropped dead in the Provost's Lodge at King's on 28 January 1905, following an attack of angina at the relatively young age of sixty-four. 'It was a quite sudden and seemingly painless death', MRJ observed. 'He was found sitting in his chair.'[158] Austen Leigh was not a distinguished scholar (his only published work had been a history of King's, which came out in 1899), but he was a great institutionalist, deeply dedicated to his College, and he had been, during his time as Tutor, a momentous yet tactful curricular reformer, significantly responsible for bringing King's into the modern world. Who should replace him? There was a lot at stake.

The date of the election was fixed for 13 May. 'The lobbying inseparable from the election of the Provost has now begun', MRJ informed his father. J. Willis Clark gave MRJ a stern talking-to, informing him 'with great severity' that he was 'the only possible person' for the role.[159] Sydney wrote from Malvern, exhorting him to run: 'The College would be safe in your hands . . . I feel that in these days of ceaseless and sometimes unnecessary chopping & changing, your influence would be conservative without bigotry.'[160] On 6 February, barely a week after Austen Leigh's death, MRJ wrote that 'The Provostship is said to be "between Walter Durnford & me" but I don't see myself in that chair. The man I want is Arthur Benson.'[161] He wrote to Arthur, telling him that he 'did not *at all* desire' the Provostship, and urging him to consider standing.[162] Arthur, who was now back in Cambridge in a full-time capacity, having been elected a Fellow of Magdalene in 1904, sent a warm reply: 'I never thought it was likely . . . that anyone so little identified with the place as myself wd appeal to the electors. So it only remains to me as another proof of your confidence & affection—of which things indeed I needed no further proof—& yet I can't help being grateful.' (Arthur's feelings towards his oldest friend were particularly complicated around this time.) Speaking candidly, Arthur tried to discourage MRJ from running for a job which 'I don't think . . . would add at all to your happiness . . . The principal use of the Head of House is to manage a lot of rather opinionated men—well, I think you would do it with great skill, but I don't think you wd like doing it.' Some aspects of the job, Arthur thought, would be a 'nightmare' for MRJ.[163] Was Arthur trying to talk MRJ out of applying for a job he knew he wanted himself? Arthur wrote in his diary that MRJ's letter had convinced him that 'I had an excellent chance . . . Well, it needed no consideration. It is difficult to imagine anything I should like better . . . It wd suit me ten times better than Eton.'[164] (In early 1905, Arthur was in fact interviewed for the Headmastership of Eton, but then categorically refused to be considered for the job.)

In the event, the 1905 Provostial (or Praeposital, in King's parlance) election was a four-horse race. Reservations notwithstanding, MRJ was persuaded to run (I suspect he didn't need very much persuasion). The other candidates were Arthur, Walter Durnford, and George Prothero. Arthur and MRJ had known Water Durnford for years, ever since he taught them at Eton. Durnford was forced to retire from Eton in 1899 due to gout, and had returned to King's where, as an unmarried man, he still held a Fellowship under the statutes of 1861. 'W.D.', Arthur thought, 'is in no sense a man of eminence, but he wd. make, I think, a *very* good Provost indeed: better than any of the others.'[165] Others shared Arthur's low opinion of Durnford as a scholar. J. H. Clapham thought that he 'viewed the idea of academical research with especial aversion'.[166] Walter Headlam was one of several friends and correspondents who wrote to MRJ expressing their concerns that Durnford was not sufficiently intellectually distinguished for the Provostship: 'What people want is not so much a business manager as a scholar with the right ideals for the College.'[167] The King's graduate Reggie Balfour agreed: 'I feel that character and mind matter much more in a Provost than facility in business or genius for entertaining.'[168] But (almost) everyone liked Walter Durnford—and on 29 March, Durnford wrote to MRJ to tell him that, while he was still standing for the election, MRJ nevertheless had his support.

George Prothero, though, was really the competition. Prothero, a historian of medieval and early modern England, was certainly a distinguished scholar, and had put King's on the map as a centre for the study of history. He had also been a very effective Tutor from 1876–94, at which point he had left Cambridge to take up a Chair of History at Edinburgh. After his return to King's in 1899, he was well placed to stand for the Provostship. He was, however, according to Nathaniel Wedd, a slightly suspicious figure to some of the College's conservatives, because of his perceived lack of orthodoxy and of deference to traditions, and so these Fellows looked for a more traditionally minded candidate.[169] There was certainly one of those knocking around—but would he run?

As institutional academic politics tend to, it was about to get more complicated. Due to anxieties about his wife's health, Prothero declined to stand for election. It seems likely that it's at this point, after Prothero had withdrawn, that MRJ allowed his name officially to go forward as a candidate. 'I have signified to the Vice Provost that I consent to be voted for as Provost', he wrote. 'The balance of duty seemed to verge that way. Certainly not of inclination. Quod bene vertat deus [May God look favourably on this].'[170] Indeed, on 24 March, Prothero wrote to MRJ expressing his support: 'the College will have good cause to congratulate itself if it gets for its Provost one on whom I always think the mantle of dear old Bradshaw has fallen.'[171] After deciding to stand, Wedd recalled, 'Monty James . . . sent to the fellows an analysis of his possible defects as Provost. It was an extraordinary exhibition of self-knowledge and honesty, and it only made his supporters more anxious to have him as Provost.'[172] Then, on 15 April, a close friend of the Protheros, Ida Darwin (Charles Darwin's daughter-in-law, and an important figure in Cambridge life), wrote to MRJ to tell him that Mrs Prothero had persuaded her husband to stand after all.[173] MRJ wrote to the Fellows, exhorting them not to feel bound by any pledges they had made to him now that Prothero was back in the race.

'The many minded Prothero has reconsidered his decision and re-entered the lists', MRJ told Herbert. 'I am just a little annoyed with Prothero for not making up his mind to more purpose at an earlier date, for he would have saved me a good deal of commotion by so doing. But he was always inclined to wobble.'[174] In the event, Prothero's perceived dithering may have cost him the Provostship. For one thing, it had afforded MRJ the opportunity to behave with integrity, even as he got involved in the inevitable lobbying and politicking. When the ballots were counted, the result was MRJ 25 votes, George Prothero 16, Walter Durnford 3, and Arthur Benson 2. 'Well, it is done; and it is a very curious thing', Arthur wrote: in a strange turn of events, Walter Durnford had voted for him (he seems to have supported everybody; it was considered bad form to vote for oneself).[175] MRJ had won with an overall majority. There was, however, some grumbling that this landslide had been secured with the aid of some of King's last remaining backwoodsmen, representatives of the old Eton-King's axis—most particularly Augustus's brother Edward Austen Leigh (the Lower Master of Eton, known as 'The Flea' for his propensity to draw blood while caning boys—an activity which, according to one authority, 'he gave every indication of enjoying'), and Sydney's great friend Frank Rawlins.[176] These, the University Librarian A. F. Scholfield recalled, were 'both Life Fellows under the old statutes who came up from Eton to vote—to the discomfiture of the rival faction!'[177]

Congratulations came flooding in, from all quarters. 'I *know* you are the right man', the archaeologist Arthur Bather wrote, 'and that King's under your guidance will be true to its best traditions and still better future.'[178] Reggie Balfour, a King's Classics graduate who, like his close friend Hugh Benson, had recently converted to Roman Catholicism, was confident that 'The College will be presided over by the best scholar and the best Christian that it claims'.[179] Henry Broadbent, who had taught MRJ at Eton, and whose views of academic administration were very much of the old school, wrote to congratulate him, and to 'hope that you new duties will not seriously interfere with your work!'.[180] Others expressed versions of the same: 'How absurd—& how magnificent!', Arthur Hort, the son of F. J. A. Hort, and most definitely an institutional reactionary, wrote from Harrow.[181] No less a figure than Richard Claverhouse Jebb wrote that 'King's is at present the foremost representative (I think) of the humanistic spirit among the Colleges of Cambridge, and no one could more fitly preside over such a society than yourself'.[182] (Jebb had a *very* conservative definition of 'the humanistic spirit'.) Of all MRJ's circle, it was Cecil Knatchbull-Hugessen who best expressed the relief that his appointment gave to traditionalists:

> If learning is of value & Greek to be encouraged, with a pass degree & a second class Archbishop of Canterbury & Headmaster of Eton, the blessed virgin was entitled to expect a proper appointment at one of her seats of learning at all events, if she still takes interest in such heretic institutions.[183]

In a rather less political vein, Augustus Austen Leigh's widow, Florence, wrote very graciously that 'You must let me be an elder sister to you'.[184] The great historian G. M. Trevelyan hoped that his new role would not stop him from writing ghost stories: 'I hope you will not be deprived of second sight, and that a Provost's Ghost Stories will be considered *de regle*.'[185] (He had no cause to worry there.) Luxmoore got in touch with some practical advice. Now was the time, he thought, given his new public-facing role, for MRJ to take an old problem in hand: 'So why not get a front tooth—I believe they are cheap second hand & you will find them good for health too & a comfort in every way.'[186]

There were rituals and formalities to be undergone. Edward King, the Bishop of Lincoln, was soon in touch to arrange dates for MRJ's formal investiture as Provost in Lincoln Cathedral. On 16 May, he was admitted to an Eton Fellowship, something which must have pleased him very much. The Provost's Lodge was his—but not quite yet.

It was only with the greatest reluctance that MRJ finally left his rooms on the top floor of the Wilkins Building. This was the end of an era. 'I simply can't bear to think of your rooms becoming Another's, & of you retreating behind a locked door', Percy Lubbock wrote, speaking for many of MRJ's friends.[187] 'Undergraduates', Arthur Hamilton-Gordon recognized, 'cannot bounce into the Lodge, throw themselves into a chair and demand a cigar and a cup of tea.'[188] It wasn't until the end of the year that he was ready to move in. He spent Christmas 1905 in Malvern with Sydney and Linda (there were no ghost stories that year), and took up residence when he got back. But it wasn't just reluctance to move: the Provost's Lodge needed extensive (and expensive) renovation. The Provost's Lodge Improvement Account handled bills for over £900, including for building a new bathroom with 'circulating water supply', a new scullery, an enlarged front hall, drainage, and much more besides (including a new dustbin).[189] He put in a new back door with a handle, so that undergraduates could come and go: 'your plan *may* enable you to keep up more or less intercourse with the undergraduates, but I am not sanguine', Hamilton-Gordon wrote.[190] He also got a new cat.

'Obviously you will now have to marry!'[191] Edward Chenevix Austen Leigh (not the E. C. Austen Leigh who had helped to vote MRJ in) was probably joking, and others unquestionably thought differently. 'Mrs. D.', a Cambridge lady, 'speaking with vexation of Monty', complained to Arthur that the new Provost 'doesn't like women; will close the Lodge to them'.[192] MRJ's reputation for misogyny was certainly, by this stage, very widespread. *The Granta* closed its profile of the incoming Provost with an anecdote:

> Although he shines in any society, he affects that of ladies only in a minor degree. A certain trio of Grey sisters with wimples will probably remember, after the lapse of 20 years, their invasion of his rooms on a collecting mission. With an alacrity that left them full of expectation, he passed into his bedroom, as if to unhoard his treasure, and it dawned upon the patient ladies only by degrees that he had made his exit by the window and transferred his embarrassment to themselves. This power of deciding and acting with promptitude has never deserted him.[193]

Writing in 1980, the King's historian L. P. Wilkinson had a go at summing up the consensus view on MRJ's Provostship from within the College:

> Everyone liked 'Monty'. As a bachelor, he made the Lodge accessible to all, fitting a new door-handle so that no one need ring the bell. The hall was equipped with decanters and syphons, tobacco and cards . . . Monty James was above all a man for peace and goodwill. He hated squabbles such as O.B. generated. But a

> distaste for controversy about college affairs is not altogether a good thing in a Head. It may lead to inertia. And in most controversies one side deserves support more than the other.[194]

Perhaps unconsciously, Wilkinson thought, MRJ was attempting to re-create the Old Etonian 'Best Set' that Nathaniel Wedd had complained about when he arrived in King's in the 1880s. These were the kinds of people around whom MRJ felt most at home.

'There is no doubt that Monty made a good Provost in his own way.'[195] This is Wedd's own verdict on MRJ's Provostship. Wedd could never shake his worries about MRJ's personal, political, aesthetic, and intellectual conservatism. He was often justified in this. MRJ's cultural views were very narrow, and so he was hardly likely to turn the College into a centre for the arts. In 1909 for example, he vetoed a performance of Elgar's *The Dream of Gerontius* in King's Chapel, because it was based on a poem by John Henry Newman, and he found it 'too papistical' (he and Arthur had an argument about this: Edward Elgar was Arthur's friend, and in 1902 the pair had collaborated to write 'Land of Hope and Glory').[196] Wedd had supported Prothero for Provost because he thought that, under his guidance and with his wife's gift for social ease, 'the Lodge would have been a centre where all subjects were discussed, fiercely and without prejudice, and men of distinction in every branch of science, art, social and political life would have met'.[197] This wasn't going to happen under MRJ's leadership. But over time Wedd came to recognize that MRJ had admirable qualities as a Provost. He was, for one thing, a surprisingly effective chair of meetings, able to exert a quiet control over some of the College's more rumbustious egos. More importantly, Wedd confided to Arthur that 'everyone feels like they have a *friend* at the head of King's, not a mere kindly man, like the late Provost, but a sympathetic friend'.[198]

Other verdicts were more hostile. The King's History don W. F. Reddaway thought that MRJ simply had no educational principles or policy, and was '*purely* emollient': 'I felt that under *no* circumstances was it conceivable that Monty should make even a tolerable Provost—it is this hateful prestige that attaches to the post: so many people wd. like it that a compromise is necessary, & it falls to the most inoffensive man.'[199] O.B., unsurprisingly, felt malevolent, complaining that King's had come under 'the influence of Monty James and Walter Durnford and has fallen into the bondage of both, and God help it!'[200] The eminent King's musicologist Edward Dent liked to cultivate beautiful young male disciples, whom he called his 'Swans', and was furious when some of them started to visit the Provost's Lodge:

> But it is too bad: as you know, Denis [Browne] is my very particular swan just at present . . . And now Clive [Carey] comes and hands him over to the Lodge! . . . you may say I ought to have personality enough to hold my friends myself—I lost Clive when Percy [Lubbock] handed him over to James . . . James hates leaders as he hates philosophers.[201]

There is a strong element of personal and sexual jealousy in Dent's complaint, a resentment that MRJ's recreated 'Best Set' was made up of too many good-looking young men (Denis Browne was a close friend of Rupert Brooke; Clive Carey's brother Gordon, whom we will meet soon, came nearer than anyone to supplying the romantic gap left in MRJ's life by McBryde's death). But there is also, and relatedly, a social and political anxiety that MRJ's Provostship would simply arrest progress.

Arthur Benson, now deep in 'the valley of humiliation', felt this too.[202] His feelings about his old friend's new role, the job he had wanted, were understandably conflicted. He recognized that 'Monty, Head of a House, in his sad robes is most refreshingly the reverse of *stiff*—always willing to get slightly intoxicated at College dinners and break into 'the voice of a drunken rustic'.[203] No one found him ponderous, pompous, intimidating, or overbearing. He performed his duties, Arthur thought, 'kindly, benevolently, disinterestedly, & faithfully'. 'But', he worried, 'he will simply be a *Head* on the old lines—reactionary, against novelty & progress. He will initiate nothing.'[204]

Arthur's concern that MRJ would simply hate the job seems to have been vindicated almost immediately. Within a few days of his election, he wrote to Billy Cropper that the role involved 'a great deal of wear and tear of plant and rolling stock as the income tax paper truly says'.[205] Again and again over the next years, Arthur's diaries record conversations in which his old friend bemoans his fate, and threatens to resign. In early 1906, he lamented, 'Well, to speak quite frankly, I find there is nothing which I do, *qua* Provost, which I don't hate'.[206] Later that year, he confessed to Arthur that 'he had no policy, desired freedom, hated business. The shadow has fallen very quickly. He said he contemplated resignation, with a Fellowship.'[207]

Arthur, though, is hardly a disinterested observer, and tends for his own reasons to accentuate the negative. MRJ did not resign the Provostship, and found plenty about it that he enjoyed: the sociability, the ceremony and ritual (he loved sitting in his special stall in the Chapel), and even the occasional moments of comedy and absurdity. He was delighted when, in September 1905, he got a letter from one Marco Conegliano, applying for the position of King's rowing coach.[208] Conegliano was a Venetian gondolier.

Christmas 1906, MRJ's first in the Lodge, was a memorable one. The snow lay deeply on the ground on Christmas Eve, and MRJ had gathered together a party of his closest friends to hear his latest ghost story. Writing on Christmas Day, Arthur captured the occasion in his diary:

> But tho' Luxmoore is as dear, as brave, as good as ever, *he is an old man*. His outline is thinned & indistinct. He has come to the end of his mental growth & he has no wish to not intention of revising his opinions . . . Tea & the conversation became occult, so I melted away, wrote a little. After dinner which was pleasant, [MRJ] told the story of the usher, *Memento putei*—a good story—& so to bed.[209]

Luxmoore was fading away, becoming ghostly. No wonder, on that snowy Christmas Day, that Arthur should be so aware of the passing of time. The story had taken him back over thirty years, to his and MRJ's shared childhood at Temple Grove School, the place MRJ had loved and Arthur hated. *Memento putei inter quatuor taxos*. 'Remember the well among the four yews.'[210] 'A School Story' was the first thing MRJ wrote for his second collection of ghost stories.

* * *

Late on a warm June evening in 1904, on the night of Walter Fletcher's wedding, MRJ was walking though the grounds of Ellergreen with Walter's best man, Eustace Talbot. The pair talked, as MRJ loved to do, about James McBryde; they discussed the shock of his death, and the great loss MRJ felt. Eustace was now working as a junior doctor in St. Bartholomew's Hospital, and his medical career had given him a new perspective on death. 'He . . . told me', MRJ recalled, 'something of what he thought and had seen of death: how easy it seemed was the process of dying: how evident it was to him that death was not the end: and how sure he had come to be that love was at the back of it all.'[211]

'This talk, however', he continued, 'was the last of its kind.'[212] On 26 May 1905, just a few days after MRJ had been elected Provost, Eustace Talbot died of the chronic pulmonary condition which had afflicted him for several years. Exactly a week earlier, he had got engaged. 'I know it will have cut deep into your large heart', a mutual friend wrote to MRJ in condolence.[213] A few years later, MRJ was able to sum up his feelings for Eustace:

> I think of him as an embodiment of life, strength, humour, and affection; a presence always hailed with delight, for whom it was impossible to outstay his welcome. He is a keystone on the structure of many lives, and, like almost all who enlist affection, he was absolutely unconscious of how much difference he made.[214]

New friends could replace at least some of MRJ's losses, assuage some of his grief, and by far the most important of these was Gordon Carey. Carey is really the last of the young men MRJ seriously took under his wing, the last to whom he can really be said to have been devoted. Gordon, in his turn, recognized that MRJ 'was indeed a great man'.[215] Gordon Vero Carey first met MRJ in 1897, as a ten-year-old chorister in King's School, and his first impression was of just how funny he was. Having failed to get an undergraduate scholarship at King's, Carey went up to Gonville and Caius in 1906 to study Classics. As an undergraduate, he became close to MRJ through his older brother Clive, an accomplished operatic baritone who, although a student at Clare, had connections with the King's circle, and was particularly close to the musicologist Edward Dent.[216] As an undergraduate, Gordon spent many evenings round at the Provost's Lodge. This he remembered very much as others did MRJ's rooms in the Gibbs and Wilkins Buildings, 'open to all comers at all times', and a riot of books and papers, with MRJ somewhere in the middle playing patience, or hammering out a piece by Purcell or Handel on his tuneless piano ('he plays with unflinching courage all that comes his way' was how *The Granta* archly summed up his piano playing at this time).[217] 'No man carried a vast store of learning more lightly than Monty James', Gordon thought, and he particularly remembered his fondness for singing music hall songs in character: '*'Ow are yer, 'ow are yer? / Very well. 'Ow's yerself?*'[218]

If Gordon Carey was an extremely good-looking young man, Rupert Brooke was *gorgeous*. Everyone who encountered him agreed on this (including, famously, W. B. Yeats, who called him 'the handsomest young man in England').[219] Brooke came up to King's from Rugby in 1906 to study Classics—but he was more concerned with making a sensation than with his studies. Almost as soon as he arrived, he went to visit MRJ, and on the steps of the Lodge he met a fellow-student who was to become one of his closest friends, the future Labour Chancellor of the Exchequer Hugh Dalton. Their friendship seems to have been platonic, or at least chaste, though it was certainly erotically charged; in 1908, Brooke wrote to Lytton Strachey with a fascinated and horrified account of the advances Dalton had made towards Lytton's brother James, 'waving an *immense* steaming penis in his face and chuckling softly'.[220]

In his first term, Brooke was a hit in the role of the Herald in that year's Greek Play, Aeschylus's *Eumenides*, directed by Walter Durnford, and also featuring A. F. Scholfield and Clive Carey among the cast. Brooke wore a very short, very tight skirt, and the audience, according to one attendee, was largely comprised of 'Hellenists and paedophiles'.[221] The following year, he played a role rather more suited to his talents and personality, Mephistophilis in Marlowe's *Dr Faustus*, alongside Geoffrey Keynes, Denis Browne, and George Mallory as the Pope. MRJ attended the opening night of *Faustus* together with J. Willis Clark and the librarian and Uranian poet Charles Sayle, who was very much a focal point for gay Cambridge life. (When Henry James visited Cambridge at Sayle's behest in 1907, he arranged for the pair of them to go punting with Brooke. It didn't go well. Sayle dropped the pole with a clang on James's head. James left after one night.)[222] Clark spent the entire performance very audibly whispering in MRJ's ear, complaining that the cast were 'pottering about in the dark', and repeatedly demanding to know why Rupert Brooke appeared to be carrying a biscuit tin (it was a casket).[223] In 1908, Brooke was spectacular in a production of Milton's *Comus*. Arthur Benson, who had been unimpressed by his performance in *The Eumenides*, was dazzled: 'Rupert Brooke—was very delightful to look at—he has beautiful arms & a radiant figure.'[224] As an undergraduate, Brooke also joined the Cambridge Apostles. Rupert Brooke was no one's idea of an intellectual, but in his case O.B., J. T. Sheppard, Lowes Dickinson, John Maynard Keynes, and the other Apostles were willing to make an exception. (Brooke generally tended to get what he wanted, and in 1908 he was even elected to a King's Fellowship.)

* * *

The Syndics of the Fitzwilliam Museum asked MRJ to stay on in the role of Director, at least for another two years, until a suitable replacement could be found. It was in fact 1908 before he stood down, to be replaced by Sydney Cockerell, a much more modern and professional Director. Even with the Fitzwilliam Directorship, MRJ's life as Provost was not exactly overburdened. While he complained to Herbert in February 1906 that 'a great quantity of meetings have been got through', the university terms were not long, and outside of them he had very little to do.[225] The following June, he listed his schedule for the week:

> Monday: Syndicate meeting in the afternoon.
> Tuesday: nothing
> Wednesday: nothing
> Thursday: Testimonial. Librarian at 3.
> Friday: French Professor and others to lunch.
> Saturday: College meeting.[226]

What this means is that MRJ still had plenty of free time to take holidays, something he never passed up an opportunity to do. He went cycling around

Lincolnshire with Walter Fletcher in 1904; in 1905, he went to stay with Willie Bridgeman in his new house in Shropshire, Leigh Manor, perched 900 feet up on a hilltop, and the pair went fishing. He was still determined, amongst other things, to see as many French cathedrals as he could. In April 1906, he and Walter went to France together, and he made a list of the new ones he visited: Nantes, Luçon, La Rochelle, Maillezais, Saintes.[227]

In December 1904, MRJ sent a copy of *Troll Hunt* to Thomas Anstey Guthrie, one of McBryde's London acquaintances. Guthrie, who published under the name 'F. Anstey', was a graduate of Trinity Hall and a successful comic novelist, whose first novel, the boarding school body-swap farce *Vice Versa*, in which a father changes places with his son, was one of the hits of 1882. Guthrie and MRJ became correspondents and friends: Guthrie sent MRJ a copy of one of the latter's favourite books as an adolescent, Francis Barrett's *The Magus*—which Guthrie thought had 'a want of lucidity in its instructions for raising demons which would I imagine drive a really earnest student distracted'.[228] In the summer of 1906, MRJ, Ramsay, and Guthrie went on the first of several holidays together, to Denmark. The crossing to Esbjerg was bumpy, as usual, and, writing from his old haunt of Preisler's Hotel in Viborg, MRJ's mind went back to the times he'd spent in Scandinavia with McBryde and Will Stone, now both dead, just a few years earlier: 'all these places full of associations', he told Herbert.[229]

His Provostial duties also left him plenty of time for reading, and in November 1905 he published an article in the *Cambridge Review* on his favourite writer, Charles Dickens. 'The Edwin Drood Syndicate' is one of many critical and creative attempts to solve the mystery of Dickens's last, unfinished novel: who kills Edwin Drood, and why? This question has provoked many ingenious responses down the years. MRJ's solution is playful but provocative, and takes place within the context of the bureaucratic university structures through which he lived his life. He reproduces the imagined report, to the University Senate, of a Syndicate set up to investigate the crime. The Syndicate's solution is that the apparently villainous John Jasper, weakened by his opium addiction, did not succeed in strangling Edwin Drood with his black silk scarf, as the surviving portion of the novel would have us believe, and that 'It is clear that Mr Drood would have been secretly conveyed away to London in all probability as soon as he could travel'.[230] To embed these speculations further within a specific institutional context, 'The Edwin Drood Syndicate' immediately follows *another* article by MRJ, a review of J. Willis Clark's new edition of David Loggan's *Cantabrigia Illustrata* (1690), a book of engravings of Cambridge Colleges, with accompanying floor-plans.[231] The great folklorist

Andrew Lang, who had just himself published an important study of *Drood*, *The Puzzle of Dickens's Last Plot*, wrote to congratulate MRJ: 'I am glad that the Syndicate's verdict is so near my own.'[232]

Set around the Cathedral of Cloisterham (a thinly fictionalized Rochester), with its Close, its crypts, and its rigidly defined sense of institutional structure and hierarchy—its various Deans, Minor Canons, Sacristans, and Sextons—it's easy to see why *Drood*, of all Dickens's novels might have appealed to MRJ. Its influence is visible, sometimes very strongly, on several of his later stories: 'The Stalls of Barchester Cathedral', 'The Residence at Whitminster', and most especially 'An Episode of Cathedral History', a tale dripping with Droodiana. All of these are stories from the 1910s: MRJ didn't let go of *Edwin Drood*, nor of the Drood Syndicate. In 1909, in fact, he brought it to life. Calling themselves the Edwin Drood Syndicate, MRJ and five friends—Henry Jackson, Arthur Shipley, H. H. Brindley of St. John's, F. A. Potts of Trinity Hall, and Dickens's grandson Pip (Philip Charles Dickens), then a student at Trinity Hall—took themselves off to Rochester that July 'to examine the possibilities of various theories on the spot'.[233]

There was something rather Dickensian about Henry Jackson, the Regius Professor of Greek. He was one of those burly, rubicund, hot-tempered, bushy-eyebrowed types who often pop up in Dickens novels. But those who knew Jackson found him warm, loveable, and kind. Jackson was even more taken by *Drood* than MRJ was (he thought it Dickens's best novel, alongside *The Pickwick Papers*), and had peppered MRJ with questions about it while he was writing 'The Edwin Drood Syndicate', which obviously grew out of intense discussions between the pair. Anstey Guthrie put Jackson onto the existence of the original *Drood* manuscript in the Victoria and Albert, and this, along with the investigations of the Drood Syndicate, led to a book, *About Edwin Drood*, published in 1911. The book was dedicated to 'the members of the "Cloisterham Syndicate" . . . in memory of our exploration of Dickensland, 3–6 July 1909.' Jackson's conclusion, in opposition to MRJ's, was that 'Drood did not escape', and that 'Jasper buried [his body] in a heap of lime in the crypt of the Cathedral'.[234] Continuing their semi-serious scholarly game, MRJ reviewed *About Edwin Drood* in *The Cambridge Review*. Jackson's book was, he thought, 'brilliant', but its conclusion was wrong: 'The titles show that the "mystery" centered, not in the manner of Edwin's disappearance, but in the question whether he was dead or living; and again I say that Dickens's answer is far more likely to have been "Alive" than "Dead".'[235]

* * *

As Arthur had realized on Christmas Day 1906, they were all getting older, he and MRJ and their friends; mortality was taking its toll. 'Such an odd effect when M. James takes off his glasses', Arthur observed at another Christmas gathering, four years later, with what seems like genuine horror; 'he becomes an old, wrinkled, furious red-faced man with a glassy stare.'[236] At a College dinner, he was sat between MRJ and Arthur Shipley, who, he suddenly noticed, had turned into a boring, fat old blowhard, perpetually harping on perceived institutional injustices and malfeasances (very much to his disgust, he had been passed over for a university Chair), and 'very different from the young, fresh, sympathetic Don of years ago'.[237]

There had been plenty of deaths, and there would be very many more. Reggie Balfour committed suicide in 1907, aged just thirty-two. Walter Headlam, himself still a young man, dropped dead after going to a cricket match in 1908. Herbert Tatham (owner of the exploding tin of Cumberland Roast Chicken at Eton, all those years ago) was killed in a climbing accident in Chamonix in August 1909. (Tatham was always good company: an 'incurably unambitious' man, according to MRJ, whose 'impassive countenance and acute sense of humour' made him 'a dreadful neighbour when anything mirth-provoking happened in school or church or any other assembly where gravity had to be preserved'; Arthur Benson thought that 'somes of my happiest Eton recollections are of long hours wasted in his company'.)[238] Willis Clark, 'J.', died in October 1910: his death, MRJ told Gwen, 'makes a great blank'.[239] On New Year's Day 1911, Fred Whitting, King's long-term Vice-Provost, one of the fixtures of the College, collapsed dead in the smoking room of his club in London.

To no one's surprise, the Reverend Herbert James died on 6 June 1909, aged eighty-six. Arthur Benson, who hadn't seen Herbert for years, met him in the Provost's Lodge in 1907, and thought he looked 'like a Blake design of God . . . I don't think I ever saw the charm of age so graciously exhibited'.[240] He had been frail and largely immobile for many years, though right up to the end he took a keen interest in his children's lives, and in the management of Great Livermere, his home for fourty-four years (a very detailed blacksmith's bill for 1907 still survives).[241] As soon as he heard the news, Sydney headed home to the Rectory: 'I found Grace and Montie—the former quite calm, natural and collected', he told an aunt. 'Perhaps there will come more of a reaction later. It's a sad break in her life. No plan for her future settle as far as I know.'[242] Luxmoore, an old and close friend of Herbert's as well as MRJ, wrote in sympathy:

> Your father's kindness to me was extraordinary from the first, and the picture of that quiet Rectory with the venerable life in it, of your father and mother, your

> sister's care, and the band of remarkable brothers, is quite one of the most helpful and reassuring memories that I take with me as a great privilege.[243]

'His life', Luxmoore wrote elsewhere, 'has been one of singular beauty & good, though the country has not used him as much as it should. But he has given his sons, no mean inheritance, to his country in return.'[244]

MRJ dined with Arthur and Oliffe Richmond after he got back from his father's funeral. Arthur found him 'tired but not depressed', and rather surprisingly 'in particularly good spirits, the sad days over, and grateful for that'.[245] He arranged for the erection of a striking monument to his parents in Livermere churchyard—a very tall, spindly cross of dark stone, enfolded by the arms of (of course) an ash tree. You can still see it there today, though the lettering has largely been eroded by the wind blowing in across the flatlands from the North Sea, or covered by moss and lichens. What remains are the words –BERT and PAX.

8

Vice-Chancellor of Cambridge University, 1913

John Maynard Keynes was the embodiment of everything MRJ disliked. Of all the 'intellects' whose presence in and around King's troubled MRJ down the years, Keynes was probably the most impressive, and certainly the most influential. He was, by any conceivable standards, one of the twentieth century's true intellectual titans. The economic historian Charles Fay, whom he met on his first day as a student at King's (they shared a staircase on King's Lane), thought him 'the most brilliant man I have ever met or can hope to meet'.[1] Isaiah Berlin, who worked with Keynes in Washington during the Second World War, also thought he was the cleverest man he'd ever met, 'intellectually awe-inspiring'.[2] 'Keynes' intellect was the sharpest and clearest I have ever known', said Bertrand Russell. 'Annihilating argument darted out of him with the swiftness of an adder's tongue.'[3] By the time the future LSE historian and *New Statesman* editor Kingsley Martin came up to Magdalene in 1919, some people had taken to referring to the University as 'Keynesbridge'.[4] Martin, who came to know Keynes well, found him intellectually arrogant and impatient, but knew that 'He could—and did—do most things better than anyone else'.[5]

Keynes, who would have been a leading light wherever he went, was a leading light in the Apostles, which he joined at age twenty, and which formed, one of his biographers writes, 'much the strongest corporate bond of his life'.[6] Famously, he was as sexually profligate as he was intellectually fecund. One of his friends and lovers referred to him as 'Maynard, the iron copulating machine'.[7] Indeed, these two aspects of his life seem indissociable: they are John Maynard Keynes. He was a member of the Bloomsbury Group—more than this, he was the great embodiment of what the critic Ann Banfield has called 'Cambridge Bloomsbury'.[8] He was given, according to his biographer Roy Harrod, to 'devastating rudeness'.[9] Keynes came up to King's in 1902, and almost straightaway announced, 'I've had a good look round the place and come to the conclusion that it's pretty inefficient'.[10] He was invited to lunch with MRJ shortly after he arrived; immediately beforehand, he had gone to Trinity to see Lytton Strachey deliver his sensational paper 'Colloquies of Senrab', which Keynes thought 'a brilliant satire on Christianity'.[11] None of this was likely to please MRJ. 'Keynes seems to be an Apostle, full of argument & with no interest in humanity', he told Arthur Benson.[12]

But MRJ and JMK were doubles as well as opposites, and this must be understood as a major aspect of their relationship. Keynes had grown up in the world of Cambridge University. Neville Keynes, Maynard's father, was a Nonconformist who had studied at UCL in the days before the lifting of the religious tests for membership of Oxford and Cambridge. The abolition of the tests in 1871 enabled Neville to take a First in the Moral Sciences Tripos in 1875, and the following year to take up a post as a Fellow and Economics don at Pembroke (though his true métier was in university administration, and in 1910 he succeeded J. Willis Clark as University Registrary). Like MRJ a generation earlier, young Maynard went to Eton as a King's Scholar. Also like MRJ, he was, throughout his life, deeply devoted to his old school. Gurney Lubbock was his tutor, and he revered H. E. Luxmoore. He was elected President of the Literary Society in 1902, as MRJ had been in 1881. Like MRJ, he believed his 'greatest schoolboy achievement' was his election to the exclusive Pop.[13]

Of course, he went up to King's. 'There is nowhere else worth going to at Cambridge', he wrote in his last year at Eton. 'And I do not want to go to Oxford at any price.'[14] He was equally devoted to his undergraduate College, which in time he served as Fellow and Bursar. The archive of his papers about King's, detailing everything from his ideas about running the College and administering its finances, to his opinions on prospective new Fellows, to his acquisitions for the College art and manuscript collections, is vast.[15]

Recruited into the Apostles, the undergraduate Keynes was heavily influenced by Lytton Strachey, then a final-year student at Trinity. Strachey's commitment to individual expression and identity, and his contemptuous scepticism for received ideas and social respectability, were the animating principles behind his iconoclastic masterpiece, *Eminent Victorians*, the great anti-Victorian diatribe he published in 1918. No less iconoclastic, no less critical of the established order, Keynes's *The Economic Consequences of the Peace* was published the following year. As an Apostle, Strachey preached the gospel of the 'Higher Sodomy', the exalted nature of sexual relations between men. For the Edwardian Apostles, writes their historian Paul Levy, 'it was obligatory to make the humorous assumption that all sexual relations were homosexual ones, so that even heterosexual love had to be treated as only a special case of the Higher Sodomy'.[16] Keynes declared himself an 'immoralist'.[17] On the recommendation of his King's friend Charles Fay—a burly, rugby-playing Lancastrian—Keynes visited 'a low sodomitical haunt in Soho . . . where guardsmen offer their services at half a crown a bottom'.[18] Ever the economist, loving his data, he kept a detailed inventory of his sexual conquests, and the various things he got up to with each of them.

Keynes studied for the Mathematical Tripos, when he had the time. He was not really interested in Mathematics for its own sake, and so his degree results were excellent rather than brilliant: he graduated with a First in Part I in 1905, but in the middle of a rather large pack of Firsts, as Twelfth Wrangler. He did not stay on to do Part II (most people didn't), but instead sat the Civil Service exam, and got the second-highest marks that year. He went to work in the India Office, and then transferred to the Revenue, Statistics, and Commerce Department, where he wrote a Blue Book report on 'The Moral and Material Progress of India': 'A special feature of this year's edition is to be an illustrated appendix on Sodomy', he wrote, obviously pleased with his wheeze. 'In the last census returns no less that 235,000 persons gave "catamite" as their trade, profession or occupation: I was quite surprised to see that quite a number were over 50 years of age.'[19] At weekends, he was generally back in Cambridge for meetings of the Apostles, which took place on Saturdays. In the evenings, he worked on his *Treatise on Probability*, with which he hoped to secure a King's Fellowship. In 1908, he left the civil service to take up a University Lectureship in Economics, and the following year he got his Fellowship.

On his return to King's, Keynes exclaimed to the artist Duncan Grant, one of his more regular sexual partners, that 'practically everyone in Cambridge, except me, is an open and avowed sodomite' ('*except me*'?).[20] It could certainly seem that way. Several participants in the King's Founder's Day Dinner on 5 December 1909 testified that matters seemed to have got out of hand that evening. The day after, Keynes wrote to Grant:

> Yesterday evening will always mark an epoch, I think, in the history of King's manners. If there was debauchery, it was private. Manners not morals gave way. Quite suddenly our rigid rules of convention that one kisses no one in public utterly collapsed—and we all kissed . . . [E]verybody was there. What our reppers [reputations] will be, heaven knows . . . We've never behaved like this before—I wonder if we ever shall again.[21]

Arthur Benson was also there that night, and it wasn't just the dons who were kissing:

> I dare say such Saturnalia do no harm. They sate, the undergrads, all massed together, interesting and attractive in many ways—the public fondling and caressing of each other, friends and lovers sitting with arms enlaced, cheeks even touching, struck me as curious, beautiful in a way, but rather dangerous.[22]

MRJ was presiding over this dinner at high table. Unsurprisingly, there is no record of what he made of the evening. Did he even notice the 'Saturnalia' going on around him? His closest friends did, as well as everybody else.

The man who lost out to Keynes in the 1909 Fellowship competition was an Old Etonian classmate and fellow King's Scholar, Stephen Gaselee, who had just taken over from Percy Lubbock as the Pepys Librarian at Magdalene. At Eton, Gaselee and Keynes played bridge together, to the accompaniment of port and cigars, brandy and soda (Keynes usually won).[23] 'Stephen Gaselee', his friend Ronald Storrs wrote in a vivid portrait, 'was already at the age of twenty what he never ceased to be, a Cambridge Personality.'[24] He played tennis in a hair net, kept Siamese cats in his rooms, and founded a dining club, the Deipnosophists, dedicated only to the finest and most unusual food. His characteristic outfit was spats, red socks, an old-fashioned tailcoat or a silk-lined burgundy smoking-jacket, and an Eton bow tie.[25] If Storrs makes Gaselee sound completely insufferable, Arthur Benson's assessment was rather more tempered: he thought him 'a fine old crusted Tory with a strong dash of the world about him'.[26] Gaselee himself worshipped MRJ, whom he thought an incomparable scholar of 'encyclopaedic knowledge, marvellous memory, vast industry, and curious *flair* . . . I consider him in *volume* of learning the greatest scholar it has been my good fortune to know'—though he confessed that 'I never greatly cared for his (or any other) ghost stories'.[27]

In 1909, there was only one King's Fellowship available, and so it came down to a straight choice between Keynes's *Treatise on Probability* and Gaselee's commentary on Petronius. Petronius was, as Gaselee's dissertation acknowledged, a controversial choice because of 'the general question of the immorality of his work': 'There can be no doubt that in the past many good scholars and many good men have looked askance at Petronius on account of his often licentious tone, and it must be admitted at once that there are very large portions which could not be read in schools.'[28] Oliffe Richmond, who was on the assessment committee, thought that this licentiousness had shocked and alienated some of the dissertation's readers, most notably the Vice-Provost, Fred Whitting. The decision was taken after a 'tremendous all-day debate', which eventually came down to MRJ's casting vote as Provost. MRJ, Richmond thought, 'was no less scared by Keynes' than Whitting was by Gaselee; but in a move which speaks well for his intellectual and institutional judgement, as well as his impartiality, he voted for Keynes.[29]

* * *

'When is the Livermere wedding going to be? Please tell', Luxmoore wrote to MRJ in January 1910.[30] Grace was getting married. Edward John Woodhouse, a graduate of Oriel College Oxford, had been Herbert's curate at Great Livermere for a decade or more, residing with the family in the Rectory. On Herbert's death he had taken over the living as Rector of Great Livermere. Edward and Grace were married by Sydney at the church of St. Andrew Undershaft in the City of London (today, it stands right underneath the Gherkin) on 29 March 1910, with MRJ as one of the witnesses. She was fifty, he forty-one. Their marriage lasted barely four years, cut short by Edward's death on 16 August 1914, at the age of forty-five.

There is, as far as I can see, no mention of Edward Woodhouse in any of the James family correspondence, other than this one brief aside from Luxmoore, and one mention in passing in a letter from Herbert to a friend.[31] Physically and especially mentally, we know Grace was very fragile, vulnerable: was the marriage primarily to enable her to continue living in the Rectory? After Herbert's death, she lived at least part of the time with MRJ at the Provost's Lodge: this is given, perhaps partly for the sake of decorum, as her home address on the marriage certificate.

Arthur, scarcely more comfortable in the company of women than MRJ, found her presence there unbearable. In March 1910 he wrote in his diary after a dinner at the Lodge:

> The horror of the evening was that Miss James was present, shrieking out the absurdest sentiments, the wildest indiscretions, & telling stories at the top of her voice about Monty's boyhood. I don't know how he can suffer such a silly old fish in the house. She must be fifty but behaves—I am bound to say *looks*—like 22. But I rather like her, dimly, if one cd. but get behind the hysterical wild foolish exterior, which she seems to regret as much as anyone.[32]

Obviously, this tells us at least as much about Arthur as it does about Grace. He was coming out of his first very long bout of depression, and had grown rather dependent on MRJ, whom he saw very often; he came greatly to appreciate his air of security and good humour. Arthur spent a lot of time at the Lodge, and a few days before the encounter with Grace, he wrote one of his most acute sketches of his old friend:

> What a strange creature Monty is! So absolutely the same, so stubbornly Tory, so inaccessible to all ideas, so hating discussion & speculation—yet so affectionate (though I don't think he would ever miss anyone) & so full of humour that he is delightful. But if it were not for his humour, he would be frozen, dull, inaccessible, the very worst kind of Don. He does carry his learning very lightly, too—I don't suppose anyone alive knows so much or so little worth knowing! He is very dear to me—but he seems to me like a person in a pleasant dream. Or is it only that he is reticent? He hates being Provost, I think—& yet I think he would hate not being P. worse.[33]

Sometimes, MRJ would come round to Arthur's rooms in Magdalene, where they would play cards and look at old photos. 'It was a *delightful* evening', Arthur wrote of one occasion, 'Monty so funny, simple, & friendly—he even did some imitations, &c.' The Dr Crippen murder case was the news sensation of 1910, and, like much of the rest of the country, Arthur and MRJ found themselves caught up in the trial. While Arthur was convinced that 'Of course he did it', he thought it would be 'horrible' to hang this 'neatly dressed, quiet, amiable doctor.' MRJ, a keen follower of trials, who always took the side of the prosecution, dismissed Arthur's views as 'sentimentality'.[34]

After their trip to Denmark in 1906, Anstey Guthrie became one of MRJ's regular travelling companions. The following year, the pair cycled through Northern France with Ramsay. 'Most of our route, little as we knew it then, lay along the fronts of the opposing armies in the Great War', Guthrie remembered years later.[35] The three went twice in 1910—to Indre and Creuse in July; and then around Poitiers and Auxerre in September. The following year, the trio were joined by the Kingsman and Eton master A. E. Conybeare, and they cycled across Germany, getting as far as Pressburg (Bratislava), on the Hungarian border—MRJ's most far-flung cycling journey. In 1912, they were back in France, over towards the French Alps, and in 1913 they cycled around Limoges, Clermont-Ferrand, and Lyon. After 1913, there would be no more cycling holidays in Europe for some years.

In the summer of 1911, cycling through Germany, MRJ stood one foggy night on the Augustus Bridge over the Elbe, looking across to the spires of Dresden Cathedral. He was alone, and became unusually introspective. The next day he wrote a long poem. 'I leaned last night upon the crazy rail' is, for MRJ, an extraordinarily revealing document, one of the very few moments in his life when he appears to acknowledge the loneliness of the scholarly calling, and the emptiness of being the man who knew so much and so little worth knowing:

I saw within a room six candles flare
As for some party bright, but no man there—
Of hats & coats a draggled wilderness,
A doctor's gown & crown, a tumbled mess
Of Grantas, catalogues, illuminated missals,
Long-buried bills, & newly found Epistles;
And oh! Inextricably clogged with these
My dissertation's maimed hypotheses.[36]

Visions of his friends come to him in dream-form—'Much-married Morley' (Walter Morley Fletcher—only married once, but *very* married), 'blameless Ram', 'Coneybee', and others—to listen to a grotesque, phantasmagoric version of his latest ghost story, in which Walter, like Anders Bjornsen in 'Count Magnus', encounters 'A suction's shape whose palpable embrace / Might leave him for his wife without a face', and 'A huddled length of London flesh / That cased a soul athirst for beauties fresh' holds up 'a bloodied fist . . . sliced and pitted', with 'avenging nails'. The story leaves his audience, back in MRJ's rooms, alternating between horror, boredom, and some sort of guilty recognition:

The legend closed at last in blood & pulp:
The Cracked throats softened with a grateful gulp;
Then eye met furtive eye, & seemed to slip
A moment's space the joy of comradeship
Within the circle strained; one nervous laughed,
One spoke of syphons, one neat whisky quaffed.
But soon the Parodist in dormouse tones
Rehearsed a drowsy tale of dead men's bones
And laurelled paths in desert garden plot:
He droned not heeding that they heeded not,
Till one by one the lids of all the rest
Were by the poppied effluence slumber-pressed.

As the poem closes, he awakens from his vision, and sees 'Dresden spires . . . his in misty shroud / The moon outblotted by a midnight cloud'.

Something in MRJ's unconscious may have been troubled by the 'maimed hypotheses' of his flamboyantly irrelevant scholarly research, and by the nature of his relationship with his friends: the vision of Walter having his face sucked away, leaving him too disfigured for his wife's love, is certainly a startling one; and who is 'the Parodist', who tells the boring sub-MRJ ghost story? It could be Arthur Benson, or one of a number of other lesser writers of the supernatural in MRJ's circle; or, perhaps more likely given that he was actually there, it could be the comic writer Anstey Guthrie, whom MRJ may not, in the end, have liked very much. But nothing in his public life or career gave any inkling of this sense of doubt or anxiety. Returning from France in the summer of 1910, he headed up to St. Andrews to be awarded an honorary degree (to go along with the one Trinity College Dublin had awarded him three years earlier), and spent a few days afterwards with Johnnie Maxwell in Dunblane, happy, successful, and reassured.

In October 1910, MRJ was invited as Provost of King's by John Neale Dalton, Canon of Windsor and King George V's Domestic Chaplain, to the opening of the tomb of Henry VI at St. George's Chapel in Windsor Castle, 'in order to put an end to all doubt as to the resting place of the remains'.[37] MRJ travelled to Windsor, along with the Professor of Anatomy, Alexander Macalister (who had worked with MRJ on the bones at Bury Abbey back in 1903), Edmond Warre, Provost of Eton, and the antiquary William St. John Hope, to witness the exhumation of the founder of Eton and King's. Opening the leaden casket, they discovered a dismembered corpse, 'a decayed mass of human bones, lying in no definite order' (in the words of Hope's report). One of the pieces of the shattered skull had hair attached to it, apparently matted in blood, which suggested that the monarch had 'died a violent death'. Also present in the casket was what turned out to be 'the humerus of a small pig', which confirmed the idea that the body had initially been buried in the earth, and then dug up and placed in the casket: the King's bones had lain in the ground at Chertsey for thirteen years, during which time they had become compounded with animal remains.[38]

* * *

'I am delighted to hear that you have got some more Ghost Stories', Edward Arnold wrote to MRJ on 8 December 1910, 'and I hope you will add to them during the Christmas Vacation, when ghosts should be abroad!' Arnold was keen to publish MRJ's second volume of ghost stories, and willing to improve the terms: a £30 advance on royalties on publication, 15% from the start, and 20% on sales over 3000. 'This assumes a 6/- volume of not less than about 60000 words as before.'[39] *More Ghost Stories of an Antiquary* appeared the following year.

'My stories have been produced (with one exception) at successive Christmas seasons', MRJ wrote in the Preface to *More Ghost Stories*.[40] The exact dates on which MRJ first wrote or read some of the stories is unclear, but it seems likely that by the time he received Arnold's proposal, he had written five of the volume's seven stories, with a sixth to follow that Christmas.[41] 'A School Story', as we know, was written in 1906. The only other story for which we have a definite date is 'The Stalls of Barchester Cathedral', which was published as 'The Stalls of Barchester Cathedral: Materials for a Ghost Story' in the Anglican periodical *The Contemporary Review* of April 1910.[42] The 'one exception' was the collection's last and longest story, 'Mr. Humphreys and his Inheritance', which 'was written to fill up the volume'.[43]

More Ghost Stories opens with 'A School Story', in which MRJ revisited his Temple Grove days. The charismatic, doomed Irishman, Mr Sampson, called up memories of MRJ's best prep school teacher, the bearded, one-armed, mysterious Charles Geoghegan. If the volume presents the stories in the chronological order of their composition (which is possible, but by no means certain), then it's likely that the next story, 'The Rose Garden', dates from Christmas 1907.[44] The occultist and charlatan Montague Summers maintained that 'the late Dr M. R. James once told me that one of his Ghost Stories—I am not sure which but I rather fancy it might be *The Rose Garden*—was suggested to him by his recollection of a particularly vivid dream'.[45] But Summers is a notoriously unreliable, not to say mendacious writer, and there's no evidence I can find that he actually met MRJ, who unquestionably did not approve of him (see Chapter 11)—so we should treat this comment with extreme caution.

'The Rose Garden' certainly demonstrates MRJ's recurring interest in seventeenth-century English history, and particularly its religious strife, its Puritan legacy, its witch trials, and its political intrigues. In 'The Ash-Tree', Sir Matthew Fell is found 'dead and black' in bed, victim of Mrs Mothersole's supernatural arachnid vengeance. But it is widely believed that 'the Squire was the victim of a recrudescence of the Popish Plot'—the alleged plot to assassinate Charles II, fabricated by the Anglican clergyman Titus Oates in 1678 to inflame anti-Catholic prejudice.[46] Similar preoccupations animate 'The Rose Garden', a story seemingly concerning the unquiet ghost of Sir William Scroggs, Charles II's Lord Chief Justice, notorious for his savage conducting of the Popish Plot trials of 1678–9. 'The Rose Garden' also alludes to the 1605 Gunpowder Plot, in that Mrs Anstruther mistakes the apparition for 'what at first she took to be a Fifth of November mask peeping out among the branches'. But closer inspection shows otherwise:

> It was not a mask. It was a face—large, smooth, and pink. She remembers the minute drops of perspiration which were starting from its forehead: she remembers how the jaws were clean-shaven and the eyes shut. She remembers also, and with an accuracy which makes the thought intolerable to her, how the mouth was open and a single tooth appeared below the upper lip.[47]

There is an obvious connection between Mrs Anstruther's glimpse of this pink, sweating face and the vision MRJ recalls in his last, fragmentary ghost story, 'A Vignette', of another glimpsed face: 'Malevolent I thought and think it was . . . It was pink and, I thought, hot'.[48] 'A Vignette', which he wrote shortly before his death, is often thought to draw on some troubling personal experience. One wonders, too, especially in the light of Arthur Benson's own disturbing glimpse of MRJ around this time as 'an old, wrinkled, furious red-faced man with a glassy stare', whether this pink, hot, toothless face might not have been one which MRJ, to his horror, saw staring back at him from a mirror. 'The Rose Garden' closes with what must be MRJ's favourite injunction, one of the phrases by which he lived his life: '*quieta non movere*', 'do not disturb quiet things'—or, leave well alone.[49]

The collection's next story, 'The Tractate Middoth', is MRJ's most *librarianly* tale, and the one that most directly draws on certain aspects of his scholarly life.[50] As the story opens, we walk through 'the swing doors leading into the vestibule of a certain library'.[51] This is Cambridge University Library, which, until the opening of Giles Gilbert Scott's new library building in 1934, was housed in the Cockerell Building, now the library of Gonville and Caius. It would make perfect sense, then, to date the story's composition around 1907 or 1908, as these were the years in which MRJ published his two-volume catalogue of the Gonville and Caius manuscripts, the years in which he had been working most intently in that College.

The story recounts the battle of wits and wills between John Eldred and his cousin Mary Simpson, both of whom are attempting to track down the will of their elderly and malicious relative, Dr Rant, which is hidden inside a book somewhere in the library. One of the questions the story raises, in fact, is: who has access to a library, and most particularly, who has access to a *university* library? As a graduate of Cambridge, John Eldred (his name an uneasy concatenation of 'eldritch' and 'dread') can simply walk in. Mary Simpson cannot. Like Virginia Woolf attempting to enter a Cambridge library at the beginning of *A Room of One's Own* (1929), her way is barred by a black-clad Fellow. In effect, this is MRJ himself, or a close analogue: an embodiment of the closed, male academic establishment: a cobwebby scholar, at the centre of things.

'The Tractate Middoth' faces, obliquely but uncomfortably, issues and concerns which were close to MRJ's heart, important parts of who he was. Like 'The Treasure of Abbot Thomas', the story is set around a cryptographic challenge. It focuses on deciphering the meaning of a very specific code, the number (or numbers) '11334'. These numbers are the only clue Dr Rant gives his niece

Mary as to the whereabouts of the codicil to his will which bequeaths his property to her rather than to Eldred. 'The Tractate Middoth' draws on the redesigning of the physical space of the Cockerell Building in 1864 by MRJ's student idol, the Cambridge librarian Henry Bradshaw.[52] Garrett deciphers the code as a library classmark, '11.3.34'. The '11' of '11.3.34' indicates its subject heading, which is Religion. Classes 1-34 in the Cockerell Building library were dedicated to religious books: 11, the story tells us, is specifically the 'Hebrew class'.[53]

The catalogue entry for 11.3.34 reads: 'Talmud: Tractate Middoth, with the commentary of Nachmanides, Amsterdam, 1707'.[54] Characteristically for MRJ, this is a combination of genuine and invented scholarship. The Middot ('measurement') is the tenth Mishnahic tractate of the order of Kodashim ('Holy Things'), the Fifth Order of the Mishna (laws), dealing with the religious ceremony of the Temple of Jerusalem. The Middot itself describes the measurements of the Second Temple of Jerusalem. Nachmanides (Moses Ben Nahman, 1194–1270) was indeed a celebrated commentator on the Talmud, although this actual work is fictional.[55] Furthermore, there is indeed a book in Cambridge University Library with the classmark 11.3.34, and it was indeed published in Amsterdam, though a century or so later than the Tractate Middoth, and it is a treatise on the persecution of Christians by the emperor Decius rather than a Talmudic commentary: Taco Hajo van den Honert, *Disputatio de Christianorum Vexatione Deciana* (Amsterdam, 1838).[56]

What is located at 11.3.34, then, is the book at the centre of the story's labyrinth—which is the library itself. At the centre of Cambridge University Library, Mr Garrett encounters a terrifying supernatural creature who is simultaneously a dry and dusty scholar—at first glance, a clergyman reading at the table—and another version of 'Canon Alberic''s spider-demon:

> 'He turned around and let me see his face—which I hadn't seen before. I tell you again, I'm not mistaken. Though for one reason or another I didn't take in the lower part of his face, I did see the upper part; and it was perfectly dry, and the eyes were very deep-sunk; and over them, from the eye-brows to the cheek-bone, there were cobwebs—thick.'[57]

As often with MRJ, explanations are left uncertain, inconclusive—but this seems to be the ghost (or the decomposing or mummified corpse) of Dr Rant himself, who was interred after his death 'sitting at a table, in his ordinary clothes, in a brick room that he'd made underground in a field near his house. Of course the country people say he's been seen about there in his old black cloak'[58]. It is implied that Dr Rant's will is a form of Satanic contract: 'I don't think you'll find the witnesses in a hurry', he tells Mary.[59]

Library encounters are also central to the collection's next story, which may be MRJ's most celebrated. 'Casting the Runes' enacts a clash between two forms of scholarship, as Karswell, the rogue independent scholar and occultist, and Dunning, the representative of institutional knowledge, disagree over the meaning and reality of the supernatural. Dunning is a reviewer for a learned journal, who at the beginning of the story rejects Karswell's submitted article; in a manner which might appeal to many academics, Karswell responds to rejection by setting a demon on his hostile reviewer. Theirs is an encounter which is played out in the British Library, where Karswell slips a demon-summoning runic parchment into Dunning's notes on MS Harley 3586, which he is studying in 'the Select Manuscript Room of the British Museum'.[60] Harley 3586 is a deliberate choice on MRJ's part—the manuscript of the story in the British Library shows MRJ initially writing 'Harley 30' and changing his mind.[61] ('Casting the Runes' is the only MRJ manuscript in the BL's possession; they acquired it deliberately because it uses the Manuscript Room as an important location.)[62] MS Harley 3586 is a cartulary, a 'register of the deeds, charters of privilege and other documents contained by landowners as evidence of their rights'.[63] It contains two monastic registers from the fourteenth century, and two letters from the seventeenth century, one from the antiquarian Thomas Blount, and one from the Balliol scholar Thomas Goad.

Three years after the publication of 'Casting the Runes', MRJ published an edition of an old favourite, the Welsh clergyman Walter Map's twelfth-century compendium *De Nugis Curialium*, which he went on to translate in 1923 as *Courtiers' Trifles*. In their 1983 parallel text of MRJ's editions, C. N. L. Brooke and R. A. B. Mynors point out that one of the works which MRJ consulted in preparing his 1914 edition was the Wormsley Priory cartulary, which contains some documents relating to Walter Map (Wormsley is in Herefordshire, on the Welsh border, and is one of the places MRJ knew about from staying with Gwen McBryde in Dippersmoor).[64] It may be that Dunning is actually in the British Museum conducting research on Walter Map, or that Dunning and MRJ are conducting *the same research*, the one which leads to the summoning of a demon.[65]

Who, if anyone, *was* Karswell, the Caster of Runes? He is a literary creation, foremost, and thus perhaps no one beyond himself. Generally, MRJ's stories have not the space nor the interest for deep character study, and so in 'Casting the Runes' Karswell is left rather blank—'a stout gentleman' and 'a very angry man'; 'a person of wealth' who terrorizes local children with his magic lantern shows at his home, Lufford Abbey in Warwickshire.[66] But what is most troubling about Karswell for MRJ, it seems, is that he practises what we might call unlicensed scholarship in the public sphere. He is 'an alchemist, apparently', and an occultist.[67] Scholars of the occult often define it as 'rejected knowledge'.[68] Karswell's paper on 'The Truth of Alchemy' is rejected for academic publication at the beginning of the story, and Dunning, the institutional expert, dismisses his self-published *History of Witchcraft* as 'quite hopeless. It deserved all the pulverizing it got.' The most 'pulverizing' review was by another establishmentarian scholar, John Harrington, on whom Karswell sets the demon as retribution. Harrington tells his brother that Karswell's book 'seemed to put the *Golden Legend* and the *Golden Bough* exactly on a par, and to believe both; a pitiable exhibition, in short'. Worse still, 'It was written in no style at all—split infinitives, and every sort of thing that makes an Oxford gorge rise'.[69] Karswell, it seems, is the wrong sort—certainly not an Oxbridge man, and most likely not even a public schoolboy. Conversely, Dunning, who hasn't actually published anything yet, is nevertheless recognized as the right sort. Indeed, it is entirely likely that Karswell is a wealthy businessman of some kind, who 'has made his money in trade' and set himself up in his Warwickshire country pile. His presence or influence in the story is frequently accompanied by the language of commerce, from the 'commercial hand' in which he writes to Harrington, to the tradesman's calendar he sends him, to the leaflets and advertising posters through which he conducts his vendetta. In the end, 'Casting the Runes' may really be a story about class.[70]

Karswell is often taken to be a representation of Aleister Crowley, the notorious black magician and self-publicist. Anthony Powell, for example, thought that MRJ drew on Crowley for Karswell, 'which implicitly suggests James as following the career of a not very desirable modern who would certainly have attracted him explicitly had Crowley been a sorcerer of the Middle Ages'.[71] (That last bit is certainly true.) There's no evidence for any of this, but it's not impossible. Edward Alexander Crowley had been a pupil at Malvern (which he left after unspecified 'abominations'), Tonbridge (from which he was expelled after contracting gonorrhoea from a Glaswegian prostitute), and finally Eastbourne (where he got into fistfights with teachers), before coming up to Trinity in 1895. His student days, according to a biographer, were 'among the happiest of his life', and he was a decent second-class student (with occasional forays into first-class results), though he left in 1898 without taking a degree: 'I had no intention of becoming a parson or schoolmaster, [so] to write B.A. after my name would have been a decided waste of ink', he wrote.[72] So, unlike Karswell, at least Crowley moved in the right social and educational circles.

More intriguing still is the possibility that MRJ may have drawn on 'a stout gentleman' of his far more proximate acquaintance in conceiving of Karswell: Oscar Browning. Again, there's no direct evidence for this, but the self-promoting O.B. certainly had a whiff of the mountebank about him, and he bore grudges like no one else MRJ knew (including grudges against MRJ himself).[73] Karswell, Dunning says, 'is very easily offended, and never forgave anybody'.[74] Which certainly sounds like Oscar Browning.

The next two stories drew heavily on some of MRJ's other longstanding interests. 'The Stalls of Barchester Cathedral' combines several characteristic preoccupations: ecclesiastical architecture, the evils of Victorian restoration, antiquarianism, manuscript cataloguing—and cats. The story's original manuscript was entitled 'The Cat of Death'. It was sold at Sotheby's on 9 November 1936—purchased along with the manuscript of 'Oh, Whistle' by James Stoddart Bain on behalf of the novelist Hugh Walpole, a good friend of Arthur Benson—but is now lost.[75]

Like King's Chapel, Barchester Cathedral (a name he obviously stole from Trollope) is a work of late-medieval perpendicular Gothic—a blend, he later explained, of Canterbury, Salisbury, and Hereford Cathedrals.[76] Modern Barchester Cathedral, the story tells us, has been restored in the neo-Gothic revival, 'odiously furnished', and featuring 'a screen of metal and coloured marbles, designed by Sir [George] Gilbert Scott'.[77] The story's narrator discovers the tale of supernatural feline vengeance carried out by the Cat of Death on the Venerable John Benwell Haynes, D.D., while he is 'cataloguing the manuscripts in the library of the college to which he belonged'.[78] Haynes is a graduate and Fellow of an unnamed Cambridge College (assuming that the story dates from around 1909, then this is the year that MRJ published his catalogue of Trinity Hall), and it's very tempting to see this as a story growing out of MRJ's experience of the self-important, rivalrous, enclosed world of academic politics, in which the ambitious and modernizing Dr Haynes, the author of 'a spirited and elegant version of the *Argonautica* of Valeruis Flaccus, [and] a volume of *Discourses upon the Several Events in the Life of Joshua*' grows increasingly frustrated by the fact that his ancient and 'incapable' superior, the nonagenarian Archdeacon Pulteney, is blocking the hitherto 'speedy preferments' of his career by refusing to die—and so takes matters into his own hands.[79]

Though set in the early nineteenth century, 'The Stalls of Barchester Cathedral' turns on the fact that the haunted stalls themselves are made from a seventeenth-century Hanging Oak; the story closes with the discovery of John Austin's verse, dated 26 February 1699: 'When I grew in the wood / I was water'd wth blood'.[80] (The haunted gibbet is one of MRJ's favourite objects, recurring in 'A View from a Hill' and again in 'Rats'.) Like 'The Ash-Tree' and 'The Rose Garden', then, 'Barchester Cathedral' draws on MRJ's fascination with the English seventeenth century. In the collection's next story, 'Martin's Close', MRJ gave this fascination its most detailed fictional expression.

MRJ was a keen student of seventeenth-century court records, about which he wrote in 1929:

> It is not until 1649 that we begin to get really lively reports. From that date till the end of the century the volumes contain the cream of the collection . . . those of the Popish Plot, the reign of James II, and the years immediately following the Revolution are undoubtedly the richest, and I should say, among them, the trials in which the figure of Jeffreys appears. Things are never dull when he is at the bar or on the bench.[81]

In reading these trials, Gwen McBryde observed, 'M. R. J.'s sympathy was rarely with the criminal'.[82] He owned, in fact, to 'a sneaking kindness for [Jeffreys] in regard of that liveliness which he infuses into proceedings, and of his undoubted ability'.[83] MRJ first conceived of the story which became 'Martin's Close' while working on the Royal Manuscripts in the British Library, and wrote an early draft (or a germ) of the story at the back of one of his notebooks.[84] This draft is very different from the published story, though it does contain the story's refrain, 'Madam, will you walk, will you talk with me?' What the draft doesn't contain as yet is the trial scene. If 'Martin's Close' proper dates from Christmas 1910, then it is around this time that MRJ and Arthur were spending their evenings arguing about the trial of Dr Crippen, whom MRJ wanted to see hanged. 'Martin's Close' is rooted in the bloody career of Judge Jeffreys, the Hanging Judge ('Things are never dull when he is . . . on the bench'), who appears as a character in the story, which is largely set on 15 May 1684. The story is intensely local and rural—set in Sampford Courtenay in Devon (where King's College owned property, which MRJ visited), it recounts the supernatural history of 'one of the smallest enclosures you are like to see—a very few yards, hedged in with quickset on all sides, and without any gate or gap leading into it'.[85] Much of the story is a transcript of the trial of George Martin for the murder of Ann Clark, as found in a 'thin bound volume' with the bookseller's catalogue entry 'JEFFREYS, JUDGE: *Interesting old MS. trial for murder*'.[86] One of the reasons MRJ was so interested in old trail reports, he said, was because 'in them alone, as far as I can see, do we find the unadorned common speech of Englishmen; the plays of the time do not afford it—they are sophisticated; still less do the novels'.[87]

'Martin's Close' allowed MRJ to indulge his great fondness for both historical forgery and for comic dialogue, from the loquacious handyman John Hill (who insists on spelling out every name) to the gleefully sadistic Jeffreys, who sits on the bench whistling folk tunes and making jokes about dancing the Tyburn jig.

Martin, and other members of the local community believe Ann Clark to have returned from the dead. The officer of the court who records the transcript 'had shew'd it to the Revd. Mr. Glanvil'—that is, Joseph Glanvill, the seventeenth-century clergyman (he was chaplain to Charles II), intellectual, and antiquary, whose *Saducismus Triumphatis; or Full and Plain Evidence Concerning Witches and Apparitions* (1681) was a major work affirming the reality of witchcraft and the supernatural, which grew out of Glanvill's earlier *Blow at Modern Sadducism* (1668), and which a modern historian has called 'a powerful defense of spiritual forces and diabolic witchcraft grounded in the most current scientific thought'.[88] MRJ, as we have seen, was very much a modern anti-Sadducee, for whom an occult-minded seventeenth-century thinker like Glanvill held enormous appeal.

'Mr. Humphreys and his Inheritance', the last story in *More Ghost Stories*, was written especially for the collection; but it has at least some of its origins in an earlier unfinished manuscript. In 'John Humphreys', as it is sometimes called, the protagonist, 'having just taken a very good degree at Cambridge', unexpectedly inherits a country house with a large library of 'something like five and twenty thousand volumes, hardly a hundred of which were later than 1830'. Humphreys, 'thoroughly fond of a library, inquisitive about old things if not deeply revering them', sets about cataloguing the library. The fragment features a loquacious head gardener, one 'Mr. Barker'.[89]

In 'Mr Humphreys', the house that the protagonist inherits contains a library and a maze, each of which is an emblem of the other, and of the universe. At the centre of the maze is a globe, covered in occult illustrations and symbols: 'Around the place of the head the words *princeps tenebrarum* [the prince of darkness] could be deciphered . . . Near the last, a man in long robes and high cap, standing in a circle and addressing two shaggy demons who hovered outside, was described as *Hostanes magus*'.[90] ('Shaggy', we remember, was MRJ's favourite adjective for the demons of illustrated manuscripts; his stories habitually exhibit a terror of hairy monsters.) MRJ was fascinated by mazes for the same reason that he loved cryptograms, codes, secret languages, jigsaw puzzles, stained glass windows—and library catalogues. On his 1899 Scandinavian trip, he was keen to visit the Trojaborg maze at Visby. In 1927, the Cambridge University Librarian A. F. Scholfield sent him a copy of

W. H. Matthews's *Mazes and Labyrinths*, which he read at the Eton Scout Camp in Worborrow, while writing 'Wailing Well'.[91] It's possible that 'Mr Humphreys''s maze was suggested to MRJ by the maze at Somerleyton Hall in Suffolk, though the maze at Hilton, not far from Cambridge, has a globe on a pillar, like the story.[92] The Hilton maze is reputed to have been designed by Capability Brown, who lived in nearby Fenstanton, though may be earlier still, cut by William Sparrow in 1660. It the centre of the Hilton maze is an obelisk with a Latin inscription—*Sic Transit Gloria Mundi*—topped by a ball or globe with a sundial gnomon.[93]

Hostanes, the figure at the centre of Mr Humphreys's maze, was the legendary mage of the Persian emperor Xerxes I, and was credited by Pliny the Elder with being the inventor of written magic, by which means he introduced sorcery to the Greek world, and 'scattered, as it were, the seeds of the hideous craft along the way, infecting the world with it'.[94] Hostanes was, according to the *Octavius* of the Latin Christian apologist Marcus Minucius Felix, 'The foremost of those Magi both in eloquence and art . . . The same Hostanes also has told us of earthly demons, wandering spirits, and enemies of mankind'.[95] These demons, according to Minucius Felix, were the source of the Magi's power: 'whatever miraculous feats they perform, they do so through demons'.[96] Like Simon Magus, Hostanes had a reputation for black magic—for ritual murder, drinking human blood, and violating corpses.[97]

Immediately on arriving at his new home, Mr Humphreys makes a resolution:

> He had all the predisposition to take interest in an old library, and there was every opportunity for him here to make systematic acquaintance with one, for he had learned from Cooper that there was no catalogue save the very superficial one made for the purposes of probate. The drawing up of a *catalogue raisonné* would be a delicious occupation for winter. There were probably treasures to be found, too: even manuscripts, if Cooper might be trusted.[98]

In parallel to cataloguing the library, Mr Humphreys also maps the maze. As he sits in the library, poring over this map, he notices a hole at the centre of it: 'But surely this was a very odd hole. It seemed to go not only through the paper, but through the table on which it lay. Yes, and through the floor below that, down, and still down, even into infinite depths.' Out of this hole, 'with the odious writhings of a wasp creeping out of a rotten apple', a figure clambers.[99]

At around the same time that he was writing the stories that formed *More Ghost Stories*, MRJ delivered a lecture on 'Black Magic and Demonology', in which he revisited some of the reading of his youth. This casts an interesting light on some of the stories in the collection, most particularly 'Casting the Runes' and 'Mr. Humphreys'.[100] MRJ is a great admirer of Walter Scott, the lecture maintains, but 'had always been rather disappointed' by his *Letters on Demonology and Witchcraft* (1830), 'inasmuch as it tells me really very little' about 'the practices of real black magic'. Rereading the work of the influential nineteenth-century French magus Éliphas Lévi, he now thought him 'nebulous, grandiloquent . . . [and] disappointing'. He now found P. L. Jacob's 1886 taxonomy of hell, *Curiosités Infernales*, and even Collin de Plancy's beloved *Dictionnaire Infernale*, 'frankly bad'. Nineteenth-century magic, he had come to believe, was an empty discourse. 'I reflect', he wrote sourly to *The Times* in 1932, responding to what he considered an example of characteristically ill-informed popular occultism, 'that persons who busy themselves about the subject of Satanism and Black Magic are rarely to be depended upon for accuracy of statement.'[101]

The middle-aged MRJ, though, was still much taken by ancient and Early Modern magic. 'Black Magic and Demonology' returns to *The Testament of Solomon*, the work which had animated 'Canon Alberic's Scrap-book', and also discusses Johan Weyer's *De praestigiis daemonium* (*On the Tricks of Demons*, 1563), and the work of the medieval intellectual Michael Scot. Weyer, or Wier, an anti-Catholic physician and theologian, sought to separate religion from magic, and attacked popular superstition, believing that witches were influenced by demons, in whose existence he unquestioningly believed.[102] MRJ encountered Scot's work in a manuscript in the John Rylands Library in Manchester. This manuscript is a 'Compendium magiae innaturalis nigrae' [Compendium of unnatural black magic], and contains, MRJ's Rylands catalogue notes, a series of instructions for the ritual summoning of demons: 'Directions for forming the circle: . . . More directions as to the wand, mitre, habit, sigil, number of operators, place, time, necessity for coolness and courage'. The spirits to be summoned are the demons 'Almuchbazar, Achundab, Balturaratz, Aghizikke, Suhub, Rabuliph, Almischack, Salhabari'.[103] Scot, MRJ writes in 'Black Magic and Demonology', had studied in Toledo, which had the reputation of being 'a school of Black Magic'.[104]

'Black Magic and Demonology' closes with a strange passage which seems to draw MRJ's scholarship and his ghost stories closer together than any other explicit statement he made:

> And now I really think you have heard enough of dark fables for one night. Still I can't avoid adding for it will probably be brought to my notice if I do not volunteer the statement, that I undertake *if necessary* in addition to the paper I had

> small hopes of writing, to read an effort in fiction which I concocted the last Christmas Eve. The apology for a paper has run to a greater length that I thought, and I honestly think you might be let off with what you have had. If you agree with me I do trust you will say so. The alternative is that you will have to resign yourselves for a further period of I think rather over half an hour of listening.[105]

This passage connects the ritual magic of the summoning of demons to another form of ritual, another form of 'Art Magic', to which it is intimately related: the occasions for telling ghost stories, the Christmas ritual at King's for MRJ and his circle. The older MRJ may have outgrown *some* of the occult influences of his younger years as a scholar, but as an imaginative source black magic and demonology were always vivid presences for him.

* * *

On 1 August 1912, MRJ celebrated his fiftieth birthday. A party of good friends gathered for dinner at the Lodge: Arthur Benson, Walter Fletcher, Percy Lubbock, Oliffe Richmond, Clive Carey, and Geoffrey Tatham. Arthur was not in the mood, and thought it 'Not a very successful party', though things brightened considerably when 'Monty sang a recitative à la Nixon from Hamlet, "Oh, Isis help". It was cruelly funny. I haven't laughed so helplessly in years—felt ill with laughter & felt I should die if I didn't stop.'[106]

A few weeks later, Arthur, to his great delight, was appointed President (Vice-Master) of Magdalene. The Master, Stuart Donaldson, had been appointed Vice-Chancellor, and needed a deputy who would take a hand in College affairs. 'It is a fitting crown for me', he wrote. 'A little sinecure, with a high-sounding name—glory without usefulness—just what I have always desired.'[107] In accepting the role, Arthur was about to get more than he had bargained for.

Perhaps to celebrate his fiftieth, after years of bother with his teeth, of which there were by now very few left, MRJ finally bit (sucked) the bullet and got himself a full set of dentures early the next year: 'how about the new dental outfit?' Sydney asked. 'Find a minute to tell us the dental tale.'[108] (Linda, we remember, was always concerned about the state of her brother-in-law's teeth.) He had, in fact, got a plate for his front teeth in 1909, and told Gwen that 'The effect of over biting is very odd. It *will* be interesting to watch the progress: I imagine you have to be always experimenting with each plate, don't you.' On 11 February 1913, he went to a London dentist and had thirteen teeth extracted.[109] (The final two he had 'torn from me . . . with no more than the inevitable bloodshed' as late as 1928.)[110] Armed with his new teeth, MRJ was about to set out on an exciting institutional adventure.

British universities are run by Vice-Chancellors, for better or worse. Cambridge did not have a full-time, permanent Vice-Chancellor until as late as 1992: by tradition, the position of Cambridge University Vice-Chancellor was a rotating one among the Heads of Colleges, normally held for a period of two years.[111] The Heads nominated two candidates to the Senate, generally based on seniority (the years in which they got their degrees), and on not having held the role already; the Senate then chose one of the nominees. The VC's duties were generally tedious, with little by way of administrative support or emoluments; the frequent necessity of public dining also placed, one historian writes, a serious 'gastric burden' on the incumbents.[112] Almost all Cambridge people—Fellows and students—felt a far closer attachment and loyalty to their Colleges than to the University as a corporate body (MRJ's memoirs are called *Eton and King's*, not *Eton and Cambridge*). The Colleges were where lives were lived, and each had their rich histories and traditions. Collectively, the Heads of Colleges held much of the institutional power. Though it certainly carried status, the Vice-Chancellorship was an onerous encumbrance, generally undertaken out of a sense of duty.

During MRJ's time at King's, the Vice-Chancellorship had been held by, among several others, Henry Montagu Butler of Trinity, and Augustus Austen Leigh of King's. In 1912, we saw, MRJ's old friend Stuart Donaldson (St. Clair's older brother), the Master of Magdalene, was appointed to the role; MRJ, eight years younger, was the second nominee that year.[113] But Donaldson's health was very poor by this point, and he stood down after only a few months in the role. He died of a stroke on 29 October 1915, in the Master's Lodge at Magdalene.[114] He was succeeded by his deputy, Arthur Benson. Arthur had finally got the institutional recognition he dreamed of, the thing he felt had eluded him throughout his professional life. He told MRJ straight away: '*please don't breathe a word of this till it is formally announced*'.[115]

And so, as MRJ wrote to Gwen, 'I have just become Vice-Chancellor at short notice—the hall is full of silver wares'.[116] 'My dear Peisthetairos', came a letter of congratulations from an old friend, Hubert Parry, 'I hope the responsibilities of the Vice-Chancellorship are as congenial to you as your never to be forgotten achievements in "The Birds" now thirty years ago—to think of it!'[117] He spent his first months as VC opening buildings, dining with visiting luminaries and dignitaries, and complaining that 'everyone is at liberty to interview me on all subjects and at all times'. Worst of all, 'the Cambridge ladies are agog to be asked here to see what I actually do with my drawing room!'[118] (Gwen told him that 'the Cambridge ladies are confusingly alike'.)[119] As VC, he gained a new sidekick and factotum, Benjamin Benham, the University's Assistant Registrary, whom no one else much liked, and who monopolized his time. Arthur Benson found him a 'tiresome little man'.[120]

Typically, it is Arthur who gives the fullest and most revealing portrait of MRJ in his early months as VC. Equally typically, it is as revealing about its author as its subject:

> I walked with Monty round Clare, M very grand in bands & silk gown, & rather proud to show himself in the streets. It was odd to think how we walked together 30 years ago as undergrads. He is the higher man, Provost & V.C.—I better known perhaps, & richer. But this is very unlike what might have been supposed. I think it wd. have been expected that I should have been more ambitious, less likely to make a literary success & certainly unlikely to make money. He wd. have been supposed likely to be Professor & scholar of note.[121]

'L[ubbock] & I saw Monty today in topper & bands walking along by the Senate House', Arthur wrote shortly after MRJ's appointment; 'he seems quite cheerful. It's an odd world.'[122]

In May 1914, the Senate of the University, which MRJ chaired, received a Memorial requesting the creation of a Syndicate 'to consider whether a certificate of efficiency in military training be obtained either before or after matriculation, should be required of Undergraduates before admission to their first Degree'.[123] That March, an article in *The Nineteenth Century and After* had advocated for compulsory military training as a requirement for a degree, and the memorial was signed by a large cohort of senior Cambridge figures and graduates, including the Masters of six Cambridge Colleges (amongst them Arthur Gray and Stuart Donaldson), and a whole host of academic luminaries, including William Ridgeway, Charles Villiers Stanford, Walter Raleigh, and R. C. Bosanquet, plus several Bishops, the Headmasters of public schools (including Edward Lyttelton of Eton), and the two figures who had been instrumental in MRJ's election as Provost of King's, Frank Rawlins and E. C. Austen Leigh. This in turn was countered by an even longer list of figures of, if anything, even greater intellectual distinction, stating 'their strong conviction that it is highly undesirable that the university should by its own authority require any form of military service from any of its members'.[124] This was signed by, amongst many others, Arthur Benson, J. H. Clapham, Sydney Cockerell, F. M. Cornford, Lowes Dickinson, Edward Dent, Arthur Eddington, Walter Fletcher, G. H. Hardy, A. E. Housman, Henry Jackson, Francis Jenkinson, Maynard Keynes, Alfred Marshall, G. E. Moore, J. E. Nixon, J. T Sheppard, Will Spens, J. J. Thomson, and Denys Winstanley. This was a group so personally and culturally diverse that it is hard to ascribe to it a uniform politics. Cambridge seemed to be bracing itself for an almighty row.

But then, within weeks, this entire subject would be rendered irrelevant.

* * *

On 28 July 1914, Archduke Franz Ferdinand was assassinated in Sarajevo by a Bosnian separatist, Gavrilo Princip, and the world changed forever. For MRJ, walking happily around Cambridge in his top hat, silk gown, and new teeth, the very personification of the place he ran, this was to be the end of the quiet, scholarly, convivial life he had known for decades, troubled by nothing worse than the occasional academic rivalry or obstreperous colleague, the odd minor professional setback. At the end of 1913, he hosted official visits from Lord Curzon, the former Viceroy of India, soon to re-enter public life in the Asquith and Lloyd George governments, and the polar explorer and naval officer Teddy Evans, a national hero for his role on the doomed Scott expedition of 1912, which he barely survived. In that legendary long, hot, glorious summer of 1914, he dined with Prince Albert, Queen Victoria's son, there to open a Physiological Laboratory and receive an honorary degree. This was the Establishment, and MRJ was a part of it.

Britain formally declared war on Germany on 4 August 1914, ostensibly to protect Belgian sovereignty. The Foreign Secretary, Edward Grey—MRJ's old rival from their Temple Grove Days—was instrumental in the declaration, and in the diplomacy leading up to it. In the words of the historian Christopher Clark, 'Grey was without doubt the most powerful foreign minister of pre-war Europe', who had the complete trust and support of the Prime Minister, Herbert Asquith, and the King, George V, to frame and carry out British foreign policy and international relations.[125] This was in spite of the fact that Grey had no interest in foreign policy and international relations, nor in foreign languages, international travel, or even politics. His greatest passion was fly-fishing on his country estate, and Cecil Spring-Rice, once MRJ's Eton fag-master, and now a senior diplomat, wished that Grey would 'spare some time from his ducks to learn French'.[126] Grey had gone on from Temple Grove to Winchester, and then to Balliol (where he graduated with a Gentleman's Third in Jurisprudence), and in him it is easy to see the uncaring damage that could be caused by the public school cult of amateurism and air of effortless, unearned superiority. To use Clark's influential term, Grey was one of the most important of the 'Sleepwalkers' who led Europe into the fiery abyss of the Great War.

MRJ was dining with Ram when they heard the news that Britain was at war, and drew up from the bottomless well of his memory these lines from Christina Rossetti:

> O thou King, terrible in strength, and building
> Thy strong future on thy past!
> Though he drink the last, the King of Sheshach,
> Yet he shall drink at the last.
> Art thou greater than great Babylon,
> Which lies overthrown?[127]

The lines are a stanza from Rossetti's 'Thy Brother's Blood Crieth', one of a pair of poems she wrote in response to the Franco-Prussian War, which were published together as 'The German-French Campaign 1870–1871'. A. F. Scholfield wrote to a puzzled Shane Leslie to explain the significance of the lines for MRJ: 'The poet is sympathizing with France which had been utterly crushed by Germany (= "the King of Sheshach") which, though victorious, would one day, in later time, drink the cup of defeat.'[128] Arthur's response that evening to the declaration of war was less poetic: 'I hope Germany will be beaten into a pulp'.[129] A few days later, Walter Fletcher wrote expressing his hopes that the War 'results in wiping out that devilish Prussian brood'.[130]

'*War*. Back to KC [King's] Monday. Meetings of Council to allow for war. Relief Committees etc', MRJ wrote in. his diary.[131] He immediately called a meeting of all the Heads of Cambridge Colleges, with Arthur deputizing for the unwell Stuart Donaldson. They unanimously agreed that the buildings and grounds of the University should be offered to the government for use 'in case of necessity'. MRJ told them he had been assured by the War Office that the Colleges would be used as hospitals 'only in case of invasion', and then only the larger Colleges—King's, Trinity, Jesus, and Downing.[132]

These assurances did not stand the test of events, and very soon Cambridge life was unimaginably different. Trinity was immediately commandeered as a military hospital, and by October, ninety nurses had moved into Bodley's buildings in King's, right next door to the Provost's Lodge (what must MRJ have thought of that?), and a large hospital was being built on the King's cricket pitch.[133] The First Eastern General Hospital, to give it its official name, was described as 'a small city on the Backs' (the large green spaces backing onto the river at the rear of the collection of Cambridge Colleges that run along King's Place and Trinity Street, roughly from King's to St. John's). Whole streets of prefabricated wooden huts were built—1700 beds in total, plus operating theatres, administrative buildings, shops, a post office, even a cinema.

The hospital published its own regular magazine. Horse-drawn and motorized ambulances, and often private cars, carried a seemingly endless line of wounded soldiers from the railway station, and the place was a hive of coal delivery, laundry workers, medical and administrative staff. From 1914–19, 70,000 casualties were treated in the hospital, which prided itself on its revolutionary medical treatments, sunlight cures, and saline baths. 'The buildings still cumber what was the fairest of all the College playing fields', MRJ wrote in 1926—the prefabs were not finally removed until 1929, having served as council houses from 1919.[134] A memorial of blood-red letters carved into a stone wall at the rear of Clare College, facing the University Library (which occupies some of the land on which the hospital stood), now commemorates the Eastern General Hospital.[135]

MRJ visited convalescing soldiers at the hospital, and had some of them for tea at the Lodge. One of these was Hope Bagenal, an Anglo-Irish stretcher bearer wounded at the Somme, who was related to the James family, and who later became a prominent architectural theorist and acoustics specialist. In a series of letters written to his niece in the 1970s, Bagenal recalled MRJ as 'a tall man with a very pleasant face and an agreeable wave of hair across his forehead . . . He had a curious charm of manner'. MRJ stood with his back to the fire, 'and carried on a reassuring conversation in a gentle rumbly voice, bending backwards and forwards and looking down at his toes'. The pair discussed synaesthesia: 'he always thought of the days of the week as a series of little squares with a bulge in Sundays. This conversation led to a good ghost story by the Provost'.[136]

Garrisons of soldiers were stationed all over Cambridge as soon as the War started, 20,000 men in total. Gonville and Caius was transformed into the headquarters of the First Army, Central Force, under the command of General Sir Bruce Hamilton, who moved into the College with eighteen of his staff.[137] The Durham Light Infantry was housed in Jesus College, in a small village of tents and marquees. College Masters and Fellows got used to the sight of officers dining in khaki at High Table, or even of commanding officers (and their wives!) moving into Provosts' Lodges, as happened to Arthur Gray in Jesus.[138] MRJ was happy to play host to a succession of convalescing officers in the Lodge as the War went on. The Dining Hall of Corpus Christi was tuned into a 'branch War Office for the issue of commissions', under the supervision of Walter Durnford.[139] In a University designed to resist change, it had all happened with stunning speed. 'We have a new Cambridge', Henry Jackson wrote on 18 October.[140]

'I have a feeling MRJ doesn't care a *rap* for the war: nor much for anything', Arthur wrote a few weeks into the War, after an evening in which the pair had dined together and played cards until eleven.[141] This was unfair, and untrue. In those early weeks, MRJ had acted with unusual decisiveness and purpose, overseeing some of the most dramatic changes Cambridge had ever witnessed. As VC, he set up a register of Cambridge dons 'who are prevented from serving in the war by various considerations, and are yet capable of rendering valuable service to the community in a civilian capacity in virtue of their knowledge of languages, their scientific attainments, or their experience in clerical or administrative work'.[142] He immediately wrote to his Oxford counterpart, Vice-Chancellor Thomas Strong, proposing that both universities should offer refuge to exiled Belgian scholars and their families—should become, in modern parlance, Universities of Sanctuary. Strong's reply was staggering, on a number of fronts:

> My general impression is that Belgians and the Latin races generally do not do so well as Germans in this University: but of course the existing circumstances make a good deal of difference to one's point of view. I will let you know as soon as I can. I know Louvain but not Liege. The only advantage I can see in the destruction of these two cities is that it enables us to see how justifiable were the Old Testament wars of extermination. Who would miss the Germans?[143]

By December, Strong had made his mind up: 'if the two universities move, they ought to move together'.[144] But by this time, Cambridge's plans were already being carried out at MRJ's instigation. The university issued an invitation to Belgian academics and their students, who were put up in Colleges, in the homes of dons, and 'under any hospitable roof that offered'.[145] When Désiré-Joseph Mercier, the exiled Cardinal of Louvain, a major voice in Belgian resistance during the War, heard the news, MRJ was told, 'His eyes filled with tears, & he said he could hardly believe in so great kindness'.[146] MRJ even welcomed Henri La Fontaine, Professor of International Law at Brussels and winner of the 1913 Nobel Peace Prize, 'Socialist—Pacifist—He brings his wife'.[147] (There *was* a war on.) On 3 November, MRJ chaired the inaugural meeting of the Belgian Relief Fund, raising money 'to restore the ruined homes and industries of Belgium'.[148] The idea for the Relief Fund originated in Jesus College, and on New Year's Day 1915, Arthur Gray hosted a packed reception for the Belgian refugees in the Master's Lodge.[149]

One of the consequences of this decision to welcome Belgian refugees was that in 1915, the thirteen-year-old Leopold, Duke of Brabant—son of King Albert of Belgium, and the future King Leopold III—was enrolled as a student at Eton, and kept up a lifelong relationship with the school.[150] At the end of the War, in January 1919, King Albert awarded MRJ the honour of Commandeur de l'Ordre de Léopold, 'in recognition of the constant and generous help given to my country in the course of the war'. The Order of Leopold is the highest rank of Belgian knighthood, and Knight Commander is the highest honour possible for a civilian, ranking above an ordinary knight. 'I wish to express in the name of my Government', the Belgian ambassador wrote, 'the sentiments of gratitude which Belgium will always feel for your personal devotion to her cause and that of her people.'[151]

The coming of war brought upheaval on an individual level, and also new and sometimes exciting experiences. Grace, widowed in the first days of the War, moved into the Lodge in December 1914, and remained there for two years, after which she moved to the Cat and Fiddle, a former drover's inn outside Presteigne on the Welsh border, where she was to live for several decades. It was Gwen McBryde who found this house for her, at a reasonable rent of £25 a year; Grace told Gwen that she thought the house was 'inhabited by ghosts'.[152] MRJ's current cat, Mrs Cat, suspected Grace's cat of being a German spy. To his amazement, MRJ saw Zeppelins over Cambridge, and realized that he had no idea to which side they belonged. For the first time in his life, Arthur saw aeroplanes, 'three of them, big biplanes . . . like vast butterflies'. Cycling out into the fens near Cambridge, MRJ could hear the boom and throb of the heavy guns echoing across the water from France.[153]

His colleague J. H. Clapham thought that the War had brought out the best in MRJ as a Vice-Chancellor, that he rose to the occasion in a role he would otherwise have found a dull administrative distraction, and that it allowed him to express or even discover aspects of his character which he had repressed or kept hidden. 'He was moved to show and communicate his emotions and his faiths', Clapham wrote. 'War he took simply and vehemently, and his love of France and distaste for things German coloured his reception of it.'[154] Not everyone who knew him agreed, either with his politics (which is understandable) or about the sincerity of his emotions (which is less so). Arthur poured scorn on Oliffe Richmond's assertion that MRJ spent hours every day in the Eastern General Hospital writing letters to the Front, and on Percy Lubbock's concern for 'Monty's silent agony & bleeding heart over the war—when he simply thinks about it as he can & is far more successful than the rest of us in forgetting it'—but this was in early 1917, when Arthur was beginning to show signs of his next bout of depression, which was to leave him incapacitated by the end of the year.[155] The musicologist Edward Dent, no friend, considered

MRJ an 'ultra-jingo'.[156] MRJ certainly loathed pacifists and conscientious objectors, as a letter of June 1916 to Clive Carey (who managed to maintain good friendships with both MRJ and Dent) makes clear:

> I'm leaving in a secret place a copy of the Daily Graphic in which is a picture of . . . Bertrand Russell leaving the court in which he has been fined £100, & followed; mark this—followed by the Elder Strachey . . . Well, well, I think this little lot are taking the back seats which they have so richly earned (if the phrase be correct) & I do not care to think of them.[157]

MRJ's distaste for Russell, Lytton Strachey, and what they stood for, is consistent with everything we know about his character and intellectual formation (they were Apostles). But he also, in the context of the War, considered their stance an affront to the unimaginable losses which Cambridge, like the rest of the country, had suffered.

Some of MRJ's Cambridge colleagues grew paranoid and jingoistic in the early years of the War. This was a dangerous, destabilizing thing in a cosmopolitan university full of international scholars and students. Siegfried Ruhemann, University Lecturer in Organic Chemistry, who had been at Cambridge for thirty years and was a naturalized British citizen, wrote to MRJ as VC resigning his position because of the attacks on him in the Cambridge press.[158] J. M. E. McTaggart, the distinguished Trinity metaphysician, saw spies and enemies wherever he looked. 'At a meeting lately', Arthur Benson recorded in 1915, 'Ridgeway called Waldstein an alien to his face.'[159] Charles Waldstein, not a mild-mannered man, replied that it was only William Ridgeway's age and infirmity that prevented the pair from coming to blows. By the end of the War, Waldstein, sick of the racist abuse his German surname attracted, had changed his name to Charles Walston.

MRJ's colleagues, students, friends, and family rushed to join up, or to aid in the war effort in other ways. Ber, now working for the War Office with the rank of Lieutenant-Colonel, went on the active list as a military doctor for the duration of the War, while Syd took up the Chaplaincy of the 2nd South Midland Brigade of the Territorial Artillery, headquartered in Essex.[160] Oliffe Richmond, a Captain in the London Regiment, was decorated with the Order of the Crown of Italy for his service. Major L. F. Giblin of the 40th (Tasmanian) Brigade of the Australian Army fought in France, was mentioned in dispatches, and awarded the DSO and the Military Cross. A. E. Conybeare, one of MRJ's companions on the epic cycling holiday through Germany in 1911, enlisted with the rank of Captain. Anstey Guthrie, age fifty-eight, joined a veterans' regiment, the 'Old Methuselahs', and spent the war on guard duty, or digging trenches in the Home Counties.[161] As soon as he heard the declaration, Stephen Gaselee joined the Naval Reserves, and 'said goodbye rather solemnly and dramatically' to Arthur—who was amused because Gaselee had enlisted as an accountant.[162] Gaselee spent the War working for the Ministry of Information, for which service he was awarded a CBE in 1919. On 2 August, Maynard Keynes was immediately drafted into the Treasury, where, acting as an advisor to the Chancellor of the Exchequer, David Lloyd George, he succeeded in 'single-handedly . . . averting monetary panic and financial collapse in the first week of the war' by dissuading mandarins from suspending the Bank Charter Act.[163]

Most of the King's Fellows, in fact, were involved in War work. The King's mathematician Arthur Berry, a longtime advocate of progressive causes and 'a notably anti-jingo Gladstonian Liberal', enlisted in the army, age fifty-three, as an Intelligence Officer. Nixon spent his last years, up to his death in February 1916, tirelessly corresponding with serving Kingsmen. J. H. Clapham stayed on for two years as College Tutor, but the College seemed empty: by 1918 there were only sixteen students.[164] 'Emptier and emptier grew the courts, and slower and duller the pace of life', MRJ wrote.[165] 'Nobody is here', he wrote to Nathaniel Wedd in September 1915.[166] In the academic year 1909–10, there had been 3699 male students registered at the University. By Michaelmas Term 1914, in the first weeks of the War, the number had more than halved, to 1658. By 1916, there were only 575. (The number of women students remailed stable throughout, around 400—which means that by the end of the War, Cambridge had almost as many women undergraduates as men—over 40%.)[167] 'They may be, they are, fewer in number than we could have wanted', MRJ said sadly, looking around him at a half-empty Dining Hall during a wartime Founder's Day speech.[168]

The pattern was the same across the University. The Kingsman R. H. Malden, an outstanding Classicist who had gone on to a Lectureship at Selwyn College before taking holy orders, served as Chaplain on board HMS Valiant, and saw action at the Battle of Jutland. Of the twenty-seven Fellows of Gonville and Caius, seven joined the forces, another seven engaged in war work of various kinds, and the Master, the physiologist Hugh Kerr Anderson, went to work for the Ministries of Munitions and Agriculture.[169] Arthur Gray vividly evoked the wartime mood in Jesus:

> Most of us helped . . . Elderly tutors and professors enrolled themselves in the O.T.C. and drilled on Jesus Close. Mr. Abbott in khaki looked fiercer that we had known him. Dons yet more elderly patrolled the streets as 'specials'. Everybody else—except the Hun spies who were everywhere, slaved for Red Cross in new lecture rooms.[170]

In October 1914, at the end of his first year as Vice-Chancellor, MRJ was called upon to give an annual formal address to the University. It is a remarkable speech—measured, principled, and completely without jingoism—and in it, MRJ mounts a defence of the University as a centre of civilized values which is both convincing and completely consistent with his own intellectual values. It was precisely through the arcane, highly specialized nature of their research, he told his colleagues, that the University best embodied civilization:

> The University meets in such circumstances as it has never known. We shall be few in number, and perpetually under the strain of a great adversity. We may be exposed to actual peril: in any case we must look forward to straitened resources and, what is more, personal sorrows. Yet there is no doubt that we are bound to carry on our work; for by it we can render definite service to the nation. Our part, while we encourage all of our students who are capable of doing so to serve their country, and while we surrender to that service many valued teachers, is to prepare more men—especially in our medical schools—for rendering active help, and to keep alive that fire of 'education, religion, learning, and research' which will in God's good time outlive the flame of war. Let us devote ourselves to making useful men of the new generation. Let us confine our own controversies within the narrowest limits, and be ready if necessary to postpone them altogether. Let our advanced work—however irrelevant it may seem to the needs of the moment—be unremittingly and faithfully pursued.[171]

The University did 'outlive the flame of war'—but at enormous cost.

The flame of war also burned MRJ's other beloved institution, Eton. The Provost of Eton, Edmond Warre, was seriously ill for much of his tenure, incapacitated by Parkinson's Disease, and the Vice-Provost was dying of cancer. So MRJ had been acting as *de facto* Provost since well before the War, chairing meetings of the Governing Body and playing an often decisive role in the running of the school. He got caught up in a scandal involving the Headmaster, Edward Lyttelton. Lyttelton, a member of a venerable Etonian dynasty, and a first-class batsman for Cambridge and Middlesex, seemed like exactly the sort the school wanted running the show—although he did have progressive ideas about abandoning compulsory Greek from the curriculum, which MRJ played his part in countering. But in March 1915 he delivered a sermon at St. Margaret's Westminster, in which he argued that it was wrong to condemn the entire German nation, and argued that the allies should be generous in any peace settlement. These sentiments were very much out of tune with the tenor of the early months of the War, and Lyttelton found himself hounded by the press.

The events that followed the speech show MRJ as a conscious actor at the centre of a political storm, and very much contradict his disclaimers that he had no aptitude for institutional politics. On the contrary: this was the water he swam in. Cis Lubbock, a member of the Governing Body and a close friend of Lyttelton's, thought that 'Eton had suffered a real injury' as a result of this recent episode, and warned Lyttelton that 'he couldn't be the Prophet and Headmaster too'.[172] MRJ's position was terse and firm: 'Keep *out* of the papers.'[173] He called an extraordinary meeting of the Governing Body, a board which included Cis Lubbock, Walter Durnford, Henry Babington Smith, and luminaries such as Lord Rosebery and Viscount Hambleden (from the family of the newsagents W. H. Smith). While no one at this time wanted Lyttelton to go, the Governing Body was very unsympathetic towards his sermon, and issued a damning statement, which MRJ drafted: 'The Provost and Fellows cannot but regard the Headmaster's recent speech and letters as detrimental to the authority and welfare of the School. They feel bound to add that their confidence in him as Headmaster of Eton has been seriously impaired.'[174] The original, longer version of the statement, also by MRJ, included stipulations for Lyttelton's continued appointment: 'We wish to point out that it is also not part of the duty of the Headmaster to make pronouncements upon public affairs.'[175] Lyttelton was an impulsive man, and his response was ill-considered. He wrote to the Governing Body expressing his unhappiness that 'the Provost and Fellows should have dealt with this matter in so severe a tone'.[176] MRJ and the Governing Body immediately withdrew their support for Lyttelton. He resigned in 1916. A couple of years later, Caroline, his wife, wrote to MRJ protesting 'the *callousness* shown to Ed by many who *were* his warm friends', and lobbying for her husband to be made the next Provost of Eton.[177] For a number of reasons, she was writing to the wrong man.

* * *

It was the students and young graduates, of course, on whom the War took the greatest toll. Walter Durnford could hardly have known, as he supervised the new Commissions Office in Corpus Christi, that he was playing a part in sending quite so many of them off to their deaths. 'The two first to whom I said goodbye at the Lodge door were of those who did not return', MRJ recalled.[178] Gordon Carey, who was wounded at Ypres, dedicated the immediate postwar years to compiling a monumental inventory of the University's combatants: *The War List of the University of Cambridge* runs to 616 pages. Over 2000 Cambridge men were killed in the War, with a further 3000 wounded. 774 Kingsmen fought in the War; 174 of these were killed.[179]

In his analysis of the lists of the war dead, the social historian J. M. Winter has shown that 'Oxford and Cambridge men of all ages suffered casualties well above the national figures'. 19.2% of Oxford servicemen were killed, and 18% of Cambridge men, compared to a national average of 12%. In King's and a small handful of other Oxbridge Colleges (including Corpus Christi, recruitment central), the fatalities were around double the national average (in King's they were 22.5%).[180] Junior Officers were slaughtered in disproportionate numbers; Oxbridge men—public school men—more disproportionately still.

There are many reasons for this, but amongst them is something we saw in earlier chapters: the fact that the Victorian public school system was deliberately designed to produce an imperial caste incapable of questioning structures of authority and power. A generation of compulsive conformists, brilliant yet safe men, marched themselves and their troops into the abattoirs of the Great War. Those giving the orders were themselves the products of the same system, a generation or two earlier. Edward Grey had no interest in politics, statesmanship, or the world. As we saw in Chapter 3, General Sir Herbert Plumer, commander of the army at Ypres and Messines, proudly admitted in an Eton dinner in 1916 that he had learned nothing at his old school. After the War, he was appointed Field Marshal, Commander of the Armies of the Rhine, and then High Commissioner of Palestine. Field Marshal Douglas Haig (Clifton College, Balliol, and Sandhurst) refused to visit the front, but insisted that all men march slowly in formation towards the German guns emplacements that cut them down. He was a believer in 'cold steel' and bayonets, rather than machine guns. Like most people responsible for the conduct of the War, he was incapable of seeing, let alone acknowledging, the horrors for which he was responsible (in the late 1920s, interviewing politicians and senior figures of all sides, the American historian B. E. Schmitt 'was struck by the apparently total immunity of his interlocutors to self-doubt').[181] Haig went to his grave in 1928 convinced of the superiority of mounted cavalry to battle tanks.[182]

Gordon Carey, now working for the University Press, walked into the Corpus Dining Hall in August 1914 to enlist. On his way in, he met Rupert Brooke (they had been in the same year as undergraduates): 'full of eagerness to join up', Gordon remembered, 'he described his promising interview with the selection board, and talked gaily of his plans and hopes.'[183] Brooke was particularly keen to get a naval commission, and wrote to MRJ on 11 September to ask for a reference: 'I'm applying for a commission in the Royal Naval Division with a very good chance of getting it. Could you give me a certificate of "good moral character", on page 3?'[184] A few months later, on 9 May 1915, MRJ got a letter from Rupert's mother:

> I am indeed almost heartbroken about Rupert, who was unceasing in his thoughtfulness to me & was I believe going to do great things. In some ways he did violence to his feelings by going to fight—but he was *firmly* convinced of the righteousness of our cause; so he went, undeterred by me I am glad to think. I am one amongst many thousands of mothers who are mourning but one's personal loss is the same. I am feeling very anxious about Alfred, who is over in France, expecting to go into the trenches every day.[185]

En route to the Gallipoli landings, Rupert was bitten by a mosquito, and the bite became infected. He died of sepsis on 23 April, on a hospital ship moored off the island of Skyros, the island on which Theseus was said to have met his death, and from which Achilles set sail for Troy. Like Hecuba, Hector's mother, Mrs Brooke was about to be driven beyond grief by the deaths of her children. Alfred Brooke, Rupert's younger brother, another Kingsman, and a Second Lieutenant in the London Regiment, was killed in action in France on 15 June 1915.[186]

While on leave for Christmas 1914, Brooke wrote some of his most celebrated work, a sequence of five sonnets written to encapsulate the mood of the first months of the War, which he called *1914*. Of these, by far the most famous is the last, 'The Soldier':

> If I should die, think only this of me:
> That there's some corner of a foreign field
> That is for ever England.[187]

1914 was published in the poetry magazine *New Numbers* in January 1915, and 'The Soldier', in particular, stuck a chord with the national mood. Brooke's fellow Kingsman W. R. Inge, now Lady Margaret's Professor of Divinity at Jesus and Dean of St. Paul's Cathedral, read the sonnet as part of his Easter Sunday service at the cathedral on 4 April. 'The Soldier' was published in *The Times* the following day, where it caused an immediate sensation. MRJ himself thought the poems of *1914* 'extremely fine', and agreed with Inge that Brooke 'was now to be numbered among the great poets'.[188]

But not all were convinced. The Scottish poet Charles Hamilton Sorley (King's School Cambridge, Marlborough, University College Oxford; killed at the Battle of Loos, October 1915) identified something important about Brooke's character, and about the worldview he so beautifully embodied: 'He is too obsessed with his own sacrifice, regarding the going to war of himself (and others) a highly intense, remarkable, and sacrificial exploit . . . He has clothed his attitude in fine words, but he has taken the sentimental attitude.'[189] This is very apparent in another of *1914*'s sonnets, one of two poems in the sequence entitled 'The Dead':

Blow out, you bugles, over the rich Dead!
There's none of these so lonely and poor of old,
But, dying, has made us rarer gifts than gold.
These laid the world away; poured out the red
Sweet wine of youth; gave up the years to be
Of work and joy, and that unhoped serene,
That men call age; and those who would have been,
Their sons, they gave, their immortality.[190]

Brooke was buried in an olive grove on Skyros, a location chosen by his close friend Denis Browne. Brooke and Browne had been at Rugby and at Cambridge together (Browne was at Clare, and was also a good friend of Clive Carey). When the war broke out, they had enlisted together in the Corpus Dining Hall. The day after he buried Brooke, Denis Browne's ship set sail for the Dardanelles. He was killed at Gallipoli on 4 June.

So many dead. Stephen Gaselee's younger brother Alec, who had graduated from King's in 1912, was killed in action at Ypres on 14 May 1915. The two students to whom MRJ had said goodbye in the Lodge at the outbreak of War, Dick Durnford and Roger Watson, were both killed on 30 July 1915.[191] On 17 July 1916, Montagu Butler's son Gordon was killed in Egypt. Overcome by grief, his father died in January 1918: 'he always said he should not get through another winter', MRJ wrote to Gwen.[192] Eric Lubbock, the Lubbock brothers' cousin, was killed at Ypres in 1917; his mother wrote to MRJ with the news, quoting one of her son's letters: 'Or task is to make the world better for those that come after us by destroying the theory that might is right and as that is a great task it can only be achieved by great sacrifice.'[193]

To MRJ's great shock, in April 1918, Harold Lubbock was killed by a shell. MRJ had gone to Harold's wedding in June 1914, where the groom was dressed as 'something of a knut' in white spats and a white waistcoat.[194] He enlisted as soon as the War started, and told MRJ in September 1914 that he was 'on the whole thoroughly enjoying being a soldier'.[195] Harold was one of MRJ's regular correspondents throughout the War; by the time of his last letter, written the month before he was killed, he had come to know that 'war is vile'.[196] 'His affection for you and dependence on your good opinions were perhaps more visible to others than to yourself', Johnnie Maxwell told MRJ when he heard the news of Harold's death. 'They were very real and were, if you are to know it, the common ground on which other friendships were built.'[197] In 1911, MRJ, Maxwell, and Harold Lubbock had gone on a 'spring expedition to France' together with another companion, the 'beloved' Trinity student Geoffrey Tatham, one of the friends with whom MRJ chose to celebrate his fiftieth birthday.[198] Geoffrey went missing in action on 30 March 1918; like very many others, his body was never recovered.[199] 'These are dark and bitter days', Walter Fletcher wrote on hearing the news of his friends' deaths.[200]

For those who survived the War, life would never be the same again. Some of the War's most celebrated literary and cultural survivors fled modernity, sickened by its implications: Robert Graves to Mallorca, David Jones to the retreats of Caldey Island or Capel-y-Ffin, H. M. Tomlinson to the Caribbean, Saunders Lewis to an imaginary medieval Wales, J. R. R. Tolkien to Middle Earth, George Mallory to his date with fate on Mount Everest. Ivor Gurney spent the last fifteen years of his life in mental hospitals, convinced the War was still raging (for him, it was).[201]

Goderic Hodges went up to King's in 1912 to study for the Theological Tripos. Just after he arrived, MRJ walked up to him in the Front Court and asked him, 'Would you like to see the Codex D?'[202] In October 1914, Hodges enlisted in the forces and, about to set sail for Gallipoli, he went to say his goodbyes at the Provost's Lodge. This was one of many such goodbyes for MRJ, often for the last time. 'I don't think I was ever so sorry for anyone', Hodges wrote to his parents. 'He came and saw me off the premises, and shook hands with me for about 2 minutes. As long as I live, I shall never forget how sad he looked as he turned back into his house.'[203] On leave in 1916, he returned to King's on a 'nasty, cold, damp evening', and met MRJ at Evensong: 'There stood James waiting in the rain. He put his arm around my shoulders and led me off to the old Lodge, as if I had been a son, a grandson. I can see him now, in the study, in his great armchair in the light of a big fire, tall, dignified, gentle, sad.'[204] Six months later, Hodges was invalided out of combat when a shell went off three feet from him, and he spent the rest of the War working with surveillance balloons, which he loved (he wrote a warm memoir about his days as a 'balloonatic').[205] But before the shell went off, before his return to the rainy chapel and the fireside armchairs at the Lodge, Goderic Hodges had fought at Gallipoli. In 1970, he wrote about his war experiences to the King's historian John Saltmarsh:

> In 1914 I had rooms on the ground floor of Gibbs, which I shared with an Old Pauline, S. S. Martin. He was killed. A year later I was on a hill in Gallipoli entirely covered with corpses, after two days they were not buried. They melted in the sun. I have been on that hill ever since. Of course I don't think about it all the time. But it's there, down inside me. In Gibbs, looking out at the lawn, it is easy to speak of the goodness of God. Surrounded by decaying corpses, it is less so.[206]

I have been on that hill ever since. Over fifty years later, Goderic Hodges was still living in the nightmare of the War.

Eric Milner-White came up to King's from Harrow in 1903 to read History, graduating with Firsts in both parts of the Tripos. Milner-White took holy orders after graduation, and was appointed King's chaplain in 1909. When the War broke out, he enlisted as a military chaplain, on the Western Front and in Italy.[207] Milner-White's division fought in nine battles on the Western Front, and as a non-combatant chaplain he went on rescue missions into no-man's-land. He wrote a series of powerful, moving letters to MRJ recounting, insofar as he could, his experiences on the Front. In October 1916, his division fought a repulse at the Somme, 'a thing of special horror . . . in the wind and the rain and the abomination of slough'. Writing from the Front, Milner-White resolved 'while I am still young enough—and idealist enough—to take the violent step of joining a [religious] community'.[208] But instead, in 1919, he returned to King's, as Fellow and Dean.

His experience at the Front had made Milner-White certain that the Church of England was badly out of step with the needs of the time. In 1917, he was one of a group of military chaplains who contributed to a volume of essays on their experience of the War, *The Church in the Furnace*. Milner-White's essay was a revolutionary (his word) call for a wholesale rethinking of church services: 'New churches, new services', with 'more and fuller and wider schemes of popular devotion . . . simple in language, intimate in feeling'.[209] He wrote to MRJ in 1916, proposing changes to the King's Chapel services after the War, including 'an "experimental" Choral Eucharist': '*the extraordinary potentialities of our Chapel for the whole religious life of England tend to be forgotten*. At the present moment of utter chaos, and of superb hope in Church, as in State, we have a chance which, boldly taken, might make Kings one of the most important churches in the land.' Such radical, modernizing language was never going to go down well with MRJ, who wrote a discouraging reply, very much to Milner-White's disappointment: 'I am so sorry you think that there will be opposition so fierce to any proposal for such a service. The grounds are incomprehensible to me.'[210]

But Milner-White did get to carry out at least some of his plans for King's Chapel. As Dean, he transformed the Side Chapel into a memorial chapel for the war dead. To help to heal the College after the War he also introduced the occasion for which King's Chapel is now best known, the Christmas Eve Festival of Nine Lessons and Carols, patiently countering the objections of King's venerable organist, Henry 'Daddy' Mann. The Festival of Nine Lessons and Carols was first developed in Truro Cathedral in 1882 by the Rev. Somerset Walpole (Hugh's father), working under the unblinking eye of Bishop Benson. But it was in King's Chapel that the Festival was to find its true home. The service was an immediate success, attracting vast crowds to the Chapel, and has from 1928 been broadcast live by the BBC as a regular part of its festive programming.[211] In one small way, at least, Eric Milner-White had succeeded in bringing the nation together.

Of all the friends, students, and colleagues who fought in the War, it was Gordon Carey to whom MRJ wrote most often. Gordon was awarded the Belgian Croix de Guerre, and finished the war with the rank of Major, first in the Rifle Brigade, and then, after Ypres, in the air force. The war for him was, he wrote, an 'Ordeal by Fire'.[212] MRJ's wartime letters to Gordon are newsy and reassuring, but they are mostly and straightforwardly love-letters written to 'my dearly beloved'.[213] 'I can't say how much I would like to be beside you when you are feeling depressed . . . But I have a confidence in you that makes me quite sure you are the right kind from one end to the other. Enough said, my dear', he wrote in August 1915.[214] 'I am no hand at expressing what I have at heart—but I do not think that matters as between you & me', he wrote the following year. 'No day & no night will pass without my thinking of you.'[215] These are sentiments which MRJ repeats throughout the War. In May 1918, reeling from the death of Harold Lubbock, and having just returned from a medal ceremony for ANZACS, he writes: 'The fact is that when I don't plunge myself into some subject quite unconnected with the present times, I am forever thinking of you.'[216]

* * *

On 22 September 1915, MRJ's term as Vice-Chancellor came to an end. He had had enough. 'I suppose it is mean to say that I relinquish the office without regret', he told Nathaniel Wedd, 'but it would be untrue to say anything else.' But, he thought, 'there is precious little of what can be called College life to get back to'.[217] He brought his tenure formally to a close with a second, valedictory Vice-Chancellor's oration. It is very different in tone from his address a year earlier—no less measured, but full of loss and grief:

> More than four hundred and seventy Cambridge men have fallen: a hundred and fifty of them, at least, should have been undergraduates still. For these no privilege that we can devise awaits. Yet the University bears them upon her heart, and will not, I know, neglect to perpetuate the memory of them in such sort that it may speak to the youth of England in time to come . . . To put into words the reverence that we owe the young who have worked and suffered and died for us

> is beyond my powers: but my heart follows our departed sons with confidence into that state of life into which it has pleased God to call them.[218]

On July 12 1916, MRJ gave an address to the Cambridge Tipperary Club, on the occasion of the unveiling of their Roll of Honour memorializing the Cambridge war dead. It is another remarkable speech: it was published and widely read during and after the War, by grieving relatives and friends, who often drew great comfort from its sentiments. 'To us Christians', MRJ said at the Tipperary Club, 'the sum of our thought about the dead is that they are alive, that they are the same persons they were on earth, and that we have a prospect of meeting them again'. This was a holy war, he asserted, 'fought in good causes under the banner of God', and the address quotes Siward's response in *Macbeth* on hearing of his son's brave death in battle: '*Why then, God's soldier be he*.' The living have an austere responsibility to the dead, one not afforded the consolations of spiritualism:

> Among much else that this war has taught us is its lesson about the dead. It has not lifted the veil and shown us what they do and what they know in the other life, but it has forced us to think about them. As we read of the hundreds who are hurried away daily, most of them men only at the beginning of life, we become sure that their story is not finished.

Those left alive have this responsibility, MRJ believed, in a sentence which encapsulates so much about his life and work, 'For the dead remember'.[219]

In 1916, a Parliamentary Committee was established to create a memento to be sent to the next of kin of all the war dead. They decided on a bronze plaque, with an accompanying scroll. Even after consulting members of the literary establishment including Rudyard Kipling, Robert Bridges, Henry Newbolt, and Laurence Binyon, finding the right wording for the scroll had proven tricky, and so Vincent Baddeley, Principal Secretary to the First Lord of the Admiralty, asked MRJ, who sent back a draft by return of post:

> He whom this scroll commemorates was numbered among the sons of the British Empire who at the bidding of their country left all that was dear to them, endured hardness, faced danger, and finally passed out of the sight of men by the path of duty and self-sacrifice, giving up their own lives that others might live in freedom.
>
> The remembrance of them shall long be honoured in the land which they loved and died to save.

This was, very substantially, the wording that was used: the word 'those' was substituted for 'the sons of the British Empire', and a final sentence was added: 'Let those who come after see to it that his name be not forgotten.' At the personal insistence of King George V, the words 'at the bidding of their country' were changed to 'at the call of King and Country'.[220]

It was reading MRJ's Tipperary Club Address that prompted Alice Lubbock to write to MRJ about the death of her son Eric in 1917, as she felt it precisely articulated his (and her) own feelings. But now, she wrote, 'This you know is not life. Our life ended last August & this is an interregnum of chaos & sin. For some life will start again after the war—but alas! for many it ended here.'[221] In the early days of the War, MRJ asked Gwen McBryde: 'What is all this love if we have to go out into the dark'? Gwen interpreted this comment positively: 'In the early days of the war when losses where very great, M.R.J. was confident that we should meet our friends again'.[222] But the consolations of faith were not always proof against the horrors of war, and MRJ increasingly found a Cambridge full of ghosts too much to bear.

On 31 July 1917, on the eve of his fifty-fifth birthday, he wrote to Gordon Carey:

> Tomorrow at an uncertain hour—towards tea-time, I believe, 55 years will have passed over my head. Unlike most people I am not sure I would not have them again up to 1914. I could have just a little more sense of proportion as to know that the troubles of early days don't matter quite so much as you think, and to see that it is worth while to take more trouble about some things than one did, I have no doubt that I would go through it again. I believe it is a highly unphilosophical attitude.[223]

The following May, he wrote to Gordon again, with the news that Edmond Warre, in chronic ill health, was resigning as Provost of Eton. Rumours immediately spread that MRJ would be offered the position. For some time, he had been chairing Eton College meetings in Warre's stead, 'But it is a far cry from that to suppose that the Crown would pick out a bachelor who has been leading the life of a University don for thirty-six years' (he thought Arthur Benson, Henry Babington Smith, or Walter Durnford would all make better candidates).[224] But the desire to escape this city of the dead and find shelter in the idealized, perpetual childhood of Eton must have been irresistible: 'To live in the midst of Eton certainly makes on the whole for cheerfulness' he wrote in 1926, from his home 'among 1,100 boys, few of whom appear to be suffering from depression of spirits'.[225] 'I imagine', E. G. Swain wrote to him in 1918, 'that no one ever grows old at Eton.'[226] Towards the end of the War, Arthur Berry wrote to MRJ, sharing his hope that the Provost could begin the hard task of rebuilding King's after the War. 'But', Berry acknowledged sadly, 'that is not to be.'[227] After thirty-six years at Kings, MRJ was going back to Eton, 'a Paradise for boys'.[228]

9

Provost of Eton, 1918

'I haven't in the least taken in that the war is over', MRJ wrote to Gwen on 12 November 1918, the day after the Armistice was signed, 'though it is beginning to percolate into my system like a healing balm.'[1] 'Is it really truly practically over', he wrote to Clive Carey a couple of days later: 'dear dear, I can't take it in, not a bit. But the boys do.'[2]

MRJ was back amongst the boys, and those who knew him well were not at all surprised. 'As Provost of Eton he swam into peaceful waters', Oliffe Richmond wrote, adding, with a characteristic touch of his own, 'Were they *all* as handsome as that at eighteen years of age?'[3] Stephen Gaselee wrote about the Provostship of Eton: 'I do not think that he had any doubt about accepting . . . [MRJ was] a great man, a man of the world in the best sense of the word . . . who loved [the boys] and every stone in the place, who had at last returned to the spot where his heart had always been.'[4] In a striking metaphor, Ronny Norman wrote on hearing the news that 'I get something of the same pleasure which the marriage of two old friends occasionally—but rarely—gives. The lady in this case is my first love, & my affection for her grows more eager & deep rooted the longer I live. And for the man I can say anyhow that time & absence do not make my heart grow any less fond.'[5]

MRJ's departure managed to unite the different factions at King's. Nathaniel Wedd, one of the College's great progressives, wrote a heartfelt letter:

> This is a hard blow. I find it little use to tell myself that I should be glad, since you must have wanted the change. The fact remains that I feel your departure as a disaster for the College and a most dismal loss for me personally. For twenty-nine years you have been the soul of the place, the chief inspiration of the things that make King's better to be in than other places: what you began as Dean & carried through as Tutor & Provost.[6]

Even more progressive, Lowes Dickinson wrote: 'I must confess that my predominant feeling is regret for the loss entailed to King's. It will not be easy for us—I think indeed it will be impossible to find anyone so admirably equipped in the qualities needed for a provost.'[7]

And not just King's. 'I'm heartily glad for your sake & for the sake of Eton', Arthur Benson wrote from the plutonian depths of his worst depressive attack, in which he stopped writing his diary for two years. 'I am sure you will be very happy there . . . & the place will prosper exceedingly in your hands. That's my prophecy. I shall miss you dreadfully at Cambridge.'[8]

MRJ gave at least some account of his mixed emotions on leaving King's in a letter to Henry Jackson. 'If I had been in your place', Jackson wrote on 30 July, 'the Provostship of Eton would have been my ambition.'[9] MRJ replied the following day:

> It is truly a very great pleasure, the prospect of being knit up so closely with Eton, which of all places holds perhaps the first place in my affections. But I begin to realize though very imperfectly that it will be a great wrench to go from here after thirty six years. But Cambridge is a place where I can keep a foot, and I refuse to think of this as a farewell.[10]

Jackson was by now more or less the last surviving remnant of an old Cambridge—almost eighty, stone deaf, largely blind, and completely immobile. The Cambridge of Nixon and Westcott, Mayor and Hort, of Montagu Butler and Fred Whitting, was passing. E. G. Swain, the former King's chaplain, thought that MRJ's departure really marked the end of this era:

> Cambridge will long be unsettled and when settlement begins, a great deal of it will be outside your main interests and sympathies . . . What many hundreds of us will feel is that this is the end, but for a few survivals, of King's as we knew it, you being a real link with the past. Your intellectual & other antecedents belonged to the King's of history, to enter into which has been the main pleasure and privilege of my life.[11]

Cambridge seemed changed utterly. The War was a radical rupture, an epistemic moment in history, which had torn the fabric of reality as MRJ had come to know it. His old friends were dying, his young friends had been slaughtered.

Almost exactly a year after he left, MRJ returned to King's to deliver a sermon, in which he attempted to sum up the complexity of his feelings:

> A year ago, when I was on the point of leaving this College to go back to its sister foundation of Eton, its tide of life had ebbed very low. Today, returning I see it as vigorous & full as of old, & fuller, and I find it offering thanks to God for a deliverance which was but beginning to dawn when I parted from it.

> Our family long scattered & sadly broken meets again not so much today to commemorate those lost members of it who are never absent from our thoughts as to acknowledge the goodness which has allowed it & the nation of which it is a part to triumph. And I who have taken part in the life of this College & of this place during the years of war & during not a few years before then am asked to speak to you in the manner suggested by the service of today.
>
> I do not find it easy.

I do not find it easy. This was not an occasion for glib words of patriotism. MRJ took his listeners back to the earliest days of the War:

> Your thought in the last days of July 1914 was probably much like mine. It is not possible, I thought, that in these days any man or group of men can be so wicked as deliberately to give the signal for an European War. They may come up to the verge of it, but surely they will have left themselves some way to step back. But it was not so . . . Then when the die was cast, you remember perhaps how everything seemed to be crumbling around you.

There were certainly times during the War itself when MRJ spoke the language of popular anti-German sentiment, rhetoric which he undoubtedly genuinely felt. He could be, as Edward Dent had thought, an 'ultra-jingo'. But here, responding formally and in the round, it is an establishment caste of sleepwalkers that MRJ holds responsible; men who lacked the imagination to find a way to step back from war. These were all, it is very likely, in MRJ's mind, *German* sleepwalkers; but he does not say this explicitly, and this is not a straightforward denunciation of the German national character. The cost of this failure, MRJ acknowledged, was immense: 'Then came the exodus of our youth. They took leave of us & went out not knowing whither they went, seeing only that for honour's sake they must go, & glad that the issue was so plain. By us whose lot it was to stay these first partings were not to be forgotten.'[12] The old world of certainties, of which he was a part, had crumbled around him. If it was to be rebuilt, it was to be rebuilt by the young.

'Well, it has materialized, this matter of the Provostry (praepositura) of Eton', MRJ wrote to one such young man.[13] Old friends were happy to see him return: 'No one will be gladder than I nor welcome you home more warmly', Henry Broadbent wrote.[14] Albert Baillie, recently appointed Dean of Windsor, was delighted that his old undergraduate acting chum would be moving in down the road.[15] Even some old enemies chipped in. Oscar Browning wrote from Rome, ostensibly to offer his congratulations while stoking up the ancient grievances that kept him going: '[Eton] College when I was in it was a Hell upon earth . . . Of course I loved my boys and my house was known to be the best and most successful at the School. But this only led to jealousy and persecution. Those who hated me hated my house worse than myself.'[16]

The Provostship of Eton is a crown appointment, arranged through the office of the Prime Minister. On 28 July, MRJ received a letter from 10 Downing Street, informing him that 'the King has been graciously pleased to approve of the Prime Minister's recommendation that you should be appointed Provost of Eton'.[17] On 24 September, Prime Minister David Lloyd George received the Warrant for MRJ's appointment, signed by the King. On 25 September, MRJ got a letter from the Home Office requesting that he send them a cheque or postal order for 10/- 'for the defrayal of the Stamp Duty on the Royal Warrant for your appointment at Eton'![18] The Warrant was forwarded to MRJ by the Home Secretary, George Cave, the following day.

There was unquestionably a politics to the appointment, given the place of Eton (then and now) at the heart of the British political establishment. Sir Ian Malcolm, the Old Etonian diplomat and Conservative MP who was at that point Arthur Balfour's Private Secretary, wrote from the Foreign Office to tell MRJ he was looking forward to attending his installation as Provost, and added: 'See that they don't overlook a psalm of thanksgiving for the final deliverance of Palestine & the Holy Land from the Turk in the excitement of welcoming you!'[19] The Balfour Declaration, which redrew the map of the Middle East along lines significantly designed by Mark Sykes, had been signed a year previously, in November 1917.

MRJ was installed as Provost on Michaelmas Day, 29 September. Knocking on the entrance door of the Eton School Yard, he was met by the Head Master, the Lower Master, and the entire staff and pupils of the school: 'a strong feeling possessed me', he wrote, 'that I had come home again.'[20] The Vice-Provost, his old teacher Frank Rawlins, led him by the hand through an avenue of boys to the statue of the founder, Henry VI, where all the Fellows of Eton were gathered (except for the 95-year-old Lord Haisbury) in the rain to greet him. At the North Porch of the Chapel, he presented his Royal Warrant (the postal order had arrived safely), and made the declarations required by the statutes. 'This was the work of less than five minutes', he wrote, 'but in that time I ceased to be a member of the Foundation of King's College.' Then there were Latin addresses from the Headmaster and the School Captain—'I replied to both addresses in the Latin tongue (old pronunciation)'.[21] They all processed into the Chapel for a service, which included a rendition of Handel's *Bright Seraphim*, one of his favourites. And then to the Hall for drinks all round.

Hugh Macnaghten was MRJ's old classmate from Eton and Cambridge. He was a prodigious scholar, though always seems to have been doomed in everyone's estimation to take second place to MRJ. In 1920, he succeeded Frank Rawlins as Vice-Provost to MRJ's Provost. 'I sincerely believe', he wrote to MRJ in 1918, 'that you are the best man imaginable for the job.' But he confessed that he had not supported him for Provost, but rather had lobbied for William Ralph Inge, another Old Etonian Kingsman, now Dean of St. Paul's and Lady Margaret's Professor of Divinity at Jesus, on account of their personal friendship and because 'to be honest for once . . . I like his wife, and rather desired a lady at the Lodge'.[22] MRJ, Inge, and Macnaghten had all been placed in the first division of the first class in Part I of the Classical Tripos in successive years, and all did brilliantly in Part II. All three were King's Scholars, Newcastle Scholars, Craven Scholars, and First Chancellor's Medallists in Classics. Macnaghten thought that MRJ and Inge were both members of an intellectually unparalleled golden generation of Eton contemporaries, along with Arthur Benson, J. K. Stephen, Henry Babington Smith, and a few others (he was too modest to include himself, but if such a category existed, he surely belonged in it).[23] Inge, according to his biographer, 'was led to think his appointment was likely' as Provost of Eton (by Macnaghten?), and wanted the job.[24] He was, it was claimed, bitterly disappointed to have finished runner up (almost forty years earlier, MRJ had beaten his record score in the King's scholarship exam too: these kinds of academic rivalries went back very far, and cut surprisingly deep). In the 1920s, Inge enjoyed a fantastically cranky public career as the 'Gloomy Dean' of St. Paul's. He was an enthusiastic nudist, an extreme eugenicist, an opponent of democracy, and a loather of Roman Catholicism. His best-known work, characteristically, was entitled *Outspoken Essays*. He spent much of his time dining on High Table at Jesus College, where he enjoyed a famously difficult relationship, largely made up of cold silences, with the Master, Arthur Gray. Both men seem to have enjoyed this rather a lot.

One of the people who was certainly glad to see MRJ leave King's was John Maynard Keynes, though he wrote a letter (the only item of correspondence between the two men) congratulating him on his new role: 'We have not seen very much of each other personally, but I shall always remember with pleasure your kindness to me when you were VC.'[25] In 1912, Keynes had complained in a circulated flysheet that 'the best qualified men are not always appointed to College staffs'.[26] Walter Durnford succeeded MRJ as Provost of King's, and one of the first things he did was to appoint Maynard Keynes as Second Bursar, and then in 1924 as Bursar. J. H. Clapham seems to have been behind this suggestion, and in 1919 Keynes took on particular responsibility for the College's accounts and investments. As one would hope he would be, he was a spectacular success in this role, turning King's into an empirical testing ground for Keynesian economics, and making a fortune for the College.

In contrast, MRJ arrived at an Eton facing financial difficulties, due to reduced income from its London properties, and the long-lasting effects of the late-Victorian agricultural depression. The College had to sell some of its property, at a disadvantageous price, just to keep going. With interest rates rising, it was struggling a little with a mortgage of £110,000.[27] The Etonian consensus is that MRJ did not manage the finances well.[28] When Keynes offered financial advice to his old school, MRJ refused to take it. But MRJ, to his credit, did oversee some important property developments at Eton, most notably a long and patient endeavour to purchase a large plot of riverside land at Boveney Court Farm, to prevent the building of a housing estate to serve the nearby Slough Trading Estate.[29] The land was purchased by the Old Etonian Association of New York, in a gesture still spoken about with gratitude today at Eton as having saved the character of the town.[30]

Eton's Headmaster under MRJ was the wonderfully named Cyril Argentine Alington. Alington had taken over the post in 1917 after the resignation of Edward Lyttelton (Alington's brother-in-law). MRJ chaired the appointment panel, and suggested they put an advert in the agony column of the *Times*:

> Dimension? say 6 by 2½ by 2
> Sober? Industrious? Willing?
> Of tidy appearance?[31]

The panel, which also included HB and Rosebery, drew up a longlist of ten possible candidates, including Lionel Ford, A. B. Ramsay, and Frank Rawlins. Ramsay was the only one who made the shortlist of five, along with Alington (Headmaster of Shrewsbury) and the Headmasters of Wellington, Tonbridge, and Dartmouth Naval College.[32] In a 6–4 split decision, the post was offered to Alington over W. W. Vaughan of Wellington.[33] (Rawlins, who had been filling in, desperately wanted the post, and was very popular with his colleagues and the boys; after much diplomacy and pride-soothing, he reluctantly accepted MRJ's offer of the Vice-Provostship as a consolation prize.)

Alington was a man of enormous drive and industry. Anthony Powell remembered him as a figure 'who had a good deal of swagger and sense of the dramatic occasion'.[34] Arthur, being Arthur, was equivocal about Alington, while providing one of his sharp pen-portraits:

> Alington has a touch of genius and is full of courage; he is not, as they say, quite a gentleman . . . But he has much character and fearlessness, and is ambitious enough to run a show well. A. poses as unconventional, but I think he is very conventional in his ambitions, and just understands the value of stimulating curiosity. I should fear him as an adversary rather than respect him as an opponent.[35]

Arthur found Alington restless, unstoppably voluble (always asking questions, but uninterested in your answers), and rather too colloquial and familiar in the pulpit for his sense of propriety. The boys didn't all like him, many regarding him as a 'sanctimonious fraud', and nicknaming him 'Creeping Jesus'.[36] But no one doubted that Eton had found in Alington a dynamic Headmaster, someone in whom MRJ could comfortably entrust the day-to-day running of the School.

* * *

The War did not really slow down MRJ's scholarship, though he didn't publish any of the great catalogues in these years. In 1917, he got involved in a seriously revealing scholarly dispute with the Newnham Classicist Jane Ellen Harrison. Harrison is a major intellectual figure in the modern development of Classics, who brought to bear on her subject recent developments in comparative mythology, anthropology, and sociology—the work of Frazer, Durkheim, and others—in her focus on the importance of ritual in understanding the Classical world and its works. Her *Prolegomena to the Study of Greek Religion* (1903) was praised by Gilbert Murray, Regius Professor of Greek at Oxford, as 'what I can only call a work of genius'.[37] In December 1916, she published an article in *The Classical Review* on 'The Head of John the Baptist'. In the story of the beheading of John the Baptist, Harrison argued,

> we have . . . a singular and instructive instance of a widespread process; we have the legend of a historical personage cast in the mould of a primitive ritual. *The dance of Herodias' daughter with the Head of John the Baptist is, mutatis mutandis, the ritual dance of Agave with the head of Pentheus.* It is the dance of the daimon of the New Year with the head of the Old Year, past and slain.[38]

Harrison connected the John the Baptist story to other ritual narratives of death and rebirth, the cycles of the seasons and years: 'Tammuz, Adonis, Osiris, Orpheus, Dionysos'.[39]

MRJ read Harrison's article, and was incensed. In the next volume of *The Classical Review*, he published his response, a denunciation of Harrison's article and her approach. 'It is confused and confusing, and in its use of certain texts most grossly misleading', he wrote, accusing Harrison of both sloppy translation from the Greek, and of misrepresenting her manuscript sources.[40] The article closes by damning Harrison for 'Loose thinking, exaggeration of resemblances, ignoring of differences, and downright falsification of evidence'.[41] He described his feelings in a letter to Gordon Carey:

> Of self: that on the evening I came back I opened the last number of the Classical Review & read in it so unscrupulous an article by Jane Harrison on the Head of John the Baptist—she said it was the Head of Pentheus, & J.B. was the Year-Daimon & all that kind of rot—that I instantly took a pen & dipped it in gall & flayed her: to appear in our next.[42]

Hope Bagenal, still convalescing in the Eastern Regional General Hospital on the cricket fields, and visiting MRJ in the Provost's Lodge, wrote an extraordinarily melodramatic letter about the controversy to his brother Nick:

> Myth Harrison, as they call her in English, seems to have attacked John the Baptist on insufficient grounds and has trespassed on some Byzantine fields that the Provost happened to know literally *all* there was to be known [sic]. The Provost, who is easily roused, seems to have been touched by the plight of John the Baptist and stirred himself. He rubbed his eyes and said: 'Damn the woman', in the most classical of language, giving all his references and taking the pages of the *Review* to say it. When said, the critics seemed to agree that there was little of [Harrison] left—that in truth she would soon be a myth and all her Comparative Mythology. Let the famous lady and her disciples look to their laurels.[43]

There is a lot going on here. There's no doubt that, in part, somewhere at the bottom of this, there is a genuine intellectual disagreement, and a clash of methods. 'I believe it to be a science, but only in the making', MRJ writes of Comparative Mythology.[44] Comparative Mythology by its nature tends to work at a high level of generalization, drawing patterns and connections across disparate cultures and historical periods, whereas MRJ was obsessed by specifics and particulars, and especially by exceptions to general rules. Harrison was also the kind of abstract, theorizing 'intellect' that MRJ distrusted, disliked, and did not understand.

But worst of all, Jane Harrison was a woman in Cambridge. MRJ was normally a mild man, and so it's worth dwelling in the violence of his rhetoric here: 'I instantly took a pen & dipped it in gall and flayed her'. 'I have not often used a pen that had gall in it', he acknowledged in *Eton and King's*, but here MRJ's pen is full of bile.[45] Ink was traditionally made from oak gall ('iron gall' ink is still manufactured, though now relatively rare as its acidity can damage pens), a growth caused by the eggs of the gall wasp. MRJ is being waspish, acidic. His pen is also a sharp knife with which he flays Harrison, as Apollo had flayed the hubristic Marsyas for daring to challenge him in a musical competition. This is what happens to women who trespass into the world of men. There are, no doubt, psychosexual overtones here too, of sexualized violence against women: MRJ is rhetorically and intellectually disfiguring Jane Harrison's naked body in this remark.

One also gets the sense of a whole conservative, male academic order egging MRJ on here. In the wake of the Jane Harrison affair, he received multiple letters of congratulation. The arch-reactionary William Ridgeway (no friend, but in this matter an ally) wrote immediately:

> I must write a line to congratulate you on the signal service you rendered to Comparative Religion by dealing drastically with Miss Harrison. I endorse every syllable that you say respecting the baneful effect of such methods on the young. Hitherto I have been a voice crying in the wilderness, for though I have got much silent support, no one has had the courage to do their part in the crusade against this most pernicious method.[46]

'I am heartily glad that you trounced her', Henry Jackson wrote. 'She deserved it.'[47] 'Let me just say with what satisfaction I have read your exposure of Miss Harrison's rubbish', Arthur Hort wrote. 'These anthropologists are, I think, a serious danger: they have covered the classical field with mares' nests, which it is not generally easy to show up.'[48] R. L. Poole, Keeper of the Archives at Oxford and the editor of the *English Historical Review*, chimed in: 'I am very glad you wrote as you did. The modern pagan is allowed too much licence in these days . . . I am grateful to you for having not only challenged but beaten Miss Harrison.'[49] Arthur Benson thought that Harrison advocated 'Free Love' at Newnham, as part of a socialist, suffragist agenda; he also thought that she was romantically interested in him. 'Poor soul', he remarked. 'She must hate mirrors.'[50] The whole episode was very unedifying, and really does not show MRJ nor any of his circle in a good light.

Jane Harrison was not the only prominent woman scholar MRJ encountered during these years. He was rather more open to the work of the Egyptologist and scholar of magic Margaret Murray. The pair corresponded in 1916, when Murray wrote from University College London to enquire about Glastonbury MSS in King's College Library: she was looking for an eighth-century manuscript, either in Arabic or in a Latin translation from Arabic, which seems to have been known at Glastonbury Abbey at the time of the dissolution, and which she thought had come from Egypt.[51] MRJ replied immediately, though his correspondence has unfortunately gone missing.[52] But we know that he asked Murray for more detail about her researches, and so she followed up with a long letter. She was researching the legend that the Grail had been brought to Glastonbury by Joseph of Arimathea, a legend which she believed to have been Egyptian in origin. The manuscript that she was looking for was known as the 'Book of Melkin', and combined, she thought, Arthurianism with Arabic influences.[53]

Famously, Margaret Murray was a practitioner as well as a scholar of witchcraft. At UCL, she was reputed to have cast spells 'to reverse academic appointments of which she disapproved'.[54] In 1921, Murray published her best-known, most influential, and most controversial work, *The Witch-Cult in Western Europe*. 'Ritual Witchcraft', Murray wrote,

> or as I propose to call it, the Dianic cult—embraces the religious beliefs and ritual of the people known in late mediaeval times as 'Witches'. The evidence proves that underlying the Christian religion was a cult practised many classes of the community, chiefly, however, by the more ignorant or those in the less thickly inhabited parts of the country. It can be traced back to pre-Christian times, and appears to be the ancient religion of Western Europe.[55]

MRJ had certainly read *The Witch-Cult in Western Europe*, and was intrigued by its possibilities. In the early 1920s, he delivered a lecture on 'Forgotten Books', in which he makes what seems like a clear (and intellectually supportive) reference to Murray's work. The 'Forgotten Books' which MRJ specifically discusses in this lecture are works of the occult. Most particularly, they are works in a collection bequeathed to Eton Library in 1754 by Nicholas Mann, Headmaster of Charterhouse: 'Books which many have heard of and not many seen. Joseph Glanvill's *Sadducismus Triumphatus*, John Beaumont's *Treatise of Spirits*, Richard Baxter's *Certainty of the World of Sprits,* Pierre de Lancre's *Tableau of the Inconstancy of Evil Angels and Daemons*, Thomas Bromhall's *Treatise of Specters.*' This, we know, is the kind of literature MRJ enjoyed, the kind that informed his ghost stories from the very beginning. Murray's scholarship, he suggests, gives a serious new historical credence to the reality of the magic:

> But Witchcraft you know has taken a step up of late and it does not do to treat the ancient tales with the levity to which we were accustomed. I am not thinking of the prevalence of occultism in the present day, but of the recent investigation of the real old paraphernalia of Sabbaths and the rest of it. I have not much doubt that Sabbaths were held, and that those who attended them were adher-

> ents of an older religion than Christianity, and that much of the confessions have a substratum of truth.[56]

While MRJ does not name Margaret Murray here, this is a paraphrase of one of the main arguments of *The Witch-Cult in Western Europe*, an argument which MRJ accepts. In fact, though he may have been something of an early adopter, there is nothing particularly unusual or *outré* in MRJ's interest in Murray's ideas. Murray's hypothesis of a widespread, organized pagan religion existing alongside Christianity in the Middle Ages before being systematically suppressed by the seventeenth century is no longer one which most modern scholars of religious history accept. But it was, in the words of the historian Ronald Hutton, the great authority on pagan Britain, 'something of a scholarly orthodoxy' in the middle decades of the twentieth century.[57]

Some of the ideas of *The Witch-Cult* also underlie one of MRJ's most interesting later stories. 'An Evening's Entertainment' (1925) is a story about the survival of pagan beliefs in England. A young man is sacrificed—dismembered and left hanging from an oak tree, dressed in a white gown, with 'a chain of some metal round the neck and a little ornament like a wheel hanging to it on the front'.[58] This is the pagan Sun Wheel, a symbol of fertility, and thus of the cycle of the year. It is a symbol which Murray discusses near the beginning of *The Witch-Cult*: 'the sun-charm of the burning wheel' is part of the fertility rituals of Candlemas.[59] This is invoked towards the end of the story by the wise man of Bascombe, who warns: 'When the sun's gathering his strength . . . and when he's in the height of it, and when he's beginning to lose his hold, and when he's in his weakness, them that haunts about the lane had best to take heed to themselves.'[60] The story is set in Dorset, under the shadow of 'that old figure cut out in the hill side'.[61] This is the priapic Cerne Abbas Giant, a figure about which MRJ wrote at length in the same year, 1925, in his book *Abbeys*:

> That the sanctuary [Cerne Abbey] is really old I have little doubt; I have always supposed that it was set up here as a counterblast to the worship of the wicked old giant who is portrayed on the side of Trendle Hill just behind the Abbey. He is surely of very great antiquity, and is perhaps the most striking monument of the early paganism of the country. Whether he is British of Saxon, who shall say? Some have thought that he represents what Caesar describes—a wicker figure in which troops of victims were enclosed and then burnt to death. On this hypothesis the figure would have been marked out by a palisade of wattles on the ground, and the victims, bound, crowded into the enclosure. In any case, here must have been an important heathen sanctuary, and a fit place consequently for champions of the new religion to set up their standard.[62]

MRJ's interest in Murray, and in the pagan underpinnings of Christian beliefs, remained with him for the rest of his life. As we will see, his postwar stories have a distinctly more folkloric emphasis than his earlier, more austerely scholarly tales. In the early 1930s, to celebrate the summer solstice, he delivered an extraordinary sermon in the Lower Chapel at Eton, ostensibly a meditation on Psalm 5:7 ('and in the fear will I worship toward thy holy temple'):

> Perhaps you have heard of some of the old customs that belonged to the day, of how on the evening before it men used to light bonfires on the hills and leap through the flames, and how they would roll from the hill-top down into the valley a burning wheel which was meant to represent the sun . . . Here at Eton, for instance . . . the old account books tell of them [Midsummer bonfires], & of how the College Hall was decked out with green boughs, and a beautiful hanging light was fixed up in it, with flowers of wax all about it. Now this was really Sun-worship: for the reason why this day was made much of was that it was counted to be the day of the summer solstice, when the sun gets to its greatest height in the heavens, and the days are longest. So in heathen times men paid honour to the sun shining in his strength, and prayed him to ripen their corn & their fruits and to go on rising every morning and drive away the powers of darkness & cold of which they were afraid.[63]

In a delicious historical coda, in 1956 Margaret Murray, then age ninety-three, was employed as a *de facto* magical consultant for Jacques Tourneur's *Night of the Demon*, a free adaptation of 'Casting the Runes'. In *Night of the Demon*, Karswell is at the head of a 'devil cult' which is clearly drawn from Murray's theories of the witch cult. Tourneur himself called Murray 'the oldest witch in England', and invited her to the opening party, from which there is a great photo of her being kissed by the film's obviously inebriated leading man, Dana Andrews.[64]

* * *

The Christmas ghost stories continued, if a little patchily and with sparser than usual attendance, throughout the war years. In December 1915, Henry Montagu Butler's son James wrote to MRJ from the Dardanelles:

> Probably the ghost story, if any, will have been read by the time this gets to you, but I will wish you a happy Christmas in any case. I can't see why the war should prevent Mr. Luxmoore and his company from finding their way to Cambridge, nor can the military age have got as low as the choir. So I hope there will be a proper King's Christmas.[65]

'There *was* a story', MRJ reassured him in his reply, 'but a very incomposite one which will require a lot of dusting to make it presentable.' (This is likely to have been either 'The Residence at Whitminster' or 'The Diary of Mr. Poynter'.)[66] But Luxmoore *wasn't* there that year:

> No, I can't come, I really can't [he wrote to MRJ]. It is not that I love you less or King's less. To lose you & to lose your chapel will leave an empty Xmas indeed but just because I enjoy it so much & look forward to it so much it seems incongruous & impossible to be so comfortable & so happy while one's boys—& men are suffering such miseries for our sake—while the country is in such peril & so distinctly asks one to forgo.[67]

In 1917, 'government regulations' prevented Luxmoore from coming to King's:

> What? Shall I pass a Xmas without 'in dulci jubilo' . . . ? without that madeira? without animal grab? & the walk in the Backs & the talk with ghosts & the sense of friendship & old days & above all the mystery of the beauty of Chapel & the fellowship of Xmas Communion?[68]

By 1919, MRJ thought he had enough material for a new collection: 'my friends have not seldom asked for the publication', he admitted.[69] And not just his friends: by now, MRJ's ghost stories had an avid international readership. In 1916, Frank Coller, Chief Justice of St. Lucia and an acquaintance of MRJ's (Coller was a fellow East Anglian, a native of King's Lynn), wrote to tell him that he had recently dined with former US President Theodore Roosevelt, who turned out to be a great admirer of MRJ's ghost stories. Roosevelt exhorted Coller: 'write to him by the next mail & tell him that he must bring out another book of ghost stories'.[70] 'I have had my doubts about the wisdom of publishing a third set of tales', MRJ acknowledged; 'sequels are, not only proverbially but actually, very hazardous things.'[71]

A Thin Ghost and Others was published by Arnold in time for Christmas 1919. It is MRJ's slightest volume, certainly in terms of length (only five stories), and perhaps also in terms of content. It was written and published in the shadow of the War: 'perhaps', he hoped, 'some one's Christmas may be the cheerfuller for a story-book which, I think, only once mentions the War.'[72] This is at the beginning of 'Two Doctors': 'it was a practice of mine before the war occasionally to buy old ledgers of which the paper was good'.[73] The War marked a kind of watershed for MRJ's ghost stories. In 1924, as he was beginning to think about the publication of *A Warning to the Curious*, MRJ wrote an introduction to *Ghosts and Marvels*, an anthology of supernatural tales, in which he made one of his relatively rare theoretical pronouncements on his chosen form: 'For the ghost story a slight haze of distance is desirable. "Thirty years ago", "Not long before the war", are very proper openings.'[74]

This may account for some of *A Thin Ghost*'s distinctive characteristics, as the volume marks the beginning of a discernible shift in MRJ's interests, away from the cosmopolitan world of occult scholarly enquiry, with its Orphic mysteries and Mithraic rituals, its devil-worshipping aristocratic Swedish vampires, its Solomonic demonologies, and its Persian magi, and towards a more local world of folklore and popular magic, Punch and Judy shows, weather prophets, and East Anglian burial mounds. This, it must be said, is a matter of drift, tendency, and emphasis, rather than an abrupt change of direction (some of the earlier stories are tales of local magic; some of the later stories are tales of the cosmopolitan occult), but it does account for the difference many readers detect between the first two volumes of ghost stories and the second two. *A Thin Ghost* contains two major stories which draw heavily on MRJ's traditional academic scholarship, his interests in demonology and ecclesiastical architecture ('The Residence at Whitminster' and 'An Episode of Cathedral History', which we have already discussed), one story which returns to MRJ's abiding fascination with the English seventeenth century ('The Diary of Mr. Poynter'), and two altogether more inconclusive, intriguing tales ('The Story of a Disappearance and an Appearance' and the very slight 'Two Doctors'). MRJ's folkloric tendencies really come to the fore in the 1920s, but more generally, in the latter half of his career, MRJ becomes a different kind of distinctively English writer, a smaller-scale regionalist.

This is most clearly in evidence in what is the volume's earliest tale, 'The Story of a Disappearance and an Appearance'. The story is set around Bicester in Oxfordshire at Christmas 1837—the first Christmas of Victoria's reign, and the year of the publication of *The Pickwick Papers*, which the narrator is reading at the time of the action, having recently finished *Sketches by Boz*. It's an MRJ story full of Dickensian allusion; but more than that, it is steeped in nineteenth-century popular culture. It has at its heart a long and literally nightmarish account of a Punch and Judy show (one of the most terrifying things MRJ ever wrote), and is full of detail about Punch and Judy lore: the beadle, the Oriental who only says 'Shallabalah' (another detail MRJ gets from Dickens, from *The Old Curiosity Shop*), the jailer, the baby, the hangman, Toby the dog.[75] 'The Story of a Disappearance and an Appearance' was first published in the *Cambridge Review* in June 1913, and so seems likely to date from as early as Christmas 1912. Gurney Lubbock, who was present for the first reading, recalled a large gathering in the drawing-room of the Lodge, and 'the silence which fell when the grim story ended'. Luxmoore, who often sounds like annoying company, broke this spell by asking 'Were there envelopes in those days?' (it's an epistolary tale). MRJ assured him that there were.[76]

The issue of a 'folkloric', let alone a 'folk horror' (to use a modern cliché) MRJ is a complex, nuanced one.[77] More so still the argument that this is a distinctive feature of his postwar writing (it is, but not uniformly: 'Disappearance and Appearance' is prewar). Not all his stories, even the later ones, are folkloric in an easily recognizable sense: 'I am not conscious of other obligations to literature or local legend, written or oral', he wrote in 1931, 'except in so far as I have tried to make my ghosts act in ways not inconsistent with the rules of folklore.'[78] As with many of his explicit pronouncements on his writing, there is something disingenuous about this. The contemporary folklorist Jacqueline Simpson has affirmed that MRJ 'was something of a folklorist too (more so than his often self-deprecating remarks on the topic imply), with a particular interest in the development and persistence of local legends and historical memories, a good knowledge of traditional beliefs, and an interest in oral narration'.[79]

Certainly in returning to Eton in 1919, MRJ as a writer also turns in on himself. He began to understand Eton itself as a folkloric or a magical space, and also consequently as a haunted one. The Midsummer sermon of the early 1930s offered pupils a vision of a pagan, sun-worshipping Eton. As we saw in Chapter 3, this received its fullest expression in the very strange 'After Dark in the Playing Fields', which conjures an Eton landscape of talking owls and invisible fairy-folk (invisible, that is, to all except MRJ, who sees them everywhere), woven together with allusions to his favourite Shakespeare plays, *A Midsummer Night's Dream* and *The Merry Wives of Windsor*, whose closing scene, set right next door in Windsor Great Forest, sees Falstaff (the role MRJ loved to play, the role he *inhabited*) transformed into the horned figure of Herne the Hunter, surrounded by 'Fairies black, grey, green and white, / You moonshine revellers and shades of night'.[80]

His own rooms as Provost were in what is now the Eton archives (just as his rooms in the Wilkins Building are now the King's archives). To get to them, then and now, you need to walk down a series of long corridors and dark stairways. 'To go to bed', he wrote to Gordon Carey, as the nights drew in that November, 'I travel dark halls & empty chambers in one of which I always expect to feel a scratch from a sharp fingernail on the sleeve of my coat.'[81]

Sharp fingernails, nail scorings, clawed demons and clawed boys. These were among MRJ's recurring images of dread, and they appear memorably in *A Thin Ghost*'s first and longest story, 'The Residence at Whitminster'. This is one of MRJ's most complex and disturbing stories, and one which has deep roots in his research. The adolescent Irish aristocrat Lord Saul has been dabbling in occult divination, a set of beliefs he has brought with him to England from his native land. This Irish setting was a very conscious decision: Shane Leslie, a native of Monaghan, pictured MRJ 'chuckling in his gazetteer of a mind to think that the most famous place in County Down associated with St. Patrick was called Saul'.[82] The Irish necromancers from whom Lord Saul learns the occult gain their power from the violation and mutilation of corpses—most particularly the corpses of children: 'I should have remarked, by the way, that on the rough walls of the enclosure I could distinguish bones, and even a skull, lying in a disorderly fashion . . . But in the town not a family but knew how he would stop out at night: and them that was with him, why they were such as would strip the skin from a child in its grave; and a withered heart makes an ugly thin ghost.'[83]

At the close of the first half of the story, Lord Saul is found dead, 'clinging desperately to the great ring of the [church] door, his head sunk between his shoulders, his stockings in rags, his shoes gone, his legs torn and bloody'.[84] What has Lord Saul's occult rite summoned? What is it that has stripped his skin? Many years later, Mary Oldys, niece of the current Senior Prebendary of Whitminster, finds a 'crystal tablet', the scrying glass which Lord Saul has used for his divination. In the glass, she sees a terrifying vision: 'Their shapes were but dimly seen, their number—three or four, perhaps—only guessed. I suppose they were on the whole more like dogs than anything else, but dogs such as we have seen they assuredly were not.'[85] As far back as his Fitzwilliam catalogue in 1895, we remember, MRJ had encountered 'Black clouds. Devils on earth. Men in eaves mourning: hell-hounds running about hills. Lurid sky.'[86]

Worse still than the hell hounds, the black magic seems to have summoned Beelzebub himself, as MRJ remembered him from the illustrations to Collin de Plancy's *Dictionnaire Infernale*—a gigantic fly. The bedroom which Lord Saul inhabited becomes infested with sawflies. Investigating a disturbance in the room at night, Dr Oldys's candle is blown out, and in the dark he brushes up against the legs of a giant insect, whose feelers explore 'all about my face, and neck, and body . . . Lord, what a size! Why, the beast must have been as tall as I am.'[87]

'How horrified James would have been', Ferdinand Mount writes in his marvellous book *English Voices*, 'to find "Lost Hearts" or "The Residence at

Whitminster" included in an anthology of gay ghost stories, but both would certainly deserve their place, especially the latter'.[88] It is hard to disagree with this assessment, although MRJ is clearly very distressed by the implications of what he writes about here. It seems most likely to me that 'Whitminster' was the ghost story of 1915, the one that needed a lot of work, 'dusting', to make it into print (it reads very much like two stories stitched together). It's tempting to speculate that MRJ uses the powerfully bodily metaphor of *flaying* at moments of agitation or discomfort (his dispute with Jane Harrison, and here the Irish sorcerers who strip dead children's skin)—there is a very disturbing rhetorical surplus to the image, a linguistic extremism very unusual in a measured, reserved writer like MRJ. We know that he didn't want to publish 'Lost Hearts', and he seems to have struggled with 'Whitminster'.

If it is a gay ghost story, it is an *extremely* troubled one. In many MRJ stories—here, and in 'Oh, Whistle', 'Abbot Thomas', and elsewhere, there is a real horror of *touch*. In 'Whitminster', this is connected to a genuinely uncomfortable sense of twisted sexuality, and of boys' play gone wrong (a nightmare of Animal Grab). The relationship between Lord Saul, aged sixteen, and Frank Sydall, eleven, recalls the 'taking up' or 'small friend' scenarios of same-sex desire which, as we saw in Chapter 3, so many Victorian schoolboy fictions and actual headmasters warned against. Saul and Frank's 'game I did not understand' has tragic consequences: Saul 'very gently laid his hand on Frank's head', a gesture which causes Frank to collapse helpless on the grass. 'Saul explained that they had been acting the tragedy of Radamistus, in which the heroine reads the future fate of her father's kingdom by means of a glass ball held in her hand, and is overcome by the terrible events she had seen.'[89] The tragedy of Rhadamistus, King of Armenia, stabbing his pregnant wife Zenobia rather than seeing her fall into the hands of the enemy, was a popular one in eighteenth-century opera and drama (the earlier part of 'Whitminster' is set in 1730), though it seems likely that MRJ is alluding to Handel's *Radamisto* (1720) here (Handel, we know, was a particular favourite). Frank, the submissive younger boy, takes the female part here, in a forbidden game which leads to the deaths of both boys, who are buried together in as stone altar tomb in Whitminster churchyard.[90]

'The Diary of Mr. Poynter' is scarcely less concerned with anxieties about touch and queer sexuality. MRJ likely got the name from the antiquary John Poynter, dismissed from Oxford University in 1732 for 'sodomitical practices'.[91] The story's protagonist has a pair of curtains made after a design which turns out to be based on the luxuriant hair of the seventeenth-century rake Sir Everard

Charlett, 'a personable young gent. but a loose atheistical companion . . . He was a very beautiful person, who constantly wore his own Hair, which was very abundant, from which, and from his loose way of living, the cant name for him was Absalom'.[92] Absalom, the son of King David, was renowned for his good looks, his blemish-free body, and most particularly the beautiful hair which proves his undoing (it becomes tangled in a tree during the battle of the Wood of Ephraim). Sir Everard is found dead in a ditch, his hair removed; but when his body is exhumed years later, the coffin is full of hair. Mr Denton's curtains summon what may be the ghost of Sir Everard Charlett, a being made entirely of hair, which is first apprehended though touch, as Denton wakes up from a doze in his armchair:

> he felt on the back of it just the slightest touch of a surface of hair, and stretching it out in that direction he stroked and patted a rounded something . . . What he had been touching rose to meet him. It was in the attitude of one that had crept along the floor on its belly, and it was, so far as could be recollected, a human figure. But of the face which was not rising to within a few inches of his own no feature was discernible, only hair.[93]

Of all things, hair sometimes seems most terrifying to MRJ and his protagonists, most emblematic of an insecure, destabilized world.[94] MRJ's own hair, as a young man, was often on the verge of being too long, and the subject of frequent comment and rebuke from his Eton masters, notably Walter Durnford ('I can still hear him proclaiming that James, K.S. [King's Scholar], must get his hair cut before five o'clock school.')[95] The hirsute 'Shavey Bardof' of his undergraduate years was the subject of Ber's recurring derision. MRJ's ghosts have hair, too much hair, hair where there should be none. Mrs Mothersole's skeleton in 'The Ash-Tree' has 'some remains of black hair', and the skeletal, child-abducting spectre of 'The Mezzotint' has 'a white dome-like forehead and a few straggling hairs'.[96] Both the demon of 'Canon Alberic' and the lamia of 'An Episode of Cathedral History' are entirely covered in hair. The entity occupying the non-existent room in 'Number 13' is glimpsed only as 'an arm . . . clad in ragged, yellowish linen, and the bare skin, where it could be seen, had long grey hair on it'.[97] The very feel of hair is unsettling: Mr Dunning in 'Casting the Runes' feels 'a mouth, with teeth, and hair about it' under his pillow; while Dr Haynes in 'The Stalls of Barchester Cathedral', putting his hand on a carved wooden choir-stall, 'was startled by what seemed a softness, a feeling as of rather rough and coarse fur'.[98]

Some of *A Thin Ghost*'s first readers responded to what they saw as a sense of slightness, and a feeling of tiredness hanging over the volume. Reginald

Farrer, the travel writer and botanist, wrote from his camp 12,000 feet up in the Himalayas to tell MRJ that 'in your preface to A Thin Ghost, as well as the thinness of the volume itself, I am horrified to note in you signs of weakening and wearying, a diffidence about "continuations"'. He entreated MRJ to continue writing, to pour his energies into the ghost stories:

> I (we) call, instead, for renewed energies, *annual* volumes, *fat* ones . . . &, perhaps, for a renewal of modern settings: Demons & 18th Century Canons & Cathedrals are all very well: but your own work has shown me how the malign supernatural doubles in conviction & horror, if it intrudes upon lives that dress & talk in just our own mode of the moment.[99]

One particular fat ghost could scarcely conceal his delight at his disappointment on reading *A Thin Ghost*:

> I know everyone in Rome [O.B. wrote to MRJ], belong to 6 clubs—and I believe I have not a single enemy—quite a new experience for me. . . . I don't care for your thin ghost, nor do I think it good. Perhaps I am not clever enough to understand it—but you have a charming style.[100]

In his correspondence (and no doubt his conversation), O.B. rarely passed up the opportunity for a sideswipe at MRJ, right up to the end. After his death in 1923, MRJ got to have the last word, in that year's King's Founders' Day Speech: 'Lately . . . the somewhat troubled life of Oscar Browning ended: in calm happiness I am glad to think. It is quite difficult for one who frankly remembers his attitude towards Eton to do complete justice to his memory.'[101]

A Thin Ghost was not the only work of supernatural fiction that MRJ planned and wrote during the war, and published in its aftermath. Visiting Grace in her home near Presteigne in September 1916, he wrote to Gwen to tell her 'I have purchased some paper with the view of writing upon it to explain to Jane what I have heard from the owls and other neighbours, and how it came about that I was able to do so: but when these matters will take shape is uncertain'.[102] This is our first sight of *The Five Jars*, a work of children's fantasy originally written for Jane, and published a few years later in 1922. It's the longest work of fiction he ever wrote, and in spite of his diffidence in the letter to Gwen, it took shape very quickly. By the end of October, Arthur had read the work in progress, and found it 'quite an enchanting story & I have little to say except that I want to hear more'.[103] Edward Arnold published *The Five Jars* in October 1922; MRJ had tried to persuade the publisher to use some of Gwen's illustrations for the book, but unfortunately, he told her, 'your pictures won't reproduce'. He wasn't happy with the illustrations Arnold did use, by the Art

Nouveau-influenced artist Gilbert James, who also designed the book's extremely stylish title-page. (The drawings are wonderful, though with their Aubrey Beardsley and Harry Clarke resonances were probably too advanced and aesthetically daring for MRJ's sensibilities.)

The Five Jars opens with a letter to Jane, very much along the same lines as MRJ's initial letter to Gwen:

> MY DEAR JANE
> You remember that you were puzzled when I told you I had heard something from the owls—or if not puzzled (for I know you have some experience of these things), you were at any rate anxious to know exactly how it happened. Perhaps the time has now come for you to be told.[104]

The narrator, 'M (or N)' (fifty-four years old, we are told—MRJ's age in September 1916—red-faced, rather overweight, and with a bit of an 'owlish expression') finds himself in a landscape 'so extraordinarily green. It seemed to have in it all the greenness that was possible', a world of talking oak trees and literally babbling brooks.[105] He eats a magical plant, which allows him to see what is buried underground (an archaeologist's fantasy), and so he unearths a hidden box, buried under a stone. The box holds five jars, each containing a magical unguent which opens his senses, allowing him to see a new, supernatural reality (a subject to which MRJ would return in 1925, in horrifying form, in his story 'A View from a Hill'). He dreams of a Romano-British alchemist and magus, the man who concocted the unguents, and comes to realize that there are forces abroad—witches, bats—who want to get their hands on the five jars.

With its talking owls and its unseen world of magical little people, *The Five Jars* has close connections with 'After Dark in the Playing Fields'. As we have seen, this story was particularly influenced by MRJ's two favourite Shakespeare plays, *A Midsummer Night's Dream* and *The Merry Wives of Windsor*. We are, in other words, firmly in the enchanted English landscapes of folklore here. As Katharine Briggs, the greatest English folklorist of the twentieth century, argued across a number of influential books, fairies are fundamental to the English imaginary, as is the sense that the land itself borders on and interpenetrates with Fairyland, a magical realm or order (borders of this and other kinds were perhaps on his mind as he began to write the book in Presteigne, right on the Welsh border, and wrote it for Jane in Dippersmoor, within sight of the same border).[106] Windsor Great Forest, the Wirral (home of the Wodwoses), Wonderland, the Great Grimpen Mire, Narnia, the Shire, Alderley Edge,

Glastonbury, Discworld. The English literary imagination (yes, even in the minds of Scottish and Northern Irish writers) constantly returns to these places which both are and are not England, which straddle the border between two realms, and two orders. This is, to borrow the title of an important book on the subject, the Land of the Green Man.[107]

The Five Jars is an oddity, a work of white magic.[108] The Modernist intellectual and occultist Mary Butts, who wrote the first sustained critical study of MRJ in 1934, considered it 'a child's classic' of the same order as Lewis Carroll's *Alice* books.[109] This would be taking things too far for most readers—but there is something fascinating about *The Five Jars*. It stands at an oblique angle to the rest of MRJ's imaginative fiction, and this allows it to cast an illuminating light on the man and his ghost stories. Nathaniel Wedd, in fact, thought that *The Five Jars* was 'the book in which the lid was partly lifted and the repressed workings of Monty's mind showed us something of what was really going on'.[110] The book tells us things about his understanding of children, his ways of communicating with them, his own childlikeness. It tells us things about his fascination with folklore and magic, and his sense as he grew older that this was, in a manner not exactly metaphorical, the world he inhabited. And it tells us things about his sense of ancient, powerful artefacts buried in the landscape, part of the sedimentary process by which the land was formed; 'surprising, too, in how many places there lie, unsuspected, bones of men.'[111]

* * *

By now, MRJ was a firm fixture amongst the great and the good, meeting and corresponding with royalty and with past, present, and future Prime Ministers and Presidents (Winston Churchill, Stanley Baldwin, Herbert Asquith, Woodrow Wilson). He was regularly invited to sit on various syndicates, committees, boards, and commissions, from the Cambridge University Press Syndicate (the body which approves all the Press's publications, of which he was a long-time and influential member, and sometime chair) to the Commission on Historical Monuments (which George Duckworth, the Commission's Secretary, co-opted him onto in 1921), to his appointment as a Trustee of the British Museum in 1925. He had become, in other words, a public figure. In 1919, he was invited to sit on the Asquith Commission, which had been established 'To consider the applications which have been made by the Universities of Oxford and Cambridge for financial assistance from the state, and for that purpose to enquire into the financial resources of the Universities and of the colleges and halls therein, into the administration and application of these resources, into the government of the Universities, and into the relations of the colleges and halls to the Universities and to each other'.[112] Traditionally economically self-sustaining through rents, fees, and benefactions, Oxford and Cambridge had taken serious financial hits during the war, which catastrophically exacerbated the long-term attritional damage caused by the agricultural depression. They had applied to the state for aid—but, if granted, would this be at the price of institutional independence?[113]

The Commission was chaired by former Prime Minister H. H. Asquith, with Gerald Balfour as his deputy. Balfour was an Old Etonian and a former Fellow and Lecturer in Classics at Trinity: it seems most likely that he suggested MRJ's membership of the Commission. He was chair of the subcommittee specifically tasked with reporting on Cambridge: the other Cambridge Commissioners were Sir Hugh Kerr Anderson, Master of Gonville and Caius, B. A. Clough, Principal of Newnham, Lord Chalmers, Master of Peterhouse, Sir Horace Darwin, Fellow of Trinity, the historian G. M. Trevelyan, and MRJ himself. It is difficult to imagine a group like this responding to the circumstances with anything really radical. Even if they were not, like MRJ, utter change-blocking conservatives, they were all heavily if not totally invested in the institution on which they reported.

The report did have things to say about governance. It recommended the appointment of Commissioners to the universities, to oversee the enactment of the Commission's report, though these turned out to be largely institutional insiders, and their mandate ceased at the end of 1925.[114] It made recommendations about teaching and research, and about opening access through an expanded system of scholarships. But it declined to mandate greater funding of the Universities by the Colleges, which would have weakened their sense of separateness and independence, not to mention their financial power. And, while the Commission's Report was in favour of the full membership of women in universities, it did not go so far as to recommend making this compulsory. Once again, the Universities were largely left to reform themselves, and the Asquith Commission's report was widely viewed as a conservative one. An editorial in *The Spectator* summed up the establishment response to the Asquith Commission report: 'The great majority of Oxford and Cambridge men must have given a sigh of relief when they saw the Report of the Royal Commission . . . Happily, the Royal Commission has decided to recommend that Oxford and Cambridge should go on being what they have always been, only more so.'[115]

* * *

The duties of the Eton Provostship were not very onerous, and left MRJ with plenty of time for research. He was still in correspondence with Henry Yates Thompson, the great book collector. But Thompson was now an old man, and had decided it was time to sell his collection. MRJ got wind of this, via Sydney Cockerell at the Fitzwilliam: 'I don't think you could have told me anything that could have pained or disgusted me more', he replied. 'Hateful, hateful.'[116] He sent Thompson an anguished and troubling letter:

> This is too sad. S.C.C. has told me now the dreadful news that you mean to sell your books. I can't say what a grief this is to me. I did think they at least were safe for England & were not, once gathered, to be dispersed again amongst Boches, Jews, & Transatlantics. If I were by you I would go down on my knees to beseech you to give up the idea.

Keeping the collection in England, MRJ argued, would be 'a real permanent service to the nation and the race . . . I beseech you by all that you hold sacred not to do this thing'.[117]

Cockerell tried to get the money together to buy the whole collection, but the price was way above the Fitzwilliam's means. 'Be reasonable', Thompson wrote to Cockerell:

> If I like you were a scholar and an expert in history & art I should probably agree that the B[ritish] Museum was the only place for the mss. at any cost. I am however only a collector of art bijoux . . . and I don't want to see mine merged in any public institution, however great.[118]

Cockerell wrote a bitter letter to MRJ:

> HYT has a heart of stone, and has never really *seen* any of his manuscripts. He does not know in the least what their eternal value is as 'life-enhancers'. They are toys that he has bought with his money and that he thinks himself justified in treating as he pleases.[119]

But Thompson did agree to donate the fourteenth-century Metz Pontifical to the Fitzwilliam, and the St. Omer Psalter to the British Museum, where the manuscript is dedicated to MRJ, Cockerell, and Sir George Warner, the Museum's Keeper of MSS.[120]

What are we to make of MRJ's remark about 'Boches, Jews, & Transatlantics' getting their hands on manuscript collections? MRJ certainly had many of the prejudices of his age, but was antisemitism one of them? There are undoubtedly traces of antisemitic stereotyping on occasion in his stories.[121] Most notably, in 'The Uncommon Prayer-Book' (1925), the unscrupulous book-collector Poschwitz is pretty clearly coded as Jewish: with his black hair, his pince-nez, and his 'little pointed beard', he is, one character asserts, not 'a reel Englishman at all'.[122] But the reality is nuanced. This is an obviously desperate, beseeching letter to Thompson, written in high agitation: 'I write at fever heat.... Nothing could have stirred me more.' Elsewhere, MRJ said, did, and was other, better things. Charles Waldstein, whom he revered, was simultaneously all three of the categories he criticizes here, a 'Boche', a Jew, and a Transatlantic. In his long introduction to *The Life and Miracles of William of Norwich*, MRJ wrote a long and highly critical analysis of the antisemitic 'blood libel' trope. But, like most Englishmen of his time and class, he could deploy what seems today like unthinking, casual antisemitic rhetoric and tropes. He once took objection to some illustrations he'd seen of the Book of Judith, 'about 4 pictures of a nasty almond-eyed Jewess with the fewest possible clothes'.[123] In a sermon he delivered at Eton at some point in the 1920s, MRJ contrasted the 'serviceable and courteous' worldwide reputation of Old Etonians with 'the qualities which makes us dislike the Jews now':

> So there is a danger in tradition as well as a safeguard. If it welded the Jews together and made it possible for them to preserve their nationality it also made them develop some very unamiable qualities—blinded their eyes and hardened their hearts—and was to no slight extent responsible for the dreadful treatment they met with from other nations. Not that I mean to excuse these other nations for the way in which they treated the Jews; only I do say that the Jews made themselves most difficult to deal with.[124]

There is, unfortunately, nothing particularly unusual in an Englishman of MRJ's time and class making such comments, nor in a man with Jewish friends (Waldstein) offering generalized denunciations of 'the Jews'. His friend Ronny Norman recounted to MRJ a meeting with two Hungarian Jews in Dresden: 'I never saw worse specimens of their noisome race.'[125] These kinds of views were hardly unusual in the kinds of circles in which MRJ moved.

* * *

The most recent and comprehensive bibliography of MRJ's work lists ninety publications of various kinds between 1918 and 1925.[126] While some of these were letters, reviews, and works of fiction, some were important works of scholarship. *The Wanderings and Homes of Manuscripts* (1919) is a guide to the world of codicological history which aims 'to tell where manuscripts were made, and how and in what centres they have been collected'.[127] He knew that manuscript collections, even ones as grand as Yates Thompson's, tended to get scattered, had their 'wanderings'. The monograph was on the subject closest to

MRJ's scholarly heart, and so it is a very revealing one, with an honest account of his own weaknesses as a cataloguer, and one which casts a strangely illuminating light on the ghost stories:

> So texts and books wander, and so do discoveries sometimes lie near our hands. The moral is: be inquisitive. See books for yourself; do not trust that the cataloguer has told you everything. I am a cataloguer myself, and I know that, try as he may, a worker of that class cannot hope to know or to see every detail that is of importance. The creature is human, and on some days his mind is less alert than on others. Nor is he interested in everything alike: an apocryphal fragment or an obscure saint will excite me, while a letter of St. Bernard which may be unpublished leaves me calm. But in spite of the imperfections of cataloguers, catalogues must be used, and they must be read and not only referred to.[128]

'The moral is: be inquisitive.' But also: 'A Warning to the Curious'. As we have seen many times, the ghost stories are imaginative but also anxious fantasies upon the implications of MRJ's own scholarly life, the dark shadows which the light of illumination inevitably casts. As MRJ writes of the doomed Mr Wraxall in 'Count Magnus', 'His besetting fault was pretty clearly that of over-inquisitiveness, possibly a good fault in a traveller, certainly a fault for which this traveller paid dearly enough in the end'.[129]

Catalogues are works of the imagination, which 'must be read and not only referred to'. In 1921, MRJ published one of his smallest but most fascinating catalogues, as he set about the task of imaginatively reconstructing and cataloguing the library of the Elizabethan magus John Dee.[130] Dee was precisely the kind of figure who fascinated MRJ most, simultaneously a magician and a bibliophile. For Dee, the former activity was dependent on the latter to such an extent that he proposed a cataloguing project of his own, the creation of a kind of British Library of Magic. 'Dee was not merely an alchemist and a spiritualist', MRJ thought, 'but a really learned man, and one who had done his best... to stimulate interest in the rescuing of MSS. from the dissolved monastic libraries and to induce the sovereign to establish a central national collection of them.' When Dee left England in 1583 for a journey to Bohemia and Poland, his neighbours in Mortlake broke into his house, stole his scientific instruments, and plundered his library. 'The cause of the raid was no doubt Dee's dealings with spirits, which not unnaturally earned him the reputation of being a sorcerer', MRJ comments.[131] Dee's library contained an extensive selection of magical and alchemical works, by Roger Bacon, Albertus Magnus, Ramon Lull, and others.

In 1924, MRJ published a book which had been many decades in the gestation, and which stands as one of his major scholarly achievements. *The Apocryphal New Testament* has its deep origins at the very beginning of MRJ's scholarly life, in the lists of apocrypha and marginalia he began to compile in his teenage notebooks, and has powerful links with his Fellowship dissertation from 1887, in which he reconstructed the contents of the lost *Apocalypse of Peter* from hints and fragments. In *The Apocryphal New Testament*, MRJ gathered together, translated, and commented upon all the textual sources for this book: the scattered quotations which formed the basis of his original argument; the Akhmîm fragment whose discovery seemed to vindicate his original hypothesis; thirteen lines from a tiny (2½ by 2 inches) and almost unreadable Bodleian manuscript; the Ancient Ethiopic text which Sylvain Grébaut had published in 1910; and a section of the *Second Book of the Sibylline Oracles* 'which is most evidently taken from the Apocalypse of Peter'.[132] Here, MRJ condenses what is effectively a whole lifetime's work into nineteen pages.

Some of MRJ's intellectual interests from this time fed very directly into his thinking on ghost stories. 'Much of my time has been spent over tracing the writings of Sheridan Le Fanu in periodicals', he wrote to Gwen in March 1922.[133] This was in preparation for publishing an edition of *Madam Crowl's Ghost and Other Tales of Mystery* in 1923, to which he appended an extensive bibliography of Le Fanu's writings in the *Dublin University Magazine* and elsewhere. The stories in *Madam Crowl's Ghost*, he wrote in the Introduction, 'have been gleaned from extinct periodicals. They are the result of a fairly long investigation'.[134] Le Fanu had been a great favourite since Temple Grove, and MRJ's account of him here sounds very much like a meditation on his own work:

> He stands absolutely in the first rank as a writer of ghost stories. That is my deliberate verdict, after reading all the supernatural tales I have been able to get hold of. Nobody sets the scene better than he, nobody touches in the effective detail more deftly. I do not think it is merely the fact of my being past middle age that leads me to regard the leisureliness of his style as a merit; for I am by no means inappreciative of the more modern efforts on this branch of fiction. No, it has to be recognized I am sure, that the ghost story is in itself a slightly old-fashioned form; it needs some deliberateness in the telling; we listen to it more readily of the narrator poses as elderly, or throws back his experience to 'some thirty years ago'.[135]

MRJ continued this preoccupation with a lecture on Le Fanu which he delivered to the Royal Institution in March 1923. 'But how does he contrive to inspire horror?' he asked. 'It is partly, I think, owing to the very skilful use of a crescendo, so to speak. The gradual removal of one safeguard after another, the victim's dim forebodings of what is to happen gradually growing clearer; these are the processes which generally increase the strain of excitement.'[136] Once again, he could have been talking about himself. 'The Familiar', 'Mr, Justice Harbottle', and 'Squire Toby's Will' were, he thought, 'the best ghost stories in the English language'.[137] Of these, it was 'Mr. Justice Harbottle', Le Fanu's tale of an eighteenth-century judge 'who had the reputation of being about the wickedest man in England', that impressed him most (MRJ loved his hanging judges).[138] He was very glad not to have read it as a schoolboy, he told Gwen, because 'it would have settled my hash'.[139]

He was also publishing rather more arcane supernatural research around this time. Reading David Casley's *A Catalogue of the Manuscripts of the King's Library* (1734), MRJ came across a brief reference to a series of what seemed to be fifteenth-century Latin ghost stories. This led him to examine the manuscript source, Royal MS 15.A.xx, in the British Museum in April 1922. What he found was a series of ghost stories written on the blank pages at the end of the manuscript by a monk at Byland Abbey, North Yorkshire—though there were parts of this manuscript which even he found unreadable.[140] His edition of 'Twelve Medieval Ghost Stories' was published in the *English Historical Review* that July.[141] MRJ thought that the stories may have originated in Scandinavia, but they are also very much tales of an intensely local folklore (these two places of origin, Scandinavia and Yorkshire, are hardly mutually exclusive given the traffic between them). The stories tell of the supernatural encounters of travellers on the lonely North Yorkshire Moors, or of ghostly appearances in Pickering, Kilburn, Ampleforth, or Cleveland—all within a few miles of Byland. The sense of the English landscape as a *haunted* one is vivid in the 'Twelve Medieval Ghost Stories'.

MRJ was back in Cambridge in the Michaelmas Term of 1923, to take up the Sandars Readership in Bibliography. Funded by a bequest from the Trinity graduate Samuel Sandars, a bibliophiliac barrister, the Readership (still very much on the go) is described by Cambridge University as 'one of the most prestigious honorary posts to which book historians, librarians and researchers can be appointed'.[142] According to the Sandars benefaction, the Reader was expected to deliver one or more lectures which 'shall embrace the subjects of Bibliography, Palaeography, Typography, Bookbinding, Book Illustration, the Science of Books and Manuscripts, and the Arts relating thereunto'.[143] This was in fact the second time MRJ had taken up this role: in 1902 he delivered a series of lectures on 'Manuscripts in Cambridge' as a last-minute replacement, and now, at the behest of the University Librarian Francis Jenkinson, he lectured on 'The Pictorial Illustration of the Old Testament from the 4th to the 16th Centuries'.[144] MRJ was paid £54 for the Sandars Readership, and complained bitterly about having to give £11 of this to the Inland Revenue: 'the cheek of the Taxers'.[145]

At Eton, MRJ became occupied by two projects in a building very near his heart, the College Chapel. In 1921, work began on transforming a part of the Chapel vestry into a War memorial Chapel. The centrepiece of this chapel is a magnificent stained glass window, executed by the artist Thomas Grylls according to a design by MRJ himself. Dominating the window is a vast red cross, as though the entire window had been drenched in blood. Christ sits in majesty at the centre of the cross, surrounded by biblical figures (King David), saints (St. Stephen, St. George, St. Alban), medieval crusaders, and, at the bottom, First World War soldiers, looking up. Surrounding the cross is the rainbow of hope. This, probably, is where we need to look to understand MRJ's feelings about the War. It is formal, public, and institutional. It offers a sense of historical continuity, of a Christian nation involved in one long struggle, a holy war. The sheer quantity of red glass symbolizes the deaths and suffering, which would be unbearable were they not mitigated by Christian faith and the belief in a just cause. Luxmoore was moved to tears by it, writing to MRJ: 'to tell the truth I was rather choked over it, it touches me very deeply & I feel that no one else cd. have done anything so fine & tender'.[146] Beneath the window sits one of Eton's great treasures, the *Libro d'oro*, the Golden Book, formally entitled *List of Etonians Who Fought in the Great War, 1914–1919*. The book is based on a list compiled by the Eton housemaster E. L. Vaughan (5660 old boys and masters fought in the War, of whom 1157 were killed), and was handwritten on vellum by the calligrapher Graily Hewitt. The names of the soldiers are bookended by two Etonian First World War poems, Julian Grenfell's 'Into Battle', which he wrote at the front not long before he was killed, and Cecil Spring-Rice's 'I Vow to Thee My Country', a poem to which we shall return.[147]

In 1847, some whitewash and wainscoting was removed from the walls of Eton College Chapel, to reveal a series of remarkable Early Modern wall paintings, two rows of scenes representing the Miracles of the Virgin and the lives of saints, painted between 1479 and 1488 in the Dutch style and credited (according to the College records) to the artist William Baker.[148] In a manner which makes one understand MRJ's animus against Victorian restoration, the top row of paintings was removed almost immediately after their rediscovery, and the rest largely covered by an organ screen. On becoming Provost, MRJ insisted on the removal of these canopies, and oversaw the reappearance of the paintings, carried out according to his strict principles. The actual work for this was done by the art historian E. W. Tristram, who 'performed little short of a miracle', according to one Eton history.[149] Time had faded the paint to a series of rather dull browns, but there was to be no renovation of the paintwork—MRJ was very clear on that, as was Luxmoore: 'The "restoration" of the pictures I dismiss—no one ventures to speak of that.'[150] But not everyone was happy with the result, which many thought made the Chapel look too dark, and even depressing. MRJ's (very) supportive Eton colleagues Lionel Byrne and E. L. Churchill had their doubts, arguing that 'the lack of colour and the long expanse of bare stone above the panels and the paintings combine to produce an impression of chill and gloom not well suited for any place of worship, and least of all for one used by a congregation of schoolboys'.[151] Others were blunter. Arthur Benson whispered to MRJ on his first sight of them that the wall paintings made the Chapel look like 'a palaeolithic cavern'.[152] MRJ himself thought that 'in these paintings Eton possesses a treasure which is, honestly, unrivalled in this country and in France'.[153] (Posterity has been more sympathetic to his views: they are, according to Pevsner, 'The most important surviving C15 wall paintings in England'.)[154] Viewing the Eton wall paintings, in fact, filled MRJ with patriotic pride: here, he thought, was an authentically great English contribution to early modern painting. 'Unless and until it is shown by very clear evidence', he wrote in the *Times*, 'that William Baker is an anglicism for Willem or Wilhelm Backer, or something of that kind, we are within our rights in claiming this painter as an Englishman.'[155]

Ecclesiastical architecture and institutions featured very heavily in MRJ's world in the first half of the 1920s. In the summer of 1924, he was approached by the Great Western Railway Company with what was a strange but, for him, appealing offer. Would he be interested in writing an antiquarian guidebook to the abbeys and monasteries of Wales and the West of England—places that an interested visitor could get to on a Great Western train? GWR would provide him with a car and driver. He certainly was interested, and in August and September of 1924 he visited as many of the abbeys as he could manage, and also a few country houses. He packed them in, generally seeing five a day—and on his busiest day, 7 August, pootling around the West Midlands, he took in Stoneleigh Abbey, Berkswell Hall, Meriden, Maxstoke Castle, Ashley, Merevale Abbey, Atherstone, and Tamworth![156] The result is one of MRJ's most enjoyable books, *Abbeys* (1925)—'a popular book', as he avows, but one with deep roots in MRJ's research and his life.[157] Some of the abbeys the book describes were very dear to him. Dore Abbey and Llanthony Priory, both on the Welsh border, were places he loved to visit while staying with Gwen in Dippersmoor. He attended services at Dore, and once read the lesson there: 'he seemed to be so much too large for the place', Gwen thought, 'it always gave me an unreal feeling, as if some saint held forth to lesser creatures and birds.'[158] Llanthony is a beautiful ruin set amongst spectacular countryside, right on the border itself. What must it be like to be able to see it as it once was? The following year he wrote a story, 'A View from a Hill', which set out to answer that question.

He took a few days out of his *Abbeys* itinerary in August to visit Dorset. His diary entry for the 19th reads 'Bettiscombe (Screaming Skull)'.[159] It's quite likely that MRJ had encountered the legend of the Screaming Skull of Bettiscombe Manor from the work of the antiquarian J. S. Udall, whose speculations on the source of the legend began a controversy which caught the attention of one of MRJ's predecessors as Provost of Eton, Charles Old Goodford. Locked in a drawer in the Manor's study was a human skull. According to legend, Udall wrote, 'if [the skull] be brought out of the house the house itself would rock to its foundations, whilst the person by whom such an act of desecration was committed would certainly die within the year'.[160] The skull was believed to be that of 'a negro servant . . . [who] had declared before his death that his spirit would not rest unless his body was taken to his native land and buried there'.[161] When his body was buried in Bettiscombe, the screaming started. Udall, a former colonial administrator, traced the story back to the slave-owning family of Azariah Pinney, exiled to Antigua by Judge Jeffreys for his part in the Monmouth Rebellion of 1685. Given his interest in Jeffreys, in the Monmouth Rebellion, and in seventeenth-century English history in general, one can see why MRJ would have been drawn to the legend of the Screaming Skull of Bettiscombe Manor. If he made any connections with his family's own West Indian slave-owning history, he kept them to himself.

In December 1924, he was asked by Randall Davidson, the Archbishop of Canterbury, to sit on a Cathedrals Commission, which would report on the future governance and financial sustainability of England's cathedrals—which, like the Oxbridge Colleges, had been jeopardized by severe fluctuations in rental income. The Commission was chaired by Cosmo Lang, then Archbishop of York, and included several bishops, as well as the patriotic man of letters Henry Newbolt. As ever, if you ensure that the right people are on a committee, you need be under no fear for their decisions—and no committee with MRJ on it was ever going to make radical suggestions. Their report emphasized the power of the Deans, proposed strengthening collegiality and fostering closer ties with the diocese, and, in a suggestion which would have pleased the Venerable John Benwell Haynes, D.D., the frustrated protagonist of 'The Stalls of Barchester Cathedral', proposed compulsory retirement at seventy, on the grounds that 'very elderly men' were 'unlikely to inspire or direct . . . the revived life of our cathedrals'.[162]

* * *

The end of the War meant that MRJ and his friends could get back to their European holidays—France was open again. In August 1920, MRJ, Ram, and A. E. Conybeare went on a bicycling holiday. From Paris, they took a night train to Bordeaux, and then cycled along the Garonne to Moissac, picking blackberries as they went, and then up through the Lot and Dordogne, to Cahors and Sarlat. The following year he went on a huge 260-mile trip with Ram and Anstey Guthrie. Montauban, Albi, Ambialey, Gaillac, Cordes, St. Antonin (where they went to an open-air cinema to watch the comedy *La Baigneuse Inconnue* [*The Unknown Bather*]), Najac, Villefranche, Rieupeyroux, Rodez, Figeac, Assier, Gramat, Rocamadour, Bretonoux, Beaulieu, Brive, Tulle, and back to Paris.[163] MRJ was a heavy smoker in his late fifties, so this is a truly impressive itinerary. They really were making up for lost time.

In April 1921, he took a holiday by himself in Aldeburgh, where he'd spent his summers as a child. This was something he would continue to do every year until the end of his life, generally around Easter. Booking into the White Lion, he would take a large supply of detective novels (Dorothy L. Sayers came to be his favourite), and happily read his way through them. More old haunts the following May, as he cycled around Kent with Johnnie Maxwell and Owen Hugh Smith. The three of them looked in on MRJ's birthplace, Goodnestone, before wending their way north, inevitably, to Aldeburgh.

In August 1922, MRJ, Ram, Conybeare, and Guthrie went to France again. They cycled through St. Yrieux and Lubersac, played Jacobi (Guthrie, who couldn't get the hang of it, was delighted when he finally won a game), and hired a lorry to take them and their bikes to Uzerche in the torrential rain. Then something very odd happened. This is how MRJ records it in a letter to Gwen:

> A sudden gloom fell upon Guthrie at Uzerche and for two or three days he confined his remarks to a minimum: we didn't know why: we guessed it might be a postcard with a pig hunting for truffles which we posted to him at Brantôme, but we never knew. It can't have been bad news from home, for he got no home letters at Uzerche. It remains a mystery.[164]

Guthrie left France on 5 September, and he and MRJ never spoke again. Every year for decades, he had sent MRJ a copy of an early Italian painting as a Christmas present—but there were no more after this. The only correspondence from Guthrie after September 1922 is a brief, rather formal note in June 1930, congratulating MRJ on being awarded the Order of Merit. 'The breach remained unmended', Gwen wrote, long after both men were dead.[165]

What can have happened? We will never know, but MRJ's story about the postcard with the pig can't be the whole story. In his memoirs, a posthumous but very public-facing document, Guthrie writes very cordially about MRJ, and goes in for warm reminiscences about their cycling holidays in France, up to and including the holiday of 1921. But the memoirs are completely silent on anything that happened to Guthrie between July 1922, shortly before the fateful trip, and early 1925, except to say this: 'For some years after the War I did no literary work whatever except two or three short stories (only one of which found itself accepted) and occasional articles for *Punch*; any dramatic ambition I ever had was effectually quenched.'[166]

Guthrie kept a diary, so we do have some sense of what was on his mind in Uzerche, and it wasn't postcards of pigs. The weather was unremittingly vile, and Conybeare decided to leave for home early. On the night of 27 August, Guthrie had what he described as a 'Humiliating dream', in which he found himself in a house with a lot of young people, being 'universally snubbed & despised'. On the night of the 29th, lying in his bed, he heard 'a woman's shriek from one of the bedrooms, followed by laughter which sounded rather hysterical—suppressed voices & more laughter'. The following night, after a day spent sightseeing, sketching, and the inevitable Jacobi (he was beginning to get good at it now), he writes, 'Fit of depression and silence all the evening. Wrote this. Shall be rather glad when the tour is over & doubt I shall ever come on another.' On 1 September, he continues: 'Still very depressed and hopeless about future'; though the following night he is 'feeling a little more cheerful'. And on 3 September: 'End of our tour. On the whole less depressed than I was, though not exactly sorry it is over.'[167] The last time the two friends ever saw one another was when they said goodbye on a railway station platform in Calais. MRJ, Guthrie notes, had bought a pair of new P. G. Wodehouse novels. At no point in his diary is there any sense of rancour, or even of irritation, with MRJ personally. (MRJ's diary for the holiday is completely unforthcoming: '*rain*. Lorry to Uzerche. 30 [August] Uzerche.')[168]

The diary entries, coupled with the blank years in the memoirs, and the inability to write or get anything published, sounds like a depressive episode:

'Still very depressed and hopeless about the future.' Guthrie's diaries are largely factual records—who he saw and where he went—but for the following weeks, when he is back in London, they are punctuated by troubled passages—more 'humiliating' dreams; images of 'General disfigurement and death' (11 September); 'Rather depressed all day' (12 September); 'Still depressed & rather dreading the week-end' (13 September). From his circle of friends and colleagues, MRJ had often encountered depression and its consequences. Arthur Benson was laid low for years at a stretch by depression, as was J. H. Middleton of the Fitzwilliam. Reggie Balfour, Marcus Dimsdale, and Hugh Macnaghten all committed suicide in the depths of depressive despair. Even closer to home, Grace suffered from lifelong mental illness, and was often unable to look after herself or deal with other people and unfamiliar surroundings: when Arthur encountered her in the Provost's Lodge in December 1924, she 'fled with cries of alarm'.[169] But MRJ was also more comfortable dealing with the implications and repercussions of comic postcards than existential anguish, a subject he may not have understood at all. What's unusual or perhaps unique about Guthrie is the cutting of ties. MRJ was usually very loyal to his friends, as they were to him. But what's also unusual about Guthrie is that this is a friendship forged without the ties of institutions. Yes, he was a Cambridge graduate, but not a Kingsman, an Old Etonian, or a College friend of any kind. This was a friendship of independent adults, and without the cement of institutions, there was nothing to keep it in place.

For his holidays the next year, MRJ was on a much surer footing. He went to Aldeburgh with Ram for Easter—and found a new Le Fanu story in an issue of the *Dublin University Magazine* at the White Lion![170] That August, he and Walter Fletcher went cycling together in Denmark, revisiting some of MRJ's old haunts from decades earlier.

* * *

Ageing, mortality, death. As MRJ moved through and beyond late middle age, these loomed larger in his life. When he went to visit MRJ in November 1923, Arthur thought his friend looked 'pursy and elderly', and rather overweight.[171] While MRJ's health was still robust enough to manage enormous cycling trips through France, he was certainly not invulnerable. In 1917, he blithely informed Gwen that 'Life has been diversified for me by an episode called the shingles'.[172] In reality, the illness was so bad that it left his waist covered in painful blisters.

Much worse was the appendix trouble that began in 1924. In December, he went to York, to give a talk on the stained glass of York Minster. He was accompanied in his journey by persistent pains, and collapsed shortly after the talk, spending the next three days in bed. The doctor was called in on 20 December and 'agreed it was the appendix giving trouble'. but assured MRJ that 'it will pass & is not serious'.[173] But it was serious, sufficiently so for MRJ, when he got back to Eton, to have to spend the whole Christmas season in bed (he read Dickens's Christmas stories), and it didn't seem to be getting any better. 'Must I be drafted off to a nursing home & cut up?' he complained to Gordon Carey on 29 December.[174] From here to the end of his life, he would be under regular nursing care.

The old problems with his teeth returned. While by this stage he didn't have many actual teeth left (there were two stragglers), his dentures no longer fitted him, and so, he wrote to Gwen in March 1925,

> More than once a week I walk or drive into Slough and something is done to the jaw. The final fitting is tomorrow, the long period of discomfort then sets in, and unexpected visitors will be apt to find me with a pink and white object beside me on the table which I shall try to cover with a handkerchief.[175]

'I'm sorry about the teeth, I don't believe they make the slightest difference to health', Arthur reassured him.[176] 'Me new teeth are in today & how beastly they are going to be I can dimly conjecture', he wrote to A. F. Scholfield on 14 March.[177] Nevertheless, he was pleased with the result: 'two gleaming clashing rows of teeth'.[178] But he still complained grimly about 'going to the dentist to be pushed round & round the room like a rat in a hayloft, shrieking for mercy while the other closes in on you with the pinchers'.[179] The ghoulish pleasure he got from witnessing the 'squelch' of Hitchcock Minor's tooth extraction in 1877 came back to haunt him many times over.

By now, MRJ's circle of friends was visibly thinning. By the time of his death in 1936, age seventy-three—an old man, but not a *very* old man—he had outlived almost all his friends and contemporaries.

Harry Cust died of a heart attack in March 1917, apparently at his London home and not, as he would surely have chosen, in the boudoir of a duchess or the garret of a maidservant. His legendary sexual appetite, though, was unquenchable to the last. In her biography of Cust and his set, Anita Leslie writes that 'So much of the Cust strain entered England's peerage that from such a number of cradles there gazed babies with eyes like large sapphires instead of the black boot-buttons of their legal fathers'.[180] One such illegitimate aristocratic offspring was certainly the future Lady Diana Cooper, the product of Cust's affair with the Duchess of Rutland. In 1888, according to

Grantham lore, he seduced a local farmgirl, Phoebe Crust.[181] Their illegitimate daughter, Beatrice, grew up to marry a local grocer and future Alderman, Alfred Roberts. Alfred and Beatrice's daughter Margaret Hilda was born in Grantham on 13 October 1925, and properly deserves a book to herself. Except to say, so persistent were these rumours (which Lady Diana Cooper and her son John Julius Norwich loved spreading), that during the 1975 Conservative leadership contest, Tory MPs delightedly circulated a garbled version of it, telling colleagues that Margaret Thatcher was in fact Harry Cust's illegitimate *daughter*, not his granddaughter.[182] She had his eyes.

In February 1918, Cecil Spring-Rice, MRJ's fagmaster at Eton, dropped dead while staying at the home of the Governor General of Canada. Not long before this, he had been abruptly dismissed from his position as Ambassador to the United States. He had been suffering from Graves' Disease, an autoimmune condition, but his doctor thought him in very sound health. The American politician Henry Cabot Lodge, a close friend, was convinced that Spring Rice had died of 'loss of the will to live . . . which in the old days used to be termed a broken heart' as a consequence of losing the Ambassadorship.[183] That October, a memorial was dedicated at Eton Chapel in honour of Spring Rice—'a great man', MRJ avowed.[184] In 1921, Spring Rice's poem 'Urbs Dei' ('The City of God') was set to music by Gustav Holst. Now known as 'I Vow to Thee My Country', it is one of the great English hymns, sung at the funerals of monarchs and Prime Ministers.

The influenza pandemic of 1918–19 took Mark Sykes at the shockingly young age of thirty-nine. He had visited MRJ at Kings several times in the past couple of years, arriving at the Provost's Lodge 'like a whirlwind' as he took a break from helping to draw up and implement the Balfour Declaration, and impressing his host with a ghost story he'd written about Templars in Yorkshire in the reign of Henry II, 'The Black Templar of York'.[185] 'Mark Sykes is certainly a cruel loss', MRJ wrote on hearing the news of his death. 'His powers were extraordinary—nobody else could really keep either a whole party or one person genuinely amused for three hours on end, but he had really solid virtues as well—took his religion seriously.'[186] 'I must always be thankful for having known him', MRJ wrote to his widow. 'However long the gaps were between our meetings he was always the same. You picked up with him where you had left off, and only found him fuller of interests and surer in grasp of things.'[187] That was the private face of Mark Sykes. For the public face, the Zionist leader Nahum Sokolow wrote: 'He was a man who has won a monument in the future pantheon of the Jewish people and of whom legends will be told in

Palestine, Arabia and Armenia. We say the rest is immortality—in the annals of Zionism.'[188]

MRJ's King's friend and colleague Marcus Dimsdale had a reputation as an eccentric, underachieving don—charming, erratic, terribly absent-minded, and rather lazy, more interested in fishing that scholarship. But in middle age, he was diagnosed with neurasthenia, or nervous exhaustion. This was a common Edwardian psychological diagnosis, and it accounted for the 'sudden collapses of energy' (what today we might call depressive episodes) which his longtime friend and colleague Nathaniel Wedd thought were characteristic of him, and which in their turn accounted for the fact that, as a scholar, 'he had left so little memorial of himself behind'.[189] On 28 July 1919, in the middle of one such depressive episode, he put a gun to his head and killed himself. The verdict was 'temporary insanity'.[190] 'I loved that man', Dimsdale had said to MRJ when they heard of the death of their friend Walter Headlam. 'Certainly', MRJ added many years later, 'there were many who could truly say the same of Marcus.'[191]

In September 1923, MRJ wrote to Gwen, 'Sir Henry Babington Smith, I very much fear, hopelessly ill, but they are not talking about it'.[192] MRJ had seen a lot of his old schoolfriend since his return to Eton—HB was on the Governing Body. And now his wife Elizabeth had written to say that he was dying. 'The measure of the loss which my world would suffer if he passed out of it helps me ever so little to imagine what it would be to you', he replied on 27 September.[193] Two days later, HB died. He had contracted encephalitis lethargica, or sleeping sickness, and his last weeks were spent in a terrible fever and unbearable pain, before he slipped into a coma. One of the side-effects of encephalitis lethargica is klazoma, or compulsive screaming, so it's no surprise that his family were not keen to discuss HB's illness, even with good friends like MRJ. 'I'm afraid I take refuge too much in silence', he wrote to Elizabeth the next month, 'but I shrink—overmuch I daresay—from the risk of saying or writing platitudes, & all words do seem very feeble'.[194] Instead, he organized a memorial for HB at Eton. 'There is no single institution or department or person with whom he had to do that was not better & stronger for his presence', MRJ thought: 'his record is wonderful.'[195]

Worst of all, Arthur Benson died of a heart attack on 17 June 1925, in the Master's Lodge at Magdalene. 'The end was absolutely peaceful. I think he had no pain at all', Fred reassured MRJ a couple of days later. 'He was always so fond of you, & we must think of the amusing & affectionate times we had together.'[196] 'His love for us was wonderful', Ram (who succeeded Arthur as

Master of Magdalene) wrote to MRJ.[197] MRJ himself struggled to find the words, to keep his emotions in check: 'It is not easy to write with balance and proportion of an old and beloved friend who has, for over fifty years, been a part of one's life'.[198]

Arthur, we know, was a troubled soul, but he had found a measure of peace and happiness in his last years. MRJ noticed 'the vivid enjoyment of life in which, to the delight and thankfulness of us all, he moved in his last two years'.[199] Arthur had his last chaste love-affair, with the dazzling young King's Fellow Dadie Rylands, and even, in his final year, started to use the word 'homosexual' to describe men like himself.[200] In one of his last letters to MRJ, a month before he died, Arthur confessed: 'I have a dream sometimes of ending my days in a nice house in the [Canterbury Cathedral] Close & becoming a dear old man full of pious resignation.' The pair had even talked about writing a book together, on Hans Andersen: 'I should be *proud* to be associated with you in a little . . . volume such as you describe', Arthur wrote.[201] His friendship with MRJ was a part of that peace: 'What a *comfortable* person Monty is, though', he wrote in his diary in October 1923; 'I am completely at ease with him as I am with few people.'[202]

10

Order of Merit, 1930

On 5 April 1925 a letter arrived, addressed from 10 Downing Street: 'It would give me great pleasure (and the pleasures of a Prime Minister are few) if you would allow me to propose you for election as a Trustee of the British Museum at the next meeting of the Trustees.' Stanley Baldwin closed his letter with a personal request: 'Should you feel any gratitude to me (which I do not expect) I would only ask you to publish another volume of ghost stories.'[1] As if in direct answer to the Prime Minister, *A Warning to the Curious and other Ghost Stories*, MRJ's fourth and final collection, was published in time for Christmas that year.

MRJ did try to continue some of the Christmas traditions when he went to Eton, serving spiced beer to the Choral Scholars (one of whom apparently tried to persuade him, to his great amusement, 'to join the Sheffield Football Club as a non-playing member') and taking snuff at High Table.[2] But on the whole, in the 1920s he felt more at home at Christmas in Cambridge, and returned there often to spend the festive season with Walter Durnford at King's, or with Arthur and Ram at Magdalene. But as the decade wore on, these visits started to remind him more and more of what, in a terribly sad phrase from 'A Neighbour's Landmark', a story he wrote in 1924, he calls 'flying Time and all it had taken out of my life'.[3] In 1928, he wrote to Gwen:

> At Cambridge I saw—not a great many of the old gang—there are in fact not many to see. Dr. Mann was too shaky after the labours of the day to dine with the rest of us: he is by no means robust. Nor did I attend the Carol Service in King's for though perfectly done it is a little too something or other—voulu [contrived] for my taste.

Plus, he observed, at Magdalene, 'The Ramsays' cat is very handsome but terribly somnolent—thinks too much of personal dignity and won't unbend'.[4]

To what must have been Stanley Baldwin's delight, the ghost stories came, if not thick and fast, then steadily throughout the 1920s. 'Do you know I have written an immense deal of stuff', MRJ joked to A. F. Scholfield, '& find myself almost incurably first-class.'[5] Not all the stories from the early 1920s found their way into *A Warning to the Curious*. He enjoyed writing stories for the boys, for publication in various Eton ephemeral magazines and pamphlets. 'After Dark in the Playing Fields' (revealing, deceptively slight), first appeared in *College Days* in June 1924.[6] 'There Was a Man Dwelt by a Churchyard' was published in *Snapdragon* the following December.[7] Both these stories take their cues from Shakespeare, who came very much to the fore of MRJ's mind as he got older. Most particularly, he became preoccupied by Shakespeare as an occult, supernatural, or folkloric writer, a writer of magic. We have already touched more than once on the influence of *A Midsummer Night's Dream* and *The Merry Wives of Windsor* on 'After Dark', and 'There Was a Man' purports to be a continuation and completion of Mamilius's unfinished Christmas ghost story in *The Winter's Tale* (it is a Christmas ghost story about a Christmas ghost story). This is, in fact, the story which gives the play its title: 'A sad tale's best for winter / I have one of sprites and goblins... There was a man—...Dwelt by a churchyard.'[8] That's as far as Mamilius gets, before Leontes breaks in and imprisons his mother, Hermione, on suspicion of infidelity. 'There is no more of the story', MRJ writes; 'Mamilius died soon after without having the chance of finishing it. Now what was it going to have been? Shakespeare knew, no doubt, and I will be bold to say that I do.'[9]

The stories of the 1920s and 1930s often carry a sense of encroaching mortality ('flying Time and all it had taken out of my life'), of the shadow of the Great War (unspoken—sometimes, we shall see, literally excised—but felt). They contain deep and personal explorations of the meaning of the local, and of the English landscape. So, when John Betjeman, for example, describes MRJ as 'that master of haunting topographical prose', or when Robert Macfarlane evokes 'the eeriness of the English countryside' in MRJ's stories, they are quite likely thinking of stories such as 'A Warning to the Curious', 'A View from a Hill', or 'A Neighbour's Landmark'.[10]

MRJ went to stay in Aldeburgh every Easter, holing up for a week or so in the White Lion Hotel with a bagful of Dorothy L. Sayers and P. G. Wodehouse novels. 'Aldeburgh suits me as very well as a place where I needn't and don't do anything', he thought.[11] 'I have now been at large for a week and I think I did right in taking a dose of sea air, for I am doing as near as nothing in the way of exercise as may be and yet feel distinctly improved', he told Gwen in April 1924.

'I walked to the Martello Tower today and viewed the Norman Keep of Orford Castle six miles away across the Alde marshes.'[12] Aldeburgh's unusually large, clover-leaf Martello Tower, a place MRJ had been visiting for years, was about to have its great moment in English fiction.

'*Aldeburgh*', MRJ wrote in 1930, '"sung" by Crabbe and figuring in Wilkie Collins's *No Name*, has a special charm for those who, like myself, have known it since childhood; but I do not find it easy to put that charm into words.'[13] What he does not say here is that he *had*, just five years previously, 'put that charm into words', in what is generally considered to be his best late story, 'A Warning to the Curious'. This is the story which, more explicitly than anything else he wrote, combines East Anglian landscape and folklore.[14]

'A Warning' opens with a long description of the topography of Seaburgh (Aldeburgh): 'Marshes intersected by dykes to the south…flat fields to the north, merging into heath; heath, fir woods, and above all gorse inland. A long sea-front and a street.'[15] Paxton, an archaeologist—'I know something about digging in these barrows. I've opened many of them down country', he says—excavates a valuable Anglo-Saxon crown from one of these barrows, unleashing dire supernatural retribution.[16]

The crown is one of the three East Anglian heraldic crowns: 'There has always been a belief in these parts in the three holy crowns', the local vicar tells Paxton. 'The old people say they were buried in different places near the coast to keep off the Danes or the French or the Germans.'[17] 'A Warning' is an extraordinarily artful combination of real and invented scholarship, folklore, and local history. The crowns themselves are not *strictly* the heraldic symbol of East Anglia, but 'unauthorized arms unofficially identified with the region'.[18] The vicar says to Paxton:

> 'Well, now, if you have read the ordinary guides and histories of this country, you will remember perhaps that in 1687 a crown, which was said to be the crown of Redwald, King of the East Angles, was dug up at Rendlesham, and alas! alas! melted down before it was even properly described or drawn.'[19]

This seems to be an allusion to Frederic Shoberl's antiquarian guide, *Suffolk* (1818): 'An ancient silver crown was found here [at Rendlesham] in the beginning of the last century, weighing about sixty ounces, which is supposed to have belonged to some of the East-Anglian kings. Thus curious piece was unfortunately disposed of for old silver, and melted down.'[20] Rendlesham, which is very close to Sutton Hoo (whose own barrows were first excavated by Basil Brown in 1938, and revealed fabulous Anglo-Saxon treasures), is closely associated, Shoberl writes, with 'Redwald, King of the East-Angles'.[21] MRJ repeats this legend in his own antiquarian guidebook to East Anglia, *Suffolk and Norfolk*: 'at Rendlesham, in Suffolk...in 1687 a silver crown, reputed to have been Redwald's, was dug up, and (it is painful to relate) was melted down almost at once, so that we know nothing of its quality'.[22]

Like 'Oh, Whistle's Burnstow, 'A Warning's Seaburgh is a place of topographical and epistemological uncertainty, on the borderland between two worlds, the land and the sea, and two orders, the material and the supernatural, and partaking of both. The second of the story's crowns was buried in 'a Saxon royal palace, which is now under the sea'.[23] This is an allusion to Dunwich, the ancient capital of East Anglia, gradually lost to the sea: 'How much of this once populous city with "fifty-two churches" is left at this moment I will not undertake to say', MRJ writes in *Suffolk and Norfolk*. 'In its time it was a bishop's see and a rich port: early in the fourteenth century the harbour was destroyed and 400 houses went. By 1550 four churches had gone, and destruction was not to be stayed: a great storm in 1740 dealt frightful havoc.'[24]

But Dunwich is not the only eroded or reclaimed supernatural coastal space in 'A Warning'. The story reaches its violent climax a mile or so down the coast from Aldeburgh, at the Martello Tower which is all now that remains of Slaughden, a fishing village finally washed into the sea in 1936: 'When you are past the tower, you know, there is nothing but shingle for a long way—not a house, not a human creature, just that spit of land, or rather shingle, with the river on your right and the sea on your left.'[25] This 'spit of land', a fast-eroding remnant of shingle, with water on either side, is Orford Ness, a narrow peninsula running south along the coast from Aldeburgh for nine miles. The Martello tower is at the entrance to Orford Ness, right on the threshold between the two worlds, where there is no solid ground. As the narrator approaches the tower, 'one of those sea-mists was coming up very quickly from the south...which all the while was getting thicker and thicker'.[26] In front of the tower is 'the old battery, close to the sea. I believe there are only a few blocks of concrete left now: the rest has all been washed away.'[27] It is here, at the foot of the tower, that the narrator discovers the mangled body of Paxton. Like 'Oh Whistle's supernatural artefact, and like the crown he has excavated, his remains are compounded with the landscape: 'His mouth was full of sand and stones, and his teeth and jaws were broken to bits.'[28]

Generally built during the Napoleonic Wars, Britain and Ireland's coastal Martello Towers are emblems of a defensive nation guarding against military assault and invasion: the ruined concrete battery next to the Slaughden Martello

Tower is a relic of nineteenth-century imperial warfare. It is symbolically fitting that 'A Warning' should come to its horrifying climax here, in front of the Tower, as the whole story is one initially conceived in the shadow of war: the 'blocks of concrete' in front of the tower are a jarring reminder that the story's concerns are modern as well as antique. The three East Anglian crowns protect the nation. The Ager family, the ancestral, supernatural guardians of the crowns, were a local Livermere family: 'Henry Ager is dead after a lingering illness to the brain', Herbert wrote to MRJ in 1874.[29] But the name also carries overtones of Agar's Plough, a section of the Playing Fields of Eton—for MRJ, the beating heart of England, where the Napoleonic Wars were proverbially won. In 1921, Aldeburgh had erected a war memorial on the front, next to the Moot Hall. Set under a Latin cross containing a sword of sacrifice, the memorial's inscription is a very close paraphrase of the words MRJ wrote in 1917 for the memorial scroll to the war dead: 'THEY WHOM THIS MONUMENT COMMEMORATES WERE HONOURED AMONG THOSE WHO AT THE CALL OF KING AND COUNTRY LEFT ALL THAT WAS DEAR TO THEM ENDURED HARDSHIP AND FINALLY PASSED OUT OF SIGHT OF MEN BY THE PATH OF DUTY AND SELF SACRIFICE...'[30]

The Ager family have guarded the last remaining crown against invasion through a series of wars: Nathaniel Ager 'camped out at the place during the whole [Franco-Prussian] war of 1870. William, his son... did the same during the South African War'. The current William Ager moved into a cottage near the barrow where the crown is buried, 'to keep the Germans from landing', but dies of consumption.[31] The manuscript of 'A Warning', in the Pierpont Morgan Library, explicitly gives the date of Ager's death as 1916, and sets the action of the story in 'April 1917', whereas the final published version settles for the vaguer '19—'.[32] With its landscape of tunnels and trenches, 'A Warning' is redolent of the War. Paxton, the archaeologist who has been digging up sites across East Anglia, undermining, may be more than a hapless amateur out of his depth: he may be a de facto traitor, or even a spy. As the aged sexton tells the narrator: 'But I tell you, if it hadn't have been for one of them 'oly crowns being there still, them Germans would a landed here time and again, they would. Landed with their ships, and killed man, woman and child in their beds.'[33] One reader of the story in 1926, the Aldeburghian Charles Mackintosh, found the story's location, wartime setting, and premise entirely believable, and wrote to MRJ:

> We should have been saved some sleepless nights in the earlier years of the war had we known of the '3 Crowns', as that legend with the exercise of a little imagin-

> ation would have comforted us much when in residence, when we daily feared that the beach at Aldeburgh was regarded as one of the best spots for a German landing.
>
> The Knoll in which (in your story) the silver crown was found, is well known to us, and when I last saw it it was partly surrounded by a deep trench, part of the efforts at fortification of the regiment in occupation of the town.[34]

'The Uncommon Prayer-Book' is the earliest of the stories from *A Warning to the Curious*: it first made its appearance in *The Atlantic Monthly* in June 1921.[35] With its large sections of dialogue, most particularly from the voluble old countryman Mr Avery, it seems certain to have been written for performance, to showcase MRJ's repertoire of comic voices—perhaps for Christmas 1920. As we have seen, the character of the dishonest Jewish book dealer, Homberger-Henderson-Poschwitz (he goes under a variety of names), who steals the titular volume, may link the story to MRJ's anxieties in 1918 about 'Boches, Jews and Transatlantics' getting their hands on priceless national treasures in the postwar years, dissipating the English national heritage. As in a number of other stories, this dissipation brings on supernatural arachnid revenge: a shrouded, 'earth-coloured' corpse with a deadly poisonous bite, 'And the eyes, well they was dry-like, and much as if there was two big spiders' bodies in the holes'.[36]

'The Uncommon Prayer-Book' is another tale of the English seventeenth century, this time with its origins in the beliefs of anti-Puritan Anglican families in Herefordshire in the years after the English Civil War. Brockstone Court is the residence of Lady Anne Sadleir—a ferocious anti-Cromwellite, and an important donor of manuscripts to the library of Trinity College. Lady Sadleir's name turns up many times across the four volumes of MRJ's Trinity manuscripts catalogue: most particularly, he thought, 'Dame Anne Sadleir merits a special expression of gratitude for her gift of an Apocalypse, which must be ranked as one of the two finest in in existence, and is certainly the most beautiful book in Cambridge'.[37] The Uncommon Prayer-Book itself is an unlicensed edition of *The Book of Common Prayer*, published and circulated during Cromwell's Protectorate, when the book was banned. 'What curious evil service was that which [Lady Anne] and a few like her had been wont to celebrate in that remote valley?'[38] Written by an Evangelical Anglican, this is a story about the persistence of Anglican Ritualism. Mr Avery repeatedly tells his son-in-law's joke about the local vicar's insistence on 'this Gregory singin' (Gregorian chants) as part of the church service—the vicar is an Anglo-Catholic High Churchman. Brockstone Chapel 'resembles some of the Oxford college chapels as much as anything'—perhaps particularly the chapel of Oriel College, the intellectual centre of the Oxford Movement. Its stained glass contains figures 'of the kind that may be seen at Abbey Dore, of Lord Scudamore's work'.[39] The Cistercian Dore Abbey in Herefordshire was one of MRJ's particular favourites—'the most surprising and delightful of all the places I have to write about', he wrote in *Abbeys*. The Scudamores are an old Herefordshire family, closely connected with Dore. This particular 'Lord Scudamore' is John Scudamore (1601–71, and so exactly contemporaneous with the post-Civil War setting), 1st Viscount Scudamore of Sligo, who restored and reconsecrated Dore in 1633–4. Scudamore, MRJ wrote, was 'an enthusiastic churchman of the Laudian type'—that is, a follower of the Archbishop of Canterbury William Laud, one of the fathers of modern Ritualism, executed under Cromwell's Long Parliament in 1645 (so perhaps Brockstone Chapel also resembles that of St. John's College, Oxford, where Laud's remains are buried).[40]

We know for certain, because MRJ tells us in the Preface to his *Collected Ghost Stories*, that 'Herefordshire was the imagined scene of "A View from a Hill"'.[41] This is the story of a pair of haunted binoculars, made with the bones of hanged men, which enables whoever looks through them to see into the past, to see things which are no longer there. As ever, we need to be careful in being too ready to assign very specific locations to fictional places, but it seems at least very likely here that MRJ had another Welsh Marches abbey in mind when he conceived of the ruins of Fulnaker Abbey in 'A View from a Hill'. Llanthony Priory, just over the Welsh border, was another of the places he visited around this time, during his various trips researching *Abbeys*, and also with Gwen McBryde, who lived nearby.[42] Llanthony, now in ruins, was, he thought, 'a very beautiful place'.[43] What must it have looked like in its twelfth-century heyday?

MRJ wasn't the only writer and cultural figure drawn to Llanthony in the mid-1920s. In 1924, the sculptor and typographer Eric Gill moved to Llanthony Abbey, a former Anglican monastery a couple of miles further up the Vale of Ewyas from the Priory, in the extraordinarily remote hamlet of Capel-y-Ffin, the Chapel on the Border. Capel-y-Ffin became something of a haven in the interwar years for Romantic Modernist artists and visionaries—Gill himself (who designed the Gill Sans and Perpetua typefaces at Capel-y-Ffin), but also David Jones and Eric Ravilious, in search of a mystical, restorative pastoralism for a waste land. Gill had initially hoped to move into Llanthony Priory itself: his wife, Mary, believed that her husband's 'mission in life' was to restore the Benedictine ruin.[44]

In October 1925, the same month that saw the publication of *A Warning to the Curious*, the Hereford archaeologist Alfred Watkins published *The Old Straight Track*, in which he outlines his influential theory of ley-lines, pre-Roman trackways criss-crossing the country. Watkins did the great majority of his research along the Welsh border, and Llanthony plays a significant role in the book, situated as it was, he believed, at the confluence of a number of ley-lines, 'a favoured spot…in the heart of the Black Mountains where primitive tracks and notches can well be studied', the best place to get 'ley-bitten'.[45] Watkins chose a photograph he took at Llanthony for the book's frontispiece. 'A View from a Hill' reaches its supernatural climax on 'Gallows Hill', where the ghosts of the hanged men whose bones have been used to make the occult binoculars through which the past can be seen, looking through dead men's eyes, return for retribution. Gallows Hill is 'in a dead line with that single tree on the top of the big ridge'.[46] There is, Watkins notes in *The Old Straight Track*, a 'gallows mound' on the ley-line between Llanthony and nearby Longtown (Ewias Lacey) Castle.[47] Others have proposed a raised, wooded landmark known as Cole's Tump for the location of the story's gallows.[48] This was certainly a place MRJ knew well. He was, in fact, Gwen testified, particularly fond of the view from *this* hill:

> The woods here are carpeted with bluebells, but the best place for them is up above my farm on Coles Tump or the thirteen trees; it is only a few fields distant, but the easiest way to reach it is by motoring round two miles. It was a favourite spot of M.R.J.'s and on this occasion we went to see the bluebells there. From the Tump you get a view of the Golden Valley and Black Mountains and the nearby Saddlebow and Garway Hills. Beyond the river you see the Skirrid or Holy mountain in the Monmouth country.[49]

'Tump', Watkins writes, is one of many names used for raised sites or structures appearing along ley-lines: 'barrow' is another.[50] Cole's Tump appears many times in Watkins's book.

While *The Old Straight Track* might perhaps be said to bear some of the impress of Frazer's *Golden Bough*, Alfred Watkins was very reluctant to make occult speculations about his ley-lines (though others, developing his work, certainly did). Nevertheless, he does concede that ritual and magic did come to form an important component of the ley-lines: 'Utility was the primary object. Later on, magic, religion and superstition blended with the system.'[51] What better place for a magus or necromancer to conduct his experiments than Llanthony?

A. E. Housman, also from the Welsh borders, thought that there was 'something wrong with the optics' in 'A View from a Hill' (isn't that the whole point of the story?). 'Well, there may be, but if these things happen, what are you going to do about it?' MRJ responded.[52] Other readers were more sympathetic to the story than the famously testy Classics professor. William McGregor Hemingway, a friend of McBryde and a regular at gatherings in MRJ's rooms in King's all those years earlier, wrote:

> How you can provide such fare without feeling the effect in yourself beats me: I shd fear to go to bed every night if my mind was charged with such devastating matter. The View from a Hill is particularly grim w/ its glasses that look through dead men's eyes & a [unreadable] from a sort of witches' cauldron. Don't you ever have appalling visions after—say—toasted cheese?[53]

From the time he was elected Provost of Eton, MRJ found himself a regular dinner guest at Windsor Castle. After his first summoning, in July 1919, he wrote to Gwen:

> You left me *distrait* at the prospect of dining at Windsor but the clothes were procured and the only real tantrum I had was when the taxi did not come and I thought I should be late, which would have been a poor thing on a first appearance, and perhaps particularly as I was the only guest outside the castle. I sat between the Queen and Princess Mary. It was not difficult and I should be less put about on another occasion. The King talks without a break, the Queen not, but has plenty to say at short intervals.[54]

After this, he found himself dining more or less annually at Windsor Castle. In 1927, after dining with the King and Queen, 'The Queen expressed her regrets to me when we parted, that we had not had one of our little talks'.[55]

In the spring of 1921, Princess Marie Louise, King George V's cousin, conceived the idea of commissioning an elaborate dolls' house for the Queen.[56] Queen Mary's Dolls' House, unveiled for the 1924 Wembley British Empire Exhibition, is one of the great British late-imperial follies. The building was designed by Sir Edwin Lutyens, with a garden by Gertrude Jekyll. It had working electricity and running water, a wine-cellar with minute bottles of vintage wine, intricate carpets and wallpaper, and tiny artworks by prominent living painters. At the heart of the Dolls' House was the library, containing over 200 volumes of miniature books, actual works of literature (many especially commissioned for the library) by a veritable Who's Who of contemporary writers, including Kipling, Housman, Yeats, Hardy, Conan Doyle, Buchan, Galsworthy, Aldous Huxley, Edith Wharton, and Rider Haggard. Arthur and Fred Benson were there too, as well as Anstey Guthrie.[57] Arthur, in particular, had been heavily involved in the conception and creation of the Dolls' House, and was the co-editor of one of two official volumes published in 1924, *The Book of the Queen's Dolls' House*. Privately, and typically, Arthur thought the whole endeavour 'ineradicably silly'.[58] But the Queen's Dolls' House was one of the last major projects he was involved with, and he marshalled a formidable cast of experts to introduce various aspects of the house: Lionel Cust on the paintings, Stephen Gaselee on the library, Edward Dent on the music, George Saintsbury on the wine-cellar, Gertrude Jekyll on the garden, and even Fred on the dolls themselves. In the grim postwar years, Arthur maintained, the Dolls' House was 'meant to have a touch of childlike fancy, of irresponsible cheerfulness, to represent the genial and leisurely side of life'.[59]

Given that he was a familiar presence at Windsor, and given Arthur's close involvement with the project, it is hardly surprising that MRJ should have been asked to contribute to the library. 'It was automatic to ask the Provost of Eton, who knows more about supernatural life than anyone living, to write a ghost story', E. V. Lucas writes in his anthology of the contents of the Dolls' House library, the companion-volume to Arthur's guidebook. 'And this is the happy result.'[60] 'The Haunted Doll's House' is, in essence, a rewriting of 'The Mezzotint', in which Mr Dillet acquires, at a knock-down price, 'a Doll's House in Strawberry Hill Gothic... "Quintessence of Horace Walpole, that's what it is; he must have had something to do with it."'[61] Walpole, a major figure in the development of the Gothic novel, and an inspiration for the Victorian Gothic Revival, haunts the tale in a number of ways, as the figures in the doll's house begin to move, re-enacting a dark family history.

There is something unusually revealing about 'A Neighbour's Landmark', which may be one of MRJ's more personal stories. It effectively opens with a kind of manifesto:

> 'Remember, if you please', said my friend, looking at me over his spectacles, 'that I am a Victorian by birth and education, and that the Victorian tree may not unreasonably be expected to bear Victorian fruit. Further, remember that an immense quantity of clever and thoughtful Rubbish is now being written about the Victorian age. Now', he went on, laying his papers on his knee, 'that article, 'The Stricken Years', in the *Times* Literary Supplement, - able, of course it is able; but, oh! my soul and body, do just hand it over here, will you?'[62]

The TLS article, 'The Stricken Years'—'clever and thoughtful Rubbish' from an undoubtedly 'able' writer—is a disparaging pastiche of the revisionist biography of Lytton Strachey's *Eminent Victorians*, a sideswipe at MRJ's old targets—Bloomsbury, the Apostles, 'intellects' (Strachey himself, we shall see, was paying attention). At around this time, he also delivered a sermon to celebrate Empire Day at Eton, in which he had another dig at Strachey: 'about the literature, art, morals, ideals of [Victoria's] age a kind of mythology has already grown up, and to say that anything is Victorian is, in the eyes of the Advanced, enough to absolve you from considering it any further'.[63]

In 1917, MRJ received a letter containing a story about Jane Dupuis, granddaughter of the former Eton Vice-Provost George Dupuis (the man who had given the teenage MRJ access to the College's manuscripts). Jane and a friend, sketching in Black Down, a wood near Taunton, Somerset, had both experienced at the same time a feeling of overwhelming dread, 'the Panic of Black Down'.[64] Could there be some supernatural explanation for this? In 'A Neighbour's Landmark', walkers in Betton Wood hear a scream which fills them with fear and despair, 'the kind of thing that makes one wonder if something has not given way in one's brain...images came to me of dusty beams and creeping spiders and savage owls up in the tower, and forgotten graves and their ugly contents below, and of flying Time and all it had taken out of my life'. A local couplet of folk-poetry provides dark hints: 'Than that which walks in Betton Woods / Knows why it walks or why it cries.'[65] (Housman, not an easy man to please, but a man who knew something about rural verse, praised MRJ for his 'good poetry' here.)[66]

The story's title is taken from the *Book of Common Prayer*, a commination (recital of divine threats against sinners): 'Cursed is he that removeth his neighbour's land-mark.' This in turn derives from Deutoronomy 19:14: 'Thou shalt not remove thy neighbour's landmark, which they of old times have set in thine inheritance, which thou shalt inherit in the land that the Lord the God giveth thee to possess it.' The folklorist Jacqueline Simpson has suggested that the story may take its inspiration from a series of 'Landmarks and Shrieking Ghosts' familiar from Scandinavian folklore (entirely plausible given MRJ's interest in Scandinavia, and particularly in the 1920s his deep engagement with Hans Andersen). Others have suggested a more local source, perhaps in Herefordshire folk-tales.[67]

However, like a number of other MRJ stories, a closer source is his interest in seventeenth-century English trials. The screaming ghost of 'A Neighbour's Landmark' is the shade of the litigious Theodosia Bryan, Lady Ivie, condemned to walk in Betton Wood for enclosing land which did not belong to her, dispossessing orphaned children. In 1929, MRJ wrote the Preface to Sir John Fox's edition of the transcript of *The Lady Ivie's Trial*. 'Lady Ivie herself', MRJ thought, 'does seem to answer to the French designation of a *triste* personnage'.[68] But Theodosia Bryan was more than a 'sad character'. The daughter of a prominent oculist, Theodosia Stepkin was a remarkable woman: great beauty who made a series of highly lucrative marriages, while also being an accomplished forger.[69] The 1684 trial was over the ownership of seven and a half acres of prime waterfront London dockland: while Bryan lost the trial, she was clearly uncowed by her appearance before Judge Jeffreys. The Victorian MRJ condemns this assertive woman to walk in Betton Woods forever over a corrupt property-claim.

The final story in *A Warning to the Curious* is the highly folkloric 'An Evening's Entertainment'. This was not a story MRJ had planned for the volume, but one he found himself having to write at the last moment. As late as 3 October, he told Gwen that 'the ghost story book is finished. I had to write another one instead of the one I was at, which would not come out.'[70] In 1929, MRJ wrote an article called 'Stories I Have Tried to Write', in which he discussed a number of his various false starts and stories 'which would not come out'.[71] He thought highly enough of this to include it in his 1931 *Collected Ghost Stories*, and its possibilities have tantalized scholars ever since. Many of these unfinished fragments survive in manuscript form, and one essentially complete story, 'The Fenstanton Witch', has been published in several editions of MRJ's stories. It is impossible to say with certainty which of these was the failed attempt in 1925.[72] One likely contender is the fragment known as 'Merfield Hall', which appears to be the story of an experiment gone horribly wrong, which summons a supernatural being. 'Merfield Hall' exists in two unfinished versions, which seems to support the idea of a story 'which would not come out'.[73] The second fragment is presented as a report to the Society for Psychical Research, and makes reference to the Roxburghe Club, the exclusive bibliophile society which produces high-end manuscript facsimiles. MRJ had been a member of the Roxburghe Club since 1909, and was particularly active during the 1920s, when he produced several volumes for the club.[74] But this is a tentative, problematic assertion, as 'Merfield Hall' may not be by MRJ at all. It's not one of the 'Stories I Have Tried to Write', and does not seem to be written in MRJ's handwriting.

* * *

In December 1925, the 'Sex Viri'—the Six Men, Cambridge University's moral guardians—published their report on an extraordinary case. J. B. S. Haldane, University Reader in Bio-Chemistry, had been found guilty of adultery in the

High Court, as part of the divorce proceedings between Jack and Charlotte Burghes. Haldane, an Old Etonian and graduate of New College Oxford, was one of the country's most high-profile scientists, a pioneering figure in modern genetics, and a significant public intellectual with connections to the Bloomsbury Group, and particularly to Aldous Huxley. He was also socialist (and later a Communist), an egomaniac, and a ferociously confrontational freethinker who loved to shock conventional morality—when a distinguished senior colleague and his wife encountered him bathing naked in the Cam as they punted along with their guests, Haldane shouted at them: 'I am now excreting the most acid urine that has ever been excreted.'[75] This kind of behaviour was entirely characteristic of Haldane, who was not a man who courted or wanted friends amongst the establishment. Haldane had been in a long-term relationship with Charlotte Burghes, and the trial was a necessary component of the divorce proceedings. 'I am going to sleep with my mistress tonight', he announced to his colleagues around the High Table at Trinity.[76] He was also given to turning up at High Table with a large jar of his own urine, a substance of which he seems to have been inordinately fond.

The Sex Viri (the Sex Weary, as he insisted on calling them), investigated Haldane for 'gross immortality'. He was urged to resign from Cambridge, but refused. The Sex Viri adjudicated 'That Mr J. B. S. Haldane be therefore, and he is hereby, deprived of his said office of Reader in Bio-chemistry'.[77] Haldane appealed, and a panel of five Judges Delegate, including MRJ and Walter Fletcher, was appointed to hear the appeal. The appeal took place on 17 March 1926 at the Royal Courts of Justice. After hearing from lawyers for both sides, the panel deliberated for 45 minutes, and produced their verdict:

> The majority of the court is of the opinion that in view of all the circumstances of this particular case, which have been more fully before us than they were before the Vice-Chancellor and the *Sex Viri*, the appeal should be allowed; but this decision is not taken as any expression of opinion that adultery may not be gross immorality within the meaning of the Statute.[78]

The verdict was on a 3–2 split decision, and it should be obvious which way MRJ's vote went. He was never going to support a flamboyant, sexually profligate, outspoken left-wing intellectual, and he didn't. But Haldane was reinstated to his Readership, which he retained until 1932, when he left to take up a Chair at UCL. He and Charlotte were married in 1926.

As MRJ and the other Judges Delegate prepared to hear the Haldane case, Britain was plunged into social upheaval and labour disputes. The 1926 General Strike formally began on 4 May; a few days later, Walter Fletcher 'brought optimistic reports from those in authority as to the duration of the strike', but MRJ himself wasn't so sure.[79] Not even the unchanging, socially secure world of Eton was completely immune from the threat of a general strike. MRJ's circle of friends and colleagues certainly knew what they thought about the industrial unrest. Luxmoore deplored 'the miserable ruinous strike', which he thought 'has set the nation back for years'.[80] MRJ, along with Cyril Alington and all the Eton masters, was enrolled as a Special Constable a couple of days before the end of the strike—though none of them had to do anything. Robert Birley, the future Eton headmaster who had just that year begun work as a History master at the school, recalled the occasion in a letter to the *Times Literary Supplement* in 1972:

> The younger masters—I was myself about the most junior among them—found the ceremony of enrolment quite delightful, especially its commencement. The police sergeant at a table said, 'Mr James, forward please.' There was no movement. Dr James had been Provost, first of King's and then of Eton, since 1905. Then there came an agitated whisper: 'Mr Provost, Mr Provost, I think he must mean you.' The Provost was then enrolled.

'Red' Robert Birley was that unusual thing, a genuine left-wing Eton master; but whatever their political differences, he revered MRJ as the most scholarly man he had ever known.[81] Birley recognized that as MRJ was by this point well into his sixties, and Alington in holy orders, 'it is doubtful, to say the least, if [any duties] would have been expected of them' as Special Constables.[82] As MRJ himself acknowledged to the librarian Eric Millar, when it came to it the strike didn't really affect his world that much: 'In the midst of all these General Strikes & what not, the pale student is still bending over his book and now wishes to know what became of two books in the Henry Perkins sale of 1873.'[83]

In November 1926, Grace came down with measles, a 'rather humiliating affliction'.[84] MRJ was unsympathetic, telling Gwen, 'Gracie has been having measles after 41 years, a silly game'.[85] He had health issues of his own. He tore a muscle during a walk, and spent the next couple of years, on and off, 'being electrocuted and massaged': 'I am a victim of the savage tribe of the *Massagetae*', he complained to Sydney Cockerell. 'One of them comes & *massages* my legs every evening. See?'[86] When Cockerell took the feminine gender of the *Massagetae* literally, MRJ had to assure him: 'not by a Female, good gracious'.[87] He had to miss the Wall Game in 1927: 'No legs as the Man said.'[88] He tried a variety of cures, from electric vibrators to elastic stockings to what he called 'ultra violent rays'. Sunshine, he thought, helped a lot—'but' he realized,

'I don't really believe I shall ever be much of a walker, particularly not on hard pavements.'[89] His doctor—'a horseleech…ghoul or vampire'—told him he had to spend Mondays in bed.[90] 'I shall probably be actually being practised upon by Drs at lunch time', he told a prospective caller in January 1928.[91]

His appendix trouble also returned in early 1927: he was bedridden that February, suffering from 'intestinal discord' and terrible heartburn.[92] He was having strange, vivid dreams, including one in which he discovered that A. E. Housman had once been in love with a Miss Mouseman ('don't tell Housman', he warned Sydney Cockerell, to whom he had related the dream; Housman rarely saw the funny side of anything).[93] He had another, that April, about J. E. Nixon: 'Recollection came upon him, and he seemed inclined to relate to an audience the story of his escape from a South African coach in which he had been confined with a ham.'[94] Nixon was never too far from his mind, and his illness seems to have brought him to the fore:

> I have just been massaged with an electric vibrator. This machine has been much improved since the early days when Henry Westcott [son of B. F. Westcott] persuaded James Nixon to buy it, & so kindly insisted on applying it himself. The voltage was at that time much in excess of what is now considered safe, and it was long before James Nixon ceased to vibrate. Had he not been gagged, doubtless he would have roused…Westcott from his reverie before the bruises had become so numerous & severe.[95]

In 'the short intervals between the times when doctors have been punching me and other persons massaging my legs', he managed to get some work done, 'and though not competent to win the Walking Race, have enough energy to describe some MSS.'[96] In 1926, MRJ embarked on what was to be by far his largest and most ambitious cataloguing project, a catalogue of the entirety of Cambridge University Library's manuscript collection up to 1500.[97] 'There are probably between two and three thousand, but without going through the five volumes, I cannot give the numbers accurately', Scholfield wrote in proposing the project to the Library Syndicate. 'Knowing Dr James's methods of work I should fancy that he could complete the task in 10 years.'[98] Scholfield suggested that 10 MSS at a time be deposited at Eton for MRJ to work on; MRJ himself proposed a locked box to transport them in—though in the event, Scholfield himself often delivered them by hand. This project was a near impossible task, especially for an old, immobile man in increasingly fragile health. Of course, it was left unfinished on his death, leaving the Cambridge archivists with 'six boxfuls of nearly illegible drafts' written on foolscap, that neither the University

Typewriting Office nor Miss Pate's typewriting agency on Trinity Street could make anything of.[99]

That year, 1926, he also published his memoir, *Eton and King's*. The scholarly publisher Williams & Norgate approached him with the proposal, and he sat down to write in August, with his notebooks and letters around him. He struggled at first, finding it 'difficult to make a beginning'; but then, 'when the pencil had begun to run along the lines, the doubt was whether I should ever be able to stop it. Doors opened in obscure parts of the brain, and people and scenes and dialogues, many more than I supposed I kept there, peeped out and insisted on being marked down.'[100] 'Reminiscences have been going on very busily', he wrote to Gwen in October 1925.[101] By the end of November, he had a completed manuscript—380 pages of pencil-written foolscap—but he couldn't stop tinkering with it, couldn't let it be.

Eton and King's is an extraordinarily frustrating book. Hard-hitting it is not; nor is it revealing. Some of MRJ's friends thought that, as he got older, he became haunted by his own vast memory. 'I think he had great difficulty in forgetting anything', Gwen wrote.[102] Shane Leslie thought that 'He simply went on remembering and remembering because perhaps he had forgotten how to forget'.[103] But when those doors opened in the far-flung corridors of his endless memory palace, it seems that they were either immediately slammed shut again, or else revealed rooms full of recollections which were, as the book's subtitle acknowledges, 'mostly trivial', full of gentle, mildly amusing anecdotes about forgotten people and incidents, funny stories about Bradshaw or Nixon. As a matter of policy, *Eton and King's* is giving nothing away: 'The tone of these recollections has been, and I foresee will be, largely rather frivolous. I have designedly kept out of them my home ties, and the expressing of emotions with which I may reasonably be thought familiar.'[104] This suggests that the repression is deliberate, and wholly conscious—that there were things hidden behind certain doors that he's not going to talk about. But hostile readers thought there was nothing there to give away in the first place. This is certainly what Lytton Strachey, who was never going to be in sympathy with the book or its author, assumed. Strachey read the book with real contempt: it was, he thought, 'a dim affair', full of 'vapid little anecdotes and nothing more. Only remarkable as showing the extraordinary impress an institution can make on an adolescent mind. It's odd that the Provost of Eton should still be aged 16. A life without a jolt.'[105]

But those readers who were going to like the book certainly liked it. Luxmoore, of course, loved it. 'I laughed more over your book than in many years put together', he told MRJ (you had to be there, I suppose). 'I can't understand how being so much with me at yr. impressionable age you escaped so completely the taint of prig, crank or idealist.'[106] The historian C. R. L. Fletcher—Old Etonian, Fellow of All Souls, biographer of Edmond Warre, and High Tory—read it on the day it came out: 'I finished it in 24 hours & cried for more. I loved every page of it.'[107] The former Prime Minister Lord Rosebery, who sat on the Governing Body of Eton alongside MRJ, was a man who understood the necessity of concealment. At Eton, he had been a favourite of William Johnson Cory, and his glittering political career was accompanied by persistent gossip about his sexuality. He was Prime Minster during the Wilde trial, in which he was implicated: the Marquess of Queensberry, one of Wilde's persecutors, called the writer 'a damned cur of the Rosebery type'.[108] Rosebery read *Eton and King's* 'with great interest and pleasure. But', he added, 'you must have been thought an extraordinary sort of sap at Eton.'[109]

In April 1926, MRJ returned to King's for Provost Walter Durnford's funeral: 'the end was not unexpected', he told Gwen.[110] MRJ had known Durnford since being taught by him at Eton, and while no one would have called him a great scholar, he had played an important role in binding the community of King's together. He had proven himself an able administrator, and had been knighted for setting up and running the officers' recruitment centre in Corpus Christi during the war. The undergraduates loved him: he dined with them, invited them to his summer house on the Isle of Wight, was keenly involved in the Amateur Dramatic Club.[111] This was the side of Walter Dunford that MRJ emphasized when he gave the address at his memorial service: 'Men like Walter Durnford... have worked to preserve the kind of family spirit that has room for normality as well as for genius—for the stupid as well as the clever, and it is your business to see that that spirit does not die.'[112]

'This is a new King's', he acknowledged in the memorial address.[113] Kings needed a new Provost. MRJ was very clear about who it should *not* be: 'An anxious question whom they will elect—as long as it is not one Maynard Keynes I think all may be well.'[114] Keynes was certainly interested in leading the College he loved, but he was not the only candidate. J. H. Clapham, the College Tutor, also put his name forward. 'Honest John' was a serious, conscientious Methodist, whom some viewed as stern and unbending in his religious and moral principles. Between the grave, rectitudinous Clapham and the brilliant, licentious Keynes, and the constituencies to whom they appealed, a rift threatened to open up in the College. To his great credit, Keynes resolved this potential impasse by proposing a compromise candidate, A. E. Brooke, the Ely

Professor of Divinity, who offended nobody. Brooke (who was Rupert's uncle) had been at Eton with MRJ, and had gone on to study for the Classical Tripos at King's, where he gained a glitteringly high First in Part I, and a disappointing Second in Part II. He was made a Fellow in 1889, and then was Dean from 1894 to 1918, at which point he relocated to the cathedral close at Ely, where he served as Canon. The undergraduates called him 'The Beetle', because of the way 'he scuttled along in his clerical black'.[115]

The Beetle was a modest man, and a self-deprecating one, rather given to musing aloud about his unfitness for this or any high office. While he was a competent administrator, many thought that the real power in the College lay with the senior team around him—Keynes and Clapham, the Bursar and Tutor; Eric Milner-White, the Dean; and J. T. Sheppard, who was (unanimously) elected Vice-Provost in 1929, and went on to succeed Brooke as Provost in 1933.

As we saw in Chapter 6, Sheppard was, by the standards of the day, fairly openly homosexual—according to future Provost Noel Annan, he was the most 'unbridled' gay man in a King's that included Maynard Keynes, which is really saying something.[116] When the Classicist L. P. Wilkinson came up to King's in the late-1920s, he arrived in a world of 'homosexual innuendos' and 'Rabelaisianism'. When he became Secretary of the Amalgamation Club, the College's major sporting and social society, Provost Brooke sent him a gentle letter of warning about demonstrative same-sex eroticism, 'but his embarrassment betrayed him into such Freudian illegibility that I could not decipher what seemed to be the operative sentence'. King's, Wilkinson concludes, 'was thus moving away from the respectability represented by the Austen Leigh—Monty James—Clapham tradition towards an ethos that had more in common with the Bloomsbury Group'.[117] As MRJ told Gwen when he heard the news of Durnford's death, 'It ends a chapter!'[118]

If MRJ needed harder evidence still of a disappearing world, it came on 11 November 1926 with the death of H. E. Luxmoore at the age of eighty-five. Luxmoore was actively involved in the life of Eton right up to the end, attending a meeting of the Shakespeare Society just a couple of days before he died. His last letter, written the day before his death, was to Henry Kennett Marten, then the School's Senior Master, complaining that the music was too loud in the School Hall and the College Chapel.[119] The following day, he went to prayers and breakfast as usual, then returned to his rooms in Baldwin's End, and slipped away. It was, MRJ wrote to Gwen, 'a dreadful loss. Dreadful from one point of view but if it was to come it couldn't have come more kindly.'

The funeral a few days later was attended by 'an extraordinary Chapelful of people'.[120] MRJ immediately wrote an appreciation of Luxmoore for the *Times*, under the heading 'A Great Etonian': 'I do not think that any more desolating loss could have befallen Eton than the removal of Henry Elford Luxmoore. For more years than I can readily reckon he has been the beloved patriarch of the place and had stood for every cause that was beautiful and kindly, noble and Christian.'[121] 'Nobody ever loved Eton more truly and faithfully than my tutor', MRJ said in an address to the Chapel the following Sunday:

> How am I to speak of him worthily, to whom I, to whom all of us owe so very much?...My friends, the simple things of life are the best, as my tutor would have told you. Let me end with simple words, the last words of a great and simple book: 'We all loved him, and somehow I think we were all better when he was near us.'[122]

One of Luxmoore's most dearly held projects at Eton was a garden he had created in the late nineteenth century on a little island in the Thames, with a wooden summerhouse overlooking a lawn, bordered by specimen trees and shrubs, and connected to the school grounds by a wooden bridge.[123] MRJ proposed formally renaming this 'Luxmoore's Garden', and launched an appeal for the £5,500 needed for its renovation and upkeep.[124] In June 1933, he presided over a formal dedication ceremony for the garden; the bust of Luxmoore presented to the College in 1921 was placed in Luxmoore's Garden, where it stands to this day. On the gate of the garden, Luxmoore placed the words which Renaissance Humanists often wrote along with their names inside their books, 'et amicorum'—'and of friends'.

* * *

A Warning to the Curious was to be MRJ's last original volume of ghost stories, but he kept writing individual tales. In June 1927, MRJ returned to Dublin for the first time in over thirty years, to give some 'very dull' lectures. 'Dublin is a dreadful place', he thought, but at least it gave him the opportunity to go on a pilgrimage to Chapelizod, in the footsteps of Sheridan Le Fanu, 'to see the House by the Churchyard, which is quite unmistakable'.[125] Communing with the shade of Le Fanu may have inspired him, a few weeks later, to write 'Wailing Well'.

On 26 July, he was driven to Worbarrow Bay in Dorset, to join colleagues and 200 boys at the Eton scout camp: 'it is further proposed that by the camp I should read them a story of a terrible nature, which I have made—contrary to my expectation'.[126] 'Wailing Well' is the story in which the wilful, disobedient schoolboy Stanley Judkins is exsanguinated by a collection of vengeful revenants, mostly women, while the actual staff of Eton all look on in horror; the story which, according to Henry Kennett Marten, one of the audience at Worbarrow, gave them all nightmares. William Hope-Jones, one of the colleagues who features in the story (it is he who discovers Stanley's corpse), remembered the evening well:

> Monty visited us and told us Wailing Well at the evening Sing-song. He didn't sleep in the Camp but returned by Car to the Hotel at Corfe Castle. In Eton next day my wife met him carrying a letter to the post and chuckling the real Monty chuckle—I'm writing to warn them, he said, not to go near the gate of their field at night. When I passed it on my way back to Corfe there was a skeleton there sharpening a long knife on its shinbone![127]

The Old Etonian poet and botanist Robert Gathorne-Hardy published 'Wailing Well' in 1928 as a limited edition (157 copies) book under his Mill House Press imprint. The Eton College Library copy of the book, no. 41, was bought by Peter Lawrence, who was in the audience at Worbarrow for the 1926 reading (he was Patrol Leader of the Third Eton College Troop), and who went on to be a long-serving Eton Master. In 1931, he had the idea of asking the story's named participants to sign their autographs in the margins of the books, next to where they appear, beginning with 'M. R. James scriptor'.[128] The one signature missing from the book is the Vice-Provost, Hugh Macnaghten.

On 11 August 1929, Macnaghten walked into the Thames at Eton and drowned himself. The coroner's verdict was 'Suicide while temporarily insane'. He had been suffering from terrible mental health problems since the end of the War, and had spent the previous autumn in a nursing home, being treated for depression. His doctor confirmed that he was in constant pain from gout, and that he believed that 'His mind was failing'.[129] Macnaghten had been for years an influential and much-loved housemaster. Fifty-three boys from his House had been killed in the War, and he never got over it.[130] While he and MRJ were never close, they had known each other as academic rivals and as colleagues for over fifty years. In a warm appreciation in the *Times*, MRJ acknowledged 'the grievous bodily and mental sufferings of his last years', but wrote: 'Few men have been more consistent in the pursuit of what is highest and best than was Hugh Macnaghten. In him, as in Henry Luxmoore, whom he greatly loved and revered, Eton has known an upholder of the purest and finest ideals, the most chivalrous of men, and one who could not condescend to any littleness.'[131]

In the late 1920s, it was obvious that MRJ's world was coming to an end. Some awareness of this may underlie his choice of subject when asked to deliver the prestigious Schweich Lectures in Biblical Archaeology to the British Academy in 1927, though in reality *The Apocalypse in Art* synthesizes decades of research on manuscripts of the Apocalypse. He wrote the lectures in between being 'poked and punched and physicked and managed' by doctors and masseurs.[132] 'I am wallowing in apocalypses and want to see all I can', he told Sydney Cockerell.[133] The monograph of the lectures, published in 1931, came with a record of MRJ's favourite scholarly pastime: an annotated catalogue of Apocalypse manuscripts.[134]

Another major research project from this period was differently personal—an edition of Hans Andersen's tales. This was the book he had planned to write with Arthur Benson just before Arthur's death: MRJ would do the scholarly heavy lifting, while Arthur would write a pleasing biographical introduction in his effortless, man-of-lettersly style. MRJ was fascinated by Scandinavian folklore, a subject which had informed both his visits to Denmark and Sweden around the turn of the century, and the stories that grew out of those visits—'Number 13', 'Count Magnus', and McBryde's *The Story of a Troll Hunt*.[135] He was very familiar with the work of the Scandinavian folklorist E. T. Kristensen, and in Cambridge he knew the Icelandic scholar and librarian Eiríkur Magnusson. Magnusson, University Lecturer in Icelandic, edited and translated a renowned series of editions of Icelandic sagas together with his former student William Morris. MRJ began to make serious inroads into his Andersen translations while staying at the White Lion in Aldeburgh in April 1927 (at the same time as he had his dream about Nixon and the South African ham). He delivered a lecture on Andersen and folklore, in which he explained to his audience his long-term fascination with his subject, dating back to the 1890s: 'I decided that I must see Andersen country. I decided too that I must read his takes in his own words: a version of a version could not be adequate.' And so, he recalled, he learnt Danish from a dictionary, with the aid of the library of the late King's Fellow and benefactor John Heath. His memories brought him back to Mr Wraxall and some of the inspiration for 'Count Magnus': 'I know not what happy chance brought to me the knowledge of a book—old-fashioned, perhaps, effusively chatty in style—may be—yet with all its faults far better than any guide book. I mean the two volumes of Horace Marryat (brother of the novelist) called *Jutland and the Danish Isles*, & published in 1860.'[136]

'In a word, they were chatty', MRJ had written in 'Count Magnus' about travel books of the Marryat variety, and around this time MRJ was presented with an opportunity to write his own 'chatty' guidebook.[137] In November 1927, 'a nice gent from the Eastern Railway made overtures about a Norfolk and Suffolk Book. I said, all being well, I might have a stab at it in April and August.'[138] *Suffolk and Norfolk: A Perambulation of the Two Counties with Notices of Their History and Their Ancient Buildings* took MRJ physically and imaginatively back to the territory of his childhood. As if literally to embed *Suffolk and Norfolk* in the region's folklore, its cover came embossed with the heraldic symbols of East Anglia, the three crowns for which he had imagined supernatural protectors in 'A Warning to the Curious'. To emphasize the point, the crowns also appeared on the title-page.

His perambulations around Suffolk and Norfolk were also a creative inspiration for him. In the splendid late story 'Rats', a Cambridge student checks into an inn 'in Suffolk, near the coast', to study for his finals in solitude.[139] Ominously, while walking nearby, he 'found himself looking at a square block of white stone fashioned somewhat like the base of a pillar, with a square hole in the upper surface. Just such another you may see at this day on Thetford Heath.'[140] Turning to MRJ's account of Thetford Heath in *Suffolk and Norfolk*, we read that 'on the west side, you may catch sight of a block of stone on the heath which I have always taken to be a gibbet: certainly the locality would have suited highwaymen'.[141]

Suffolk and Norfolk is obviously a very personal project, 'I have many early associations which endear these two great counties to me, and the attempt to expound some of their manifold attractions to those who live in them and those who visit them has been a pleasant task', MRJ explains in the preface.[142] When the book arrives at Great Livermere, MRJ writes: 'The reader will forgive a little expansiveness here: from 1865 to 1909, the rectory was my home, if not my dwelling place.' But even here, far from centres of civilization, the world was changing: 'Livermere Hall is gone, and many oaks in its park are cut down. "It must needs be that," let us say, changes "come." '[143]

* * *

'Rats' takes part of its inspiration from Dickens, with its epigraph from 'Tom Tiddler's Ground' about 'mouldy bedclothes a-heaving and a-heaving like seas...with the rats underneath 'em'.[144] This was MRJ's literary world, and it was not the modern world. Modern thinkers and writers upset him: Keynes,

Strachey, and the Bloomsbury Group, Bertrand Russell, J. B. S. Haldane. He didn't approve of 'that unspeakable Aldous Huxley', and condemned James Joyce as 'that prostitutor of our language' and 'a charlatan'.[145] While getting his portrait painted by Gerald Kelly in the 1930s, the pair got into a discussion of Alfred Jarry's symbolist masterpiece *Ubu Roi*. Kelly lent MRJ his copy. He was not impressed: 'I am afraid Ubu Roi has not clicked with me', he told the artist, 'and as for the sentences quoted from Jarry's later... pamphlet—I can only say I am glad he's dead, & hope it hurt.'[146] Even the *Cambridge Review*, he complained, had become 'full of stories of obscure authors who would appear to be superior to any one since Shakespeare but the quotations do not in my judgement support this view'.[147]

In November 1928, MRJ got a letter from Rubinstein, Nash, and Co., solicitors. Radclyffe Hall's lesbian classic, *The Well of Loneliness*, had been banned by the Director of Public Prosecution, and was in danger of having all copies seized and destroyed. The novel, the solicitors assured MRJ, came with a foreword by Havelock Ellis, praising its 'notable psychological and sociological significance, apart from its fine qualities as a novel by a writer of accomplished art'. A number of literary and cultural luminaries, including Leonard and Virginia Woolf, Rose Macaulay, Julian Huxley, and Sheila Kaye-Smith had agreed to testify that the book was not obscene: 'We venture to believe that you will be taking a sympathetic interest in the matter, and we shall be very glad to know that we may add your name to the list.'[148]

What were they thinking, Rubinstein, Nash, and Co.? This is MRJ's reply, sent the following day:

> I believe Miss Hall's book is chiefly about birth control or some kindred topic, isn't it? I find it difficult to believe either that it is a good novel or that its suppression causes any loss to Literature. I am quite sure that if nine tenths of the novels, biographies, critical studies, poems, that come out every week were barked, nobody but publishers and authors would be the poorer. If I read this particular sex novel I should probably be bored & disgusted. It is perfectly idle for Mr. Havelock Ellis or any one else to talk of 'notable psychological and sociological significance'. These easy panegyrics mean nothing. As for your cloud of witnesses, they do not impress me. They are writers not readers.[149]

This is a crass, foolish letter. Like his response to Jane Harrison, the combination of ignorance and vitriol on display here seems, alas, too characteristic of MRJ's attitude to intellectual women.[150] A couple of months later, he was fulminating over the 'disheartening' news that the Cambridge Amateur Dramatic Club 'is to execute itself... by admitting women to membership'.[151]

But it wasn't just literary Modernism that drew MRJ's ire. He didn't like modern developments in supernatural fiction, either. Most particularly, he didn't like the subgenre of the weird tale, with its characteristic pulpy narratives of transdimensional entities, cosmic indifference, and inhuman morphology. He was ambivalent towards the weird tale's great pioneer, Arthur Machen, whom he believed 'has a nasty after-taste. Rather a foul mind I think, but as clever as they make 'em.'[152] In a 1931 essay, 'Ghosts—Treat Them Gently!', he writes: 'On the whole, then, I say you must have horror and also malevolence. Not less necessary, however, is reticence.' He disliked Christine Campbell Thomson's pulpish *Not at Night* series, whose stories were largely anthologized from *Weird Tales* magazine, 'which sin glaringly against this law' of reticence.[153] He was dismissive of the outrageously diegetic autodidact H. P. Lovecraft: in a letter of 1928, he informed Nico Llewelyn Davies, Old Etonian and ward of J. M. Barrie, that he has been reading 'a disquisition of nearly 40 pages of double columns on Supernatural Horror in Literature by one H. P. Lovecraft, whose style is of the most offensive. He uses the word cosmic about 24 times.'[154] In January 1929, he received a letter from 'a native of Wisconsin', asking for recommended reading on antiquarian subjects, 'as comprehensive as it is possible to make it'. 'He is evidently one of those who feel there is no harm in asking', he told Gwen.[155] The 'native of Wisconsin' seems to have been August Derleth, Lovecraft's friend, collaborator, and publisher, who was at the time working on his honours thesis on 'The Weird Tale in English since 1890'. MRJ replied, though with an account of his own stories rather than a long antiquarian bibliography: 'I think perhaps in its proportions the View from the Hill is to be preferred, but Count Magnus pleased me a little more when I wrote it.' Derleth, it seems, had terrible trouble deciphering MRJ's handwriting.[156]

* * *

Established in 1902 by King Edward VII, the Order of Merit is the most prestigious and exclusive of all British honours.[157] The OM is awarded, according to its official website, 'to such persons, subject of Our Crown, as may have rendered exceptionally meritorious service in Our Crown Services or towards the advancement of the Arts, Learning, Literature, and Science or such other exceptional service as we are fit to recognise'.[158] Membership is strictly limited to twenty-four people, and the original awardees in 1902 included Lords Roberts, Kitchener, Rayleigh, Lister, and Kelvin. Honorary awardees have included Dwight D. Eisenhower, Albert Schweitzer, Mother Teresa of Calcutta, and Nelson Mandela. This was the most exclusive club imaginable, the establishment's establishment, and MRJ was invited to join in 1930, alongside the philosopher Samuel Alexander and the historian G. M. Trevelyan.

MRJ got a letter from Buckingham Palace, informing him of the award, bestowed 'to recognise your pre-eminent position as a medievalist, your unique knowledge of illuminated manuscripts, medieval literature, ecclesiastical architecture and stained glass windows: and also your contribution as a specialist on the Apocryphal literature of the Bible'.[159] Walter Fletcher was visiting at the time, and MRJ excitedly showed him the letter. 'I expect the chaps will be cheering him in School Yard today', Walter wrote to his son, Charles Montague, MRJ's godson.[160] But MRJ complained that 'the Lower Boys can't be disabused of their impression that O.M. stands for Old Man, & say that it tells them nothing new'.[161] He confessed, though, when pushed, 'I won't deny that the affair gives me pleasure'.[162] Congratulations poured in. 'Makes me proud to be one, though an unworthy one, myself', J. M. Barrie (OM, 1922) wrote.[163] When he heard the news, Fred Benson got in touch with a little panegyric: 'Let us laud three glorious names / Montague and Rhodes and James. / Alleluia.'[164] Willie Bridgeman, newly ennobled after retiring from parliament (he was now Viscount Bridgeman of Leigh in the County of Shropshire), proposed that Eton should celebrate 'the honour of your O.M.' by making a donation to the Conservative Party.[165] Even Anstey Guthrie thawed out enough at the news to break his years of silence to write a short note of congratulation, 'Not of course that any title can add to your distinction'.[166]

II

Nunc dimittis

Provost's Lodge, Eton, 12 June 1936

It would be the last time so many of them were gathered together. On 18 March 1929, a dinner was held for Old Etonians at the Mansion House in London. After a lavish meal, beginning with Russian caviar and including Trout Meunière, smoked beef tongue, and stuffed quail *en croustade*, MRJ gave an address to an appreciative audience of diners that included Willie Bridgeman, Owen Hugh Smith, George Duckworth, Ronny Norman, Cis Lubbock, and A. E. Conybeare. Hugh Macnaghten was there too, a few months before his tragic end, sitting at the corner of the top table. Near him was Edward Lyttelton, somewhat reconciled with the institution that had treated him so badly in the febrile years of the Great War.[1] This was the world MRJ had built around him, and it was now a world of old men. For his seventieth birthday on 1 August 1932, the Eton Collegers sent him a poem. There were seventy Collegers allowed for according to the Founder's Statutes, so this was a symbolic Etonian number:

No Provost ever guided
With more paternal eye
The Colleges confided
To his supremacy:

But Art must seek perfection
In everything, and so, sir,
You seek in sheer affection
To draw your children closer:

And seventy Collegians
Will pay you, as is due,
Still more devout allegiance,
When you are seventy too.[2]

MRJ spent the 1930s in often severe pain, and was increasingly immobile. Age, it must be said, did not soften his views. In February 1930, he went to an Italian art exhibition in London (he was particularly keen to see the Canalettos), where he was annoyed by 'herds of dwarfish women of hideous aspect, and art students of unspeakable dirge'.[3] He was very unhappy with the work of the Magdalene English don I. A. Richards and his collaborator C. K. Ogden (also a Magdalene graduate) on a simplified auxiliary language, dismissing their *Basic English* (1930) as 'one of several devices intended to enable obscure foreigners to think they know our language'.[4] (Basic English was an aspect of a progressive internationalizing agenda that MRJ was never going to like: Richards was an advanced literary theorist with deep interests in psychology, and a devotee of the League of Nations; Ogden had connections with Edward Dent and Lowes Dickinson, was widely viewed as a pacifist during the war, and was a champion of Joyce and Wittgenstein.). When Gandhi came to speak at Eton in 1931, MRJ wrote: 'I declined to attend.'[5]

Cyril Alington, who as Headmaster worked closely alongside MRJ, began to notice a touch of petulance, 'the childlike pout of a disgruntled moment'.[6] This is an aspect of his personality in later years that comes most to the fore in his communications with Eric Millar, Keeper of Manuscripts at the British Museum, with whom he had been in regular correspondence since the war. In writing to Millar, MRJ allowed himself to give rein to a testiness we don't see too often elsewhere, in a series of unpleasantly toned, sometimes sarcastic letters. This, from March 1931, is a very unhappy MRJ complaining about his unrecognized scholarship on a medieval manuscript:

> I won't [mention] the fact that once again, in the face of all the sniffs and snubs I receive when I make *any* suggestion of *any* kind, the truth when investigated is found to be with me: I just leave it there. Perhaps another time... but no, I won't say a word more: only it *is* hard to forget the *scornful guffaw* which greeted the words *Hortus deliciarum*. But there—let it rest—[7]

When MRJ accused Millar of blackmailing him about an overdue cheque for one guinea towards a memorial volume, it was pretty obviously a joke, albeit a pointed one: 'But let me warn you that any repetition of your demand will result in my placing the whole series of documents... in the hands of the police.'[8] But the joke contained memories of an event three years earlier, when Millar felt he had to apologise for his plain-spokenness in asking MRJ for a previous overdue cheque.[9] If ever MRJ was feeling particularly grouchy, he would remind Millar that, as a librarian at the British Museum, he was a denizen of Bloomsbury.

He found plenty of things to irk him. In January 1932, MRJ and Scholfield went to see an exhibition of French paintings at Burlington House on Piccadilly, and were both struck by the fifteenth-century triptych known as the 'Aix Annunciation'. They weren't the only ones. On 21 January, an article appeared in the *Times* entitled 'A Satanist Picture', which maintained that the Aix Annunciation 'is acknowledged to be the work of a Satanist painter…a demoniacal painter living at the Papal Court at the time of the Great Schism…insinuating hell into every detail while preserving the pious appearance of the picture'.[10] MRJ read this, and wrote to Scholfield: 'Since we looked at the Aix Annunciation an ass has written to the Times calling it a Satanist picture, and I have asked some questions about it on the same organ, which you may see.' In a later handwritten note in the margin of the letter, Scholfield identifies the anonymous author of this article as the notorious self-publicist and fake scholar Montague Summers.[11] (He certainly was an ass.) MRJ's letter takes issue with every point the article makes, on its way to a devastating conclusion in the penultimate paragraph:

> Sir,—May I question the accuracy of your correspondent of January 21 on the subject of 'A Satanist Picture'?
>
> Did Mistral really speak of trefoil festoonery, writhing pillars and whirling capitals? And if so, what did he mean? What is the conclusion as to the date of the picture? We have mention of a demoniacal painter at the court of Avignon (how many such were there?), and of two 'conceivable' donors, of the fourteenth century; then we are told that the costumes of Virgin and Angel fix the work to the fifteenth century; then the reign of Louis XIII (1610) is hinted at. The rays on which the figure of the Diving Child is conveyed do not do more than pass over the lectern on which the finial is a monkey; he does not crouch on the edge of it. Where are the bats and vampires that flutter in the groining? I see none, and do not know how a vampire is portrayed. The word properly means an animated corpse, and is used as the nickname of a bat found only in America.
>
> Will a botanist assure us of the presence of venomous plants in the lilypot? The thumb of the Father is not 'advanced between his third and middle fingers'; it is in fact scarcely seen; nor is that of the Angel, who is not blessing at all. The 'two pious figures' on the wings whose titles 'we shall never know' are two prophets. The name of one, *Jeremias propheta*, is legibly inscribed below him. Isaiah's happens to have been cut off. May we have a reference to the medieval demonologists who state that the Devil often opened Sabbaths with a certain gesture?

> More might be said, but I reflect that persons who busy themselves about the subject of Satanism and the Black Mass are rarely to be depended upon for accuracy of statement. They should not, however, be allowed without protest to blacken gratuitously the name and work of a fine painter.
>
> Since Aix-en-Provence is concerned, it may be as well to mention that its beautiful tapestries (Nos. 27, 32) have been shown to have decorated the choir of Canterbury Cathedral, not St. Paul's, until they were sold under the Commonwealth.[12]

MRJ was better-placed than anyone else to conduct such a controversy about medieval iconography and demonology, and it was dangerous to disagree with him on this territory (though, to give Summers his due, the painting does contain what looks to me like a winged devil and a bat in the trefoil arch to the left of the centrepiece; and he may also be right about the position of God's thumb, if not about its symbolic significance). 'A botanist' did indeed write in to comment upon the allegedly venomous plants in the lily pot. Arthur W. Hill, Director of the Royal Botanic Gardens at Kew, and a Kingsman and former university lecturer in Botany at Cambridge, concluded that we were looking at lilies, columbine, roses, and catkins: 'I can see nothing sinister in the picture and all the plants have some particular significance in connexion with the Virgin Mary.'[13] The heraldic scholar Hilda Barron joined in along similar lines, and also took issue with Summers's wobbly chronology; Margaret Murray wrote in from UCL, unhappy with his use of 'Satanism' to describe what was, for her, a painting full of pre-Christian symbols of fertility.[14] On 28 January, Summers wrote to the *Times*, effectively admitting defeat:

> I agree with Dr. James that in this case, as in others, occult appearances may not be able to bear scientific tests. I hold no brief for my statements being so firmly rooted local tradition. Singly, each detail described might pass as mere ornament. It is the accumulation of abnormal features on the same canvas, taken in connexion with the history of the region where it originated, that has won for the picture in its native land a mysterious reputation. This seemed to me sufficiently interesting to warrant its presentation to the British public at a time when the picture was being shown in London.[15]

MRJ was not magnanimous in victory, and wrote to Millar: 'Yes, it's a wool-headed animal that wrote that stuff about Satanism . . . But probably, like the Lindisfarne Gospel and . . . Shakespeare's plays & Alice in Wonderland it's all Satanist—& pretty certainly by Lord Bacon. I'm very anxious to see your show—also full of Satanism—at the B. M.'[16]

* * *

One consistent source of happiness for MRJ in the second half of his life was Shakespeare. As a student, he had been one of the founders of the Eton Shakespeare Society, with Luxmoore as its first president. After Luxmoore's death in 1926, MRJ took over the role, which he carried out with dedication and real enthusiasm. His correspondence is full of news about Shakespeare Society events, and of discussions of Shakespeare's works more generally. 'One of my solaces now is the Shakespeare Society', he wrote to Nathaniel Wedd in 1927.[17] He kept a record of the Shakespeare Society readings for his first year, 1926–7, often with accompanying comments on the plays. The session began on 26 November with a reading of *Anthony and Cleopatra*, followed by *As You Like It* on February 1. This was followed in turn by *Hamlet* from 22 February, and then *The Comedy of Errors* ('an odd play', he thought). After that came what was for MRJ an ill-advised foray into modern theatre, with Lady Gregory's *The Workhouse Ward*, the play which he found 'full of the vilest language', before getting back on track in May with *King John*. Then came his favourite, *The Merry Wives of Windsor*, in which of course he read the part of Falstaff: 'Evidently the play hits the fancy', he wrote, 'and I for one cannot resent the change in Falstaff which troubles many people.' Next came *Macbeth* and his other favourite, *A Midsummer Night's Dream*. The season ended in September with *The Winter's Tale*, 'that most attractive and tortuous play'.[18] Though perhaps not quite this intensively, he kept the Shakespeare Society readings going until near the end. The last Shakespeare Society events he attended were reading groups for *Richard III* in September 1935, and *Hamlet* the following month. An earlier reading of *Richard III* in 1930 had him musing to Scholfield: 'I may be old-fashioned, but I cannot think him…no, no. He seems to me at the moment downright vicious. Well I suppose it takes all sorts to make a world, but I did think of speaking seriously to the boys on the dangers of *want of principle*.'[19] One Eton student testified to MRJ's intense absorption in the plays: 'The reading of a comedy would reduce him to helpless laughter: at the culmination of a Tragedy it was almost painful to witness the emotions.'[20]

MRJ was very much of the opinion that Shakespearean performance should be an all-male affair. Most particularly, he and Percy Lubbock were strongly of a mind that, when it came to the Comedies, 'No woman ought to touch them'.[21] At Christmas 1932, he wrote to Scholfield about a horrible prospect: 'Soon, too soon, I have to go to a performance of Macbeth, I am told done entirely by females. I can hardly credit this, & if it proves to be true, may I not sit it out.'[22]

In 1917, MRJ read an article on *Hamlet* by the former Trinity librarian W. W. Greg, whose implications disturbed him, but which marked the beginning of a long and serious engagement with the play. 'Hamlet's Hallucination' is a materialist counter-reading of the tragedy, arguing that Shakespeare's attitude to ghosts in general was 'frankly sceptical', and attempting to debunk 'the genuineness and objectivity of the Ghost in *Hamlet*'.[23] MRJ, with his deep investment in the reality of the supernatural, wasn't having this, and wrote at length to Gordon Carey, then on active service in the Royal Flying Corps:

> I have also read an article by a man called Greg who used to be Librarian at Trinity, to show that the ghost in Hamlet is not genuine. At present I can't believe it; but he tries to make out that in the play scene the King was not frightened by the representation of his own crimes on the stage, but by Hamlet's mad behaviour. He makes a great deal of the difficulty of supposing that the King could've sat through the dumb show unmoved... and no doubt that is difficult. He goes on to say that the play (which was an old one, not written for this occasion) was what suggested to Hamlet the idea that Claudius had killed old Hamlet by pouring poison in his ear: Claudius had indeed poisoned him but not in this way, & therefore was not nervous when he saw the play. *But* the Ghost told Hamlet that this was how he had been killed: *ergo* the Ghost's revelation is not a genuine one but the product of Hamlet's brain. He throws cold water on Horatio's evidence about the Ghost. But he does not offer any explanation of the fact that the Ghost appears to the sentinels before Hamlet turns up—& all that. Enough: I have been reading Shakes so much of late, & Hamlet in particular, that it has interested me, this article.[24]

Because a part of MRJ's vindication of a supernatural *Hamlet* rests on the appearance of the ghost of Hamlet's father to the sentinels at Elsinore when Hamlet is not present, he also took issue in a very particular way with T. S. Eliot's influential account of the play in 'Hamlet and His Problems' (1919). Eliot notoriously claimed that *Hamlet* was 'most certainly an artistic failure' because of its inability to find an 'objective correlative' for Hamlet's madness: that is, 'a set of objects, a situation, a chain of events which shall be the formula of that *particular* emotion; such that, when the external facts, which must terminate in sensory experience are given, the emotion is immediately evoked'.[25] Unlike Modernist literary critics, MRJ doesn't seem to have paid much attention to the objective correlative. What troubled him about 'Hamlet and His Problems' was the assertion that Shakespeare had left in 'superfluous and inconsistent scenes'; and while Eliot doesn't specify which scenes these are, he immediately goes on to quote disparagingly from Act I Scene I, the scene in which the ghost appears on the battlements of Elsinore, so the implication is obvious.[26] MRJ was still unhappy with this in 1935, when he read *Hamlet* with the Shakespeare

Society for what he must surely have known was the last time: 'We read Act 1 of Hamlet last night and I continue to feel that the opening of it is about the best thing that could be desired: certainly not what T. S. Eliot calls "an artistic failure".'[27]

At Christmas 1920, the season of ghosts, he read the twelfth-century Danish historian Saxo Grammaticus's *Gesta Danorum*, one of the major sources for *Hamlet*, which he found 'very instructive'.[28] But it wasn't until the 1930s that he found a major voice in Shakespeare scholarship to give support to his beliefs about *Hamlet*. He remained on the Cambridge University Press syndicate, and was very supportive of John Dover Wilson's New Shakespeare editions, which began to be published in 1921. Most particularly, he admired Dover Wilson's edition of *Hamlet*, published in 1934, and recommended it warmly to Gwen.[29] Dover Wilson's long introduction delves deeply into issues of sources and analogues, including a detailed disquisition on Saxo Grammaticus, is curtly dismissive of modern psychoanalytical readings (most particularly Ernest Jones's famous Oedipal interpretation of the play), and maintains flatly, *contra* W. W. Greg, that 'Practically everyone in that age, including probably Shakespeare himself, believed in ghosts'.[30] All of this would greatly have pleased MRJ.

He was even more pleased with Dover Wilson's next book. *What Happens in Hamlet* (1935) opens with '*an epistle dedicatory to* WALTER WILSON GREG': 'You will not agree with this book; I am not at all sure you will like it; but it is yours whether you like it or not.'[31] Like MRJ, Dover Wilson had been fascinated and shocked by Greg's 'Hamlet's Hallucination', which he read while stuck on a stationary train in Sunderland in November 1917. This started Dover Wilson on a long path of disagreement and refutation, which culminated in *What Happens in Hamlet*. The book contains a long section, 'Ghost or Devil?', in which Dover Wilson contextualizes the play in Early Modern supernaturalism and demonology, from King James and Thomas Browne to Ludwig Lavater and Reginald Scot—exactly the kind of material that MRJ had devoted so much of his life to studying. Shakespeare, Dover Wilson concludes, 'spent much thought upon this unique creature of his imagination; he made it an epitome of the ghost lore of his age'. Whether or not the actual historical Shakespeare 'believed in ghosts' may now be unknowable, but 'Certainly as a poet he believed in *this* ghost, and determined that his audience should believe in it likewise'.[32] In 1936, in his very last letter to Gwen, MRJ tells her 'I have been reading *What Happens in Hamlet* with improvement to the mind'.[33] It was the last book we know that he read.

* * *

Edward Arnold published MRJ's *Collected Ghost Stories* in April 1931. He spent much of February working on the proofs, and was taken aback by how long it was: 'we are at p. 448 and I think should run to nearly 600, which seems a lot'.[34] In its various forms and editions, the book has never been out of print. In 1947, reviewing a later reprint, John Betjeman latched onto something powerful and distinctive in MRJ's stories. He was, Betjeman thought (as others have done after him), one of the great writers of the English landscape:

> If you have any love of English scenery, particularly East Anglia and the West Country; of you like a well-told story redolent of the England of horse-carriages and branch railway lines; if old churches and old houses delight you... buy this book... Here are thirty unforgettable ghost stories... They awaken your eyes to English scenery and are better, for that purpose, than any guide-book.[35]

There would be three more stories after this, and they usually find their way into modern editions of the *Collected Ghost Stories*. 'The Experiment', subtitled 'A New Year's Eve Ghost Story', appeared in the *Morning Post* on 31 December 1931. 'The Experiment' is a tale of East Anglian necromancy, in which the body of the recently deceased Squire Bowles is exhumed and enjoined through black magic to reveal the location of his hidden treasure to his wife and son, who have conspired in his death. 'The Experiment' itself, the spell to command the dead to speak, is, we are told, from the library of the Bishop of Ely, John Moore (1646–1714), whose vast collection of 30,000 volumes was donated to Cambridge University Library by George I, where it is now known as the King's Library. In 1926, early in his CUL cataloguing project, MRJ came upon a fifteenth-century manuscript containing details of 'An experimēt most ofte proued true to find out treasure hiddē in ye ground, theft, manslaughter or anie other thynge'.[36] The text of the 'experiment', which MRJ reproduces at the end of the story, is taken verbatim from this manuscript.

The second story, 'The Malice of Inanimate Objects', was published in *The Masquerade*, one of the Eton ephemerals for which MRJ enjoyed writing stories, in June 1932. This is a much more modern story. In many ways, in fact, it is a story which expresses frustration with the modern world of aeroplanes, motorbikes, and telephones, in which the shaky-handed protagonist, Mr Burton, finds himself increasingly thwarted, and eventually done in, by the material stuff of his life: pipes, inkstands, books, razors. This, of course, was the material stuff of the increasingly shaky-handed MRJ's life too. Towards the end, he was no longer able to use a cut-throat razor: 'Now I ought to be shaving with a safety razor whose movement I do not understand', he told Eric Millar.

'But it has not yet cut me.'[37] His fictional counterpart, the pipe smoking, inky, bookish Mr Burton, is not so lucky. 'My hand's so shaky...I really daren't shave this morning', he tells a friend—but at the end of the story he is found dead in a railway compartment, his throat cut: 'apparently someone tried to shave Mr Burton in the train, and did not succeed overly well'.[38] What would Shavey Bardolf Barker have made of that?

The third story is the one that comes at the very end.

The ghost stories were beginning to receive sustained critical attention, as well as positive reviews. In February 1934, Mary Butts published 'The Art of Montagu James' in the Modernist periodical *The London Mercury*.[39] MRJ was not happy: 'a fulsome article on *my* art—save the mark—I knew not that I had any', he commented diffidently. It certainly didn't help that Butts's article was 'cheek by jowl' in the *Mercury* with 'a mean philippic' by Aldous Huxley and 'a panegyric on James Joyce'.[40] Nor, probably, that Butts had misspelled his name in her title (MRJ reciprocated by calling her 'Mary Butt').[41] Butts was an experimental novelist, a sexual liberationist, a disciple of Crowley and a friend of Cocteau, moved in circles that included Ezra Pound and Wyndham Lewis, and had her work championed by H.D. and published by T. S. Eliot. MRJ would hardly have been in personal or intellectual sympathy with Mary Butts—especially had he read her diary for 5 November 1927: 'Left to myself I should suspect that Professor James had once been in contact with an elemental, & built most of his stories on that.'[42]

That said, Butts's essay is full of astute commentary based on genuine love for MRJ's work. She first discovered his stories as a child, when she read Lost Hearts in the *Pall Mall Magazine* in the library of 'an old house'. She believed that if MRJ 'had chosen to write stories about any other subject under the sun, he would be considered the greatest classic short story writer of our time'.[43] (Even I think that's a bit strong.) Her journals testify to her deep and abiding fascination with MRJ (his name is dotted all over them), which grew in part out of a visit she had paid to St. Bertrand de Comminges in 1920, before she had even read him. St. Bertrand gave her occult visions of 'the magical acts of the grimoire... the abyss & the counter-abyss & the union of the pairs of opposites', and she believed she saw in MRJ a like-minded fellow-traveller in supernatural realms.[44] When she did read him, she was entranced: 'I halted several years, in the perfections of Professor James', she wrote in 1927; his 'faultless style, invention & learning, make him a great master.'[45] Butts was the first commentator to engage seriously with MRJ's great power as a writer of English landscape and climate. She recognized that 'the essence of his art is a sudden, appalling shock of visibility... unspeakably real, solid, *present*', to create 'something terse and poignant and durable'. But above all else, she maintained, surely correctly, as a writer 'Doctor James is pitiless'.[46]

Of course, MRJ was not often happy with women writers and intellectuals. The *only* woman writer about whom he was consistently and unequivocally positive is Dorothy L. Sayers, whose work he loved. For obvious reasons, he was particularly keen on *The Nine Tailors*, Sayers's campanological murder mystery set amongst the snowy East Anglian fens: 'an excellent thriller', he thought.[47] It probably helped that this novel features the bibliophiliac Old Etonian Lord Peter Wimsey, but not the 'Shrewsbury' (Somerville) College graduate Harriet Vane, with her First in English. Confined to bed in the last year of his life, he reread as many of her novels as he could get his hands on: 'the Nine Tailors, the Unpleasantness at the Bellona Club, the Unnatural Death, Clouds of Witness and others procurable at 2/6. She is a remarkably successful writer I must say; though ever and anon she does introduce intolerable people like Dian de Momerie in Murder must Advertise. I could do no less than congratulate her on having that lady's throat cut.'[48] (Pitiless to the end.)

The admiration was, in fact, mutual. *The Nine Tailors* closes with allusions to two MRJ stories, 'The Mezzotint' (which turns on the narrative of the decayed East Anglian Gawdy family, originally from Redenhall, Norfolk, but now fallen on hard times and resettled in Essex), and 'The Treasure of Abbot Thomas': '*The voice of the bells of Fenchurch St. Paul: Gaude, Gaudy Domine in laude... Abbot Thomas set me here and bade me ring both loud and clear.*'[49] Sayers, whose father was rector of Bluntisham in the Cambridgeshire fens, first read *Ghost Stories of an Antiquary* as a student at Somerville in 1913, and loved its 'very gruesome grue... very nice and nasty!' In 1928, she included 'Martin's Close' in the first volume of her anthology *Great Short Stories of Detection, Mystery and Horror*.[50] In 1937, Sayers wrote a letter to the *Eton Chronicle*, purporting to be from a seventeenth-century ancestor of Peter Wimsey, Lord Charles Wimsey, who has witnessed the events of 'Martin's Close': 'Mr Coffyn told me what I had not known before, that Ann Clark met her death by drowning in a pond, being about the middle of May last.'[51]

MRJ was less impressed when he read Lois Austen Leigh's *The Incredible Crime: A Cambridge Mystery* (1931). Lois was the niece of Augustus Austen Leigh, and her murder mystery is set amongst the Fellows of 'Prince's College', a thinly disguised King's. Prudence Pinsent, the novel's heroine, is 'the only child of the Master of Prince's College, a retired bishop'.[52] Knowing his taste for detective fiction, she sent a copy to MRJ, asking whether he would review it for the *Eton Chronicle*. The response was not encouraging:

> I've read it and written to tell her I don't like the heroine at all. The scene is partly at Cambridge which seems very conventionally done and partly in East Anglia which isn't so bad. Anyhow the heroine who's the daughter of a retired Bishop, Master of a College, has a great facility on swearing and on one occasion, lunching at a hotel with an old friend, a gent, takes occasion to swear solidly for two whole minutes: the language isn't reported, but I can't imagine anyone being able to swear for 2 minutes without trespassing a good deal over the limits.[53]

* * *

'I went on Monday to see my brother the Colonel', MRJ told Gwen in January 1932, '—very much under the weather, has been most of a month in bed—but was up again'.[54] Ber had taken 'very sick', and was confined to a nursing home in Boscastle, Cornwall until that summer: 'The sunshine, bless it, gives the aged a chance.'[55] Ber remained on active duty, though his health was badly compromised: he was hospitalized again in 1934.

As Ber was lying ill in hospital in January 1932, MRJ got news of Leo Maxse's death. In *Eton and King's*, MRJ had remembered the pair's student friendship with great fondness and humour, and they continued to meet up throughout the 1920s. As a self-described 'intelligent conservative', MRJ certainly disapproved of the radical political direction in which Maxse took the *National Review*, and his support of Mussolini: 'As for old Mussolini's proceedings', he wrote to Gwen, 'one watches them with horror but has a sneaking hope that he may crash.'[56]

Much more shocking losses were to follow. Lionel Ford had fallen sick at Christmas 1931, and then faded away at the Deanery of York Minster, seemingly barely aware of where he was and what was happening: 'L. Ford is hopelessly ill', MRJ wrote to Scholfield '—but I doubt if he knows it, and it isn't supposed to be spoken of freely. Dreadful!'[57] But Lionel did know that he was dying, and in his last weeks his often-repeated entreaty was that he be allowed to live until Easter. He died on Easter Sunday 1932, to the sounds of the hymn that had been sung at his wedding, 'Jesus Christ is risen to-day. Alleluia!'[58]

Walter Fletcher had been plagued by pulmonary congestion since the early 1920s, and in May 1932 was treated in Brompton Hospital for emphysema, and an abscess on the lungs. On 29 May he went in for an operation which, he told MRJ, 'I hope will make a radical cure & put a final end to all this bother. So I'm not a bit depressed. I've got this big last hurdle to jump & there I am.' The operation turned out to be much more serious than anyone anticipated, and was not a success. He died a few days later. 'I do resent having missed one of the best springs of my lifetime. So few springs left', he wrote from hospital in his last letter to MRJ. 'I have thought so much of you in recent difficulties.'[59]

MRJ went to the funeral at Cambridge, and afterwards wrote about it to Eric Millar. Walter's death had left 'a dreadful gap', but 'I now hear that possibly mischief in the form of an abscess was likely to come to the brain. If so, better an end than loss of mind.'[60] Not long after, MRJ gave the address at his old friend's memorial service:

> There are many who will be wishing to say how much the cause of healing has lost in Sir Walter Fletcher: let a word be added by one of those who hardly know how to do without him as a friend. These have known him (I for over forty years) as the truest & kindest of counsellors & sympathizers, magnificently keen in enjoyment of the best & simplest pleasures of life... We others who knew well his solid excellencies keep very bright memories of his humour, his ever multiplying hobbies (including collecting of old playing cards and wool-weights!) and his unrivalled qualities as a travelling companion, especially when things went slightly wrong; and for all these things and for him we are thankful.[61]

On 10 February 1934, Sydney died in a nursing home at Leatherhead, Surrey. At the end of the war, in June 1919, Sydney had been awarded the CBE for his work as a Territorial Army chaplain. In 1921, he took up the role of Archdeacon of Dudley, attached to the See of Worcester. He and Linda lived at the White Couse, College Green, next to Worcester Cathedral, on the banks of the Severn, a 'singularly peaceful and quiet' place: 'we have a splendid view of the Malvern Hills from our windows, so that my new home and my old home are within sight of each other'.[62] MRJ visited often, on his way to and from staying with Gwen. Sydney and Linda even sailed to South Africa for three months in 1930, on a family visit. Sydney's children had continued the James family's colonial tradition: his oldest son, Sydney Herbert Rhodes James, was appointed Rector of Mafeking in 1936; his younger son, Philip Montague Rhodes James, emigrated to Rhodesia, and died in Salisbury (Harare), in 1953. Ber, too, sailed for Southern Africa, in the mid-thirties, and lived out his final years in Harare. MRJ was one of the executors of Sydney's estate, valued at £11,257.[63]

Willie Bridgeman was next, in August 1935. He and MRJ always saw a lot of each other, and Willie was heavily involved with the life of his old school as a member of the Eton Governing Body. In February 1935, they had worked closely together on the delicate diplomatic matter of appointing a new Vicar of

Eton: it came down to a choice between a geriatric Freemason and a reactionary Ulsterman. In his letters, Willie was keen to tell MRJ all about his grandchildren, and about the new house he was having built. The pair last met up three weeks before Willie's death, and MRJ knew that something was wrong: he found his old friend 'full of rheumatical venom, and hardly his old self'.[64]

Henry Broadbent taught MRJ at Eton; the pair first encountered one another in 1876, and had remained friends ever since. When MRJ returned as Provost, the pair developed a daily ritual—every morning from the mid-1920s on, as he wrote to Gordon Carey, both would do 'the Daily Telegraph crossword puzzle, which rears its ugly head day by day', and then Broadbent would call round and they would compare their answers.[65] (The pupils put it about that MRJ finished the crossword every morning while his egg was boiling, and he liked his eggs soft-boiled.) But Broadbent's health was failing badly, and while MRJ was 'desolated' by his death in November 1935, 'it was no more than we had expected for a longish time'.[66] 'It is of a truth a grievous gap that the death of Henry Broadbent makes', he wrote to Shane Leslie. 'What a lot I owe him in the matter of reading, and I hope a conception of how little I know and how much there was to be known.'[67]

The worst news of all came for MRJ on 7 December 1935, when he heard of the death of St. Clair Donaldson. 'A real crusher came in this morning in the shape of the news of the Bishop of Salisbury's death whom I reckon to have known since 1881! though there have been long gaps when he was in Australia and places', he told Gwen. 'He is about the oldest friend I've had and one of the best of men.'[68] He was particularly devastated by St. Clair's death because it took him back to the beloved Eton of his youth. Arthur Benson, Harry Cust, HB, and now St. Clair. They were all gone. Only MRJ was left.

A few weeks later, MRJ wrote to a mutual friend, Walter Frere, Bishop of Truro, asking for his memories of St. Clair. The reply is very moving. Frere takes down an old photograph, taken in 1885 just before sitting their Classical Tripos exam: 'I see there St. Clair, tall, very fair, with a light moustache, a lithe frame & rather specially square & solid shoulders, from bright blue eyes looking out on our prospects; - simple, strong, resolute and gentle.'[69]

* * *

MRJ's own health was now fading badly too. He spent more and more time bedridden, either with leg trouble or with recurring problems with what he termed his 'interior economy'.[70] From 1928 on, he was prescribed to 'partake of a gloomy drink of which the avowed purpose is to change the flora of the intestine'.[71] In February 1933, it was 'a chill on the liver' that incapacitated him; he was laid low again that autumn, out of action for three months, though 'in good care'.[72]

By May 1934, he wrote to Millar: 'I have been horribly supine because for weeks or months now I have gradually but distinctly lost my capacity for walking, and half a mile or so is as much as I can contemplate.' He went to Aldeburgh that Easter for the last time, alone, not speaking to anyone for days on end, doing his light reading, and 'pacing short distances along the sea front'.[73] 'Did little being infirm', he confessed in his diary.[74] By September, he complained to Sydney Cockerell, 'I am much disinclined to do anything—in fact ain't allowed to. Can't walk about... Nothing specific. I eat well & sleep well, but once I get a sight of a job of work I go all of a twitter.'[75] He found himself quoting often a remark from Wodehouse's *A Damsel in Distress*: 'Sad piece of human wreckage that you are, you speak like an educated man.'[76] 'Legs very infirm' was how he put it in his diary.[77]

Grace moved into the Lodge permanently to look after her brother, who complained that she was 'a prey to apprehension' on every subject imaginable, from bus timetables to fog.[78] A nurse was employed—'the Dragon of the Bedchamber'—who wheeled him about in a wheelchair and tried to prevent him from writing letters when he needed to rest.[79] He never stopped being a heavy smoker. He was taken to Herefordshire to stay with Gwen and Jane, and then went to stay with Vincent Yorke and his wife. He proposed that A. F. Scholfield edit a collection of his writings, entitled *Truth, Wit and Wisdom* ('but perhaps better not').[80] He had plenty of visitors at the Lodge: Scholfield, Owen Hugh Smith, Ronny Norman, Ted Butler, J. H. Clapham, Sydney Cockerell, Eric Millar, E. G. Swain and others all came to see him in his last months. Ram, perhaps his most faithful friend, he saw more than anyone. The pair had even planned to go to Lord's to see the cricket for one last time in the summer of 1935, but in the end MRJ wasn't up to it. When Shane Leslie paid what was to be his last visit to the Lodge on Founder's Day, 6 December 1935, the pair found themselves talking about Eton and King's, the past, old friends, and ghosts—the stuff of MRJ's life:

> Though a sick man he laughed aloud. We talked of old King's... And also the story of the ghost on Gibbs' buildings. A Fellow called Brocklebank died there in 1878 in great trouble. He was the College ghost. His voice was heard shouting by Henry Luxmoore, also the sounds of drops of water in the night. Luxmoore was susceptible to outer sounds. He had heard music when his mother died. About ghosts the Provost added: Yes there are such things but we don't know the rules.[81]

He was still mentally sharp and engaged, though, in the last couple of years of his life. He continued where he could to oversee Eton's affairs, alongside the Vice-Provost and the Bursar. In October 1934, by this point very frail and sick, he was invited to give a speech at a dinner to commemorate the opening of Giles Gilbert Scott's magisterial new University Library, a great monument of Assyrian Modernism (MRJ *can't* have liked it!). The library was built on the land formerly occupied by the Eastern General Hospital, the field hospital erected during the War—where MRJ had visited Hope Bagenal and so many other wounded soldiers. Not surprisingly, the occasion found him musing again on flying time and all it had taken from his life:

> Surely then, this is a day to be much observed throughout our generations. Wisdom hath builded her a new house, & long may she dwell therein. But wisdom will not expect the men of my generation or of several later ones to leave without a sore pang of regret the old home, redolent to them of the personalities of Bradshaw, Robertson Smith, & Jenkinson (& of how many other cherished names). Each of them has left his mark—& a great one—upon the Library, for good.[82]

The last catalogue he published in his lifetime, of the medieval manuscripts of Ipswich Public Library, came out in 1934, and he started work on his last scholarly projects, on the Canterbury Psalter and the manuscripts of Leicester Abbey.[83] He tried to edit Walter Fletcher's letters, but this was too much for him. 'Paralysis of the will', he complained.[84] There were to be no diary entries after 1934. His last words, on 16 September, were exactly what you'd expect: 'back to Eton'.[85]

He found himself very engaged, though, by the 1935 General Election, which returned an overall Conservative majority and saw Stanley Baldwin back as Prime Minister at the head of a National Government. He was pleased by the result, and particularly pleased that Clement Attlee's Labour Party had not performed as strongly as he had feared they might: 'So the election is happily over', he said to Gwen. 'I own I was apprehensive of swings of the pendulum and of extremists getting their way to a much greater extent than they have.'[86]

In 1931, MRJ became President of the Penn-Gray Society, an organization dedicated to raising £30,000 for the purchase of the land surrounding the churchyard of Stoke Poges, a village four miles north of Eton. (The Society was named in honour of Stoke Poges's two most famous sons, William Penn and Thomas Gray; way back in 1875, in his first-ever ghost story, written while recovering from a fever at Temple Grove, MRJ had fictionalized the village as 'Stockton-cum-Podgers'.) His name appears in the Society's membership book directly below Horlick's Malted Milk Co. Ltd of Slough. On 23 May 1935, he went to the dedication ceremony of the Stoke Poges Memorial Gardens. The photograph taken that day was the amongst last ones ever taken of him.[87]

There was to be one last portrait, too—a great one. The artist Gerald Kelly was commissioned to paint him in 1934. But the process was a long one, as MRJ was too sick to sit for long at a time, and found himself having to leave considerable gaps between sittings. But artist and subject got on very well, arguing about Alfred Jarry and discussing the possibility of a posthumous portrait of Walter Fletcher. MRJ even liked Gerald Kelly's wife! The portrait was finally delivered on 6 June 1936, and shows MRJ, looking serious and understandably a little grim, dressed in blazing scarlet doctoral gown in front of shelves of books. It now occupies pride of place in the study of the Provost's Lodge at Eton.

There were to be no more Christmases at Cambridge. For his health, he was taken to Torquay for Christmas 1934, which he found 'very sophisticated, a mass of gardens and asphalte paths'.[88] He spent his time there reading *Right Ho, Jeeves* and the letters of Pliny the Younger. In 'more than Scythian' cold, he spent the Christmas of 1935, his last, at the Lodge:

> The festive season now obviously near—going to be very soberly kept—we shall stay here, 'the world forgetting, by the world forgot' and adopt the Scrooge attitude, none of your caperings and skippings hither and yon, but probably purchasing the new Wodehouse if favourable, and not without regret renouncing Cambridge attractions.[89]

What exactly it was in his 'interior economy' that finally failed is somewhat unclear. It may have been prostate cancer—though he may also have suffered a heart attack in early 1936, from which he never recovered. The apparent paralysis of the left side of the face and the left hand in the final photograph taken of MRJ might also suggest a stroke, though it is impossible to say with certainty[90] In January 1936, he decided to go on one last jaunt to attend a gathering of friends at Kew organized by the botanist Arthur Hill, though 'not without searchings of the heart (and other organs): however the attractions of the Old Gang are paramount, and I should be able at least to sit in a chair, though I'm not much for company'.[91] But at Kew he collapsed, seriously ill, and was immediately driven home to Eton. The eminent cardiologist Sir Maurice Cassidy, who was also physician to the King, was called in to examine him on January 16, and recommended a month in bed. Cassidy's presence, and the fact that Grace explicitly describes him as 'the heart specialist', suggests the possibility of a heart attack; Sydney Cockerell's observation after visiting him for the last time in May 1936 that 'the heart trouble...frustrated him and made life hardly worth living' suggests its likelihood.[92] Further plans for that season—a trip to King's to stay with J. T. Sheppard, the Old Etonians' Dinner at the House of Commons, lunch with Gerald Kelly and his wife—all had to be shelved. Cassidy recommended surgery, but MRJ, who had seen James McBryde, Eustace Talbot, and Walter Fletcher all die after operations, refused: 'I hate the knife', he had told Gwen before Walter's operation.[93] (Charles Montague Fletcher, Walter's son and MRJ's godson, was adamant that, had his father been alive, he would have urged his old friend to have the surgery.)[94]

From the early months of 1936, MRJ's handwriting—never remotely a model of clarity—becomes almost unreadable: his hands, at times, were shaking too much to write. From this we can trace quite closely the rate of his deterioration. A letter he writes to Sydney Cockerell on 1 April is (by his standards) perfectly legible, and even finds him planning one last visit 'to the bleak shore of Aldeburgh'.[95] But this was not to be. In his next letter to Cockerell, on 22 April, his handwriting is *very* shaky, and his mood very low: 'I go on grovelling in bed & there seems no definite end...I don't feel useful, & am much bored.'[96] His last letter to Eric Millar, on 22 May, is shakier still. It finds MRJ wanting to make amends for those moments of testiness: 'No friend could have been more faithful than Eric Millar: prodigal in gifts and visits.'[97] He forgot to sign his name, or couldn't sign it, or couldn't finish the letter. He started dictating his correspondence to a typist. The last public sighting of MRJ was on 4 June. His nurse pushed him in his wheelchair around the Playing Fields of Eton for one last time.[98] A photograph taken that day, in which he is talking to a smiling schoolboy, is the very last one ever taken of him.

In those last weeks, his friends clubbed together to get him a gramophone. Confined to bed in January, MRJ was bored, and Millar recommended 'the newest H.M.V. model, which really is almost incredible'.[99] The gramophone arrived on 20 February, with greetings from a large group of 'conspirators': Millar himself, plus almost all the surviving Old Gang.[100] It was a gift he appreciated enormously: 'Solace is brought by Bach, & other choral composers', he told Cockerell, who thought the music might even nurse him back to health.[101] The gramophone was set up in the Election Hall, and every evening after dinner Grace wheeled MRJ in to listen to it, 'with his pipe in his mouth, & matches strewn around, listening so intently, & beating time with his hand to the music'.[102]

MRJ died on 12 June 1936. Grace was with him at the end:

> He passed... so peacefully, at 3p.m.—just as they were playing the Nunc Dimittis in Chapel—
>
> And if you could have seen him, afterwards, you would have rejoiced—Every line gone, looking a young man again, and a most beautiful profile—and strangely enough—& yet not strange—a great likeness to my mother appeared—I feel sure that he looks like that in Paradise.[103]

Nunc dimittis. Lord, now lettest thou thy servant depart in peace.

* * *

MRJ's funeral took place in the bright sunshine on 16 June, attended by hundreds of Old Etonians: a service in Eton Chapel, followed by a procession to the grave itself in Eton Cemetery. Stephen Gaselee was there, and found the choir singing the Founder's Prayer 'one of the most affecting things in my memory'.[104]

> Domine Jhesu Christe, qui mi creasti, redemisti, et preordinasti ad hoc quo sum, tu scis quid de me fecere vis: fac de me secundum voluntatem tuam cum misericordia. *Amen.*
>
> O Lord Jesus Christ, who hast created and redeemed us, and hast brought us unto that which now we are; thou knowest what thou wouldst do with us, according to thy will, for thy tender mercy's sake. *Amen.*[105]

As the coffin was taken from the chapel, followed by the Headmaster, Masters, and boys, Handel's Dead March from *Saul* was played.

At the cemetery, prayers were offered by Cyril Alington, recently installed as Dean of Durham Cathedral. As the earth was placed over the grave, the mourners sang one last hymn, 'Jesus lives! No longer now / Can thy terrors, death, appal us'. Oliffe Richmond, who had travelled down from Edinburgh for the funeral, was overcome by a sense not only of desolation, but of loneliness:

> He was buried in the modern cemetery on the outskirts of Eton. His sister stood alone by the grave. There was no one to tell the old happy stories of him, as he had done of Whitting years ago. There seemed to be no one else there of our generation of King's men. No one spoke to me; no one asked any friend to go and stand by his sister at the grave of one beloved of so many. I went thanking Monty from my heart for all his life had given me; I came away with a sense of utter frustration. Surely, I kept thinking, Eton's so distinguished and so devoted son should have been buried in the Cloisters, where his heart had been.[106]

Richmond was wrong. There were plenty of old friends at the funeral: Stephen Gaselee, we've seen, and also Cis Lubbock, Ronny Norman, Eric Millar, Albert

Baillie, A. F. Scholfield, Ted Butler, Clive Carey, Owen Hugh Smith, Maisie Fletcher, A. E. Conybeare, and many others.[107] Some of those who couldn't make the funeral, like J. H. Clapham or Arthur Tilley, attended the memorial service held at the same time in King's. Eric Milner-White, officiating at the memorial, read MRJ's own prayer for the institutions which had shaped his life:

> Let thy blessing, O Lord, be on the Colleges of thy servant King Henry the Sixth, designed to thy praise and built for thy work: and as thou hast appointed unto them diversities of gifts, grant them also the same spirit: that they may together serve thee to the welfare of this realm, the benefit of all men, and thy honour and glory: through Jesus Christ our Lord. *Amen.*[108]

As the choir processed out of King's Chapel, the organ played Handel's 'I know that my Redeemer liveth'.

Ram was at the funeral, of course, and felt very differently about it from Richmond. For him, the loss of MRJ was like 'the death of a brother': 'Life will be quite a different thing without his personal touch & inspiration. But I am not going to be wretched, because grief always distressed him. Also I know that longer life was not to be desired for him.'[109]

Oliffe Richmond wrote his recollections of MRJ in a typescript in 1964. At the end of the typescript, he wrote in by hand the words: 'But he had chosen to lie where Luxmoore lay before him.' The grave of Montague Rhodes James, OM, Born August 1 1862 Died June 12 1936, Provost of King's College Cambridge 1905 to 1918, Provost of Eton 1918 to 1936, lies near the back wall of Eton's public cemetery. It is not easy to find. H. E. Luxmoore's grave is nearby, and his old travelling companion A. E. Conybeare is in the next row. On MRJ's grave are the words from Ephesians that he had used himself to memorialize James McBryde, binding the pair together in death: 'No longer a sojourner, but a fellow citizen with the saints and of the household of God.'

* * *

THIS IS THE LAST WILL

\- of me -

MONTAGUE RHODES JAMES O.M., Litt.D., of the Lodge, Eton College, Provost of Eton College aforesaid.

1. I REVOKE all prior Wills and testamentary depositions made by me.

2. I APPOINT my friends ALLEN BEVILLE RAMSAY Master of Magdalene College, Cambridge and CLARENCE HENRY KENNETT MARTEN, Vice-Provost of Eton College to be EXECUTORS of this my Will.[110]

MRJ drew up his last will and testament in February 1934. At the time of his death, he had £641 in his current account in the Westminster Bank at Eton, and a life insurance policy for £689. The total value of his estate, as per the final Executorship Account drawn up in August 1937, was £6094 in securities, £7583 in cash.[111] The duty payable on the estate was £91.5.9.[112]

Quite a bit of the cash value of the estate was in books and manuscripts. 'I will not draw up a list of the friends whom I desire to be remembered in the distribution of books', he wrote in his will. 'My Executors must exercise their discretion in the matter...I am afraid I am asking a good deal of their patience but I believe they will know in what spirit I ask it, and will also know what messages to Eton and King's I desire to leave.' The value of the books and MSS left to Eton and King's was estimated at £348. Some of his books and manuscripts, including the manuscripts of some of the ghost stories, were sold at Sotheby's in October 1936, with £760 going to the estate. The remainder of his books were sold separately, and fetched £810.

Whatever MRJ and John Maynard Keynes thought of one another personally, they both loved their Colleges. In October 1936, Keynes wrote to the antiquarian book-dealer Ernest Maggs (whose shop at 50 Berkeley Square was reputed to be the most haunted house in London), arranging for the purchase of some of the manuscripts of MRJ's stories, which Maggs had got from the Sotheby's auction, including 'Canon Alberic's Scrap-book' and 'Count Magnus', for King's College library.[113] You can read them today in the King's archive, the very rooms at the top of the Wilkins Building where MRJ first read 'Oh, Whistle' and 'Count Magnus' to James McBryde, Walter Fletcher, H. E. Luxmoore, and all the others, all those Christmases ago.

He left a small number of bequests to specific people. First and foremost, he was very clear that he wanted to give 'To the Provost and Fellows of Eton College the silver-gilt copy of Archbishop Parker's salt cellar given to me by Corpus Christi College, Cambridge and the silver tankard given to me by Gonville and Caius College, Cambridge'. With that out of the way, £100 went to his housekeeper, Jane Maplethorpe, and £50 each to the maidservants, Mary and Ethel Halls. Everything besides went to Grace. When the various donations, debts, and duties were cleared, she inherited £2591.

His notebooks went to Sydney Cockerell at the Fitzwilliam, and they're still there. Finally, he wrote in his will, 'As to my correspondence, there is a mass of it roughly classified in my bedroom. It should probably be destroyed.' Fortunately for posterity, and for the labouring biographer, Ram and Kennett Marten did not do this. Instead, his papers found their way to the Manuscript

Room of Cambridge University Library. 'Similarly, sermons, addresses and such are in drawers in the table-desk in the study on the first floor; mostly illegible and not worth keeping.' He was right about the legibility, wrong about the value.

* * *

But that is not the place to end, with wills and executors, securities and bequests. There was one last ghost story—though 'A Vignette' is hardly a story at all. It is an inconclusive fragment, like the memory of a dream—which indeed it may be. The story was published a few months after MRJ's death, in the *London Mercury*. He had written the story in early December 1935, at the behest of Owen Hugh Smith, who had asked him 'to try to recapture the mood in which he wrote *Ghost Stories of an Antiquary*'.[114] He sent a manuscript, handwritten in pencil, to the *Mercury*, but was reluctant at first to see it published. 'I am ill satisfied with what I enclose', he wrote to R. A. Scott James, the magazine's editor. 'It comes late and is short and ill written. There have been a good many events conspiring to keep it back, besides a growing inability…I send it because I was enjoined to do something by Mr Owen Hugh Smith.'[115]

'A Vignette' takes us back to Great Livermere, and to the imagination of a child and the dreams we never forget: 'I do seem to remember looking out of a window…and questioning whether there was or was not any appearance of a moving form among the trees. . . . I began to be visited by dreams which I would much rather not have had—which, in fact, I came to dread acutely; and the point around which they centred was the Plantation gate.' It is through this gate that the narrator, who is MRJ as both a small child and a dying man, has the glimpse of a face which haunts him to the last, 'monstrous…malevolent…pink…hot.'[116] This both is and is not the face of MRJ himself.

What does 'A Vignette' mean? 'Do not press me with questions', MRJ's narrator says. But the story closes, as I will, with MRJ's last word. It is a vision of the haunted, supernatural England he had been vouchsafed, the other world that he could see, but you could not:

> Are there here and there sequestered places which some curious creatures still frequent, whom once on a time anybody could see and speak to as they went about on their daily occasions, whereas now only at rare intervals in a series of years does one cross their paths and become aware of them; and perhaps that is just as well for the peace of mind of simple people.[117]

Requiescat, Monty James.

Endnotes

PREFACE

1. MRJ, lecture on 'Two Ancient Scholars', Notebooks 19.II.
2. Jo Grimond, *Memoirs* (London: Heinemann, 1979), p. 46.
3. LF, pp. 108–9.
4. Pfaff, p. 426.
5. MRJ, *Apocryphal New Testament*, p. 113. For the shepherds, see Note Book, CUL MS Add. 7517. In a note inserted amongst the leaves of this notebook, he identifies the shepherds as 'Asher, Zebulon, Justus, Nicodemus, Joseph, Barshabba & Jose'. His source for this is Solomon of Akhlat's 13th-century Syriac text *The Book of the Bee*.
6. MRJ, 'Occult Sciences', supplement to *The Ghosts and Scholars M. R. James Newsletter*, 5 (February 2004), p. 18. The original manuscript is at CUL MS Add. 7874/1.90.
7. Patrick Strong, letter to A. N. L. Munby, 28 October 1972, ECL COLL/P6/32.
8. For a longer version of the speculations in this and subsequent paragraphs, see Darryl Jones, 'M. R. James: Towards a New Biography', *Ghosts and Scholars M. R. James Newsletter*, vol. 40 (2021), pp. 8–15.
9. LF, p. 123.
10. Darryl Jones, 'Introduction' to CGS, p. xii.
11. H. E. Luxmoore, letter [first page missing—no date or addressee], CUL MS Add. 7481/L340.
12. Oliffe Richmond, letter to Shane Leslie, 9 November 1964, letter inserted into Leslie's annotated copy of E&K, ECL Lp.2.24.

CHAPTER I

1. MRJ, letter to parents, 1 May 1887. CUL MS Add. 7480/D6/284.
2. Hugh Paget, 'The Early History of the Family of James of Jamaica', *The Jamaican Historical Review*, vol. 1, no. 3 (December 1948), 260.
3. BRJ, 'Some Notes on the Family of James', JFP.
4. Nathaniel Wedd, Memoir, KCC NW 1/17, p. 38.
5. Paget, 'James Family of Jamaica', p. 263.
6. Ibid., p. 265.
7. William Rhodes James I, UCL Legacies of British Slavery database: https://www.ucl.ac.uk/lbs/person/view/2146662347
8. For MRJ and Montague Vidal James, see *The Eton Register, Part IV: 1871–1880* (Eton: Spottiswood and Co., 1907), pp. 125, 130.
9. E. N. Geijer, letter to MRJ, 20 May 1927, CUL MS Add. 7481/G9; Paget, 'James Family of Jamaica', p. 271.
10. William Rhodes James I, UCL Legacies of British Slavery database: https://www.ucl.ac.uk/lbs/person/view/2146662347
11. Will of Haughton James I, 1737, JFP.
12. Haughton James, letter to Dr Haughton, 30 December 1787, JFP.
13. Haughton James, letter to Dr Haughton, 2 October 1789, JFP.
14. Mary Williamson, letter, 26 October 1809, JFP.

15. JFP.
16. https://historicengland.org.uk/listing/the-list/list-entry/1269728
17. JFP, Box 4a.
18. JFP.
19. JFP.
20. Jamaica Hanover 566 (Haughton Tower Estate), UCL Legacies of British Slavery database: https://www.ucl.ac.uk/lbs/claim/view/23860
21. JFP/Box 4d.
22. JFP/Box 4e.
23. Jamaica Trelawny 107 (Steelfield), UCL Legacies of British Slavery database: https://www.ucl.ac.uk/lbs/claim/view/15119
24. William Rhodes James IV, UCL Legacies of British Slavery database: https://www.ucl.ac.uk/lbs/person/view/23186
25. William Rhodes James, letter to HJ, January 1844, CUL MS Add. 7480/D1/3.
26. '1103. James, William Rhodes', in Lieut. Col. D. G. Crawford, *Roll of the Indian Medical Service, 1615–1930* (London: W. Thacker & Co. 1930), p. 336.
27. Thomas James, letter to HJ, 10 April 1849, CUL MS Add. 7480/D1/11.
28. Harry James, letter to HJ, 5 February 1848, CUL MS Add. 7480/D1/10.
29. 1881 England Census, Class: RG11; Piece: 1882; Folio: 108; Page: 25; GSU roll 1341454.
30. See Mona Sakr, 'A Life's Work: Minnie James and Images of the Woman Librarian', https://blue-stocking.org.uk/2010/12/01/a-life's-work-minnie-james'-and-images-of-the-woman-librarian/
31. CUL MS Add. 7480/B9.
32. CUL MS Add. 7480/B7.
33. CUL MS Add. 7480/B17.
34. See F. Clark, *The East India Register and Army List for 1854* (London: Wm. H. Allen & Co. 1854), p. 271; BRJ, 'Some Notes on the Family of James'.
35. J. R. Tanner, ed. *The Historical Register of the University of Cambridge, Being a Supplement to the Calendar with a Record of University Offices Honours and Distinctions to the Year 1910* (Cambridge: Cambridge University Press, 1917), p. 270.
36. Pfaff, p. 2.
37. Edward Falconer, letter to HJ, 24 February 1894, CUL MS Add. 7480/D5/27.
38. In my account of the Evangelical movement here, I draw on Owen Chadwick, *The Victorian Church, Part I*, Third Edition (London: Adam & Charles Black, 1971), pp. 440–55; Alec R. Vidler, *The Church in an Age of Revolution* (London and Harmondsworth: Penguin, 1971), pp. 33–44.
39. Vidler, p. 36.
40. Ibid., p. 49.
41. Chadwick, p. 445.
42. Vidler, p, 37.
43. Charles Dickens, *Bleak House*, ed. George Ford and Sylvère Monod (New York: W. W. Norton, 1977), Chapter 4.
44. Chadwick, p. 443.
45. HJ, *The Country Clergyman and his Work: Six Lectures on Pastoral Theology Delivered in the Divinity School, Cambridge, May Term, 1889* (London: Macmillan, 1890), pp. 18, 16.
46. Ibid., p. 156.
47. Ibid., p. 151.
48. Ibid., pp. 65–6.

49. Ibid., p. 57.
50. Ibid., p. 9.
51. Ibid., p. 13.
52. Ibid., p. 12.
53. E&K, p.87. Throughout, I refer to this edition: MRJ, *Eton and King's: Recollectiions, Mostly Trivial 1875–1925* (Ashcroft, British Volumbia: Ash-Tree Press, 2005).
54. Chadwick, p. 441.
55. MRJ, letter to HJ [no date], CUL MS Add. 7480/D6/56.
56. Edward Henry Bickersteth, *Yesterday, To-day, and For Ever* (New York: Robert Carter, 1875), p. 316.
57. Percy Lubbock, letter to MRJ, 23 January 1923, CUL MS Add. 7481/L84.
58. HJ, letter to Montagu James [1854], CUL MS Add. 7480/B25.
59. MEJ, letter to HJ, 9 October 1854, CUL MS Add. 7480/D2/1. For their correspondence during their engagement, see JFP.
60. MEJ, letter to HJ, 9 October 1854, CUL MS Add. 7480/D2/1.
61. JFP.
62. John Marshall, 'Joshua Sydney Horton, Esq. [Post-Captain of 1800]', in *Royal Naval Biography: Containing Memoirs of all the Flag-Officers of His Majesty's Fleet Now Living* (London: Longman, Hurst, Rees, Orme and Brown, 1823), Vol. 2, pp. 247–50.
63. *The Navy List, Corrected to 20 March 1834* (London: John Murray, 1834), p. 5.
64. *The Navy List, Corrected to 20 December 1835* (London: John Murray, 1836), p. 168.
65. Ashworth P. Burke, *Burke's Family Records* (London: Harrison and Sons, 1897), p. 335.
66. BRJ, 'Some Notes on the Family of James'.
67. 'Introduction to Mary Emily James (née Horton) Scrap & Visitors Card Book', JFP.
68. See Mary Emily James, Diary of Travels in Italy, 1840–43. JFP.
69. John Stevenson, letter to HJ [1854], CUL MS Add 7480/D5/10.
70. MEJ, letter to HJ, 8 June [1854], JFP.
71. MEJ, letter to HJ, 29 February 1864, CUL MS Add. 7480/D2/10.
72. SRJ, *Seventy Years: Random Reminiscences and Reflections* (London: Williams & Norgate, 1926), pp. 2–3.
73. CGS, p. 401.
74. For an earlier version of this section, see Darryl Jones, 'M. R. James and Folk Horror', in Robert Edgar and Wayne Johnson, eds. *The Routledge Companion to Folk Horror* (London: Routledge, 2024), pp. 57–8.
75. George Ewart Evans, *The Pattern Under the Plough: Aspects of the Folk Life of East Anglia* (1966; Toller Fratrum: Little Toller Books, 2013), p. 242. Evans was careful to qualify this statement: 'in writing *primitive* I am not making a value judgement and using the word as a synonym for backward'.
76. Ibid., pp. 19–21.
77. Rob Lewis, 'The Pattern Under the Plough', *Sight and Sound*, 20:8 (August 2010), 16–22.
78. M. H. James, *Bogie Tales of East Anglia*, with an introduction by Francis Young (Peterborough: St. Jurmin Press, 2019), p. 47.
79. See Katharine M. Briggs, 'Black Dogs', in *A Dictionary of British Folk-Tales in the English Language, Part B: Folk Legends*, Vol. 1 (London: Routledge and Kegan Paul, 1971), pp. 3–19.
80. See Patricia Dale-Green, *Dog* (London: Rupert Hart-Davis, 1966).
81. James, *Bogie Tales of East Anglia*, p. 21.
82. Beryl Dyson, *Great Livermere: A Parish with Ghosts* (Ely: Melrose Books, 2016), p. 7.

83. Edward Parnell, *Ghostland: In Search of a Haunted Country* (London: William Collins, 2019), p. 6.
84. MRJ, letter to family, 17 January 1888, CUL MS Add. 7480 D6/299.
85. MRJ, letter to family, 8 March 1891, CUL MS Add. 7480/D6/329.
86. Dyson, *Great Livermere*, p. 14.
87. CGS, p. 402.
88. MRJ, 'Magic: Its Possibilities' [1884]. Notebooks 2.III.
89. MRJ, letter to Henry Kennet Marten, 27 May 1927, CUL MS Add. 7481/MISC.
90. MRJ, sermon delivered at Eton, 9 December 1933, CUL MS Add. 7485/22.

CHAPTER 2

1. MGSA, pp. 5–6.
2. Meston Batchelor, *Cradle of Empire: A Preparatory School through Nine Reigns* (London and Chichester: Phillimore, 1981), p. 20.
3. Vyvyen Brendon, Prep School Children: A Class Apart over Two Centuries (London: Continuum, 2009), p. 9.
4. E&K, p. 8.
5. MRJ letter to parents, no date [?January 1874], CUL MS. Add. 7480/D6/40.
6. MRJ letter to MEJ, 26 January 1874, CUL MS. Add. 7480/D6/6.
7. MEJ, letter to MRJ, 27 January 1874, CUL MS. Add. 7480/E2/1.
8. GRJ, letter to MRJ, 28 January 1874, JFP.
9. MRJ letter to parents, 31 January 1874, CUL MS. Add. 7480/D6/7.
10. Notebooks 3.I, pp. 1–2.
11. MRJ, letter to MEJ [no date], CUL MS Add. 7480/D6/55.
12. LF, p. 14.
13. GSA, p. 19.
14. GSA, p. 111. MRJ, letter to James McBryde, 3 March 1904, CUL MS Add. 7481/M120*.
15. MGSA, pp. 59–9.
16. MGSA, p. 270.
17. E&K, p. 8.
18. This description of Temple Grove is drawn from Batchelor, *Cradle of Empire*, pp. 2–7. See also Simon Wright, *Waterfield's School: A Preparatory School in Its Victorian Heyday* (Guildford: The Heron's Ghyll Press, 1994), pp. 85–94. Pearson had relatively little formal education (he was admitted to Cambridge, but never went), though he was a gifted astronomer and ended up a Fellow of the Royal Society.
19. Batchelor, p. 4; Wright, p. 92. Wellington's sons were at Temple Grove from 1813 to 1817.
20. See Batchelor, p. 46 for these costs.
21. Benjamin Disraeli, *Coningsby, or: The New Generation* (1844; London: Dent, 1911), p. 10. For 'that wretched Pinkney' see Batchelor, p. 7. Wright, p. 99, also supports the view of Pinckney as a sycophant.
22. Henry J. Coke, *Tracks of a Rolling Stone* (London: Smith, Elder, & Co., 1905), p. 9.
23. ACB, *Memories and Friends* (London: John Murray, 1924), p. 44.
24. Batchelor, p. 13; Wright, p. 106. The author of these words was Arthur Hailstone.
25. [Clarendon Commission], *Report of Her Majesty's Commissioners Appointed to Inquire into the Revenues and Management of Certain Colleges and Schools and the Studies Pursued and the Instruction Given Therein with an Appendix and Evidence* (London: George E. Eyre and William Spottiswoode for Her Majesty's Stationery Office, 1864), vol. 1, p. 42.

26. Arthur Marwick, *The Sixties: Cultural Revolution in Britain, France, Italy, and the United States, c.1958–c.1974* (Oxford: Oxford University Press, 1998), pp. 30–1.
27. See John Chandos, *Boys Together: English Public Schools 1800–1844* (Oxford: Oxford University Press, 1985), Chapter 4.
28. H. E. Luxmoore, *Communion* (London: Society for Promoting Christian Knowledge, 1906), p. 21.
29. Thomas Hughes, *Tom Brown's Schooldays*, ed. Andrew Sanders (1857; Oxford: Oxford University Press, 1989), p. 173.
30. [Clarendon Commission], *Report*, p. 43.
31. [Clarendon Commission], *Report*, p. 44.
32. Charles Darwin, *Autobiographies*, ed. Michael Neve and Sharon Messenger (London: Penguin, 2002), p. 10.
33. J. R. de S. Honey, *Tom Brown's Universe: The Development of the Victorian Public School* (London: Millington, 1977), pp. 218, 224.
34. See, for example, Kevin Waite, 'Beating Napoleon at Eton: Violence, Sport and Manliness in England's Public Schools, 1783–1815', *Cultural and Social History*, vol. 11, no. 3 (2013), 407–24.
35. See Chandos, p. 97; Lawrence James, *Raj: The Making of British India* (London: Abacus, 1998), pp. 257–60.
36. Batchelor, p. 35.
37. Chandos, p. 76. For accounts of schools and Muscular Christianity, see, for example, David Newsome, *Godliness and Good Learning: Four Studies on a Victorian Ideal* (London: John Murray, 1961).
38. For an influential example of this last argument, see Ian Gibson, *The English Vice: Beating, Sex and Shame in Victorian England and After* (London: Duckworth, 1978).
39. Chandos, pp. 237–8.
40. Batchelor, p. 41.
41. Batchelor, pp. 53–4. This particular teacher was Albert Cheese, who was, like O. C. Waterfield and MRJ, a Scholar of Eton and King's. According to past pupils of Temple Grove, he never smiled.
42. Wright, pp. 4, x.
43. Coke, p. 9.
44. Brendon, p. 19.
45. Ciaran Brady, *James Anthony Froude: An Intellectual Biography of a Victorian Prophet* (Oxford: Oxford University Press, 2013), p. 47.
46. Brendon, p. 16.
47. Brady, p. 48.
48. Christopher Hollis, *Eton: A History* (London: Hollis and Carter, 1960), p. 232.
49. Brendon, p. 12.
50. See Rupert Hart-Davis, *Hugh Walpole* (Gloucester: Sutton, 1997), pp. 17–18.
51. Chandos, pp. 82, 95.
52. Alex Renton, *Stiff Upper Lip: Secrets, Crimes, and the Schooling of a Ruling Class* (London: Weidenfeld and Nicolson, 2017), pp. 29, 196–7; Renton, 'School of Hard Knocks: The Dark Underside to Boarding School Books', *Guardian*, 8 April 2017: https://www.theguardian.com/books/2017/apr/08/school-boarding-secrets-crimes-alex-renton-kipling-rowling-dahl-churchill
53. See Lucy Bending, *The Representation of Bodily Pain in Late Nineteenth-Century English Culture* (Oxford: Clarendon Press, 2000), Chapter 6.

54. Honey, p. 212. Capitals in original.
55. Chandos, p. 70.
56. See Kasia Boddy, *Boxing: A Cultural History* (London: Reaktion, 2008).
57. For Francis Ashley's death, see Chandos, pp. 142–8.
58. Hollis, p. 231.
59. Gervase Morley, *The History of Temple Grove School*: http://www.templegrove.org.uk/UserFiles/File/TG History Nov 09.pdf
60. E&K, p. 11.
61. Waterfield's descendant, the diplomat J. P. Waterfield, wrote: 'Ottiwell Charles Waterfield, who was son of Charles, a barrister and younger brother of Thomas Nelson, my great grandfather, made Temple Grove a distinguished preparatory school in the 19th century . . . I think there was a feeling in my immediate family that the Waterfields who descended from the barrister, Charles, were "grander" and more "society" than our lot': J. P. Waterfield, *Some Memories*: http://www.tamburlane.co.uk/resources/Some%20memories%20for%20my%20grandchildren.pdf, p. 15.
62. ACB, *Memories and Friends*, pp. 27–54.
63. ACB, *Memories and Friends*, p. 41; E. F. Benson, *Our Family Affairs* (New York: George H. Doran, 1921), p. 81.
64. ACB, *Memories and Friends*, p. 41.
65. For a fascinating study of the Benson family, see Simon Goldhill, *A Very Queer Family Indeed: Sex, Religion, and the Bensons in Victorian Britain* (Chicago and London: University of Chicago Press, 2017).
66. ACB, *Memories and Friends*, pp. 27, 28.
67. E&K, p. 8.
68. ACB, *Memories and Friends*, p. 42.
69. ACB, *Memories and Friends*, p. 44.
70. [Joseph Haythorne Edgar], *General Rules for the Conduct of Temple Grove School* (Richmond: Hiscoke and Sons, 1880), p. 5.
71. Batchelor, pp. 18–19; E. F. Benson, *Our Family Affairs*, p. 81.
72. O. C. Waterfield letter to Herbert James, *c.*25 November 1874, CUL MS. Add. 7480 D4/29.
73. MRJ, letter to MEJ, 20 July 1876, CUL MS. Add. 7480/D6/32.
74. MRJ, letter to MEJ, no date [Autumn 1874], CUL MS. Add. 7480/D6/17; Mary Emily James, letter to MRJ, 4 December 1874, CUL MS. Add. 7480/E2/7.
75. MRJ, letter to HJ, no date [Autumn 1874], CUL MS. Add. 7480/D6/18.
76. William Brown, letter to ACB, 16 July 1924, ECL MS. 590.
77. ACB, *Memories and Friends*, p. 45.
78. L. S. R. Byrne and E. L. Churchill, *Changing Eton: A Survey of Conditions based on the History of Eton since the Royal Commission of 1862–64* (London: Jonathan Cape, 1937), p. 9.
79. Byrne and Churchill, p. 2.
80. Batchelor, p. 19; ACB, *Memories and Friends*, p. 43; Wright, p. 138.
81. Byrne and Churchill, p. 11.
82. Coke, p. 10. It could, I suppose, have been worse: George Orwell recalled finding 'a human turd' floating in his bathwater at St. Cyprian's. See Orwell, 'Such, such were the joys', in *Essays*, ed. John Carey (London: Everyman, 2002), p. 1310.
83. Wright, p. 156.
84. Batchelor, pp. 31–2; Byrne and Churchill, p. 12; ACB, *Memories and Friends*, p. 50.
85. ACB, Memories and Friends, pp. 43–4.
86. ACB, Memories and Friends, pp. 34–5.

87. MRJ, letter to MEJ, November 1875, CUL MS. Add. 7480/D/24.
88. Batchelor, p. 24.
89. Wright, p. 156.
90. Benson, *Our Family Affairs*, p. 85.
91. ACB, *Memories and Friends*, p. 32.
92. Wright, pp. 160–1.
93. MRJ, letter to GRJ, [23 May 1875], CUL MS. Add. 7480/E5/7.
94. Coke, p. 9.
95. Eleanor Hoare, 'A spoonful of brimstone and treacle', *Eton College Collections*: https://etoncollegecollections.wordpress.com/2017/01/31/a-spoonful-of-brimstone-and-treacle/. Accessed 16 October 2019.
96. [Robert Kemp Philp,], *The Dictionary of Daily Wants* (London: Houlston and Wright, 1859), APA-APE.
97. Coke, pp. 9–10.
98. Ibid., p. 10; E. F. Benson, *David Blaize* (London: Hogarth Press, 1989), p. 59.
99. Benson, *David Blaize*, p. 80.
100. Byrne and Churchill, pp. 4–5.
101. Benson, *David Blaize*, p. 12.
102. Brady, p. 47.
103. Arthur Gray, 'Some Memories of Fifty Years', *The Chanticlere*, LXXI (Lent Term 1922), p. 11.
104. Byrne and Churchill, p. 4.
105. E&K, p. 9.
106. Charles Geoghegan was admitted to TCD on 8 July 1854, according to the College Entrance Book: TCD MUN V 24/4 (1848–1868), Folio 46v. *Alumni Dublinenses*, a register of TCD graduates from 1593–1860, has no record of his graduation, though he may have graduated after 1860.
107. Wright, pp. 77–8.
108. Honey, p. 113.
109. E&K, p. 12. See also ACB, *Memories and Friends*, p. 39, where he is pseudonymously referred to as 'Mr. Abbot'.
110. MGSA, p. 7.
111. MRJ, letter to GRJ, 2 October [1874], CUL MS. Add. 7480/E5/5.
112. MRJ, letter to parents, [Autumn 1874], CUL MS. Add. 7480/D6/17.
113. Wright, p. 144.
114. MRJ, letter to MEJ, no date, CUL MS. Add. 7480/D6/41.
115. Byrne and Churchill, p. 22.
116. Wright, p. 150.
117. Byrne and Churchill, p. 22. *Principia Latina* was a fairly common title for Latin textbooks, and a number with this title were published in the later nineteenth century, though there is no record of one by Waterfield. Batchelor (p. 26) says that the book was published and distributed privately, so it may well have been written by Waterfield—though he calls it *Elementa Latina*, which may be conflating it with W. H. Morris's widely used 1902 Latin grammar of that title.
118. See *Sertum, A Greek Reading Book for the Use of the Fourth Form at Eton: With Notes* (Eton College: E. P. Williams & Son, 1869).
119. John Lawson and Harold Silver, *A Social History of Education in England* (London: Methuen, 1973), p. 198.

120. Chandos, p. 248.
121. Coke, p. 13.
122. ACB, *Memories and Friends*, p. 33.
123. [Clarendon Commission], *Report*, p. 32
124. See Batchelor, pp. 25–6.
125. Stephen Gaselee, 'Montague Rhodes James, 1862–1936', *Proceedings of the British Academy*, 22 (1936), p. 433. Gaselee was Pepys Librarian and Fellow of Magdalene College, Cambridge, and Librarian and Keeper of Papers at the Foreign Office.
126. E&K, pp. 5–6.
127. Temple Grove school report, 16 October 1873, CUL MS. Add. 7480/D4/1.
128. Temple Grove school report, 27 July 1874, CUL MS. Add. 7480/D4/8.
129. Temple Grove school report, 24 February 1875, CUL MS. Add. 7480/D4/12.
130. O.C. Waterfield, letter to HJ, 4 March 1875, CUL MS. Add. 7480/D4/31.
131. O.C. Waterfield, letter to HJ, 5 March [1875], CUL MS. Add. 7480/D4/32.
132. MRJ, letter to HJ, 5 March 1875, CUL MS. Add. 7480/D6/20.
133. HJ, letter to MRJ, 6 March 1875, CUL MS. Add. 7480/E1/3.
134. MRJ, letter to HJ [?Spring 1875], CUL MS. Add. 7480/D6/30.
135. MRJ, letter to HJ, [September–October 1875], CUL MS. Add. 7480/D6/29.
136. Viscount Grey of Fallodon [Edward Grey], *Twenty-Five Years: 1892–1916* (New York: Frederick A. Stokes, 1925), p. 20.
137. E&K, p. 9.
138. Reports of the Classical Examiner, Temple Grove School archive, East Sussex Record Office, Brighton: TGS 7/1.
139. MRJ, letter to HJ, May/June 1876. CUL MS. Add. 7480/D6/25.
140. ACB, *Memories and Friends*, pp. 49–50.
141. David Newsome, *On the Edge of Paradise: A. C. Benson: The Diarist* (London: John Murray, 1980), p. 23.
142. MRJ, letter to HJ, 4 May 1875. CUL MS Add. 7480/D6/22.
143. MRJ, lecture at Eton [no date], CUL MS Add. 7484/2.28.
144. Byrne and Churchill, p. 6.
145. Wright, p. 162.
146. HJ, letter to O. C. Waterfield, 28 July 1875. CUL MS. Add. 7480/D4/38.
147. S. G. Lubbock, *A Memoir of Montague Rhodes James* (Cambridge: Cambridge University Press, 1939), p. 7.
148. MRJ, address to Royal Grammar School, Worcester, 12 May 1915, CUL MS Add. 7484/2.2; E&K, pp. 9–10.
149. Details of books borrowed from Temple Grove Library, April 1872-December 1873. Temple Grove School archive, East Sussex Record Office, Brighton: TGS 8/1/2. Unfortunately, no library records survive for the rest of MRJ's time at Temple Grove.
150. Robert Curzon, *Visits to Monasteries in the Levant* (London: John Murray, 1849), p. 120.
151. Curzon, *Visits*, p. 122–3.
152. Ibid., pp. 124–5.
153. GSA, pp. 4–5.
154. MRJ, letter to MEJ, [November 1873], CUL MS. Add. 7480/D6/4.
155. MRJ, letter to HJ, 25 July 1874, CUL MS. Add. 7480/D6/14.
156. MRJ, letter to HJ, 9 June 1875, CUL MS. Add. 7480/D6/26.
157. Aunt Rachel, letter to MRJ [no date], JFP; E&K, p. 9. Vonones II of Parthia, in modern-day Iran, ruled from 11–51 AD.

158. MGSA, p. 7.
159. MRJ, letter to HJ [no date]; CUL MS Add. 7480/D6/60.
160. ACB, *Memories and Friends*, p. 36.
161. L. S. R. Byrne, letter to MRJ, 31 July 1918; CUL MS. Add. 7481/B409.
162. E&K, p. 13.
163. Temple Grove Divinity paper, October 1873; CUL MS. Add. 7480/D6/4.
164. MRJ, letter to MEJ, no date, CUL MS. Add. 7480/D6/38.
165. F. W. Farrar, *St. Winifred's, or The World of School* (1862; London and Melbourne: Ward, Lock & Co. 1920), p. 76.
166. Wright, p. 167.
167. Benson, *David Blaize*, p. 10.
168. LF, 111.
169. MRJ, 'Ghosts – Treat Them Gently!', *Evening News*, 17 April 1931, in CGS, p. 418.
170. E&K, p. 10.
171. E&K, p. 11.
172. MRJ, letter to BRJ [1875], JFP.
173. MRJ, letter to HJ, no date, CUL MS. Add.7480/D6/52.
174. O.C. Waterfield, letter to HJ, July 1875, CUL MS. Add. 7480/D4/35.
175. O.C. Waterfield, letter to HJ, 24 July 1875, CUL MS. Add. 7480/D4/36.
176. HJ, letter to O.C. Waterfield, 21 January 1876, CUL MS. Add. 7480/D4/42; SRJ, letter to HJ [no date], JFP.
177. HJ, letter to O.C. Waterfield, 13 March 1876, CUL MS. Add. 7480/D4/44.
178. O.C. Waterfield, letter to HJ, 14 March 1876, CUL MS. Add. 7480/D4/45.
179. MRJ, letter to HJ and GRJ, [July 1876], CUL MS. Add. 7480/D6/33.
180. Temple Grove school report, 1 August 1867, CUL MS. Add. 7480/D4/24.
181. O.C. Waterfield, Name Book, 1859–80. Temple Grove School archive TGS 2/2.1.

CHAPTER 3

1. Tim Card, *Eton Renewed: A History of Eton from 1860 to the Present Day* (London: John Murray, 1994), p. 107.
2. Anthony Powell, *Under Review: Further Writings on Writers 1946–1989* (London: Heinemann, 1991), p. 275.
3. MRJ, *Eton College. St. Andrew's Day 1921, 11.30 A.M. Election Hall* (Eton College: Spottiswoode, Ballantyne & Co., Ltd, 1921), p. 6.
4. MRJ, preface to H. E. Luxmoore, *Letters of H. E. Luxmoore* (Cambridge: Cambridge University Press, 1929), pp. v-vi.
5. *Eton College, St. Andrew's Day 1921*, p. 6; WTC, p. 71.
6. H. E. Luxmoore, *St. George's Guild Address, May 31, 1922* (Liverpool: Lyceum Press, 1922), p. 27.
7. 'Mr. H. E. Luxmoore: A Great Etonian', *Times*, 12 November 1926, p. 19.
8. H. E. Luxmoore, letter to HJ, 16 September 1876, CUL MS. Add. 7480/D4/61.
9. E&K, p. 14.
10. *Eton College Chronicle*, 2380 (Thursday, June 18, 1936), p. 165.
11. MRJ, address at Eton, no date, CUL MS Add. 7484/1/29.
12. MRJ, letter to Herbert James, May 1877, CUL MS. Add. 7480/D6/75.
13. LF, pp. 12, 15.
14. CGS, pp. 378, 380.
15. CGS, pp. 389–90.

16. *Eton College Chronicle*, 2380 (Thursday, 18 June 1936), p. 166.
17. E&K, p. 63.
18. Christopher Hollis, *Eton: A History* (London: Hollis & Carter, 1960), p. 1; Eton College Foundation Charter, 1441, ECL/SLIDE 091/Archives: Foundation Charter.
19. Hollis, pp. 5–6.
20. Hollis, p. 209.
21. Anon., 'Collegers v. Oppidans: A Reminiscence of Eton Life', *Cornhill Magazine*, XXIV (July–December 1871), pp. 688–717. John Chandos identifies the author of this story as Eustace Clare Grenville Murray: Chandos, *Boys Together: English Public Schools 1800–1844* (Oxford: Oxford University Press, 1985).
22. Shane Leslie, *The Oppidan* (London: Chatto and Windus, 1922).
23. MRJ, letter to parents, no date [?1877], CUL MS Add. 7480/D6/72.
24. E. C. Chambers, letter to MRJ, 17 November 1926, CUL MS Add. 7481/C19.
25. Hollis, p. 11.
26. For Rosewall, see Hollis, p. 116. For Heath, see Hollis, p. 179. For Keate, see Hollis, pp. 191, 200–1; Chandos, p. 177.
27. All these are phrases from public school historians: Hollis, p. 172; Chandos, Preface, n.p.; J. R. de S. Honey, *Tom Brown's Universe: The Development of the Victorian Public School* (London: Millington, 1977), p. 20.
28. Hollis, p. 235.
29. SRJ, *Seventy Years*, p. 4.
30. Chandos, pp. 122–3, 131.
31. Card, p. 46.
32. Charles Allix Wilkinson, *Reminiscences of Eton (Keate's Time)* (London: Hurst and Blackett, 1888), p. 3.
33. Honey, p. 228.
34. Hollis, pp. 249–50; Elisabeth Leedham-Green, 'Afterword', in Jonathan Smith and Christopher Stray, eds, *Teaching and Learning in Nineteenth-Century Cambridge* (Woodbridge: Boydell Press/Cambridge University Library, 2001), pp. 208–9; L. S. R. Byrne and E. L. Churchill, *Changing Eton: A Survey of Conditions based on the History of Eton since the Royal Commission of 1862–64* (London: Jonathan Cape, 1937), p. 35; Card, p. 8. For a study of the teaching of Classics in this period, see Christopher Stray, *Classics Transformed: Schools, Universities, and Society in England, 1830–1960* (Oxford: Clarendon Press, 1998).
35. Card, pp. 7–8.
36. Byrne and Churchill, p. 32; [George Nugent-Bankes], An Eton Boy, *A Day of My Life; or, Every Day Experiences of Eton* (London: Sampson Low, Marston, Searle, & Rivington, 1877), p. 40.
37. Card, p. 15; Byrne and Churchill, pp. 152–3.
38. Card, pp. 33–4.
39. E&K, p. 55; Chandos, pp. 320, 245.
40. Byrne and Churchill, pp. 37, 41, 70, 169; Card, p. 48.
41. SRJ, *Seventy Years*, p. 67.
42. Nugent-Bankes, p. 34.
43. E&K, p. 14.
44. E&K, p. 14.
45. MRJ, letter to HJ, 12 Oct 1877, CUL MS. Add. 7480/D6/79.
46. David Newsome, *On the Edge of Paradise. A. C. Benson: The Diarist* (London: John Murray, 1980), p. 30.

47. E&K, p. 14.
48. MRJ, letter to HJ, 12 Oct 1877, CUL MS. Add. 7480/D6/79.
49. C. H. M. *Recollections of an Eton Colleger 1898–1902* (Eton College: Spottiswoode and Co., 1905), p. 52.
50. J. M. Barrie, letters to MRJ, 14 May 1925, 3 July 1927, CUL MS Add. 7480/B44, B45. Captain James Hook certainly was an Old Etonian.
51. Philip S. Potter, 'Bilious Attacks in Children', *Boston Medical and Surgical Journal*, vol. 163 (1910), 55. See also Angel Money, 'Bilious Attacks', *The Lancet*, vol. 133, no. 3433 (15 June 1889), 1187.
52. E&K, p. 53.
53. GRJ, letter to MRJ, 8 November 1876, JFP.
54. MRJ, letters to father, no date, CUL MS. Add. 7480/D4/80–81; Mary Emily James, letter to MRJ, 27 October 1876, CUL MS. Add. 7480/E2/10.
55. MEJ, letter to MRJ, 23 February 1877, CUL MS. Add. 7480/E2/13.
56. MEJ, letter to MRJ, 18 May 1877, CUL MS. Add. 7480/E2/10.
57. MEJ, letter to MRJ, 19 March 1877, CUL MS. Add. 7480/E2/14.
58. E&K, p. 53.
59. MRJ, letter to HJ, no date [?1877], CUL MS. Add. 7480/D6/81.
60. MRJ, letter to HJ, no date, CUL MS. Add. 7480/D6/101.
61. MRJ, letter to parents, 26 Feb 1877, CUL MS. Add. 7480/D6/70; MRJ, letter to parents, no date [?1877], CUL MS. Add. 7480/D6/72; MRJ, letter to HJ, no date [?1877], CUL MS. Add. 7480/D6/81.
62. Nugent-Bankes, pp. 36, 27.
63. MRJ, letter to parents, 26 February 1877, CUL MS. Add. 7480/D6/70; E&K, p. 53.
64. MRJ, letter to parents, 26 February 2877, CUL MS. Add. 7480/D6/70; MRJ, letter to HJ, May 1877, CUL MS. Add. 7480/D6/74.
65. E&K, p. 45.
66. MRJ, letter to parents [?Autumn 1879], CUL MS. Add. 7480/D6/125.
67. For the Bensons' graphomania, see Simon Goldhill, *A Very Queer Family Indeed: Sex, Religion, and the Bensons in Victorian Britain* (Chicago and London: University of Chicago Press, 2016), Chapter 1.
68. St. Clair Donaldson, letter to MRJ, 29 May [?1888], CUL MS. Add. 7481/D77.
69. William C. Lubenow, 'Smith, Sir Henry Babington', ODNB online: https://www-oxforddnb-com.elib.tcd.ie/view/10.1093/ref:odnb/9780198614128.001.0001/odnb-9780198614128-e-36144?rskey=Ct8v1Y&result=1
70. E&K, pp. 33, 47.
71. Shane Leslie papers, KCC MS SJRL/1/2.
72. ACB, 'Utrumque Nostrum Incredibili Modo Consentit Astrum', *The Poems of A. C. Benson* (London: John Lane, The Bodley Head, 1908), pp. 148–51.
73. E&K, p. 46.
74. Eton Society records: ECL MS/SCH/SOC/ES/1880, p. 58.
75. Newsome, p. 333.
76. ACB, Diary v. 158 f. 44, March 1916, Pepys Library, Magdalene College Cambridge.
77. ACB, Diary v. 54 f. 2, 14 June 1904.
78. ACB, Diary v. 158 f. 44, March 1916.
79. Powell, *Under Review*, p. 275.
80. Canon Adrian Carey, interviewed by Mark Gatiss, *M. R. James: Ghost Writer*, BBC TV, first broadcast 25 December 2013.

81. For changing attitudes to homosexuality in the wake of the Wilde trial, see Michael S. Foldy, *The Trials of Oscar Wilde: Deviance, Morality, and Late-Victorian Society* (New Haven: Yale University Press, 1997).
82. Goldhill, p. 13.
83. William Bridgeman, letter to MRJ, 14 February 1888, CUL MS Add. 7481/B241; Walter Morley Fletcher, letters to MRJ, 8 October 1903, 10 October 1914, 15 April 1918, CUL MS Add. 7481/F26, F30, F35. In using the term queer is this specific institutional context, I am borrowing from Simon Goldhill, *Queer Cambridge* (Cambridge: Cambridge University Press, 2025).
84. Card, p. 66.
85. Ibid., p. 64. MRJ's comment on Johnson is from a sermon delivered in Trinity College Cambridge in 1929: CUL MS Add. 7485/47.
86. Card, p. 68–9; Chandos, p. 287.
87. Honey, p. 300.
88. MRJ, letter to parents, 12 March 1889, CUL MS Add. 7480/D6/308.
89. H. E. Luxmoore, *Communion* (London: Society for Promoting Christian Knowledge, 1906), pp. 6–7.
90. Ibid., pp. 14–15.
91. Ibid., pp. 14, 21.
92. Timothy d'Arch Smith, *Love in Earnest: Some Notes on the Lives and Writings of English 'Uranian' Poets from 1889 to 1930* (London: Routledge and Kegan Paul, 1972), p. 2.
93. Thomas Hughes, *Tom Brown's Schooldays*, ed. Andrew Sanders (1857; Oxford: Oxford University Press, 1989).
94. Frederic William Farrar, *Eric; or Little by Little* (1858; New York: Rudd & Careton, 1859), pp. 90, 106.
95. Farrar, *St. Winifred's, or The World of School* (1862; London and Melbourne: Ward, Lock & Co. 1920), pp. 230–1
96. George Orwell, 'Boys' Weeklies', in *Essays*, ed. John Carey (London: Everyman, 2002), p. 190.
97. Simon Wright, *Waterfield's School*, p. 175.
98. Goldhill, *A Very Queer Family Indeed*, p. 13.
99. Benson, *David Blaize*, p. 116.
100. Honey, p. 184.
101. Ibid., p. 171.
102. MRJ, sermon delivered at Eton, 16 December 1928, CUL MS Add. 7485/34.
103. H. E. Luxmoore, letter to HJ, 30 March 1877, CUL MS. Add. 7480/D4/63.
104. MRJ, letter to parents, 26 February 1877, CUL MS. Add. 7480/D6/70.
105. MRJ, letter to parents, no date [?1877], CUL MS. Add. 7480/D6/72.
106. F. H. Rawlins, school report, March 1877, CUL MS. Add. 7480/D4/63.
107. E&K, p. 25.
108. MRJ school report [1876–7], CUL MS Add. 7481/L376; H. A. Chignell, school report, [1877–78], CUL MS. Add. 7480/D4/64.
109. Ronald Norman, letter to MRJ, 28 December [no year], CUL MS Add. 7481/N58.
110. E&K, p. 35.
111. MRJ school reports, CUL MS Add. 7481/L341, L344.
112. Edmond Warre, school report [?1879], CUL MS. Add. 7480/D4/65.
113. H. E. Luxmoore, letter to HJ, no date [c.1879], CUL MS. Add. 7480/D4/66.
114. H. E. Luxmoore, letter to HJ, July 1879, CUL MS. Add. 7481/L347.

115. E&K, pp. 2607.
116. E. C. Austen Leigh, letter to MRJ, 14 August 1885, CUL MS. Add. 7481/A40.
117. E. H. Ryle, letter to MRJ, 12 August 1925, ECL M. R. James Miscellanies vol. II/E&K Inserts 3.
118. MRJ, letter to HJ, May 1877, CUL MS. Add. 7480/D6/75.
119. MRJ, letter to HJ, 18 December 1877, CUL MS. Add. 7480/D6/86.
120. MRJ, letter to GRJ, 2 October 1877, MS Add. 7480/E5/8.
121. MRJ, letter to parents, 29 July 1877, CUL MS. Add. 7480/D6/77.
122. E&K, p. 25.
123. MRJ, letter to parents, ?Autumn 1877, CUL MS. Add. 7480/D6/78.
124. School report, unsigned and undated, CUL MS. Add. 7480/D4/74.
125. MRJ, letter to HJ, 18 March 1878, CUL MS. Add. 7480/D6/92.
126. MRJ, letter to HJ, 21 July 1877, CUL MS Add. 7480/D6/76.
127. MRJ, letter to GRJ, 2 October 1877, MS Add. 7480/E5/8.
128. MRJ, letter to HJ, 29 March 1878, CUL MS Add. 7480/D6/93.
129. MRJ, letter to HJ, 29 March 1878, CUL MS Add. 7480/D6/93.
130. MRJ, letter to HJ, 23 October 1878, CUL MS Add. 7480/D6/106.
131. MRJ, letter to HJ, 23 October 1878, CUL MS Add. 7480/D6/106.
132. MRJ, letter to HJ, 21 February [1878], CUL MS Add. 7480/D6/90.
133. E&K, p. 100.
134. E&K, p. 18.
135. Lubbock, *Memoir of Montague Rhodes James*, p. 25; KCC MS SJRL/1/1.
136. LF, p. 17.
137. Leslie Papers, KCC MS SJRL/1/1.
138. E. F. Benson, *Our Family Affairs*, p. 228.
139. A. E. Housman, letter to MRJ, 23 September 1930, CUL MS. Add. 7481/H133. MRJ thought he was referring to *Martin Chuzzlewit*, but Housman concluded he had misremembered or dreamt the quotation.
140. TG, p. 115.
141. Eton College, Remove English Literature Prize, 2 December 1926. KCC SJRL 1/1.
142. E&K, p. 18.
143. MEJ, letter to MRJ, 18 May 1877, CUL MS Add. 7480/D6/106; GRJ, letter to MRJ, 27 May 1877, JFP.
144. SRJ, letter to parents, 6 July [1879], JFP.
145. SRJ, *Seventy Years*, p. 55.
146. MRJ, letter to BRJ [no date], JFP.
147. BRJ, letters to MRJ, 27 June 1876, 7 Nov [1880], 24 June [1881], CUL MS Add. 7480/E4/3, 5, 7.
148. Lubbock, p. 28.
149. MRJ, letter to BRJ, [July ?1881], CUL MS Add. 7480/E4/1.
150. BRJ, postcard to MRJ, no date, CUL MS Add. 7480/E4/26.
151. Lubbock, p. 29.
152. MRJ, letter to family, 7 July 1878, CUL MS. Add. 7480/D6/98; E&K, p. 39.
153. Chandos, p. 352.
154. CGS, p. 379.
155. MRJ, letter to MEJ, 30 November [?1877], CUL MS. Add. 7480/D7/85.
156. E&K, p. 17. E&K renders this year as 1882: this may be a misprint or a misremembering, as MRJ had left Eton by November 1882.

157. Powell, p. 274.
158. E&K, p. 50.
159. MRJ, letter to MEJ, 23 October 1878, CUL MS. Add. 7480/D6/105.
160. H. E. Luxmoore, letter to HJ, 20 December 1878, CUL MS. Add. 7481/L350.
161. Lubbock, p. 12.
162. Thomas Anstey Guthrie, Diaries, Vol. CXI, 14 August 1906, BL Add. MS 63564.
163. MRJ, letter to HJ, 8 November 1878, CUL MS Add. 7480/D6/109.
164. MRJ, letter to HJ, [December 1881], CUL MS Add. 7480/D6/155.
165. H. E. Luxmoore, letter to HJ, 20 December [1876], CUL MS Add. 7481/L350.
166. Edward Austen Leigh, MRJ school report 1878, CUL MS. Add. 7481/L345.
167. MRJ school report 1879, CUL MS. Add. 7480/D4/66.
168. John W. Fortescue, letter to MRJ, 3 June 1930, CUL MS. Add. 7481/F/84.
169. H. E. Luxmoore, letter to HJ, 9 April 1881, CUL MS. Add. 7481/L349.
170. E&K, p. 19.
171. Stephen Gaselee, 'Montague Rhodes James 1862-1936', in S. T. Joshi and Rosemary Pardoe, eds. *Warnings to the Curious: A Sheaf of Criticism on M. R. James* (New York: Hippocampus Press, 2007), p. 15. Gaselee's obituary was first published in *Proceedings of the British Academy*, 22 (1936), pp. 418–33.
172. MRJ school report 1879, CUL MS. Add. 7480/D4/66.
173. MRJ, letter to GRJ, [?January 1879], CUL MS Add. 7480/E5/10.
174. Notebooks 9.II.
175. SRJ, *Seventy Years*, p. 55.
176. E&K, p. 31.
177. Notebooks 9.III.
178. MRJ, letter to HJ, CUL MS Add. 7480/D/117.
179. E&K, p. 31. The translation survived in notebook form, with the title page reading 'Liber hic traductio est ex Æthiopica lingua in Anglicani a M. R. James' (This book is translated from the Ethiopic language into English by M. R. James): Notebooks 9.III.
180. H. E. Luxmoore, letter to HJ, [March 1879], CUL MS Add. 7480/E3/6; Luxmoore, letter to HJ, 8 August 1879, CUL MS. Add. 7481/L346.
181. MRJ, letter to HJ, 30 March [1879], CUL MS Add. 7480/D6/94.
182. Notebooks 9.III.
183. MRJ, letters to HJ, [March 1879], CUL MS Add. 7480/D6/118; 2 April 1879, CUL MS Add. 7480/D6/119.
184. H. E. Luxmoore, letter to HJ, [March 1879], CUL MS Add. 7480/E3/6.
185. HJ, letter to SRL [March 1879], CUL MS Add. 7480 E3/6.
186. H. E. Luxmoore, letter to HJ, [March 1879], CUL MS Add. 7480/E3/6.
187. MRJ, letter to HJ, 2 April 1879, CUL MS Add. 7480/D6/119.
188. MRJ, *Old Testament Legends: Being Stories out of Some of the Less-Known Apocryphal Books of the Old Testament* (London: Longmans, Green and Co. 1913); MRJ, ed. *The Lost Apocrypha of the Old Testaments: Their Titles and Fragments* (London: SPCK, 1920).
189. GSA, p. 33.
190. E&K, p. 65.
191. H. E. Luxmoore, letter to HJ, 8 August [1881], CUL MS Add/D4/69.
192. Pfaff, p. 36. This is a collated list from several of MRJ's notebooks.
193. MRJ, letter to HJ, [July 1879], CUL MS Add. 7480/D6/124.
194. MGSA, p. 270; WTC, p. 195.

195. E&K, p. 12; Francis Barrett, *The Magus, or Celestial Intelligencer; Being a Complete System of Occult Philosophy* (1801; York Beach, Maine: Samuel Weiser, 2000). This is a full-size facsimile of the 1801 first edition, and reproduces the colour plates between pp. 104 and 105.
196. GSA, p. 19.
197. MRJ, letter to parents, 4 December 1878, CUL MS Add. 7480/D6/110.
198. MRJ, letter to HJ, [May 1880], CUL MS Add. 7480/D6/135.
199. [MRJ], 'Ghost Stories', *The Eton Rambler*, 2 (18 May 1880), p. 10.
200. [MRJ], 'Ghost Stories', *The Eton Rambler*, 4 (21 June 1880), p. 25.
201. MRJ, letters to HJ, May 28 [1881], and [December 1881], CUL MS Add. 7480/D6/152, 155.
202. E&K, p. 64.
203. [MRJ], 'Clarence *Mi.*'s Dream', *Eton College Chronicle*, 10 November 1881, p. 1353. *Eton College Chronicle* articles are generally anonymous, but L. V. Harcourt's annotated set, in ECL, identifies many of the authors.
204. [MRJ], 'Things Not Generally Known at Eton', *Eton College Chronicle*, 29 October 1881, p. 1348. L. V. Harcourt set, ECL.
205. E&K, p. 64.
206. E&K, pp. 39–40.
207. E&K, p. 39. Ruskin gave this address on 6 November 1880.
208. *Eton College Chronicle*, 340 (15 December 1881), p. 1362.
209. E&K, p. 40.
210. MRJ, letter to Herbert James, [April-May 1880], CUL MS Add. 7480/D6/134.
211. *Eton College Chronicle*, 327 (24 March 1881), p. 1310.
212. MRJ, 'Occult Sciences', CUL MS Add. 7480/1.90. The lecture has been transcribed, annotated, and published: MRJ, 'Occult Sciences', ed. Rosemary Pardoe, Subscriber's Supplement to *Ghosts and Scholars M. R. James Newsletter*, 5 (February 2004). This is the text I use here. See p. 7 for this quotation.
213. François Lenormant, *Chaldean Magic: Its Origin and Development*, trans. William Ricketts Cooper (London: Samuel Bagster, [1877]), p. 31.
214. GSA, pp. 28–9.
215. MRJ, 'Occult Sciences', p. 10.
216. TG, pp. 92, 106.
217. For MRJ on *The Testament of Solomon*, for example, 'The Testament of Solomon', *The Guardian*, March 15 1899, p. 367; 'Solomon and the Demons', in *Old Testament Legends*, pp. 107–19; *Lost Apocrypha*, pp. 51–3; 'The Testament of Solomon', *Journal of Theological Studies*, vol. 24 (1923), pp. 467–8. In the 1920s, MRJ corresponded with the great historian of magic Lynn Thorndike, helping him with some of the details for his chapter on Solomonic magic in Volume II of his eight-volume *History of Magic and Experimental Science*: see Thorndike, *A History of Magic and Experimental Science*, Volume II (New York: Columbia University Press, 1923), p. 281n.5.
218. GSA, p. 16.
219. MRJ, 'Occult Sciences', p. 12.
220. TG, pp. 11, 34.
221. Eton Literary and Scientific Society Journal, vol. II, p. 146, ECL MS SCH/SOC/LS/1/2.
222. MRJ, letter to Herbert James, [March 1879], CUL MS Add. 7480/D6/118.
223. C. E. Doble, letter to MRJ, 11 July 1879, CUL MS. Add. 7481/D52.
224. MRJ, letter to HJ, July 1879, CUL MS Add. 7480/D6/124.
225. MRJ, 'A Latin Fragment of Plutarch's Sertorius', *The Academy*, vol. 16 (26 July 1879), p. 68.

226. Pfaff, p. 33.
227. E. C. Doble, letter to MRJ, 8 August 1879, CUL MS Add. 7481/D53.
228. E&K, p. 64.
229. Eric Parker, *Playing Fields: School Days at Eton* (London: Philip Allan, 1922), p. 308.
230. E. C. Chambers, letter to MRJ, 17 November 1926, CUL MS Add. 7481/C19.
231. Byrne and Churchill, p. 249; Hollis, p. 208.
232. MRJ, letter to MEJ, [October-November 1878], CUL MS Add. 7480/D6/108.
233. Eton College Debating Society Records, vol. 13: Eton College Library MS SCH/HOUSE/03 COLL/02/13, pp. 257, 261.
234. Ibid., p. 333.
235. Eton College Debating Society Records, vol. 14: Eton College Library MS SCH/HOUSE/03/COLL/02/14, p. 56.
236. Cox, p. 43.
237. Eton College Debating Society Records, vol. 14, p. 56.
238. Eton College Debating Society Records, vol. 13, pp. 379–81.
239. Eton College Debating Society Records, vol. 14, p. 141.
240. Cox, p. 43.
241. MRJ, letter to HJ, 28 September 1880, CUL MS. Add. 7480/D6/142.
242. E&K, p. 38.
243. CGS, pp. 379–80.
244. Nugent-Bankes, pp. 85ff; E&K, p. 37.
245. MRJ, letter to HJ, 28 Sept [1880], CUL MS Add. 7480/D6/142; E&K, p. 37.
246. MRJ, letter to MEJ, 3 February 1881, CUL MS Add. 7480/D6/149.
247. E. P. Rouse, school report 1881, CUL MS Add. 7481/L349A.
248. Eton Society Records: ECL MS SCH/SOC/ES/1881, p. 75.
249. MRJ, letter to MEJ, 23 Jan 1880, CUL MS Add. 7480/D6/132.
250. Hollis, p. 292. See also Hilary Newman, *James Kenneth Stephen: Virginia Woolf's Tragic Cousin* (London: Cecil Woolf, 2008).
251. Newman, p. 28.
252. ACB, *The Leaves of the Tree: Studies in Biography* (London: Smith, Elder & Co., 1911), p. 89.
253. Shane Leslie papers, KCC MS SJRL/1/2.
254. See Theo Aronson, *Prince Eddy and the Homosexual Underworld* (London: John Murray, 1994).
255. See, for example, Deborah McDonald, *The Prince, His Tutor, and the Ripper* (Jefferson, NC: McFarland, 2007).
256. Newman, p. 38.
257. J. K. Stephen, 'Coll. Regal.', in *Lapsus Calami and Other Verses* (1891; Cambridge: Macmillan and Bowes, 1898), p. 14.
258. H. E. Luxmoore, letter to MRJ, January 1880, CUL MS. Add. 7481/L337.
259. H. E. Luxmoore, letter to HJ [*c.* 1879], CUL MS Add. 7480/D4/66.
260. MRJ, letter to HJ, [?July 1881], CUL MS Add. 7480/D6/153.
261. *Eton College Chronicle*, 347 (I June 1882), pp. 1388, 1389.
262. MRJ, letter to Henry Babington Smith, 12 January 1882, Wren Library, Trinity College Cambridge MS. HBS/71/123(1).
263. MRJ, letters to HJ, [July 1882], 28 June 1882, CUL MS Add. 7480/D6/172, 169; Cox, p. 46.
264. MRJ, letter to Henry Babington Smith, 7 September 1882, Wren Library, Trinity College Cambridge MS HBS/71/117.
265. MRJ, latter to family [May-June 1882], CUL MS Add. 7480/D6/171; E&K, 64.

266. Card, pp. 7, 11.
267. H. C. Tait, letter to MRJ, 18 July 1879, CUL MS Add. 7481/T1.
268. E&K, p. 43; MRJ, letter to parents, 5 August 1880, CUL MS Add 7480/D6/141.
269. Luxmoore, letter to HJ, 8 August [1881], CUL MS Add 7480/D4/69.
270. J. E. C. Welldon, letter to HJ, 25 January 1882, CUL MS Add 7480/D5/19.
271. Herbert Ryle, letter to HJ, 25 January 1882, CUL MS Add 7480/D5/18.
272. Luxmoore, letter to MRJ, 22 June [no year], CUL MS. Add. 7481/L262.
273. Notebooks 11.I loose leaves.
274. Luxmoore, letter to HJ, 2 February [1882], CUL MS Add 7480/D4/70.
275. Luxmoore, letters to HJ, 6 April [1882], CUL MS Add. 7481/L355; 2 February [1882], CUL MS Add 7480/D4/70.
276. BRJ, letter to MRJ, 22 May 1882, CUL MS Add. 7480/E4/9.
277. MRJ, letters to family, 17 April 1882, 23 April 1882, CUL MS Add. 7480/D/161, 162; E&K, p. 43.
278. MRJ, letter to Henry Babington Smith, 2 May 1882, Wren Library, Trinity College Cambridge MS. HBS/2/10(1).
279. E&K, p. 47.
280. Eton College Debating Society records, vol. 13: Eton College Library MS SCH HOUSE 03 Coll 02 13, p. 292.
281. E&K, p. 48.
282. Card, p. 148.
283. MRJ, letter to Henry Babington Smith, 12 August 1882, Wren Library, Trinity College Cambridge, MS HBS/71/115(1).
284. HJ, letter to MRJ, 31 July 1882, CUL MS Add 7480/E1/25.
285. ACB, letter to MRJ [1882], CUL MS Add 7481 B145.

CHAPTER 4

1. MRJ, letter to HJ, 14 October [1882], CUL MS. Add. 7480/D6/176.
2. Nathaniel Wedd, *The University* [unpublished memoir], p. 78. KCC MS. NW/1/15.
3. E&K, p. 91.
4. Wedd, *Memoir* [unpublished], p. 3. KCC MS. NW/1/17.
5. Wedd, *The University*, pp. 3–4.
6. L. P. Wilkinson, *A Century of King's 1873–1972* (Cambridge: King's College, 1980), p. 25.
7. Christopher Morris, *King's College: A Short History* (Cambridge: King's College, 1989), p. 54; Wilkinson, *A Century of King's*, p. 25.
8. Morris, p. 1.
9. E&K, p. 71.
10. Wilkinson, p. 1; Morris, p. 4. For the seventy disciples, see Luke 10: 1.
11. Christopher N. L. Brooke, *A History of the University of Cambridge Vol. IV 1870–1990* (Cambridge: Cambridge University Press, 1993), p. 34; Morris, p. 38.
12. Morris, p. 33.
13. Brooke, pp. xv, 26.
14. Leslie Stephen, *Sketches from Cambridge by A Don* (London and Cambridge: Macmillan, 1865), pp. 39, 41, 31, 17.
15. Cambridge University Library website: https://www.lib.cam.ac.uk/university-archives/glossary/poll-men
16. Peter Searby, *A History of the University of Cambridge Volume III 1750–1870* (Cambridge: Cambridge University Press, 1997), pp. 4, 96.

17. Stephen, p. 84.
18. Searby, p. 434. For the Graham Commission, see Searby, Chapter 14.
19. Ibid., p. 506.
20. Brooke, p. 83.
21. See William Austen Leigh, ed. *Augustus Austen Leigh, Provost of King's College Cambridge: A Record of College Reform* (London: Smith, Elder, & Co., 1906).
22. Wilkinson, p. 6; Brooke, p. 35.
23. E. N. Wix, letter to MRJ, 31 December 1926, CUL MS Add. 7481/W91.
24. Denys Arthur Winstanley, *Later Victorian Cambridge* (Cambridge: Cambridge University Press, 1947), pp. 37–8. For religious tests in Cambridge, see Winstanley, Chapter 3; Brooke, Chapter 4.
25. Brooke, p. 99.
26. Ibid., pp. 252–3; Wilkinson, p. 22.
27. Stephen, pp. 94, 144.
28. Brooke, pp. 252–3; Wilkinson, pp. 22–3.
29. E&K, pp. 89–90.
30. Patrick J. Murphy, *Medieval Studies and the Ghost Stories of M. R. James* (University Park, PA: Pennsylvania State University Press, 2017).
31. See Graham Parry, *The Trophies of Time: English Antiquarians of the Seventeenth Century* (Oxford: Oxford University Press, 1996).
32. MEJ, letter to MRJ, 18 October [1882], CUL MS Add. 7480/E2/24.
33. Prescot Manor had been granted to Kings by Henry VI in 1445: KCL MS PRE/5. King's living of Prescot dates from 1448, when William, Bishop of Coventry and Lichfield, endowed it to Ralph Dukworth, Professor of Theology: KCL MS PRE/8.
34. SRJ, letters to MRJ, 16 & 28 October 1882, CUL MS. Add. 7480/E3/10/11.
35. GRJ, letter to MRJ, [*c.* October 1882], CUL MS Add. 7480/E3/31.
36. BRJ, letter to MRJ, 12 November 1882, CUL MS Add. 7480/E4/10.
37. BRJ, letter to MRJ, 19 November [1882], CUL MS. Add. 7480/E4/11.
38. Morris, p. 39.
39. BRJ, letters to MRJ, [March-April 1883], [Autumn 1883], CUL MS. Add. 7480/E4/17.
40. Wilkinson, p. 59.
41. E&K, p. 92.
42. J. E. C. Welldon, letter to HJ, 29 January 1883, CUL MS. Add. 7480/D5/20.
43. Walter Headlam, *Walter Headlam: His Letters and Poems, with a Memoir by Cecil Headlam and a Bibliography by L. Haward* (London: Duckworth and Co., 1910), p. 145.
44. E&K, p. 93.
45. See John Henderson, *Juvenal's Mayor: The Professor who Lived on 2d a Day* (Cambridge: Cambridge Philological Society, 1998), p. 59.
46. E&K, p. 118; MRJ, letter to HJ, 24 October [1883], CUL MS. Add. 7480/D6/205; MRJ, letter to MEJ, [4 November 1883], CUL MS. Add. 7480/D6/206. For MRJ's notes to Mayor's lectures, see Notebooks 2.III.
47. ACB, *The Leaves of the Tree: Studies in Biography* (London: Smith, Elder, & Co., 1911), p. 22.
48. HJ, letter to MRJ, 27 May 1883, CUL MS. Add. 7480/E1/47.
49. Brooke, p. 137.
50. Brooke Foss Westcott, *Social Aspects of Christianity* (London and Cambridge: Macmillan and Co., 1897).
51. HJ, *Country Clergyman*, p. 7; HJ, letter to MRJ, 27 May 1883, CUL MS. Add. 7480/E1/47.
52. MRJ, letter to HJ, 3 March 1883, CUL MS Add. 7480/D6/191.

53. E&K, p. 80.
54. E&K, p. 96.
55. E&K, p. 80.
56. Newsome, *On the Edge of Paradise*, pp. 192–3.
57. *Basileon: Being the Fourth Book of King's*, 11 (June 1909), inside front cover.
58. CUL MS Add. 7481/S288.
59. Oscar Wilde, letter to Robert Ross, c 13 October 1881, in *The Complete Letters of Oscar Wilde*, ed. Merlin Holland and Rupert Hart-Davis (London: Fourth Estate, 2000), p. 360.
60. E. M. Butler, letter to MRJ, 26 January 1888, CUL MS Add. 7481/B337.
61. Virginia Woolf, *A Room of One's Own and Three Guineas*, ed. Anna Snaith (Oxford: Oxford University Press, 2015), p. 41.
62. G. V. Carey, *Nobody's Business: An Eightieth Year Report* (Eastbourne: Eastbourne College Arnold Embellishers, 2007), p. 23.
63. Richard Holmes, *Sidetracks: Explorations of a Romantic Biographer* (London: Harper Perennial, 2005), p. 165.
64. For MRJ on Nixon, see E&K, pp. 81–7.
65. P. P. Dickinson, letter to MRJ, 9 July 1926. CUL MS. Add. 7481/D37.
66. E. F. Benson, letter to MRJ [1890], CUL MS Add. 7481/B168.
67. MRJ, 'The Interlude as Performed', CUL MS Add 7484/2/7.
68. Jack Tilley, letter to MRJ, 10 January 1927, CUL MS Add. 7481 T26.
69. Norton G. Lawson, letter to MRJ, 18 November 1926, CUL MS Add. 7481/L11.
70. MRJ, letter to Clive Carey, 1 June 1930. KCC MS MRJ/D/Carey/13.
71. Cyril Alington, *Lionel Ford* (London: Society for Promoting Christian Knowledge, 1934), pp. 19–20.
72. MRJ, letter to Gordon Carey, 10 February 1923, KCC MS. MRJ/F/4.
73. G. W. Prothero, *A Memoir of Henry Bradshaw: Fellow of King's College, Cambridge, and University Librarian* (London: Kegan Paul, Trench & Co., 1888), p. 314.
74. See Brett W. Walwyn, 'M. R. James and Changing Methods of Incunable Description', in Lynda Dennison, ed. *The Legacy of M. R. James: Papers from the 1995 Cambridge Symposium* (Donington: Shaun Tyas, 2001), p. 213.
75. MRJ, *A Descriptive Catalogue of the Manuscripts other than Oriental in the Library of King's College, Cambridge* (Cambridge: Cambridge University Press, 1895), p. xiv.
76. Prothero, p. 390.
77. E&K, p. 75.
78. E&K, p. 74.
79. Prothero, p. 390.
80. E&K, p. 73.
81. E&K, p. 79.
82. MRJ, letters to HJ and MEJ, 1, 7, 12 December 1882, CUL MS. Add. 7480/D6/186, 187, 188.
83. MRJ, letter to HJ, 12 March [1883], CUL MS. Add. 7480/D6/192. For the Previous Examination results of MRJ and his cohort, see *Cambridge University Reporter*, 19 December 1882, pp. 259–60.
84. MRJ, letter to MEJ, 12 December 1882, CUL MS. Add. 7480/D6/183.
85. MRJ, letter to Henry Babington Smith, 29 December 1882, Wren Library, Trinity College Cambridge, MS. HBS/71/121(1).
86. MRJ kept a diary of his movements over this busy Christmas: see Notebooks 14.I.
87. Ibid.
88. H. E. Luxmoore, letter to MRJ, 26 January 1883, CUL MS. Add. 7481/L242.

89. SRJ, letter to MRJ, 26 November 1882, JFP.
90. J. E. C. Welldon. letter to HJ, 29 January 1883, CUL MS. Add. 7480/D5/20.
91. J. E. C. Welldon, letter to HJ, 27 January 1883, CUL MS. Add. 7480/D5/21.
92. MRJ, letter to HJ, 27 January 1883, CUL MS. Add. 7480/D6/187.
93. SRJ, letter to MRJ, 28 January 1883, CUL MS. Add. 7480/E3/13.
94. This account of the holiday is taken from SRJ, *Seventy Years*, pp. 84–7, and from MRJ's contemporaneous diary: see Notebooks 14.I.
95. E&K, p. 99.
96. MRJ, letters to parents, 30 May & 11 June 1883, CUL MS. Add. 7480/D/196/199.
97. MRJ, letter to MEJ, 17 June 1883, CUL MS. Add. 7480/D6/200.
98. MRJ, *A Guide to the Windows of King's College Chapel* (1899; Cambridge: Cambridge University Press, 2010). For an account of the provenance of the story, see Michael Halls, 'A Night in King's College Chapel: Introduction', *Ghosts and Scholars*, 7 (1985), p. 1.
99. MRJ, 'A Night in King's College Chapel', KCC MS. MRJ/A/14a; the story was first published in *Ghosts and Scholars*, 7 (1985), pp. 1–5.
100. MRJ, letter to HJ, 3 March 1883, CUL MS. Add. 7480/D6/191.
101. Minutes of the Meetings of the Chit-Chat Club, vol. 1, CUL MS. SOC.65.1. For an excellent anthology of Chit-Chat Club writings, see Robert Lloyd Parry, ed. *Ghosts of the Chit-Chat* (Dublin: The Swan River Press, 2020).
102. Minutes of the Meetings of the Chit-Chat Club, vol. 4, p. 86, CUL MS. SOC.65.4.
103. See James A. Secord, *Visions of Science: Books and Readers at the Dawn of the Victorian Age* (Chicago: University of Chicago Press, 2014), pp. 11–19.
104. MRJ, 'Useless Knowledge', CUL MS Add. 7481/2.27.
105. MRJ, ed. and trans., *The Apocryphal New Testament* (Oxford: Oxford University Press, 1924), pp. xi–xii.
106. MRJ, 'Magic. Its Possibilities', Notebooks 2.III.
107. For MRJ's many papers, see Minutes of the Meetings of the Chit-Chat Club, vols 4–5, Cambridge University Library MS. SOC.65.4–5.
108. MRJ, 'The Education of a Gentleman', CUL MS Add. 7481/MISC. See Minutes of the Meetings of the Chit-Chat Club, vol. 4, pp. 188–9. The discussion took place on 30 November 1889.
109. MRJ, letter, 23 September 1918, pasted to the inside cover of Minutes of the Meetings of the Chit-Chat Club, vol. 1, CUL MS. SOC.65.1.
110. Minutes of the Meetings of the Chit-Chat Club, vol. 5, p. 70, CUL MS. SOC.65.5.
111. E&K, p. 159.
112. MEJ, letter to MRJ, 15 October 1884, CUL MS. Add. 7480/E2/38.
113. E&K, p. 105.
114. MRJ, letter to HJ, 16 October 1884, CUL MS. Add. 7480/D6/237.
115. LF, p. 10. Leavis's Piano Shop, 19–25 Regent Street, was a regular advertiser in several Cambridge periodicals.
116. Arthur Somervell, letter to MRJ, no date, CUL MS Add. 7481/S110.
117. E&K, p. 104.
118. Shane Leslie's annotated copy of E&K p. 159, Eton College Library Lp.2.24. As far as I am aware, Patrick J. Murphy was the first modern commentator to begin to solve the mystery of the King's College ghost: see Murphy, pp. 156, 229.
119. Leslie papers, KCC MS SJRL/1/1.
120. KCC MS MRJ/D/Brocklebank/4.
121. Thomas Brocklebank, letter to Herbert James, 5–6 January 1846. KCC MS MRJ/D/Brocklebank/1.

122. W. H. Macaulay, letter to MRJ, 24 December 1896, KCC MS MRJ/D/Macaulay.
123. William [Johnson] Cory, *Extracts from the Letters and Journals of William Cory, Author of 'Ionica'*, selected and arranged by Francis Warre-Cornish (Oxford: Printed for the Subscribers, 1897), p. 151.
124. For Uranianism, see Timothy d'Arch Smith, *Love in Earnest*; Jennifer Ingleheart, *Masculine Plural: Queer Classics, Sex, and Education* (Oxford: Oxford University Press, 2018). Smith, in particular, understands Arthur Benson as at least a Uranian fellow-traveller.
125. Newsome, *On the Edge of Paradise*, p. 250.
126. Anstruther, *Oscar Browning*, p. 77.
127. O. R. Vassall-Phillips, letter to MRJ, 26 December 1926, ECL M. R. James Miscellany vol. II/*Eton and King's* Inserts 2. It seems very unlikely that the ghost was James Wilson, who was a student at Trinity, and had died in 1879—but Vassall-Phillips's emotions are obviously very powerful.
128. Details of this production, including some wonderful photographs of MRJ, can be found at: https://www.cambridgegreekplay.com/plays/1883/birds
129. Charles Villiers Stanford, *Pages from an Unwritten Diary* (London: Edward Arnold, 1914), p. 187.
130. Charles Villiers Stanford, letter to MRJ, 7 October 1913, CUL MS Add. 7481/S126.
131. For these and many other reviews (all glowing), see MRJ's scrapbook of *The Birds*, KCC MS MRJ/F/5.
132. E&K, p. 98.
133. MRJ, letter to family, 7 December 1883, CUL MS Add. 7480/D6/210.
134. E&K, p. 97.
135. Newsome, *On the Edge of Paradise*, p. 221; A. E. Shipley, *'J.' A Memoir of John Willis Clark: Registrary of the University of Cambridge and Sometime Fellow of Trinity College* (London: Smith, Elder, & Co., 1913), p. 228.
136. E&K, p. 118.
137. E&K, p. 117.
138. Leslie papers, KCC MS SJRL/1/1. The same documents show that MRJ did, however, admire Synge's *Playboy of the Western World* and its 'admirable language'.
139. Alington, *Lionel Ford*, p. 12.
140. E&K, 114–5. MRJ's King's contemporary, the future Eton master Arthur Goodhart, wrote to him in 1926 after reading E&K, claiming that it was he, and not Lionel Ford, who accompanied MRJ on this raucous duet: A. M. Goodhart, letter to MRJ, 18 November 1926, CUL MS. Add. 7481/G54.
141. Alington, p. 12.
142. E. F. Benson, *Our Family Affairs* (New York: George H. Doran, 1921), p. 226.
143. E&K, p. 111; Benson, *Our Family Affairs*, p. 226; Nigel Jones, *Rupert Brooke: Life, Death & Myth* (London: Richard Cohen, 1999), p. 74.
144. See Hermione Lee, *Virginia Woolf* (London: Vintage, 1997), pp. 246–7.
145. Charles Tennyson, *Cambridge from Within* (London: Chatto and Windus, 1913), p. 76.
146. [Shane Leslie], 'Walter Headlam', *The Academy*, 8 October 1910, p. 351. For a fascinating account of Headlam's various disagreements with colleagues, see Simon Goldhill, *Who Needs Greek: Contests in the Cultural History of Hellenism* (Cambridge: Cambridge University Press, 2002), pp. 231–43.
147. Headlam, *Letters and Poems*, p. 159.
148. MRJ, 'Headlam, Walter George (1866-1908)', DNB: https://www-oxforddnb-com.elib.tcd.ie/view/10.1093/odnb/9780192683120.001.0001/odnb-9780192683120-e-33784
149. Goldhill, *Who Needs Greek?*, p. 237.

150. Alington, p. 16. See p. 15 for MRJ's impersonations.
151. MRJ, letter to parents, 19 June 1885, CUL MS. Add. 7480/D6/250.
152. MRJ, letter to MEJ, 14 March 1885, CUL MS. Add. 7480/D6/244.
153. Albert Victor Baillie, *My First Eighty Years* (London: John Murray, 1951), pp. 46–7.
154. Baillie, p. 47.
155. LF, p. 12.
156. Leo Maxse, letter to MRJ, 21 November 1887, CUL MS Add. 7481/M201.
157. E&K, p. 106..
158. Shane Leslie, *Long Shadows* (London: John Murray, 1966), p. 101.
159. E&K, p. 107.
160. Leo Maxse, letter to MRJ, 31 January 1886, CUL MS Add. 7481/M197.
161. G. C. Webber, *The Ideology of the British Right, 1918–1939* (New York: St. Martin's Press, 1986), p. 28. For a detailed study of Maxse and the *National Review*, see John A. Hutcheson, *Leopold Maxse and the National Review, 1893–1914: Right-Wing Politics, Journalism, and the Edwardian Era* (New York and London: Garland, 1989).
162. MRJ, letters to parents, 7 & 27 May 1884, CUL MS Add. 7480/D6/223, 226.
163. E&K, p. 103.
164. Leslie papers, KCC SJRL/1/1.
165. J. H. B. M., 'The Expense of an University Education', *The Cambridge Review*, 18 May 1893, p. 344.
166. For this figure of £250, see Searby, p. 80.
167. J. J. Hornby, letter to MRJ, 15 March 1883, CUL MS. Add. 7481/H98.
168. *The Historical Register of the University of Cambridge, Being a Supplement to the Calendar with a Record of University Offices Honours and Distinctions to the Year 1910*, ed. J. R. Tanner (Cambridge: Cambridge University Press, 1917), p. 259.
169. Wedd, *The University*, p. 40; St. Clair Donaldson, letter to MRJ, 15 June [1884], CUL MS. Add. 7481/D85.
170. GRJ, letter to MRJ, 10 February 1884, CUL MS Add. 7480/E5/30.
171. Here and throughout the chapter, for information on the Classical Tripos on the 1880s, I draw on C. A. Stray, 'Renegotiating Classics: The Politics of Curricular Reform in Later Victorian Cambridge', *Classical Views/Echos du monde Classique*, vol. 42 no. 3 (1998). I am very grateful to Dr Stray for sharing with me a longer version of this article, with unpublished material.
172. MRJ, letters to HJ, 12 May–6 June 1884, CUL MS. Add. 7480/D6/224-7; Albert Baillie, letter to MRJ, 25 Feb [?1885], CUL MS. Add. 7481/B6.
173. MRJ, letter to HJ, October 1900, CUL MS. Add. 7480/D6/433.
174. Richard Okes, letter to HJ, 31 March 1885, KCC MS. MRJ/D/Okes.
175. MEJ, letters to MRJ, 22 June 1885, CUL MS. Add. 7480/E2/34
176. MRJ, letter to HJ, 22 May 1884, CUL MS. Add. 7480/D6/225.
177. Leonard Huxley, *Life and Letters of Thomas Henry Huxley* (London: Macmillan, 1908), Vol. II, p. 355.
178. MRJ, postcard to parents, 24 June 1884, CUL MS. Add. 7480/D6/231.
179. Notebooks 14.II.
180. MRJ, postcard to parents, 28 June 1884, CUL MS. Add. 7480/D6/232.
181. Notebooks 14.II.
182. MEJ, letter to MRJ, 10 July 1884, CUL MS. Add. 7480/E3/37.
183. MRJ, letter to family, 8 July 1884, CUL MS. Add. 7480/D6/234.
184. St. Clair Donaldson, letter to MRJ, 26 September 1884. CUL MS. Add. 7481/D88.

185. Historical Register, pp. 330–1.
186. E&K, p. 83.
187. MRJ, letter to Henry Babington Smith, 21 September 1882, Wren Library, Trinity College Cambridge MS HBS/71/118(1).
188. See W. M. Beard, 'The Invention (and Reinvention) of "Group D': An Archaeology of the Classical Tripos, 1879–1984", in C. A. Stray (ed.), *Classics in Cambridge* (*PCPS* supp. Vol.) (Cambridge, 1999).
189. MRJ, letter to MEJ, 14 March 1885, CUL MS add. 7480/D6/244.
190. Beard, 'Group D'.
191. Baillie, p. 48.
192. 'Obituary. The Late Sir Charles Walston', *The Times*, 24 March 1927, p. 16. For MRJ's notes on Waldstein's lectures, see Notebooks 13.I–IV.
193. MRJ, letter to HJ, May 1885, CUL MS. Add. 7480/D6/248.
194. MEJ, letter to MRJ, 5 November 1884, CUL MS. Add. 7480/E2/40.
195. Cecil Baring, letter to MRJ, 7 June 1885, CUL MS. Add. 7481/B32.
196. MRJ, letter to parents, 19 June 1885, CUL MS. Add. 7480/D6/250.
197. Alington, p. 16.
198. *Historical Register*, p. 652.

CHAPTER 5

1. Morris, *King's College*, p. 48.
2. Stephen, *Sketches from Cambridge*, pp. 37–8.
3. Brooke, *History of the University of Cambridge*, pp. 78–9; Morris, p. 48; Searby, *History of the University of Cambridge*, p. 138; Wilkinson, *A Century of King's*, pp. 3–4.
4. ACB, Diaries, v. 93 p. 28, 28 May 1907. Pepys Library, Magdalene College, Cambridge.
5. For the fullest account of the meaning and provenance of *The Apocalypse of Peter*, see Pfaff, pp. 70–2.
6. J. Armitage Robinson and MRJ, *The Gospel According to Peter, and The Revelation of Peter: Two Lectures on the Newly Recovered Fragments together with the Greek Texts* (Cambridge: Cambridge University Press, 1892), p. 40.
7. E&K, p. 129.
8. MRJ, Note Book, p. 13r. CUL MS Add. 7517.
9. William Smith, ed. *Dictionary of the Bible: Comprising its Antiquities, Biography, Geography, and Natural History* (1860; London: John Murray, 1893), Vol. II, p. 810. The entry on Peter is written by F. C. Cook.
10. Cecil Baring, letter to MRJ, 15 June 1885, CUL MS. Add. 7481/B32.
11. MRJ, letter to family, 30 July 1885, CUL MS Add. 7480/D6/252.
12. MRJ, letter to HJ, 13 August 1885, CUL MS Add. 7480/D6/254.
13. MRJ, letter to family, 1 September 1885, CUL MS Add. 7480/D6/255.
14. Marquis of Hamilton, letter to MRJ, 17 November 1885, CUL MS. Add. 7481/H5. For MRJ's inventory of the trip, see CUL MS Add. 7481/MISC: the tutoring fee was £30, the expenses £45.12.8.
15. MRJ, letter to GRJ, 17 January 1886, CUL MS Add. 7480/E5/12.
16. Mary Anna Hamilton [Duchess of Abercorn], letter to MRJ, [1886], CUL MS. Add. 7481/H12; MRJ, letter to MEJ, 3 February 1886, CUL MS. Add. 7480/D6/263.
17. Francis Ford, letter to MRJ, 20 July [no year], CUL MS Add. 7481/F55.
18. MRJ, letter to HJ [October 1886], CUL MS Add. 7480/D6/255.
19. E&K, p. 13.

20. E. M. Butler, letter to MRJ, 4 September 1887, CUL MS Add. 7481/B326.
21. MRJ, letter to family, 14 May 1887, CUL MS Add. 7480/D6/285.
22. ACB, letter to MRJ [no date], CUL MS Add. 7481/B149.
23. Pfaff, pp. 192–3.
24. William Bridgeman, letter to MRJ, 7 March 1886, CUL MS. Add. 7481/B238. for information about the 1885 *Eumenides* production, including photographs and playbills, see https://www.cambridgegreekplay.com/plays/1885/eumenides
25. MRJ, letter to family, 8 March 1886, CUL MS. Add. 7480/D6/264.
26. '"Œdipus Tyrannus" at Cambridge', *Daily Telegraph*, 24 November 1887, p. 17.
27. MRJ, letter to HJ, 25 October 1885, CUL MS. Add. 7480/D6/257.
28. *Historical Register*, p. 291.
29. MRJ, letter to family, 25 January 1886, CUL MS. Add. 7480/D6/262; MEJ, letter to MRJ, 9 March 1886, CUL MS. Add. 7480/E2/45; Cecil Baring, letter to MRJ, 9 March [1886], CUL MS. Add. 7481/B35.
30. J. E. C. Welldon, letter to MRJ, 12 September 1885, CUL MS Add. 7481/W53.
31. MRJ, letters to family, 25 January, 3 February, 8 March 1886, CUL MS. Add. 7480/D6/262/263/264.
32. MRJ, address to University College School, 28 July 1921, CUL MS Add. 7484/2/1.
33. MRJ, letter to family, 15 April 1886, CUL MS. Add. 7480 D6/265.
34. MRJ, letter to HJ, 23 April 1886, CUL MS. Add. 7480 D6/266.
35. MRJ, letter to HJ, CUL MS. Add. 7480/D6/267.
36. ACB, *From a College Window* (London: Smith, Elder, & Co., 1909), p. 58.
37. MRJ, letter to HJ, 22 May 1884: CUL MS. Add. 7480/D6/225.
38. The argument for an occultist MRJ was put forward by Terry Hale, 'M. R. James and French fin-de-siècle Occultism', *M. R. James: Through a Glass Darkly* conference, York, 26–27 September 2018. For a pantheist MRJ, see Rosemary Pardoe, 'Some Thoughts on M. R. James's World View', *Ghosts & Scholars*, 18 (1994), pp. 42–3.
39. Notebooks 2.III [1883].
40. CGS, p. 404.
41. HJ, letter to MRJ, 31 July 1886, CUL MS. Add. 7480/E1/72.
42. HEL, letter to MRJ, 18 February [1889], CUL MS. Add. 7481/L244.
43. HJ, letters to MRJ, 31 July 1883, 1 August 1891, CUL MS. Add. 7480/E1/50, 95.
44. William Bridgeman, letters to MRJ, 27 December 1885, 4 October 1886, CUL MS Add. 7480/B235, 237; MRJ, letter to family [1886], CUL MS. Add. 7480/D6/274.
45. MRJ, letter to Herbert James, 31 October 1885. CUL MS Add. 7480/D6/258.
46. E. F. Benson, *Our Family Affairs*, p. 228.
47. Brian Masters, *The Life of E. F. Benson* (London: Chatto and Windus, 1992, p. 85.
48. E. F. Benson, Diary 1886–81, p. 181: 25 June 1889. Magdalene College Cambridge MS MCPP//EFB/1.
49. Owen Hugh Smith, letter to MRJ, 20 November 1902, CUL MS Add. 7481/S76.
50. I. Keith-Falconer, letter to MRJ, 8 August 1886, CUL MS. Add. 7481/K2.
51. Pierre Batiffol, 'Le Livre de la Prière d'Asénath', *Studia Patristica*, 1–2 (1889–90).
52. Robinson and MRJ, *Peter*, p. 40.
53. Robinson and MRJ *Peter*, p. 8; F. J. A. Hort, letter to MRJ, 26 November 1888, CUL MS. Add. 7481/H121.
54. MRJ, sermon, 1926: CUL MS Add. 7485/53.
55. F. J. A. Hort, letter to MRJ, 17 March 1887, CUL MS. Add. 7481/H123.
56. Leo Maxse, letter to MRJ, 21 November 1887, CUL MS Add. 7481/M201.

57. MRJ, Note Book, p. 69. CUL MS Add. 7517.
58. MRJ, ed. *The Apocryphal New Testament, being the Apocryphal Gospels, Acts, Epistles, and Apocalypses* (Oxford: Clarendon Press, 1924), pp. 504–24.
59. MEJ, letter to MRJ, 18 November 1886, CUL MS. Add. 7480/E2/51.
60. MRJ, letter to MEJ, 23 January 1887, CUL MS Add. 7480 D6/275.
61. MRJ, letters to family, 29 March, 2 April 1887, CUL MS. Add. 7480/D6/281, 282.
62. Notebooks 4.I, p. 67.
63. William Bridgeman, letter to MRJ, 6 April 1887, CUL MS. Add. 7481/B240.
64. MRJ, letter to family, 21 May 1887, CUL MS Add. 7480/D6/286.
65. [MRJ], 'E. S. Merganser', *Athens in the Fourteenth Century. An Inedited Supplement to Sir John Maundeville's Travels. Published from the Rhodes MS. No. 17* (Cambridge: Macmillan and Bowes, 1887). The edition I use here is Nicholas Rogers, 'Four Extracts from M. R. James's Early Writings', in Dennison, ed. *The Legacy of M. R. James*, pp. 230–8.
66. *Athens in the Fourteenth Century*, pp. 236–7.
67. MRJ, letter to family, [October 1886], CUL MS. Add. 7480/D6/270.
68. Augustus Austen Leigh, letter to MRJ, May 26 [1887], CUL MS. Add. 7481/A38.
69. E&K, p. 148.
70. For MRJ's lectures, see Pfaff, p. 78.
71. F. J. A. Hort, letter to MRJ, 9 March 1892, CUL MS. Add. 7481/H17.
72. Alexander Roberts and James Donaldson, eds. *The Anti-Nicene Fathers: The writings of the fathers down to A.D. 325*, vol 8 (Peabody, Mass.: Hendrickson, 1995), p. 100. This translation is exactly contemporaneous with our story, first appearing in 1886.
73. GSA, p. 50.
74. MRJ, letter to family, 12 March 1877, CUL MS. Add. 7480/D6/279.
75. Ber, letter to MRJ, [no date], CUL MS. Add. 7480/E4/18.
76. HJ, letters to MRJ, 14, 21 November 1887, CUL MS. Add. 7480/E1/82, 83; MEJ, letter to MRJ, 1 December 1887, CUL MS. Add. 7480/E2/64; SRJ, letter to MRJ, 21 November 1887, CUL MS. Add. 7480/E3/18.
77. MRJ, letter to family, 12 December 1887, CUL MS. Add. 7480/D6/292.
78. St. Clair Donaldson, letter to MRJ, 7 January 1888. CUL MS. Add. 7481/D65.
79. MRJ, letter to SRJ, 18 December 1887, CUL MS Add. 7480/E3/4.
80. Lionel Ford, letter to MRJ, 27 December 1887, CUL MS. Add. 7481/F74.
81. E. M. Butler, letter to MRJ, 3 January 1888. CUL MS. Add. 7481/B335.
82. H.E. Luxmoore, letter to MRJ, December 1887, CUL MS Add. 7481/L157.
83. MRJ, letter to family, 12 December 1887, CUL MS. Add. 7480 D6/292.
84. MRJ, letters to family, 17 January, 4 February, 15 February 1887, CUL MS. Add. 7480 D6/293, 294, 295.
85. See D. G. Hogarth, M. R. James, R. Elsey Smith and E. A. Gardner, 'Excavations in Cyprus, 1887–88. Paphos, Leontari, Amagetti', *Journal of Hellenistic Studies*, 9 (1888), 147–271. For MRJ's notes on Cyprus, including the results of his many games of cribbage with Ber and with his colleagues on the dig, see Notebooks 13.V.
86. MRJ, 'Cyprus', lecture delivered c. December 1892, CUL MS Add. 7484/2/6.
87. MRJ, letters to family, 17 January, 4 February, 15 February 1888, CUL MS. Add. 7480/D293, 294, 295.
88. Luxmoore, *Letters*, p. 13.
89. D. G. Hogarth, *Accidents of an Antiquary's Life* (London: Macmillan, 1910), p. 11.
90. MRJ, letter to family, 17 January 1888, CUL MS. Add. 7480/D6/293.
91. Lionel Ford, letter to MRJ, 27 December 1887, CUL MS. Add. 7481/F74.

92. MRJ, letter to family, 13 November 1887, CUL MS. Add. 7480/D6/291.
93. GSA, p. 14.
94. Oliffe Legh Richmond, letter to MRJ, [1905], CUL MS Add. 7481/R47.
95. MRJ, *The Wanderings and Homes of Manuscripts* (London: SPCK, 1919), p. 79.
96. D. G. Hogarth, letter to MRJ, 17 May 1888, CUL MS. Add. 7481/H79.
97. Goldhill, *Very Queer Family*, p. 54.
98. MRJ, letter to family, [1888], CUL MS. Add. 7480/D6/302.
99. MEJ, letter to MRJ, 19 June 1889, CUL MS. Add. 7480/E2/72.
100. MRJ, letter to family, 1 December 1889, CUL MS. Add. 7480/D6/317.
101. Emily Koley, 'Virginia Woolf's Cousin J. K. Stephen: Forgotten But Not Gone', *English Literature in Transition, 1880–1920*, 15(2) (2016), 192.
102. Hermione Lee, *Virginia Woolf*, p. 124.
103. Walter Headlam, letter to MRJ, 18 September 1889, CUL MS. Add. 7481/H47.
104. MRJ, letter to MEJ, [September-October 1886], CUL MS. Add. 7480/D6/313.
105. Pfaff, p. 61.
106. ACB, *From a College Window*, p. 60.
107. J. H. Clapham, letter to MRJ, 9 April 1905, CUL MS Add. 7481/C48.
108. Oliffe Richmond, letter to MRJ, 19 December 1905, CUL MS Add. 7481/R45.
109. Owen Hugh Smith, letter to MRJ, 28 March 1903, CUL MS Add. 7481/S78.
110. LF, pp. 7, 22.
111. MRJ, letter to HJ, 21 February 1889, CUL MS. Add. 7480 D6/307.
112. MRJ, letter to HJ, 21 February 1889, CUL MS. Add. 7480 D6/307.
113. 'The Coming Dean', *The Granta*, vol. 1, no. 9 (1 March 1889), 3.
114. 'Those in Authority: Mr. Montague Rhodes James', *The Granta*, vol. II, no. 14 (31 May 1889), 10.
115. MRJ, 'A Miscellany', CUL MS Add. 7481/MISC.
116. *Pall Mall Gazette*, 7480 (8 March 1889), 1.
117. 'The Coming Dean', p. 3.
118. MRJ, letter to family, 12 March 1889, CUL MS. Add. 7480/D6/308. All of MRJ's thoughts on the matter are from this long letter. For the fullest account of the Robbie Ross affair, see Maureen Borland, *Wilde's Devoted Friend: A Biography of Robert Ross* (Luton: Lennard, 1990), pp. 21ff.
119. 'Moonlighting in King's', *The Granta*, vol. 1, no. 9 (15 March 1889), p. 2.
120. E. F. Benson, Diary 1885–91, p. 171, 6 March 1887. Magdalene College Cambridge MS MCPP/EFB/1.
121. Leo Maxse, telegram to MRJ, 12 March 1889, CUL MS Add. 7481/M211.
122. Oscar Browning, letter to Members of the Governing Body, 22 November 1889, KCC MS. MRJ/D/Nixon.
123. Francis Ford, letter to MRJ, [1889], CUL MS. Add. 7481/F56.
124. J. E. Nixon, letter to MRJ, 8 February 1890, King's College Cambridge MS. MRJ/D/Nixon.
125. 'Moonlighting in King's', p. 1; 'Ad Regis Sanguines: A Challenge to the King's Rowdies', *The Granta*, vol. 1, no. 9 (15 March 1889), p. 6.
126. Nathaniel Wedd, *The University* [unpublished memoir], KCC MS NW/1/15, pp. 128–9.
127. *The Granta*, vol. 1, no. 9 (15 March, 1889), p. 6.
128. J. H. Clapham, 'The Provost of Eton', *The Cambridge Review*, 9 October 1936, p. 6.
129. Cox, p. 91.
130. MRJ, letter to family, 12 March 1889, CUL MS. Add. 7480/D6/308.
131. J. H. Doncaster, letter to MRJ, 18 February 1927, CUL MS Add. 7481/D111.

132. [Charles Waldstein], *The Jewish Question and the Mission of the Jews* (1889; New York: Harper and Brothers, 1894); Sir Charles Walston (Waldstein), *Eugenics, Civics and Ethics: A Lecture Delivered at the Summer School of Eugenics, Civics and Ethics on August 8th, 1919, in the Arts School, Cambridge* (Cambridge: Cambridge University Press, 1920).
133. E&K, p. 137.
134. MRJ, letter to F. J. H. Jenkinson, 4 June 1889, CUL MS Add. 6483/1171.
135. See L. H. Cust, revised by Richard Smail, 'Middleton, John Henry (1846–1896)', *Oxford Dictionary of National Biography*: https://www-oxforddnb-com.elib.tcd.ie/view/10.1093/ref:odnb/9780198614128.001.0001/odnb-9780198614128-e-18676?rskey=5VD9gh &result=8
136. Lionel Ford, letter to MRJ, [1889], CUL MS. Add. 7481/F75; E. M. Butler, letter to MRJ, 17 November 1889, CUL MS Add. 7481/B350; MRJ, letter to HJ, 23 October 1889, CUL MS. Add. 7480/D6/316.
137. H. Montagu Butler, letter to MRJ, 3 December 1887, CUL MS. Add. 7481/B370.
138. MEJ, letter to MRJ, 10 May 1889. CUL MS. Add. 7480/E2/69.
139. MEJ, letter to MRJ, 4 June 1889, CUL MS. Add. 7480/E2/71.
140. MRJ, letter to GRJ, 29 May 1889, CUL MS. Add. 7480/E5/13.
141. GRJ, letters to MRJ, May 1889, CUL MS. Add. 7480/E5/49, 50.
142. GRJ, letter to MRJ, [August 1889], CUL MS. Add. 7480/E5/53.
143. E. F. Benson, *Our Family Affairs*, pp. 244.
144. E. F. Benson, letter to MRJ, [1890], CUL MS. Add. 7481/B168.
145. E. F. Benson, *Our Family Affairs*, p. 245.
146. E&K, p. 134.
147. For MRJ's notes on the Brent Eleigh MSS, see Note Book, pp. 147r-151r. CUL MS Add. 7517.
148. Ibid., p. 134.
149. Augustus Jessopp, letter to MRJ, 13 November 1891, CUL MS. Add. 7481/J43.
150. Joseph Jacobs, letter to MRJ, 16 June 1892, CUL MS. Add. 7481/J18. The MS. is excerpted in Joseph Jacobs, *The Jews of Angevin England: Documents and Records from Latin and Hebrew Sources* (London: David Nutt, 1893), pp. 19–21.
151. Augustus Jessopp, letter to MRJ, 13 June 1892, CUL MS. Add. 7481/J49.
152. Augustus Jessopp, 'An Antiquary's Ghost Story', *The Athenæum*, no. 2724 (10 January 1880), p. 54.
153. Augustus Jessopp, letter to MRJ, 13 November 1891, CUL MS. Add. 7481/J43.
154. Thomas of Monmouth, *The Life and Miracles of William of Norwich*, ed. Augustus Jessopp and Montague Rhodes James (Cambridge: Cambridge University Press, 1896), p. v.
155. Ibid., pp. lxii–lxiii.
156. Philip Schaff and Henry Wace, eds. *Nicene and Post-Nicene Fathers Volume 2. Socrates, Sozomenus: Church Histories* (Peabody, MA: Hendrickson, 1995), p. 78.
157. GSA, p. 33. For a good account of the influence of William of Norwich on 'Lost Hearts', see Robert Lloyd Parry, *Ghosts of the Chit-Chat*, pp. 7–10.
158. Thomas of Monmouth, *William of Norwich*, p. lxxxv.
159. MRJ, letter to family, 7 November 1890, CUL MS. Add. 7480/D6/327.
160. Newsome, *On the Edge of Paradise*, p. 49.
161. MRJ, letter to family, February 1891, CUL MS. Add. 7480/D6/328.
162. For an account of the last months of Stephen's life, see Newman, *J. K. Stephen*, pp. 34–9.
163. Lee, *Virginia Woolf*, p. 65.
164. J. K. Stephen, *The Living Languages: A Defence of the Compulsory Study of Greek at Cambridge* (Cambridge: Macmillan and Bowes, 1891), p. 3.

165. Winstanley, *Later Victorian Cambridge*, p. 179.
166. ACB, letter to MRJ, 30 September 1902, CUL MS Add. 7481/B88.
167. Minutes of the Meetings of the Chit-Chat Club, vol. 4, p. 140, CUL MS. SOC.65.4. The vote took place on 4 February 1887.
168. Goldhill, *Who Needs Greek?*, pp. 240–1.
169. James Adam, letter to MRJ, 27 November 1891, CUL MS. Add. 7481/A12.
170. MRJ, letter to family [March 1892], CUL MS. Add. 7480/D6/337.
171. MRJ, letter to family, 1 April 1892, CUL MS. Add. 7480/D6/338.
172. For the notes MRJ took during his visit to St. Bertrand, see Notebooks 12.I, pp. 18–26.
173. GSA, p. 3.
174. MRJ, letter to MEJ, 18 July 1892, CUL MS. Add. 7480/D6/340. MRJ's account of his Irish trip is all taken from this long letter.
175. GSA, pp. 39–40.
176. MRJ, letter to MEJ, 9 November 1888, CUL MS. Add. 7480/D6/305.

CHAPTER 6

1. MRJ, 'Foreword' to Maisie Fletcher, *The Bright Countenance: A Personal Biography of Walter Morley Fletcher* (London: Hodder and Stoughton, 1957), p. 9.
2. Ibid., pp. 23–4.
3. Ibid., p. 44.
4. Notebooks 5.VI.
5. Oliffe Richmond, unpublished memoir of MRJ (1964), KCC MRJ/x/1/3 [Misc. 19/10], p. 1.
6. MRJ, 'Foreword' to Fletcher, p. 10.
7. Walter Fletcher, letter to MRJ, 31 July 1918, CUL MS Add. 7481/F36.
8. ACB, Diaries, v.7 f.1, 4 August 1901.
9. Godfrey Locker-Lampson, letter to MRJ, 18 May 1905, CUL MS Add. 7481/L36. This refers specifically to his rooms in the Wilkins Building.
10. 'Those in Authority: The Provost of King's', *The Granta*, vol. XVIII (8 June 1905), p. 11.
11. Sir Charles Tennyson, *Stars and Markets* (London: Chatto and Windus, 1957), pp. 92–4.
12. ACB, Diaries, v.44 f.33, December 1903.
13. ACB, Diaries, v.38 ff. 11–12, September 1903.
14. Leslie papers, KCC SJRL/1/2.
15. Oliffe Richmond, unpublished memoir of MRJ (1964), KCC MRJ/x/1/3 [Misc 19/10], p. 6; Fletcher, p. 73.
16. ACB, Diaries, v. 46 f. 11, 27 January 1904.
17. ACB, Diaries, v.39 ff.75–6, October 1903.
18. J. H. Clapham, 'The Provost of Eton', *The Cambridge Review*, 9 October 1936, p. 6.
19. Ibid., p. 6.
20. Wedd, *King's in 1883*, unpublished memoir, KCC NW 1/16, p. 36.
21. MRJ, Foreword to Fletcher, p. 9.
22. E&K, p. 143.
23. MRJ, undated letter of reference for James McBryde, CUL MS Add. 7481/M26.
24. MRJ, undated letter of reference for James McBryde, CUL MS Add. 7481/MISC.
25. MRJ, Introduction to James McBryde, *The Story of a Troll-Hunt* (Cambridge: Cambridge University Press, 1904), n.p.
26. Fletcher, p. 38.
27. James McBryde, letter to MRJ, 22 March 1898, CUL MS Add. 7481/M68.
28. MRJ, letter to James McBryde, 9 December 1899, KCC MRJ/E/2.

29. Minutes of the Meetings of the Chit-Chat Club, vol. 5, p. 37. CUL MS SOC 65.5.
30. *The Testament of Solomon*, trans. F. C. Conybeare, *The Jewish Quarterly Review*, vol. 11, no. 1 (October 1898), reprinted in *The Three Magical Books of Solomon* (Bristol: Mockingbird Press, 2017), pp. 268–9.
31. Notebooks 10.I.
32. See A. S. G. Edwards, 'M. R. James, 'Canon Alberic's Scrap-book', and 'Dennistoun', *Notes and Queries*, vol. 58, no. 1, March 2011, pp. 104–5.
33. GSA, pp. 16–18. For a close reading of the story which persuasively identifies 'Canon Alberic''s demon as Ornias, see Helen Grant, 'The Nature of the Beast: The Demonology of 'Canon Alberic's Scrap-book', in Joshi and Rosemary Pardoe, eds. *Warnings to the Curious*, pp. 227–37.
34. Arthur E. Shipley, *Zoology of the Invertebrata* (London: Adam and Charles Black, 1893), p. 415. For more on this, see Murphy, *Medieval Studies and the Ghost Stories of M. R. James*, p. 9.
35. GSA, pp. 18–19.
36. Notebooks 10.I.
37. It is impossible to reconstruct these gatherings year by year, or even to be certain of which stories MRJ told. Some very incomplete lists of his Christmas visitors are dotted throughout the diary he kept in the large notebook in which he also wrote his notes on the Greek New Testament: CUL MS Add. 5517, pp. 22–43.
38. E&K, pp. 155–6.
39. This is a composite of a number of eyewitness accounts, including MRJ's own: see E&K, pp. 155–6; S. Lubbock, *Memoir*, pp. 38–9; Oliffe Richmond, Unpublished memoir of MRJ (1964), KCC MRJ/x/1/3 [Misc 19/10], pp. 7–9.
40. H. E. Luxmoore, letters to MRJ, 17–18 January [no year], 28 December [no year], 23 June 1917 CUL MS Add. 7481/L239, 314, 217.
41. H. E. Luxmoore, letter to A. T. Loyd, 24 December [1902], *Letters*, p. 110.
42. https://www.wopc.co.uk/delarue/animal-grab.
43. Cyril Connolly, *Enemies of Promise* (1948; Chicago: University of Chicago Press, 2008), p. 253.
44. Ibid., p.218.
45. GSA, p. 24.
46. GSA, pp. 48, 42.
47. For an earlier version of this argument, see Darryl Jones, Introduction to CGS, p. xxiii.
48. Notebooks 1.III [1878].
49. W. H. Macaulay, letter to MRJ, 24 December 1896, KCC MRJ/D/Macaulay.
50. Luxmoore, letter to A T. Loyd, *Letters*, p. 113.
51. ACB, Diaries, v.44 f. 42–3, December 1903.
52. For a splendid anthology, see Lloyd-Parry, *Ghosts of the Chit-Chat*.
53. Leo Maxse, letter to MRJ, 8 January 1894, CUL MS Add. 7481/M206.
54. MRJ, 'The Scrap-Book of Canon Alberic', *The National Review*, 25 (March 1895), pp. 132–41.
55. Arthur Machen, letter to MRJ, 15 March 1895, CUL MS Add. 7481/M145. Later in his life, Machen revised this initially positive view: see Rosemary Pardoe, 'M. R. James and Arthur Machen', in *The Black Pilgrimage*, pp. 173–8.
56. For an earlier version of the argument that follows. see Jones, Introduction to CGS, pp. xciii–xx.
57. Janet Oppenheim, *The Other World: Spiritualism and Psychical Research in England, 1850–1914* (Cambridge: Cambridge University Press, 1985).

58. Jarlath Killeen, *Gothic Literature, 1914–1925* (Cardiff: University of Wales Press, 2009), pp. 124, 129.
59. Julia Briggs, *Night Visitors: The Rise and Fall of the English Ghost Story* (London: Faber and Faber, 1977), p. 124.
60. MRJ, Preface to *Collected Ghost Stories*, CGS, p. 419.
61. MRJ, Preface to MGSA, pp. v-vi.
62. MRJ, Introduction to V. H. Collins, ed. *Ghosts and Marvels* (Oxford: Oxford University Press, 1924), CGS, p. 407.
63. MRJ, 'Ghosts—Treat Them Gently!', *Evening News*, 17 April 1931, CGS, p. 416.
64. ACB, Diaries, 6 May 1905, v.69 f.13.
65. Leslie papers, KCC SJRL/1/1.
66. Leslie papers, KCC SJRL/1/1; Leslie, 'Montague Rhodes James', p. 35.
67. Wedd, *King's in 1883*, pp. 37–8. For Matthew Arnold and Celtic magic, see 'On the Study of Celtic Literature', *Selected Criticism of Matthew Arnold*, ed. Christopher Ricks (New York: Signet, 1972), pp. 118–39.
68. Peter Davidson, *The Idea of North* (London: Reaktion, 2016), p. 164.
69. Wedd, *King's in 1883*, p. 36.
70. E&K, p. 80.
71. MRJ, *A Descriptive Catalogue of Manuscripts in the Fitzwilliam Museum* (Cambridge: Cambridge University Press, 1895), p. 38.
72. Ibid., pp. 46, 50.
73. See, for example, Ibid., pp. 113, 120, 153.
74. GSA, p. 18.
75. Ibid., p. 79.
76. MRJ, sermon delivered at Eton, no date, CUL MS Add. 7485/3.
77. William James, *Varieties of Religious Experience*, in *Writings 1902–1910* (New York: Library of America, 1987), p. 55.
78. MEJ, letters to MRJ, 29 September 1896, and undated, CUL MS Add. 7480/E2/125, 139.
79. MEJ, letter to MRJ, 20 March 1896, CUL MS Add. 7480/E2/118.
80. BRJ, unpublished memoir, p. 18, JFP.
81. BRJ, 'A Report on the Epidemic of Bubonic Plague which Occurred in Hong Kong in the Months of May, June, and July 1894, with Six Diagrams', Army Medical Department, Appendix to Report for 1893: Appendix V.
82. SRJ, letter to MRJ, [1894], CUL MS Add. 7480/E3/22.
83. MEJ, letter to MRJ [Autumn 1894], CUL Ms Add. 7480/E2/103.
84. SRJ, *Seventy Years*, p. 132.
85. SRJ, Diary, 20–25 January 1897, JFP.
86. Linda Hoare, Diary, 23 January 1897.
87. 'A Great Head: Memories of Eton and Malvern', anonymous review of SRJ, *Seventy Years*, JFP; ACB, reference for SRJ, 25 May 1897, JFP. Sydney's other referees were a heavyweight crew: R. Carr Bosanquet, Edmond Warre, Henry Jackson, Edward Lyttelton, and J. J. Hornby.
88. SRJ, letters to MRJ, 12 March 1913, and undated, CUL MS Add. 7480 E3/31, 37; Fletcher, p. 87.
89. Linda James, letter to MRJ, 31 January 1904, CUL MS Add. 7480/E3/38.
90. Linda James, letter to MRJ, 21 February 1904, CUL MS Add. 7480/E3/39.
91. MRJ, Note Book, p. 37. CUL MS Add. 7517.
92. Lionel Ford, letter to MRJ, 30 December [1888], CUL MS Add. 7481/F77.
93. Kate Lushington, letter to MRJ, 1 Aug [1889], CUL MS Add. 7481/L111.

94. GRJ, letter to MRJ [June 1899], CUL MS Add. 7480/E5/51.
95. GRJ, letter to MRJ, 20 May 1903, CUL MS Add. 7480/E5/60.
96. Goldhill, *A Very Queer Family Indeed*, p. 248.
97. MRJ, letter to HJ, 31 January 1905, CUL MS Add. 7480/D6/518; Cox, p. 152.
98. Charles Scott Kilner, letter to MRJ, 16 November 1905, CUL MS Add. 7481/K19.
99. Pfaff, p. 115.
100. MRJ, letter to Francis Jenkinson, 19 November 1892, CUL MS Add. 6463/2197.
101. MRJ, letter to John Peile, 19 November 1892, CUL MS Add. 2594.20/7.
102. For the records of the 1892 competition for the Disney Chair, see CUL MS Cam/EA/49.
103. MRJ, letter to John Peile, 19 November 1892, CUL MS Add. 2594.20/7.
104. Robert Burn, letter to John Peile, 17 October 1892, CUL MS Add. 2594.20/1; Augustus Jessopp, letter to John Peile, 24 November 1892, CUL MS Add. 2594.20/10.
105. ACB, Diaries, v.153 f.6. 2 June 1915.
106. MRJ, Note Book, p. 29v. CUL MS Add. 7517.
107. MRJ, letter to family, May 1893, CUL MS Add. 7480/D6/342.
108. HJ, letter to MRJ, 15 November 1893, CUL MS Add. 7480/E1/101.
109. J. H. Middleton letter to MRJ, CUL MS Add. 7481/M234.
110. Edmund Gosse, letter to MRJ, 20 November 1893, CUL MS Add. 7481/G60.
111. Wilfrid Blunt, *Cockerell: Sydney Carlyle Cockerell, Friend of Ruskin and William Morris and Director of the Fitzwilliam Museum*, Cambridge (London: Hamish Hamilton, 1964), p. 136.
112. MRJ, letter to Sydney Cockerell, 31 May 1908. BL Add. MS 52728/16.
113. Lucilla Burn, *The Fitzwilliam Museum: A History* (Cambridge: The Fitzwilliam Museum, 2016), p. 110.
114. MRJ, *A Descriptive Catalogue of the Manuscripts in the Fitzwilliam Museum*, p. xvii.
115. Burn, p. 110.
116. R. C. Bosanquet, letters to MRJ, 6 Sept 1901, 23 July 1903, CUL MS Add. 7481/B226, 227.
117. MEJ, letter to MRJ, 25 January 1895, CUL MS Add. 7480/E2/104; MRJ, letter to family, 26 November 1895, CUL MS Add. 7480/D6/369.
118. GSA, pp. 55, 57, 62.
119. MRJ, *The Sculptures in the Lady Chapel at Ely* (London: D. Nutt, 1895); *On the Abbey of S. Edmund at Bury*, Cambridge Octavo Publications, XXVIII (1895).
120. 'Ruins of the Abbey of St. Edmondsbury: Suggestions for excavations made by Dr. Montague Rhodes James and Sir Ernest Clarke as the result of a personal inspection made on May 26th, 1902', 30 May 1902. CUL MS Add. 7481/C72.
121. MRJ, letter to *Times*, 7 January 1903.
122. MRJ, *Suffolk and Norfolk*, p. 36.
123. MRJ Lectures and Addresses, CUL MS Add. 7484/2.5.
124. MRJ Lectures and Addresses, CUL MS Add. 7484/1.87.
125. MRJ, letter to HJ [Summer Term 1894], CUL MS Add. 7480/D6/356.
126. Owen Hugh Smith, letter to MRJ, 12 October 1894, CUL MS Add. 7481/S63.
127. J. H. Middleton, letter to MRJ, 24 April 1895, CUL MS Add. 7481/M236.
128. Prunella Scales, 'Introduction' to E. F. Benson, *Dodo: An Omnibus* (London: Hogarth Press, 1986), n.p.
129. Brian Masters, *The Life of E. F. Benson* (London Chatto and Windus, 1991), p. 99.
130. Scales, 'Introduction', n.p.
131. Newsome, *On the Edge of Paradise*, p. 56.
132. Owen Hugh Smith, letter to MRJ, 22 December 1892, CUL MS Add. 7481/S57.

133. ACB, letter to MRJ, [1893], CUL MS. Add. 7481/B157.
134. GSA, p. 184.
135. Ibid., p. 185.
136. For an analysis of the unstable landscape of MRJ's East Anglian stories, see Lucie Armitt, 'Ghost-al Erosion: Beaches and the Supernatural in Two Stories by M. R. James', in Lisa Fletcher, ed. *Popular Fiction and Spatiality: Reading Genre Settings* (Basingstoke: Palgrave Macmillan, 2016), pp. 95–108.
137. GSA, p. 196.
138. For analyses of the meaning of these unstable landscapes of fear, see, for example, Catherine Wynne's chapter 'Colonial Topographies: Bogs, Moors and Shifting Grounds', in *The Colonial Conan Doyle: British Imperialism, Irish Nationalism, and the Gothic* (Westport, CT: Greenwood, 2002), 65–99; Nicholas Daly, *Modernism: Romance and the Fin de Siècle: Popular Fiction and British Culture, 1880–1914* (Cambridge: Cambridge University Press, 1999), pp. 53–84.
139. GSA, p. 222.
140. Cecil Knatchbull-Hugessen, letter to MRJ, 29 January 1891, CUL MS Add. 7481/K25.
141. MRJ, letter to MEJ, January 1894, CUL MS Add. 7480/D6/354; MRJ, letter to HJ, January-February 1898, CUL MS Add. 7480/D6/388.
142. Carey, *Nobody's Business*, p. 14.
143. MRJ, *The Tragedy of Henry Blew Beard, Esq*, CUL MS Add. 7484/2.60.
144. MRJ, *Alex Barber and the Forty Thieves,* CUL MS Add. 7482/34.
145. ACB, Diaries, v.39 f.55–6, October 1903.
146. Leslie papers, KCL/SJRL/1/1.
147. A. B. Ramsay, 'In Memoriam, M. R. J.', *Montague Rhodes James: Praepositus necnon amicus 1862–1936* (Cambridge: King's College, 1936), p. 27.
148. E&K, p. 110.
149. Wilkinson, *Kingsmen of a Century 1873–1972* (Cambridge: King's College Cambridge, 1980), p. 190.
150. Leslie papers, KCC SJRL/1/1; E&K, p. 110.
151. Dimsdale, 'On Shaving with a Bradshaw', *Happy Days* (Cambridge: W. Heffer and Sons, 1921), pp. 12–13.
152. GSA, p. 31.
153. Gwendolen Stephenson, Walter Morley Fletcher, and MRJ, *Eustace Talbot: Some Recollections* (Cambridge: Privately published, 1908), p. 39.
154. Ibid., pp. 14–15.
155. MRJ, letter to Shane Leslie, 2 October 1921, Leslie papers KCC SJRL/1/1.
156. Mark Sykes, letter to MRJ [1905], CUL MS Add. 7481/S286.
157. Mark Sykes, letter to MRJ [no date], CUL MS Add. 7481/S297.
158. E&K, p. 145.
159. Shane Leslie, *Mark Sykes: His Life and Letters* (London: Cassell, 1923), p. 55.
160. Rebecca Tessier, *Ad Montem: Eton's Lost Procession* (Eton: Eton College, 2023), p. 4.
161. See *Montem Lists from 1773 to 182, Inclusive* (Eton: T. Ingalton and Son).
162. 'The Fresher's Guide to College Clubs and Societies', *Basileon: Being the Fourth Book of King's* (June 1909), p. 19.
163. Noel Annan, *The Dons: Mentors, Eccentrics and Geniuses* (London: HarperCollins, 1999), p. 115.
164. Annan, 'The Cult of Homosexuality in England 1850–1950', *Biography*, vol. 13, no. 3 (Summer 1990), 189–202.

165. L. P. Wilkinson, the King's historian, writes that the College had 'a reputation for homosexuality' right up to the 1970s, when women were admitted: *A Century of King's*, p. 18. For a full-length study, see Goldhill, *Queer Cambridge*.
166. MRJ, letter to family, May 1899, CUL MS Add. 7480/D6/399.
167. Lubbock, *Memoir*, p. 20.
168. Leslie papers, KCC SJRL/1/1.
169. Lord Acton, letter to MRJ, 2 December 1896, CUL MS Add. 7481/A3.
170. Clapham, 'The Provost of Eton', p. 6.
171. Lord Acton, letter to MRJ, 29 July 1900, CUL MS Add. 7481/A7.
172. E&K, p. 101.
173. MRJ, Note Book, p. 23. CUL MS Add. 7517.
174. Lubbock, p. 31; E&K, p. 100.
175. MRJ, letter to parents, 8 September 1895, CUL MS Add. 7480/D6/367.
176. E&K, p. 144.
177. MRJ, letter to parents, 8 September 1895, CUL MS Add. 7480/D6/367.
178. E&K, p. 144.
179. Lord Stanmore, letter to MRJ, 22 June 1901, CU MS Add. 7481/S138.
180. Lord Stanmore, letter to MRJ, 20 January 1896, CUL MS Add. 7481/S128.
181. MRJ, letter to family, 4 October 1896, CUL MS Add. 7480/D6/381.
182. Percy Lubbock, *Mary Cholmondeley: A Sketch from Memory* (London: Jonathan Cape, 1928), pp. 61, 59.
183. Goldhill, *Queer Cambridge*, p. 82.
184. SRJ, *Seventy Years*, p. 16.
185. George Santayana, *The Middle Span: Vol. II Persons and Places* (New York: Charles Scribner's Sons, 1945), pp. 118, 120.
186. ACB Diaries, v.1 f.40, 20 September 1896.
187. ACB, *Memories and Friends*, pp. 277–8, 275–6
188. Goldhill, *Queer Cambridge*, p. 83.
189. ACB, Diaries, v.1 f.40, 20 September 1896.
190. For this section, I draw heavily on Rita McWilliams Tullberg, *Women at Cambridge* (Cambridge: Cambridge University Press, 1998). See also Edward Shils and Carmen Blacker, eds. *Cambridge Women: Twelve Portraits* (Cambridge: Cambridge University Press, 1996). Ann Kennedy Smith's remarkable blogsite *Women at Cambridge* contains a wealth of information: https://akennedysmith.com
191. *Historical Register*, p. 558.
192. For the vote of 1897 and surrounding events, see Tullberg, Chapter 8.
193. 'To the Members of the Senate: Notice of a Non-Placet', 9 March 1896, CUL Cam/H/41.
194. Cecil Lubbock, letter to MRJ [no date], CUL MS Add. 7481/L59.
195. *Report of the Degrees for Women Syndicate*, 1 March 1897, CUL Cam/H/41.
196. See Tullberg, pp. 108, 210n.35.
197. 'Proposed Titles of Degrees for Women', 27 March 1897, CUL Cam/H/41. On 10 May, MRJ also signed a 'formal notice of **non-placet**'.
198. MRJ, 'Speech in Senate House on Admission of Women', CUL MS Add. 7484/2.62.
199. Tullberg, p. 92.
200. 'Women's Degrees', *The Granta*, vol. X, no. 208 (24 April 1897), pp. 263–4.
201. J. E. Nixon, 'Proposed Titles of Degrees for Women', Flysheet, 11 May 1897, KCC MRJ/D/Nixon/6.

202. 'Votes Recorded at the Congregation on Friday, 21 May, 1897', Special Supplement to *The Cambridge Review*, 3 June 1897, CUL Cam/H/41.
203. James McBryde, letter to MRJ, 17 November 1902, CUL MS Add. 7481/M105.
204. Kennedy Smith, '"No Women at Cambridge": The 1897 Protests', https://akennedysmith.com/tag/1897/
205. For this and much other information on the 1897 campaign, see the CUL exhibition 'The Rising Tide: Women at Cambridge', https://cudl.lib.cam.ac.uk/collections/therisingtide.
206. Kennedy Smith, 'The 1897 Protests, Part Two: The Women in the Photograph': https://akennedysmith.com/2022/01/20/the-1897-protests-part-2-the-women-in-the-photograph/
207. KCC MRJ/F/1.
208. 'Votes Recorded at the Congregation on Friday, 21 May, 1897', CUL Cam/H/41.
209. CUL Cam/H/41. See also Tullberg, p. 116.
210. Ronald Norman, letter to MRJ [no date], CUL MS Add. 7481/N41.
211. MEJ, letter to MRJ, 24 March 1898, CUK MS Add. 7480/E2/137.
212. MRJ, letter to MEJ, September 1898, CUL MS Add. 7480/D6/393.
213. Lubbock, pp. 6–7.
214. Ibid., p. 6. This letter does not appear in any archive of MRJ's correspondence, and was quite possibly sent to a member of the Lubbock family.
215. Owen Hugh Smith, letter to MRJ, 10 December 1918, CUL MS Add. 7481/S101.
216. F. Harrison, *The Painted Glass of York: An Account of the Medieval Glass of the Minster and the Parish Churches* (London: SPCK, 1927), pp. 2, viii.
217. Harrison, p. 177; Peter Gibson, 'The Stained and Painted Glass of York', in Alberic Stacpoole et al, eds. *The Noble City of York* (York: Cerialis Press, 1972), p. 168; Allan B. Barton, *A Guide to the Church of All Saints North Street, York* (York: Maxiprint, n.d.), p. 10.
218. Ralph Hanna and Sarah Wood, ed. *Richard Morris's 'Prick of Conscience': A Corrected and Amplified Text*, Early English Text Society O.S. 342 (Oxford: Oxford University Press, 2013). Line references are to this edition. The Fitzwilliam *Prick of Conscience* is MS McClean 131: see MRJ, *A Descriptive Catalogue of the McClean Collection of Manuscripts in the Fitzwilliam Museum* (Cambridge: Cambridge University Press, 1912), p. 278.
219. Jacobus de Voragine, *The Golden Legend: Readings on the Saints*, trans. William Granger Ryan (Princeton, NJ: Princeton University Press, 1993), I: 53.
220. GSA, p. 171.
221. Simon MacCulloch, 'The Toad in the Study: M. R. James, H. P. Lovecraft, and Forbidden Knowledge', in Joshi and Pardoe, eds. *Warnings to the Curious*, p. 96.
222. Notebooks, 4V. The notes for all of the twelve York churches MRJ visited in 1898 can be found here.
223. Charles Kightly, *The Church of St. Denys Walmgate, York: History and Guide* (York, 2018) p. 30.
224. GSA, p. 38. This hurdy-gurdy played a significant, and terrifying, role in Lawrence Gordon Clark's 1973 television version of 'Lost Hearts', part of the BBC's *Ghost Story for Christmas* series.
225. Harrison, p. 160.
226. Ibid., pp. 198, 139, 140.
227. Augustus Austen Leigh, letter to MRJ, 28 November 1899, KCC MRJ/D/Augustus Austen Leigh/1.
228. MRJ, letter to HJ, November–December 1899, CUL MS Add. 7480/D6/495.
229. Richmond, Unpublished memoir of MRJ (1964), KCC MRJ/x/1/3 [Misc 19/10], p. 1.

230. MRJ, letter to Henry Babington Smith, 18 February 1903, TCC HBS/71/127.
231. MRJ, letter to HJ, 30 November 1900, CUL MS Add. 7480/D6/436.
232. Augustus Austen Leigh, letter to MRJ, 30 May 1901, KCC MRJ/D/Augustus Austen Leigh/5–7.
233. A. H. Cooke, letter to Augustus Austen Leigh, included with Austen Leigh, Letter to MRJ, 1 April 1901, KCC MRJ/D/Augustus Austen-Leigh/2.
234. For Macaulay as Tutor, see Wilkinson, *A Century of King's*, pp. 43–5.
235. E&K, p. 144.
236. Ibid., p. 144.
237. Ibid., p. 144.
238. MRJ, letter to GRJ, August 1899, CUL MS Add. 7480/E5/15.
239. McBryde, *Troll-hunt*, p. 1.
240. MRJ, Address on Hans Andersen, CUL MS Add. 7484/1.63.
241. MRJ, letter to family, 13 August 1900, CUL MS Add. 7481/D6/428.
242. GSA, p. 115.
243. MRJ, letter to family, 19 August 1900, CUL MS Add. 7481/D6/429.
244. MRJ, letter to family, 27 August 1900, CUL MS Add. 7480/D6/430.
245. W. J. Stone, letter to Ruth Stone, August 1900, in *The Letters and Memorials of William Johnson Stone* (Eton College: Spottiswoode and Co., Ltd, 1904), pp. 108–9.
246. W. J. Stone, letter to MRJ, 10 September 1900, CUL MS Add. 7481/S250.
247. W. J. Stone, letter to Lucy Stone 13 October 1900, *Letters and Memorials*, p. 113.
248. W. J. Stone, letter to father, 16 February 1901, *Letters and Memorials*, p. 120.
249. MRJ, letter to HJ, 26 February 1901, CUL MS Add. 7480/D6/443.
250. MRJ, letter to family, 18 August 1901, CUL MS Add. 7480/D6/453.
251. GSA, pp. 153, 152, 170, 171.
252. Ibid., p. 166.
253. MRJ, letter to family, 18 August 1901, CUL MS Add. 7480/D6/453.
254. John Lindow, *Swedish Legends and Folktales* (Berkeley: University of California Press, 1978), p. 45.
255. GSA, p. 148.

CHAPTER 7

1. LF, p. 7.
2. Walter Fletcher, letter to MRJ, 17 July 1903, CUL MS Add. 7481/F24.
3. MRJ, letter to GRJ, 19 July 1903, CUL MS Add. 7480/E5/20.
4. MRJ, letter to HJ, 17 June 1903, CUL MS Add. 7480/D6/481.
5. MRJ, letter to HJ, 7 August 1903, CUL MS Add. 7480/D6/482.
6. MRJ, letter to HJ, 19 January 1904, CUL MS Add. 7480/D6/488.
7. MRJ, letter to HJ, 20 February 1904, CUL MS Add. 7480/D6/492.
8. Julia Hilton, letter to MRJ, 6 June 1904, CUL MS Add. 7481/H69.
9. Walter Fletcher, letter to Maisie Fletcher: Fletcher, *The Bright Countenance*, p. 84.
10. Henry Vaughan, 'The Garland', in *The Oxford Authors: George Herbert and Henry Vaughan*, ed. Louis L. Martz (Oxford: Oxford University Press, 1986), p. 364.
11. ACB, letter to MRJ, 15 June 1904, CUL MS Add. 7481/B95.
12. ACB, Diaries, v.5 f.1–2, 14 June 1904.
13. ACB, Diaries, v.5 f.2, 14 June 1904.
14. Lionel Ford, letter to MRJ, 19 June 1904, CUL MS Add. 7481/F70.
15. H. E. Luxmoore, letter to MRJ, 11 June 1904, CUL MS Add. 7481/L184.

16. S. G. Lubbock, letter to MRJ, 7 June 1904, CUL MS Add. 7481/L95.
17. John Stirling Maxwell, letter to MRJ, 17 June 1904, CUL MS Add. 7481/S189.
18. See, for example, *The Victorian Language of Flowers: Occasional Papers from the RHS Lindley Library*, vol. 10 (April 2013).
19. Fletcher, *The Bright Countenance*, p. 84.
20. Julia Hilton, letter to MRJ [1904], CUL MS Add. 7481/H70.
21. MRJ, Introduction to McBryde, *Troll-Hunt*, n.p.
22. Vaughan, 'As time one day by me did pass', *Oxford Authors*, p. 386.
23. MRJ, letter to HJ, 6 December 1904, CUL MS Add. 7480/D6/513.
24. Gwendolen McBryde, letter to MRJ, 13 December 1904, CUL MS Add. 7481/M11.
25. LF, p. 29.
26. MRJ, letter to HJ, 27 May 1905, CUL MS Add. 7481/D6/537.
27. Maisie Fletcher, letter to Shane Leslie [no date], inserted into Leslie's annotated copy of E&K, Eton College Library Lp.2.24.
28. Leslie papers, KCC SJRL/1/1.
29. Richmond, Unpublished memoir of MRJ (1964), KCC MRJ/x/1/3, p. 10.
30. LF, pp. 9–10.
31. For the Cat and Mouse letters, see CUL MS Add. 7481/M127-32; LF, pp. 53ff.
32. Christian Stirling-Maxwell letter to MRJ, 28 March 1923, CUL MS Add. 7481/S177.
33. MRJ, letter to HJ, 7 July 1904, CUL MS Add. 7480/D6/502.
34. Newsome, *On the Edge of Paradise*, p. 212.
35. Richmond, Memoir, p. 10.
36. Fletcher, *The Bright Countenance*, p. 48.
37. Ibid., p. 55.
38. MRJ, letter to HJ, 30 June 1904. CUL MS Add. 7480/D6/501.
39. Fletcher, *The Bright Countenance*, p. 72.
40. Leslie Papers, KCC SJRL 1/1.
41. Fletcher, *The Bright Countenance*, p. 73.
42. MRJ, letter to Sibyl Cropper, no date, CUL MS Add. 7481/C179.
43. Sibyl Cropper, letter to MRJ, 29 January 1903, CUL MS Add. 7481/C165.
44. Sibyl Cropper, letter to MRJ, 25 January [no year], CUL MS Add 7481/C173.
45. ACB, Diaries, v.158, f.44, March 1916.
46. Newsome, *On the Edge of Paradise*, p. 53. This seems to have taken place in 1907, when MRJ was occupied with the Corpus Christi catalogue: his very sketchy notebook diary records: '1907 *Lent*. Corpus. N. Lyttelton. O. Smith.' Note Book, p. 126. CUL MS Add. 7517.
47. ACB, Diaries, v.44, f.44, 21 December 1903.
48. H. E. Luxmoore, letter to MRJ, 28 December [1912], CUL MS Add. 7481/L313.
49. ACB, Diaries, v.122 F.49, 19 July 1911.
50. Dominick Spring-Rice, letter to MRJ, 3 January 1927, CUL MS Add. 7481/S120.
51. Richmond, Memoir, p. 4.
52. Richmond, letters to MRJ, 31 March [1904], and [*c.*1905], CUL MS Add. 7481/R49, R47.
53. Ethel Richmond, letter to MRJ [no date], JFP.
54. Richmond, letter to MRJ [c.1905], CUL MS Add. 7481/R47.
55. Newsome, *On the Edge of Paradise*, p. 201.
56. Goldhill, *A Very Queer Family Indeed*, p. 146.
57. Newsome, *On the Edge of Paradise*, p. 201.
58. Luxmoore, letter to MRJ, 28 December [1912], CUL MS Add. 7481/L313.
59. L. F. Giblin, letter to MRJ, 12 March 1904, CUL MS Add. 7481/G19.
60. Edward Arnold, letter to MRJ, 19 November 1902, CUL MS Add. 7481/A30.

61. MRJ, 'The Christian Renaissance', in Lord Acton, ed. *The Cambridge Modern History vol. I: The Renaissance* (Cambridge: Cambridge University Press, 1902), pp. 585–619.
62. Edward Arnold, letter to MRJ, 5 March 1903, CUL MS Add. 7481/A31.
63. Edward Arnold, letter to MRJ, 27 June 1904, KCC MRJ/D/Arnold/1; James McBryde, letter to MRJ, 11 March 1904, CUL MS Add. 7481/M120.
64. MRJ, *Old Testament Legends* (London: Longmans, Green and Co, 1913).
65. MRJ, letter to James McBryde, 13 March 1904, CUL MS Add. 7481/M120*.
66. Edward Arnold, letter to MRJ, 22 June 1904, KCC MRJ/D/Arnold/2.
67. Edward Arnold, letter to MRJ, 27 June 1904, KCC MRJ/D/Arnold/1.
68. Edward Arnold, letter to MRJ, 22 June 1904, KCC MRJ/D/Arnold/2.
69. See Cox, p. 139 for this suggestion.
70. MRJ, letter to James McBryde, 13 March 1904, CUL MS Add. 7481/M120*.
71. Richmond, Memoir, p. 6.
72. MRJ, letter to HJ, 26 May 1883, CUL MS Add. 7480/D6/194.
73. Simon Bradley and Nikolaus Pevsner, *The Buildings of England: Cambridgeshire* (New Haven and London: Yale University Press, 2014), p. 132.
74. Robert Willis and John Willis Clark, *The Architectural History of the University of Cambridge*, vol. 1 (Cambridge: Cambridge University Press, 1886), p. 498.
75. MRJ, *A Guide to the Windows of King's College Chapel*, p. 5. See also Stephen Clare, 'The Great Glass Vista: A Survey of the Stained Glass in King's College Chapel', in Jean-Michel Massing and Nicolette Zeeman, eds. *King's College Chapel 1515–2015: Art, Music and Religion in Cambridge* (London: Harvey Miller, 2014), pp. 136–7.
76. See Willis and Clark, pp. 501–8.
77. MRJ, *King's College Chapel*, p. 19. For Hedgeland's restoration, see also Clare, 'The Great Glass Vista', p. 150.
78. E&K, pp. 148–9.
79. Leslie papers, KCC SLRL/1/1/Envelope 3.
80. Arthur Gray, letter to MRJ [no date], CUL MS Add. 7481/G72. But see also Gray and Frederick Brittain, *A History of Jesus College, Cambridge* (London: Heinemann, 1960), p. 163:'These windows display Pre-Raphaelite work at its best, and together form one of the most striking and brilliant features of the chapel. Fortunately for the College, the chapel has been restored, repaired, and embellished for more than a century by dons, architects, and builders who have loved it.' This book was published twenty years after Gray's death, and this passage may have been written by the considerably more ameliorative Freddie Brittain.
81. John Ruskin, *The Seven Lamps of Architecture* (London: Smith, Elder, & Co., 1849), p. 179.
82. Simon Goldhill, *The Buried Life of Things: How Objects Made History in Nineteenth Century Britain* (Cambridge: Cambridge University Press, 2015), p. 5.
83. Ibid., p. 49.
84. MRJ, letter to Raymond Pelly, 25 October [c.1900], CUL MS Add. 7481/MISC.
85. Thackeray Turner, letter to MRJ, 28 September 1900, CUL MS Add. 7481/T49.
86. TG, p. 82.
87. GSA, p.230.
88. Dundas Harford, letters to MRJ, 24 July 1903, 19 August 1903, CUL MS Add. 7481/H18, 19.
89. For an invaluable account of MRJ, Nikola Reinartz, and the Ashridge glass, on which I draw here, see Helen Grant, 'M. R. James and the Lost Treasure of Father Reinartz: A detective in search of a ghost story' (2016), https://www.rlf.org.uk/showcase/m-r-james-and-the-lost-treasure-of-father-reinartz/. See also Nicholas Connell, 'A Haunting Vision: M. R. James and the Ashridge Stained Glass', in Joshi and Pardoe, eds. *A Warning to the Curious*, pp. 253–7.

90. MRJ, *Notes of Glass in Ashridge Chapel* (Grantham: Leayton and Eden, 1906), n.p.
91. Grant, 'MRJ and the Lost Treasure of Father Reinartz'.
92. Nikola Reinartz, letter to MRJ, 20 September 1908, CUL MS Add. 7481/R36.
93. Nikola Reinartz, letter to MRJ, 2 October 1908, CUL MS Add. 7481/R37.
94. See Bernard Rackham, 'The Mariawald-Ashridge Glass', *The Burlington Magazine for Connoisseurs*, vol. 85, no. 500 (November 1944), 266–73.
95. https://collections.vam.ac.uk/item/O65284/panel-rensig-everhard/
96. Connell, 'A Haunting Vision', p. 254
97. See, amongst many examples, his account of the windows of Chartres Cathedral from 1889: Notebooks 4.II, p. 126.
98. MRJ, *The Apocalypse in Art* (London: British Academy, 1931), p. 17.
99. Harrison, *The Painted Glass of York*, pp. 214–17.
100. Gibson, 'The Stained and Painted Glass of York', p. 77.
101. Charles Cropper, letter to Sydney Cockerell, 31 January 1912, BL Add. MS 52728/36. Reproduced in monochrome in Lubbock, *Memoir*, facing p. 20. The original is in JFP, along with Charles Cropper's drawing of Walter Fletcher.
102. Gibson, p. 77.
103. E. Milner-White, 'The Restoration of the East Window at York Minster', *The Antiquaries Journal*, vol. 30, no. 3–4 (July–October 1950), 181.
104. E&K, p. 149.
105. Edward Arnold, letter to MRJ, 14 July 1904. CUL MS Add. 7481/A32.
106. Owen Davies, *The Haunted: A Social History of Ghosts* (London: Palgrave Macmillan, 2007), pp. 8–9.
107. This is a much-condensed version of an argument I have made elsewhere: see Darryl Jones, *Sleeping With the Lights On: The Unsettling Story of Horror* (Oxford: Oxford University Press, 2018), pp. 78–9.
108. Andrew Lang, *Cock Lane and Common Sense* (London: Longmans, Green, & Co., 1894), p. 95.
109. William Shakespeare, *Hamlet*, Act 1, Scene 1.
110. See Parry, *The Trophies of Time.*
111. See Philippa Levine, *The Amateur and the Professional: Antiquarians, Historians and Archaeologists in Victorian England, 1838–1886* (Cambridge: Cambridge University Press, 1986).
112. Edward Arnold, Memorandum of Agreement, 25 July 1904, KCC MRJ/D/Arnold/3.
113. MRJ, letter to HJ, 21 October 1904, CUL MS Add. 7481/D6/509.
114. SRJ, letter to MRJ, 6 November 1904, CUL MS Add. 7480/E3/26.
115. GSA, p. vii.
116. Lubbock, *Memoir*, p, 39.
117. James McBryde, letter to MRJ, 6 May 1904, CUL MS Add. 7481/M122.
118. MRJ, letter to James McBryde, 19 November 1903, JFP.
119. Gwen McBryde, letter to MRJ, 11 June 1904, CUL MS Add. 7481/M7.
120. James McBryde, letter to MRJ, 6 May 1904, CUL MS Add. 7481/M122.
121. Ronald Norman, letter to MRJ, 18 December 1904, CUL MS Add. 7481/N33.
122. ACB, letter to MRJ, 25 November 1904, CUL MS Add. 7481/B97.
123. H. G. W. Tatham, letter to MRJ, 18 December 1904, CUL MS Add. 7481/T6.
124. Eustace Talbot, letter to MRJ, 26 December 1904, CUL MS Add. 7481/T2.
125. Edith Cropper, letter to MRJ, December 1904, CUL MS Add. 7481/C156.
126. Sibyl Cropper, letter to MRJ, 23 December 1904, CUL MS Add. 7481/C181.

127. Baron Stanmore [Arthur Hamilton-Gordon], letter to MRJ, 15 January 1905, CUL MS Add. 7481/S144.
128. Mark Sykes, letter to MRJ, [1904], CUL MS Add. 7481/S281.
129. Mark Sykes, letter to MRJ [no date], CUL MS Add. 7481/S285.
130. Herbert Warren, letter to MRJ, 20 October 1913, CUL MS Add. 7481/W39.
131. Iris Osborne Morgan, letter to Shane Leslie, 14 October 1951, in Shane Leslie's annotated copy of E&K. Eton College Library Lp.2.24.
132. William K. Dickson, letter to MRJ, 19 May 1907, CUL MS Add. 7481/D38.
133. A. E. Housman, letter to Thomas Hardy, 4 November, 1913; Hardy, letter to Housman, 15 November 1913, in *The Letters of A. E. Housman*, ed. Archie Burnett (Oxford: Clarendon Press, 2007), vol: 1, p. 316.
134. Florence Hardy, letter to MRJ, 25 March [?1914], CUL MS Add. 7481/H16.
135. 'Our Library Table', *The Athenaeum*, 17 December 1904, p. 842.
136. 'Ghost Stories', *The Spectator*, 4017 (24 June 1905), p. 925.
137. 'The Ghost Collector', *New York Times*, 22 July 1905, p. 483.
138. CUL MS Add. 7484/2.25.
139. KCC MS MRJ/B/4. In a development which would have delighted MRJ, the librarians at King's, who may be in on the joke, have catalogued this as 'Pencil MS in an unidentified hand expressing sentiments appreciative of MRJ's *Ghost Stories of an Antiquary*, 1904.'
140. MRJ, letter to Israel Gollancz, 3 December 1903, CUL MS Add. 7481/G53.
141. I am grateful to Marlene Arnese for sharing with me her paper 'M. R. James: A Life in Manuscripts', which I heard delivered at the symposium 'Sequestered Places, Heaving Seas: The Life and Works of M. R. James', University of Suffolk, Ipswich, 30 April 2024.
142. For MRJ and Thompson, see Pfaff, pp. 192–4.
143. See Christopher De Hamel, *The Posthumous Papers of the Manuscript Club* (London: Allen Lane, 2022), p. 429.
144. MRJ, letter to HJ, 22 November 1904, CUL MS Add. 7480/D6/512.
145. Newsome, *On the Edge of Paradise*, p. 160.
146. ACB, Diaries, v.62, f. 15–16, December 1904.
147. ACB, Diaries, v. 61, f.62, October 1904.
148. ACB, Diaries, v.62, f.29, December 1904.
149. ACB, open letter, 24 November 1904, CUL MS Add.7481/B96.
150. Newsome, *On the Edge of Paradise*, p. 160.
151. Ibid., p. 194.
152. H. E. Luxmoore, letter to MRJ, 2 April 1905, CUL MS Add. 7481/L189.
153. ACB, Diaries, v.52, f. 67, May 1904.
154. ACB, Diaries, v.71 f.79, 11 July 1905.
155. ACB, Diaries, v.39, f. 75–6, October 1903.
156. ACB Diaries, v.68, f. 54, April 1905.
157. E&K, p. 157.
158. MRJ, letter to HJ, 30 January 1905, CUL MS Add. 7480/D6/519.
159. MRJ, letter to HJ, February 1905, CUL MS Add, 7480/D6/522.
160. SRJ, letter to MRJ, 24 March 1905, CUL MS Add. 7480/E5/29.
161. MRJ, letter to HJ, 6 February 1905, CUL MS Add. 7480/D6/521.
162. ACB, Diaries, v.56, f. 85, February 1905.
163. ACB, letter to MRJ, 23 March 1905, CUL MS Add. 7481/B101.
164. Newsome, *On the Edge of Paradise*, p. 178.
165. ACB, Diaries, v.65, f.16, January 1905.

166. MRJ, 'Durnford, Sir Walter (1847-1926)', ONDB: https://www-oxforddnb-com.elib.tcd.ie/display/10.1093/ref:odnb/9780198614128.001.0001/odnb-9780198614128-e-32942?rskey=KqCZPj&result=3
167. Walter Headlam, letter to MRJ, 22 March 1905, KCC MS MRJ/D/Headlam.
168. Reggie Balfour, letter to MRJ, 5 April 1905. CUL MS Add. 7481/B19.
169. Wedd, *King's in 1883,* pp. 34–5.
170. MRJ letter to HJ, 26 March 1905, CUL MS Add.7480/D6/528.
171. George Prothero, letter to MRJ, 24 March 1905, KCC MS MRJ/D/Prothero/3.
172. Wedd, *King's in 1883,* p. 35.
173. Ida Darwin, letter to MRJ, 15 April 1905. KCC MS MRJ/D/Darwin/1.
174. MRJ, letter to HJ, 9 May 1905. CUL MS Add. 7480/D6/531.
175. ACB, Diaries, v.68, f.31, May 1905.
176. Honey, *Tom Brown's Universe*, p. 197. This is Edward Compton Austen Leigh, Augustus's brother—not to be confused with MRJ's friend Edward Chenevix Austen Leigh.
177. Leslie papers, KCC SJRL/1/1.
178. Arthur J. Bather, letter to MRJ, 20 May 1905, CUL MS Add. 7481/B53.
179. Reggie Balfour, letter to MRJ, 5 April 1905, CUL MS Add. 7481/B19.
180. Henry Broadbent, letter to MRJ, 13 May 1905, CUL MS Add. 7481/B275.
181. Arthur F. Hort, letter to MRJ, 14 May 1905, CUL MS Add 7481/H114.
182. R. C. Jebb, letter to MRJ, 16 May 1905, CUL MS Add. 7481/J26.
183. Cecil Knatchbull-Hugessen, letter to MRJ, 15 May 1905, CUL MS Add. 7481/K26.
184. Florence Austen Leigh, letter to MRJ, 13 May 1905, CUL MS Add. 7481/A43.
185. G.M. Trevelyan, letter to MRJ, 14 May 1905, CUL MS Add. 7481/T34.
186. HEL, letter to MRJ, 2 April 1905, CUL MS Add. 7481/L189.
187. Percy Lubbock, letter to MRJ, 28 May 1905, CUL MS Add. 7481/L81.
188. Baron Stanmore [Arthur Hamilton-Gordon], letter to MRJ, 13 May 1905, CUL MS Add. 7481/S146.
189. For this list, see Pfaff, p. 211n.4.
190. Baron Stanmore [Arthur Hamilton-Gordon], letter to MRJ, 26 October 1905, CUL MS Add. 7481/S147.
191. E. C. Austen Leigh, letter to MRJ, 15 May 1905, CUL MS Add. 7481/A41.
192. ACB, Diaries, v.69, f.16, 6 May 1905.
193. 'Those in Authority: The Provost of King's', *The Granta*, vol. XVIII (8 June 1905), p. 11.
194. Wilkinson, *A Century of King's*, pp. 49–50.
195. Wedd, *King's in 1883*, pp. 35–6.
196. ACB, Diaries, v.106, f.96, 6 February 1909.
197. Wedd, *King's in 1883*, p. 39.
198. ACB, Diaries, v. 76 f.4, 12 November 1905.
199. ACB, Diaries, v.87 f.8, 4 November 1906.
200. Oscar Browning, letter to C. A. Fay, 13 December 1912, CUL MS Add.7461/5.
201. Goldhill, *Queer Cambridge*, p. 196.
202. ACB, Diaries, v.76 f.27, 27 November 1905.
203. ACB, Diaries, v.102, f.16, 9 July 1908.
204. ACB, Diaries, v. 71 f.79, 11 July 1905.
205. MRJ, letter to Sibyl Cropper, 18 May 1905, KCC MS MRJ/x/3.
206. ACB, Diaries, v.78, f.27, 1906.
207. ACB, Diaries, v.86, f.53, 19 October 1905.
208. Marco Conegliano, letter to MRJ, 11 September 1905, KCC MS MRJ/D/Conegliano.

209. ACB, Diaries, v.88 f.34, 25 December 1906. ACB's handwriting has been (understandably) mistranscribed by some commentators as 'the story of the ashes': see MRJ, *A Pleasing Terror: The Complete Supernatural Writings*, ed. Christopher Roden and Barbara Roden (Aschroft: British Columbia: The Ash-Tree Press, 2001), p. 121.
210. MGSA, 9–10.
211. Stephenson, Fletcher, and MRJ, *Eustace Talbot*, pp. 42–3
212. Ibid., p.43.
213. Vincent S. Jones, letter to MRJ, 1 June 1905, CUL MS Add. 7481/J91.
214. *Eustace Talbot*, p. 43.
215. G. V. Carey, *Nobody's Business*, p. 61.
216. For a record of their long friendship, see Hugh Carey, *Duet for Two Voices: An Informal Biography of Edward J. Dent compiled from his letters to Clive Carey* (Cambridge: Cambridge University Press, 1979).
217. 'Those in Authority: The Provost of King's', p. 11.
218. For Carey's account of the Provost's Lodge, see *Nobody's Business*, p. 61.
219. Nigel Jones, *Rupert Brooke*, p. 304. Yeats also thought that he wore 'the most beautiful shirts'.
220. Michael Bloch, *Closet Queens: Some 20th Century British Politicians* (London: Abacus, 2015), p. 228.
221. Jones, *Rupert Brooke*, p. 46.
222. For Sayle, see D'Arch Smith, *Love in Earnest*, pp. 78–81; Goldhill, *Queer Cambridge*, pp. 86–7.
223. E&K, p. 117.
224. ACB, Diaries, v.102 f.15, 9 July 1908.
225. MRJ, letter to HJ, 2 February 1906, CUL MS Add. 7481/D6/549.
226. MRJ, letter to HJ, June 1906, CUL MS Add. 7481/D6/556. This list is a close paraphrase.
227. MRJ, letter to HJ, 8 April 1906, CUL MS Add. 7481.
228. Anstey Guthrie, letter to MRJ, 23 July 1906, CUL MS Add. G106.
229. MRJ, letter to HJ, 12 August 1906, CUL MS Add. 7481/D6/561.
230. MRJ, 'The Edwin Drood Syndicate', *The Cambridge Review*, 30 November 1905, p. 125.
231. MRJ, 'Cantabrigia Illustrata Rediviva', *The Cambridge Review*, 30 November 1905, p. 123.
232. Andrew Lang, letter to MRJ, 9 September 1906, CUL MS Add. 7481/L6.
233. E&K, p. 141.
234. Henry Jackson, *About Edwin Drood* (Cambridge: Cambridge University Press, 1911), p. 89.
235. MRJ, 'About Edwin Drood', *Cambridge Review*, 9 March 1911, pp. iv, 346–7.
236. ACB, Diaries, v.117 f.45–6, December 1910.
237. ACB, Diaries, v.130 f.21, 16 April 1912.
238. E&K, pp. 46–7; ACB, 'Memoir', in H. F. W. Tatham, *The Footprints in the Snow and Other Tales* (London: Macmillan, 1910), p. xiii. For a warm and valuable account of Tatham, see Joseph Hinton, 'H. F. W. Tatham: An Outlier of the James Gang', *Ghosts & Scholars*, 34 (October 2018), pp. 22–30.
239. LF, p. 37.
240. ACB, Diaries, v.97, f.20, October 1907.
241. I am very grateful to Beryl Dyson, a lifelong resident of Great Livermere, whose father was the village blacksmith, for showing me the family ledgers and bills for the Rectory.
242. SRJ, letter, 15 June 1909, JFP.
243. H. E. Luxmoore, letter to MRJ, 21 June 1909, CUL MS Add. 7481/L200.
244. H. E. Luxmoore, letter to MRJ, June 1909. CUL MS Add. 7481/L333.
245. ACB, Diaries, v.52 f.106, 19 June 1909.

CHAPTER 8

1. C. R. Fay, 'King's College Cambridge, 1902–6', *The Dalhousie Review*, vol. 30, no. 4 (1951), 332.
2. Richard Davenport-Hines, *Universal Man: The Seven Lives of John Maynard Keynes* (London: William Collins, 2015), p. 6.
3. Ibid., p. 245.
4. Kingsley Martin, *Father Figures: The Evolution of an Editor, 1897–1931* (Chicago: Henry Regnery, 1970), p. 103.
5. Davenport-Hines, p. 13.
6. Ibid., p. 51.
7. Ibid., p. 229.
8. Ann Banfield, 'Cambridge Bloomsbury', in Victoria Rosner, ed. *The Cambridge Companion to the Bloomsbury Group* (Cambridge: Cambridge University Press, 2014), pp. 33–53.
9. R. F. Harrod, *The Life of John Maynard Keynes* (London: Penguin, 1972), p. 65.
10. Fay, p. 334.
11. Harrod, p. 79.
12. ACB, Diaries, v.46 f.55, 2 February 1904.
13. Davenport-Hines, p. 46.
14. Harrod, p. 52.
15. For the King's Keynes archive, see KCC GBR/0272/JMK.
16. Paul Levy, *Moore: G. E. Moore and the Cambridge Apostles* (London: Weidenfeld & Nicholson, 1979), p. 140.
17. W. C. Lubenow, *The Cambridge Apostles 1820–1914* (Cambridge: Cambridge University Press, 1998), p. 19.
18. Davenport-Hines, p. 213.
19. Ibid., p. 68.
20. D. E. Moggridge, *Maynard Keynes: An Economist's Biography* (London: Routledge, 1992), p. 181.
21. Robert Skidelsky, *John Maynard Keynes, Volume One: Hopes Betrayed 1883–1920* (London: Macmillan, 1983), p. 235.
22. Newsome, *On the Edge of Paradise*, p. 246.
23. Harrod, p. 53.
24. Ronald Storrs, *Orientations* (London: Ivor Nicholson & Watson, 1937), pp. 15–16.
25. Storrs, 'Gaselee, Sir Stephen (1882–1943)', *Oxford Dictionary of National Biography*: https://www-oxforddnb-com.elib.tcd.ie/display/10.1093/ref:odnb/9780198614128.001.0001/odnb-9780198614128-e-33347?rskey=oRYeEM&result=4
26. Newsome, *On the Edge of Paradise*, p. 228.
27. Gaselee, 'Montague Rhodes James 1862–1936', in Joshi and Pardoe, eds, *Warnings to the Curious*, pp. 16, 27, 25.
28. Stephen Gaselee, 'The Bibliography of Petronius', *The Library*, vol. TBS-10, no. 1 (1909), 142.
29. Richmond, Memoir, p. 9.
30. H. E. Luxmoore, letter to MRJ, 31 January 1910, CUL MS Add. 7481/L201.
31. HJ, letter to Mrs Paley, 25 March 1902, JFP.
32. ACB, Diaries, v.110 f. 45–6, 4 March 1910.
33. ACB, Diaries, v.110 f.36–7. 26 February 1910.
34. ACB, Diaries, v.116 f.17, 28 October 1910.
35. F. Anstey [Thomas Anstey Guthrie], *A Long Retrospect* (London and New York: Oxford University Press, 1936), p. 289.

36. MRJ, 'I leaned last night upon the crazy rail'. CUL MS Add. 7481/MISC.
37. John N. Dalton, letter to MRJ, 17 October 1910, CUL MS Add. 7481/D3.
38. See W. H. St. John Hope, *The Discovery of the Remains of King Henry VI in St. George's Chapel, Windsor Castle* (Oxford: Horace Hart, for the Society of Antiquaries of London, 1911), pp. 535–41.
39. Edward Arnold, letter to MRJ, 8 December 1910, CUL MS Add. 7481/A34.
40. MGSA, p. vi.
41. For a chronology of MRJ's stories, see Rosemary Pardoe, 'A Chronological Listing of M. R. James's Ghost Stories', *Ghosts and Scholars*, http://www.users.globalnet.co.uk/~pardos/MRJStories.html.
42. MRJ, 'The Stalls of Barchester Cathedral: Materials for a Ghost Story', *Contemporary Review XCVII*, no. 35 (April 1910), pp. 449–60.
43. MRJ, Preface to CGS, p. 420.
44. The volume's chronology is not straightforward. If the stories date from successive Christmases, as MRJ's Preface maintains, then either one of the stories dates from Christmas 1905, and so predates 'A School Story', meaning that the stories are not presented in chronological order, or MRJ wrote two ghost stories for one of the Christmases between 1906 and 1910. Either explanation is possible, as is the explanation that not *all* the stories were written for successive Christmases.
45. Montague Summers, *The Gothic Quest: A History of the Gothic Novel* (London: Fortune Press, 1938), p. 409.
46. GSA, pp. 91, 96.
47. MGSA, p. 42.
48. CGS, p. 404.
49. MGSA, p. 44.
50. For a longer article on MRJ's ghost stories and their libraries, on which I draw here for my readings of 'The Tractate Middoth', 'Casting the Runes', and 'Mr. Humphreys and his Inheritance', see Darryl Jones, 'M. R. James's Libraries', in Alice Crawford and Robert Crawford, eds, *Libraries in Literature* (Oxford: Oxford University Press, 2022), pp. 114–27.
51. MGSA, p. 47.
52. See Henry Bradshaw, 'List of Library Classes Showing in which Room Each Class Stands' (1864), https://exhibitions.lib.cam.ac.uk/royal/artifacts/finding-your-books/ for a reproduction of Bradshaw's original design. I am very grateful to Liam Sims of the Rare Books Department of Cambridge University Library for helping me decipher the mystery of 11.3.34.
53. MGSA, p. 48.
54. Ibid., p. 48.
55. See CGS, p. 440n129.
56. The Cambridge University Library cataloguing record for this book, including the clas mark 11.3.34, can be found at https://idiscover.lib.cam.ac.uk/primo-explore/fulldisplay?docid=44CAM_ALMA21480032410003606&context=L&vid=44CAM_PROD&search_scope=SCOP_CAM_ALL&tab=cam_lib_coll&lang=en_US
57. MGSA, pp. 58–9.
58. Ibid., p. 62.
59. Ibid., p. 65.
60. Ibid., p. 107.
61. MRJ, Manuscript version of 'Casting the Runes', BL MS Egerton 3141.
62. Andrew Dunning, 'The Medieval Cartulary Behind a Ghost Story', *British Library Medieval Manuscripts Blog*, 27 August 2017: 'The British Museum's curators were so

delighted by James' story that, in November 1936, they purchased the autograph manuscript of the tale in his memory': https://blogs.bl.uk/digitisedmanuscripts/2017/08/the-medieval-cartulary-behind-a-ghost-story.html.

63. BL MS Harley 3586.
64. Walter Map, *De Nugis Curialium/Courtiers' Trifles*, ed. and trans. M. R. James; revised by C.N.L. Brooke and R.A.B. Mynors (Oxford: Clarendon Press, 1983), p. ii.
65. See Murphy, *Medieval Studies and the Ghost Stories of M. R. James*, p. 73.
66. MGSA, pp. 108, 89.
67. Ibid., p. 89.
68. James Webb, *The Occult Underground* (La Salle, PS: Open Court, 1974), p. 191. For modern scholarship, see for example Wouter J. Hanegraaff, *Esotericism and the Academy: Rejected Knowledge in Western Culture* (Cambridge: Cambridge University Press, 2012); Christopher Partridge, ed. *The Occult World* (London and New York: Routledge, 2016).
69. MGSA, pp. 98–9, 120–1.
70. See Mike Pincombe, 'Class War in "Casting the Runes"', *The Ghosts and Scholars M. R. James Newsletter*, 9 (March 2006), pp. 4, 6.
71. Powell, *Under Review*, pp. 275–6.
72. For Crowley's school and university days, see Lawrence Sutin, *Do What Thou Wilt: A Life of Aleister Crowley* (New York: St. Martin's Press, 2000), pp. 32–5.
73. See Murphy, pp. 60–1.
74. MGSA, p. 91.
75. See Rosemary Pardoe, 'Bain', *The Ghosts and Scholars M. R. James Notebook*, 3 (January 2003), pp. 37–8. The 'Oh, Whistle' MS is now at the King's School, Canterbury, Walpole's alma mater.
76. CGS, p. 419.
77. MGSA, p. 144.
78. Ibid., p. 141.
79. Ibid., pp. 139, 148, 138.
80. Ibid., p. 166.
81. MRJ, Preface to Sir John Fox, ed. *The Lady Ivie's Trial: For the Great Part of Shadwell in the County of Middlesex before Lord Chief Justice Jeffreys in 1684* (Oxford: Clarendon Press, 1929), p. v.
82. LF, p. 15.
83. MRJ, *Lady Ivie's Trial*, p. v.
84. Notebooks 6.VI. I am very grateful to Patrick J. Murphy and Fred Porcheddu for drawing my attention to this draft story, tucked away at the back of the notebook.
85. MGSA, p. 172.
86. Ibid., p. 175.
87. MRJ, *Lady Ivie's Trial*, p. viii.
88. Michael D. Bailey, 'Diabolic Magic', in David J. Collins, S.J., ed. *The Cambridge History of Magic and Witchcraft in the West: From Antiquity to the Present* (Cambridge: Cambridge University Press, 2015), p. 387.
89. KCC MS MRJ/A/11.
90. MGSA, pp. 256–7.
91. MRJ, letter to A. F. Scholfield, 21 July 1927, CUL MS Add. 7894/34. See W. H. Matthews, *Mazes and Labyrinths: A General Account of their History and Development* (London: Longmans, Green & Co., 1922).

92. See Rosemary Pardoe, 'Introduction to *The Ghosts and Scholars Book of Mazes*', *The Black Pilgrimage 2: Further Explorations in Supernatural Fiction* (Birmingham: Shadow Publishing, 2023), pp. 259–61. Matthews, *Mazes and Labyrinths*, p. 140, reproduces an image of the Somerleyton maze.
93. For a detailed account of the Hilton maze, see Nigel Pennick, *Mazes and Labyrinths* (London: Robert Hale, 1990), pp. 68–71. Matthews has a photograph of the Hilton maze, with obelisk and ball: *Mazes and Labyrinths*, facing p. 84.
94. Thorndike, *A History of Magic and Experimental Science*, Volume I (New York: Columbia University Press, 1923), pp. 22, 58–9; Davies, *Grimoires*, p. 7.
95. CGS, p. 447. Hostanes was something of a favourite figure for MRJ: see Martin Hughes, 'A Maze of Secrets in a Story by M. R. James,', in Joshi and Pardoe, eds, *Warnings to the Curious*, pp. 258–78; Rosemary Pardoe, 'Hostanes Magus', in *The Black Pilgrimage & Other Explorations: Essays on Supernatural Fiction* (King's Norton: Shadow Publishing, 2018), pp. 43–9.
96. Thorndike, *A History of Magic and Experimental Science*, Vol. I, p. 465.
97. Ibid., p. 61.
98. MGSA, p. 243.
99. Ibid., pp. 269–70.
100. MRJ, Lecture on Black Magic and Demonology, CUL MS Add. 7484/2.32. For the dating of the lecture (after 1904), see Murphy, *Medieval Studies and the Ghost Stories of M. R. James*, p. 190n.30.
101. MRJ, letter to *The Times*, 25 January 1932.
102. Thorndike, *A History of Magic and Experimental Science*, Vol. VI, p. 515. See also Frances Yates, *Giordano Bruno and the Hermetic Tradition* (London: Routledge, 2002), p. 158.
103. MRJ, *A Descriptive Catalogue of the Latin Manuscripts in the John Rylands Library at Manchester*, vol. 1 (Manchester: Manchester University Press; London: Longmans, Green & Company; London: Bernard Quaritch Limited, 1921), p. 188.
104. MRJ, Lecture on Black Magic and Demonology.
105. MRJ, Lecture on Black Magic and Demonology.
106. ACB, Diaries, v.131 f.62, August 1912.
107. Newsome, *On the Edge of Paradise*, p. 294.
108. SRJ, letter to MRJ, 12 March 1913, CUL MS Add. 7480/E3/34.
109. LF, pp. 35, 44.
110. MRJ, letter to Eric Millar, 19 January 1928, BL Add. MS 54320/134.
111. For the appointment of the Vice-Chancellor, on which I draw here, see Searby, *History of the University of Cambridge Vol. III*, pp. 47–9.
112. Ibid., p. 47.
113. See H. Montagu Butler, letter to MRJ, 1 June 1912, CUL MS Add. 7481/B389. Butler apologizes for not having supported MRJ's candidacy: he had already promised his vote to Donaldson.
114. Stuart Alexander Donaldson obituary, *Times*, 30 October 1915, p. 10.
115. ACB, letter to MRJ, 11 November 1915, CUL MS Add. 7481/B115.
116. LF, p. 46.
117. C. Hubert Parry, letter to MRJ, 12 November 1913, CUL MS Add. 7481/P8.
118. Leslie papers, KCC SJRL/1/1.
119. Gwen McBryde, letter to MRJ, 12 October 1912, CUL MS Add. 7481/M40.
120. ACB, Diaries, v.149 f.9, 29 October 1914.

121. ACB, Diaries, v.141 f.28–9, 28 October 1913.
122. ACB, Diaries, v.141 f.19, 18 October 1914.
123. 'Report of the Council of the Senate on the suggested appointment of a Syndicate on Military Training as a requirement for proceeding to a Degree', *Cambridge University Reporter*, 6 October 1914, p. 49.
124. Ibid., p. 52.
125. Christopher Clark, *The Sleepwalkers: How Europe Went to War in 1914* (London: Penguin, 2013), p. 200.
126. Ibid., p. 202.
127. Christina Rossetti, 'The German-French Campaign 1870–1871', in *Poems and Prose*, ed. Simon Humphries (Oxford: Oxford University Press, 2008), p. 209.
128. Leslie papers, KCC SJRL/1/1.
129. ACB Diaries, v.147 f.15, 2 August 1914.
130. Walter Fletcher, letter to MRJ, 9 August 1914, CUL MS Add. 7481/F29.
131. MRJ, Note Book, p. 31. CUL MS Add. 7517.
132. ACB Diaries, v. 147 f. 23–4, August 1914.
133. LF, pp. 50–1.
134. E&K, p. 171.
135. For the story of the Eastern General Hospital, on which I draw here, see 'From the Front to the Backs: The Story of the First Eastern Hospital': https://www.cam.ac.uk/research/news/from-the-front-to-the-backs-story-of-the-first-eastern-hospital. See also the extraordinary accompanying video: https://www.youtube.com/watch?v=pAU9rzL9SME&t=588s.
136. Hope Bagenal, *Letters to a Niece and Letters to a Brother: Two Autobiographical Fragments*, ed. Patience Bagenal (Privately published, 2010), pp. 33, 68.
137. Brooke, *History of the University of Cambridge*, p. 333.
138. See Arthur Gray, 'The College in War Time', *The Chanticlere*, LVI (Michaelmas term 1919), pp. 7–11.
139. E&K, p. 171.
140. Brooke, *History of the University of Cambridge*, pp. 333.
141. ACB, Diaries, v.148 f.7, 11 September 1914.
142. BL Add. MS 52728/54.
143. Thomas B. Strong, letter to MRJ, 31 August 1914, CUL MS Add. 7481/S254.
144. T. B. Strong, letter to MRJ, 9 December 1914, CUL MS Add. 7481/S255.
145. Gray, 'The College in War Time', p. 9.
146. Arthur P. Barnes, letter to MRJ, 13 September 1914, CUL MS Add. 7481/B42.
147. J. G. Stewart, letter to MRJ, 3 November 1914, CUL MS Add. 7481/S167.
148. J. G. Stewart, letter to MRJ, 3 November 1914, CUL MS Add. 7481/S167.
149. Gray, 'The College in War Time', p. 153.
150. See https://findoes.etoncollege.com/leopold-iii-of-belgium/
151. Legation de Belgique, letter to MRJ, 25 January 1919, CUL MS Add. 7481/M259.
152. Gwen McBryde, letter to MRJ, 18 January 1916, CUL MS Add. 7481/M34.
153. See LF, pp. 51–2, 55; ACB, letter to MRJ, 6 June 1915, CUL MS Add. 7481/B114; E&K, p. 171.
154. Clapham, 'Obituary: The Provost of Eton', p. 7.
155. ACB, Diaries, v.161, v. 43, 1 September 1916; v.164 f.25, 19 March 1917.
156. Carey, *Duet for Two Voices*, p. 83.
157. MRJ, letter to Clive Carey, 14 June 1916, KCC MRJ/D/Carey/8.
158. Siegfried Ruhemann, letter to MRJ, 25 May 1914, CUL MS Add. 7481/R135.
159. ACB, Diaries, v.153 f.6, 2 June 1915.

160. SRJ, *Seventy Years*, p. 194.
161. Guthrie, *Long Retrospect*, p. 345.
162. ACB, Diaries, v.147, f.15, 2 August 1914.
163. Davenport-Hines, p. 3. For a more general account of Keynes and the War, see Harrod, pp. 229–96.
164. See Wilkinson, *A Century of King's*, p. 66, for King's during the War.
165. E&K, p. 171.
166. MRJ, letter to Nathaniel Wedd, 20 September 1915, KCC NW/2/31.
167. For these figures, see Brooke, *History of the University of Cambridge*, p. 331.
168. MRJ, Founder's Day Speech [World War 1], CUL MS Add. 7484/1.5.
169. See Brooke, *History of the University of Cambridge*, p. 332.
170. Gray, 'The College in War Time', pp. 7–8. Edwin Abbott was a Fellow in Classics, and the College Tutor.
171. MRJ, Vice-Chancellor's Address, *Cambridge University Reporter*, 2 October 1914, p. 420.
172. Cecil Lubbock, letter to Walter Durnford, 4 April 1915, ECL COLL/P6/7/1a.
173. Cecil Lubbock, letter to MRJ, 6 April 1915, ECL COLL/P6/7/3.
174. Card, *Eton Renewed*, p. 138.
175. MRJ, handwritten draft of censure for Edward Lyttelton, April 1915, ECL COLL/P6/7/12.
176. Edward Lyttelton, letter to MRJ, 27 April 1915, ECL COLL/P6/7/18.
177. Caroline Lyttelton, letter to MRJ, 12 June 1918, CUL MS Add. 7481/L377.
178. E&K, p. 171.
179. See G. V. Carey, ed. *The War List of the University of Cambridge 1914–1918* (Cambridge: Cambridge University Press, 1921); Brooke, *History of the University of Cambridge*, p. 334; Wilkinson, *A Century of King's*, p. 68.
180. For these figures, see J. M. Winter, 'Britain's "Lost Generation" of the First World War', *Population Studies*, vol. 31, no. 3 (November 1977), pp. 449–66.
181. Clark, *The Sleepwalkers*, p. xxii.
182. See Wade Davis, *Into the Silence*, pp. 15–16.
183. Carey, *Nobody's Business*, p. 95.
184. Rupert Brooke, letter to MRJ, 11 September 1914, CUL MS Add. 7481/B288.
185. R. M. Brooke, letter to MRJ, 9 May 1915, CUL MS Add. 7481/B287.
186. Carey, *War List*, p. 194.
187. Rupert Brooke, 'The Soldier', in *The Poems of Rupert Brooke*, ed. Michael Croland (Mineola, NY: Dover, 2020), p. 112.
188. LF, p. 54.
189. Jones, *Rupert Brooke*, p. 403.
190. Brooke, 'The Dead', *Poems*, p. 110.
191. MRJ, letter to Gordon Carey, 6 August 1915, KCC MRJ/F/4.
192. LF, p. 76.
193. Alice Lubbock, Baroness Avebury, letter to MRJ, 17 April 1917, CUL MS Add. 7481/A48.
194. Harold Lubbock, letter to MRJ, 22 May 1914, CUL MS Add. 7481/L68.
195. Harold Lubbock, letter to MRJ, 5 September 1914, CUL MS Add. 7481/L71.
196. Harold Lubbock, letter to MRJ, 18 March 1918, CUL MS. Add 7481/L76.
197. John Stirling Maxwell, letter to MRJ, 26 May 1918, CUL MS Add. 7481/S232.
198. E&K, p. 147.
199. Walter Durnford, letter to MRJ, 10 April 1918, CUL MS Add. 7481/D140.
200. Walter Fletcher, letter to MRJ, 15 April 1918, CUL MS Add. 7481/F35.

201. See Davis, *Into the Silence*, p. 108 and *passim* for these and other reactions to surviving the War.
202. Goderic Hodges, letter to John Saltmarsh, 8 July 1970, KCC MRJ/x/1/2/2.
203. Goderic Hodges, letter to parents, 18 October 1914, KCC MRJ/x/1/2/1.
204. Goderic Hodges, letter to John Saltmarsh, 8 July 1970, KCC MRJ/x/1/2/2.
205. Goderic Hodges, *Memoirs of an Old Balloonatic* (London: William Kimber, 1972).
206. Goderic Hodges, letter to John Saltmarsh, 8 July 1970, KCC MRJ/x/1/2/2.
207. See Natalie K. Watson, 'Milner-White, Eric (1884–1963)', ODNB: https://www-oxforddnb-com.elib.tcd.ie/display/10.1093/ref:odnb/9780198614128.001.0001/odnb-9780198614128-e-47849?rskey=APyf18&result=1
208. Eric Milner-White, letter to MRJ, 28 October 1916, KCC MRJ/D/Milner-White.
209. Eric Milner-White, 'Worship and Services', in F. B. Macnutt, ed. *The Church on the Furnace: Essays by Seventeen Temporary Church of England Chaplains on Active Service in France and Flanders* (London: Macmillan, 1917), pp. 175, 179.
210. Eric Milner-White, letter to MRJ, 13 July 1916, KCC MRJ/C/4.
211. See Nicholas Nash, '"A Right Prelude to Christmas": A History of *A Festival of Nine Lessons and Carols*', in Massing and Zeeman, eds. *King's College Chapel*, pp. 323–46.
212. See Carey, *Nobody's Business*, Chapter 7.
213. MRJ, letter to Gordon Carey, 19 April 1917, KCC MRJ/F/4/7.
214. MRJ, letter to Gordon Carey, 6 August 1917, KCC MRJ/F/4/2.
215. MRJ, letter to Gordon Carey, 23 October 1916, KCC MRJ/F/4/3.
216. MRJ, letter to Gordon Carey, 24 May 1918, KCC MRJ/F/4/16.
217. MRJ, letter to Nathaniel Wedd, 20 September 1915, KCC NW/2/31.
218. MRJ, Vice-Chancellor's Address, *Cambridge University Reporter*, 2 October 1915, p. 43.
219. MRJ, *Address at the Unveiling of the Roll of Honour or the Cambridge Tipperary Club on July 12, 1916* (Cambridge: Cambridge University Press, 1916), pp. 2–4.
220. Vincent Baddeley, 'The Provost and the Scroll', *Times*, Friday 19 June 1936, p. 17.
221. Alice Lubbock, Baroness Avebury, letter to MRJ, 17 April 1917, CUL MS Add. 7481/A48.
222. LF, pp. 25–6.
223. MRJ, letter to Gordon Carey, 31 July 1917, KCC MRJ/F/4/10.
224. MRJ, letter to Gordon Carey, 18 May 1918, KCC MRJ/F/4/15.
225. E&K, p. 173.
226. E. G. Swain, letter to MRJ, 31 August 1918, CUL MS Add. 7481/S261.
227. Arthur Berry, letter to MRJ, 4 August 1918, CUL MS Add. 7481/B201.
228. E&K, p. 174.

CHAPTER 9

1. LF, p. 85.
2. MRJ, letter to Clive Carey, 14 November 1918, KCC MRJ/D/Carey/10.
3. Richmond, Memoir, pp. 10–11.
4. Gaselee, 'Montague Rhodes James 1862-1936', pp. 23–4.
5. Ronald Norman, letter to MRJ, 31 July 1918, CUL MS Add. 7481/N35.
6. Nathaniel Wedd, letter to MRJ, 7 August 1918, CUL MS Add. 7481/W46.
7. G. Lowes Dickinson, letter to MRK, 8 August 1918, CUL MS Add. 7481/D36.
8. ACB, letter to MRJ, 2 August 1918, CUL MS Add. 7481/B132. His last diary entry for almost two years was on 18 June.
9. Henry Jackson, letter to MRJ, 30 July 1918, CUL MS Add. 7481/J16.
10. MRJ, letter to Henry Jackson, 31 July 1918, Trinity College Cambridge Add. MS *c*.34/5.

11. E. G. Swain, letter to MRJ, 31 August 1918, CUL MS Add. 7481/S261.
12. MRJ, sermon delivered in KCC, 1919, CUL MS Add. 7485/6.
13. MRJ, letter to Gordon Carey, 8 August 1918, KCC MRJ/F/4/18.
14. Henry Broadbent, letter to MRJ, 20 July 1918, CUL MS Add. 7481/B279.
15. Albert Baillie, letter to MRJ, 14 September 1917, CUL MS Add. 7481/B154.
16. Oscar Browning, letter to MRK, 22 June 1919, CUL MS Add. 7481/B299.
17. J. I. Davies, letter to MRJ, 29 July 1918, ECL COLL/P6/38/5.
18. A. J. Eagleton, letter to MRJ, 25 September 1918, CUL MS Add. 7481/E1.
19. Ian Malcolm, letter to MRJ, 23 September 1918, CUL MS Add. 7481/M181.
20. E&K, pp. 172–3.
21. MRJ, letter to Gordon Carey, 30 September 1918, KCC MRJ/F/4/20.
22. Hugh Macnaghten, letter to MRJ, 2 August 1918, CUL MS Add. 7481/M165.
23. Hugh Macnaghten, *Fifty Years of Eton, in Prose and Verse* (London: George Allen & Unwin, 1924), p. 101.
24. Adam Fox, *Dean Inge* (London: John Murray, 1960), p. 139.
25. John Maynard Keynes, letter to MRJ, 1918, CUL MS Add. 7481/K16.
26. John Maynard Keynes, *Organization of Teaching and Research in the University and Colleges*, 25 October 1912, KCC JMK/KC/2/6.
27. P. A. Martindoe [Eton College Bursar], letter to MRJ, 22 September 1920, Provost James Papers: ECL/COLL/P6/4/39.
28. P. R. Quarrie, 'M. R. James at Eton', in Dennison, ed. *The Legacy of M. R. James*, p. 20.
29. Provost James papers: ECL COLL P6/4/89.
30. Provost James papers: ECL COLL/P6/46/1a.
31. Leslie papers, KCC SJRL/1/2.
32. MRJ, 'Report of the Committee on the Head Mastership', 1916. Provost James papers: ECL COLL/P6/9/1. Others not shortlisted included the Headmasters of Charterhouse and Haileybury. The Headmaster of Rugby was shortlisted, but declined to come for interview.
33. MRJ, 'Memorandum of proceedings at the Election of the Headmaster', 1916, Provost James papers: ECL COLL/P6/10/1b.
34. Powell, *To Keep the Ball Rolling, Vol. 1: Infants of the Spring* (London: Heinemann, 1976), p. 74.
35. Newsome, *On the Edge of Paradise*, p. 338.
36. Card, *Eton Renewed*, p. 159.
37. Mary Beard, *The Invention of Jane Harrison* (Cambridge, MA, and London: Harvard University Press, 2000), p. 4.
38. Jane Harrison, 'The Head of John the Baptist', *The Classical Review*, vol. 30, no. 8 (December 1916), p. 216.
39. Ibid., p. 217.
40. MRJ, 'Some Remarks on "The Head of John the Baptist"', *The Classical Review*, vol. 31, no. 1 (February 1917), p. 1.
41. Ibid., p. 4.
42. MRJ, letter to Gordon Carey, 28 January 1917, KCC MRJ/F/4/5.
43. Bagenal, *Letters to a Niece and Letters to a Brother*, pp. 71–2.
44. MRJ, 'Some Remarks on "The Head of John the Baptist"', p. 4.
45. E&K, p. 4.
46. William Ridgeway, letter to MRJ, 15 February 1917, CUL MS Add. 7481/R58.
47. Henry Jackson, letter to MRJ, 26 March 1917, CUL MS Add. 7481/J16.
48. Arthur F. Hort, letter to MRJ, 10 February 1917, CUL MS Add. 7481/H114.

49. R. L. Poole, letter to MRJ, 3 March 1917, CUL MS Add. 7481/P33.
50. Newsome, *On the Edge of Paradise*, pp. 245, 212.
51. M. A. Murray, letter to MRJ, 20 January 1916., CUL MS Add. 7481/M328.
52. See Margaret A. Murray papers, National Archive, Kew, MS Add. 155. I am grateful to Rafael C. Siodor of Special Collections, UCL library, for his help in attempting to track down the MRJ-Murray correspondence.
53. M. A. Murray, letter to MRJ, 22 January 1916. CUL MS Add. 7481/M329.
54. Max Mallowan, revised by R. S. Simpson, 'Murray, Margaret Alice (1863–1963), ODNB': https://www-oxforddnb-com.elib.tcd.ie/display/10.1093/ref:odnb/9780198614128.001.0001/odnb-9780198614128-e-35169?rskey=505lrV&result=4
55. Margaret Alice Murray, *The Witch-Cult in Western Europe: A Study in Anthropology* (Oxford: Clarendon Press, 1921), pp. 11–12.
56. MRJ, 'Lecture on "Forgotten Books"', CUL MS Add. 7484/2.12.
57. Ronald Hutton, *Pagan Britain* (New Haven and London: Yale University Press, 2013), p. 373.
58. WTC, p. 188–9.
59. Murray, *Witch-Cult*, p. 13.
60. WTC, pp. 198–9.
61. WTC, p. 183.
62. MRJ, *Abbeys* (London: Great Western Railway, 1925), p. 149.
63. MRJ, Sermon, Lower Chapel, Eton, 21 June [early 1930s], CUL MS Add 7485/65.
64. Jacques Tourneur, 'Interview' [with Bertrand Tavernier], in Claire Johnston and Paul Willemen, eds. *Jacques Tourneur* (Edinburgh: Edinburgh Film Festival, 1975), p. 54. The photograph of Margaret Murray and Dana Andrews is reproduced in Tony Earnshaw. *Beating the Devil: The Making of The Night of the Demon* (Bradford: National Museum of Photography, Film and Television, 2005), p. 33.
65. J. R. M. Butler, letter to MRJ, 3 December 1915, CUL MS Add. 7481/B405.
66. 'The Story of a Disappearance and an Appearance' and 'An Episode of Cathedral History' had already been published by Christmas 1915. Rosemary Pardoe, in her chronology of MRJ's stories, believes that 'Two Doctors' was 'probably written in 1919 to fill up [*A Thin Ghost*]', which would certainly tally with what we know about the publication of MRJ's books of ghost stories generally: he always found himself having to write at least one new story. So, from the stories written during these years, that only leaves 'Whitminster' and 'Mr. Poynter'. See Pardoe, 'Chronological Listing'.
67. HEL, letter to MRJ, 13 December [1915], CUL MS Add. 7481/L303.
68. HEL, letter to MRJ, 23 December 1917, CUL MS Add. 7481/L216.
69. MRJ, 'Preface' to TG, n.p.
70. Frank H. Coller, letter to MRJ, 1 March 1916, CUL MS Add. 7481/C114.
71. MRJ, 'Preface' to TG.
72. Ibid.
73. TG, p. 137.
74. CGS, pp. 407–8.
75. See Charles Dickens, *The Old Curiosity Shop* (1840), Chapter 16: 'the foreign gentleman who not being familiar with the language is unable in the representation to express his ideas other than by the utterance of the word "Shallabalah" three distinct times.'
76. Lubbock, *Memoir*, p. 39.
77. See, for example, Darryl Jones, 'M. R. James and Folk Horror', and Peter Bell, 'Terror in the Landscape: Folk Horror in the Stories of M. R. James', both in Robert Edgar and Wayne Johnson, eds. *The Routledge Companion to Folk Horror* (London: Routledge, 2024), pp. 55–64, 101–10.

78. CGS, p. 418.
79. Jacqueline Simpson, '"The Rules of Folklore" in the Ghost Stories of M. R. James', in Joshi and Pardoe, eds. *Warnings to the Curious*, p. 142.
80. William Shakespeare, *The Merry Wives of Windsor*, V.v.37–8, *The Riverside Shakespeare*, ed. G. Blakemore Evans (Boston: Houghton Mifflin, 1974), p. 319.
81. MRJ, letter to Gordon Carey, 14 November 1918, KCC MRJ/D/Carey/10.
82. Leslie papers, KCC SJRL/1/1.
83. TG, pp. 25, 44.
84. TG, p. 19.
85. TG, pp. 24, 26–7.
86. MRJ, *Catalogue of Manuscripts in the Fitzwilliam Museum*, p. 46.
87. TG, pp. 33–4.
88. Ferdinand Mount, *English Voices: Lives, Landscapes, Laments 1985–2015* (London: Simon and Schuster, 2016), p. 146.
89. TG, p. 11.
90. TG, p. 19.
91. See Murphy, *Medieval Studies and the Ghost Stories of M. R. James*, p. 15.
92. TG, pp. 69–70.
93. TG, pp. 67–8.
94. For an earlier version of this argument, see CGS, pp. xxxii–xxix.
95. E&K, p. 25.
96. GSA, pp. 112, 75.
97. GSA, p. 143.
98. MGSA, pp. 112, 155.
99. Reginald Farrer, letter to MRJ, 25 August 1920, CUL MS Add. 7481/F4.
100. Oscar Browning, letter to MRJ, 9 February 1920, KCC MRJ/D/Browning.
101. MRJ, KCC Founder's Day speech, 1923, CUL MS Add. 7484/1.22.
102. LF, p. 64.
103. ACB, letter to MRJ, 30 October 1916, CUL MS Add. 7481/B125.
104. MRJ, *The Five Jars* (London: Arnold, 1922), p. 11.
105. Ibid., pp. 172, 118, 19. 'M (or N)' may be a private joke between MRJ and Jane (M = Monty, or perhaps Mouse; his relationships with children were full of such jokes), though in a letter to the *Ghosts and Scholars Newsletter* (vol. 4, August 2003, p. 40), Steve Duffy points out that 'N or M' appears in *Brewer's Phrase and Fable* as 'The answer given to the first question in the Church of England Catechism. It means that here the person catechized gives his or her names, Latin *nomen vel nomina*.' *Brewer's Phrase and Fable*, 18th edition, ed. Camilla Rockwood (London: Chambers Harrap, 2009), p. 909.
106. See, amongst several others, Katharine Briggs, *The Fairies in Tradition and Literature* (1967; London and New York: Routledge, 2002). For an illuminating contemporary account, see Francis Young, *Twilight of the Godlings: The Shadowy Beginnings of Britain's Supernatural Beings* (Cambridge: Cambridge University Press, 2023).
107. See Carolyne Larrington, *The Land of the Green Man: A Journey Through the Supernatural Landscapes of the British Isles* (London: I. B. Tauris, 2015).
108. Holmes, *Sidetracks*, p. 163.
109. Mary Butts, 'The Art of Montagu James', in *Warnings to the Curious*, p. 54. First published in *London Mercury*, 29 (February 1934), pp. 306–17.
110. Wedd, Memoir [King's in 1883], p. 37.
111. MRJ, *The Five Jars*, p. 101.

112. 'Universities of Oxford and Cambridge Bill [H.L.], *Hansard*, 19 April 1923, vol. 53, cc734-55, https://api.parliament.uk/historic-hansard/lords/1923/apr/19/universities-of-oxford-and-cambridge
113. For accounts of the Asquith Commission, on which I draw here, see Brooke, *History of the University of Cambridge Vol. IV*, pp. 341–69; John Prest, 'The Asquith Commission, 1919–1922', in Brian Harrison, ed., *The History of the University of Oxford Vol. VIII: The Twentieth Century* (Oxford: Oxford University Press, 1994), pp. 26–43.
114. Universities of Oxford and Cambridge Act 1923, https://www.legislation.gov.uk/ukpga/Geo5/13-14/33/enacted/data.xht?view=snippet&wrap=true
115. 'The Royal Commission on Oxford and Cambridge', *The Spectator*, 1 April 1922, p. 6.
116. MRJ, letter to Sydney Cockerell, 4 September 1918, BL Add. MS 52728/69.
117. MRJ, letter to Henry Yates Thompson, 3 September 1918, H.Y. mss/LMC 2014/Box 1/1917–18, Lilly Library, Indiana University, Bloomington, Indiana.
118. J. Q. Bennett, 'Portman Square to New Bond Street, or, How to Make Money Though Rich', *The Book Collector*, 16/3 (1967), pp. 323–39.
119. Sydney Cockerell, letter to MRJ, 7 September 1918. CUL MS Add. 7481/C106.
120. For this episode, see Laura Cleaver and Olivia Baskerville, 'The Purchase of the *Life of St. Cuthbert* for the Nation', in Vinni Lucherini and Cécile Voyer, eds. *Le live enluminé medieval instrument politique* (Rome: Viella, 2021), p. 380.
121. For a balanced account see Murphy, *Medieval Studies and the Ghost Stories of M. R. James*, p. 151.
122. WTC, pp. 52, 59.
123. LF, p. 153.
124. MRJ, Sermon delivered at Eton [no date], CUL MS Add. 7485/46.
125. Ronald Norman, letter to MRJ, 9 September [no year], CUL MS Add. 7481/N55.
126. Nicholas Rogers, 'A Bibliography of the Published Works of Montague Rhodes James', in Dennison, ed. *The Legacy of M. R. James*, pp. 239–67.
127. MRJ, *The Wanderings and Homes of Manuscripts* (London: SPCK, 1919), p. 3.
128. Ibid., p. 95.
129. GSA, p. 153.
130. This section on Dee draws heavily on Jones, 'M. R. James's Libraries', p. 117.
131. James, *List of the Manuscripts Formerly Owned by John Dee, with Preface and Identifications* (Oxford: Oxford University Press, 1921), pp. 3, 4.
132. MRJ, *The Apocryphal New Testament*, p. 521.
133. LF, p. 112.
134. MRJ, Introduction to Joseph Sheridan Le Fanu, *Madam Crowl's Ghost and Other Tales of Mystery*, collected and edited by M. R. James (London and Glasgow: G. Bell & Sons, 1923), p. viii.
135. Ibid., p. vii.
136. MRJ, lecture on Sheridan Le Fanu, Royal Institution, 16 March 1923, published in *Ghosts and Scholars*, 7 (1985), p. 27. The original MS of this can be found in KCC MS MRJ A/15.
137. Ibid., p. 26.
138. Sheridan Le Fanu, 'Mr Justice Harbottle', in *In a Glass Darkly*, ed. Robert Tracy (Oxford: Oxford University Press, 1993), p. 88.
139. LF, p. 112.
140. MRJ's notes on the MS, dated 27 April 1922, can be found in Notebooks 3.VIII, pp. 73–84.
141. MRJ, 'Twelve Medieval Ghost Stories', *English Historical Review*, 37 (July 1922), pp. 413–22. For an English translation, see MRJ, *The Haunted Doll's House and Other Ghost Stories*, ed. S. T. Joshi (London: Penguin, 2006), pp. 222–45.

142. https://www.lib.cam.ac.uk/sandars/sandars-lectures-2022-2023
143. https://www.lib.cam.ac.uk/about-library/sandars-readership-bibliography/duties-sandars-reader
144. MRJ, 'The Pictorial Illustration of the Old Testament from the 4th to the 16th Centuries', Sandars Lectures 1923. CUL MS CCB/10/2. For the 1902 lectures, see CUL MS Add. 4229.
145. MRJ, letter to A. F. Scholfield, 11 December 1924, 11 December 1924, CUL MS Add. 7894/7.
146. HEL, letter to MRJ, 9 August 1922, CUL MS Add. 7481/L274. For a superb analysis of this window, see Robert Lloyd Parry's remarkable documentary *Dim Presences*: https://www.youtube.com/watch?v=Ne2kYzwvHOI
147. See Rachel Bond, 'Remembering the First World War: The *Libro d'oro*': https://collections.etoncollege.com/remembering-the-first-world-war-the-libro-doro/
148. See MRJ, 'Old Wall Paintings in Eton College Chapel', *Country Life*, 8 September 1923, pp. 303–5. For a modern account, see Nikolaus Pevsner and Elizabeth Williamson, *The Buildings of England: Buckinghamshire* (New Haven and London: Yale University Press, 2003), p. 306.
149. Byrne and Churchill, *Changing Eton*, p. 174.
150. H. E. Luxmoore, letter to MRJ [1923], ECL COLL P6/19/6.
151. Byrne and Churchill, *Changing Eton*, p. 174.
152. M. R. James and E. W. Tristram, 'The Wall Paintings in Eton College Chapel and in the Lady Chapel of Winchester Cathedral', *The Volume of the Walpole Society*, Vol. 17 (1928–29), p. 12.
153. E&K, p. 60.
154. Pevsner and Williamson, *Buckinghamshire*, p. 306.
155. MRJ, 'Eton Wall Paintings: The Hand of a Master', *Times*, 27 September 1923, p. 13.
156. MRJ's notes for this trip, which took place between 5 August and 22 September 1924, can be found in Notebooks 18.II.
157. MRJ, *Abbeys* (London: Great Western Railway, 1925), p. v.
158. LF, p. 18.
159. MRJ, Note Book, p. 37v. CUL MS Add. 7517.
160. J. S. Udall, 'The Story of the Bettiscombe Skull', *Proceedings of the Dorset Natural History and Antiquarian Field Club*, XXXI (1910), 177. This article includes a summary of Udall's work on this subject going back to 1872. MRJ was not the only ghost-story writer drawn to screaming skull legends: see, for example, F. Marion Crawford, 'The Screaming Skull' (1911); Eleanor Scott, 'Unburied Bane' (1929).
161. Ibid., p. 178.
162. Garth Turner, *Cathedrals and Change in the Twentieth Century: Aspects of the Life of the Cathedrals of the Church of England with Special Reference to the Cathedral Commissions of 1925; 1958; 1992*, PhD thesis, University of Manchester, 201, pp, 20–1.
163. For this itinerary, see LF, pp. 106–7.
164. LF, p.118.
165. LR, p. 19.
166. Guthrie, *Long Retrospect*, p. 375.
167. Guthrie, Diaries, Vol. CXXII, December 1921-October 1922. BL Add. MS 63575.
168. MRJ, Note Book, p. 35. CUL MS Add. 7517.
169. ACB, Diaries, v. 178, 12 December 1924.
170. LF, p. 121.
171. ACB, Diaries, v.176 f.6, November 1924.
172. LF, p. 67.

173. MRJ, letter to Eric Millar, 22 December 1924, BL Add. MS 54320/82; H. E. Luxmoore, letter to E. W. Grazebrook, 20 December 1924, ECL SCH/M/HEL/7/5.
174. MRJ, letter to Gordon Carey, 29 December 1924, KCC MRJ/F/4/28.
175. LF, 131.
176. ACB, letter to MRJ, 2 March 1925, ECL *Eton and King's* Inserts 3/7.
177. MRJ, letter to A. F. Scholfield, 14 March 1925, CUL MS Add. 7894/9.
178. MRJ, letter to A. F. Scholfield, 7 November 1925, CUL MS Add. 7894/8.
179. MRJ, letter to A. F. Scholfield, 27 June 1927, CUL MS Add. 7894/32.
180. Anita Leslie, *The Marlborough House Set* London: Dell, 1973, p. 248.
181. 'Beatrice Ethel Roberts (1888–1960)', https://www.granthammatters.co.uk/roberts-beatrice/
182. Jonathan Aitken, *Margaret Thatcher: Power and Personality* (London: Bloomsbury, 2013), p. 25.
183. Stephen Gwynn, ed. *The Letters and Friendships of Sir Cecil Spring Rice: A Record* (Boston and New York: Houghton Mifflin, 1929), Vol II, p. 435.
184. LF, p. 55.
185. LF, pp. 73, 76–7.
186. LF, p. 89.
187. Leslie, *Mark Sykes*, p. 298.
188. Ibid., p. 293.
189. Nathaniel Wedd, 'Marcus Southwell Dimsdale (A Memoir)', in Dimsdale, *Happy Days*, pp. xiii–iv.
190. MRJ's note, appended to Marcus Dimsdale, letter to MRJ, 31 July 1918, CUL MS Add. 7481/D46.
191. E&K, p. 111.
192. LF, p. 69.
193. MRJ, letter to Elizabeth Babington Smith, 27 September 1923, Trinity College Cambridge MS HBS/92/42.
194. MRJ, letter to Elizabeth Babington Smith, 19 October 1923, Trinity College Cambridge MS HBS/92/43.
195. MRJ, letter to Elizabeth Babington Smith, 29 September 1923, Trinity College Cambridge MS HBS/12/9.
196. E. F. Benson, letter to MRJ, 19 June 1925, CUL MS Add. 7481/B160.
197. A. B. Ramsay, letter to MRJ, 13 November 1926, CUL MS add. 7481/R16.
198. MRJ, 'Trivial Reminiscences, Early and Late', in E. H. Ryle, ed. *Arthur Benson as Seen by Some Friends* (London: G. Bell and Sons, 1925), p. 3.
199. Ibid., p. 19.
200. See Goldhill, *A Very Queer Family Indeed*, pp. 201–300, 13.
201. ACB, letter to MRJ, 2 May 1925, ECL MS 588/8.
202. ACB, Diaries, v.172 f.22, 30 October 1923.

CHAPTER 10

1. Stanley Baldwin, letter to MRJ, 5 April 1925, CUL MS Add. 7481/B16.
2. Leslie papers, KCC SJRL 1/1.
3. WTC, p. 81.
4. LF, p. 151.
5. MRJ, letter to A. F. Scholfield, 19 October 1925, CUL MS Add. 7894/11.
6. MRJ, 'After Dark in the Playing Fields', *College Days*, 10 (28 June 1924), pp. 311–12, 314.
7. MRJ, 'There Was a Man Dwelt by a Churchyard', *Snapdragon* (6 December 1924), pp. 4–5.

8. Shakespeare, *The Winter's Tale*, II, i, 25–30.
9. CGS, p. 368.
10. John Betchman [Betjeman], letter to Shane Leslie [no date], inside Leslie's annotated copy of E&K, ECL Lp.2.24/8; Robert Macfarlane, 'The eeriness of the English countryside', *The Guardian*, 10 April 2015: https://www.theguardian.com/books/2015/apr/10/eeriness-english-countryside-robert-macfarlane
11. MRJ, letter to Eric Millar, 26 April 1932, BL Add. MS 54320/200.
12. LF, pp. 126–7.
13. MRJ, *Suffolk and Norfolk*, p. 102.
14. For an earlier version of the reading of this story, see Darryl Jones, 'M. R. James and Folk Horror', pp. 59–61.
15. WTC, p. 138.
16. Ibid., p. 151.
17. Ibid., p. 146.
18. Jennifer Westwood and Jacqueline Simpson, *The Lore of the Land: A Guide to England's Legends, from Spring-Heeled Jack to the Witches of Warboys* (London: Penguin, 2005), p. 683.
19. WTC, pp. 146–7.
20. Frederic Shoberl, *Suffolk; or, Original Delineations, Topographical, Historical, and Descriptive, of That County. The Result of Personal Survey* (London: J. Harris, 1818), p. 308. Westwood and Simpson, p. 682, also note 'the so-called "crown" actually dug up at Rendlesham, according to one of William Camden's editors, in 1687'.
21. Shoberl, p. 308.
22. MRJ, *Suffolk and Norfolk*, p. 11.
23. WTC, p. 147.
24. Ibid., p. 104.
25. WTC, p. 172.
26. Ibid., pp. 170–1.
27. Ibid., p. 172.
28. Ibid., p. 173.
29. HJ, letter to MRJ, 27 June 1874, CUL MS Add. 7480/E1/2.
30. https://www.iwm.org.uk/memorials/item/memorial/5407. For a reading of 'A Warning' and the War with many parallels to my own here, see Murphy, *Medieval Studies and the Ghost Stories of M. R. James*, pp. 169–73. See also Lloyd Parry, *Dim Presences*, for an excellent account of the story's context.
31. WTC, pp. 148, 144.
32. MRJ, 'A Warning to the Curious: Autograph Manuscript', Morgan Library and Museum, New York, MS James 6/MA 1165.
33. WTC, p. 144.
34. Charles Mackintosh, letter to MRJ, 30 May 1926, CUL MS Add. 7481/M149.
35. 'The Uncommon Prayer-Book', *Atlantic Monthly*, vol. 127, no. 6 (June 1921), pp. 756–65.
36. WTC, pp. 66–7.
37. MRJ, *The Western Manuscripts in the Library of Trinity College, Cambridge: A Descriptive Catalogue, Volume II* (Cambridge: Cambridge University Press, 1901), pp. vi–vii. Historically, Lady Anne Sadleir lived in Hertfordshire and Staffordshire, not in Herefordshire. While the story is deliberately geographically vague, there are good reasons for placing it in Herefordshire: see MRJ, *Casting the Runes and Other Ghost Stories*, ed. Michael Cox (Oxford: OUP, 1987), p. 331.
38. WTC, p. 54.

39. Ibid., pp. 39, 44, 45. For a reading of the story in the context of 1920s Anglo-Catholicism, see George R. Featherston, 'In Defence of "The Uncommon Prayer-Book"', *The Ghosts and Scholars M. R. James Newsletter*, 14 (September 2008), pp. 30–1.
40. For Dore Abbey and the Scudamores, see MRJ, *Abbeys*, p. 116.
41. CGS, p. 419.
42. For a convincing argument connecting Fulnaker with Llanthony, on which I draw here, see Rosemary Pardoe and Darroll Pardoe, 'The Herefordshire of "A View from a Hill"', *The Black Pilgrimage*, pp. 89–100. See also LF, p. 22.
43. MRJ, *Abbeys*, p. 134.
44. Fiona MacCarthy, *Eric Gill* (London: Faber and Faber, 1989), p. 180.
45. Alfred Watkins, *The Old Straight Track: Its Mounds, Beacons, Moats, Sites, and Mark Stones* (1925; London: Methuen, 1948), pp. 76, 258.
46. WTC, p. 108.
47. Ibid., p. 71.
48. See Pardoe and Pardoe, 'The Herefordshire of "A View from a Hill"', pp. 90–1.
49. LF, p. 25.
50. Watkins, *Old Straight Track*, p. 1.
51. Ibid., p. 279.
52. MRJ, letter to A. F. Scholfield, 19 October 1925, CUL MS Add. 7894/11.
53. William McGregor Hemingway, letter to MRJ, 18 January 1927, ECL M. R. James Miscellanies, vol. II/Eton and King's Inserts I/3.
54. LFMC, p. 92. LF has 'bad time' instead of 'tantrum'.
55. LF, p. 143.
56. For the commissioning and building of Queen Mary's Dolls' House, see Mary Stewart-Wilson, *Queen Mary's Dolls' House* (London: Ebury Press, 1995), pp. 10–21; *Queen Mary's Dolls' House: Official Guidebook* (London: Royal Collection, 2004); Lucinda Lambton, *The Queen's Dolls' House* (London: Royal Collection, 2010).
57. For a complete list of the contents of the library, as well as all the artists, musicians, designers, craftspeople, and organizations who contributed to the Dolls' House, see Lambton, pp. 114–23.
58. Newsome, *Another Side of Paradise*, p. 357.
59. ACB, Introduction to ACB and Sir Lawrence Weaver, eds. *The Book of the Queen's Dolls' House* (London: Methuen, 1924), p. 6.
60. E. V. Lucas, ed. *The Book of the Queen's Dolls' House Library* (London: Methuen, 1924), p. 171. 'The Haunted Dolls' House' is on pp. 171–81, and had previously been published in *The Empire Review*, vol. XXXVIII, no. 265 (February 1923), pp. 91–101.
61. WTC, pp. 14–15.
62. WTC, p. 71.
63. MRJ, Empire Day sermon [no date], CUL MS Add. 7485/9.
64. W. Wyndham, letter to MRJ, 29 December 1917, CUL MS Add. 7481/W102.
65. WTC, pp. 80–1, 75.
66. Cox, p. 145.
67. See Jacqueline Simpson, 'Landmarks and Shrieking Ghosts', and Rosemary Pardoe, 'Addendum', in Pardoe and Joshi, eds, *Warnings to the Curious*, pp. 316–20.
68. MRJ, *Lady Ivie's Trial*, p. vi.
69. Elizabeth Jenkins, 'The Lady Ivie', in *Six Criminal Women* (London: Sampson Low, 1949), pp. 57–80.
70. LF, p. 135.

71. MRJ, 'Stories I Have Tried to Write', *The Touchstone*, 2 (30 November 1929), pp. 46–7. Reprinted in CGS, pp. 408–10.
72. The fragments have (almost) all now been published, though not in easily-available editions. They were first put together in Rosemary Pardoe, ed. *The Fenstanton Witch and Others* (Chester: Haunted Library, 1999), and then appeared in *A Pleasing Terror*. Neither volume discusses dates for the fragments.
73. For the manuscript of the story, see KCC MRJ A/13.
74. https://www.roxburgheclub.org.uk/clubBooks/
75. Samanth Subramanian, *A Dominant Character: The Radical Science and Restless Politics of J. B. S. Haldane* (London: Atlantic Books, 2020), p. 106.
76. Ibid., p. 154.
77. 'Communication from the Sex Viri', *Cambridge University Reporter*, 22 December 1925, p. 443.
78. *Cambridge University Reporter*, 18 March 1926, p. 790.
79. LF, p. 138.
80. HEL, letter to E. W. Grazebrook, 12 May 1926, ECL SCH/M/HEL/7/12.
81. For Birley and MRJ, see Tim Card, *Eton Renewed*, p. 151,
82. Robert Birley, 'The General Strike', *TLS*, 10 November 1972, p. 1369.
83. MRJ, letter to Eric Millar, 5 May 1926, BL Add. MS 54320/107.
84. Arthur F. Hort, letter to MRJ, 11 November 1926, CUL MS Add. 7481/H116.
85. LF, p. 140.
86. MRJ, letter to Sydney Cockerell, 9 November 1927, BL Add. MS 52728/156.
87. MRJ, letter to Sydney Cockerell, 14 November 1927, BL Add. MS 52728/157.
88. MRJ, letter to A. F. Scholfield, 29 November 1927, CUL MS Add. 7894/44.
89. MRJ, letter to Eric Millar, 19 Jan 1928, BL Add. MS 54320/134.
90. MRJ, letters to A. F. Scholfield, 27 January & 8 February 1928, CUL MS Add. 7894/48, 49.
91. MRJ, letter to Sydney Cockerell, 27 January 1928, BL Add. MS 52728/160.
92. MRJ, letter to A. F. Schofield, 2 February 1927, CUL MS Add. 7894/20.
93. MRJ, letter to Sydney Cockerell, 11 August 1926, BL Add. MS 52728/135.
94. MRJ, letter to A. F. Schofield, 6 April 1927, CUL MS Add. 7894/23.
95. MRJ, letter to A. F. Schofield, 4 July 1928, CUL MS Add. 7894/64.
96. MRJ, letters to A. F. Schofield, 7 November 1927 & 15 January 1928, CUL MS Add. 7894/42, 47.
97. For an account of this project, see Jayne Ringrose, 'The Legacy of M. R. James in Cambridge University Library', in Dennison, ed. *The Legacy of M. R. James*, pp. 23–36.
98. A. F. Scholfield, 'Revision of the Old Catalogue of MSS, 1856–67', 9 November 1925, CUL MS Library Syndicate/Appendix to Minutes 1924-.
99. Ringrose, p. 35.
100. E&K, p. 3.
101. LF, p. 134.
102. LF, p. 20.
103. KCC SLRJ 1/1.
104. E&K, p. 64.
105. Michael Holroyd, *Lytton Strachey Volume II: The Years of Achievement 1910–1932* (London: Heinemann, 1968), pp. 530–1.
106. H. E. Luxmoore, letter to MRJ, 9 July 1926, CUL MS Add. 7481/L322.
107. C. R. L. Fletcher, letter to MRJ, 25 October 1925, CUL MS Add. 7481/F18.
108. Michael Bloch, *Closet Queens*, p. 29.

109. Lord Rosebery, letter to MRJ, 26 January 1927, CUL MS Add. 7481/R126.
110. LF, p. 137.
111. Wilkinson, *A Century of King's*, pp. 71–2.
112. MRJ, 'Walter Durnford: An Address by the Provost of Eton on the occasion of the Memorial Service in King's Chapel', in J. H. Clapham, ed. *Walter Durnford: Praepositus necnon amicus 1918–1926* (Cambridge: Cambridge University Press, 1926), p. 31.
113. Ibid., p. 31.
114. LF, p. 137.
115. Wilkinson, *A Century of King's*, p. 79.
116. Noel Annan, 'The Cult of Homosexuality in England 1850–1950', *Biography*, vol. 13, no. 3 (Summer 1990), p. 195.
117. Wilkinson, *A Century of King's*, pp. 91–2, 80.
118. LF, p. 137.
119. H. E. Luxmoore, letter to Henry Kennett Marten, 10 November 1926, ECL SCH/M/HEL/8.
120. LF, p. 140.
121. MRJ, 'Mr. H. E. Luxmoore: An Appreciation', *Times*, 12 November 1926, p. 19.
122. MRJ, 'Henry Elford Luxmoore', address given on Sunday 14 November 1926, *Eton College Chronicle*, 6 December 1926, pp. 133–4.
123. For an account of the garden and its history, see https://www.parksandgardens.org/places/eton-college-provosts-fellows-and-luxmores-garden
124. MRJ, 'Mr. Luxmoore's Garden', *Times*, 2 June 1928, p. 8.
125. LF, p. 144.
126. LF, p. 144.
127. KCC SJRL 1/1.
128. MRJ, *Wailing Well* (Stanford Dingley: Mill House Press, 1928); Peter Lawrence's copy can be found at ECL MS 344.
129. 'Vice-Provost of Eton: Body Recovered from the Thames', *Times*, 14 August 1929, p. 7.
130. For a list of the war dead from Macnaghten's House, see E. Millington-Drake, ed. *Hugh Macnaghten's House Record: Eton 1899–1920* (Eton College: Spottiswoode, Ballantyne & Co., for the Savile Press, 1930), p. xxv.
131. MRJ, letter, *Times*, 16 August 1929, p. 11.
132. LF, p. 147.
133. MRJ, letter to Sydney Cockerell, 30 January 1926, BL Add. MS 52728/123.
134. MRJ, *The Apocalypse in Art* (London: British Academy, 1931).
135. For an important essay on MRJ and Scadinavian folklore, on which I draw here, see Jacqueline Simpson, '"The Rules of Folklore" in the Ghost Stories of M. R. James', in *Warnings to the Curious*, pp. 142–61.
136. MRJ, lecture on Hans Andersen, CUL MS Add. 7484/1.63.
137. GSA, p. 152.
138. LF, p. 147.
139. CGS, p. 371.
140. Ibid., p. 372.
141. MRJ, *Suffolk and Norfolk*, p. 66.
142. Ibid., p. vii.
143. Ibid., p. 71.
144. CGS, p. 371
145. MRJ, letter to Eric Millar, 5 February 1934, BL Add. MS 54320/236; KCC SJRL 1/1/.

146. MRJ, letter to Gerald Kelly, 21 February 1935, ECL COLL/P6/26/9.
147. MRJ, letter to A. F. Scholfield, 14 May 1930, CUL MS Add.7894/96.
148. Rubinstein, Nash, and Co., letter to MRJ, 5 November 1928, CUL MS Add. 7481/R134.
149. MRJ, letter to Rubinstein, Nash, and Co., 6 November 1928, CUL MS Add. 7481/R134A.
150. It is only fair to say that there are a couple of exceptions, the American librarian Belle Da Costa Greene and the Danish historian Ellen Jørgensen, both of whom he evidently held in high regard: 'Ah!' he wrote after receiving a letter from Jørgensen. 'If more people could write Latin as good—as smart—as hers!'). MRJ, letter to Eric Millar, 17 December 1926, BL Add. MS 54320/116.
151. MRJ, letter to A. F. Scholfield, 23 February 1929, CUL MS Add. 7494/78.
152. MRJ, letter to Nicholas Llewellyn Davies, 12 January 1928, in *A Pleasing Terror*, p. 642.
153. CGS, p. 418.
154. MRJ, letter to Nicholas Llewellyn Davies, 12 January 1928, p. 641.
155. LF, p. 152.
156. MRJ, letter to August Derleth, 13 November 1929, Wisconsin Historical Society, University of Wisconsin-Madison Wis Mss WO/Box 26, Folder 7. For an account of the MRJ-Derleth correspondence, on which I draw here, see Pardoe, 'M. R. James and "The Native of Wisconsin"', in *The Black Pilgrimage*, pp. 179–82.
157. For a history of the Order of Merit, see Stanley Martin, *The Order of Merit: One Hundred Years of Matchless Honour* (London: I. B. Tauris, 2007).
158. https://www.royal.uk/order-of-merit
159. Baron Stamfordham [Arthur Bigge], letter to MRJ, 22 May 1930, JFP.
160. Maisie Fletcher, *The Bright Countenance*, p. 256.
161. MRJ, letter to Sydney Cockerell, 6 June 1930, BL Add. MS 52728/175.
162. MRJ, letter to A. F. Scholfield, 9 June 1930, CUL MS Add. 7894/97.
163. J. M. Barrie, letter to MRJ, 5 June 1930, CUL MS Add. 7481/B47.
164. E. F. Benson, letter to MRJ, 5 June 1930, CUL MS Add. 7481/B164.
165. William Bridgeman, letter to MRJ, 16 July 1930, CUL MS Add. 7481/B250.
166. Thomas Anstey Guthrie, letter to MRJ, 3 June 1930, CUL MS Add. 7481/G130.

CHAPTER 11

1. ECL COLL/P6/38/12.
2. 'Lines. Found near Cloister Pump on August 1st 1932', ECL COLL/P6/37/7.
3. MRJ, letter to Sydney Cockerell, 6 June 1930, BL Add. MS 52728/161.
4. MRJ, Founder's Day address, KCC, 1930s, CUL MS Add. 7484/1.24.
5. MRJ, letter to Gwen McBryde, 16 November 1931, KCC MRJ/F/9b.
6. KCC SJRL 1/1.
7. MRJ, letter to Eric Millar, 17 March 1931, BL Add. MS 54320/174.
8. MRJ, letter to Eric Millar, 18 February 1933, BL Add. MS 54320/217.
9. Eric Millar, letter to MRJ, 8 June 1930, CUL MS Add, 7481/M133.
10. 'A Satanist Picture', *Times*, 21 January 1932, p. 15.
11. MRJ, letter to A. F. Scholfield, 23 January 1932, CUL MS 7894/108.
12. MRJ, letter to the *Times*, 25 January 1932, p. 15.
13. Arthur W. Hill, letter to the *Times*, 27 January 1932, p. 15.
14. Hilda Barron, letter to the *Times*, 25 January 1932, p. 15; M. A Murray, letter to the *Times*, 27 January 1932, p. 15.
15. [Montague Summers], letter to the *Times*, 28 January 1932, p. 6.
16. MRJ, letter to Eric Millar, 25 January 1932, BL Add. MS 54320/190.

17. KCC SJRL 1/1.
18. KCC SJRL 1/1.
19. MRJ, letter to A. F. Scholfield, 29 January 1930, CUL MS 7894/71.
20. KCC SJRL 1/1.
21. Percy Lubbock, letter to MRJ, 23 January 1923, CUL MS Add. 7481/L84.
22. MRJ, letter to A. F. Scholfield, 17 December 1932, CUL MS 7894/113.
23. W. W. Greg, 'Hamlet's Hallucination', *Modern Language Review*, vol. 12, no. 4 (October 1917), p. 395.
24. MRJ, letter to Gordon Carey, 23 October 1917, KCC MRJ F4/11A.
25. T. S. Eliot, 'Hamlet' ['Hamlet and His Problems'], in *Selected Essays* (London: Faber and Faber, 1951), pp. 143, 145.
26. Ibid., p. 143.
27. LF, p. 217.
28. MRJ, letter to Eric Millar, 30 December 1930, BL Add. MS 54320/18.
29. LF, p. 189.
30. William Shakespeare, *Hamlet*, ed. John Dover Wilson (Cambridge: Cambridge University Press, 1934), p. l.
31. John Dover Wilson, *What Happens in Hamlet* (Cambridge: Cambridge University Press, 1935), p. 3.
32. Ibid., pp. 52–3.
33. MRJ, letter to Gwen McBryde [1936], KCC MRJ/9b.
34. LF, p. 170.
35. John Betjeman, review of *Collected Ghost Stories*, *Daily Herald*, 27 April 1947.
36. CUL MS Dd.11.45/f.144r. In an ingenious piece of intellectual archaeology, this connection was spotted by Patrick J. Murphy, *Medieval Studies and the Ghost Stories of M. R. James*, pp. 126–32.
37. MRJ, letter to Eric Millar, 14 April 1936, BL Add. MS. 54320/264.
38. CGS, p. 400.
39. Mary Butts, 'The Art of Montagu James', *London Mercury*, 29 (February 1934), pp. 306–17, reprinted in *Warnings to the Curious*, pp. 53–65.
40. MRJ, letter to Eric Millar, 5 February 1934. BL Add. MS. 54320/236.
41. LF, p. 201.
42. *The Journals of Mary Butts*, ed. Nathalie Blondel (London: Yale University Press, 2002), p. 169.
43. Butts, 'The Art of Montagu James', pp. 53, 54.
44. Butts, *Journals*, p. 153
45. Ibid., pp. 268–9.
46. Butts, 'The Art of Montagu James', pp. 54, 64.
47. LF, p. 187.
48. LF, p. 217.
49. Dorothy L. Sayers, *The Nine Tailors* (1934; London: Hodder and Stoughton, 2016), p. 374. See also Roger Johnson, 'Gaudy, Gawdy, Domini in Laude', *The Ghosts and Scholars M. R. James Newsletter*, 15 (May 2009), pp. 30–1.
50. Dorothy L. Sayers, *The Letters of Dorothy L. Sayers 1899–1936: The Making of a Detective Novelist*, ed. Barbara Reynolds (London: Sceptre, 1995), p. 71; Dorothy L. Sayers, ed. *Great Short Stories of Detection, Mystery and Horror* (London: Gollancz, 1928).
51. Dorothy L, Sayers, letter to the *Eton Chronicle*, 28 December 1936. The letter was published in the *Eton Chronicle*, 4 February 1837. See also 'Martin's Close: The Wimsey Connection', *Ghosts and Scholars*, 12 (1990), pp. 32–4.

52. Lois Austen Leigh, *The Incredible Crime: A Cambridge Mystery* (1931; London: British Library, 2017), p. 16.
53. LF, p. 171.
54. LF, p. 178.
55. MRJ, letters to Eric Millar, 28 May, 6 June 1932, BL Add. MS 54320/202, 203.
56. MRJ, lecture to Salisbury Club, no date, CUL MS Add. 7484/2.11. LF, p. 217.
57. MRJ, letter to A. F. Scholfield, 27 February 1932, CUL MS. Add. 7894/109.
58. Alington, *Lionel Ford*, p. 142.
59. Walter Fletcher, letter to MRJ, 29 May 1933, CUL MS Add. 7481/F42.
60. MRJ, letter to Eric Millar, 10 June 1933, BL Add. MS 54320/223.
61. MRJ, address at memorial service for Walter Fletcher [1933], CUL MS Add. 7484/1.49.
62. SRJ, *Seventy Years*, pp. 219–20.
63. *England and Wales, National Probate Calendar (Index of Wills and Administrations), 1858–1995*, 1934: Haab-Kyte. https://www.ancestry.com/imageviewer/collections/1904/images/31874_222761-00464?pId=3411280
64. LF, p. 215.
65. MRJ, letter to Gordon Carey, 4 November 1929, KCC MRJ/F/4/33.
66. LF, p. 219.
67. MRJ, letter to Shane Leslie, 6 November 1935, pasted to the back of Shane Leslie's annotated copy of E&K, ECL Lp.2.24.
68. LFMC, p. 221.
69. Walter Frere, letter to MRJ, 31 Jan 1936, CUL MS Add. 7481/F95.
70. MRJ, letter to Eric Millar, 23 December 1935, BL Add. MS 54320/261.
71. MRJ, letter to Eric Millar, 28 January 1928, BL Add. MS 54320/138.
72. MRJ, letter to Gwen McBryde, 12 February 1933, KCC MRJ/E/2; Hugh Fraser Stewart, letter to A. F. Scholfield, 13 November 1933, CUL MS Add. 7894/120.
73. MRJ, letter to Eric Millar, 28 May 1934, BL Add. MS 54320/239.
74. MRJ, Note Book, p. 42r. CUL MS Add. 7517.
75. MRJ, letter to Sydney Cockerell, 26 September 1934, BL Add. MS 52728/176.
76. MRJ, letter to Gwen McBryde, 21 January 1935, KCC MRJ/F/9b. See also MRJ, letter to Gordon Carey, 24 January 1935. KCC MRJ/F/4/34.
77. Note Book, p. 43v. CUL MS Add. 7517.
78. MRJ, letter to Eric Millar, 23 December 1935, BL Add. MS 54320/261.
79. J. H. Clapham, letter to MRJ, 26 January 1936, CUL MS Add. 7481/C53.
80. MRJ, letter to A. F. Scholfield, 12 February 1935, CUL MS Add. 7894/128.
81. Leslie papers. KCC SJRL 1/1.
82. 'Speech delivered by Dr. M. R. James at a lunch in Pembroke College on 22 October 1934 before the giving of Honorary Degrees on the occasion of the opening of the new University Library by King George V'. CUL MS ULIB 9/4/18. Robertson Smith was University Librarian from 1886–89.
83. MRJ, 'Description of the Ancient Manuscripts in the Ipswich Public Library', *Proceedings of the Suffolk Institute of Archaeology and Natural History*, vol. XXII, Part 1 (1934). See also MRJ, 'Catalogue of the Library of Leicester Abbey', *Transactions of the Leicestershire Archaeological Society*, 19 (1936–37), pp. 111–61, 377–440; 21 (1939–41), pp. 1–88; MRJ, 'Four Leaves of an English Psalter, 12th century, and an English Picture-Book of the Late 13th Century', *Walpole Society*, 25 (1936–37), pp. 1–30.
84. LF, p. 216.
85. MRJ, Note Book, p. 43r. CUL MS Add. 7517.
86. LF, p. 219.

87. See Duncan J. Rule, 'M. R. James, Stoke Poges, and the Pen-Gray Society', *The Ghosts and Scholars M. R. James Newsletter*, 41 (2022), pp. 7–11.
88. LF, p. 209.
89. LF, p. 222.
90. Both Pfaff (p. 409) and Cox (p. 232) maintain that MRJ died of prostate illness, though Pfaff also suggests the possibility of a stroke. My thanks to Professor Joseph Harbison of TCD School of Medicine for his advice on the symptoms of strokes.
91. Pfaff, p. 419.
92. GRJ, letter to Eric Millar, 22 January 1936, BL Add. MS 54320/274; Sydney Cockerell, letter to Eric Millar, 7 May 1936, BL Add. MS 54320/273.
93. LF, p. 194.
94. Cox, p. 232.
95. MRJ, letter to Sydney Cockerell, 1 April 1936, BL Add. MS 52728/204.
96. MRJ, letter to Sydney Cockerell, 22 April 1936, BL Add. MS 52728/205.
97. MRJ, letter to Eric Millar, 22 May 1936, BL Add. MS 54320/266.
98. Leslie papers, KCC SJRL 1/1.
99. Eric Millar, letter to MRJ, 24 January 1936, CUL MS Add. 7481/M250.
100. Eric Millar, letter to MRJ, 20 February 1936, CUL MS Add. 7481/M251.
101. MRJ, letter to Eric Millar, 22 April 1936, BL Add. MS 52728/205.
102. GRJ, letter to Eric Millar, 18 June 1936, BL Add. MS 54320/275.
103. GRJ, letter to Eric Millar, 18 June 1936, BL Add. MS 54320/275.
104. Gaselee, 'Montague Rhodes James', p, 24.
105. MRJ, Funeral Order of Service, 16 June 1936, BL Add. MS 52728/206.
106. Oliffe Richmond, unpublished memoir of MRJ, KCC MRJ/x/1/3, p. 11.
107. 'The Late Dr. Montague James', unattributed newspaper clipping, JFP.
108. 'King's College Chapel: Montague Rhodes James, Provost of King's 1905–1918, Provost of Eton 1918–1936. 1 August 1862–12 June 1926', Memorial Service, Tuesday 12 June 1936, 2.30pm, pp. 5–6.
109. A. B. Ramsay, letter to Eric Millar, 19 June 1936, BL Add. MS 54320/276.
110. MRJ's will, February 1934, ECL COLL/P6/27.
111. MRJ, Executorship Account, 16 August 1937, ECL COLL/P6/38/15/5.
112. ECL COLL/P6/38/15/2.
113. John Maynard Keynes, letter to E. U. Maggs, 30 October 1936, KCC MRJ/A2.
114. R. A. Scott James, preface to 'A Vignette', *London Mercury*, 35 (November 1936), p. 18.
115. Ibid., p. 18.
116. CGS, pp. 412, 404.
117. CGS, p. 405.

Index

For the benefit of digital users, indexed terms that span two pages (e.g., 52–53) may, on occasion, appear on only one of those pages.